London

First published 2001 by

Philip's
a division of Octopus Publishing Group Ltd
2–4 Heron Quays
London E14 4JP

First edition 2001
Fourth impression with revisions 2003

ISBN 0 540 07813-1 (perfect -bound)
ISBN 0 540 08222-8 (spiral-bound)

© Philip's 2003

This product includes mapping data
licensed from Ordnance Survey®, with the
permission of the Controller of Her Majesty's
Stationery Office.© Crown copyright 2003.
All rights reserved.
Licence number 100011710

This product contains driver restriction
information derived from Teleatlas
©TeleatlasDRI

Printed and bound in Spain
by Cayfosa-Quebecor.

Contents

II Key to map pages

IV Administrative and Postcode boundaries

VI Key to map symbols

1 Street maps

77 Keys to enlarged map pages and symbols

78 Enlarged street maps

174 Index

267 List of numbered locations

280 *London Underground*

282 *Central London theatres and cinemas*

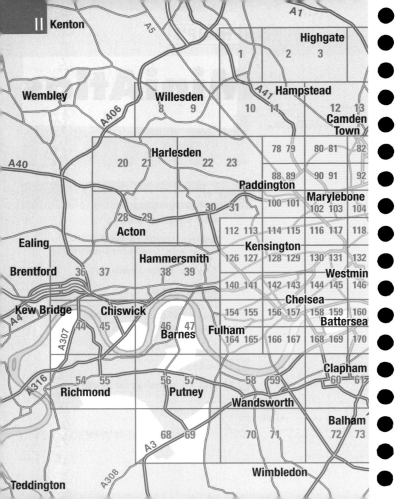

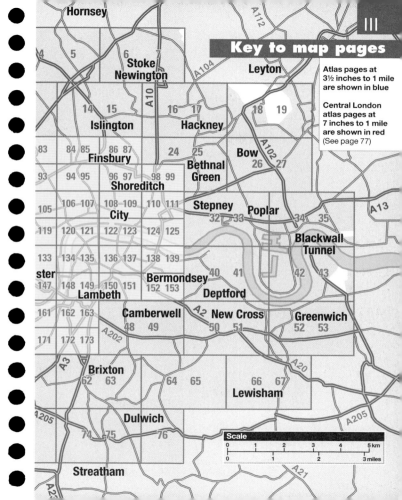

III

Key to map pages

Atlas pages at
3½ inches to 1 mile
are shown in blue

Central London
atlas pages at
7 inches to 1 mile
are shown in red
(See page 77)

Hornsey

A112

Stoke
Newington

A104

Leyton

4 5 6 7

14 15 16 17

18 19

Islington

A10

Hackney

A102

Bow

83 84 85 86 87 24 25 26 27

Finsbury

Bethnal
Green

93 94 95 96 97 98 99

Shoreditch

105 106 107 108 109 110 111

City

Stepney

Poplar

32 33 34 35

A13

119 120 121 122 123 124 125

Blackwall
Tunnel

133 134 135 136 137 138 139

40 41 42 43

ster

147 148 149 150 151 152 153

Bermondsey

Deptford

Lambeth

161 162 163

Camberwell

48 49

A2

New Cross

50 51

Greenwich

52 53

171 172 173

A202

A3

Brixton

62 63

64 65

66 67

A20

Lewisham

A205

Dulwich

74 75 76

A205

Scale					
0	1	2	3	4	5 km
0	1	2		3 miles	

Streatham

A21

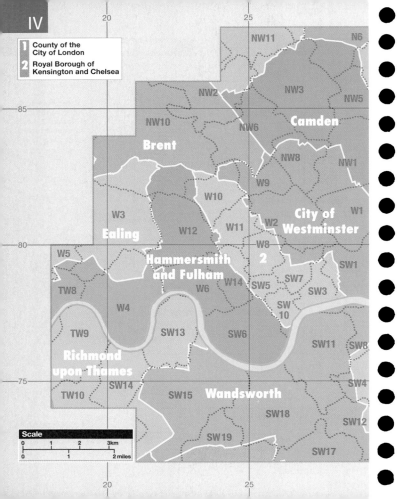

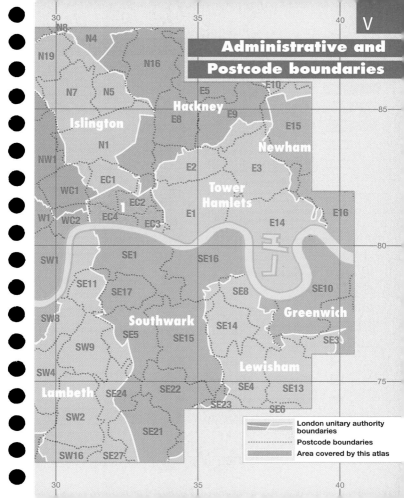

Administrative and Postcode boundaries

	London unitary authority boundaries
	Postcode boundaries
	Area covered by this atlas

Key to map symbols

(22a)	Motorway with junction number	Ambulance, police, fire station
	Primary route – single, dual carriageway	H ✚ Hospital, accident and emergency entrance
	A road – single, dual carriageway	Market, public amenity site
	B road – single, dual carriageway	ℹ PO Information centre, post office
	Through-route – single, dual carriageway	VILLA House Roman, non-Roman antiquity
	Minor road – single, dual carriageway	100 · House number, spot height 304 – in metres
	Road under construction	✚ Christian place of worship
	Rural track, private road or narrow road in urban area	☾★ ✡ Mosque, synagogue
	Path, bridleway, byway open to all traffic, road used as public path	◘ Other place of worship
	Tunnel, covered road	Houses, important buildings
	Gate or barrier, car pound	Woods, parkland/common
P P&R	Parking, park and ride	65 Adjoining page number
Three Legged Cross	Junction name	NW6 Postcode boundaries
	Pedestrianised area	City of Westminster Unitary authority boundaries
	Restricted access area	
⇌	Railway with station	Barking Creek Tidal water
⊖	London Underground station	River or canal – major, minor
D	Docklands Light Railway station	Stream
●	Bus or coach station	Water

Scale

3½ inches to 1 mile   1:18103

0	220yds	440yds	660yds	½ mile

0	250m	500m	750m	1km

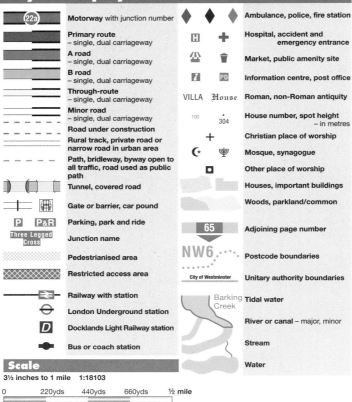

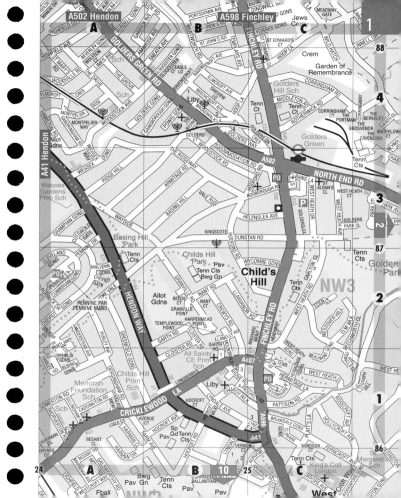

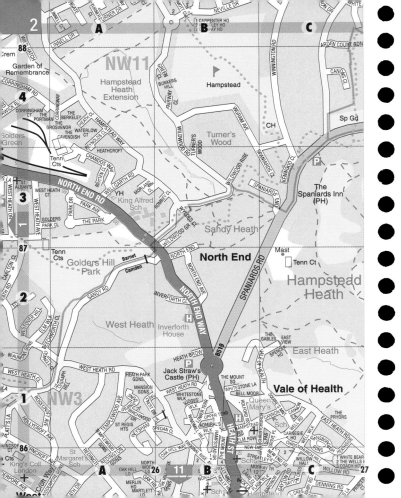

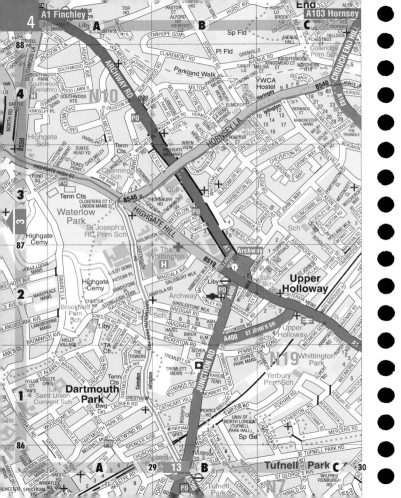

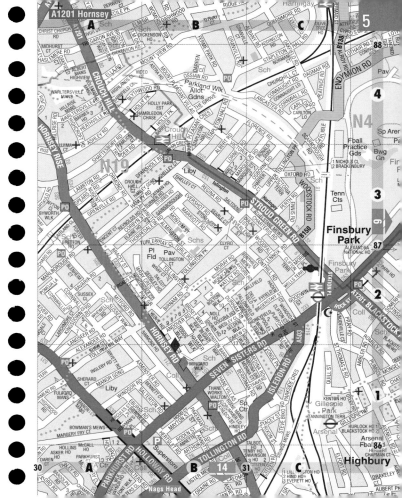

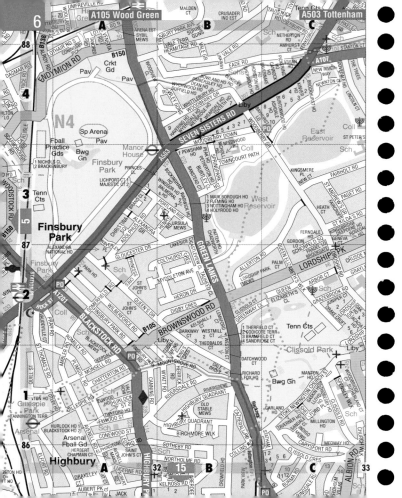

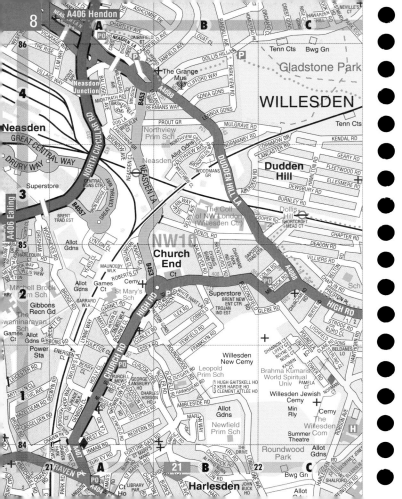

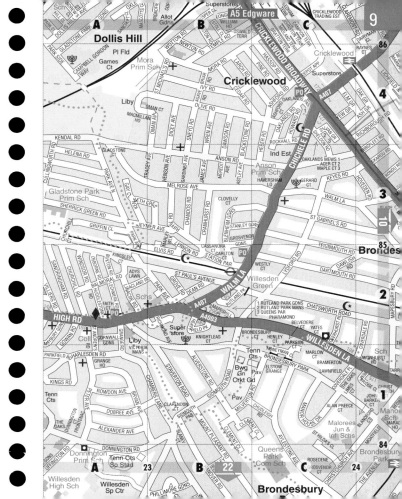

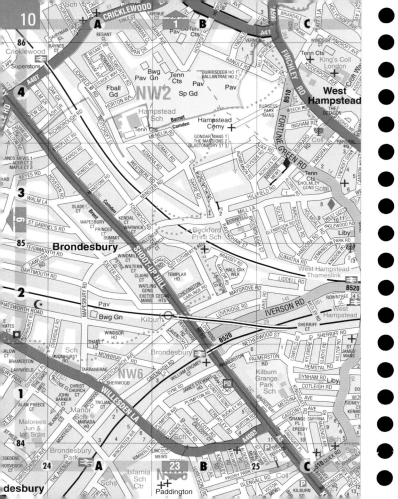

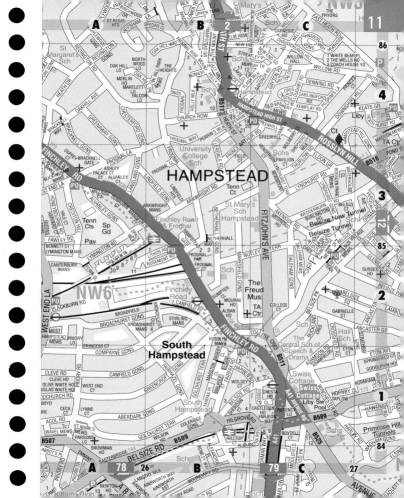

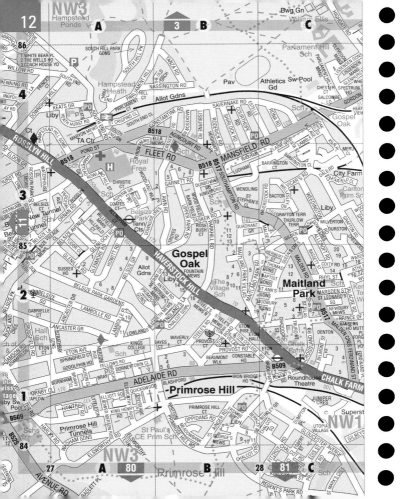

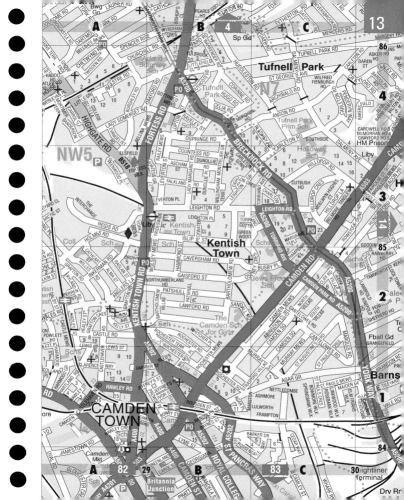

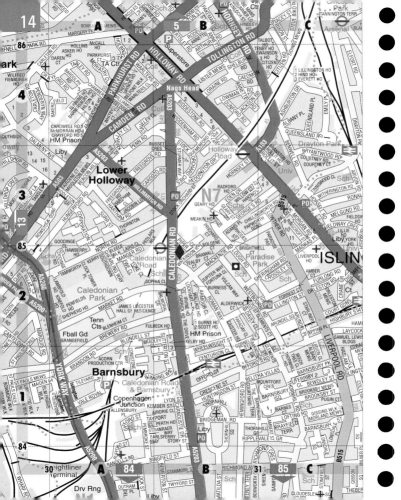

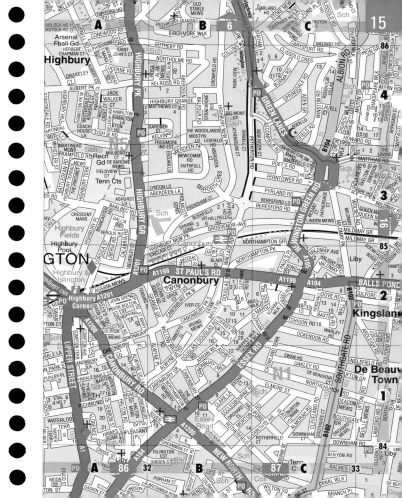

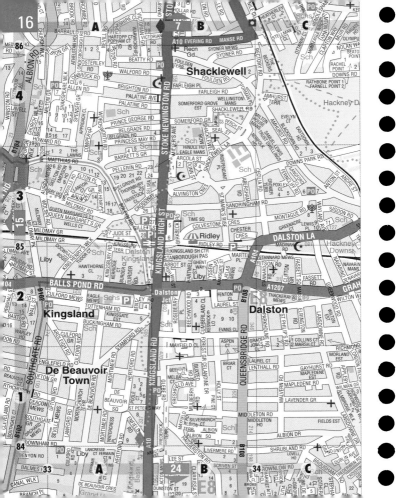

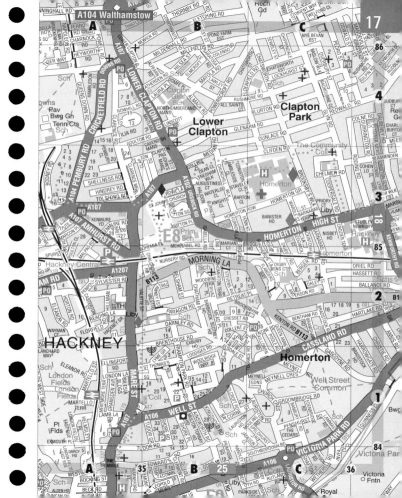

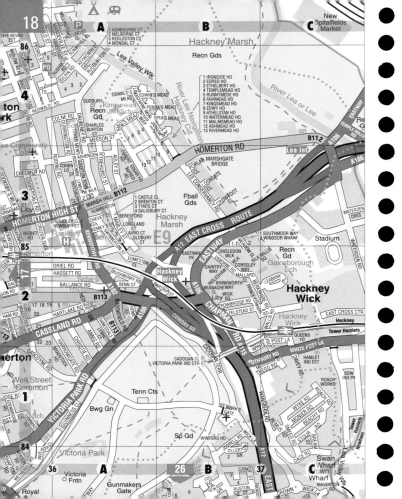

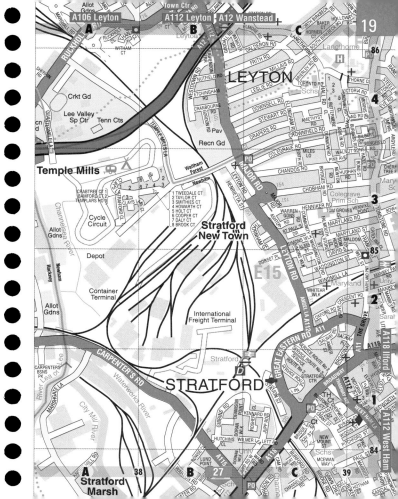

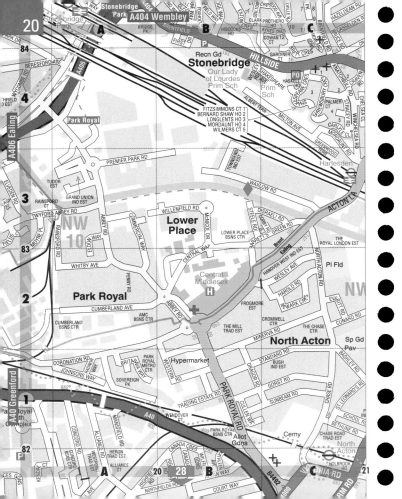

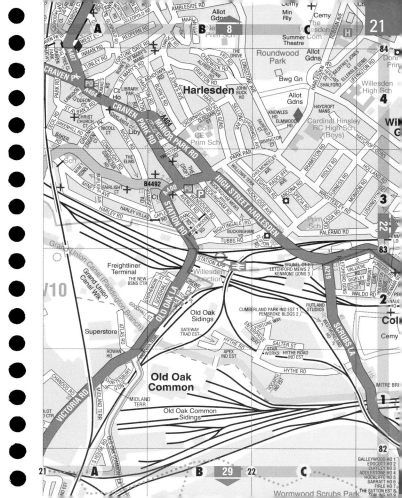

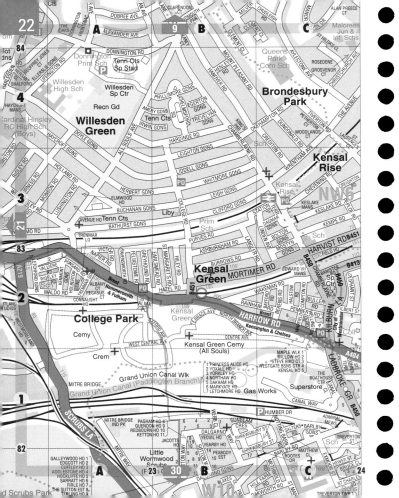

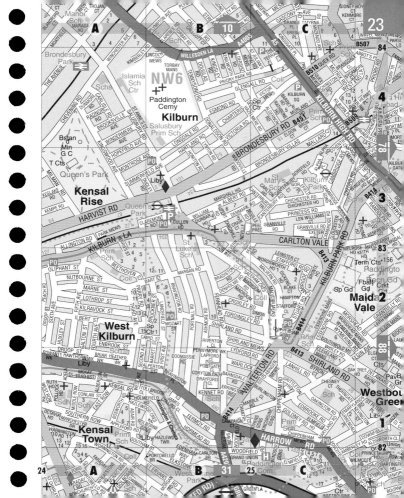

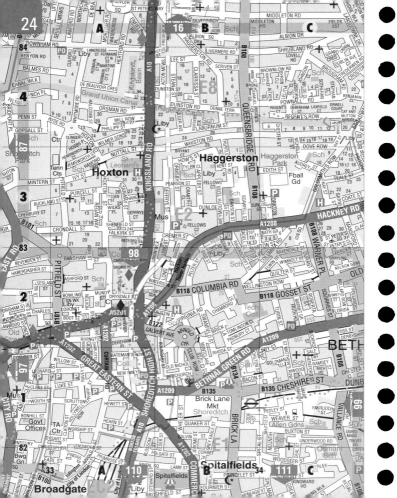

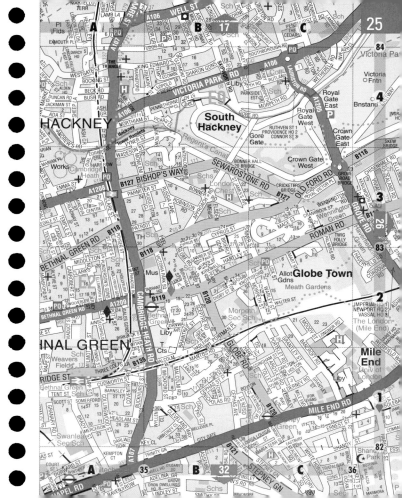

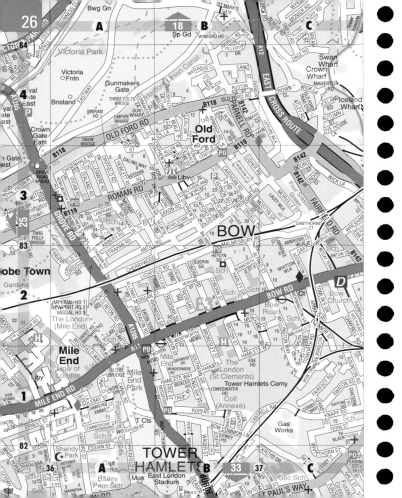

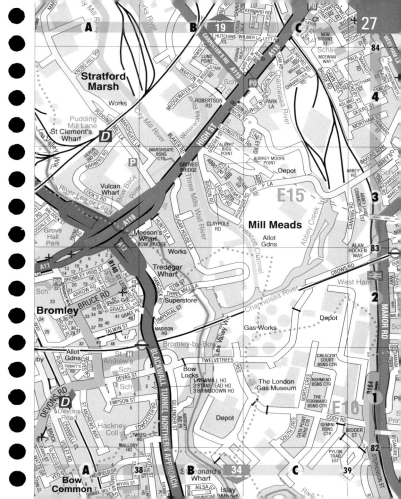

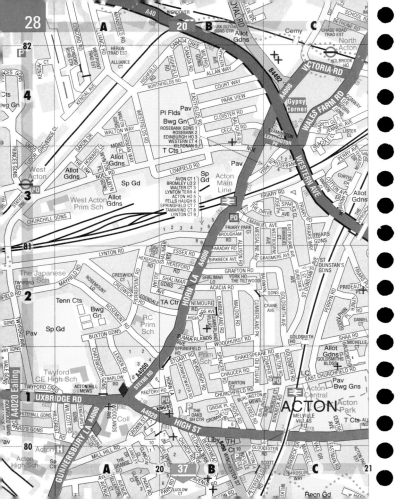

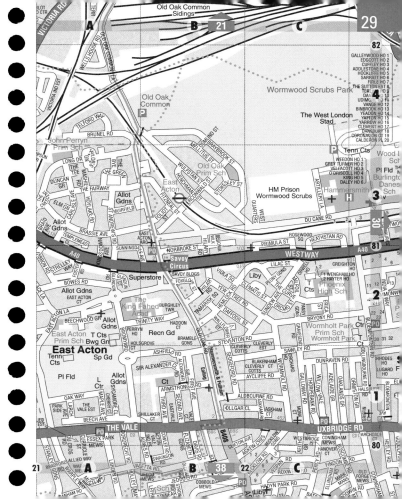

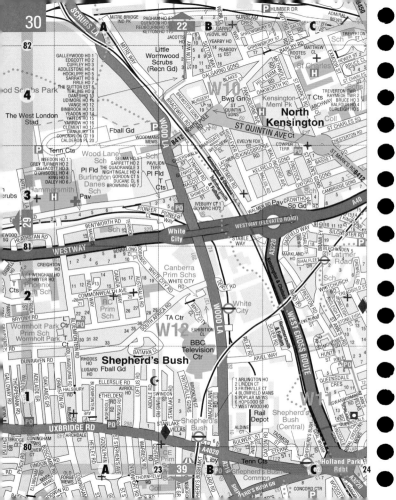

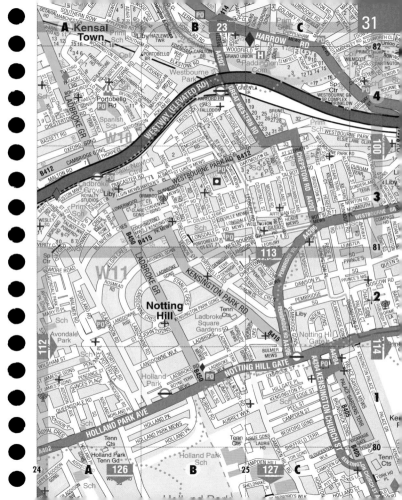

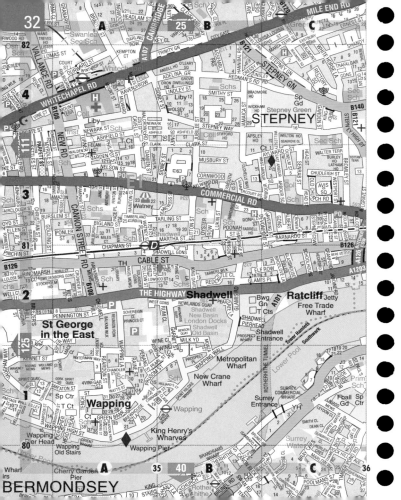

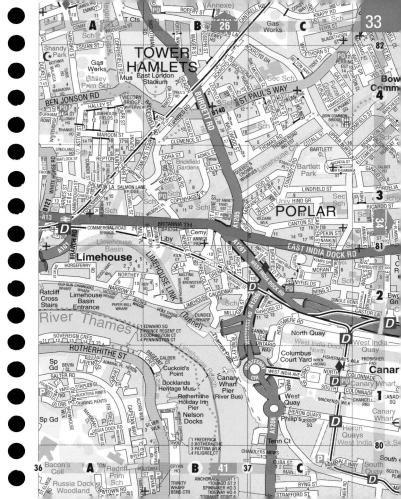

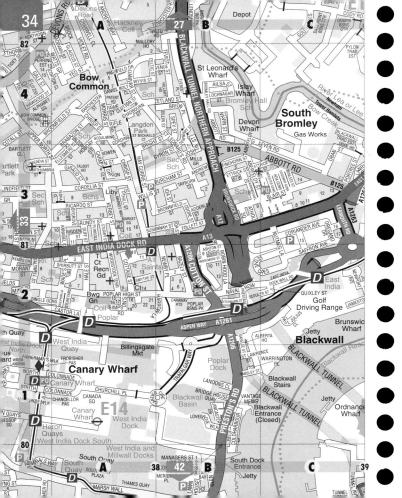

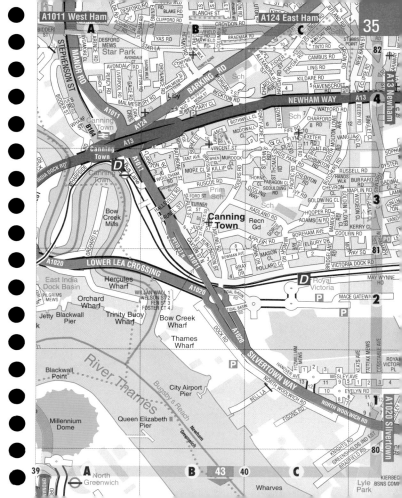

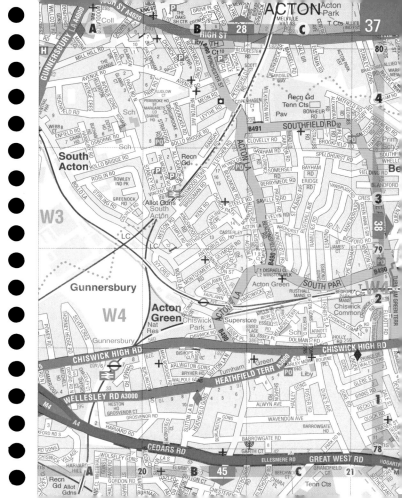

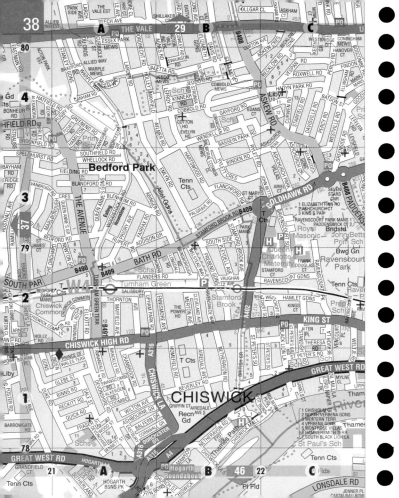

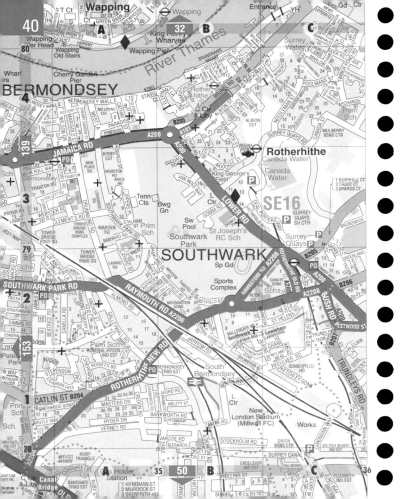

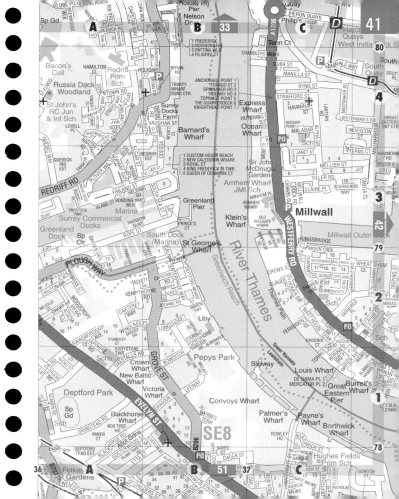

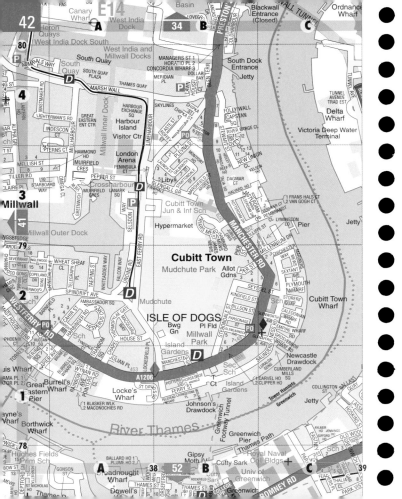

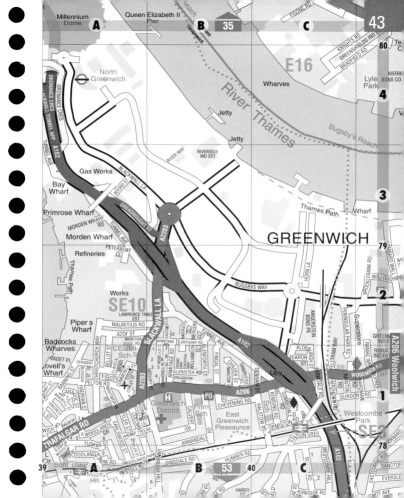

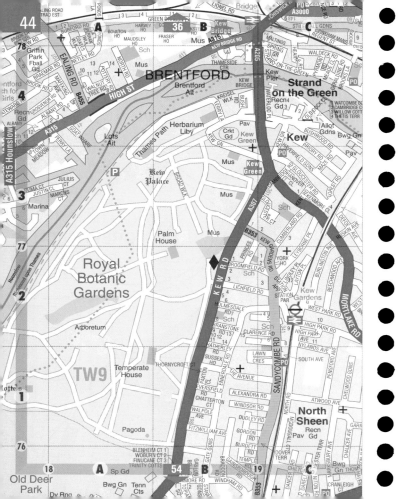

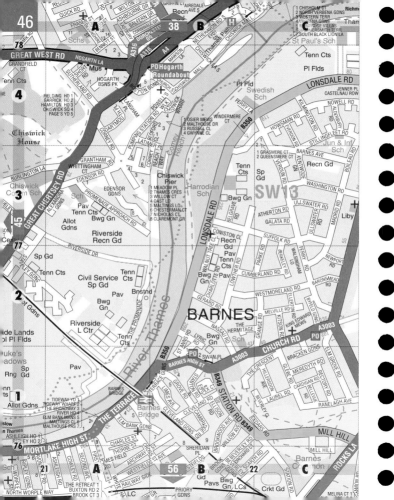

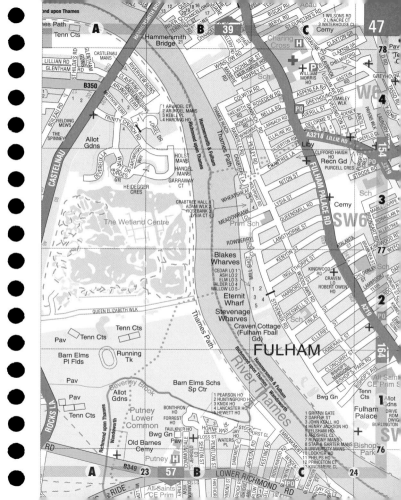

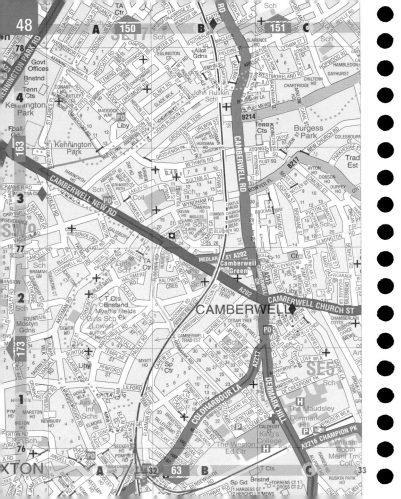

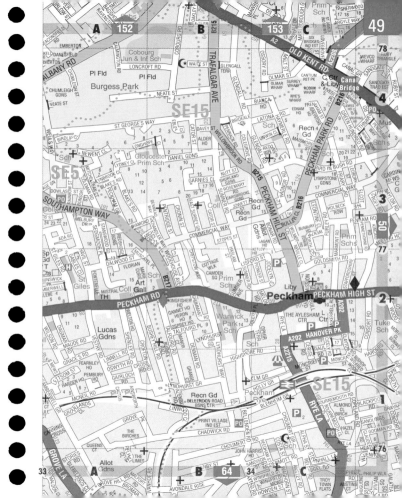

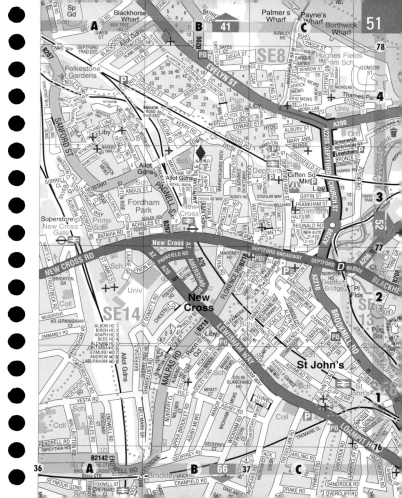

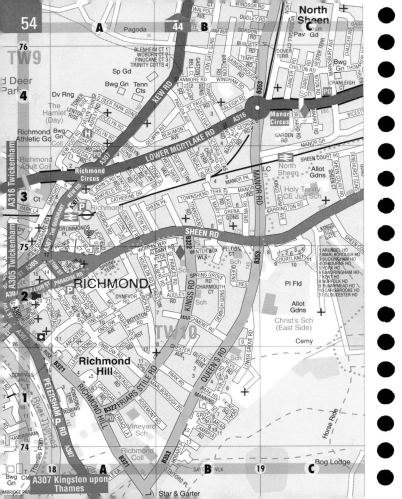

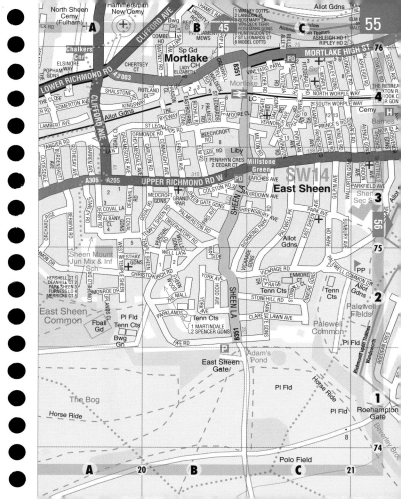

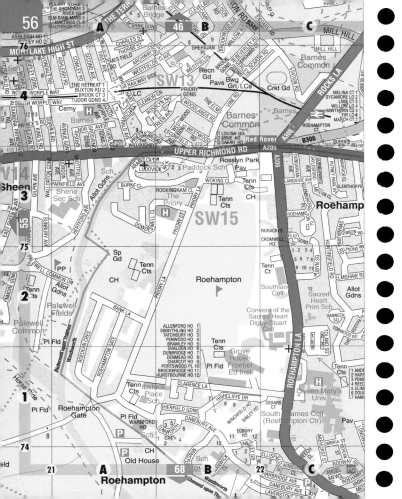

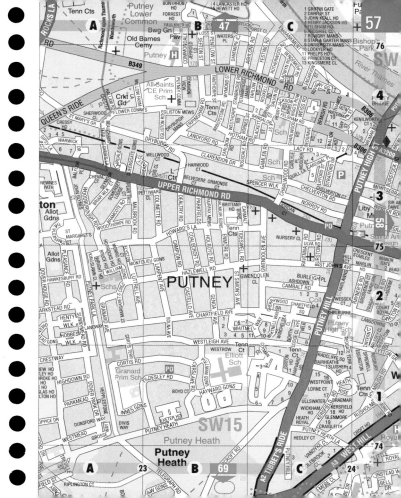

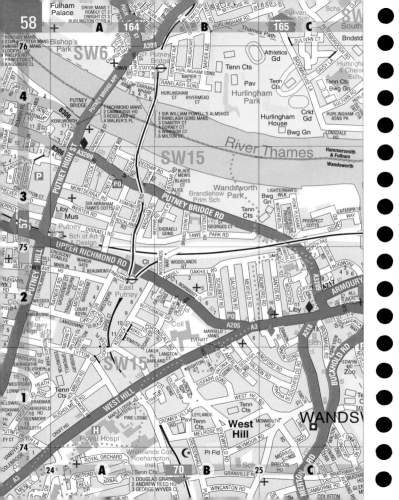

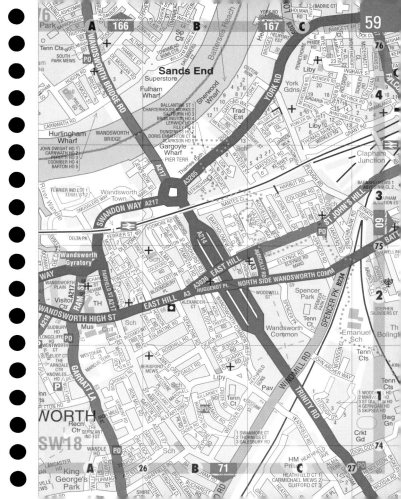

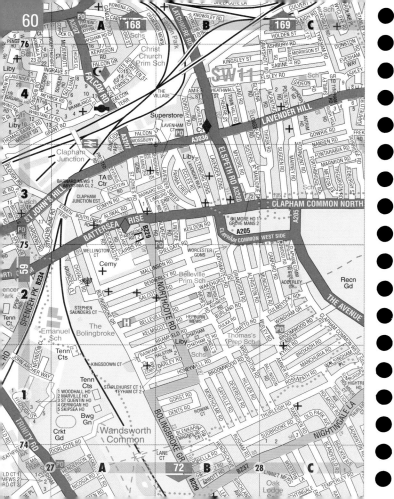

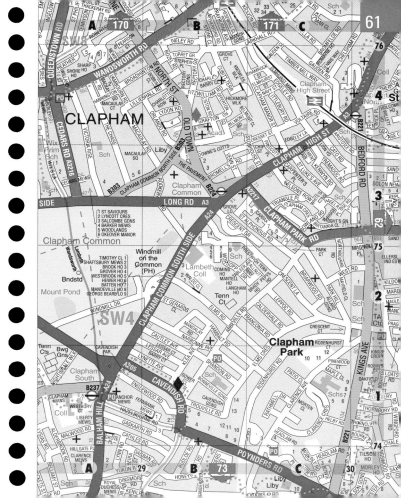

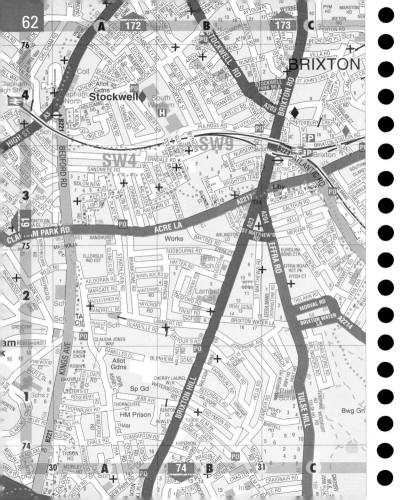

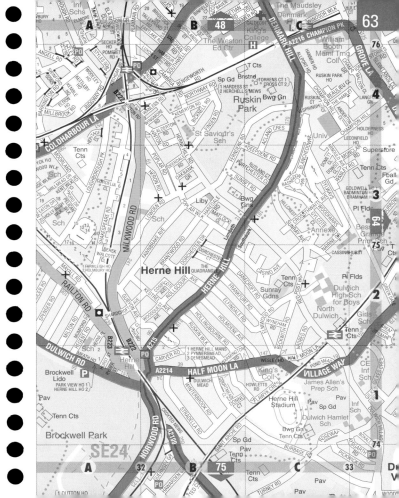

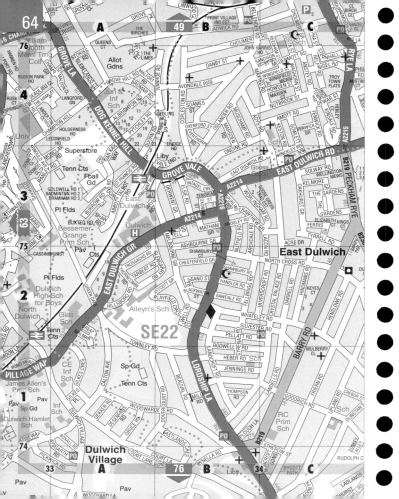

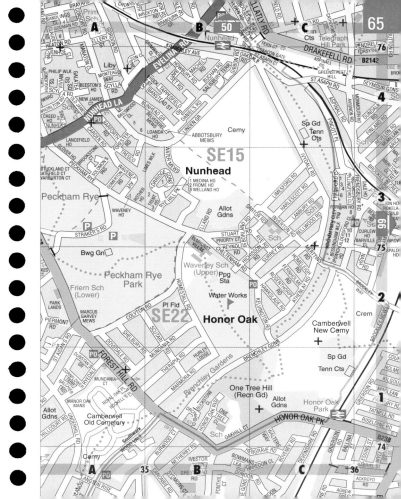

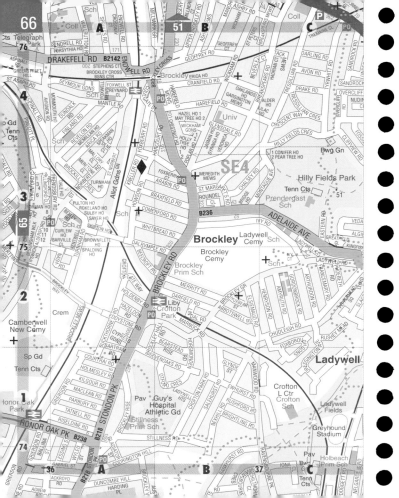

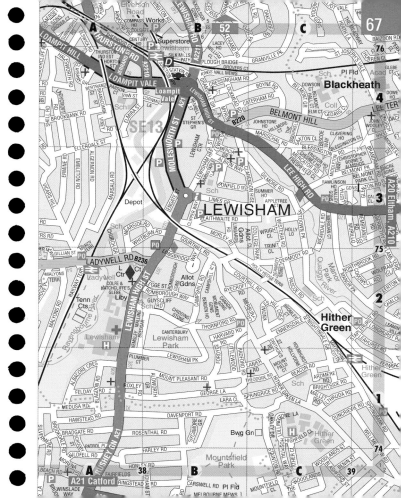

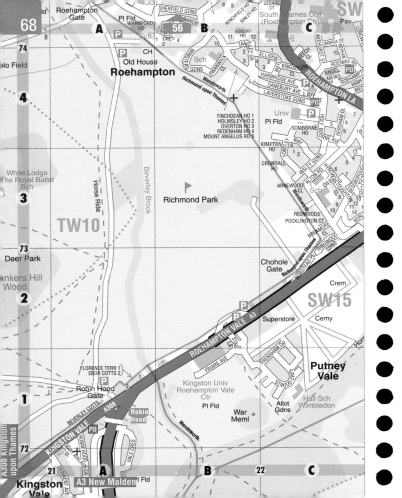

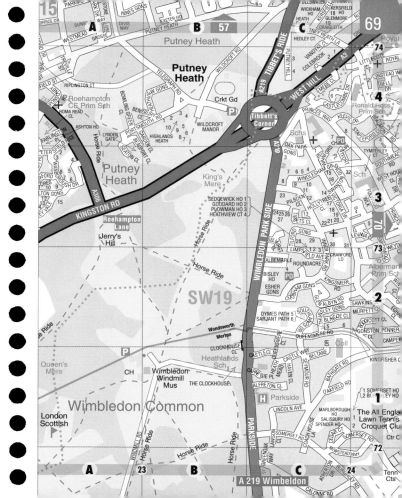

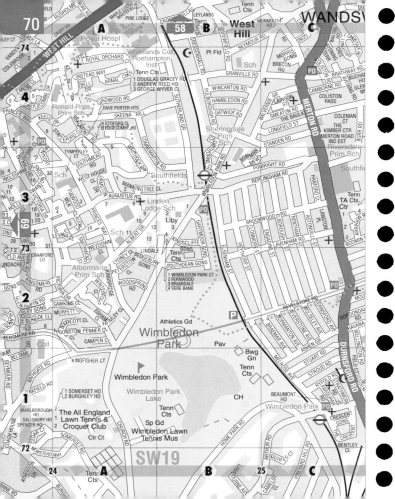

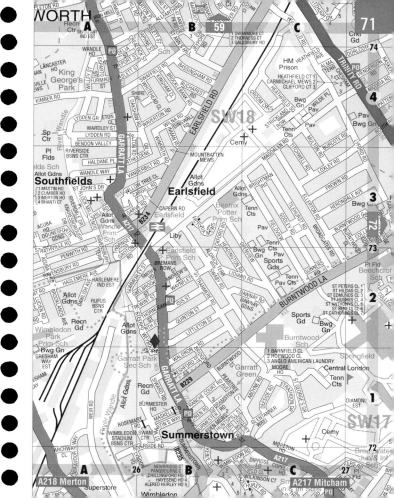

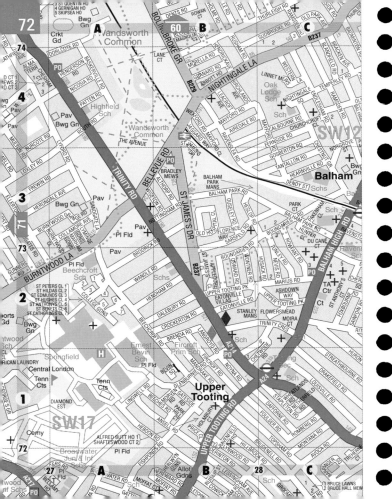

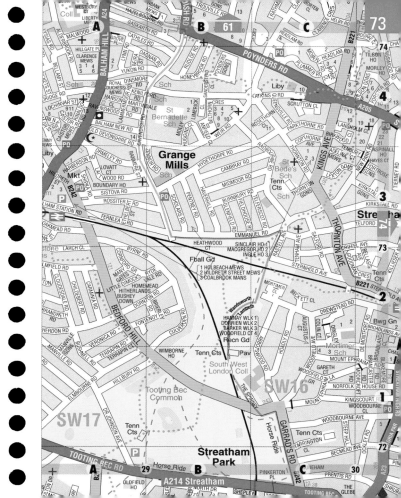

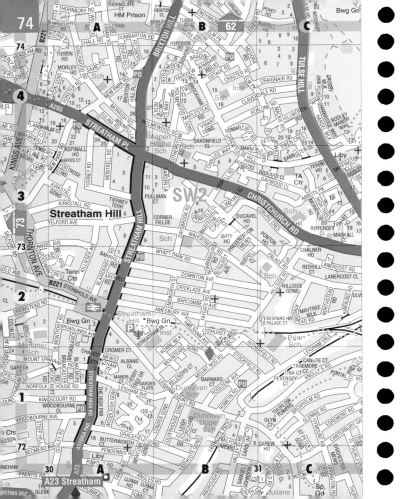

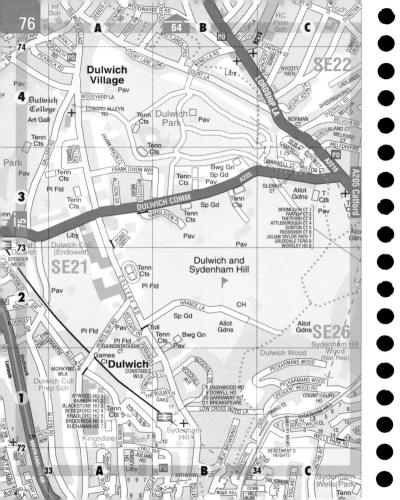

Key to enlarged map pages

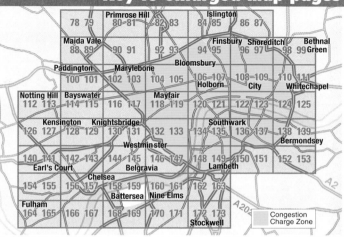

78 79	Primrose Hill 80 81	82 83	Islington 84 85	86 87	
Maida Vale 88 89	90 91	92 93	Finsbury 94 95	Shoreditch 96 97	Bethnal 98 99 Green
Paddington 100 101	Marylebone 102 103	Bloomsbury 104 105	106 107 Holborn	108 109 City	110 111 Whitechapel
Notting Hill 112 113	Bayswater 114 115	116 117	Mayfair 118 119	120 121	122 123	124 125
Kensington 126 127	Knightsbridge 128 129	130 131	132 133	Southwark 134 135	136 137	138 139 Bermondsey
140 141 Earl's Court	142 143	Westminster 144 145	146 147	148 149 Lambeth	150 151	152 153
154 155 Fulham	Chelsea 156 157	Belgravia 158 159	160 161 Battersea Nine Elms	162 163	
164 165	166 167	168 169	170 171	172 173 Stockwell	

Congestion Charge Zone

Additional symbols on enlarged maps

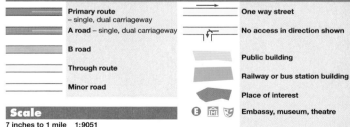

Primary route – single, dual carriageway

A road – single, dual carriageway

B road

Through route

Minor road

One way street

No access in direction shown

Public building

Railway or bus station building

Place of interest

Embassy, museum, theatre

All other symbols may be found on page VI

Scale

7 inches to 1 mile   1:9051

0   110yds   220yds   330yds   **440 yards**

0   125m   250m   325m   **500 metres**

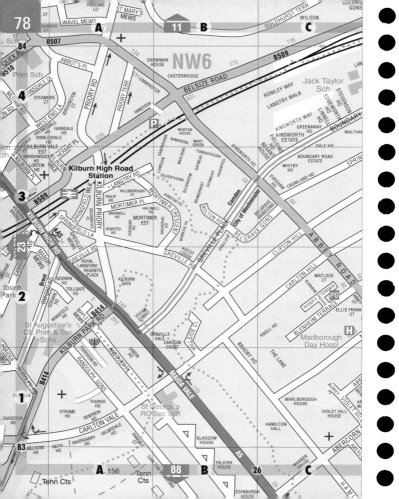

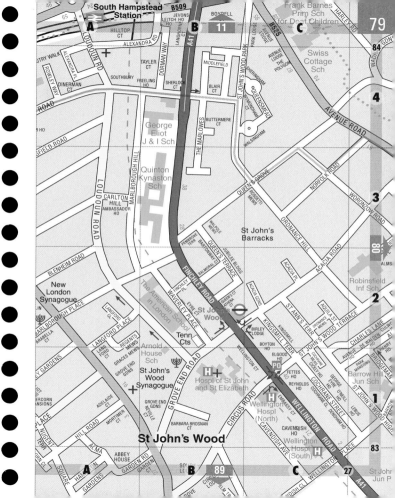

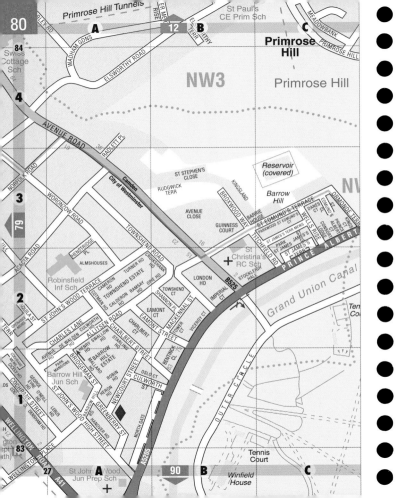

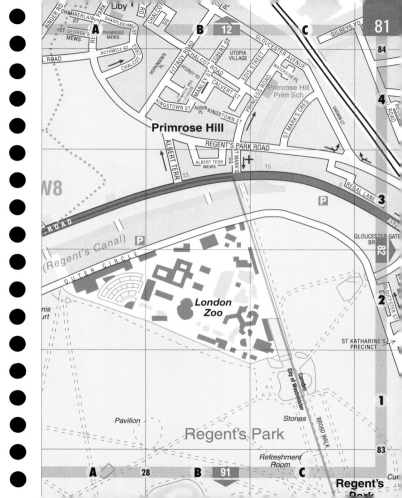

AINGER RD
CHAMBERLAIN ST
SHARPLES HAL
ST GEORGE'S MEWS
A
RE PARK
PRIMROSE MEWS
Liby
CHALCO
SQ
B
12
C
GILBEYS YD
84

ROTHWELL ST
L ROAD
HOPKINSON'S PL
FITZROY RD
CHALCOT RD
EGBERT ST
MANLEY ST
CHALCOT CRES
CALVERT ST
UTOPIA VILLAGE
EDIS STREET
WATERSIDE PL
GLOUCESTER AVENUE
Primrose Hill
Prim Sch
ST MARK'S CRES
DARWIN CT

KINGSTOWN ST
AUDEN PL
KINGSTOWN ST
PRINCESS ROAD
4
RO

Primrose Hill

REGENT'S PARK ROAD
ST MARK'S SQ

ALBERT TERR
ALBERT TERR MEWS
23
15
REGAL LANE
A520
3

W8

(Regent's Canal)
ROAD
P
P
OUTER CIRCLE
GLOUCESTER GATE
BR
82
GLOUCESTER GT

nis
urt

London Zoo

ST KATHARINE'S PRECINCT
2

Camden
City of Westminster

1

Pavilion

Stones

BROAD WALK

83

Regent's Park

Refreshment Room

A
28
B
91
C

Regent's
Park

Cur

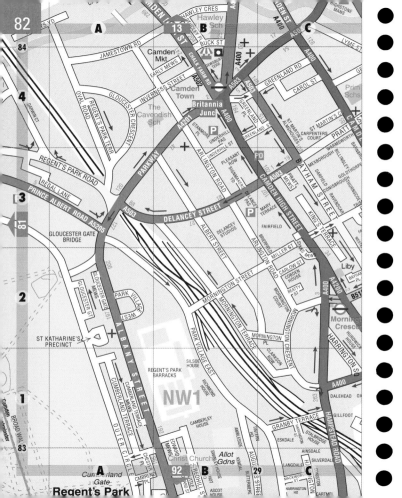

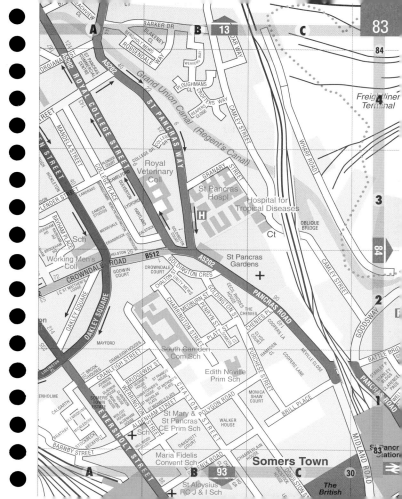

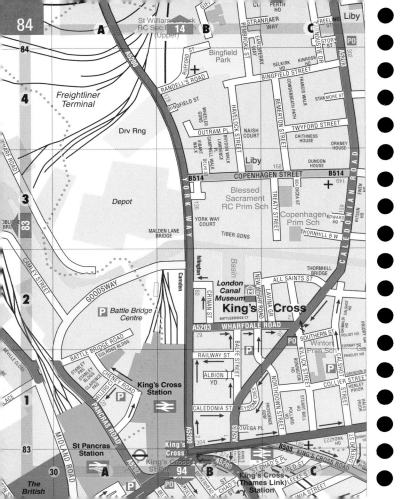

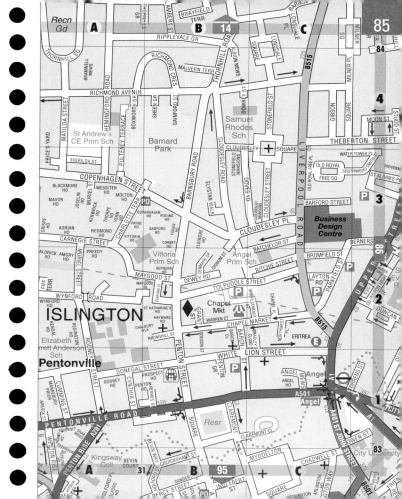

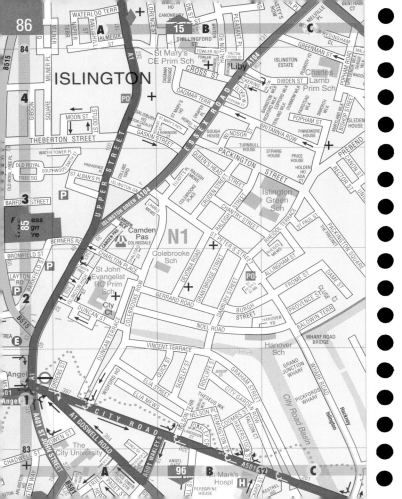

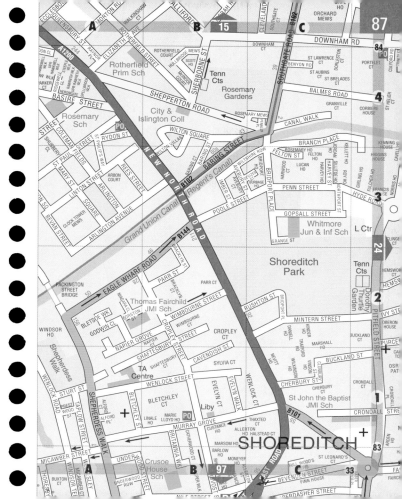

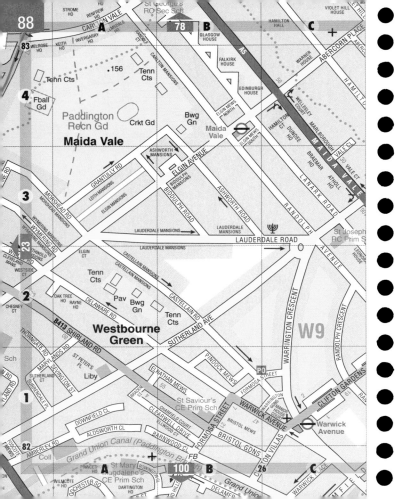

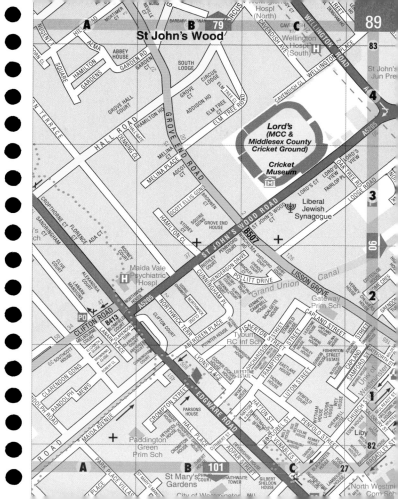

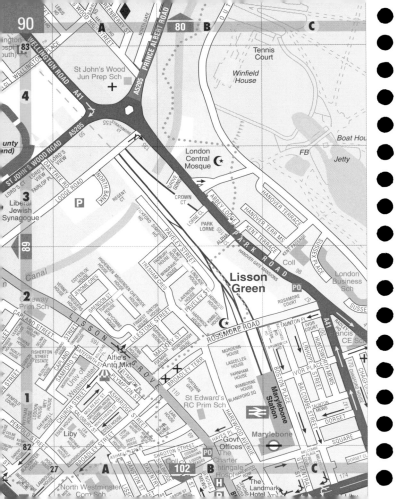

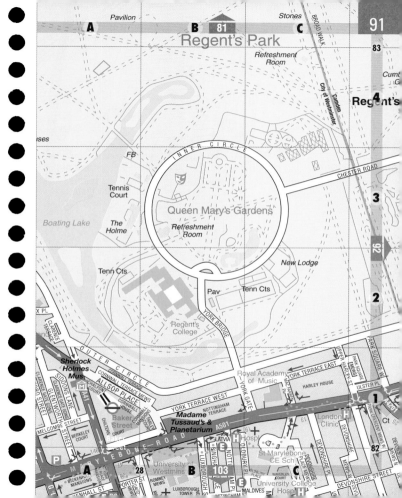

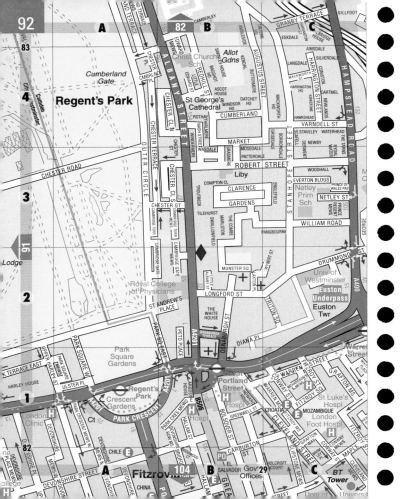

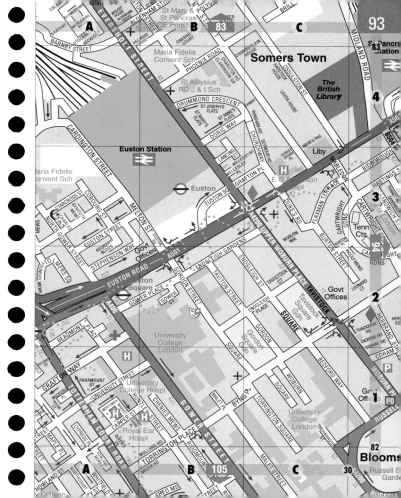

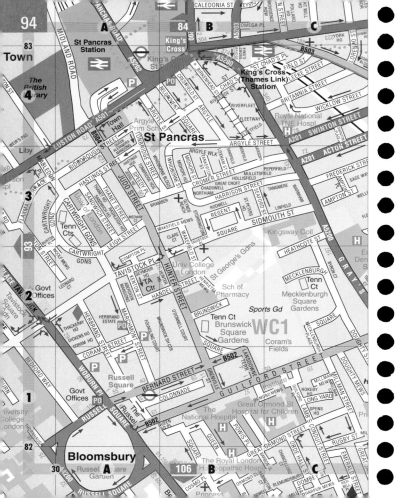

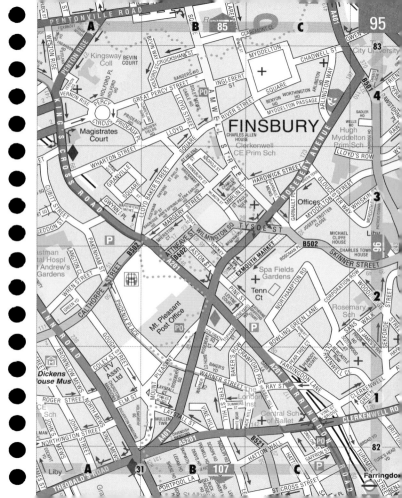

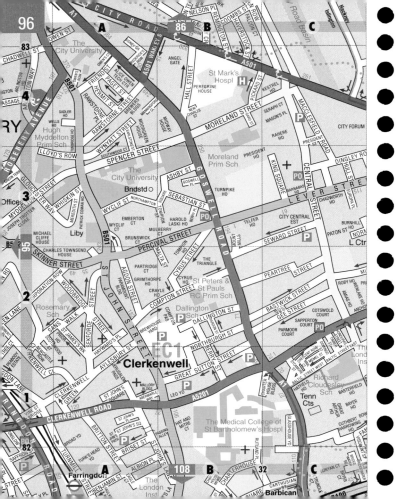

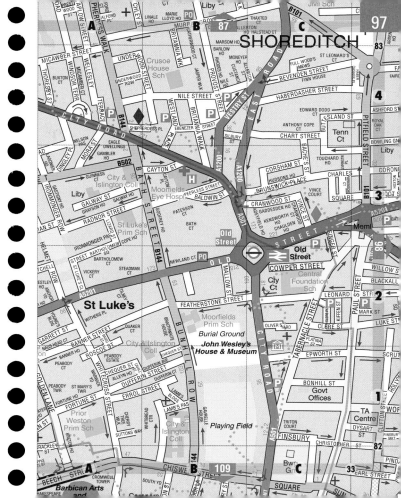

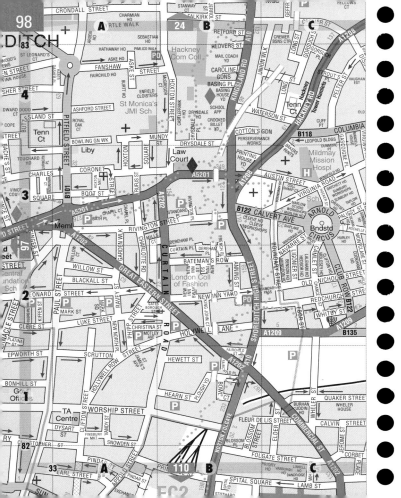

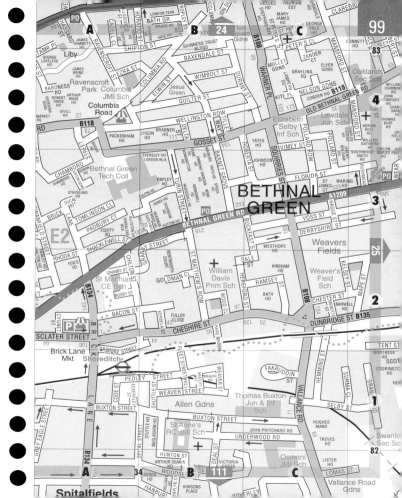

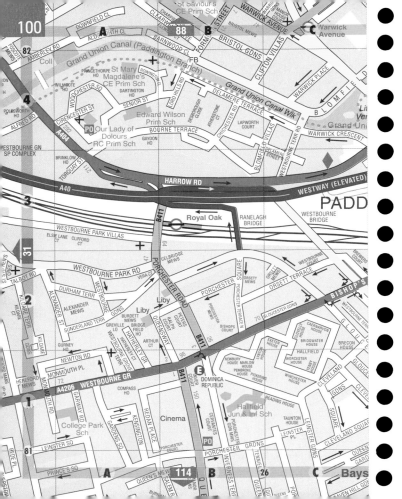

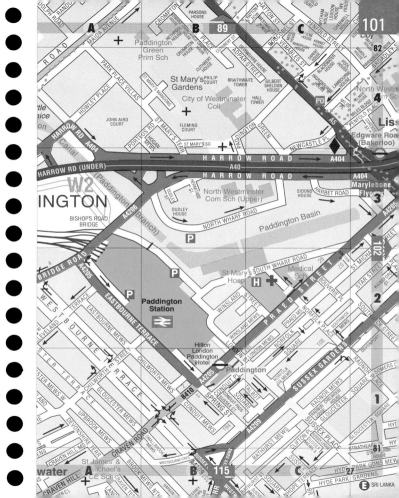

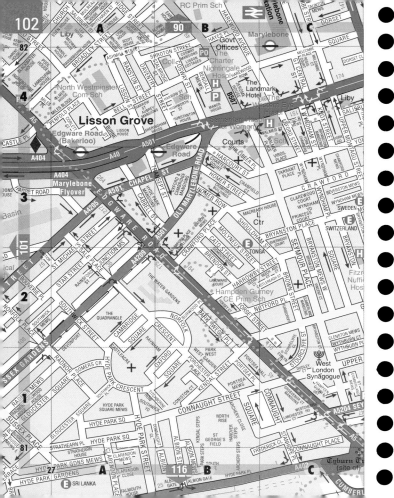

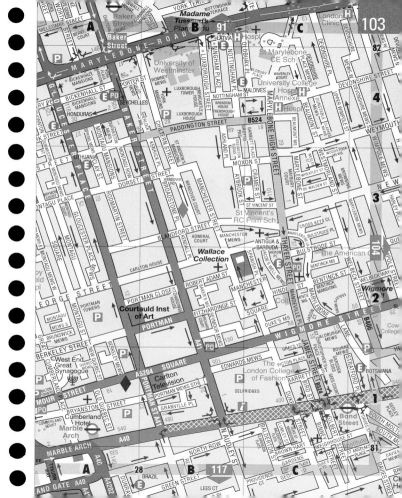

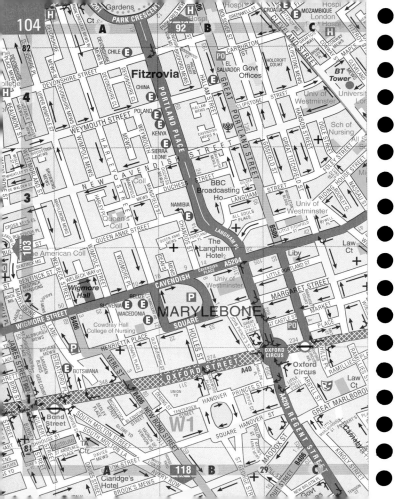

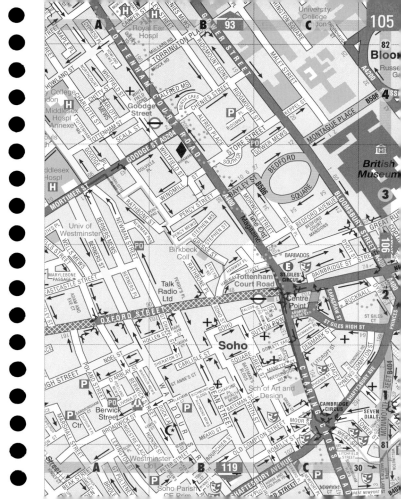

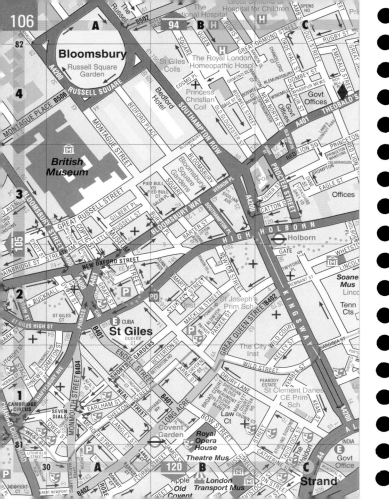

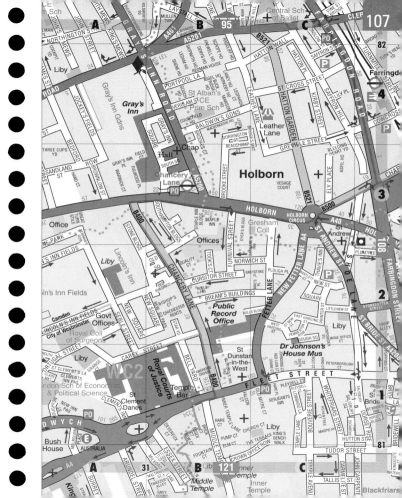

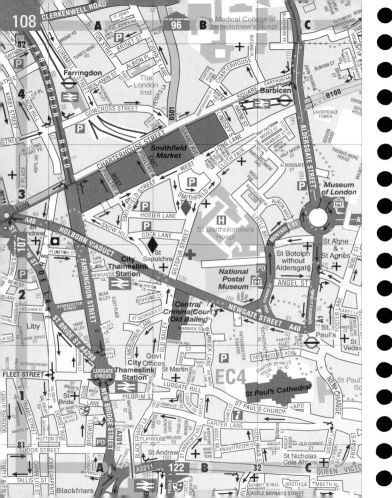

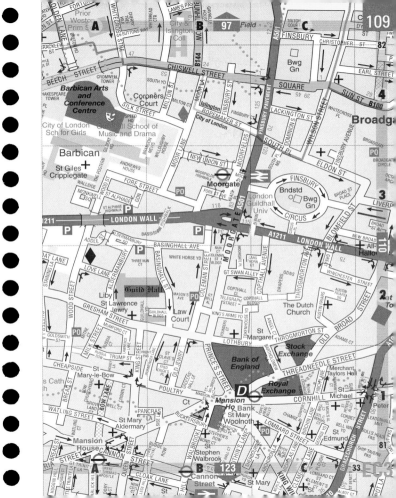

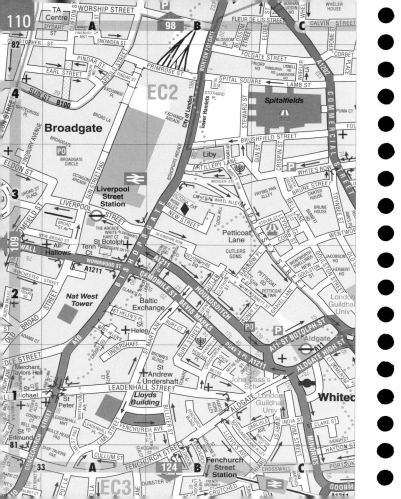

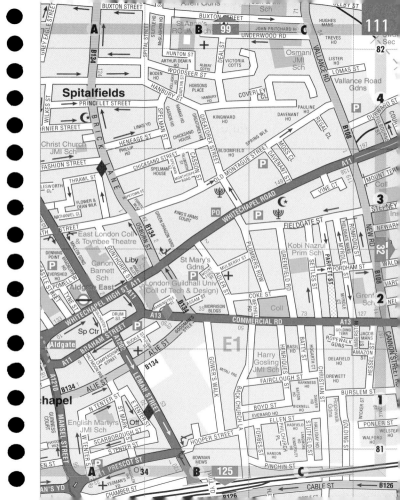

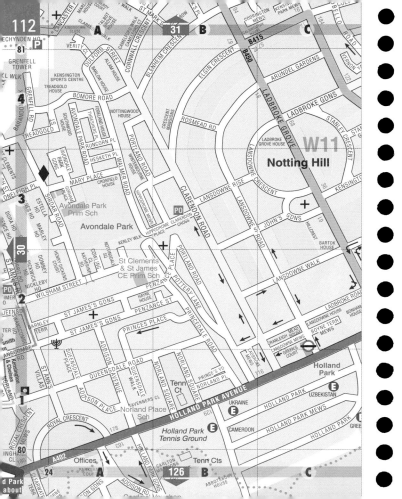

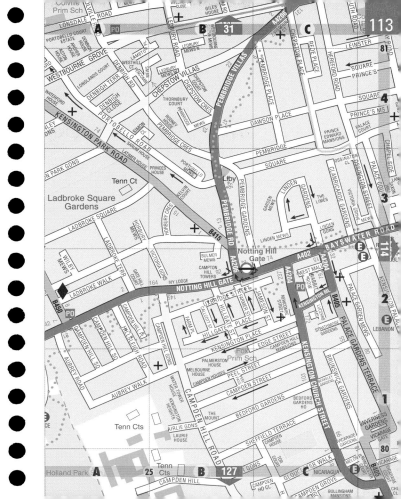

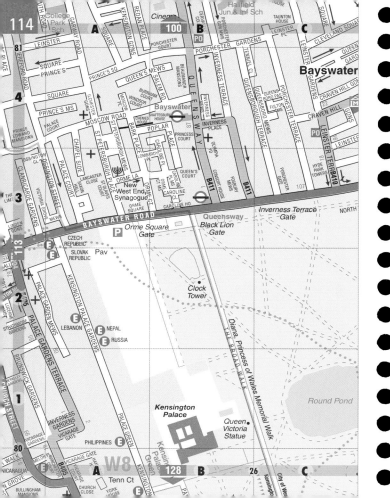

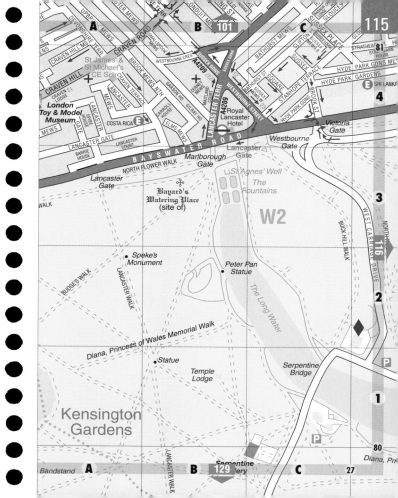

A · B · **101** · C

UPPER · TER MEWS · CONDUIT ME · ING ST · GLOUCES

DEVONSHIRE TERR · CRAVEN ROAD · SMALLBROOK · A4209

CRAVEN HILL GDNS · CRAVEN HILL · St James' & St Michael's CE Sch · BROOK MEWS NTH · CRAVEN TERRACE · WESTBOURNE CRES · SUSSEX GDNS · BATHURST MEWS · CLIFTON PLACE · SUSSEX PLACE · STRATHEA · 81 · STRA STARN HOUSE

CRAVEN HILL · London Toy & Model Museum · MEWS · CRAVEN HILL LODGE · SPIRE HOUSE · LANCASTER TERRACE · LANCASTER MEWS · CARROLL HOUSE · GILBEY RD · GLANSON HO · MAITLAND HO · SUSSEX SQUARE · BATHURST ST · STANHOPE TERRACE · HYDE PARK GDNS ME · HYDE PARK GARDENS · SRI LANKA/ · **E**

COSTA RICA · **E** · LANCASTER TERR · ELMS MEWS · A4209 · Royal Lancaster Hotel · HYDE PARK GDNS · BROOK ST · **4**

BARRIE HOUSE · LANCASTER COURT · Lancaster Gate · Victoria Gate

BAYSWATER ROAD · Marlborough Gate · Lancaster Gate · Westbourne Gate

NORTH FLOWER WALK · Lancaster Gate · St Agnes' Well · The Fountains

Bayard's Watering Place (site of) · **W2** · **116** · WEST CARRIAGE DRIVE · NORTH

Speke's Monument · Peter Pan Statue · **3**

BUDGE'S WALK · LANCASTER WALK · The Long Water · BUCK HILL WALK · **2**

Diana, Princess of Wales Memorial Walk · Statue · Temple Lodge · Serpentine Bridge · P · **1**

Kensington Gardens · LANCASTER WALK · P · **80** · Diana, Pri

Bandstand · **A** · **B** · **129** · Serpentine ery · **C** · **27**

101 · 116 · 129 · 80 · 27

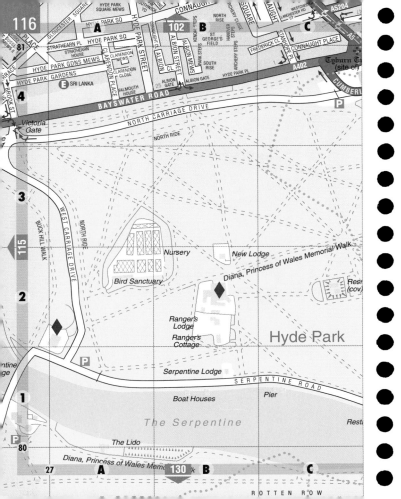

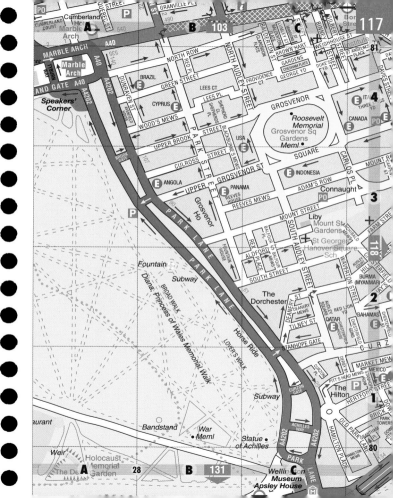

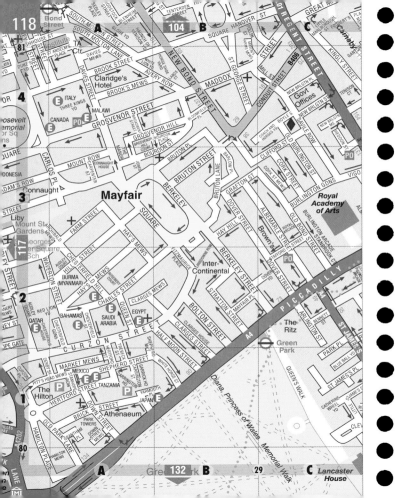

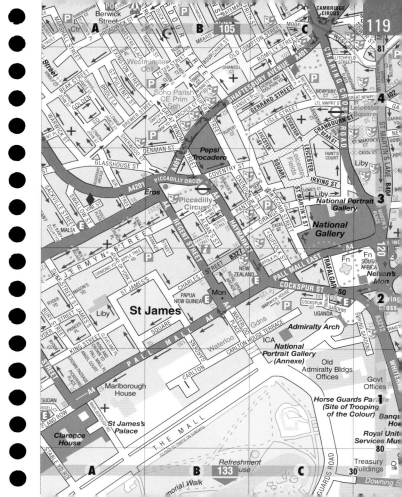

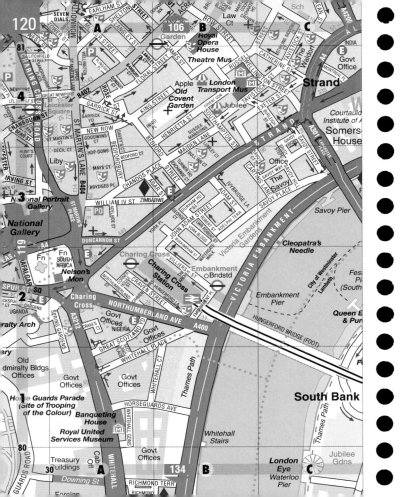

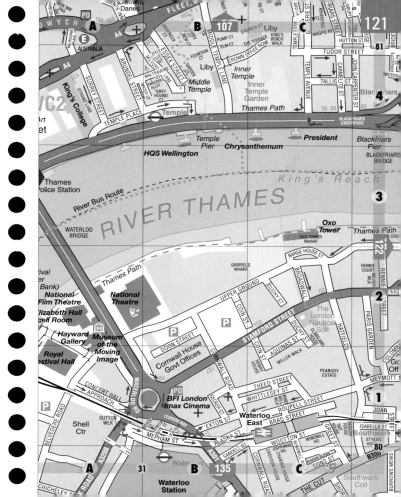

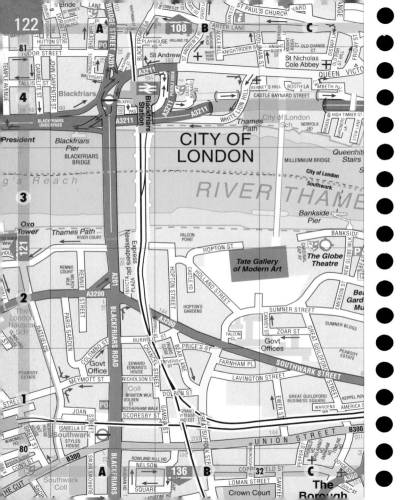

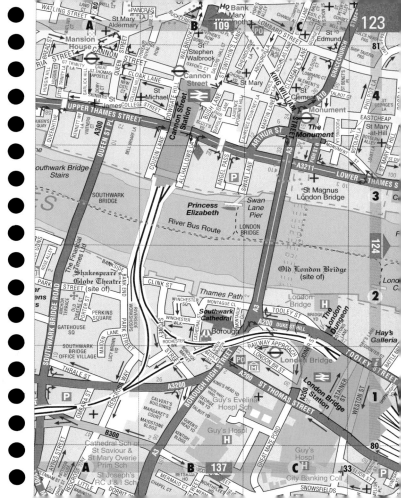

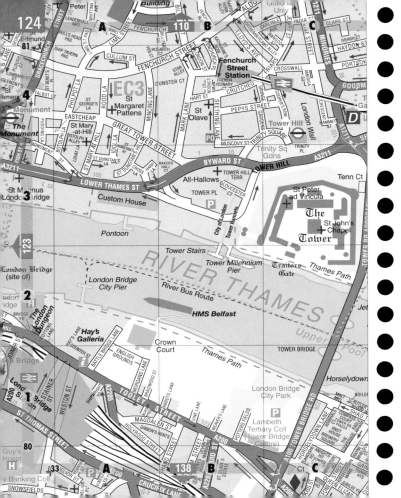

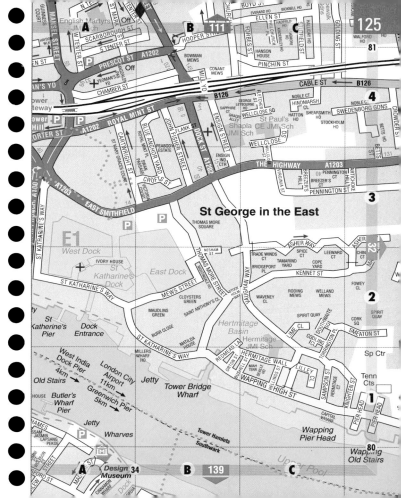

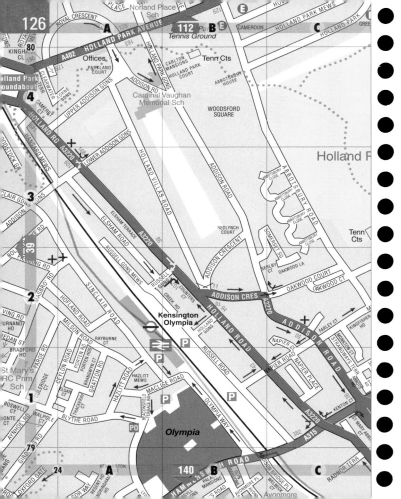

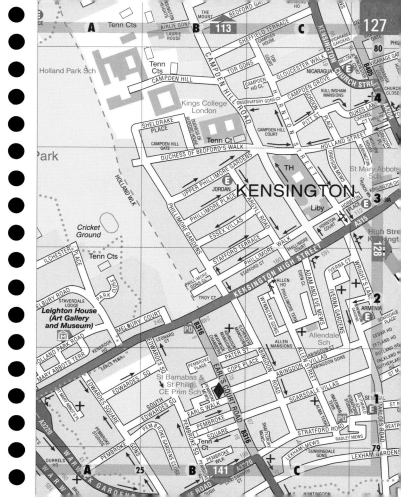

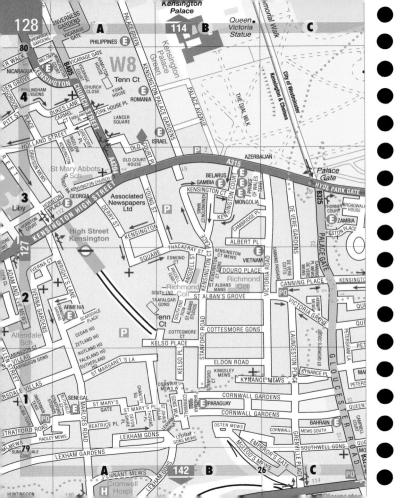

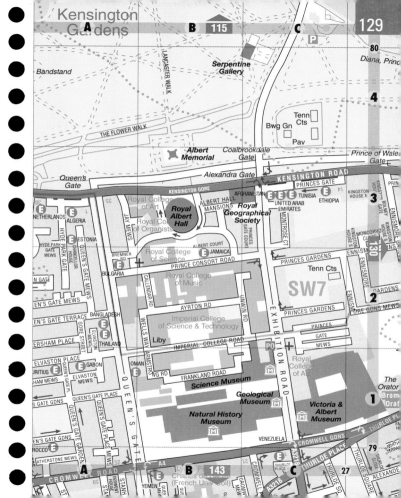

P

80

Diana, Princ

Bandstand

Serpentine Gallery

4

LANCASTER WALK

THE FLOWER WALK

Tenn Cts

Bwg Gn

Pav

Albert Memorial

Coalbrookdale Gate

Prince of Wale Gate

Queen's Gate

Alexandra Gate

KENSINGTON ROAD

KENSINGTON GORE

PRINCES GATE

Royal College of Art

ALBERT HALL MANSIONS

Royal Albert Hall

AFGHANISTAN

E E E

TUNISIA

E

KINGSTON HOUSE N

PRIN

3

NETHERLANDS

E ALGERIA

JAY MEWS

Royal College of Organists

Royal Geographical Society

UNITED ARAB EMIRATES

ETHIOPIA

PRINCES GATE COURT

MONTROSE CT.

KINGSTON HOUSE S

KINGSTON HOUSE MIDDLE

MONCORVO CLOSE

KINGSTON GATE

HYDE PARK GATE MEWS

CHANCERY

E ESTONIA

BREMNER

Royal College of Science

ALBERT COURT

E JAMAICA

ENNISMORE

2

N GATE

QUEEN'S GATE MEWS

BULGARIA

PRINCE CONSORT ROAD

PRINCES GARDENS

Tenn Cts

SW7

ENNISMORE GARDENS

EEN'S GATE MEWS

CALLENDAR RD

Royal College of Music

WELLS WAY

UNWIN RD

PRINCES GARDENS

ENNISMORE GDNS MEWS

EN'S GATE TERRACE

BANGLADESH

E E

THAILAND

ELVASTON MEWS

AYRTON RD

Imperial College of Science & Technology

Liby

EXHIBITION ROAD

ARMSTRO

PRINCES GATE MEWS

ERSHAM PLACE

IMPERIAL COLLEGE ROAD

PO

ELVASTON PLACE

E GABON

OMAN

E

NG RD

FRANKLAND ROAD

Royal College of Ar

1

URITIUS

E

QUEEN'S GATE

ELVASTON MEWS

Science Museum

The Orator Brom Orat

HAM MEWS

Geological Museum

S GATE GDNS

QUEEN'S GATE PLACE MEWS

Natural History Museum

Victoria & Albert Museum

THURLOE PL

EN'S GATE GDNS

ROCCO

E

ATHERSTONE MEWS

VENEZUELA

CROMWELL GDNS

79

NORTH TERRAC

THURLOE PLACE

THURLOE CLOSE

ALEXANDE

YEMEN

E

Charles d (French Univ Coll)

THURLOE SQUARE

130

129

115

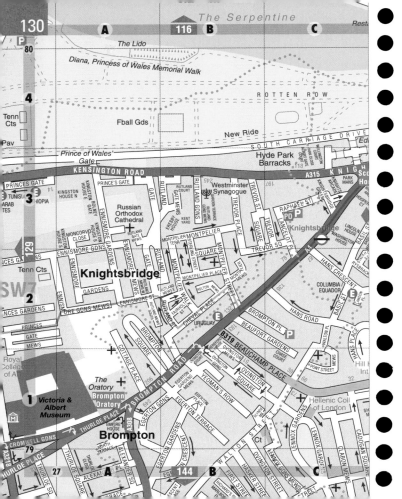

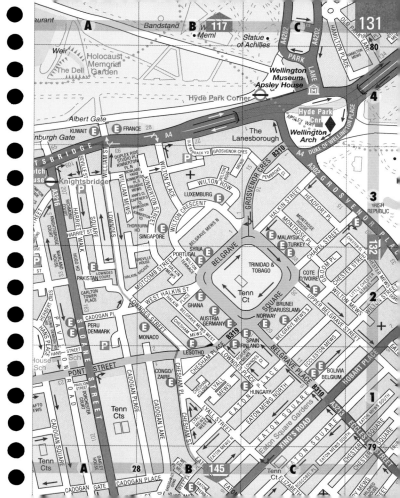

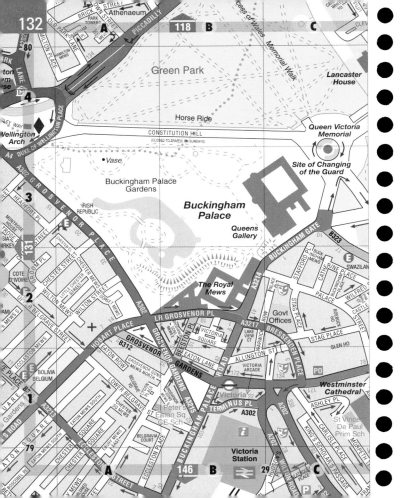

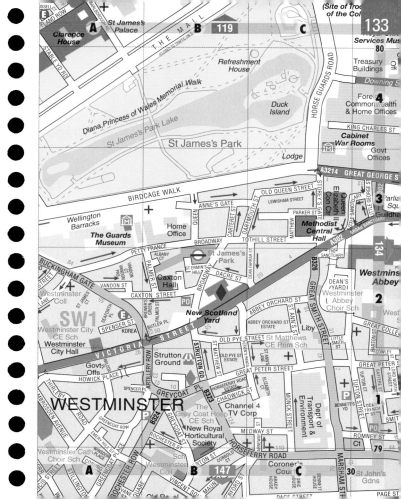

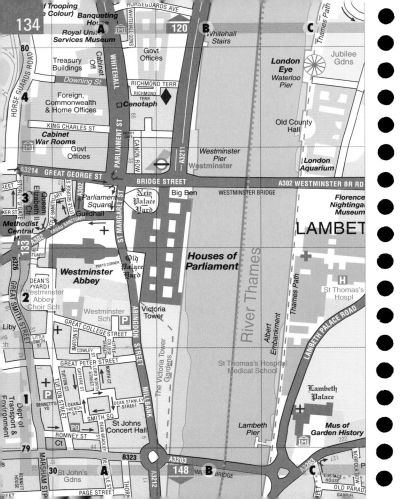

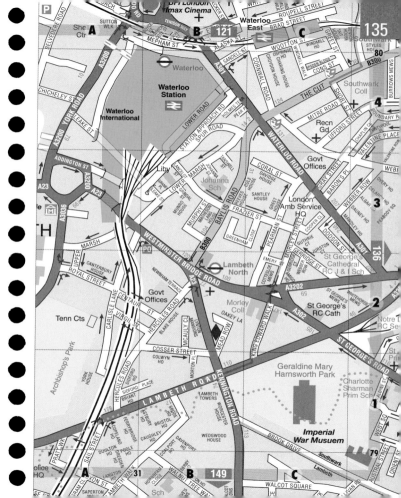

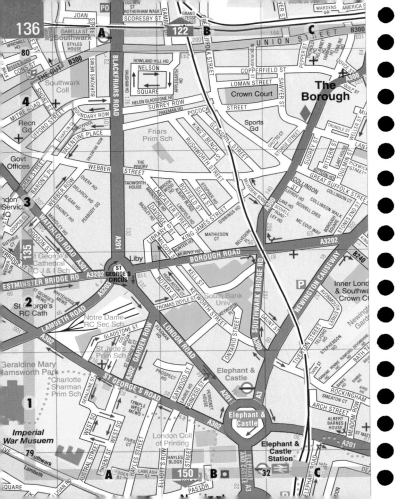

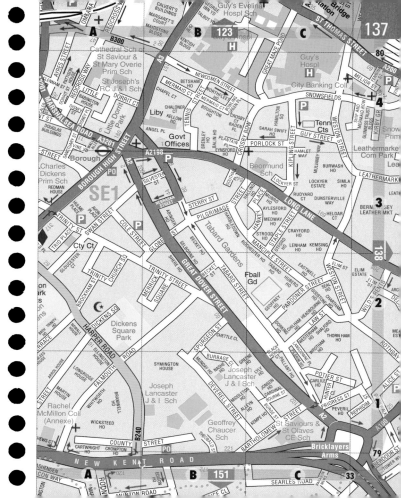

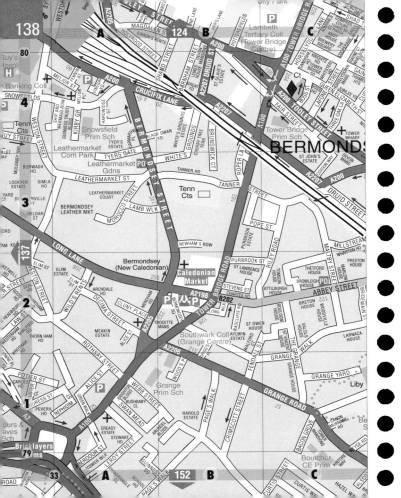

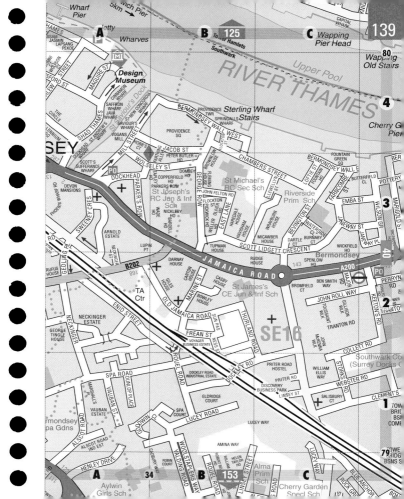

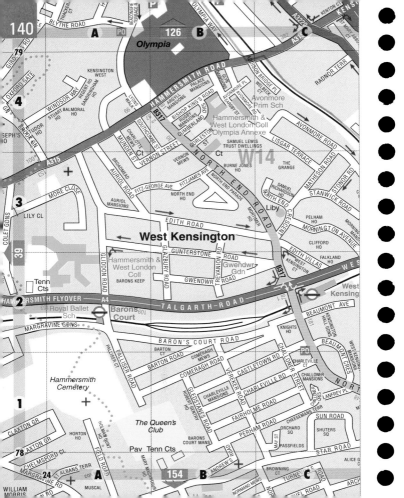

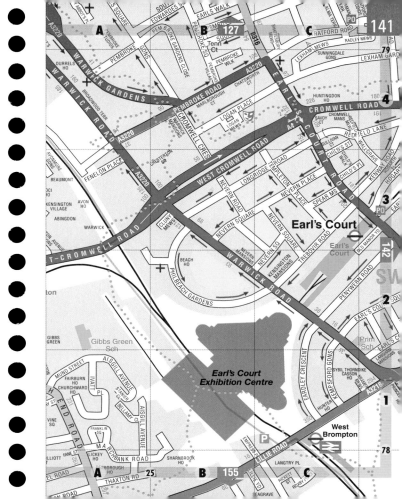

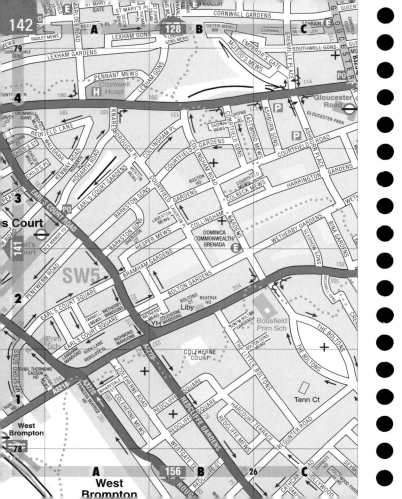

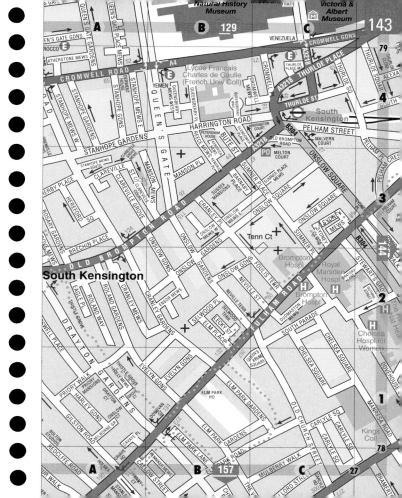

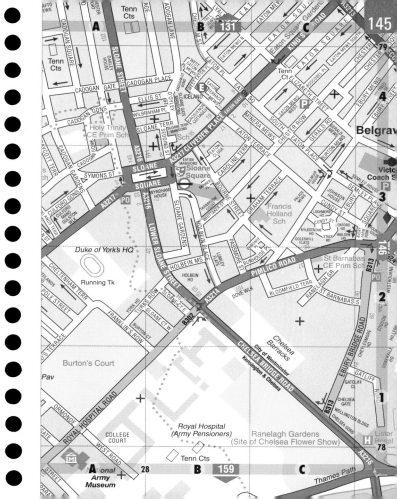

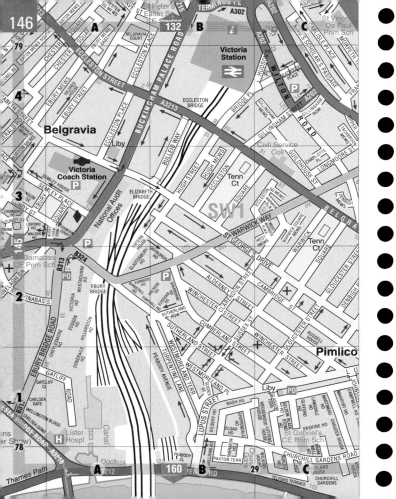

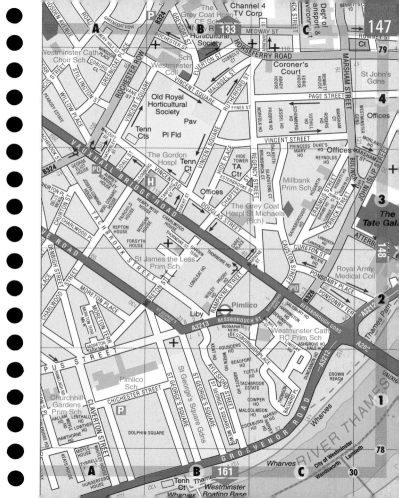

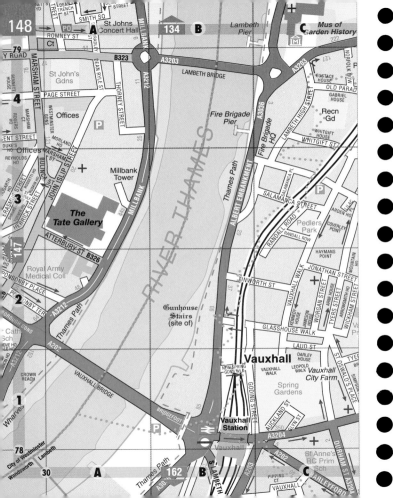

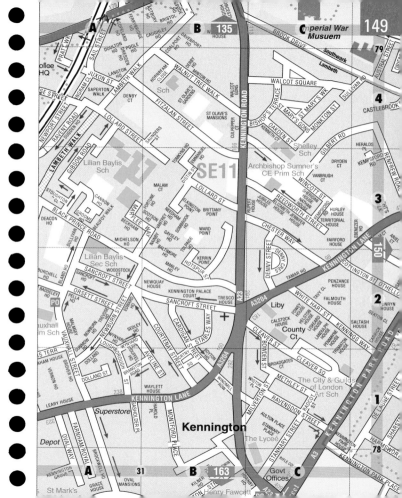

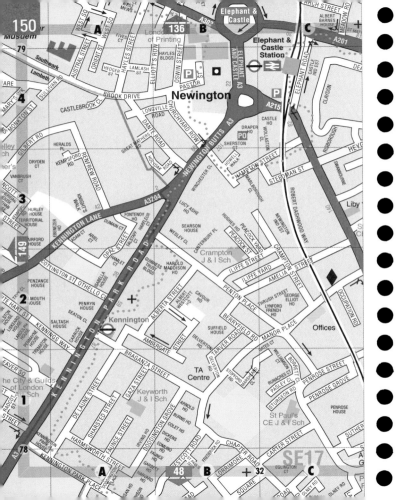

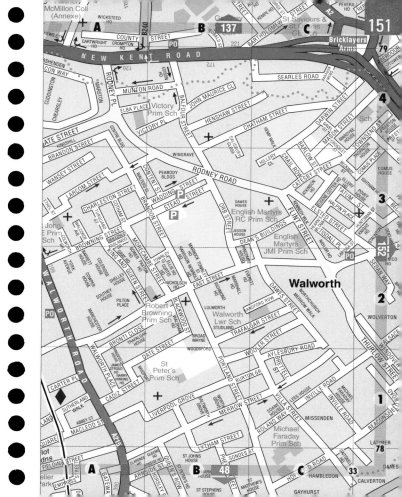

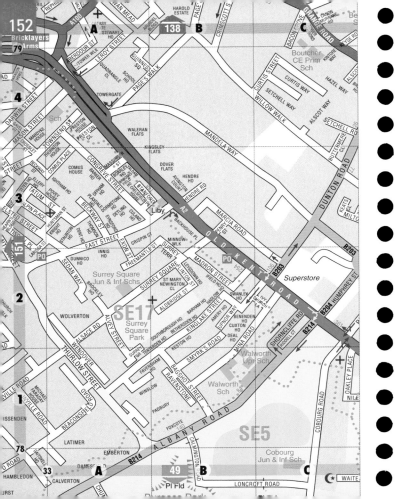

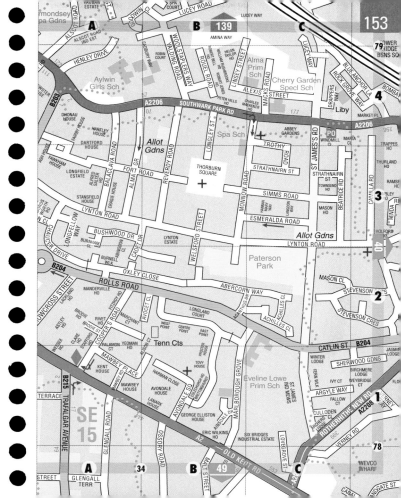

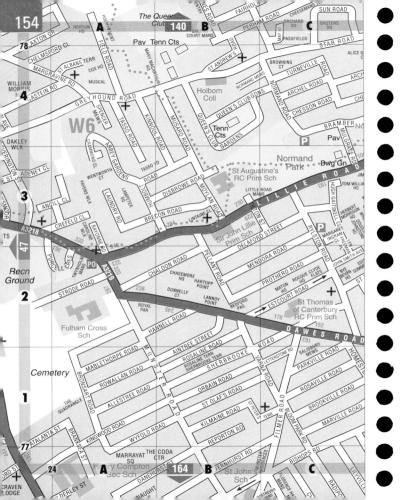

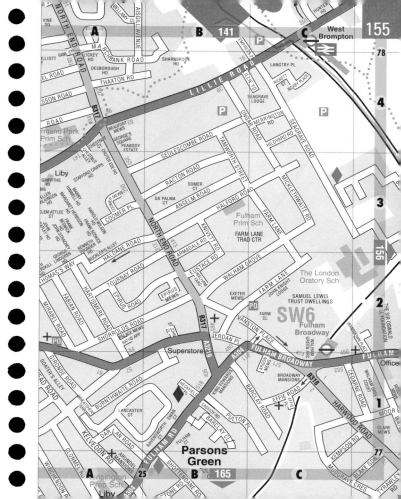

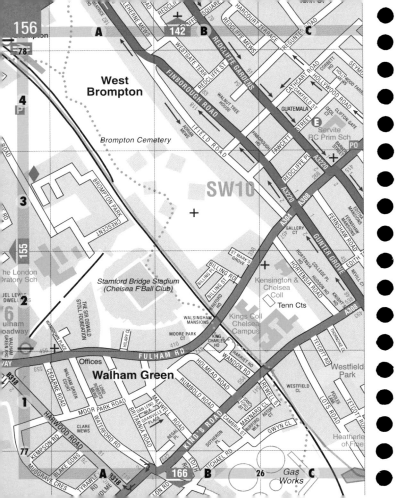

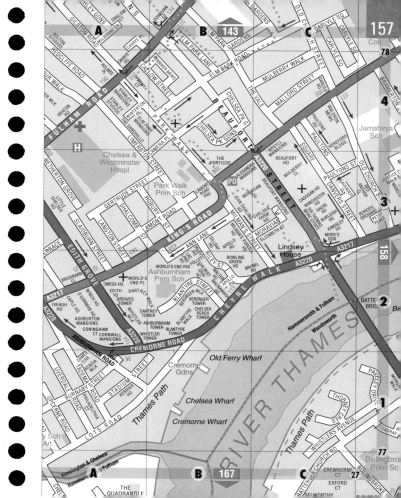

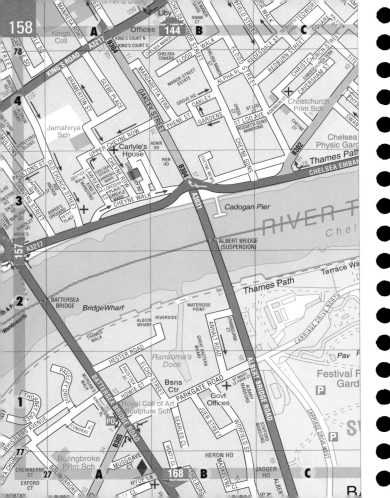

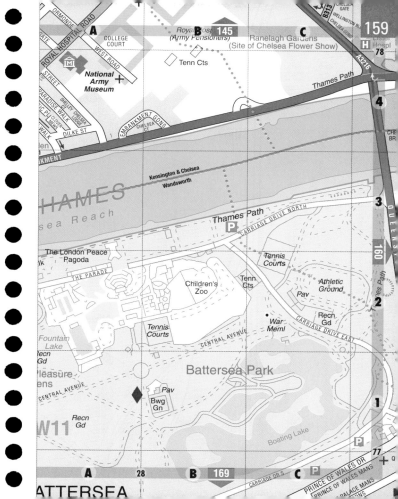

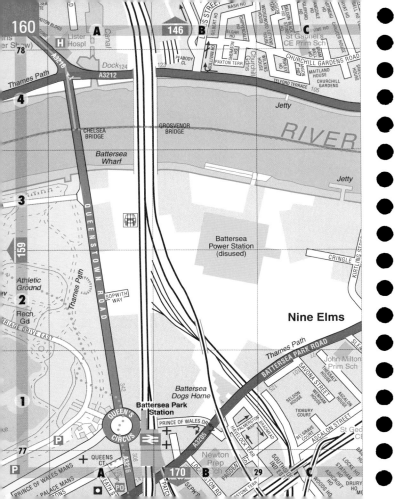

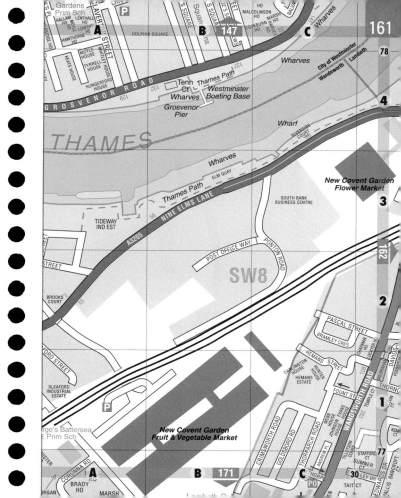

Gardens
Prim Sch

HALLAM LENTHALL
HO HO
MOYLE
HO

SLATERS
STREET

HAWTHORNE
HO

MOYLE
HOUSE
WHITE HO

TYRRELL
HOUSE

KEATS HOUSE

HUNGERFORD
HOUSE

A STREET
DOLPHIN SQUARE

Square

S SQUARE

B 147

MALCOLMSON
HO

MARSH
HO

COOKBURN HO

BALVE

C Wharves

78

Wharves

City of Westminster
Wandsworth Lambeth

GROSVENOR ROAD

Tenn
Ct
Wharves

Grosvenor
Pier

Thames Path
Westminster
Boating Base

4

Wharf

RIVERSIDE
COURT

THAMES

Wharves

Thames Path ELM QUAY

NINE ELMS LANE

SOUTH BANK
BUSINESS CENTRE

*New Covent Garden
Flower Market*

3

A3205

TIDEWAY
IND EST

POST OFFICE WAY

PONTON ROAD

162

STREET

SW8

BROOKS
COURT

PASCAL STREET

BRAMLEY CRES

2

FORD STREET

HEMANS STREET

DARLINGTON
HOUSE
HUNTER
HOUSE

CHAPMAN
HO

LOCKYER HO

DAVILS

THORNO

SLEAFORD
INDUSTRIAL
ESTATE

P

WEBB
HOUSE
JOHNSTON
HOUSE
EVANS
HOUSE
HUNTER
HOUSE

FOUNT ST

TEMPLE CT

1

rge's Battersea
E Prim Sch

*New Covent Garden
Fruit & Vegetable Market*

CRIMSWORTH ROAD

GOLDSBORO RD

THORPARCH ROAD

ANDREW PL

TILLISTON

STAFFORD
CT
SUMNER
CT

WANDSWORTH ROAD

KEMD

77

MINSTER

CORUNNA RD

BRADY
HO

MARSH

A

B 171

C

EDWARDS DR

30 LEY DR

TAIT CT

THORP

PO

BANCROFT

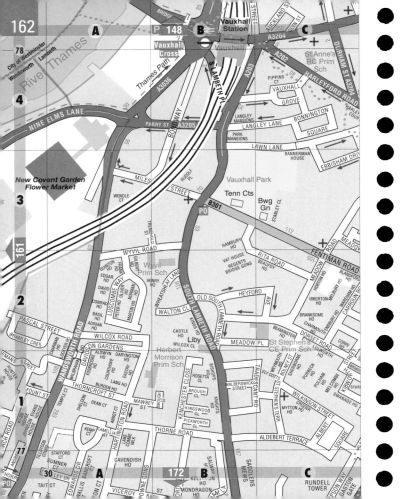

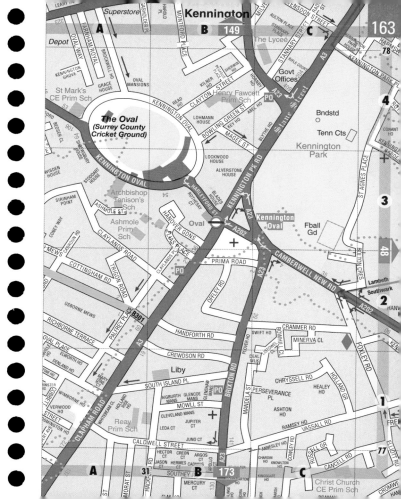

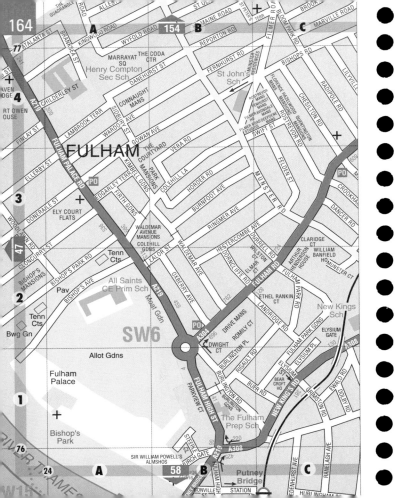

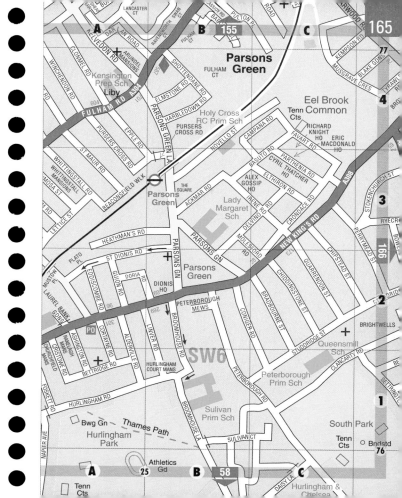

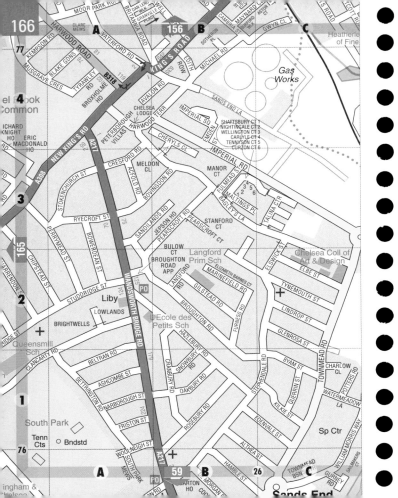

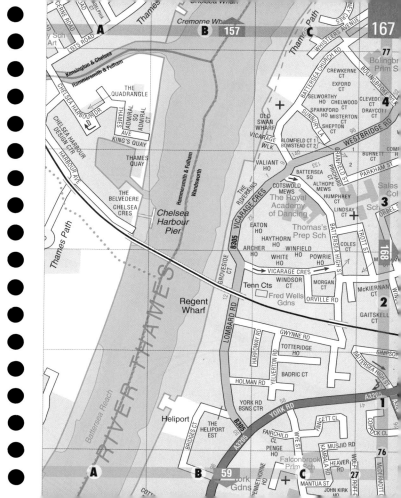

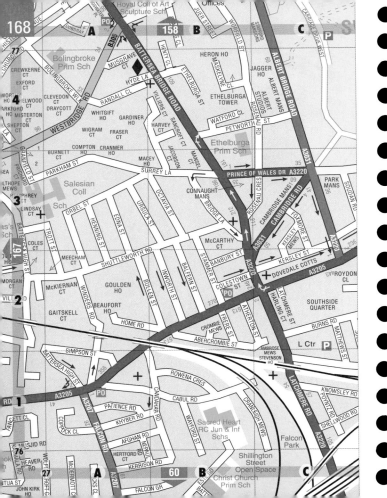

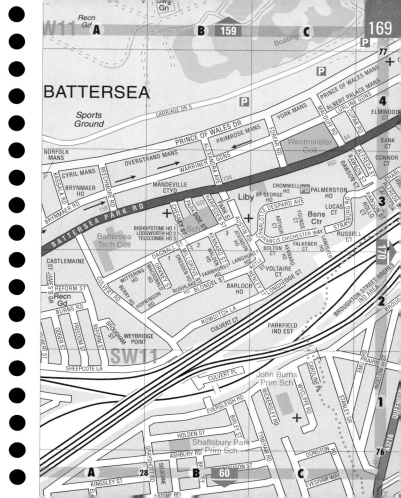

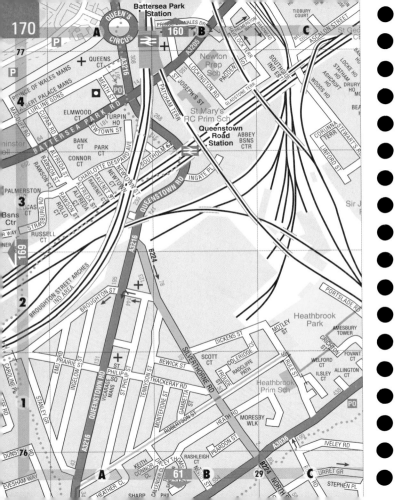

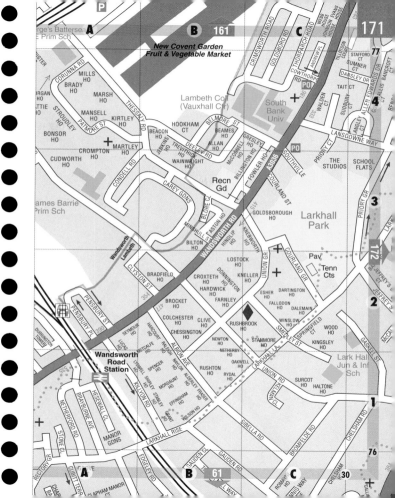

New Covent Garden Fruit & Vegetable Market

Lambeth Coll (Vauxhall Ctr)

South Bank Univ

P

Larkhall Park

Recn Gd

Lark Hall Jun & Inf Sch

Wandsworth Road Station

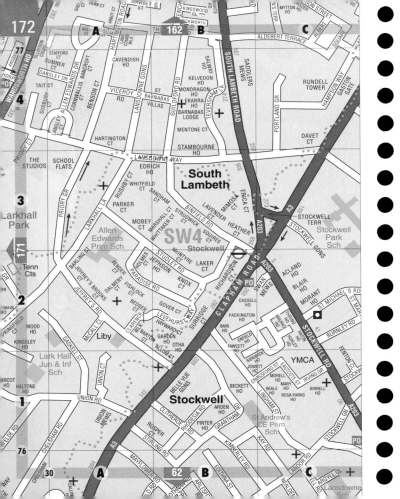

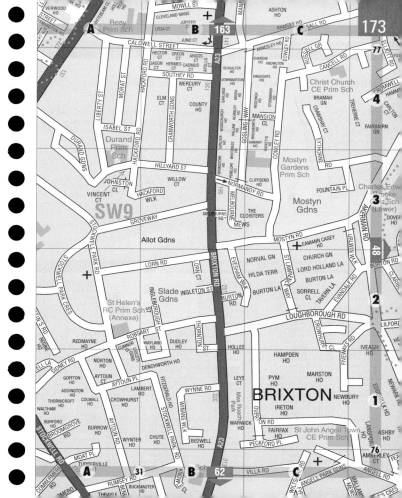

Index

Church Rd **6** Beckenham BR2..........**53** C6 **228** C6

Place name	Location number	Locality, town or village	Postcode district	Standard scale reference	Enlarged scale reference
May be abbreviated on the map	Present when a number indicates the place's position in a crowded area of mapping	Shown when more than one place (outside London postal districts) has the same name	District for the indexed place	Page number and grid reference for the standard mapping	Page number and grid reference for the central London enlarged mapping, underlined in red

Public and commercial buildings are highlighted in magenta
Places of interest are highlighted in blue with a star★

Index of localities, towns and villages

A
Acton 28 C1
Acton Green 37 B2

B
Balham 72 C2
Barbican 109 A3
Barnes 46 B2
Barnsbury 14 A1
Battersea 169 A4
Bayswater 114 C4
Bedford Park 38 A3
Belgravia 146 A4
Belsize Park 12 A3
Bermondsey 40 A4
Bethnal Green 25 A2
Blackheath
  Vale 53 B1
Blackwall 34 C2
Bloomsbury 106 A4
Borough The 136 C4
Bow 26 B3
Bow Common 34 A4
Brixton 62 C4
Broadgate 110 A4
Brockley 66 B3
Bromley
  (Tower Hamlets) .27 A2
Brompton 130 A1
Brondesbury 10 A2
Brondesbury
  Park 22 C2
Brook Green 39 C2

C
Camberwell 48 B2
Camden Town 13 A1
Canary Wharf 34 A1
Canning Town 35 B3
Canonbury 15 B2
Chelsea 144 B1
Child's Hill 1 C6
Chiswick 38 B1
Church End
  (Brent) 8 B2
City of London ...122 B4
Clapham 61 A4
Clapham
  Common 61 A3
Clapham Junction .60 A3
Clapham Park 61 C2
Clapton Park 17 C4
Clerkenwell 96 A1
College Park 22 A2
Covent Garden ...120 B4
Cricklewood 9 B4
Cubitt Town 42 B2

D
Dalston 16 C2
Dartmouth Park 4 A1
De Beauvoir Town .16 A1
Deptford 50 C3
Dollis Hill 9 A4
Dudden Hill 8 C3
Dulwich 76 A2
Dulwich Village ...76 A4

E
Earl's Court 141 C3
Earlsfield 71 B3
East Acton 29 A1
East Dulwich 64 C2
East Sheen 55 C3
Euston 93 A3

F
Finsbury 95 C4
Finsbury Park 5 C3
Fitzrovia 104 A4
Fulham 47 C1

G
Globe Town 25 C2
Gospel Oak 12 B2
Greenwich 53 A4
Grove Park
  (Hounslow) 45 B2
Gunnersbury 37 A2

H
Hackney 17 A2
Hackney Wick 18 C2
Haggerston 24 B3
Hammersmith 39 B2
Hampstead 11 B3
Harlesden 21 B4
Herne Hill 63 B2
Highbury 15 A4
Highgate 3 C1
Holborn 107 C3

I
Isle of Dogs 42 B2
Islington 14 C2

K
Kennington 149 B1
Kensal Green 22 B2
Kensal Rise 22 C3
Kensal Town 23 A1
Kensington 127 C5
Kentish Town 13 B2
Kew 44 C4
Kilburn 23 B4
King's Cross 84 C2
Kingsland 16 A2
Knightsbridge ...130 A1

L
Ladywell 66 C1
Lambeth 134 C3
Lewisham 67 B3
Leyton 19 C4
Limehouse 33 A2
Lisson Green 90 B2
Lisson Grove 102 A4
Lower Clapton 17 B4
Lower Holloway ...14 A3
Lower Place 20 B3

M
Maida Vale 88 A4
Maitland Park 12 C2
Marylebone 104 B2
Mayfair 118 A3
Mile End 26 A1
Mill Meads 27 C3
Millwall 41 C3
Mortlake 55 B4

N
New Cross 51 B2
New Cross Gate ...50 C2
Newington 150 B4
Nine Elms 160 C2
North Acton 20 C2
North End 2 B2
North Kensington .30 C4
North Sheen 44 C1
Notting Hill 112 C3
Nunhead 65 B3

O
Old Ford 26 B4
Old Oak Common ..21 B1

P
Paddington 100 C3
Park Royal 20 A2
Parsons Green ...165 B4
Peckham 49 A2
Pentonville 85 A1
Pimlico 146 C1

Poplar	33 C3	Shepherd's Bush	30 A1	St James	119 B2
Primrose Hill	12 B1	Shoreditch	87 C1	St John's	51 C1
Putney	57 B2	Soho	105 B1	St John's Wood	79 B1
Putney Heath	57 B1	Somers Town	93 C4	St Luke's	97 A2
Putney Vale	68 C1	South Acton	37 A3	St Pancras	94 B4
		South Bank	120 C1	Stamford Hill	7 A3
R		South Bromley	34 C4	Stepney	32 C4
Ratcliff	32 C2	South Hackney	25 B4	Stockwell	62 A4
Regent's Park	92 A4	South Hampstead	11 B1	Stoke Newington	7 A2
Richmond	54 A2	South		Stonebridge	20 B4
Richmond Hill	54 A1	Kensington	143 A3	Strand	120 C4
Roehampton	68 A4	South Lambeth	172 B3	Strand on	
Rotherhithe	40 C3	Southfields	71 A3	the Green	44 C4
		Southwark	40 B2	Stratford	19 B1
S		Spitalfields	110 A4	Stratford Marsh	27 A4
Sands End	59 B4	St George in		Stratford New Town	19 B3
Shacklewell	16 B4	the East	32 A2	Streatham Hill	74 A3
Shadwell	32 B2	St Giles	106 A2	Summerstown	71 B1

T		Wandsworth	58 C1
		Wapping	32 A1
Temple Mills	19 A3	Waterloo	135 B4
Tower Hamlets	33 B4	West Brompton	156 A4
Tufnell Park	13 C4	West Dulwich	75 A2
Tulse Hill	75 A4	West Hampstead	10 C4
		West Hill	58 B1
U		West Kensington	140 B3
Upper Holloway	4 C2	West Kilburn	23 A2
Upper Tooting	72 B1	West Norwood	75 B1
		Westbourne Green	88 A2
V		Westminster	133 A1
Vale of Health	2 C1	Whitechapel	110 C1
Vauxhall	148 B1	Willesden	8 C4
		Willesden Green	22 A4
W		Wimbledon Park	70 B2
Walham Green	156 A1		
Walworth	151 C2		

Abbreviations used in the index

Acad	Academy	Ent Pk	Enterprise Park	Orch	Orchard
App	Approach	Est	Estate	Par	Parade
Arc	Arcade	Ex Ctr	Exhibition Centre	Pas	Passage
Art Gall	Art Gallery	Ex Hall	Exhibition Hall	Pav	Pavilion
Ave	Avenue	Fst	First	Pk	Park
Bglws	Bungalows	Gdn	Garden	Pl	Place
Bldgs	Buildings	Gdns	Gardens	Prec	Precinct
Bsns Ctr	Business Centre	Gn	Green	Prep	Preparatory
Bsns Pk	Business Park	Gr	Grove	Prim	Primary
Bvd	Boulevard	Gram	Grammar	Prom	Promenade
Cath	Cathedral, Catholic	Her Ctr	Heritage Centre	RC	Roman Catholic
CE	Church of England	Ho	House	Rd	Road
Cemy	Cemetery	Hospl	Hospital	Rdbt	Roundabout
Cir	Circus	Hts	Heights	Ret Pk	Retail Park
Circ	Circle	Ind Est	Industrial Estate	Sch	School
Cl	Close	Inf	Infant	Sec	Secondary
Cnr	Corner	Inst	Institute	Sh Ctr	Shopping Centre
Coll	College	Int	International	Sp	Sports
Com	Community	Intc	Interchange	Specl	Special
Comm	Common	Jun	Junior	Sports Ctr	Sports Centre
Comp	Comprehensive	Junc	Junction	Sq	Square
Con Ctr	Conference Centre	La	Lane	St	Street, Saint
Cotts	Cottages	L Ctr	Leisure Centre	Sta	Station
Cres	Crescent	Liby	Library	Stad	Stadium
Cswy	Causeway	Mans	Mansions	Tech	Technical/Technology
Ct	Court	Mdw/s	Meadow/s	Terr	Terrace
Ctr	Centre	Meml	Memorial	Trad Est	Trading Estate
Crkt	Cricket	Mid	Middle	Twr/s	Tower/s
Ctry Pk	Country Park	Mix	Mixed	Univ	University
Cty	County	Mkt	Market	Wlk	Walk
Ctyd	Courtyard	Mon	Monument	Yd	Yard
Dr	Drive	Mus	Museum		
Ent Ctr	Enterprise Centre	Obsy	Observatory		

A

Abady Ho SW1 ....147 C4
Abbess Cl SW2 ....75 A3
Abbeville Mews **3**
SW4 ....61 C3
Abbeville Rd SW4 ....61 B2
Abbey Bsns Ctr
SW8 ....170 B4
Abbey Ct NW8 ....78 C2
SE17 ....151 A1
6 W12 ....38 A3
Abbey Gdns NW8 ....79 A1
SE16 ....153 C4
W6 ....154 A3
Abbey La E15 ....27 C3
Abbey Lo NW8 ....90 B3
Abbey Orchard St
SW1 ....133 C2
Abbey Orchard Street
Est SW1 ....133 C2
Abbey Rd NW8 ....78 C2
NW6 ....11 A1
NW10 ....20 A3
Abbey St SE1 ....138 C2
Abbeyfield Rd SE16 ....40 B2
Abbot Cl SW1 ....162 A1
Abbot Ho 13 E14 ....34 A2
Abbot St E8 ....16 B2
Abbot's Pl NW6 ....78 A4
Abbots Ho W14 ....126 C1
SW1 ....147 B1
Abbots La SE1 ....124 B1
Abbots Pk SW2 ....74 C3
Abbotsbury Cl
W14 ....126 C3
E15 ....27 B3
Abbotsbury Ho
W14 ....126 B4
Abbotsbury Mews
SE15 ....65 B4
Abbotsbury Rd
W14 ....126 C3
Abbotshade Rd 13
SE16 ....32 C1
Abbotstone Ho 4 E5 7 C2
Abbotstone Rd
SW15 ....57 B4
Abbotswell Rd SE4 ....66 B2
Abbotswood Rd
SE22 ....64 A3
SW16 ....73 C1
Abbott Ho SW12 ....72 B4
Abbott Rd E14 ....34 C3
Abbotts Cl N1 ....15 B2
Abchurch La EC2,
EC4 ....123 C4
Abchurch Yd EC4 ....123 B4
Abdale Rd W12 ....30 A1
Abel Ho SE1 ....163 B4
Aberavon Rd E3 ....26 A2
Abercorn Cl NW8 ....88 C4
Abercorn Mans
NW8 ....79 A1
Abercorn Pl NW8 ....78 C1
Abercorn Way SE1 ....153 B2
Abercrombie Ho
W12 ....30 A2
Abercrombie St
SW11 ....168 B2

Aberdale Ct 22 ....40 C4
Aberdare Gdns
NW6 ....11 A1
Aberdeen Ct W2 ....89 B1
N5 ....15 B3
Aberdeen La N5 ....15 B3
Aberdeen Mans
WC1 ....94 A2
Aberdeen Pk N5 ....15 B3
Aberdeen Pl NW8 ....89 B2
Aberdeen Rd NW10 ....8 B3
N5 ....15 B4
Aberdeen Terr SE3 ....52 C1
Aberdour St SE1 ....152 A4
Aberfeldy Ho SE5 ....48 A3
Aberfeldy St E14 ....34 B3
Abersham Rd E8 ....16 B3
Abingdon W14 ....141 A3
Abingdon Cl SE1 ....153 A2
NW1 ....13 C2
Abingdon Ct W8 ....127 C1
Abingdon Gdns
W8 ....127 C1
Abingdon Ho E2 ....98 C2
Abingdon Mans
W8 ....127 B2
Abingdon Rd W8 ....127 C1
SW1 ....134 A2
Abingdon Villas
W8 ....127 C1
Abinger Gr SE8 ....51 B4
Abinger Ho 1 SE1 ....137 B3
Abinger Mews W9 ....23 C1
Abinger Rd W4 ....38 A3
Ablett St SE16 ....40 B1
Abney Park Cemetery*
N16 ....7 B2
Abney Pk Ct N4 7 B2
Aboyne Rd SW17 ....71 C1
Aborfield 6 NW5 ....13 B3
Abyssinia Cl SW11 ....60 A3
Abyssinia Rd SW11 ....60 A3
Acacia Cl SE8 ....41 A2
Acacia Gdns NW8 ....79 C2
Acacia Gr SE21 ....75 C2
Acacia Ho N16 ....6 C2
Acacia Pl NW8 ....79 C2
Acacia Rd NW8 ....79 C2
W3 ....28 B2
Acacia Wlk SW10 ....157 A1
Academy Ct 13 E2 ....25 B2
Academy The 2 N19 ....4 B3
Acanthus Dr SE1 ....153 B2
Acanthus Rd SW11 ....60 C4
Accommodation Rd
NW11 ....1 B3
Acer Ct NW2 ....9 C4
Acfold Rd SW6 ....166 A3
Achilles Cl SE1 ....153 C2
Achilles Ho 13 E2 ....25 A3
Achilles Rd NW6 ....10 C3
Achilles St SE14 ....51 A3
Achilles Way W1 ....117 C1
Acklam Rd W10 ....31 B4
Ackmar Rd SW6 ....165 B3
Ackroyd Dr E3 ....33 C4
Acland Burghley Sch
NW5 ....13 A4
Acland Cres SE5 ....63 C4
Acland Ho SW9 ....172 C2
Acland Rd NW2 ....9 A2
Acol Ct 13 NW6 ....10 C1
Acol Rd NW6 ....11 A1
Acorn Gdns W3 ....28 C4
Acorn Par 7 SE15 ....50 A3

Acorn Production Ctr
N7 ....14 A1
Acorn Wharf SE1 ....49 C4
Acorns The 21
SW19 ....69 C3
Acre Dr SE22 ....64 C3
Acre La SW2 ....62 B3
Acris St SW18 ....59 B2
Acton Central Ind Est 4
W3 ....28 A1
Acton Central Sta
W3 ....28 C1
Acton High Sch W3 ....36 C4
Acton Hill Mews
W3 ....28 A1
Acton Ho 18 E8 ....24 B4
5 W3 ....28 B3
Acton Hospl W3 ....36 C4
Acton La NW10 ....20 C3
W4 ....37 B2
W3 ....37 B4
Acton Mews E8 ....24 B4
Acton Park Est W3 ....37 C4
Acton St WC1 ....94 C3
Acton Town Sta W3 ....36 C4
Acton Vale Ind Pk
W3 ....29 B1
Acuba Ho SW18 ....71 A3
Acuba Rd SW18 ....71 A2
Ada Ct N1 ....86 C3
W9 ....89 A3
Ada Gdns E14 ....34 C3
Ada Ho 22 E2 ....24 C4
Ada Kennedy Ct 6
SE10 ....52 B3
Ada Pl E2 ....24 C4
Ada Rd SE5 ....49 A3
Ada St E8 ....25 A4
Adair Ho SW3 ....158 B4
Adair Rd W10 ....23 A1
Adair Twr 7 W10 ....23 A1
Adam & Eve Ct
W1 ....105 A2
Adam & Eve Mews
W8 ....127 C2
Adam Ct SE11 ....150 A3
W7 ....120 B3
Adam Wlk SW6 ....47 B3
Adam's Row W1 ....117 C3
Adamfields NW3 ....11 C1
Adams Ct EC2 ....109 C2
Adams Gardens Est 5
SE16 ....40 B4
Adams Ho 3 E14 ....34 C3
Adams Pl N7 ....14 B3
Adamson Rd NW3 ....11 C1
E16 ....35 C3
Adare Wlk SW16 ....74 B1
SW2 ....74 B3
Adderley Gr SW11 ....60 C2
Adderley St E14 ....34 B3
Added Stanhope Lds
SE14 ....51 C2
Addey Ho SE8 ....51 B3
Addington Ct 7
SW14 ....55 C4
Addington Ho
SW9 ....173 A1
Addington Rd E3 ....26 C2
Addington Sq SE5 ....48 C3
Addington St SE1 ....135 A3
Addison Ave
W11 ....31 A1 112 A1

Addison Bridge Pl
W14 ....140 C4
Addison Cres W14 ....126 B2
Addison Gdns
W14 ....126 A3
W14 ....39 C3
Addison Gr W4 ....38 A3
Addison Ho NW8 ....89 B4
Addison Park Mans 12
W14 ....39 C3
Addison Pl
W11 ....31 A1 112 A1
Addison Prim Sch
W14 ....39 C3
Addison Rd W14 ....126 C2
Addle Hill EC4 ....108 B1
Addle St EC2 ....109 A3
Addlestone Ho W10 ....30 B4
Addy Ho SE16 ....40 B2
Adela Ho W6 ....39 B1
Adela St W10 ....23 A1
Adelaide Ave SE4 ....66 C3
Adelaide Ct NW8 ....79 A1
Adelaide Gr W12 ....29 C1
Adelaide Ho NW3 ....12 A1
Richmond TW9 ....54 B3
2 SW18 ....59 C3
Adelaide St WC2 ....120 A3
Adelaide Wlk SW9 ....62 C3
Adelina Gr E1 ....32 B4
Adelina Mews
SW12 ....73 C3
Adeline Pl WC1 ....105 C3
Adelphi Cl 20 SE16 ....40 C4
Adelphi Terr WC2 ....120 B3
Aden Gr N16 ....15 C4
Aden Ho 12 E1 ....32 C4
Aden Lo N16 ....15 C4
Adeney Cl W6 ....47 C4
Adeyfield Ho EC1 ....97 C3
Adie Rd W6 ....39 B3
Adisham Ho 4 E5 ....17 A3
Adler St E1 ....111 B2
Adley St E5 ....18 A3
Admiral Ct W1 ....103 B3
SW10 ....167 A4
Admiral Hyson Ind Est
SE16 ....40 A1
Admiral Mews W10 ....22 C1
Admiral Pl SE16 ....33 A1
Admiral Sq SW10 ....167 A4
Admiral St SE8 ....51 C2
Admiral Wlk W9 ....31 C4
Admiral's Wlk NW3 ....2 B1
Admirals Ct SE1 ....124 C1
2 SW19 ....69 C3
Admirals Way E14 ....41 C4
Admiralty Arch*
SW1 ....119 C2
Admiralty Cl 1 SE8 ....51 C2
Adolphus Rd N4 ....6 A3
Adolphus St SE8 ....51 B3
Adpar St W2 ....101 B4
Adrian Bolt Ho 2
E2 ....25 A2
Adrian Ho N1 ....85 A3
SW8 ....162 A2
Adrian Mews
SW10 ....156 B4
Adriatic Ho 18 E1 ....25 C1
Adron Ho 9 SE16 ....40 B2
Aelstock Ho 8 N1 ....15 A1
ADT Coll SW15 ....58 B2
Adys Lawn NW2 ....9 A2
Adys Rd SE15 ....64 B4
Affleck St N1 ....85 A1

Afghan Rd SW11 ....168 A1
Agamemnon Rd
NW6 ....10 B3
Agar Gr NW1 ....13 C1
Agar Pl NW1 ....13 B1
Agar St WC2 ....120 B3
Agate Rd W6 ....39 B3
Agatha Cl E1 ....32 B1
Agave Rd NW2 ....9 B4
Agdon St EC1 ....96 A2
Agincourt Rd NW3 ....12 B4
Agnes Ct 18 SW18 ....59 C3
Agnes Ho 13 W11 ....30 C2
Agnes Rd W3 ....38 B4
Agnes St E14 ....33 B3
Aigburth Mans
SW9 ....163 B1
Ailsa St E14 ....34 B4
Ainger Mews NW3 ....12 B1
Ainger Rd NW3 ....12 B1
Ainsdale NW1 ....153 B1
Ainsley St E2 ....25 A2
Ainsty St 14 SE16 ....40 B4
Ainsworth Cl SE5 ....49 A1
Ainsworth Est NW8 ....78 B3
Ainsworth Ho NW8 ....78 B3
Ainsworth Rd E9 ....17 B1
Ainsworth Way
NW8 ....78 C4
Aintree St SW6 ....154 B2
Air St W1 ....119 A3
Aird Ho SE1 ....136 C1
Airdrie Cl N1 ....14 B1
Airedale Ave W4 ....38 B1
Airedale Ave S W4 ....38 B1
Airedale Rd SW12 ....72 B4
Airlie Gdns
W8 ....31 C1 113 B1
Aisgill Ave W5 ....141 A1
Aiten Pl W6 ....38 C2
Aithan Ho 12 E14 ....33 B3
Aitken Cl E8 ....24 C4
Ajax Ho 13 E2 ....25 A3
Ajax Rd NW6 ....10 C3
Akbar Ho 7 E14 ....42 A2
Akehurst St SW15 ....58 C4
Akenside Ct 3
NW3 ....11 C3
Akenside Rd NW3 ....11 C3
Akerman Rd SW9 ....48 A2
Akintaro Ho 7 SE8 ....51 B4
Al Sadiq & Al Zahra
Schs NW6 ....23 C4
Alan Preece Ct NW6 ....9 C1
Aland Ct SE16 ....41 A3
Alaska St SE1 ....121 B1
Alba Pl W11 ....31 B3
Albacore Cres SE13 ....67 A1
Alban Ho NW3 ....11 B2
Albans Cl SW16 ....74 A1
Albany W1 ....118 C3
Albany Cl SW14 ....55 A3
Albany Ct 13 NW8 ....79 B1
Albany Ctyd W1 ....119 A3
Albany Ho 6 TW8 ....44 A4
Albany Mans SW11 ....158 B1
Albany Mews N1 ....14 C1
SE5 ....48 B4
Albany Par 4 TW8 ....44 A4
Albany Pl N7 ....14 C4
Albany Rd SE5 ....49 A4
Richmond TW10 ....54 A2
Albany St NW1 ....92 B4
Albany Terr 6
TW10 ....54 B2

Albemarle St W19 ... 69 C2
Albemarle Ho SE8 ... 41 B2
Albemarle Mans
NW3 .... 11 A4
Albemarle St W1 .. 118 C3
Albemarle Way EC1 . 96 A1
Albermarle Ho 3
SW9 .... 62 C4
Albermarle Prim Sch
SW19 .... 70 A3
Albermarle Prim Sch
(Annexe) SW19 ... 70 A3
Albert Ave SW8 ... 162 C1
Albert Barnes Ho
SE1 .... 136 C1
Albert Bigg Point
E15 .... 27 B4
Albert Bridge Rd
SW11 .... 158 C1
Albert Cl 11 E9 .... 25 A4
Albert Cotts E1 .. 111 B4
Albert Ct SW7 .... 129 B3
9 SW19 .... 70 A3
Albert Dr SW19 .... 70 A3
Albert Emb SE1 .. 148 B3
Albert Gate Ct
SW1 .... 130 C3
Albert Gdns E1 ... 32 C3
Albert Gray Ho
SW10 .... 157 B2
Albert Hall Mans
SW7 .... 129 B3
Albert Mans SW11 168 C4
N8 .... 5 A4
Albert Memorial★
.... 129 B3
Albert Mews W8 .. 128 C2
Albert Palace Mans
SW11 .... 169 C4
Albert Pl N4 .... 5 B4
NW6 .... 23 B3
Richmond TW10 ... 54 B2
Albert Sq SW8 ... 162 C1
Albert St NW1 .... 82 B3
Albert Starr Ho 7
SE8 .... 40 C2
Albert Studios
SW11 .... 168 C4
Albert Terr NW1 .. 81 B3
NW10 .... 20 C4
Albert Terr Mews
SE17 .... 150 B2
Alberta Ct 1 TW10 54 B2
Alberta Ho E14 .... 34 B1
Alberta St SE17 .. 150 B2
Albion Ave SW8 .. 171 B1
Albion Cl W2 ...... 116 B4
Albion Dr E8 .... 16 C1
Albion Est SE16 ... 40 B4
Albion Gate W2 .. 116 B4
Albion Gdns 1 E8 39 A2
Albion Gr N16 ..... 16 A4
Albion Jun & Inf Sch
SE16 .... 40 B4
Albion Mews N1 ... 85 B4
W2 .... 102 A2
6 W6 .... 39 A2

Albion Sq E8 .... 16 B1
Albion St W2 ..... 102 B1
SE16 .... 40 B4
Albion Terr E8 ..... 16 B1
Albion Way EC1 .. 108 C3
SE13 .... 67 B3
Albion Wharf
SW11 .... 158 A2
Albion Yd N1 .... 84 B1
Albon Ho SE14 .... 51 B2
SW18 .... 59 A1
Albrighton Rd SE5,
SE22 .... 64 A4
Albury Bldgs SE1 . 136 B3
Albury Lo 7 SW2 .. 74 B4
Albury St SE8 ...... 51 C4
Alconbury Rd E5 ... 7 C2
Aldbourne Rd W12 29 C1
Aldbridge St SE17 152 B2
Aldburgh Mews
W1 .... 103 C2
Aldbury Ho SW3 . 144 A3
Aldebert Terr SW8 162 C1
Aldeburgh St SE10 43 C1
Alden Ho E8 .... 25 A4
Aldenham Ho NW1 83 B1
Aldenham St NW1 . 83 B1
Aldensley Rd W6 .. 39 A3
Alder Ho 1 NW3 .. 12 B2
SE15 .... 49 B4
Alder Lo SW6 ...... 47 C2
Alder Mews 3 N19 . 4 B2
Alder Rd SW14 .... 55 C4
Alderbrook Prim Sch
SW12 .... 73 A4
Alderbrook Rd
SW12 .... 61 A1
Alderbury Rd SW13 46 C4
Aldergrove Ho 3 E5 .7 C2
Alderholt Way 9
SE15 .... 49 A3
Alderley Ho SW8 . 171 B1
Alderman's Wlk
EC2 .... 110 A3
Aldermanbury EC2 109 A2
Aldermanbury Sq
EC2 .... 109 A3
Alderney Ho 16 N1 15 B2
Alderney Rd E1 .... 25 C1
Alderney St SW1 . 146 B2
Aldersford Cl SE4 . 65 C3
Aldersgate EC1 ... 108 C3
Aldersgate St EC1 108 C2
Aldershot Rd NW6 . 23 B4
Alderson St W10 .. 23 A1
Alderton Rd SE24 . 63 B4
Alderville Rd SW6 145 A1
Alderwick Ct N7 ... 14 B2
Aldgate EC3 ...... 110 B1
E1 .... 110 B1
Aldgate East Sta
E1 .... 111 A2
Aldgate High St
EC3 .... 110 C1
Aldgate Sta EC3 . 110 C1
Aldham Ho SE4 ... 51 B2
Aldine Ct W12 ..... 30 B1
Aldine St W12 ..... 39 B4
Aldington Ct 1 E8 . 16 C1
Aldred Rd NW6 ... 10 C3
Aldren Rd SW17 .. 71 B1
Aldrich Terr SW18 . 71 B2

Aldrick Ho N1 ..... 85 A2
Aldridge Ct 8 W11 31 B4
Aldridge Rd Villas
W11 .... 31 B4
Aldsworth Cl W9 .. 88 A1
Aldworth Gr SE13 . 67 B1
Aldwych WC2 .... 107 A1
Aldwych Bldgs
WC2 .... 106 B2
Aldwyn Ho SW8 .. 162 A1
Alex Gossip Ho
SW6 .... 165 B3
Alexander Ct 6
Alexander Ct SE3 . 53 C1
SW18 .... 59 B2
Alexander Ho 5
E14 .... 41 C3
Alexander Mans
SW3 .... 157 B3
6 SW3 .... 157 B3
Alexander Mews 6
W2 .... 100 A2
Alexander Pl SW7 144 A4
Alexander Rd N19 .. 5 A2
Alexander Sq SW3 144 A4
Alexander St W2 .. 31 C3
Alexandra Ave
SW11 .... 169 B3
Alexandra Cotts
SE14 .... 51 B2
Alexandra Ct W9 . 89 A2
4 N16 .... 16 B4
Alexandra Gdns W4 46 A3
Alexandra Gr N4 ... 6 A3
Alexandra Ho 13
W6 .... 39 B1
Alexandra Mans
SW3 .... 157 B3
6 NW6 .... 10 C3
Alexandra National Ho
N4 .... 6 A2
Alexandra Pl NW8 . 79 A4
Alexandra Rd NW8 11 C1
SW14 .... 55 C4
Richmond TW9 .... 44 B3
SW14 .... 55 C4
Alexandra St E16 . 35 C4
8 SE14 .... 51 A3
Alexis St SE16 .... 153 C4
Alfearn Rd E5 ..... 17 B4
Alford Ct N1 .... 87 A1
Alford Pl N1 .... 87 A1
Alfred Butt Ho
SW17 .... 72 B1
Alfred Cl W4 ...... 37 C2
Alfred Ho E9 ...... 18 A3
Alfred Mews W1,
WC1 .... 105 B4
Alfred Nunn Ho
NW10 .... 21 B4
Alfred Pl WC1 .... 105 B4
Alfred Rd W3 ...... 28 B1
W2 .... 31 C4
Alfred Salter Ho
SE1 .... 153 A3
Alfred St E3 .... 26 B2
Alfreda Ct SW11 . 170 A3
Alfreda St SW11 . 170 A3
Alfreton Cl SW19 .. 69 C1
Alfriston Rd SW11 . 60 B2
Algar Ho SE1 ..... 136 A3
Algarve Rd SW18 . 71 B3
Algernon Rd NW6 . 23 C4
SE13 .... 67 A3
Algiers Rd SE13 ... 66 C3
Alice Ct SW15 ..... 58 B3

Alice Gilliott Ct
W14 .... 155 A4
Alice La E3 .... 26 B4
Alice Owen Tech Ctr
EC1 .... 96 A4
Alice Shepherd Ho 7
E14 .... 42 B4
Alice St SE1 ...... 138 A1
Alice Walker Cl 6
SE24 .... 63 A2
Alie St E1 .... 111 A1
Alison Ct SE1 .... 153 B3
Aliwal Rd SW11 ... 60 A3
Alkerden Rd W4 ... 38 A1
Alkham Rd N16 .... 7 B2
All England Lawn Tennis
& Croquet Club The
SW19 .... 70 A1
All Saints CE Prim Sch
SW6 .... 164 A2
E3 .... 26 C2
SW15 .... 57 B4
All Saints Ct E5 .... 7 C2
6 E1 .... 32 B2
All Saints Dr SE3 .. 53 B1
All Saints Rd W11 . 31 B3
All Saints Rd W3 .. 37 B3
All Saints St N1 ... 84 C2
All Saints' CE Prim Sch
NW2 .... 1 B2
SE3 .... 53 A1
All Saints' Rd W3 . 37 B3
All Souls CE Prim Sch
W1 .... 104 C4
All Souls' Ave NW10 22 A4
Allam Ho W11 .... 112 A4
Allan Ho SW8 .... 171 B4
Allan Way W3 ..... 28 B4
Allanbridge N16 .... 7 A4
Allard Gdns SW4 . 61 C2
Allardyce St SW4,
SW9 .... 62 B3
Allbrook Ho 4
SW15 .... 68 C4
Allcroft Rd NW5 ... 12 C3
Allen Edwards Dr
SW8 .... 172 A4
Allen Edwards Prim Sch
SW4 .... 172 A3
Allen Ho W8 ..... 127 C2
Allen Rd N16 ...... 16 A4
E3 .... 26 B3
Allen St W8 ...... 127 C1
Allendale Cl SE5 .. 48 C2
Allendale Sch W8 127 C2
Allenford Ho 1
SW15 .... 56 B1
Allensbury Pl
7 NW1 .... 13 C1
NW1 .... 14 A1
Allenswood 12
SW19 .... 70 A3
Allerdale Ho 2 N4 .. 6 C4
Allerton Ho N1 .... 87 C1
Allerton Rd N16 ... 6 C2
Allerton St N1 ..... 97 C4
Allerton Wlk 11 N7 . 5 B2
Allestree Rd SW6 154 B1
Alleyn Cres SE21 . 75 C2
Alleyn Ho SE1 .... 137 B1
Alleyn Pk SE21 ... 76 A1
Alleyn Rd SE21 ... 76 A1
Alleyn's Sch SE22 . 64 A2

Allfarthing La SW18 59 B1
Allfarthing Prim Sch
SW18 .... 59 B1
Allgood St 10 E2 .. 24 B3
Allhallows La EC4 . 123 B3
Alliance Ct W3 .... 28 A4
Alliance Rd W3 .... 29 A4
Allied Ind Est SW7 38 A4
Allied Way W3 ..... 38 A4
Allingham St NW3 . 12 A3
Allingham St N1 ... 86 C2
Allington Ct SW8 . 170 C1
Allington Rd W10 . 23 A3
Allington St 1
SW1 .... 132 B1
Allison Cl SE10 .... 52 B2
Allison Gr SE21 ... 76 A3
Allison Rd W3 ..... 28 B2
Alliston Ho 2 ...... 99 A3
Allitsen Rd NW8 ... 80 A2
Allnutt Way SW4 .. 61 C2
Alloa Rd SE8 ...... 41 A1
Allom Ct SW4 .... 172 B1
Allonby Ho E14 .... 33 A4
Alloway Rd E3 ..... 26 A2
Allport Ho SE5 .... 63 C4
Allsop Pl NW1 ..... 91 A1
Alma Birk Ho 1
NW6 .... 10 B1
Alma Gr SE1 ..... 153 A3
Alma Pl NW3 ...... 22 A4
Alma Pl NW10 ..... 22 A2
Alma Prim Sch
SE16 .... 153 C4
Alma Rd SW18 .... 59 B2
Alma Sq NW8 ..... 89 A4
Alma St NW5 ...... 13 A2
E15 .... 19 C2
Alma Terr W8 .... 127 C1
SW18 .... 71 C4
Almack Rd E5 ..... 17 B4
Almeida St 10 N1 . 15 A1
Almeric Rd SW11 . 60 B3
Almington St N4 ... 5 B3
Almond Ave W5 ... 36 A3
Almond Cl SE15 ... 49 C1
Almond Ho SE4 ... 51 B1
Almond Rd SE16 .. 40 A2
Almondsbury Ct 7
SE15 .... 49 A3
Almorah Rd N1 .... 15 C1
Almshouses NW8 . 80 A4
Alperton St W10 .. 23 B1
Alpha Cl NW1 ..... 90 B3
Alpha Ct 3 NW5 .. 13 A2
Alpha Gr E14 ...... 41 C4
Alpha Ho NW6 .... 23 C3
Alpha Pl SW3 .... 158 B4
SW3 .... 158 B4
Alpha Rd SE14 .... 51 B2
Alpha St SE15 ..... 49 C1
Alphabet Sq E3 ... 33 C4
Alpine Rd SE16 .... 40 C1
Alroy Rd N4 .... 5 C4
Alsace Rd SE17 .. 152 A2
Alscot Rd SE1 .... 139 A1
SE1 .... 139 A1
Alscot Road Ind Est
SE1 .... 139 A1
Alscot Way 1 SE1 152 C4
Altenburg Gdns
SW11 .... 60 B4
Althea St SW6 .... 59 A4

Althope Mews
SW11 ....167 C3
Althorp Rd SW17 ....72 B3
Alton Ho 3 E3 ....27 A2
Alton Rd
Richmond TW10,TW9 ..54 A3
SW15 ....68 C3
Alton St E14 ....34 A4
Alumni Ct SE1 ......139 A4
Alvanley Ho SW9 ....11 A3
Alvanley Gdns NW6 ..11 A3
Alvanley Ho SW9 ...173 B4
Alverstone Ave
SW18,SW19 ....70 C2
Alverstone Ho
SE11 ....163 B3
Alverstone Rd NW2 ...9 B1
Alverton St SE8 .....51 B4
Alvey St SE17 ......152 A2
Alvington Cres E8 ..16 B3
Alwyn Ave W4 ....37 C1
Alwyn Gdns W3 ......28 A3
Alwyne La N1 ....15 A1
Alwyne Pl N1 ....15 B1
Alwyne Rd N1 ....15 B1
Alwyne Sq N1 ....15 B2
Alwyne Villas N1 ....15 A1
Alzette Ho 🟥 E2 ....25 C3
Amazon St E1 ....32 A3
Ambassador Ct 🟥
NW6 ....10 C3
Ambassador Ho
NW8 ....79 A3
Ambassador Sq E14 .42 A2
Amber Ct N7 ....14 C2
Amber St E1 ....19 C2
Ambergate St
SE17 ....150 B2
Amberley Ct 🟥
SW9 ....63 A4
Amberley Rd W9 ....31 C4
Ambler JMI Sch N4 ...6 A2
Ambler Rd N4 ....6 A1
Ambleside NW1 ....82 B1
🟥 SW19 ....70 A3
Ambleside Cl 🟥 E9 ..17 B3
Ambleside Point 🟥
SE15 ....50 B3
Ambleside Rd NW10 ..8 B1
Ambrosden Ave
SW1 ....133 A1
Ambrose Ho 🟥 E14 .33 C4
Ambrose Mews
SW11 ....168 C2
Ambrose St SE16 ....40 A2
Ambrose Wlk 🟥 E3 ..26 C3
AMC Bsns Ctr NW10 ..20 C2
Amelia Ho 🟥 W6 ....39 B1
Amelia St SE17 ....150 C2
Amen Cnr EC4 ......108 B1
Amen St EC4 ....108 B1
America Sq EC3 ....124 C4
America St SE1 .....122 C1
American Coll The
W1 ....103 C2
American Sch in London
The NW8 ....79 B2
Amerland Rd SW18 .58 B1
Amersham Gr SE14 .51 B3
Amersham Rd SE14 .51 B3
Amersham Vale
SE14,SE8 ....51 B3
Amery Gdns NW10 ..22 A4

Amery Ho SE17 ....152 B2
Ames Cotts 🟥 E3 ...33 A4
Ames Ho 🟥 E2 ......25 C3
Amesbury Ave SW2 .74 B2
Amesbury Twr
SW8 ....170 C2
Amethyst Rd E15 ...19 C4
Amhurst JMI Sch
E8 ....16 C3
Amhurst Ct N4 ....6 C4
Amhurst Par N16 ....7 B4
Amhurst Pk N4,N16 ..7 A4
Amhurst Rd E8,N16 .16 C4
Amhurst Terr E8 ...16 C4
Amias Ho EC1 ....96 C2
Amies St SW11 ......60 B4
Amigo Ho SE1 .....135 C2
Amina Way SE16 ..139 B1
Amner Rd SW11 ....60 C1
Amor Rd W6 ....39 B3
Amory Ho N1 ....85 A2
Amott Rd SE15 ......64 C4
Amoy Pl E14 ....33 C2
Ampton Pl WC1 ......94 C3
Ampton St WC1 .....94 C3
Amstel Ct 🟥 SE15 .49 B3
Amsterdam Rd E14 .42 B3
Amwell St EC1 ....95 B4
Amyruth Rd SE4 ....66 C2
Anatola Rd N19 ......4 B2
Anchor Ho EC1 ......96 C2
Anchor Mews SW12 .61 A1
Anchor St SE16 .....40 A2
Anchor Terr SE1 ...123 A2
Anchor Yd EC1 ....97 A2
Anchorage Point
E14 ....41 C4
Ancill Cl W6 ....154 A3
Ancona Rd NW10 ...21 C3
Andalus Rd SW9 ....62 A4
Andaman Ho 🟥 E1 .33 A4
Anderson Cl W3 ....28 C3
Anderson Ho 🟥 E14 .34 B2
Anderson Rd E9 ....17 C2
Anderson St SW3 .144 C2
Anderton Cl SE5 ....63 C4
Andover Ho 🟥 N7 ...5 B2
Andover Pl NW6 ....78 A1
Andover Rd N7 ....5 B2
Andoversford Ct 🟥
SE15 ....49 A4
Andre St E8 ....16 C3
Andrew Borde St
WC2 ....105 C2
Andrew Ho SE4 .....51 B1
SW15 ....56 C2
N16 ....16 A4
Andrew Marvell Ho 🟥
SW8 ....171 C4
Andrew Reed Ho
SW18 ....70 A4
Andrew St E14 ......34 B3
Andrew's Rd E8 ....25 A4
Andrewes Ho EC2 .109 A3
Andrews Crosse
WC2 ....107 B1
Andrews Wlk SE17 .48 A4
Anfield Cl SW12 ....73 B4
Angel N1 ....85 C1
Angel Alley E1 .....111 A2
Angel Ct EC2 ....109 C2
SW1 ....119 A1
Angel Gate EC1 .....96 B4
Angel Ho N1 ....85 C1
Angel La E15 ....19 C2

Angel Mews N1 .....85 C1
E1 ....32 A2
SW15 ....68 C4
Angel Pas EC4 .....123 B3
Angel Pl SE1 ....137 B4
Angel Prim Sch N1 .85 C2
Angel St EC1 ....108 C2
Angel Sta EC1 ....86 A1
Angel Wlk W6 ....39 B2
Angela Davis Ind Est 🟥
SW9 ....63 A3
Angelina Ho 🟥
SE15 ....49 C2
Angell Park Gdns 🟥
SW9 ....62 C4
Angerstein Bsns Pk
SE10 ....43 C2
Angerstein La SE3 ..53 B2
Anglebury 🟥 W2 ...31 C3
Anglers La NW5 .....13 A2
Anglesey Ho 🟥 E14 .33 C3
Anglia Ho 🟥 E14 ...33 A3
Anglo American Laundry
SW17 ....71 B1
Anglo Rd 🟥 E3 ......26 B3
Angrave Ct 🟥 E8 ...24 B4
Angrave Pas 🟥 E8 .24 B4
Angus Ho 🟥 SW12 .72 B4
Angus St SE14 ......51 A3
Anhalt Rd SW11 ...158 B2
Ankerdine Cres SE18 .77 C3
Anley Rd W14 ....39 C4
Ann La SW10 ....157 B3
Ann Moss Way SE16 .40 B3
Ann's Cl SW1 ....131 B3
Ann's Pl E1 ....110 C3
Anna Cl E8 ....24 B4
Annabel Cl E14 ......34 A3
Annandale Prim Sch
SE10 ....43 B1
Annandale Rd W4 ..38 A1
SE10 ....43 C1
Anne Goodman Ho 🟥
E1 ....32 B3
Anne Kerr Ct 🟥
SW19 ....70 C3
Annesley Ho SW9 .163 C1
Annesley Wlk N19 ...4 B2
Annette Cres 🟥 N1 .15 B1
Annette Rd N7 ....5 B1
Annette Rd N7 ......14 A4
Annie Besant Cl E3 .26 B4
Anning St E2 ....98 B2
Annis Rd E9 ....18 A2
Ansdell Rd SE15 ....50 B1
Ansdell St W8 ......128 B2
Ansdell Terr W8 ...128 B2
Ansell Ho E1 ....32 B4
Ansell Rd SW17 ....72 B1
Anselm Rd SW6 ...155 B3
Ansleigh Pl W11 ....30 C2
Anslie Wlk 🟥 SW12 .73 A4
Anson Ho SW1 .....160 C4
🟥 E1 ....26 A1
Anson Prim Sch NW2 .9 C3
Anson Rd N7 ....9 B3
N7 ....5 C1
Anstey Ct 🟥 W3 ....37 A4
Anstey Ho 🟥 E9 ....25 B4
Anstey Rd SE15 .....64 C4
Anstice Cl W4 ....46 A3
Antenor Ho 🟥 E2 ...25 A3
Anthony Cope Ct
N1 ....97 C4
Anthony Ho NW8 ...90 A1
Anthony St E1 ....32 A3

Antill Rd E3 ....26 A2
Antill Terr 🟥 E1 ....32 C3
Anton St E8 ....16 C3
Antony Ho 🟥 SE16 .40 B2
SE14 ....50 C3
Antrim Gr NW3 .....12 B2
Antrim Ho 🟥 E3 ....26 A2
Antrim Mans NW3 .12 A2
Antrim Rd NW3 .....12 B2
Antrobus Rd W4 ....37 B3
Apex Ind Est NW10 .21 B1
Aphrodite Ct 🟥 E14 .41 C2
Apollo Ct SW9 .....173 B4
Apollo Ho SW10 ...157 B3
🟥 N6 ....3 B4
🟥 E2 ....25 A3
Apollo Ind Bsns Ctr 🟥
SE8 ....50 C4
Apollo Pl SW10 ...157 B2
Apollo Studios 🟥
NW5 ....13 C3
Apothecary St EC4 .108 A1
Appach Rd SW2 ....62 C1
Apple Mkt WC2 ...120 B4
Apple Tree Yd
SW1 ....119 A2
Appleby Rd E8 ......16 C1
E16 ....35 C3
Appleby St E2 ....24 B3
Appledore Cl SW12,
SW17 ....72 B2
Appleford 🟥 W5 ...13 B3
Appleford Ho 🟥
W10 ....23 A1
Appleford Rd W10 .23 A1
Applegarth Ho SE1 .136 B4
🟥 SE15 ....49 C3
Applegarth Rd W14 .39 C3
Appleshaw Ho 🟥
SE5 ....64 A4
Appletree Ct SE13 .67 C3
Appold St EC2 .....110 A4
Apprentice Way 🟥
E5 ....17 A4
Approach Cl N16 ...16 A4
Approach Rd E2 ....25 B3
Approach The W3 ..28 C3
April Ct 🟥 E2 ....24 C3
April St E8 ....16 B4
Apsley Ho E1 ....32 B4
Apsley Way W1 ....131 C4
Aquila St NW8 ....79 C2
Aquinas St SE1 ....121 C1
Arabella Ct NW8 ....79 A2
Arabella Dr SW15 ..56 A3
Arabian Ho 🟥 E1 ...26 A1
Arabin Rd SE4 ....66 B3
Aragon Twr SE8 ....41 B2
Arakan Ho 🟥 N16 .15 C4
Aral Ho 🟥 E1 ....25 C1
Arapiles Ho 🟥 E14 .34 C3
Arbery Rd E3 ....26 A3
Arbon Ct N1 ....87 A3
Arbor Ct N16 ....6 C2
Arborfield Ho 🟥
E14 ....33 C2
Arbour Ho 🟥 E1 ....32 C3
Arbour Sq E1 ....32 C3
Arbourfield Cl SW2 .74 B3
Arbuthnot Rd SE14 .50 C1
Arbutus St E8 ....24 B4
Arcade The EC2 ...110 A3
🟥 N7 ....14 A4
Arcadia St E14 ......33 C3
Arch St SE1 ....136 C1

Archangel St SE16 ..40 C4
Archbishop Michael
Ramsey Tech Coll
SE5 ....48 A3
Archbishop Sumner's
CE Prim Sch
SE11 ....149 C3
Archbishop Tenison's
Sch SE1 ....163 A3
Archbishop's Pl 🟥
SW2 ....74 B4
Archdale Ct W12 ...30 A1
Archdale Ho SE1 ..138 A2
Archdale Rd SE22 ..64 B3
Archel Rd W14 .....154 C4
Archer Ho N1 ....110 A4
SW11 ....167 C3
🟥 N1 ....24 A4
Archer Sq SE14 ....51 A4
Archer St W1 ....119 B4
Archers Lo SE16 ..153 C2
Archery Cl W2 ....102 B1
Archery Fields Ho
WC1 ....95 B4
Archery Steps 🟥 W2 .116 B4
Arches The WC2 ...120 B2
Archibald Mews
W1 ....118 A3
Archibald Rd N7 ....13 C4
Archibald St E3 .....26 C2
Archie St SE1 ......138 B3
Archway N19 ....4 B2
Archway Bsns Ctr 🟥
N19 ....4 C1
Archway Cl W10 ....30 C4
Archway Hts 🟥 N19 .4 B3
Archway Rd N6 ....4 A3
Archway St SW13,
SW14 ....56 A4
Archway Sta N19 ....4 B2
Arcola St E8 ....16 B3
Arctic St NW5 ....13 A3
Ardbeg Rd SE24 ....63 C2
Arden 🟥 SW19 .....69 C3
Arden Cres E14 .....41 C2
Arden Ho SE11 ....148 C3
🟥 SW9 ....172 B1
🟥 N1 ....24 A3
Ardent Ho 🟥 E3 ....26 A3
Ardilaun Rd N5 ....15 B4
Ardleigh Rd N1 .....16 A2
Ardlui Rd SE27 .....75 B2
Ardmere Rd SE13 ..67 C1
Ardshiel Cl SW15 ..57 C4
Ardwell Rd 🟥 SW2 .74 A2
Ardwick Rd NW2 ...10 C4
Ares Ct 🟥 E14 ......41 C2
Arethusa Ho 🟥 E14 .42 A2
Argon Mews SW6 .155 C1
Argos Ct 🟥 SW9 ..173 B4
Argos Ho 🟥 E2 .....25 A3
Argosy Ho W1 ....92 B1
🟥 SE8 ....41 A2
Argyle Ho E14 ......42 B3
Argyle Pl W6 ....39 A2
Argyle Prim Sch
WC1 ....94 A4
Argyle Rd E1 ....25 C1
Argyle Sq WC1 ......94 B4
Argyle St WC1 ....94 B4
Argyle Way SE16 .153 C1
Argyle Wlk WC1 ....94 B3
Argyll Cl SW9 ....62 B4
Argyll Ct 🟥 SW2 ...74 A4
Argyll Mans W14 ..140 B4
SW3 ....157 C4
Argyll Rd W8 ....127 C3

Argyll St W1 ...104 C1
Arica Ho SE16 ...40 A3
Arica Rd SE4 ...66 A4
Ariel Ct SE11 ...150 A3
  W12 ...30 A1
Ariel Ho NW6 ...10 C2
Ariel Way W12 ...30 B1
Aristotle Rd SW4 ...61 C4
Arkansas Ho 17 N1 ...24 A4
Arklow Ho SE17 ...48 C4
Arklow Rd SE14 ...51 B4
Arklow Road Trad Est
  SE14 ...51 B4
Arkwright Ho 22
  SW2 ...74 A4
Arkwright Mans
  NW3 ...11 B3
Arkwright Rd NW3 ...11 B3
Arlesey Cl SW15 ...58 A2
Arlesford Rd SW9 ...62 A4
Arlingford Rd SW2 ...62 C1
Arlington Ave N1 ...87 A3
Arlington Gdns W4 ...37 B1
Arlington Ho EC1 ...95 C4
  W12 ...30 A1
  8 SE8 ...51 B4
Arlington Lo 9 SW2 ...62 B3
Arlington Park Mans 3
  W4 ...37 B1
Arlington Pl 7
  SE10 ...52 B3
Arlington Rd NW1 ...82 B3
Arlington Sq N1 ...87 A3
Arlington St SW1 ...118 C2
Arlington Way EC1 ...95 C4
Armada Ct 11 SE8 ...51 C4
Armada St 10 SE8 ...51 C4
Armadale Rd SW6 ...155 B3
Armagh Rd E3 ...26 B4
Arminger Rd W12 ...30 A1
Armitage Rd NW11 ...1 B3
  SE10 ...43 B1
Armour Cl N7 ...14 B2
Armoury Rd SE8 ...52 A1
Armoury Way SE18 ...58 C2
Armsby Ho 15 E1 ...32 B4
Armstrong Ho 8
  SW15 ...57 C1
Armstrong Rd
  SW7 ...129 B1
  W3 ...29 B1
Arnal Cres SW18 ...70 A4
Arncliffe NW6 ...78 B3
Arne Ho SE11 ...148 C2
Arne St WC2 ...106 B1
Arneway St SW1 ...133 C1
Arnewood Cl SW15 ...68 C3
Arnhem Pl E14 ...41 C3
Arnhem Way 3
  SE22 ...64 A2
Arnhem Wharf E14 ...41 C3
Arnhem Wharf JMI Sch
  E14 ...41 C3
Arnold Cir E2 ...98 C3
Arnold Est SE1 ...139 A3
Arnold Ho SE17 ...150 B1
  9 N16 ...7 A1
Arnold House Sch
  NW8 ...79 B1
Arnold Rd E3 ...26 C2
Arnot Ho 27 SE5 ...48 B3
Arnould Ave SE5 ...63 C3
Arnside Ho 2 SE17 ...48 C4
Arnside St SE17 ...48 B4
Arodene Rd SW2 ...62 B1

Arragon Rd SW18 ...70 C3
Arran Ho N16 ...7 B3
Arran Wlk N1 ...15 B1
Arrol Ho SE1 ...137 A1
Arrow Ho 23 N1 ...24 A4
Arrow Rd E3 ...27 A2
Arrowe Ct 7 E5 ...17 A4
Arrowsmith Ho
  SE11 ...148 C2
Arsenal Sta N5 ...5 C1
Artemis Ct 6 E14 ...41 C2
Artesian Rd W2 ...31 C3
Arthur Ct W2 ...100 A2
  SW11 ...169 C3
  10 W10 ...30 C3
Arthur Deakin Ho
  E1 ...111 B4
Arthur Henderson Ho
  SW6 ...164 C2
Arthur Newton Ho 20
  SW11 ...59 C4
Arthur Rd N7 ...14 B4
  SW19 ...70 C1
Arthur St EC4 ...123 C4
Arthur Wade Ho E2 ...99 A4
Arthurdon Rd SE4 ...66 C2
Artichoke Hill 8 E1 ...32 A2
Artichoke Mews 5
  SE5 ...48 C2
Artichoke Pl SE5 ...48 C2
Artillery La 1 ...110 B3
  W12 ...29 C3
Artillery Row SW1 ...133 B1
Artizan St E1 ...110 B2
Arton Wilson Ho 12
  SW15 ...56 C2
Arts Educational Schs
  The W4 ...38 A2
Arundel Bldgs SE1 ...138 B1
Arundel Cl SW11 ...60 A2
Arundel Ct SW3 ...144 B2
  SW13 ...47 A4
  W11 ...31 B2 112 C4
Arundel Gdns
  W11 ...31 B2 112 C4
Arundel Gr N16 ...16 A3
Arundel Ho N1 ...86 B4
  3 W3 ...37 A4
  Richmond TW10 ...54 C2
Arundel Mans
  SW6 ...165 A4
  SW13 ...47 A4
Arundel Pl N1,N7 ...14 C2
Arundel Sq N7 ...14 C2
Arundel St WC2 ...121 A4
Arundel Terr SW13 ...47 A4
Arvon Rd N5 ...14 C3
Asaph Ho SE1 ...51 B2
Ascalon Ct 18 SW2 ...74 B4
Ascalon Ho SW8 ...160 C1
Ascalon St SW8 ...160 C1
Ascham St NW5 ...13 B3
Ascot Ct SW4 ...89 B3
  5 W4 ...38 A1
Ascot Ho NW1 ...92 B4
  1 W9 ...31 C4
  4 W3 ...37 B1
Ascot Lo NW6 ...78 B2
Ascot Par 9 SW4 ...62 A3
Ascott Ave W5 ...36 A4
Ascham Cl SW11 ...107 C2
Ash Ct W1 ...102 B1
  N19 ...4 C3
  SW11 ...60 C2
Ash Gr NW2 ...10 A4

Ash Gr continued
  E8 ...25 A4
  ...36 A3
Ash Ho SE1 ...153 A3
  14 E14 ...42 B4
Ash Lo SW6 ...47 C2
Ashbourne Ct E5 ...18 A4
Ashbourne Gr W4 ...38 A1
  SE22 ...64 B3
Ashbridge St NW8 ...90 A1
Ashbrook Rd N19 ...4 C2
Ashburn Gdns
  SW7 ...142 C4
Ashburn Pl SW7 ...142 C4
Ashburnham Gr
  SE10 ...52 A3
Ashburnham Pl
  SE10 ...52 A3
Ashburnham Prim Sch
  SW10 ...157 A1
Ashburnham Rd
  SW10 ...157 A1
  NW10 ...22 B2
Ashburnham Retreat 6
  SE10 ...52 A3
Ashburnham Twr
  SW10 ...157 B2
Ashburton Gr N7 ...14 C4
Ashburton Mans
  SW10 ...157 A2
Ashburton Rd E16 ...35 C3
Ashby Ct NW8 ...89 C2
Ashby Gr N1 ...15 B1
Ashby Ho N1 ...15 B1
  8 SW9 ...48 A1
Ashby Mews SE4 ...51 B1
Ashby Rd SE4 ...51 B1
Ashby St EC1 ...96 B3
Ashchurch Ct W12 ...38 C3
Ashchurch Gr W12 ...38 C3
Ashchurch Park Villas
  W12 ...38 C3
Ashchurch Terr
  W12 ...38 C3
Ashcombe Ct 4 ...38 A2
Ashcombe Ho 39 E3 ...27 A2
Ashcombe St SW6 ...166 A1
Ashcroft Ho SW8 ...170 C4
Ashcroft Rd E3 ...26 A2
Ashcroft Sq W6 ...39 B2
Ashdale Ho N4 ...6 C4
Ashdene 6 SE15 ...50 A3
Ashdown Ct SW15 ...57 C2
Ashdown Cres NW5 ...12 C3
Ashdown Ho 5 E7 ...7 C2
Ashdown Rd NW10 ...21 B4
Ashdown Way
  SW17 ...72 C2
Ashdown Wlk 18
  E14 ...41 C2
Ashen Gr SW19 ...70 C2
Ashenden SE17 ...151 A4
Ashenden Rd E5 ...18 A3
Ashentree Ct EC4 ...107 C1
Asher Way E1 ...125 C3
Ashfield Ho N5 ...15 B3
Ashfield Rd W3 ...29 B1
Ashfield St E1 ...32 A4
Ashford Ct NW2 ...9 C4
Ashford Ho 8 SE1 ...51 B4
  SW9 ...63 A3
Ashford Rd NW2 ...9 C4
Ashford St N1 ...98 A4
Ashgrove Ct 9 ...31 C4
Ashgrove Ho SW1 ...147 C2

Assam SE1 ...125 A1
Assam St E1 ...111 B2
Assata Mews N1 ...15 A2
Assembly Pas E1 ...32 B4
Astbury Ho SE11 ...135 B1
Astbury Rd SE15 ...50 B2
Aste St E14 ...42 B4
Astell Ho 3 N1 ...15 B1
Astey's Row 3 N1 ...15 B1
Astle St SW11 ...169 C2
Astley Ave NW2 ...9 B3
Astley Ho 1 SE1 ...153 A2
  4 SW18 ...59 C3
Aston Ho W11 ...113 A3
  SW8 ...171 B3
Aston St E14 ...33 A4
Astonville St SW18 ...70 C3
Astor Ct SW6 ...156 C1
Astoria Mans 5
  SW16 ...74 A1
Astoria Par SW16 ...74 A1
Astoria Wlk SW9 ...62 C4
Astra Ho N4 ...5 B4
  4 E3 ...26 B2
Astrop Mews W6 ...39 B3
Astrop Terr W6 ...39 B3
Astwood Mews
  SW7 ...142 C4
Asylum Rd SE15 ...50 A3
Atalanta St SW6 ...154 A1
Atheldene Rd SW18 ...71 B3
Athelstan Gdns 6
  NW6 ...10 A1
Athelstan Ho E9 ...18 B3
Athelstan Gr E3 ...26 B3
Athelstane Mews N4 ...5 C3
Athena Ct NW8 ...79 B2
Athenia Ho 7 E14 ...34 C3
Athenlay Rd SE15 ...65 C2
Atheneeum Ct N5 ...15 B4
Athens Gdns W9 ...23 C1
Atherden Rd E5 ...17 B4
Atherfield Ct SW18 ...59 A1
Atherfold Rd SW9 ...62 A4
Atherstone Ct W2 ...100 B4
Atherstone Mews
  SW7 ...143 A4
Atherton Rd SW13 ...46 C3
Atherton St SW11 ...168 B2
Athlone Cl 24 E5 ...17 A3
Athlone Ho 18 NW5 ...12 C2
  9 E1 ...32 B3
Athlone House (The
  Middlesex Hospl)
  ...3 B3
Athlone Rd SW2 ...74 C4
Athlone St NW5 ...12 C2
Athol Sq E14 ...34 B3
Atholl Ho W9 ...88 C3
Atkins Rd SW4,SW12 ...73 C4
Atkinson Ho SE17 ...151 C3
  SW11 ...169 B3
  4 E2 ...24 C3
Atlantic Ho 4 E1 ...33 A4
  4 SW15 ...58 B2
Atlantic Rd SW2,
  SW9,SE24 ...62 C3
Atlas Mews E8 ...16 B2
  N7 ...14 B2
Atlas Rd NW10 ...21 A2
Atley Rd E3 ...26 C4
Atney Rd SW15 ...58 A3
Atterbury St SW1 ...148 A3
Attilburgh Ho SE1 ...138 C2

Attneave St WC1 .....95 B3
Atwater Cl SW2 .....74 C3
Atwell Rd 4 SE15 .....49 C1
Atwood Ave TW9 .....44 C1
Atwood Ho SE21 .....76 A1
Atwood Rd W6 .....39 A2
Aubert Ct N5 .....15 A4
Aubert Pk N5 .....15 A4
Aubert Rd N5 .....15 A4
Aubrey Beardsley Ho
  SW1 .....147 A3
Aubrey Mans NW1 .....102 A4
Aubrey Moore Point
  E15 .....27 B3
Aubrey Pl NW8 .....78 C1
Aubrey Rd
  W14 .....31 B1 113 A1
Aubrey Wlk
  W14 .....31 B1 113 A1
Auburn Cl SE14 .....51 A3
Aubyn Sq SW15 .....56 C2
Auckland Ho 11
  W12 .....30 A2
Auckland Rd SW11 .....60 A3
Auckland St SE11 .....148 C1
Auden Pl NW1 .....81 B4
Audley Cl W11 .....118 A2
Audley Ct W1 .....118 A2
Audley Ho SW4 .....54 B2
Audley Sq W1 .....117 C2
Audrey St E2 .....24 C3
Augustas Cl W12 .....39 A3
Augustine Rd W14 .....39 C3
Augustines Ct E9 .....17 B3
Augustus Cl
  3 SW3 .....70 A3
  SW16 .....73 C1
Augustus Rd SW19 .....70 A3
Augustus St NW1 .....92 B4
Aulton Pl SE11 .....149 C1
Auriga Mews N1 .....15 C3
Auriol Mans W14 .....140 A3
Auriol Rd W14 .....140 A3
Austen Ho 2 NW6 .....23 C2
Austin Friars EC2 .....109 C2
Austin Friars Sq
  EC2 .....109 C2
Austin Ho 1 SE14 .....51 B3
  6 SW2 .....62 B2
Austin St E2 .....98 C3
Austins Ct SE15 .....64 C4
Austral St SE11 .....150 A4
Australia Rd W12 .....30 A2
Autumn St E3 .....26 C4
Avalon Rd SW6 .....166 A4
Ave Maria La EC4 .....108 B1
Avebury Ct N1 .....87 B3
Avebury St N1 .....87 B3
Aveline St SE11 .....149 B1
Avenell Mans N5 .....15 A4
Avenell Rd N5 .....6 A1
Avenfield Ho 1 W1 .....117 A4
Avening Rd SW18 .....70 C4
Avening Terr SW18 .....70 C4
Avenue Cl NW8 .....80 B3
Avenue Cres W3 .....37 A4
Avenue Ct SW3 .....144 C3
  NW2 .....1 B1
Avenue Gdns 3 .....37 A4
  SW14 .....56 A4
Avenue Ho NW8 .....80 A1
  N16 .....16 A4
  NW10 .....22 A3

Avenue Lo NW8 .....79 C4
12 NW8 .....79 C4
Avenue Mans NW3 .....11 A3
Avenue Park Rd
  SE21,SE27 .....75 A2
Avenue Rd NW8 .....80 A4
  N6 .....
  NW10 .....21 B3
  W3 .....37 A4
Avenue The NW6 .....23 A4
  W4 .....38 A3
  Richmond TW9 .....44 B1
  SW4 .....
  SW13,SW14 .....72 A4
Averill St W6 .....47 C4
Avery Farm Row
  SW1 .....146 A3
Avery Row W1 .....118 B4
Avery Hill Coll (Mile End
  Annexe) E3 .....26 B1
Aviary Ct E1 .....35 B2
Avigdor (Jewish) JMI
  Sch N16 .....
Avignon Rd SE4 .....65 C4
Avington Ct SE1 .....152 B3
Avis Sq E1 .....32 C3
Avoca Rd SW17 .....72 C1
Avocet Cl SE1 .....153 B3
Avon Ct 11 SW15 .....58 A2
  W3 .....28 B3
Avon Ho W14 .....141 A3
  14 N16 .....15 C4
Avon Pl SE1 .....137 A3
Avon Rd SE4 .....66 C4
Avondale Ct E16 .....35 A4
  6 SW14 .....55 C4
  11 SW14 .....55 C4
Avondale Mans
  SW6 .....164 C4
Avondale Park Gdns
  W11 .....31 A2 112 A4
Avondale Park Prim Sch
  W11 .....31 A2 112 A4
Avondale Rd E16 .....35 A4
  SW14 .....55 C4
Avondale Rise SE15 .....64 B4
Avondale Sq SE1 .....153 B1
Avonhurst Ho NW6 .....10 A1
Avonley Rd SE14 .....50 B3
Avonmore Gdns
  W14 .....141 A3
Avonmore Pl W14 .....140 B4
Avonmore Prim Sch
  .....140 B4
Avonmore Rd W14 .....140 C4
Avonmouth St SE1 .....136 C2
Avriol Ho W12 .....30 A1
Avro Ct E9 .....18 A3
Axford Ho SW2 .....75 A3
Axminster Rd N7 .....5 B1
Aybrook St W1 .....103 B3
Aycliffe Rd W12 .....29 C1
Aylesbury Ho 15
  SE15 .....49 C4
Aylesbury Rd SE17 .....151 C1
Aylesbury St EC1 .....96 A1
  NW10 .....8 A4
Aylesford Ho SE1 .....137 C3
Aylesford St SW1 .....147 B1
Aylesham Centre The
  SE15 .....49 C2
Aylestone Ave NW6 .....22 C4
Aylmer Ho SE10 .....42 C1
Aylmer Rd W12 .....38 B4
Aylton Est 22 SE16 .....40 B4

Aylward St E1 18 E14 .....33 A4
Aylward St E1 .....32 C3
Aylwin Est SE1 .....138 B2
Aylwin Girls Sch
  SE1 .....153 A4
Aynhoe Mans W14 .....39 C3
Aynhoe Rd W14 .....39 C3
Ayres St SE1 .....137 A4
Ayrsome Rd N16 .....7 A1
Ayrton Gould Ho 9
  E2 .....25 C2
Ayrton Rd SW7 .....129 B2
Aysgarth Rd SE21 .....76 A4
Ayston Ho 10 SE8 .....40 C2
Ayton Ho SE5 .....48 C3
Aytoun Ct SW9 .....173 A1
Aytoun Pl SW9 .....173 A1
Aytoun Rd SW9 .....173 A1
Azalea Ho SE14 .....51 B3
Azenby Rd SE15 .....49 B1
Azof St SE10 .....43 A2
Azov Ho 9 E1 .....26 A1

B

Baalbec Rd N5 .....15 A3
Babington Ho SE1 .....137 A4
Babmaes St SW1 .....119 B3
Bacchus Wlk 17 N1 .....24 A3
Bache's St N1 .....97 C3
Back Church La
  E1 .....111 B1
Back Hill EC1 .....95 C1
Back La NW3 .....11 B4
Backhouse Pl SE1 .....152 B3
Bacon Gr SE1 .....138 C1
Bacon St E2 .....24 C1 99 A2
Bacon's Coll SE16 .....41 A4
Bacon's La N6 .....3 C3
Bacton NW5 .....12 C3
Bacton St E2 .....25 B2
Baddeley Ho SE11 .....149 A2
Baddow Wlk (off
  Popham Rd) N1 .....86 C4
Baden Pl SE1 .....137 B4
Badminton Ct 9 N4 .....6 B4
Badminton Ho SE22 .....64 A3
Badminton Mews 10
  E16 .....35 C1
Badminton Rd
  SW12 .....60 C1
Badric Ct SW11 .....167 C1
Badsworth Rd 3
  SE5 .....48 B2
Bagley's La SW6 .....166 B3
Bagnigge Ho WC1 .....95 B3
Bagshot Ho NW1 .....92 B4
Bagshot St SE17 .....152 B1
Baildon 21 E2 .....25 B3
Baildon St SE8 .....51 B3
Bailey Ct 9 W12 .....38 C4
Bailey Mews W4 .....45 A4
Bain Ho SW9 .....172 B2
Bainbridge St
  WC1 .....105 C2
Baird Ho 10 W12 .....30 A2
Baird St EC1 .....97 A2
Baizdon Rd SE3 .....53 A1
Baker Ho 12 E3 .....27 A2
Baker Rd NW10 .....21 A4
Baker St 11 .....91 A1
Baker St W1 .....103 A4
Baker Street Sta
  NW1 .....91 A1
Baker's Mews W1 .....103 B2
Baker's Row EC1 .....95 B1

Baker's Yd EC1 .....95 B1
Bakers Field N7 .....14 A4
Bakers Hall EC3 .....124 B3
Balaclava Rd SE1 .....153 A3
Balchier Rd SE22 .....65 A1
Balcombe Ho NW1 .....90 C2
  3 SW2 .....74 B3
Balcombe St NW1 .....90 C1
Balcorne St E9 .....17 B1
Balderton Flats
  W1 .....103 C1
Balderton St W1 .....103 C1
Baldock Ho 20 SE5 .....48 B1
Baldock St E3 .....27 A3
Baldrey Ho 10 SE10 .....43 B1
Baldwin Cres SE5 .....48 B2
Baldwin Ho 15 SW2 .....74 C3
Baldwin St EC1 .....97 B3
Baldwin Terr N1 .....86 C2
Baldwin's Gdns
  EC1 .....107 B4
Baldwyn Gdns W3 .....28 C2
Bales Coll W10 .....22 C2
Balfe St N1 .....84 B1
Balfern Gr W4 .....38 A1
Balfern St SW11 .....168 B2
Balfour Ho W10 .....30 C4
Balfour Mews W1 .....117 C2
Balfour Pl W1 .....117 C3
  SW15 .....57 A3
Balfour Rd N5 .....15 B4
  W3 .....28 B4
Balfour St SE17 .....151 B4
Balfron Twr 2 E14 .....34 B3
Balham Gr SW12 .....72 C4
Balham High Rd
  SW12,SW17 .....72 C3
Balham Hill SW12 .....61 A1
Balham New Rd
  SW12 .....73 A4
Balham Park Mans
  SW12 .....72 B3
Balham Park Rd
  SW12,SW17 .....72 B3
Balham Station Rd
  SW12 .....73 A3
Balin Ho SE1 .....137 B4
Balkan Wlk 1 E1 .....32 A2
Ball Ct EC3 .....109 C1
Ball's Pond Pl 2
  N1 .....15 C2
Ball's Pond Rd N1 .....16 A2
Ballance Rd E9 .....18 A2
Ballantine St SW18 .....59 B3
Ballantrae Ho NW2 .....10 B4
Ballard Ho SE10 .....52 A4
Ballast Quay SE10 .....42 C1
Ballater Rd SW2,
  SW4 .....62 A3
Ballin Ct 9 E14 .....42 B4
Ballina St SE23 .....65 C1
Ballingdon Rd
  SW11 .....60 C1
Ballinger Point 13
  E3 .....27 A2
Balliol Ho 11 SW15 .....57 C1
Balliol Rd W10 .....30 C3
Ballogie Ave NW10 .....8 A4
Ballow Cl 25 SE5 .....49 A3
Balman Ho 3 SE16 .....40 C2
Balmer Rd E3 .....26 B3
Balmes Rd N1 .....87 C4
Balmoral Cl 1
  SW15 .....57 C1
Balmoral Ct NW8 .....79 B2

Balmoral Ct continued
  21 SE16 .....32 C1
Balmoral Gr N7 .....14 B2
Balmoral Ho W14 .....140 A4
  4 E14 .....42 A3
Balmoral Mews
  W12 .....38 B3
Balmoral Rd NW2 .....9 A2
Balmore St N19 .....4 A2
Balmuir Gdns SW15 .....57 B3
Balnacraig Ave
  NW10 .....8 A4
Balniel Gate SW1 .....147 C2
Balsam Ho 8 E14 .....34 A2
Baltic Cl SW19 .....71 A1
Baltic Ho 5 SE5 .....48 B1
Baltic St E EC1 .....96 C1
Baltic St W EC1 .....96 C1
Baltimore Ho SE11 .....149 B2
Balvaird Pl SW1 .....147 C1
Balvernie Gr SW18 .....70 C4
Bamborough Gdns 18
  W12 .....39 B4
Bamford Ct E15 .....19 A3
Banbury Ct WC2 .....120 A4
Banbury Ho 5 E9 .....17 C1
Banbury Rd E9 .....17 C1
Banbury St SW11 .....168 B2
Bancroft Ct SW8 .....172 A4
Bancroft Ho 2 E1 .....25 B1
Bancroft Rd E1 .....25 C1
Banff Ho 1 NW3 .....12 A2
Bangabandhu JMI Sch
  .....25 B2
Bangalore St SW15 .....57 C4
Banim St W6 .....39 A2
Banister Ho SW8 .....171 A4
  E9 .....17 C3
  10 W10 .....23 A2
Banister Rd W10 .....22 C2
Bank Ct SW11 .....170 A4
Bank End SE1 .....123 A2
Bank La SW15 .....56 A2
Bank of England
  EC2 .....109 B1
Bank Sta EC3 .....109 C1
Bank The N6 .....4 A3
Banks Ho SE1 .....136 C1
Bankside 1 SE1 .....122 C3
  .....123 A2
Bankside Pier SE1 .....122 C3
Bankton Rd SW2 .....62 C3
Banner Ho EC1 .....97 A1
Banner St EC1 .....97 A2
Bannerman Ho
  SW8 .....162 C3
Banning Ho 4
  SW19 .....69 C3
Banning St SE10 .....43 A1
Bannister Cl SW2 .....74 C3
Bannister Ho 28
  SE14 .....50 C4
Banqueting House*
  SW1 .....120 A1
Banstead Ct N4 .....6 B3
Banstead St SE15 .....65 B4
Bantock Ho 10 W10 .....23 A2
Bantry Ho 8 E1 .....25 C1
Bantry St SE5 .....48 C3
Banyan Ho 8 NW3 .....11 A2
Banyard Rd SE16 .....40 A3
Baptist Gdns NW5 .....12 C2
Barandon Wlk 9
  W11 .....30 C2
Barb Mews W6 .....39 B3
Barbanel Ho 11 E1 .....25 B1

Barbara Brosnan Ct NW8 .....79 B1
Barbauld Rd N16 .....7 A3
Barber Beaumont Ho ⬛ E1 .....25 C2
Barbers Rd E15 .....27 A3
Barbican★ EC2 .....103 A3
Barbican Arts & Con Ctr EC2 .....109 A4
Barbican Sta EC1 .....108 C4
Barbon Cl WC1 .....106 C4
Barbrook Ho E9 .....17 B2
Barchard St SW18 .....59 A2
Barchester St E14 .....34 A4
Barclay Cl SW6 .....155 B1
Barclay Ho 21 E9 .....17 B1
Barclay Rd SW6 .....155 C1
Barcombe Ave SW2 .....74 B2
Bard Rd W10 .....30 C2
Bardell Ho E1 .....139 B3
Bardolph Rd N7 .....14 A4
  Richmond TW9 .....54 B4
Bardsey Pl 35 E1 .....25 B1
Bardsey Wlk 2 N1 .....15 B2
Bardsley Ho 5 SE10 .....52 B4
Bardsley La SE10 .....52 B4
Barents Ho 10 E1 .....25 C1
Barfett St W10 .....23 B1
Barfleur Ho SE8 .....41 B2
Barford Ho 19 E3 .....26 B3
Barford St N1 .....85 C3
Barforth Rd SE15 .....65 A4
Barge House St SE1 .....121 C2
Barham Ho SE17 .....152 B2
Baring Ct N1 .....87 B3
Baring Ho 10 E14 .....33 C3
Baring St N1 .....87 B3
Bark Pl W2 .....114 A4
Barker Dr NW1 .....13 C1
Barker Ho SE17 .....152 A1
  SE21 .....76 A1
Barker Mews SW4 .....61 A3
Barker St SW10 .....156 C4
Barker Wlk SW16 .....73 C1
Barkston Gdns SW5 .....142 A3
Barkway Ct N4 .....6 B2
Barkwith Ho 27 SE14 .....50 C4
Barkworth Rd SE16 .....40 B1
Barlborough St SE14 .....50 C3
Barlby Gdns W10 .....22 C1
Barlby Prim Sch W10 .....22 C1
Barlby Rd W10 .....30 C4
Barley Mow Pas EC1 .....108 B3
  W4 .....37 C1
Barleycorn Way E14 .....33 B2
Barling 3 NW1 .....13 A1
Barling Ct SW4 .....172 A2
Barlings Ho 2 SE4 .....65 C3
Barloch Ho W12 .....169 B2
Barlow Ho N1 .....97 B4
  W11 .....112 A4
  14 SE16 .....40 A2
Barlow Pl W1 .....118 B3
Barlow Rd NW6 .....10 B2
  W3 .....28 A1
Barlow St SE17 .....151 C3
Barmouth Ho 6 N7 .....5 B2
Barmouth Rd SW18 .....59 B1
Barn Cl 19 NW5 .....13 C3

Barn Field NW3 .....12 B3
Barn St N16 .....7 A1
Barnabas Ho EC1 .....96 C3
Barnabas Lo SW8 .....172 B4
Barnabas Rd E9 .....17 C3
Barnaby Pl SW7 .....143 B3
Barnard Ct SW16 .....74 B1
Barnard Ho 17 E2 .....25 A2
Barnard Lo 10 W9 .....31 C4
Barnard Mews SW11 .....60 A3
Barnard's Inn EC4 .....107 C2
Barnardo Gdns 1 E1 .....32 C2
Barnardo St E1 .....32 C3
Barnbrough N1 .....82 C3
Barnby St NW1 .....93 A4
Barnersbury Ho N7 .....14 A4
Barnes Ave SW13 .....46 C3
Barnes Bridge Sta SW13 .....46 A1
Barnes Common SW13 .....56 C4
Barnes High St SW13 .....46 B1
Barnes Ho N19 .....4 C4
  14 E2 .....25 B3
  28 SE14 .....50 C4
Barnes Hospl SW14 .....56 A4
Barnes St E14 .....33 A3
Barnes Sta SW13 .....56 C4
Barnes Terr SE8 .....41 B1
Barnet Gr 2 .....24 C2 99 B3
Barnet Ho 38 SE5 .....48 B1
Barnett Ho E1 .....110 C3
Barnett St 8 E1 .....32 A3
Barnfield Pl E14 .....41 C2
Barnham St SE1 .....138 B4
Barnsbury Gr N1 .....14 B1
Barnsbury Ho 12 SW4 .....61 C1
Barnsbury Pk N1 .....14 C1
Barnsbury Rd N1 .....85 B3
Barnsbury Sq N1 .....14 C1
Barnsbury St N1 .....14 C1
Barnsbury Terr N1 .....14 B1
Barnsdale Ave E14 .....41 C2
Barnsdale Rd W9 .....23 B1
Barnsley St E1 .....25 A1
Barnstaple La SE13 .....67 B3
Barnston Wlk N1 .....86 C4
Barnwell Ho 1 SE5 .....49 A2
Barnwell Rd SW2 .....62 C2
Barnwood Cl W9 .....88 B1
Baron Cl N1 .....85 B2
Baron St N1 .....85 B2
Baron Wlk E16 .....35 B4
Baron's Court Rd W14 .....140 B2
Baron's Pl SE1 .....135 C3
Baroness Rd E2 .....99 A4
Barons Court Mans W14 .....140 B1
Barons Court Sta W14 .....140 A1
Barons Gate 10 W4 .....37 B3
Barons Keep W14 .....140 A2
Barons Lo 8 E14 .....42 B2
Baronsmead Rd SW13 .....46 C2
Baronsmede W5 .....36 B4

Barque Mews SE8 .....51 C4
Barratt Ho 1 N1 .....15 A1
Barratt Ind Pk E3 .....27 A1
Barret Ho NW6 .....23 C4
  2 SW9 .....62 C4
Barrett Ho 12 SE17 .....151 A2
Barrett St W1 .....103 C1
Barrett's Gr N16 .....16 A3
Barrett's Green Rd NW10 .....20 C3
Barrhill Rd SW2 .....74 A2
Barridge Mews NW6 .....10 C3
Barrie Ho NW8 .....80 B3
  W2 .....115 A3
  8 N16 .....7 A3
  W3 .....37 B4
Barriedale SE14 .....51 A1
Barrington Cl NW5 .....12 C3
Barrington Ct NW5 .....12 C3
Barrington Rd SW9 .....63 A4
Barrow Hill Est NW8 .....80 A1
Barrow Hill Jun Sch NW8 .....80 A1
Barrow Hill Rd NW8 .....80 A1
Barrowgate Ho W4 .....37 C1
Barrowgate Rd W4 .....37 C1
Barry Ct SW4 .....61 B1
Barry Ho 4 SE16 .....40 A1
Barry Lo N4 .....5 B4
Barry Par SE22 .....64 C3
Barry Rd SE22 .....64 C2
Barset Rd SE15 .....65 B4
Barston Rd SE27 .....75 B1
Barstow Cres SW2 .....74 B3
Bartell Ho SW2 .....62 C1
Barter St WC1 .....106 B3
Bartholomew Cl EC1 .....108 C3
  SW18 .....59 B3
Bartholomew Ho 20 SE5 .....48 B1
Bartholomew La EC2 .....109 C1
Bartholomew Pas EC1 .....108 B3
Bartholomew Pl EC1 .....108 C3
Bartholomew Rd NW5 .....13 B2
Bartholomew Sq 16 EC1 .....97 A2
Bartholomew St SE1 .....137 C1
Bartholomew Villas NW5 .....13 B2
Bartle Rd W11 .....31 A3
Bartlett Cl E14 .....33 C3
Bartlett Ct EC4 .....107 C2
Bartok Ho W11 .....112 C3
Bartolomew Sq EC1 .....97 A2
Barton Cl E9 .....17 B3
  SE15 .....65 A4
Barton Ct W14 .....140 B2
  SW4 .....172 A2
Barton Ho N1 .....15 A1
  8 E3 .....27 A2
  5 SW6 .....58 C4
Barton Rd W14 .....140 B2
Barton St SW1 .....134 A2
Bartonway NW8 .....79 B2
Bartram Rd SE4 .....66 A1
Bartrip St E9 .....18 B2

Barville Cl SE4 .....66 A3
Barwell Ho 2 .....99 B2
Barwick Ho 7 W3 .....37 B3
Bashley Rd NW10 .....20 C1
Basil Ho E1 .....111 C2
  SW8 .....162 A2
Basil Mans SW1 .....130 C3
Basil St SW1,SW3 .....130 C2
Basing Ct 12 SE15 .....49 B2
Basing Hill NW11 .....1 B3
Basing House Yd E2 .....98 B4
Basing Pl E2 .....98 B4
Basing St W11 .....31 B3
Basingdon Way SE5 .....63 C3
Basinghall Ave EC2 .....109 B2
Basinghall St EC2 .....109 B2
Basire St N1 .....87 A4
Baskerville Gdns NW10 .....8 A4
Baskerville Rd SW18 .....72 A4
Baslow Wlk E5 .....17 C4
Basnett Rd 8 SW11 .....60 C4
Basque Ct 20 SE16 .....40 C4
Bassano St SE22 .....64 B2
Bassein Park Rd W12 .....38 B4
Bassett Rd W10 .....30 C3
Bassett St NW5 .....12 C2
Bassingbourn Ho 3 N1 .....15 A1
Bassingham Rd SW18 .....71 B4
Bassishaw Highwalk EC2 .....109 B3
Basswood Cl SE15 .....65 A4
Basterfield Ho EC1 .....96 C1
Bastwick St EC1 .....96 C2
Basuto Rd SW6 .....165 C3
Batavia Ho 1 SE14 .....51 A3
Batavia Mews 3 SE14 .....51 A3
Batavia Rd SE14 .....51 A3
Batchelor St N1 .....85 C3
Bate St 10 E14 .....33 B2
Bateman Ho 8 SE17 .....48 A4
Bateman St W1 .....105 B1
Bateman's Bldgs W1 .....105 B1
Bateman's Row EC2 .....24 A1 98 B2
Bath Cl SE15 .....50 A3
Bath Ct EC1 .....95 B1
  8 SE26 .....76 C1
Bath Gr E2 .....24 C3
Bath Ho E2 .....24 C1 99 B2
  SE1 .....137 A2
Bath Pl EC2 .....98 A3
  14 W6 .....39 B1
Bath Rd W4 .....38 A2
Bath St EC1 .....97 B3
Bath Terr SE1 .....136 C2
Bathgate Ho 8 SW9 .....48 A2
Bathgate Rd SW19 .....69 C1
Baths App SW6 .....155 A3
Bathurst Gdns NW10 .....22 A3
Bathurst Ho 12 W12 .....30 A2
Bathurst Mews W2 .....101 C1

Bathurst Mews continued 115 C4
Bathurst St W2 .....115 C4
Batley Pl 3 N16 .....7 B1
Batley Rd N16 .....7 B1
Batman Cl W12 .....30 A1
Batoum Gdns W6 .....39 B3
Batson Ho E1 .....111 C1
Batson St W12 .....38 C4
Batten Ho 8 W10 .....23 A2
  4 SW4 .....61 B2
Batten St SW11 .....60 A4
Battersea Bridge Rd SW11 .....158 A1
Battersea Church Rd SW11 .....167 C4
Battersea Dogs Home SW8 .....160 B1
Battersea High St SW11 .....167 C3
SW11 .....168 A3
Battersea Park★ SW11 .....159 A1
Battersea Park Rd SW11 .....169 C3
Battersea Park Sta SW8 .....160 B3
Battersea Power Station (dis) SW11 .....160 B3
Battersea Rise SW11 .....60 B3
Battersea Sq SW11 .....167 C3
Battersea Tech Coll SW11 .....168 B3
Battishill St N1 .....15 A1
Battle Bridge Ctr N1 .....84 A2
Battle Bridge La SE1 .....124 A2
Battle Bridge Rd NW1 .....84 A2
Battle Ho 5 SE15 .....49 C4
Battlebridge Ct NW1 .....84 B2
Battledean Rd N5 .....15 A3
Batty St E1 .....111 C2
Baty Ho SW2 .....74 B3
Baulk The SW18 .....70 C4
Bavaria Rd N19 .....5 A2
Bavent Rd SE5 .....48 B1
Bawdale Rd SE22 .....64 B2
Bawtree Rd SE14 .....51 A3
Baxendale St E2 .....24 C2 99 B4
Baxter Ho 11 E3 .....27 A2
Baxter Rd N1 .....15 C2
Bay Ct 7 E1 .....25 C1
  W5 .....36 A3
Baycliffe Ho 8 E9 .....17 C2
Bayer Ho EC1 .....96 C1
Bayes Ct NW3 .....12 B1
Bayfield Ho 5 SE4 .....65 C3
Bayford Rd NW10 .....22 C2
Bayford St 5 E8 .....17 A1
Bayford St Ind Ctr 4 E8 .....17 A1
Bayham Pl NW1 .....83 A3
Bayham Rd W4 .....37 C3
Bayham St NW1 .....82 C3
Bayhurst Lo N4 .....6 B4
Bayley St WC1 .....105 B3
Baylis Rd SE1 .....135 B3

Baynes Mews **2**
NW3 ....11 C2
Baynes St NW1 ...13 B1
Bayon Ho **20** N19 ....4 C4
Bayonne Rd W6 ...154 A3
Bayston Rd N16 .....7 B1
Bayswater Rd W2 ...115 B3
Bayswater Sta W2 ...114 A4
Baythorne St **3** E3 ...33 B4
Bayton Ct **5** E8 .....16 C1
Baytree Rd SW2 ....62 B3
Bazalgette Ho NW8 ..89 C2
Bazeley Ho SE1 ....136 A3
Bazely St E14 ......34 B2
BBC Television Ctr
W12 ....30 B1

Beach Ho SW5 .....141 B2
Beachy Rd E3 ......18 C1
Beacon Gate SE14 ..65 C4
Beacon Hill N7 .....14 A3
Beacon Ho SW8 ...171 B4
19 SE5 ....49 A3
Beacon Rd SE13 ....67 C1
Beaconfield Terrace Rd
W14 ....126 A1
Beaconsfield Cl W4 ..37 B1
SE3 ....53 C4
Beaconsfield Rd
SE17 ....152 A1
NW10 ....8 B2
W4 ....37 C3
SE3 ....53 C3
Beaconsfield Wlk
SW6 ....165 A3
Beadon Rd W6 .....39 B2
Beak St W1 ....119 A4
Beale Ho SW9 ....172 C1
Beale Pl E3 ....26 B3
Beale Rd E3 ......26 B4
Beames Ho SW8 ..171 B4
Beaminster Ho
SW8 ....162 C2
Beamish Ho **5**
SE16 ....40 B2
Beanacre Cl E9 ....18 B2
Bear Alley EC4 ....108 A2
Bear Croft Ho
SW6 ....164 C1
Bear Gardens Mus
SE1 ....122 C2
Bear Gdns SE1 ...122 C2
Bear La SE1 ......122 B1
Bear St WC2 .....119 C4
Beardsley Way W3 ..37 C4
Bearstead Rise SE4 .66 B2
Beatrice Ho **4** W6 ..39 B1
1 SW2 ....62 B2
Beatrice Pl W8 ...128 A1
Beatrice Rd SE1 ..153 C3
N4 ....5 C4
2 Richmond TW10 ..54 B2
Beatrice Tate Sch
E2 ....25 A2
Beatrice Webb Ho **3**
E3 ....26 A3
Beatrix Ho SW5 ..142 B2
Beatrix Potter Prim Sch
SW18 ....71 B3
Beattie Ho SW8 ..171 A4
Beatty Ho E14 ....41 C4
Beatty St NW1 ....82 C2
Beauchamp Cl **16**
W4 ....37 B3

Beauchamp Pl
SW3 ....130 B1
Beauchamp Rd
SW11 ....60 B3
Beauchamp St EC1 .107 B3
Beauchamp Terr
SW15 ....57 A4
Beauclerc Rd W6 ...39 A3
Beauclerk Ho **10**
SW16 ....74 A1
Beaufort Cl SW19 ..69 A4
Beaufort Gdns
SW3 ....130 B2
Beaufort Ho SW1 .147 B1
SW3 ....157 C3
SW11 ....168 A2
Beaufort Mans
SW3 ....157 C3
Beaufort Mews
SW6 ....155 A4
Beaufort St SW3 ..157 C3
Beaufoy Ho SW8 ..162 C2
3 SE27 ....75 A1
Beaufoy Wlk SE11 .149 A3
Beaulieu Cl SE5 ...63 C4
Beaulieu Pl W4 ....37 B3
Beaumanor Mans
W2 ....114 B4
Beaumaris Twr **2**
W3 ....37 A4
Beaumont W14 ...141 A3
SW15 ....58 A2
Beaumont Ave
W14 ....140 C2
Richmond TW9 ....54 B4
Beaumont Bldgs
WC2 ....106 B1
Beaumont Cres
W14 ....140 C1
Beaumont Ct **19** W4 ..37 B1
Beaumont Gdns NW3 ..1 C1
Beaumont Gr E1 ...25 C1
Beaumont Ho SW19 .70 C1
1 SW7 ....74 A3
Beaumont Mews
W1 ....103 C3
Beaumont Pl NW1,
WC1,W1 ....93 A2
Beaumont Rd W4 ...37 B3
SW15,SW19 ......70 A4
Beaumont Rise N19 ..4 C3
Beaumont Sq E1 ...32 C4
Beaumont St W1 ..103 C4
Beaumont Wlk NW3 .12 B1
Beavis Ho N16 .....7 A1
Beavor La W6 .....38 C1
Beccles St E14 ....33 B2
Beck Cl SE13 ......52 A2
Beck Ho N16 ....7 A1
Beck Rd E8 ....25 A4
Beckers The N16 ...16 C4
Becket Ho SE1 ...137 B3
Becket St SE1 ....137 B2
Beckett Cl NW10 ...8 A2
SW16 ....73 C2
Beckett Ho SW9 ..172 B1
12 E1 ....32 B4
Beckfoot NW1 .....83 A1
Beckford Ho **10** N16 .16 A3
Beckford Prim Sch
NW6 ....10 B3
Beckham Ho SE11 .149 A3
Beckington **10** NW5 .12 C2
Beckley Ho E3 .....26 B1

Becklow Gdns W12 ..29 C1
1 W12 ....38 C4
Becklow Mews **7**
W12 ....38 C4
Becklow Rd W12 ...38 C4
Beckton Rd E16 ....35 B2
Beckway St SE17 ..152 A3
Beckwith Ho **22** E2 ..25 A3
Beckwith Rd SE24 ..63 C2
Bective Pl SW15 ...58 B3
Bective Rd SW15 ...58 B3
Bedale St SE1 ....123 B1
Bede Ho SE14 .....51 B2
5 SW15 ....57 C1
Bedefield WC1 .....94 B3
Bedford Ave WC1 .105 C3
9 Richmond TW9 ...54 B3
Bedford Gardens Ho
W8 ....113 C1
Bedford Gdns
W8 ....31 C1 113 C1
Bedford Hill SW12 ..73 A2
Bedford Ho **8** SW4 ..62 A3
2 SW4 ....62 A3
Bedford Park Cnr **9**
W4 ....38 A2
Bedford Park Mans
W4 ....37 C2
Bedford Pas SW6 ..154 B2
Bedford Pl WC1 ...106 A4
Bedford Rd W4 ....38 A3
SW2,SW4 ....62 A3
Bedford Row WC1 ..107 A3
Bedford Sq WC1 ..105 C3
Bedford St WC2 ..120 B3
Bedford Way WC1 ..93 C1
Bedfordbury WC2 ..120 A3
Bedgebury Gdns
SW19 ....70 A2
Bedser Cl SE11 ...163 A4
Bedser Ct SW4 ...172 A2
Bedwell Ho SW9 ..173 B1
Beech Ave W3 .....29 A1
Beech Cl SE8 .....51 B4
SW15 ....68 C4
Beech Croft Ct N5 ..15 A4
Beech Ct W1 .....102 C2
NW2 ....1 A2
Beech Gdns W5 ...36 A3
Beech Ho **5** N16 ....6 C2
6 NW3 ....11 C3
13 SE16 ....40 B4
Beech St EC2 ....109 A4
Beech Tree Cl N1 ..14 C1
Beechcroft Ave
NW11 ....1 B4
Beechcroft Ct **3**
1 ....1 B4
Beechcroft Rd
SW14 ....55 B4
SW17 ....72 A2
Beechcroft Sch
SW17 ....72 A2
Beechcroft Way N19 ..4 C3
Beechdale Rd SW2 ..62 B1
Beechdene **4** SE15 ..50 A2
Beeches **4** SW17 ...72 C1
Beeches Ho SE15 ..49 B3
Beeches Rd SW17 ..72 B1
Beechey Ho **11** E1 ..32 A1
Beechmore Rd
SW11 ....169 A3

Beechwood Ave
TW9 ....44 C2
Beechwood Ct N16 ..7 A4
Beechwood Gr W3 ..29 A2
Beechwood Ho **7**
E2 ....24 C3
Beechwood Rd E8 ..16 B2
Beechworth Cl NW3 ..1 C2
Beecroft Rd SE4 ...66 A2
Beehive Cl E8 .....16 B1
Beehive Pl SW9 ...62 C4
Beeston Cl **8** E8 ...16 C3
Beeston Pl SW1 ..132 B2
Beeston's Ho SE15 .65 A4
Beethoven St W10 ..23 A2
Begbie Ho SW9 ...173 A2
Begonia Wlk W12 ..29 B3
Beira St SW12 ....73 A4
Beis Rachel D'Satmar
Girls Sch N16 .....7 A4
Bekesbourne St **10**
E14 ....33 A3
Beldanes Lo NW10 ..8 C1
Belenoyd Ct SW16 ..74 B1
Belfast Rd N16 .....7 B2
Belfont Wlk N7 ....14 A4
Belford Ho **7** E8 ...24 B4
Belfort Rd SE15 ...50 B1
Belfry Cl **15** SE16 ...40 A1
Belgrade Ho N16 ..16 A4
Belgrade Rd N16 ..16 A4
Belgrave Cl **1** W3 ..37 B4
Belgrave Ct SW8 ..160 C1
8 E14 ....33 A2
Belgrave Gdns NW8 .78 C3
Belgrave Mans
NW8 ....78 C3
Belgrave Mews N
SW1 ....131 B3
Belgrave Mews S
SW1 ....131 C2
Belgrave Mews W
SW1 ....131 B2
Belgrave Pl SW1 ..131 C1
Belgrave Rd SW1 .146 C3
SW13 ....46 B3
Belgrave Sq SW1 .131 B2
Belgrave St E1 ....32 C3
Belgravia Ct SW1 .132 A1
Belgravia Ho **11**
SW4 ....61 C1
Belgrove St WC1 ...94 B4
Belham Wlk **13** SE5 .48 C2
Belinda Rd **8** SW9 ..63 A4
Belitha Villas N1 ...14 C1
Bell Ct SE13 ......70 A4
Bell Ho SE10 .....52 B4
10 SW2 ....74 C4
Bell Ind Est **2** W4 ..37 B2
Bell Inn Yd EC3 ...109 C1
Bell La E1 ....110 C3
E16 ....35 C1
Bell Moor NW3 .....2 B1
Bell St NW1 ......102 A4
Bell Wharf La EC4 .123 A4
Bell Yd WC2 ......107 B1
Bellamy Cl SW5 ..141 A1
E14 ....41 C4
Bellamy St SW12 ..73 A4
Bellamy's Ct **18**
SE16 ....32 C1
Bellasis Ave SW2 ..74 A2
Belle Vue Gdns
SW9 ....172 B1
Bellefields Rd SW9 .62 B4

Bellenden Prim Sch
SE15 ....49 B1
Bellenden Rd SE15 .49 B1
Bellenden Road Bsns
Ctr SE15 ....49 B1
Belleville Prim Sch
SW11 ....60 B2
Belleville Rd SW11 ..60 B2
Bellevue Pl E1 ....25 B1
Bellevue Rd SW13 ..46 C1
SW17 ....72 B3
Bellgate Mews NW5 ..4 A1
Bellina Mews NW5 ..13 B4
Bello Cl SE24,SW2 ..75 A3
Bellot Gdns **1** SE10 .43 A1
Bellot St SE10 ....43 A1
Bellwood Rd SE15 ..65 C3
Belmont Cl SW4 ...61 B4
N20 ....7 A3
Belmont Ct N5 ....15 B4
Belmont Gr SE13 ..67 C4
Belmont Hall Ct
SE13 ....67 C4
Belmont Hill SE13 ..67 C4
Belmont Jun & Inf Sch
Belmont Pk SE13 ..67 C3
Belmont Pk Cl SE13 .67 C3
Belmont Rd SW4 ..61 B4
Belmont St NW1 ...12 C1
Belmont Terr W4 ...37 C2
Belmore Ho N7 ...13 C3
Belmore St SW8 ..171 B4
Beloe Cl SW11 ....55 C3
Belsham St E9 ....17 B2
Belsize Ave NW3 ..12 A3
Belsize Court Garages
1 NW3 ....11 C3
Belsize Cres NW3 ..11 C2
Belsize Ct NW3 ...11 C3
Belsize Gr NW3 ...12 A2
Belsize La NW3 ...11 C3
Belsize Mews NW3 .11 C2
Belsize Park Gdns
NW3 ....12 A2
Belsize Park Mews **1**
NW3 ....11 C2
Belsize Park Sta
NW3 ....12 A3
Belsize Pk NW3 ...11 C3
Belsize Pl NW3 ...11 C3
Belsize Rd NW6 ...78 B4
Belsize Sq NW3 ...11 C2
Belsize Terr NW3 ..11 C2
Beltane Dr SW19 ..69 C1
Belthorn Cres SW12 .73 B4
Belton Rd NW2 .....8 C2
Belton Way E3 ....33 C4
Beltran Rd SW6 ..166 A1
Belvedere Bldgs
SE1 ....136 B3
Belvedere Ct NW2 ..9 C2
SW15 ....57 B3
7 SW4 ....61 C1
Belvedere Mews
SE15 ....65 B4
Belvedere Pl SE1 .136 B3
Belvedere Rd SE1 .121 A1
Belvedere The
SW10 ....167 A3
Belvoir Lo SE22 ...76 C4
Belvoir Rd SE22 ...76 C4
Bembridge Cl NW6 .10 A1
Bembridge Ho
6 SE8 ....41 B2
SW18 ....59 A1

Bemerton St N1 .... 84 C4
Bemish Rd SW15 .....57 C4
Ben Ezra Ct SE17 ... 151 A3
Ben Jonson Ct 30 SE1
............24 A3
Ben Jonson JMI Sch
E1 ....26 C2
Ben Jonson Rd E1 ...33 A4
Ben Smith Way
SE16 ....139 C2
Benabo Ct 8 E8 ....16 C3
Benbow Ho 19 SE8 ..51 C4
Benbow Ho 15 SE8 ..51 C4
Benbow Rd W6 .....39 A3
Benbow St SE8 .....51 C4
Bence Ho 13 SE8 ...41 A2
Bendall Mews
NW1 ....102 B4
Bendemeer Rd
SW15 ....57 C4
Benden Ho SE13 ....67 B2
Bendon Valley
SW18 ....71 A4
Benedict Rd SW9 ...62 B4
Benenden Ho 17 SE17 152 B2
Benfleet Ct 6 E8 ...24 B4
Bengal Ct EC3 ......109 C1
Bengal Ho EC1 ......25 C1
Bengeworth Rd SE5 .63 B4
Benham Cl 1 SW11 59 C4
Benham's Pl 8
NW3 ....11 B4
Benhill Rd SE5 .....48 C2
Benjamin Cl E8 ....24 C4
Benjamin St EC1 ...108 A4
Benledi St E14 .....34 C3
Benn Ho E2 ....99 B3
Benn St E9 ....18 A2
Bennelong Cl W12 ..30 A3
Bennerley Rd SW11 .60 B2
Bennet's Hill EC4 ..122 B4
Bennett Ct 7 N1 ....5 B2
NW6 ....11 B2
7 W3 ....37 A4
Bennett Gr SE13 ...52 A2
Bennett Ho SW1 ...147 C4
2 SW4 ....73 C4
Bennett St SW1 ....118 C2
W4 ....38 A1
Bennett's Yd SW1 ..133 C1
Bensbury Cl SW15 ..69 B4
Benson Ct SW8 ....172 A4
N19 ....13 B4
Benson Ho E2 ......98 C2
SE1 ....121 C1
Benson Quay E1 ...32 B2
Benthal Ct N16 .....7 C1
Bentham JMI Schs
N16 ....7 C1
Benthal Rd N16 .....7 C1
Bentham Ct 10 N1 .15 B1
Bentham Rd E9 ....17 C2
Bentinck Cl NW8 ...80 B1
Bentinck Ho 4
W12 ....30 A2
Bentinck Mans
W1 ....103 C2
Bentinck Mews
W1 ....103 C2
Bentinck St W1 ....103 C2
Bentley Cl SW19 ...70 C1
Bentley Ho 5 SE5 ..49 A2
4 E1 ....32 B3
Bentley Rd N1 .....16 A2
Bentworth Ct E2 ...99 B2

Bentworth Prim Sch
W12 ....30 A3
Bentworth Rd W12 .30 A3
Benville Ho SW8 ...163 A1
Benwell Rd N7 .....14 C3
Benwick Cl SE16 ...40 A2
Benworth St E3 ....26 B2
Benyon Ho EC1 ....95 C4
Benyon Rd N1 .....87 C4
Beormund Sch
SE1 ....137 C3
Berber Rd SW11 ...60 B2
Berberis Ho 3 E3 ..26 C1
Bere St 1 ....32 C2
Berebinder Ho 17
E3 ....26 B3
Berenger Twr
SW10 ....157 B2
Berenger Wlk
SW10 ....157 B2
Berens Rd NW10 ...22 C2
Beresford Ct E9 ...18 A3
Beresford Ho 21 SE5 76 A1
Beresford Lo N4 ...15 C3
Beresford Rd N5 ...15 C3
Beresford Terr 3
N5 ....15 B3
Berestede Rd 3
W6 ....38 B1
Bergen Ho 1 SE5 ..48 B1
Bergen Sq SE16 ....41 A3
Berger JMI Sch E9 .17 C2
Berger Rd E9 ......17 C2
Berghem Mews
W14 ....39 C3
Bergholt Cres N16 ..7 A4
Bergholt Mews 4
NW1 ....13 C1
Bering Sq E14 .....41 C1
Berisford Mews
SW18 ....59 B1
Berkeley Ct NW1 ...91 A1
1 NW11 ....1 B4
19 SW2 ....74 C3
Berkeley Gdns W8 .113 C1
Berkeley Ho 17 E3 .26 C2
8 SE8 ....41 B1
Berkeley Mews
W1 ....103 A1
Berkeley Rd SW13 .46 C2
Berkeley St W1 ....118 B3
Berkeley St W1 ....118 B2
Berkeley The NW11 .2 A4
Berkeley Wlk 1 N7 .5 B2
Berkerley Ct SW15 157 C2
Berkley Gr NW1 ...12 C1
Berkley Rd NW1 ...12 B1
Berkshire Rd E9 ...18 B2
Berkeley Ct NW10 ..8 A4
Bermans Way NW10 .8 B4
Bermondsey Leather
Mkt SE1 ....138 A3
Bermondsey Mkt *
SE1 ....138 A3
Bermondsey Sq
SE1 ....138 B2
Bermondsey St
SE1 ....138 B2
Bermondsey Trad Est
SE16 ....40 B1
Bermondsey Wall E
SE16 ....40 A4
Bermondsey Wall W
SE1,SE16 ....139 B4

Bermonsey Sta
SE16 ....139 C2
Bernard Angell Ho 4
SE10 ....52 C4
Bernard Cassidy St 4
E16 ....35 B2
Bernard Shaw Ct 3
NW1 ....13 B1
Bernard Shaw Ho 2
NW10 ....20 C4
Bernard St WC1 ...94 B1
Bernay's Gr SW9 ..62 B3
Berners Ho N1 .....85 B2
Berners Mews W1 .105 A3
Berners Pl W1 .....105 A2
Berners Rd N1 .....86 A3
Berners St W1 .....105 A2
Bernwood Ho 7
N4 ....6 C4
Berridge Ho 1
SE17 ....151 A2
Berriman Rd N7 ....5 B1
Berry Cl NW10 .....8 A1
Berry Ho SW11 ....169 A2
21 E1 ....25 A1
Berry Pl EC1 ......96 B3
Berry St EC1 ......96 B1
Berry Way W5 .....36 A3
Berryfield Rd SE17 150 B2
Berrymead Gdns
W3 ....37 B4
Berrymede Inf Sch
W3 ....37 A4
Berrymede Jun Sch
W3 ....37 A4
Berthon St SE8 ....51 C3
Bertie Rd NW10 ....8 C2
Bertram House Sch
SW17 ....72 C2
Bertram St N19 ....4 A2
Bertrand Ho 11
SW16 ....74 A1
Bertrand St SE13 ..67 A4
Berwick St W1 .....105 A1
Berwyn Ho 3 N16 ..7 B3
Berwyn Rd
SW14,TW10 ....55 A3
SE24 ....75 A3
Beryl Rd W6 ......39 C1
Besant Cl NW2 ....1 A1
Besant Ct N1 ......6 C3
Besant Ho NW8 ....78 C3
Besant Rd NW2 ....10 A4
Besant Wlk N7 .....5 B2
Besford Ho 25 E2 ..24 C3
Bessant Dr TW9 ...45 A2
Bessborough Gdns
SW1 ....147 C2
Bessborough Pl
SW1 ....147 B2
Bessborough Rd
SW15 ....68 C3
Bessborough St
SW1 ....147 B2
Bessemer Ct 5
NW1 ....13 B1
Bessemer Grange Prim
Sch SE5 ....64 A3
Bessemer Park Ind Est
3 SE24 ....63 A3
Bessemer Rd SE5 ..48 B1
Bessingham Wlk
SE4 ....65 C2
Besson St SE14 ....50 C2
Bessy St E2 ....25 B2
Bestwood Ho SE8 ..40 C2

Beswick Mews 1
NW6 ....11 A2
Betchworth Ho 8
N7 ....13 C3
Bethersden Ho
SE17 ....152 B2
Bethlehem Ho 13
E14 ....33 B2
Bethnal Green Museum
of Childhood * 2 E2 25 A2
Bethnal Green Rd
E2 ...24 B1 99 B3
Bethnal Green Sta
E2 ....25 A1
Bethnal Green Tech Coll
E2 ....25 A1
Bethune Rd N16 ...7 A4
NW10 ....20 C1
Bethwin Rd SE5 ...48 B3
Betsam Ho SE1 ....137 B4
Betterton Ho WC2 106 B1
Betterton St WC2 ..106 B1
Bettridge Rd SW6 .165 A1
Betts Ho E1 ....32 A2
Betts St E1 ....32 A2
Betty May Gray Ho 1
E14 ....42 B2
Bev Callender Cl 4
SW8 ....61 A4
Bevan St N1 ....87 A3
Bevenden St N1 ...97 C4
Beverley Cl SW13 ..46 C1
6 SW11 ....59 C3
Beverley Cotts
SW15 ....68 A1
Beverley Ct N5 ....15 A2
4 W4 ....37 B1
5 SE4 ....51 B1
SE4 ....66 B4
Beverley Gdns NW11 1 A4
3 SW13 ....56 B4
Beverley Lo 8
TW10 ....54 A2
Beverley Path 8
SW13 ....46 B1
Beverley Prim Sch
SE10 ....43 B3
Beverley Rd W4 ...38 B1
SW13 ....56 B4
Beversbrook Rd N19 4 C1
Beverston Mews
NW1 ....102 C3
Bevin Cl SE16 .....33 A1
Bevin Ct WC1 .....95 A4
Bevin Ho 2 E3 ....26 C2
7 E2 ....25 B2
Bevin Sq SW17 ....72 B1
Bevin Way WC1 ....95 B4
Bevington Prim Sch
W10 ....31 A4
Bevington Rd W10 .31 A4
Bevington St SE16 133 C3
Bevis Marks EC3 ..110 B2
Bewdley Ho N4 ....6 B4
Bewdley St N1 .....14 C1
Bewick Mews SE15 .50 A3
Bewick St SW8 ....170 B1
Bewley Ho 7 E1 ...32 A2
Bewley St E1 ......32 A2
Bexhill Rd SW14 ..55 B4
SE4 ....66 B1
Bexley Ho SE4 ....66 A3
BFI London Imax
Cinema SE1 ......121 B1
Bianca Rd SE1,SE15 49 C4
Bicester Rd TW9 ...55 A4
Bicknell Mans
W1 ....103 A4
Bicknell Ho E1 ....103 A4
Bickerton Rd N19 ..4 B2
Bicknell Ho E1 ....111 C1
Bicknell Rd SE5 ...63 B4
Bicknor Ho 25 E5 .17 A3
Bidborough St N1,
WC1 ....94 A3
Biddenham Ho 18
SE16 ....40 C2
Bidder St E16 .....35 A4
Biddesden Ho
SW3 ....144 C3
Biddestone Rd N7 .14 B4
Biddulph Man W9 ..88 B3
Biddulph Rd W9 ...88 B3
Bidwell St SE15 ...50 A2
Big Ben * SW1 ....134 B3
Bigg's Row SW15 ..57 C4
Biggerstaff Rd E15 27 B4
Biggerstaff St N4 ..5 C2
Bigland Green JMI Sch
E1 ....32 A3
Bigland St E1 .....32 A3
Bilberry Ho 12 E3 .33 A4
Billing Ho 2 E1 ...32 C3
Billing Pl SW10 ...156 B2
Billing Rd SW10 ...156 B2
Billing St SW10 ...156 B2
Billingford Cl SE4 .65 C3
Billingley NW1 ....82 C3
Billingsgate Mkt
E14 ....34 A1
Billington Ho SW8 171 C3
Billington Rd SE14 50 C3
Billiter Sq EC3 ....110 B1
Billiter St EC3 .....110 B1
Billson St E14 .....42 B2
Bilton Ho SW8 ....171 B3
Bilton Twrs W1 ....103 A1
Bina Gdns SW5 ...142 C3
Binbrook Ho W10 ..30 B4
Binden Rd W12 ....38 B3
Binfield Ct SE5 ....48 B1
Binfield Rd SW4 ..172 B3
Bingfield St N1 ....84 C4
Bingham Pl W1 ....103 B4
Bingham St N1 ....15 C2
Binley Ho SW15 ...56 B1
Binney St W1 ......103 C1
Binnie Ho SE1 ....136 C1
Binns Rd W4 ......38 A1
Binns Terr 3 W4 ..38 A1
Binstead Ho SW18 59 A1
Binyon Ho 8 N16 ..16 A4
Birch Cl N19 ......4 B2
SE15 ....49 C1
SW15 ....57 A3
Birch Ho 14 SE14 ..51 B2
6 SW2 ....62 C1
Birch Vale Ct NW8 89 C2
Bircham Path SE4 ..65 C3
Birchdown Ho 23
E3 ....27 A2
Birches The SE5 ...49 A1
Birchfield Ho 4
E14 ....33 C2
Birchfield St E14 ..33 C2

Birchin La EC3 ....109 C1
Birchington Ct NW6 .78 A4
Birchington Ho 1
E5 ....17 A3
Birchington Rd
NW6 ....23 C4
Birchlands Ave
SW12 ....72 B4
Birchmere Lo 18
SE16 ....40 A1
Birchmere Row SE3 53 B1
Birchmore Wlk N5 .6 B1
Birchwood Dr NW3 .2 A1
Bird In Bush Rd
SE15 ....49 C3
Bird St W1 ....103 C1
Bircage Wlk SW1 133 B3
Birdhurst Rd SW18 .59 B2
Birdlip Cl SE15 ....49 A4
Birdsall Ho 5 SE5 ..64 A4
Birdsfield La E3 ......26 B4
Birkbeck Ave W3 ...28 B2
Birkbeck Coll W1 .105 B2
Birkbeck Ct W3 ......28 C1
Birkbeck Gr W3 ......27 C4
Birkbeck Hill SE21 ..75 A3
Birkbeck Mews 5
E8 ....16 B3
Birkbeck Pl SE21 ...75 B2
Birkbeck Rd E8 ......16 B3
W3 ....28 C1
Birkbeck St E2 ....25 A2
Birkdale Cl 1 SE16 .40 A1
Birkenhead Ho 11
N7 ....14 C3
Birkenhead St WC1 .94 B4
Birkwood Cl SW12 .73 C4
Birley Ho NW8 ....79 C2
Birley St SW11 .....169 B1
Birnam Rd N4 ....5 B2
Birrell Ho SW9 ......172 C1
Birse Cres NW10 ......8 A4
Birtwhistle Ho 5
E3 ....26 B4
Biscay Ho 11 E1 ......25 C1
Biscay Rd W6 ....39 C1
Biscoe Way SE13 ...67 C4
Biscott Ho 3 E3 ......27 A1
Bisham Gdns N6 .....3 C3
Bishop Challoner Sec
Sch 1 ....32 B3
Bishop Duppa's
Almshouses 7
TW10 ....54 A2
Bishop King's Rd
W14 ....140 B4
Bishop St N1 ....86 C4
Bishop Way NW10 ...8 A1
Bishop Wilfred Wood Cl
SE15 ....49 C1
Bishop's Ave SW6 .164 A2
Bishop's Bridge Rd
W2 ....100 C2
Bishop's Ct N19 .....4 C2
Bishop's Ct WC2 ...107 B2
EC4 ....108 A2
Bishop's Mans SW6 .47 C1
Bishop's Park Rd
SW6 ....47 C1
Bishop's Park Rd
SW6 ....164 A2

Bishop's Terr
SE11 ....149 C4
Bishop's Way E2 ....25 B3
Bishopsgate 55 N1 ..24 A4
Bishops Ci W4 ....37 B1
Bishops Ct W2 ......100 B2
Bishops Ho SW8 ...162 B1
Bishops Mead SE5 .48 B3
Bishops Rd SW6 ...164 C4
Bishopsdale Ho 8
N4 ....6 C4
Bishopsgate EC2 ...110 A2
Bishopsgate Arc
E1 ....110 B3
Bishopsgate Church Yd
EC2 ....110 A2
Bishopstone Ho
SW11 ....169 B2
Bishopswood Rd N6 .3 B4
Bisley Ho SW19 .....69 C2
Bisserelle Ho SE22 .64 C1
Bisson Rd E15 ....27 B3
Bittern Ct 8 SE8 ....51 C4
Bittern Ho SE1 ......136 C3
Bittern St SE1 ....136 C3
Black Friars La
EC4 ....108 A1
Black Horse Ct
SE1 ....137 C2
Black Lion La W6 ...38 C2
Black Lion Mews 4
W6 ....38 C2
Black Prince Rd
SE1,SE11 ....149 A3
Black Roof Ho 9
SE5 ....48 A2
Black Swan Yd
SE1 ....138 A4
Black's Rd W6 ....39 B2
Blackall St EC2 ......98 A2
Blackburn Rd NW6 .11 A2
Blackburne's Mews
W1 ....117 B3
Blackdown Ho E8 ..16 C4
Blackett St SW15 ...57 C4
Blackfriars Bridge
EC4 ....122 A3
Blackfriars Ct EC4 122 A3
Blackfriars Pas
EC4 ....122 A3
Blackfriars Pier
EC4 ....122 A3
Blackfriars Rd SE1 122 A2
Blackfriars Sta
EC4 ....122 A3
Blackfriars Underpass
EC4 ....121 C3
Blackheath SE3 ......53 A2
Blackheath Ave SE3 53 A2
Blackheath Bsns Est
SE10 ....52 B2
Blackheath Gr SE3 .53 B1
Blackheath High Sch
SE3 ....53 C3
Blackheath High Sch
(Girls) SE3 ....53 B3
Blackheath High Sch
GPDST (Jun Dept)
SE3 ....53 C1
Blackheath Hill
SE10 ....52 B2
Blackheath Pk SE3 .53 C1
Blackheath Rd SE10 52 A2
Blackheath Rise
SE13 ....52 B1

Blackheath Vale
SE3 ....53 A1
Blackheath Village
SE3 ....53 B1
Blackhorse Rd SE8 .51 A4
Blacklands Terr
SW3 ....144 C3
Blackmore Ho N1 ...85 A3
2 SW18 ....59 A2
Blackmore Twr 3
SW11 ....59 C3
Blackpool Rd SE15 .50 A1
Blackstock Ho N5 ...6 A1
Blackstock Mews N4 .6 A1
Blackstock Rd N4,N5 .6 A2
Blackstone Ho
SW1 ....146 C1
SE21 ....76 A1
Blackthorn Ct
4 E15 ....19 C3
5 SE15 ....49 B3
Blackthorn St E3 ...26 C1
Blacktree Mews 1
SW9 ....62 C4
Blackwall La SE10 ..43 B2
Blackwall Trad Est
E14 ....34 B2
Blackwall Tunnel
E14,SE10 ....34 C1
Blackwall Tunnel App
SE10 ....43 A4
Blackwall Tunnel
Northern Approach
E14,E3 ....27 B1
Blackwall Way E14 .34 B2
Blackwater Ho
NW8 ....101 C4
Blackwater St SE22 .64 B2
Blackwell Cl 10 E5 .17 C4
Blackwell Ho 3
SW4 ....61 C1
Blackwood Ho 1
E1 ....25 A1
Blackwood St
SE17 ....151 B2
Blade Mews SW15 .58 B3
Bladen 4 E1 ....32 C3
Blades Ct SW15 .....58 A4
Blades Ho SE11 ......163 B3
Blagdon Rd SE13 ...67 A1
Blagrove Rd 3 W10 .31 B4
Blair Cl N1 ....15 B2
Blair Ct NW8 ....79 B4
Blair Ho SW9 ....172 C2
Blair St E14 ....34 C3
Blairderry Rd SW2 .74 A2
Blake Ct SW6 ....23 C2
4 SE16 ....40 A1
Blake Gdns SW6 ...166 A4
Blake Ho N11 ....135 B2
1 N19 ....13 C3
14 N16 ....16 A4
2 SE8 ....51 C4
Blake's Rd SE15 .....49 A3
Blakemore Rd
SW16 ....74 A1
Blakeney Cl 5 NW1 13 C1
4 E8 ....16 C3
Blakenham Rd
SW12 ....30 A1
Blaker Rd E15 ....27 B4
Blakes Cl W10 ....30 B4
Blanca Ho 11 N1 ....24 A3
Blanch Cl SE15 ......50 B3
Blanchard Way E8 .16 C2

Blanche Ho NW8 ....90 A1
Blanchedowne SE5 .63 C3
Bland Ho SE11 ......149 A2
Blandfield Rd SW12 72 C4
Blandford Ct NW6 ..10 A1
6 N1 ....16 A1
Blandford Ho SW8 162 C2
Blandford Rd W4 ...38 A3
Blandford Sq NW1 .90 C1
Blandford St W1 ...103 B3
Blaney Pl 1 N7 ......14 C3
Blantyre St SW10 .157 B2
Blantyre Twr
SW10 ....157 B2
Blantyre Wlk
SW10 ....157 B2
Blashford NW3 ......12 B1
Blasker Wlk E14 ....42 A1
Blaxland Ho 12 W12 30 A2
Blechynden Ho 17
W10 ....30 C3
Blechynden St W10 30 C2
Bledlow Ho NW8 ....89 C1
Bleeding Heart Yd
EC1 ....107 C3
Blemundsbury
WC1 ....106 C4
Blendworth Point 4
SW15 ....69 A3
Blendworth Way E5
SE15 ....49 A3
Blenheim 28 SW19 .70 A3
Blenheim Cres
W11 ....31 A3 112 B4
Blenheim Ct N19 ....5 A2
N7 ....14 A2
59 SE16 ....32 C1
Richmond TW9 ......54 B4
Blenheim Gdns NW2 .9 B3
SW2 ....62 B1
Blenheim Gr SE15 ..49 C1
Blenheim Pas NW8 .78 C2
Blenheim Rd NW8 ..79 A2
W4 ....38 A3
Blenheim St W1 ...104 A1
Blenheim Terr NW8 .78 C2
Blenkarne Rd SW11 60 B1
Blessed John Roche RC
Sec Sch E14 ....33 C3
Blessed Sacrament RC
Prim Sch N1 ....84 C3
Blessington Cl SE13 67 C4
Blessington Rd
SE13 ....67 C3
Bletchley Ct N1 ......87 B1
Bletchley St N1 ......87 A1
Bletsoe Wlk N1 ......87 A2
Blick Ho 5 SE16 .....40 B3
Blincoe Cl SW19 ....69 C2
Blissett St SE10 ......52 B2
Blisworth Ho 12 E2 .24 C4
Blithfield St W8 ....128 A1
Bloemfontein Ave
W12 ....30 A1
Bloemfontein Rd
W12 ....30 A2
Blomfield Ct W9 .....89 A2
SW11 ....167 C4
Blomfield Mans
W12 ....30 B1
Blomfield Rd W9 ....88 C1
Blomfield St EC2 ..109 C3
Blomfield Villas

Bloom Gr SE27 ....75 A1
Bloom Park Rd
SW6 ....154 C1
Bloomburg St
SW1 ....147 A3
Bloomfield Ho 11 ..111 B3
Bloomfield Pl W1 ...118 B4
Bloomfield Terr
SW1 ....145 C2
Bloomsbury Ct
WC1 ....106 B3
Bloomsbury Ho 10
SW4 ....61 C1
Bloomsbury Pl
WC1 ....106 B3
SW18 ....59 B2
Bloomsbury Sq
WC1 ....106 B3
Bloomsbury St
WC1 ....105 C3
Bloomsbury Way
WC1 ....106 B3
Blore Cl SW8 ....171 B3
Blore Ct W1 ....119 B4
Blossom Cl W5 ......36 A4
Blossom Pl E1 ....98 B1
Blossom St
E1 ....24 A1 98 B1
Blount Ho 10 E14 ...33 A3
Blount St E14 ....33 A3
Blucher Rd SE5 .....48 B3
Blue Anchor Alley 1
TW9 ....54 A3
Blue Anchor La
SE16 ....40 A2
Blue Ball Yd SW1 .118 C1
Blue Gate Field JMI
Schs 1 ....32 B2
Blundell St N7 ....14 A2
Blurton Rd E5 ....17 C4
Blyth Cl 1 E14 ....42 C2
Blyth's Wharf E14 ..33 A2
Blythe Ho SE11 .....163 C4
Blythe Mews 2
W14 ....39 C3
Blythe Rd W14 .....126 A1
Blythe St E2 ....25 A2
Blythendale Ho 9
E2 ....24 C3
Blythwood Rd N4 ....5 A4
Boadicea St N1 ......84 C3
Boarley Ho SE17 ...152 A3
Boat Lifter Way 10
SE16 ....41 A2
Boathouse Ctr The
W10 ....22 C1
Bob Marley Way 1
SE24 ....62 C3
Bobbin Cl 1 SW4 ...61 B4
Bobington Ct WC1 106 B4
Bocking St E8 ....25 A4
Boddicott Cl SW19 .70 A2
Boddington Ho
SE14 ....50 B2
Boden Ho 6 E1 ....111 B4
Bodeney Ho 10 SE5 .49 A2
Bodington Ct 2
W12 ....39 C4
Bodley Manor Way
SE24 ....74 C4
Bodmin St SW18 ...70 C3
Bodney Mans 8 E8 .17 A3
Bodney Rd E5,E8 ...17 A3
Bohemia Pl 1 1 E8 ..17 A2

Boileau Rd SW13 . . . . .47 A4
Boilerhouse SE1 . . . .124 C1
Boisseau Ho 27 E1 . .32 B4
Bolden St SE8 . . . . . . .52 A1
Boldero Pl NW8 . . . . . .90 A1
Boleyn Rd N16 . . . . . . .16 A3
Bolina Rd SE16 . . . . . .40 B1
Bolingbroke Gr
SW11 . . . . .60 B2
Bolingbroke Hospl The
SW11 . . . . .60 A2
Bolingbroke Prim Sch
SW11 . . . . .60 A3
Bolingbroke Rd
W14 . . . . .39 C3
Bolingbroke Wlk
SW11 . . . . .168 A4
Bollo Bridge Rd W3 . . .37 B4
Bollo Ct 2 W3 . . . . . . .37 B3
Bollo La W3 . . . . .37 A4
Bolney Gate SW7 . . . .130 A3
Bolney St SW8 . . . . . .162 C1
Bolsover St W1 . . . . . .92 B1
Bolt Ct EC4 . . . . .107 C1
Bolton Cres SE5 . . . . .48 A3
Bolton Ct 1 SW9 . . . .169 C2
Bolton Gdns SW5 . . . .142 B2
NW10 . . . . .22 C3
Bolton Gdns Mews
SW10 . . . . .142 C2
Bolton Ho 4 SE10 . . .43 A1
Bolton Rd NW8 . . . . . .78 B3
NW10 . . . . .21 A4
W4 . . . . .45 B3
Bolton St W1 . . . . . . .118 B2
Bolton Studios
SW10 . . . . .143 A1
Bolton Wlk N7 . . . . . . .5 B2
Boltons Ct SW5 . . . . .142 B2
Boltons The SW10 . . .142 C2
Bombay St SE16 . . . . .40 A2
Bomore Rd
W11 . . . . . .31 A2 112 A4
Bonar Rd SE15 . . . . . .49 C3
Bonchurch Rd W10 . . .31 A4
Bond Ct EC4 . . . . .109 B1
Bond Ho 4 NW6 . . . . .23 C3
Bond Street Sta
W1 . . . . .103 C1
Bonding Yard Wlk
SE16 . . . . .41 A3
Bondway SW8 . . . . . .162 B4
Bonfield Rd SE13 . . . .67 B3
Bonham Ho W11 . . . .112 C3
Bonham Rd SW2 . . . . .62 B2
Bonheur Rd W4 . . . . . .37 C4
Bonhill St EC2 . . . . . . .97 C1
Bonington Ho N1 . . . . .84 C1
Bonner Ho 3 SW15 . . .56 C2
Bonner JMI Sch E2 . .25 B2
Bonner St E2 . . . . .25 B3
Bonneville Gdns
SW4 . . . . .61 B1
Bonneville Prim Sch
SW4 . . . . .61 B2
Bonnington Sq
SW8 . . . . .162 C4
Bonny St NW1 . . . . . . .13 B1
Bonsor Ho SW8 . . . . .171 A4
Bonsor St SE5 . . . . . . .49 A3
Bonthron Ho SW15 . . .47 B1
Booker CI 18 E3 . . . . .33 B4
Boot St N1 . . . . .98 A3
Boot St N1 . . . . .98 A3
Booth CI 10 E9 . . . . . .25 A4

Booth Ho 2 SW2 . . . .74 C4
Booth La EC4 . . . . . . .122 C4
Booth's Pl W1 . . . . . . .105 A3
Boothby Rd N19 . . . . . .4 C2
Bordon Wlk 3
SW15 . . . . .68 C4
Boreas Wlk N1 . . . . . . .86 B1
Boreham Ave E16 . . . .35 C3
Boreman Ho 10
SE10 . . . . .52 B4
Borland Rd SE15 . . . . .65 B3
Borneo St SW15 . . . . .57 B4
Borough High St
SE1 . . . . .123 B1
Borough Mkt* . . . .
SE1 . . . . .123 B1
Borough Rd SE1 . . . . .136 B2
Borough Sq SE1 . . . . .136 C3
Borough Sta SE1 . . . .137 A3
Borrett CI SE17 . . . . . .150 C1
Borrodaile Rd SW18 . .59 A1
Borrowdale NW1 . . . . .92 C3
Borthwick St SE8 . . . .41 C1
Boscastle Rd NW5 . . . .4 A1
Boscobel Ho 4 E8 . . .17 A2
Boscobel Pl SW1 . . . .145 C4
Boscobel St NW8 . . . .89 C1
Boscombe CI E5 . . . . .18 A3
Boscombe Rd W12 . . .38 C4
Boss Ho SE1 . . . . .138 C4
Boss St SE1 . . . . .138 C4
Boston Gdns W4 . . . . .46 A4
Boston Ho NW1 . . . . . .90 C2
SE1 . . . . .142 B3
SE5 . . . . .48 B1
Boston Pl NW1 . . . . . . .90 C1
Boswell Ct WC1 . . . . .106 B4
9 W14 . . . . .39 C3
Boswell Ho W10 . . . . .23 A1
Boswell St WC1 . . . . .106 B4
Bosworth Ho 4
W10 . . . . .23 A1
Bosworth Rd W10 . . . .23 A1
Bothnia Rd E1 . . . . . . .25 C1
Bothwell CI E16 . . . . . .35 B2
Bothwell St 4 W6 . . . .47 C4
Botolph Alley EC3 . . .124 A4
Botolph La EC3 . . . . .124 A4
Bott's Mews W2 . . . . . .31 C3
Boughton Ho SE1 . . . .137 B4
Boulcott St E1 . . . . . . .32 C3
Boulevard The 4
SW17 . . . . .72 C2
Boulogne Ho SE1 . . . .138 C2
Boulter Ho SE14 . . . . .50 C2
Boulton Ho TW8 . . . . .36 A1
Boundaries Mans 5
SW12 . . . . .72 C3
Boundaries Rd
SW12 . . . . .72 C3
Boundary Ho 1 SE5 . .48 B3
Boundary La SE17 . . . .48 B4
Boundary Pas E2 . . . . .98 C2
Boundary Rd NW8 . . . .79 A4
Boundary Rd Est
NW8 . . . . .78 C4
Boundary Row
SE1 . . . . .136 A4
Boundary St
E2 . . . . . .24 B1 98 C2
Bourchier St W1 . . . . .119 B4
Bourdon Pl W1 . . . . . .118 B4
Bourdon St W1 . . . . . .118 B3

Bourke CI NW10 . . . . . .8 A2
SW4 . . . . .62 A1
Bourlet CI W1 . . . . . . .104 C3
Bourne Ct W4 . . . . . . .45 B4
Bourne Ho 5 SW4 . . .61 B3
Bourne Mews W1 . . . .103 C1
Bourne PI W4 . . . . .37 C1
Bourne St SW1 . . . . . .145 B3
Bourne Terr W2 . . . . .100 B4
Bournemouth CI
SE15 . . . . .49 C1
Bournemouth Rd
SE15 . . . . .142 C2
Bousfield Prim Sch
SE1 . . . . .152 C4
Boutflower Rd
SW11 . . . . .60 A3
Bouverie Mews N16 . .7 A2
Bouverie Pl W2 . . . . . .101 C2
Bouverie Rd N16 . . . . .7 A2
Bouverie St EC4 . . . . .107 C1
Boveney Rd SE23 . . . .65 C1
Bovingdon CI 3 N19 . .4 B2
Bovingdon Rd
SW6 . . . . .166 B3
Bow Boys Sec Sch
E3 . . . . .26 C2
Bow Brook The 20
E2 . . . . .25 C3
Bow Church Sta 3 . .26 C2
Bow Churchyard
EC2,EC4 . . . . .109 A1
Bow Common La
E3 . . . . .33 C4
Bow Ind Pk E15 . . . . . .18 C1
Bow La EC2,EC4 . . . .109 A1
Bow Rd E3 . . . . .26 C2
Bow Road Sta E3 . . . .26 C2
Bow St WC2 . . . . .106 B1
Bow Triangle Bsns Ctr
3 . . . . .26 C2
Bowater CI SW2 . . . . . .62 A1
Bowater Ho EC1 . . . . . .97 A1
Bowden Ho 28 E2 . . . .25 C2
Bowden St SE11 . . . . .149 C1
Bowditch SE8 . . . . .41 B1
Bowen Ct 2 N5 . . . . . .15 A4
Bowen Dr SE21 . . . . . .76 A1
Bowen St E14 . . . . .34 A3
Bower Ave SE3 . . . . . .53 C3
Bower Ho SE14 . . . . . .50 C2
Bower St E1 . . . . .32 C3
Bowerdean
SW6 . . . . .166 A3
Bowerman Ave
SE14 . . . . .51 A4
Bowerman Ct 1 N19 . .4 C2
Bowes Rd W3 . . . . .29 A2
Bowfell Rd W6 . . . . . . .47 B4
Bowhill CI SW9 . . . . . .163 C2
Bowie CI SW4 . . . . .73 C4
Bowl Ct EC2 . . . . .98 B1
Bowland Ho N4 . . . . . . .6 B4
Bowland Rd SW4 . . . . .61 C3
Bowland Yd SW1 . . . .131 A3
Bowles Rd 1 SE1 . . . .49 C4
Bowley Ho SE16 . . . . .139 B2
Bowley St E14 . . . . . . .33 A2
Bowling Green CI
SW19 . . . . .69 A4
Bowling Green Ho
SW10 . . . . .157 B2

Bowling Green La
EC1 . . . . .95 C2
Bowling Green Pl
SE1 . . . . .137 B4
Bowling Green St
SE11 . . . . .163 B4
Bowling Green Wlk
N1 . . . . .98 A4
Bowman Ave E16 . . . .35 B2
Bowman Mews E1 . . .125 B4
SW18 . . . . .70 B3
Bowman's Mews N7 . .5 A1
Bowman's PI N7 . . . . . .5 A1
Bowmore Wlk NW1 . .13 C1
Bowness CI 7 E8 . . . .16 B2
Bowness Ho SE15 . . . .50 B3
Bowood Rd SW11 . . . .60 C2
Bowry Ho 14 E14 . . . .33 B4
Bowsprit Point 1
E14 . . . . .41 C3
Bowstead Ct SW11 . .167 C3
Bowyer Ho 23 N1 . . . .24 A4
SW18 . . . . .59 A2
Bowyer PI SE5 . . . . . . .48 B3
Bowyer St 15 SE5 . . .48 B3
Box Tree Ho SE8 . . . . .41 A1
Boxall Rd SE21 . . . . . .64 A1
Boxley Ho 8 E5 . . . . . .17 A3
Boxmoor Ho 10 E2 . . .24 C4
8 W11 . . . . .30 C1
Boxworth Gr N1 . . . . . .85 A4
Boyce Ho 6 W10 . . . . .23 B2
Boyce St SE1 . . . . .121 B1
Boyd Ct SW15 . . . . . . .57 B1
Boyd St E1 . . . . .111 C1
Boyfield St SE1 . . . . . .136 B3
Boyle St W1 . . . . .118 C4
Boyne Ct NW10 . . . . . .8 C1
Boyne Rd SE13 . . . . . .67 C4
Boyne Terr Mews
W11 . . . . . .31 B1 112 C2
Boyson Rd 9 SE17 . . .48 C4
Boyton CI E1 . . . . .25 C1
Boyton Ho NW8 . . . . . .79 C2
SE11 . . . . .149 B1
Brabazon St E14 . . . . .34 A3
Brabner Ho 22 E2 . . . .99 B4
Brabourn Gr SE15 . . . .50 B1
Bracer Ho 1 N1 . . . . . .24 A3
Bracewell Rd W10 . . . .30 B4
Bracey St N4 . . . . .5 A2
Bracken Ave SW12 . . .72 C4
Bracken Gdns SW13 . .46 C1
Bracken Ho 14 E3 . . . .33 C4
Brackenbury
W6 . . . . .39 A3
Brackenbury Gdns
W6 . . . . .39 A3
Brackenbury Prim Sch
W6 . . . . .39 A3
Brackenbury Rd
W6 . . . . .39 A3
Brackley Ct NW8 . . . . .89 C2
Brackley Rd W4 . . . . . .38 A1
Brackley St EC1 . . . . .109 A4
Brackley Terr 6
W4 . . . . .38 A1
Bracklyn Ct N1 . . . . . . .87 B2
Bracklyn St N1 . . . . . . .87 B2
Bracknell Gate
NW3 . . . . .11 A3
Bracknell Gdns
NW3 . . . . .11 A4
Bracknell Way NW3 . .11 A4
Brad St SE1 . . . . .121 C1
Bradbeer Ho 24 E2 . . .25 B2

Bradbourne St
SW6 . . . . .165 C2
Bradbury Ct 2 SE3 . .53 C3
Bradbury Ho 1 . . . . . .111 A2
Bradbury St 28 N16 . .16 A3
Bradby Ho NW8 . . . . . .78 B1
Braddon Rd TW9 . . . . .54 B4
Braddyll St SE10 . . . . .43 A1
Braden St W9 . . . . .88 A1
Bradenham 11 SE17 . .48 C4
Bradenham CI SE17 . .48 C4
Bradfield Ct 14
NW1 . . . . .13 A1
Bradfield Ho 5 SW8 . .171 B2
Bradfield Rd E16 . . . . .43 C4
Bradford Ho 4
W14 . . . . .39 C3
Bradford Rd W3 . . . . . .38 A4
Bradgate SE6 . . . . .67 A1
Brading Rd SW2 . . . . .74 B4
Brading Terr W12 . . . . .38 C3
Bradiston Rd W9 . . . . .23 B2
Bradley CI N7 . . . . .14 B2
Bradley Ho 4 E3 . . . . .27 A2
6 E3 . . . . .25 A1
SE16 . . . . .40 A2
Bradley Mews SW12 . .72 B3
Bradley's CI N1 . . . . . . .85 C2
Bradlord Ho SE21 . . . .76 A1
Bradmead SW8 . . . . .160 C1
Bradmore Ho 1 . . . . . .32 B4
Bradmore Park Rd
W6 . . . . .39 A2
Bradstock Ho E9 . . . . .18 A1
Bradstock Rd E9 . . . . .17 C2
Bradwell Ho NW6 . . . .78 A3
Brady Ho SW8 . . . . . .171 A4
SW4 . . . . .61 C2
Braefoot Ct SW15 . . . .57 C2
Braemar SW15 . . . . . .57 C1
Braemar Ave
SW19 . . . . .70 C2
Braemar CI 5 SE16 . .40 A1
Braemar Ho W9 . . . . . .88 E3
Braemar Mans W8 . . .128 B1
Braemore Ho 21
SE15 . . . . .49 B3
Braes St N1 . . . . .15 A1
Braganza St SE17 . . . .150 A1
Braham Ho SE11 . . . . .149 A2
Braham St E1 . . . . . . .111 A2
Brahma Kumaris World
Spiritual Univ NW10 . .8 C1
Braid Ave W3 . . . . .29 A3
Braidwood Ho SE1 . . .52 B2
Braidwood St SE1 . . .124 A1
Brailsford Rd SW2 . . . .62 C1
Braintree Ho 6 E1 . . . .25 B1
Braintree St E2 . . . . . .25 B2
Braithwaite Ho EC1 . . .97 B2
14 E14 . . . . .34 C3
Braithwaite Twr
W2 . . . . .101 B4
Bramah Gn SW9 . . . .173 C4
Bramall Ct N7 . . . . . . .14 B2
Bramber WC1 . . . . .94 A3
Bramber Ct TW8 . . . . .36 A2
Bramber Rd W14 . . . .154 C4
Bramble Gdns W12 . . .29 B2
Bramble Ho 22 E3 . . . .33 C4
Brambledown 4 N4 . . .5 A4
Brambling 25
SE8 . . . . .51 B4

Bramcote Gr SE16 . . 40 B1
Bramcote Rd SW15 . . 57 A3
Bramerton NW6 . . . . . 9 C1
Bramerton St SW3 158 A4
Bramfield Ct N4 . . . . . . 6 B2
Bramfield Rd SW11 . . 60 B2
Bramford Rd SW18 . . 59 B3
Bramham Gdns
SW5 . . . . 142 B2
Bramham Ho SE22 . . 64 A3
Bramlands Cl SW11 . 60 A4
Bramley Cres SW8 161 C2
Bramley Ho ⑩ W10 . 30 C3
⑤ SW15 . . . . 56 B1
Bramley Rd W10 . . . . 30 C2
Bramshaw Rd E9 . . . . 17 C2
Bramshill Gdns NW5 . . 4 A1
Bramshill Rd NW10 . 21 B3
Bramshot Ave SE3 . . 52 C4
Bramshurst NW8 . . . . 78 B3
Bramston Rd NW10 . 22 A3
SW17 . . . . 71 B1
Bramwell Ho 137 A1
SW1 . . . . 160 C4
Bramwell Mews N1 . 85 A4
Brancaster Ho N5 . . 15 B3
⑳ E1 . . . . 25 C2
Brancaster Rd
SW16 . . . . 74 A1
Branch Pl N1 . . . . . . 87 C4
Branch Rd E14 . . . . . 33 A2
Branch St SE15 . . . . . 49 A3
Brand Cl N4 . . . . 6 A3
Brand St SE10 . . . . . . 52 B3
Brandlehow Prim Sch
SW15 . . . . 58 B3
Brandlehow Rd
SW15 . . . . 58 B3
Brandon Mews
EC2 . . . . 109 B4
Brandon Rd N7 . . . . . 14 A1
Brandon St SE17 . . 151 A3
Brandrams Wharf
SE16 . . . . 40 B4
Brandreth Rd SW17 . 73 A2
Brangton Rd SE11 149 A1
Brangwyn Ct W14 126 A1
Branksea St SW6 . . 154 A1
Branksome Ho
SW8 . . . . 162 C2
Branksome Rd SW2 . 62 A2
Bransby Ct N4 . . . . 6 A3
Branscombe NW1 . . 83 A3
Branscombe St
SE13 . . . . 67 A4
Bransdale Cl NW6 . . 23 C4
Branston Ho N7 . . . . 14 C3
Branstone St ⑨
TW9 . . . . 44 B2
Branstone Rd TW9 . . 44 B2
Brantwood Ho ⑨
SE5 . . . . 48 B3
Brantwood Rd SE24 . 63 B2
Brass Talley Alley ⑥
SE16 . . . . 40 C4
Brassey Ho ① E14 . . 42 A2
Brassey Rd NW6 . . . 10 B2
Brassey Sq SW11 . . . 60 C4
Brassie Ave W3 . . . . 29 A3
Brathay NW1 . . . . . . 83 A1
Brathway Rd SW18 . 70 C4
Bratley St E1 . . . . 99 B1
Bravington Pl W9 . . 23 B1

Bravington Rd W9 . . 23 B2
Brawne Ho ⑫ SE17 . 48 A4
Braxfield Rd SE4 . . . 66 B3
Bray NW3 . . . . 12 A1
Bray Cres SE16 . . . . . 40 C4
Bray Dr E16 . . . . 35 B2
Bray Pl SW3 . . . . . . 144 C3
Brayard's Rd SE15 . . 50 A1
Braybrook St W12 . . 29 B3
Brayburne Ave
SW4 . . . . 171 A1
Braydon Rd N16 . . . . . 7 C3
Brayfield Terr N1 . . . 14 C1
Brayford Sq ⑥ E1 . . 32 B3
Bread St EC2,EC4 . . 109 A1
Breakspeare SE21 . . 76 B1
Breakspears Mews
SE4 . . . . 51 C1
Breakspears Rd SE4 66 C4
Breakwell Ct ⑯
W10 . . . . 23 A1
Bream St E3 . . . . 18 C1
Bream's Bldgs
EC4 . . . . 107 B2
Breamore Cl SW15 . . 68 C3
Breasley Cl SW15 . . . 57 A3
Brechin Pl SW7 . . . 143 A3
Brecknock Prim Sch
NW1 . . . . 13 C2
Brecknock Rd N19 . . 13 C3
Brecon Ho ⑩ W2 . . 100 C2
N16 . . . . 7 B3
SW18 . . . . 70 C4
Brecon Rd W6 . . . . . 154 B3
Bredel Ho ① E14 . . . 33 C4
Bredgar SE13 . . . . . . 67 A2
Bredgar Rd N19 . . . . . 4 B2
Bredinghurst SE22 . 76 C4
Bredinghurst Sch
SE15 . . . . 65 C3
Breer St SW6 . . . . . . 59 A4
Breezer's Cl E1 . . . . 125 C3
Breezer's Hill E1 . . . 125 C3
Bremans Row SW18 71 B2
Bremner Rd SW7 . . 129 A2
Brenchley Gdns
SE15,SE22,SE23 . . . 65 C1
Brenda Rd SW17 . . . . 72 B2
Brendon Ave NW10 . . 8 A4
Brendon Ho N1 . . . 103 B4
Brendon St W1 . . . 102 B2
Brenley Ho SE1 . . . 137 B4
Brent Ho ⑮ E9 . . . . 17 B2
Brent New Ent Ctr
NW10 . . . . 8 B2
Brent Rd E16 . . . . . . 35 C4
Brent Trad Est NW10 . 8 A3
**Brentford Fountain
Leisure Centre** W4 36 C1
Brenthouse Rd E9 . . 17 B2
Brenthurst Rd NW10 . 8 B2
Brenton Ct E9 . . . . . . 18 A3
Brenton St E14 . . . . . 33 A3
Brentwick Gdns
TW8 . . . . 36 A2
Brereton Ho ⑩
SW2 . . . . 74 C4
Bressenden Pl
SW1 . . . . 132 C2
Breton Ho EC2 . . . . . 97 A1
SE1 . . . . 138 C2
Brett Cl N16 . . . . 7 A2
Brett Cres NW10 . . . 20 C4
Brett Ho ① SW15 . . 69 C4

Brett House Cl ②
SW15 . . . . 69 C4
Brett Manor E8 . . . . 17 A3
Brett Pas ⑩ E8 . . . . 17 A3
Brett Rd E8 . . . . 17 A3
Brettell St SE17 . . . 151 C1
Brettinghurst SE1 . 153 B1
Bretton Ho N19 . . . . . 5 A3
Brewer St W1 . . . . . 119 A4
Brewer's Gn SW1 . . 133 B2
Brewers Bldgs EC1 . 96 A4
Brewers Ct W2 . . . . 100 C2
Brewery Rd N7 . . . . . 14 A2
Brewery Sq SE1 . . . 124 C1
Brewhouse La E1 . . . 32 A1
Brewhouse St SW15 58 A4
Brewhouse Wlk
SE16 . . . . 33 A1
Brewhouse Yd EC1 . 96 A2
Brewster Gdns W10 30 B4
Brewster Ho EC1 . . 153 A4
E14 . . . . 33 B2
Briant Ho SE1 . . . . . 135 A1
Briant St SE14 . . . . . 50 C3
Briar Ct E8 . . . . 16 B1
Briar Rd NW2 . . . . 9 B4
Briar Wlk W10 . . . . . 23 A1
SW15 . . . . 57 A3
Briardale SW19 . . . . 70 B3
Briardale Gdns NW3 . 1 C1
Briardale Ho N16 . . . . 7 A3
Briarwood Rd SW4 . 61 C2
Briary Cl NW3 . . . . . 12 A1
Brick Ct EC4 . . . . . . 107 B1
Brick Farm Cl TW9 . 45 A2
Brick La E1 . . . . 99 A2
⑫ 24 B2 99 A3
Brick St W1 . . . . 118 A1
Brickbarn Cl SW10 157 A2
Bricklayers Arms
SE1 . . . . 137 C1
Brickworth Ho ⑥
SW9 . . . . 173 C4
Bride La EC4 . . . . . . 108 A1
Bride St N7 . . . . 14 B2
Brideale Cl SE15 . . . 49 B4
Bridewain St SE1 . . 138 C2
Bridewell Pl EC4 . . 108 A1
⑳ E1 . . . . 32 A1
Bridford Mews W1 104 B4
Bridge App NW1 . . . 81 B4
Bridge Ave W6 . . . . . 39 B1
Bridge Avenue Mans ①
W6 . . . . 39 B1
Bridge Cl ⑱ W10 . . 30 C3
Bridge Field Ho
W2 . . . . 100 A2
Bridge Ho ① NW1 . 12 C1
E9 . . . . 17 B3
SE4 . . . . 66 B3
Bridge House Quay
E14 . . . . 34 B1
Bridge La SW11 . . . 168 B3
Bridge Meadows
SE14 . . . . 50 C4
Bridge Pk ⑦ SW18 . 58 C2
Bridge Rd NW10 . . . 20 C4
E15 . . . . 27 C4
Bridge St SW1 . . . . 134 B3
W4 . . . . 37 C2
Bridge Terr E15 . . . . 19 C1
Bridge Wharf ⑱ E2 . 25 C3
Bridge Yd SE1 . . . . 123 C2
Bridgefoot SE1 . . . 148 B1

Bridgeland Rd E16 . . 35 C2
Bridgeman Ho ⑲
E9 . . . . 17 B1
Bridgeman Rd N1 . . 14 B1
Bridgeman St NW8 . 80 A1
Bridgen Ho ⑭ E1 . . 32 A3
Bridgend Rd SW18 . 59 B3
Bridgeport Pl E1 . . 125 C2
Bridges Ct SW11 . . 167 B1
Bridges Ho ⑮ SE5 . 48 C3
Bridgeview ② W6 . . 39 B1
Bridgewater Rd E15 27 B4
Bridgewater Sq
EC2 . . . . 108 C4
Bridgewater St
EC2 . . . . 108 C4
Bridgeway St NW1 . 83 A1
Bridgford St SW17,
SW18 . . . . 71 B1
Bridgman Rd W4 . . . 37 B3
Bridgnorth Ho ⑩
SE15 . . . . 49 C4
Bridgwater Ho W2 100 C2
Bridle La W1 . . . . . . 119 A4
Bridlington Ho
SW18 . . . . 59 B3
Bridport SE17 . . . . . 151 A1
Bridport Ho N1 . . . . 87 C3
Bridport Pl N1 . . . . . 87 C3
Bridstow Pl W2 . . . . 31 C3
Brief St SE5 . . . . 48 A2
Brierfield NW1 . . . . . 82 C3
Brierley Rd E11 . . . . 19 C4
SW12 . . . . 73 B2
Brierly Gdns E2 . . . . 25 B3
Brig Mews SE8 . . . . . 51 C4
Brigade St SE3 . . . . . 53 B1
Briggeford Cl ⑤ E5 . . 7 C2
Briggs Ho ② 99 A4
Bright St E14 . . . . . . 34 A4
Brightling Rd SE4 . . 66 B1
Brightlingsea Pl ⑤
E14 . . . . 33 B2
Brightman Rd SW18 71 C3
Brighton Bldgs
SE1 . . . . 138 A1
Brighton Ct SW15 . . 58 B1
Brighton Gr SE14 . . 51 A2
Brighton Ho ⑦ SE5 . 48 C2
Brighton Rd N16 . . . 16 A4
Brighton Terr SW9 . 62 B3
Brightside Rd SE13 . 67 C1
Brightwell Ct N7 . . . 14 B3
Brightwells SW6 . . 166 A2
Brigstock Ho SE5 . . 48 B1
Brill Pl NW1 . . . . 83 C1
Brimsdown Ho E3 . . 27 B1
Brindley Ho ㉒
SW12 . . . . 74 A4
Brindley St SE14 . . . 51 B2
Brine Ho ⑮ E3 . . . . . 26 A3
Brinklow Ho W2 . . 100 A3
Brinkworth Way E9 . 18 B2
Brinsley Ho ⑰ E1 . . 32 B3
Brinsley St ⑪ E1 . . . 32 A3
Brinton Wlk SE1 . . 122 A1
Brion Pl E14 . . . . 34 B4
Brisbane Ho ③
W12 . . . . 30 A2
Brisbane St SE5 . . . . 48 C3
Briset St EC1 . . . . . . 96 A1
Briset Way N7 . . . . . . 5 B2
Bristol Gdns W9 . . . . 88 B1
Bristol Ho SE11 . . . 135 B1
Bristol Mews W9 . . . 88 B1
Britannia Cl SW4 . . . 61 B3

Britannia Gate ⑫
E16 . . . . 35 C1
Britannia Junc NW1 82 B4
Britannia Rd SW6 . 156 A1
⑪ E14 . . . . 41 C2
Britannia Row N1 . . 86 C4
Britannia St WC1 . . . 94 C4
Britannia Way
NW10 . . . . 20 A1
Britannia Wlk N1 . . . 97 B4
British Gr W4 . . . . . . 38 B1
British Grove Pas ②
W4 . . . . 38 B1
British Grove S ③
W4 . . . . 38 B1
British Library The ★
WC1 . . . . 93 C4
British Mus ★ WC1 106 A3
British St E3 . . . . 26 B2
British Wharf Ind Est
SE14 . . . . 50 C4
Brinley Ho ⑩ SE1 . . 137 A3
Brittany Ho SW15 . . 57 B3
Brittany Point
SE11 . . . . 149 B3
Britten Cl NW11 . . . . . 2 A3
Britten House
SW3 . . . . 144 B2
Britten St SW3 . . . . 144 A2
Britton St EC1 . . . . . 96 A1
Brixton Day Coll
SW9 . . . . 62 B4
Brixton Hill SW2 . . . 62 B1
Brixton Hill Ct ⑧
SW2 . . . . 62 B2
Brixton Hill Pl SW2 . 74 A4
Brixton Mkt SW9 . . . 62 C3
Brixton Oval ⑦
SW2 . . . . 62 C3
Brixton Rd SW9 . . . 173 B2
Brixton Sta SW9 . . . 62 C3
Brixton Station Rd
SW9 . . . . 62 C4
Brixton Water La
SW2 . . . . 62 B2
Broad Bridge Cl
SE3 . . . . 53 C3
Broad Common Est
N16 . . . . 7 C3
Broad Ct WC2 . . . . . 106 B1
Broad La EC2 . . . . . 110 A4
Broad Sanctuary
SW1 . . . . 134 A3
Broad St Ave EC2 . . 110 A3
Broad St Pl EC2 . . . 109 C3
Broad Wlk NW1 . . . . 81 C1
W1 . . . . 117 B2
Hackney TW9 . . . . . . 44 B3
Broad Wlk The W8 114 B1
Broad Yd EC1 . . . . . . 96 A1
Broadbent Cl N6 . . . . 4 A3
Broadbent St W1 . . 118 A4
Broadfield NW6 . . . . 11 A2
Broadfield La NW1 . . 14 A1
Broadfields Way
NW10 . . . . 8 B3
Broadford Ho ⑳ E1 . 26 A1
Broadgate EC2 . . . . 110 A4
Broadgate Circ
EC2 . . . . 110 A3
Broadgates Rd
SW18 . . . . 71 C3
Broadhinton Rd
SW4 . . . . 61 B4

Broadhurst Cl NW6 ...11 B2
  9 Richmond TW10 ...54 B2
Broadhurst Gdns
NW6 ...11 A2
Broadhurst Mans
NW6 ...11 A2
Broadlands N6 ...3 C4
Broadlands Ave
SW16 ...74 A2
Broadlands Cl N6 ...3 C4
SW16 ...74 A2
Broadlands Cl TW9 ...44 C3
Broadlands Lo N6 ...3 B4
Broadlands Mans 2
SW16 ...74 A2
Broadlands Rd N6 ...3 B4
Broadley St NW8 ...102 A4
Bradley Terr NW1 ...90 B1
Broadmayne SE17 ...151 B2
Broadmead W14 ...140 A3
Broadoak Ct 9
SW9 ...62 C4
Broadoak Ho NW6 ...78 B3
Broadstone Ho
SW8 ...162 C1
Broadstone Pl W1 ...103 B3
Broadwalk Ho
SW7 ...128 C3
Broadwalk La NW11 ...1 B4
Broadwall SE1 ...121 C2
Broadway SW1 ...133 B2
E15 ...19 C1
Broadway Arc 3
W6 ...39 B2
Broadway Ho E2 ...8 B2 C4
Broadway Mans
SW6 ...155 C1
Broadway Market
E8 ...25 A4
Broadway Market Mews
21 E8 ...24 C4
Broadway Mews E5 ...7 B4
Broadway The W3 ...36 C4
SW13 ...46 A1
Broadwick St W1 ...105 A1
Broadwood Terr
W14 ...141 A4
Brocas Cl NW3 ...12 A1
Brock Ho NW1 ...105 B4
Brock Pl E3 ...27 A1
Brock St SE15 ...65 B4
Brockbridge Ho 11
SW15 ...56 B1
Brocket Ho SW8 ...171 B2
Brockham Dr SW2 ...74 B4
Brockham Ho NW1 ...83 A3
11 SW2 ...74 B4
Brockham St SE1 ...137 A2
Brockhurst Ho N4 ...6 C4
Brockill Cres SE4 ...66 A3
Brocklebank Rd
SW18 ...71 B4
Brocklehurst St
SE14 ...50 C3
Brockley Cross SE4 ...66 B4
Brockley Cross Bsns Ctr
SE4 ...66 B4
Brockley Gdns SE4 ...51 B1
Brockley Gr SE4 ...66 C2
Brockley Hall Rd
SE4 ...66 A2
Brockley Mews SE17 ...152 A2
Brockley Prim Sch
SE4 ...66 B2
Brockley Rd SE4 ...66 B2

Brockley Sta SE4 ...66 A4
Brockley Way SE4 ...66 A2
Brockmer Ho 5 E1 ...32 A2
Brockweir 20 E2 ...25 B3
Brockwell Ct 2
SW2 ...62 C2
Brockwell Ho
SE11 ...163 A4
Brockwell Park
SE24 ...62 C2
Brockwell Park Gdns
SW2 ...62 C1
Brockwell Prim Schs
SW2 ...62 C2
Broderick Rd SE21 ...76 A1
Brodia Rd N16 ...7 A1
Brodick Ho 11 E3 ...26 B3
Brodie Ho SE1 ...153 A2
Brodie St SE1 ...153 A2
Brodlove La E1 ...32 C2
Brodrick Rd SW17 ...71 C2
Broke Wlk 8 ...24 B4
1 E8 ...24 B4
Broken Wharf EC4 ...122 C4
Brokesley St E3 ...26 B2
Bromar Rd SE5 ...64 A4
Bromehead St 5
E1 ...32 B3
Bromell's Rd SW4 ...61 B3
Bromfelde Rd
SW4 ...171 C1
Bromfield Ct SE16 ...139 C2
Bromfield St N1 ...85 C2
Bromleigh Ho SE1 ...138 C2
Bromley Ct SE13 ...67 C2
Bromley Hall Rd
E14 ...34 B4
Bromley High St
E3 ...27 B2
Bromley Lo 2 W3 ...28 B3
Bromley Pl W1 ...104 C4
Bromley St E1 ...32 C3
Bromley-by-Bow Sta
E3 ...27 A2
Brompton Arc
SW1 ...131 A3
Brompton Hospl
SW3 ...143 C2
Brompton Oratory
SW3 ...130 A1
Brompton Park Cres
SW6 ...156 A3
Brompton Pl SW3 ...130 B2
Brompton Rd SW3 ...130 A1
Brompton Sq SW3 ...130 A2
Bromstone Ho
SW9 ...173 B3
Bromwich Ave N6 ...3 C2
Bromwich Ho 3
TW10 ...54 A1
Bromyard Ave W3 ...29 A2
Bromyard Ho 3
SE15 ...50 A3
Bron Ct NW6 ...23 C4
Brondesbury Ct NW2 ...9 C2
Brondesbury Mews 11
NW6 ...10 C1
Brondesbury Park Sta
NW6 ...23 A4
Brondesbury Pk NW6 ...9 C1
Brondesbury Rd
NW6 ...23 C3
Brondesbury Sta
NW6 ...10 B1

Brondesbury Villas
NW6 ...23 C3
Bronsart Rd SW6 ...154 A1
Bronte Ct 8 W14 ...39 C3
Bronte Ho 6 N16 ...16 A3
NW6 ...23 C2
Bronti Cl SE17 ...151 A2
Bronwen Ct NW8 ...89 B3
Bronze St SE8 ...51 C3
Brook Cl SW14 ...56 A4
E15 ...76 B3
Brook Dr SE11 ...150 A5
Brook Gate W1 ...117 A3
Brook Gdns SW13 ...56 B4
Brook Gn W6 ...39 C2
Brook Green Flats 11
W6 ...39 C2
Brook Ho 6 W3 ...36 C4
4 W6 ...39 B2
3 SW4 ...61 B2
Brook Hos NW1 ...83 A1
Brook Mews N W2 ...115 A4
Brook St W2 ...115 C4
W1 ...118 A4
Brook's Mews
W1 ...118 A4
Brookbank Rd SE13 ...67 A4
Brookdale Rd SE6 ...67 A1
Brooke Rd E5,N16 ...7 C1
Brooke St EC1 ...107 B3
Brooke's Mkt EC1 ...107 C4
Brooke St EC1 ...107 B3
Brookfield N6 ...3 C1
11 N4 ...5 C2
Brookfield Pk NW5 ...4 A1
Brookfield Prim Sch
N19 ...4 A2
Brookfield Rd E9 ...18 A2
W4 ...37 C4
Brookgate N16 ...6 C2
Brooklands Ave
SW18 ...71 A2
Brooklands Court
Apartments 3
NW6 ...10 B1
Brooklands Ct 6
NW6 ...10 B1
Brooklyn Ct W12 ...30 B1
Brookmarsh Ind Est
SE10 ...52 A3
Brookmill Rd SE8 ...51 C2
Brooks Ct 8 SW4 ...161 A2
SW4 ...172 A2
Brooks Ho 6 SW2 ...74 C3
Brooks La W4 ...44 C4
Brooksbank Ho 7
E9 ...17 B2
Brooksbank St 9
E9 ...17 B2
Brooksby Mews N1 ...14 C1
Brooksby St N1 ...14 C1
Brooksby's Wlk E9 ...17 C3
Brookside Rd N19 ...4 B2
Brookstone Ct SE15 ...65 A3
Brooksville Ave
NW6 ...23 A4
Brookville Rd SW6 ...154 C1
Brookwood Ave
SW13 ...46 B1
Brookwood Ho
SE1 ...136 B3
Brookwood Rd
SW18 ...70 C3
Broome Ct 3 TW9 ...44 C2
Broome Ho 7 E5 ...17 A3

Broome Way SE5 ...48 C3
Broomfield 7 NW1 ...12 C1
Broomfield Ho
SE17 ...152 A3
Broomfield House Sch
TW9 ...44 B2
Broomfield Rd TW9 ...44 B2
Broomfield St E14 ...34 A4
Broomgrove Rd
SW9 ...173 A1
Broomhill Rd SW18 ...58 C2
Broomhouse La
SW6 ...58 C4
Broomhouse Rd
SW6 ...165 B3
Broomsleigh St
NW6 ...10 B3
Broomwood Rd
SW11 ...60 C2
Brough Cl SW8 ...162 B1
Brough St SW8 ...162 B1
Brougham Rd E8 ...24 C4
W3 ...28 B3
Brougham St
SW11 ...169 A2
Broughton Dr 20
SW9 ...63 A3
Broughton Rd
SW6 ...166 B2
Broughton Road App
SW6 ...166 A2
Broughton St SW8 ...170 A2
Broughton Street
Arches Ind Area
SW11 ...170 A2
Brouncker Rd W3 ...37 B4
Brown Hart Gdns
W1 ...103 C1
W1 ...117 C4
Brown St W1 ...102 C2
Browne Ho 13 SE8 ...51 C3
Brownfield St E14 ...34 B3
Brownflete Ho SE4 ...66 A3
Browning Cl W9 ...89 A1
Browning Ct W14 ...154 C4
Browning Ho
16 N16 ...16 A4
W12 ...30 B3
Browning Mews
W1 ...103 C3
Browning St SE17 ...151 A3
Brownlow Ho SE16 ...139 B3
Brownlow Mews
WC1 ...95 A1
Brownlow Rd NW10 ...8 A1
E8 ...24 C4
Brownlow St WC1 ...107 A3
Brownswood Rd N4 ...6 B2
Broxash Rd SW11 ...60 C1
Broxbourne Ho 7
E3 ...27 A1
Broxholm Rd SE27,
SW16 ...74 C1
Broxholme Ho
SW6 ...166 A4
Broxwood Way
NW8 ...80 B3
Bruce Cl W10 ...30 C4
Bruce Glasier Ho 13
N19 ...4 C4
Bruce Ho W10 ...30 C4
SW15 ...57 A2
4 SW4 ...61 C1
Bruce Rd E3 ...27 A2

Bruckner St W10 ...23 B2
Brudenell Rd SW17 ...72 C1
Bruges Pl 13 NW1 ...13 B1
Brune Ho E1 ...110 C3
Brune St E1 ...110 C3
Brunel Cl NW10 ...21 C2
3 SW13 ...47 A4
Brunel Est W2 ...31 C4
Brunel Ho SW10 ...157 C2
4 NW5 ...13 A4
E14 ...42 A1
25 SW2 ...74 A4
Brunel Rd W3 ...29 A4
SE16 ...32 B1
Brunel St E16 ...35 B1
Brunlees Ho SE1 ...137 A1
Brunswick Ct EC1 ...96 A3
SE1 ...138 B4
SW1 ...147 C3
Brunswick Gdns
W8 ...31 C1 113 C1
Brunswick Ho NW1 ...90 C2
2 E2 ...24 B3
Brunswick Mews
W1 ...103 A2
Brunswick Park Prim
Sch SE5 ...48 C3
Brunswick Pk SE5 ...49 A2
Brunswick Pl N1 ...97 C3
Brunswick Quay
SE16 ...40 C3
Brunswick Rd E14 ...34 B3
Brunswick Sh Ctr
WC1 ...94 B2
Brunswick Sq WC1 ...94 B2
Brunswick Villas 2
SE5 ...49 A2
Brunton Pl E14 ...33 A3
Brushfield St E1 ...110 C4
Brushwood Ho 4
E14 ...34 A4
Brussels Rd SW11 ...59 C3
Bruton La W1 ...118 B3
Bruton Pl W1 ...118 B3
Bruton St W1 ...118 B3
Bryan Ave NW10 ...9 A1
Bryan Ct W1 ...102 C2
Bryan Ho SE16 ...41 B4
Bryan Rd SE16 ...41 B4
Bryanston Ct W1 ...102 C2
Bryanston Ho 11
SE15 ...49 B2
Bryanston Mans
W1 ...102 C4
Bryanston Mews E
W1 ...102 C3
Bryanston Mews W
W1 ...102 C2
Bryanston Pl W1 ...102 C3
Bryanston Sq W1 ...102 C2
Bryanston St W1 ...103 A1
Bryant Ct E2 ...24 B3
W3 ...28 B1
Bryantwood Rd N5,
N7 ...14 C3
Bryce Ho 5 SE14 ...50 C4
Brydale Ho 8 SE16 ...40 C2
Brydges Pl WC2 ...120 A3
Brydges Rd E15 ...19 C3
Brydon Wlk N1 ...84 B4
Bryer Ct EC2 ...108 C4
Bryett Rd N7 ...5 A1
Bryher Ho W4 ...37 B1
Brymay Cl E3 ...26 C3

Brymon Ct W1 ....103 A3
Brynmaer Ho
SW11 ....169 A3
Brynmaer Rd
SW11 ....169 A3
Bryony Rd W12 ....29 C2
BT Tower* W1 ....104 C4
Buccleuch Ho E5 ....7 C4
Buchan Ho W3 ....37 A4
Buchan Rd SE15 ....65 B4
Buchanan Ct 18
SE16 ....40 C2
Buchanan Gdns
NW10 ....22 A3
Buchanan Ho SW18 ....70 C4
SE21 ....76 A1
Bucharest Rd SW18 ....71 B4
Buck Hill Wlk W2 ....115 C3
Buck St NW1 ....13 A1
Buckfast St
E2 ....24 C2 99 C3
Buckhold Rd SW18 ....58 C1
Buckhurst Ho 10 N7 ....13 C3
Buckhurst St E1 ....25 A1
Buckingham Gate
SW1 ....133 A2
Buckingham Ho N4 ....6 B3
   Richmond TW10 ....54 C2
Buckingham Mans
NW6 ....11 A3
Buckingham Mews
SW1 ....132 C2
NW10 ....21 B3
Buckingham Palace*
SW1 ....132 C3
Buckingham Palace Rd
SW1 ....146 B4
Buckingham Pl
SW1 ....132 C2
Buckingham Rd N1 ....16 A2
NW10 ....21 B3
Buckingham St
WC2 ....120 B3
Buckingham Yd
NW10 ....21 B3
Buckland Cres NW3 ....12 A2
Buckland Ct 6 N1 ....24 A3
Buckland St N1 ....87 C1
Buckland Wlk 2
W3 ....37 B4
Buckle St E1 ....111 A2
Buckler's Alley
SW6 ....155 A2
Bucklersbury EC2,
EC4 ....109 B1
Buckley Ct 5 NW6 ....10 B1
Buckley Rd NW6 ....10 B1
Buckley St SE1 ....121 B1
Buckmaster Ho
1 N7 ....14 B4
Buckmaster Cl 4
SW9 ....62 C4
Buckmaster Rd
SW11 ....60 A3
Bucknall St WC1 ....106 A2
Bucknell Cl SW2 ....62 B3
Bucknall Rd SW2 ....62 B3
Buckridge Ho EC1 ....107 B4
Buckshead Ho 10
W2 ....31 C4
Buckstone Cl SE23 ....65 B1
Buckters Rents
SE16 ....33 A1
Buckthorne Rd SE4 ....66 A2

Budge Row EC4 ....109 B1
Budd's Wlk W2 ....115 B1
Budleigh Ho 10
SE15 ....49 C3
Buer Rd SW6 ....164 C1
Bugsbys Way SE10 ....43 B3
Buick Ho 4 E3 ....26 C1
Bulinca St SW1 ....147 C3
Bull Inn Ct WC2 ....120 B3
Bull Yd SE15 ....49 C2
Bull's Gdns SW3 ....144 B4
Bullace Row SE5 ....48 C2
Bullards Pl 18 E2 ....25 C2
Bulleid Way SW1 ....146 B3
Bullen Ho 13 E1 ....25 A1
Bullen St SW11 ....168 B2
Buller Cl SE15 ....49 C3
Buller Rd NW10 ....22 C2
Bullfinch Ct 3 SE21 ....75 C2
Bullingham Mans
W8 ....127 C4
Bullivant St 9 E14 ....34 B2
Bulls Alley SW14 ....45 C1
Bulls Head Pas
EC3 ....110 A1
Bulmer Mews
W11 ....31 C1 113 B2
Bulow Ct 5 SW6 ....166 B3
Bulstrode Pl W1 ....103 C3
Bulstrode St W1 ....103 C2
Bulwer St W12 ....30 B1
Bunbury Ho SE15 ....49 C3
Bunhill Row EC1 ....97 B1
Bunhouse Pl SW1 ....145 C2
Bunkers Hill NW11 ....2 B4
Bunning Ho N7 ....14 A4
Bunning Way N7 ....14 B1
Bunsen Ho 1 E3 ....26 A3
Bunsen St 2 E3 ....26 A3
Bunyan Ct EC2 ....108 C4
Buonaparte Mews
SW1 ....147 B2
Burbage Cl SE1 ....137 B1
Burbage Ho N1 ....87 C3
16 SE14 ....50 C4
Burbage Rd SE21,
SE24 ....75 C4
Burcham St E14 ....34 B3
Burchell Ho SE11 ....149 A2
Burchell Rd SE15 ....50 A2
Burcote Rd SW18 ....71 C4
Burden Ho SW8 ....162 A1
Burdenshott Ave
TW10 ....55 A3
Burder Cl N1 ....16 A2
Burder Rd N1 ....16 A2
Burdett Coutts CE Prim
Sch SW1 ....147 B4
Burdett Mews W2 ....100 A2
Burdett Rd E3 ....33 B4
   Richmond TW9 ....54 B4
Burford Ho SW9 ....173 A1
1 Brentford TW8 ....36 A1
Burford Rd E15 ....27 C4
   Brentford TW8 ....36 A1
Burford Wlk SW6 ....156 B1
Burgate Ct 10 SW9 ....62 C4
Burge St SE1 ....137 C1
Burges Gr SW13 ....47 A3
Burgess Ho 3 SE5 ....48 B3
Burgess Park Mans
NW6 ....10 C4
Burgess St E14 ....33 C4
Burgh St N1 ....86 B2

Burghley Ho SW19 ....70 A1
Burghley Rd NW5 ....13 A4
Burghley Twr W3 ....29 B2
Burgon St EC4 ....108 B1
Burgos Gr SE10 ....52 A2
Burgoyne Rd SW9 ....62 B4
Burhan Uddin Ho
E1 ....98 C1
Buriton Ho 9 SW15 ....69 A3
Burke Cl SW15 ....56 A3
Burke Ho 6 SW11 ....59 C3
Burke St E16 ....35 B2
Burland Rd SW11 ....60 B2
Burleigh Ho SW3 ....157 C3
   W10 ....30 C4
Burleigh Pl SW15 ....57 C2
Burleigh St WC2 ....120 C4
Burlington Arc W1 ....118 C3
Burlington Ave TW9 ....44 C2
Burlington Cl W9 ....23 C1
Burlington Ct W4 ....45 B3
Burlington Danes Sch
W12 ....30 A3
Burlington Gdns
W1 ....118 C3
SW6 ....164 B1
W3 ....28 B1
W4 ....37 B1
Burlington Ho NW3 ....11 C3
Burlington La W4 ....45 C3
Burlington Mews
1 SW15 ....58 B2
Burlington Pl SW6 ....164 B1
Burlington Rd
SW6 ....164 B1
W4 ....37 B1
Burma Rd N16 ....15 C4
Burmarsh 8 NW5 ....12 C2
Burmester Ho SW17 ....71 B1
Burmester Rd SW17 ....71 B1
Burn's Ho NW10 ....21 A4
Burn's Rd NW10 ....21 B4
Burnaby Cres W4 ....45 B4
Burnaby Ct 5 SE16 ....139 C3
Burnaby Gdns W4 ....45 A4
Burnaby St SW10 ....157 A1
Burnand Ho 8 W14 ....39 C3
Burnaston Ho 5 E5 ....7 C1
Burnbury Rd SW12 ....73 B3
Burne Jones Ho
W14 ....140 B3
Burne St NW1 ....102 A4
Burnell Ho 10 SW2 ....74 C3
Burnell Wlk SE1 ....153 A2
Buress Cl N7 ....14 B2
Burnett Cl E9 ....17 B3
Burnett Ho 5 SE13 ....52 B1
Burney St SE10 ....52 B3
Burnfoot Ave SW6 ....164 B3
Burnham NW3 ....12 A1
Burnham Cl SE1 ....153 A3
Burnham Ct W2 ....114 B4
Burnham Est 8 E2 ....25 B2
Burnham St E2 ....25 B2
Burnhill Ho EC1 ....96 C3
Burnley Rd SW9 ....172 C2
   NW10 ....8 C3
Burns Ho SE17 ....150 B1
N7 ....14 A4
18 E2 ....25 B2
Burns Rd SW11 ....168 C2
Burnsall St SW3 ....144 B2

Burnside Cl SE16 ....32 C1
Burnthwaite Rd
SW6 ....155 A1
Burntwood Cl SW18 ....72 A3
Burntwood Ct SW17 ....71 B1
Burntwood Grange Rd
SW18 ....72 A3
Burntwood La
SW17 ....71 C2
Burntwood Sch
SW17 ....71 C2
Buross St E1 ....32 A3
Burr Cl E1 ....125 B2
Burr Rd SW18 ....70 C3
Burrage Ct 17 SE16 ....40 C2
Burrard Ho 11 E2 ....25 B3
Burrard Rd NW6 ....10 C4
Burrell's Wharf Sq
E14 ....42 A1
Burrhill Ct SE16 ....40 C3
Burrow Ho SW9 ....173 A1
Burrow Rd SE22 ....64 A3
Burrow Wlk SE21 ....75 B4
Burrows Mews
SE1 ....136 A4
Burrows Rd NW10 ....22 C2
Bursar St SE1 ....124 A1
Burstock Rd SW15 ....58 A3
Burston Rd SW15 ....57 C2
Burtley Cl N4 ....6 B3
Burton Bank N1 ....15 C1
Burton Ct SW3 ....145 A2
Burton Gr SE17 ....151 B1
Burton Ho 6 SE16 ....40 A4
   SE5 ....48 A2
Burton La SW9 ....173 C2
Burton Lo 5 SW15 ....58 B2
Burton Mews SW1 ....145 C3
Burton Pl WC1 ....93 C3
Burton Rd SW9 ....173 B2
   SW9 ....48 A1
Burton Road SW9 ....48 A1
Burton St WC1 ....93 C3
Burtons Ct E15 ....19 C1
Burtonwood Ho N4 ....6 C4
Burtt Ho N1 ....98 A4
Burwash Ho SE1 ....137 C3
Burwell Cl 22 E1 ....32 A3
Burwell Wlk 4 E3 ....26 C1
Burwood Cl SE22 ....65 B1
Burwood Ho 11
SW9 ....63 A3
Burwood Pl W2 ....102 B2
Bury Cl SE16 ....32 C1
Bury Ct EC3 ....110 B2
Bury Pl WC1 ....106 B3
Bury St EC3 ....110 B2
   SW1 ....119 A2
Bury Wlk SW3 ....144 A2
Busbridge Ho 16
E14 ....33 C4
Busby Ho SW16 ....73 C1
Busby Pl NW5 ....13 C2
Busby St E2 ....99 A2
Bush Cotts 12 SW18 ....58 C2
Bush Ct 7 W12 ....39 C4
Bush La EC4 ....123 B4
Bush Rd E8 ....25 A4
   SE8 ....40 C2
   Richmond TW9 ....44 C4
Bushbaby Cl SE1 ....138 A1
Bushberry Rd E9 ....18 A2
Bushell Cl SW2 ....74 B2
Bushell St E1 ....125 C1
Bushey Down SW12 ....73 A2
Bushey Hall SE5 ....49 B2

Bushey Hill Rd SE5 ....49 B2
Bushey Ho NW6 ....11 A3
Bushnell Rd SW17 ....73 A1
Bushwood Dr SE1 ....153 A3
Bushwood Rd TW9 ....44 C4
Business Design Ctr*
N1 ....85 C3
Buspace Studios 3
W10 ....23 A1
Butcher Row E1 ....32 C3
Butchers Rd E16 ....35 C3
Bute Gdns W6 ....39 C2
Bute House Prep Sch
W6 ....39 C2
Bute St SW7 ....143 B4
Butfield Ho 6 E9 ....17 B2
Butler Ho 32 E2 ....25 B2
   14 E14 ....33 B3
   5 SW9 ....48 A2
Butler Pl SW1 ....133 B2
Butler Rd NW10 ....8 B1
Butler St 33 E2 ....25 B2
Butler's Wharf W
SE1 ....124 C1
Butterfield Cl 1
SE16 ....40 A4
Butterfly Wlk 2
SE5 ....48 C2
Buttermere NW1 ....92 B4
Buttermere Cl SE1 ....152 C3
Buttermere Ct NW8 ....79 B4
Buttermere Dr
SW15 ....58 A2
Buttermere Ho 11
E3 ....26 B2
Buttermere Wlk 9
E8 ....16 B2
Butterwick W6 ....39 B2
Butterworth Ct
SW16 ....74 A1
Buttesland St N1 ....97 C4
Buxted Rd E8 ....16 B1
   SE22 ....64 A3
Buxton Ct N1 ....97 A4
Buxton Gdns W3 ....28 A2
Buxton Ho 3 SW11 ....59 C3
Buxton Rd N19 ....4 C3
   NW2 ....9 A2
   SW14 ....56 A4
Buxton St E1 ....24 C1 99 B1
Byam Shaw Sch of Art
N19 ....4 C2
Byam St SW6 ....166 C1
Byards Ct SE16 ....40 C3
Byas Ho 6 E3 ....26 B2
Bye The W3 ....29 A3
Byefield Cl SE16 ....41 A4
Byelands Cl 12 SE16 ....32 C1
Byeway The SW14 ....55 B4
Byfeld Gdns SW13 ....46 C2
Bygrove Prim Sch
E14 ....34 A3
Bygrove St E14 ....34 A3
Byng Pl WC1 ....93 B1
Byng St E14 ....41 C4
Byrne Ho 11 SW2 ....62 B2
Byrne Rd SW12 ....73 A2
Byron Cl E8 ....24 C4
Byron Ct 4 W1 ....94 C2
   SW3 ....144 B3
   3 NW6 ....11 B1
   W9 ....23 C1
   SE21 ....76 C3
Byron Mews NW3 ....12 A4

Byron St E14 ......34 B3
Bythorn St SW9 ....62 B3
Byward St EC3 ....124 B3
Bywater Pl SE16 ...33 A1
Bywater St SW3 ...144 C2
Bywell Pl W1 ......104 C3
Byworth Wlk N19 ...5 A3

C

Cabbell St NW1 ...102 A3
Cabinet Office SW1 ....134 A4
Cabinet War Rooms ★ SW1 ....133 C3
Cable Ho WC1 .....95 B4
Cable Pl SE10 .....52 B2
Cable St E1 ....32 A2
Cabot Ct SE16 .....40 C3
Cabot Sq E14 ......33 C1
Cabul Rd SW11 ...168 B1
Cactus Cl SE5 .....49 A1
Cadbury Way SE16 .153 B4
Caddington Rd NW2 ..1 A1
Cade Rd SE10 .....52 C2
Cade Tyler Ho SE10 ....52 C2
Cadell Cl E2 ......24 B3
Cadell Ho 15 E2 ...24 B3
Cader Rd SW18 ....59 B1
Cadet Dr SE1 .....153 A2
Cadet Pl SE10 .....43 A1
Cadiz St SE17 ....151 A1
Cadmore Ho 4 N1 ..15 A1
Cadmus Ct SW9 ...173 B4
Cadnam Point 15 SW15 ....69 A3
Cadogan Cl E9 ....18 B1
Cadogan Ct SW3 ..144 C3
Cadogan Ct Gdns SW1 ....145 B4
Cadogan Gate SW1 ....145 A4
Cadogan Gdns SW3 ....145 A3
Cadogan Ho SW3 ..157 C3
Cadogan La SW1 ..131 B1
Cadogan Pl SW1 ..131 A1
Cadogan Sq SW1 ..131 A1
Cadogan St SW3 ..144 C3
Cadogan Terr E9 ...18 B1
Caedmon Rd N7 ...14 B4
Caernarvon Ho W2 ....100 C2
Cahill St EC1 ......97 A1
Cahir St E14 ....42 A2
Caine Ho W3 ....37 B4
Caird St W10 ......23 B2
Cairns Ho 3 N7 ...14 B4
Cairns Rd SW11 ...60 A2
Caister Ho N7 .....14 B2
10 SW12 ......73 A4
Caistor Mews SW12 .73 A4
Caistor Rd SW12 ..73 A4
Caithness Ho N1 ..84 C4
Caithness Rd W14 ..39 C3
Calabria Rd N5 ...15 A3
Calais Gate SE5 ...48 A2
Calais St SE5 .....48 A2
Calbourne Rd SW12 .72 C4
Calcraft Ho 2 E2 ..25 B3
Caldecot Ct SE5 ...48 B1
Caldecot Rd SE5 ..48 B1
Calder Ct SE16 ...33 B1
Calderon Ho NW8 ..80 A2
Calderon Pl W10 ..30 B4

Caldervale Rd SW4 .61 C2
Caldew St SE5 .....48 C3
Caldwell St SW9 ..163 B1
Caldy Wlk 16 N1 ...15 B2
Cale St E1 ....32 A2
Cale St SW3 ......144 A2
Caleb St SE1 .....137 A4
Caledonia Ho 17 E14 ....33 A3
Caledonia St N1 ...84 B1
Caledonian Market SE1 ....138 B2
Caledonian Rd N1 ..84 C3
N7 ....14 B2
Caledonian Road & Barnsbury Sta N7 ..14 B1
Caledonian Road Sta N7 ....14 B2
Caledonian Wharf Rd E14 ....42 C2
Caletock Way SE10 .43 B1
Calgarth NW1 .....83 A1
Calgary Ct 24 SE16 .40 B4
Caliban Twr 9 N1 ..24 A3
Calico Ho 4 SW11 .59 B4
Calico Row 5 SW11 .59 B4
Calidore Cl SW2 ...62 B1
Callaby Terr 11 N1 ..15 C2
Callahan Cotts 8 E1 ....32 B4
Callcott Ct NW6 ...10 B1
Callcott Rd NW6 ...10 B1
Callcott St W8 ...113 B2
Callendar Rd SW7 129 B2
Callingham Cl 17 E14 ....33 B4
Callingham Ho 4 SW4 ....172 A2
Callow St SW3 ....157 B4
Calmington Rd SE5 ....152 B1
Calmore Mews SE15 ....50 A2
Calshot Ho N1 ....84 C2
Calshot St N1 .....84 C1
Calstock NW1 .....83 B3
Calstock Ho SE15 149 C2
Calthorpe St WC1 ..95 A2
Calton Ave SE21 ...64 A1
Calver 13 NW5 .....13 A4
Calverley Gr N19 ...4 C3
Calvert Ct 2 N19 ...4 B3
5 Richmond TW9 ...54 B4
Calvert Ho 6 W12 ..30 A2
Calvert Rd SE10 ...43 B1
Calvert St NW1 ....81 B4
Calvert's Bldgs SE1 ....123 B1
Calverton SE5 .....49 A4
Calvin St E1 ..24 B1 98 C1
Calypso Way SE8, SE16 ....41 B2
Cam Ct 2 SE15 ....49 B4
Cam Rd E15 ......27 C4
Cambalt Ho 3 SW15 ....57 C2
Cambalt Rd SW15 ..57 C2
Cambell Wlk N1 ...84 B4
Camber Ho 6 SE15 .50 B4
Camberley Ho NW1 ..82 B1
Camberwell Church St SE5 ....49 A2
Camberwell Coll of Arts SE5 ....49 A2
SE15 ....49 A3

Camberwell Glebe SE5 ....49 A2
Camberwell Gn SE5 .48 C2
Camberwell Gr SE5 .49 A1
Camberwell Green SE5 ....48 B2
Camberwell New Rd SE5 ....163 C2
SW9 ....48 B3
Camberwell Rd SE5 .48 B3
Camberwell Station Rd SE5 ....48 B2
Camberwell Trad Est SE5 ....48 B2
Camborne Rd SW18 70 C4
Cambourne Mews 6 W11 ....31 A3
Cambray Rd SW12 ..73 B3
Cambria Ho 14 E14 ..33 A3
Cambria Rd SE5 ...63 B4
Cambria St SW6 ..156 B1
Cambrian Cl SE27 ..75 A1
Cambrian Rd TW10 .54 B1
Cambridge Ave NW6 ....23 C3
Cambridge Cir WC2 ....105 C1
Cambridge Cotts TW9 ....44 C4
Cambridge Cres 20 E2 ....25 A3
Cambridge Ct 14 N16 ....7 A4
22 E2 ....25 A3
NW6 ....23 C3
W2 ....102 A2
Cambridge Gate NW1 ....92 A3
Cambridge Gate Mews NW1 ....92 A3
Cambridge Gdns 10 N1 ....23 C3
W10 ....31 A3
Cambridge Gr W6 ..39 A2
Cambridge Heath Rd E1, E2 ....25 A3
Cambridge Heath Sta E2 ....25 A3
Cambridge Ho SW6 .58 A4
Cambridge Mans SW11 ....168 C3
Cambridge Pas 8 E9 ....17 B1
Cambridge Pl W8 128 B3
Cambridge Rd SW11 ....168 C3
SW13 ....46 B1
NW6 ....23 C3
Richmond TW9 ..44 C3
SW13 ....46 B1
Cambridge Rd N W4 ....37 A1
Cambridge Rd S 4 W4 ....37 A1
Cambridge Sch W6 .39 A2
Cambridge Sq W2 102 A2
Cambridge St SW1 146 C2
Cambridge Terr NW1 ....92 B3
Cambridge Terr Mews NW1 ....92 C3
Cambus Rd E16 ....35 C4
Camden Gdns NW1 .13 A1
Camden High St NW1 ....82 C3
Camden Ho 6 SE8 .41 B1
Camden Lock Pl NW1 ....13 A1

Camden Mews NW1 13 C2
Camden Mkt ★ NW1 82 B4
Camden Park Rd NW1 ....13 C2
Camden Pas N1 ...86 A3
Camden Rd NW1 ...82 C4
Camden Road Sta NW1 ....13 B1
Camden Row SE3 ..53 A1
Camden Sch for Girls The NWS 13 B2
Camden Sq NW1 ...13 C2
SE15 ....49 B2
Camden St NW1 ...83 A4
Camden Studios NW1 ....83 A3
Camden Town Sta NW1 ....82 B4
Camden Wlk N1 ...86 A3
Camdenhurst St E14 ....33 A3
Cameford Ct 20 SW2 ....74 A4
Camelford NW1 ...83 A3
Camelford Ct 1 W11 ....31 A3
Camelford Ho SE1 148 B1
Camelford Wlk 6 W11 ....31 A3
Camellia Ho SE8 ..51 B3
Camellia St SW8 .162 A1
Camelot Ho 6 NW1 .13 C2
Camelot Prim Sch SE15 ....50 B3
Camera Ho 6 SE10 157 A4
Cameret Ct 6 W11 .39 C4
Cameron Ct 3 SW19 ....70 A3
Cameron Ho NW8 ..80 A2
SE5 ....48 B3
Camerton Cl 8 E8 .16 B2
Camilla Rd SE16 ...40 A2
Camlet St E2 ......98 C2
Camley St NW1 ...83 C2
Camomile St EC3 .110 B2
Campaign Ct W9 ..23 B1
Campana Rd SW6 165 C4
Campbell Ct SW7 .128 C1
SE22 ....76 C3
Campbell Gordon Way NW2 ....9 A4
Campbell Ho W2 ...89 B1
SW1 ....146 C1
30 W12 ....30 A2
Campbell Rd E3 ...26 C2
Campbell Rd N7 ....4 C1
Campden Gr W8 ..127 C4
Campden Hill W8 .127 B3
Campden Hill Ct W8 ....127 C4
Campden Hill Gate W8 ....127 C4
Campden Hill Gdns W8 ....113 B2
Campden Hill Mans W8 ....113 C2
Campden Hill Rd W14 ....113 A2
Campden Hill Sq W14 ....31 B1 113 A2
Campden Hos 2 W8 ....113 B1
Campden House Cl W8 ....127 C4

Campden St W8 ...31 C1 113 B1
Campen Cl SW19 ..70 A2
Camperdown St E1 ....111 A1
Campion Ho 15 N16 .16 A3
Campion Rd SW15 .57 B2
Camplin St SE14 ...50 C3
Campshill Pl SE13 .67 B2
Campshill Rd SE13 67 B2
Campton Hill Towers W8 ....113 B2
Camsey Ho 3 SW2 .62 B2
Canada Cres 2 W3 .20 B1
Canada Gdns SE13 .67 B2
Canada Rd W3 ....28 B4
Canada Sq E14 ....34 A1
Canada St SE16 ...40 C4
Canada Way W12 ..30 A2
Canal App SE8 ....51 A4
Canal Bridge SE15 .49 C4
Canal Cl W10 .....22 C1
E1 ....26 A1
Canal Gr SE15 ....50 A4
Canal Path 22 E2 ..24 B4
Canal Rd E3 ......33 A4
Canal Side Wlk W9 ....90 A2
Canal St SE5 .....48 C4
Canal Way W10 ...22 C1
Canal Wlk N1 .....87 C4
Canalside Studios 81 N1 ....24 A4
Canary Wharf ★ E14 34 A1
Canary Wharf Pier (River Bus) E14 ...33 B1
Canary Wharf Sta W12 ....30 A2
Canberra Prim Schs W12 ....30 A2
Canbury Mews SE26 ....76 C1
Cancell Rd SW9 ..173 C4
Candahar Rd SW11 ....168 B1
Candida Ct 9 NW1 .13 A1
Candishe Ho SE1 .138 C4
Candover St W1 ..104 C3
Candy St E3 ......26 B4
Canfield Gdns NW6 .11 A1
Canfield Pl NW6 ..11 B2
Canford Rd SW11 ..60 C2
Canham Rd W3 ....38 A4
Canning Cross SE5 .49 A1
Canning Ho 23 W12 .30 A2
Canning Pas W8 ..128 C2
Canning Pl W8 ...128 C2
Canning Pl Mews W8 ....128 C2
Canning Rd N5 ....6 A1
Canning Town E16 .35 A4
Canning Town Sta E16 ....35 A4
Cannizaro Rd SW19 5 C2
Cannock Ho N4 ....6 C4
Cannon Dr 1 E14 ..33 C2
Cannon Hill NW6 ..10 C3
Cannon Ho SE11 .149 A3
Cannon La NW3 ....2 C1
Cannon Pl NW3 ....2 C1
Cannon St EC4 ...123 A4
Cannon Street Rd E1 ....32 A3

Cannon Street Sta EC4 ... 123 B4
Cannon Wharf Bsns Ctr **15** SE8 ... 41 A2
Canon Barnett CE Prim Sch E1 ... 111 A2
Canon Beck Rd SE16 ... 40 B4
Canon Murnane Rd SE1 ... 138 C1
Canon Row SW1 ... 134 A3
Canon St N1 ... 86 C3
Canonbury Cres N1 ... 15 B1
Canonbury Cres **21** N1 ... 15 B1
Canonbury Gr N1 ... 15 B1
Canonbury La N1 ... 15 B1
Canonbury Pk N N1 ... 15 B2
Canonbury Pk S N1 ... 15 B2
Canonbury Pl N1 ... 15 A2
Canonbury Prim Sch N1 ... 15 A1
Canonbury Rd N1 ... 15 A1
Canonbury Sq N1 ... 15 A1
Canonbury St N1 ... 15 B1
Canonbury Sta N1, N5 ... 15 B3
Canonbury Villas N1 ... 15 A1
Canons Cl N2 ... 2 C4
Canrobert St E2 ... 25 A2
Cantelowes Rd NW1 ... 13 C2
Canterbury SE13 ... 67 B2
Canterbury Cl **10** SE5 ... 48 B1
Canterbury Cres SW9 ... 62 C4
Canterbury Ct NW6 ... 23 C3
Canterbury Gr SE27, SW16 ... 74 C1
Canterbury Ho SE1 ... 135 A2
6 E3 ... 27 A2
Canterbury Ind Pk **18** SE15 ... 50 B4
Canterbury Mans NW6 ... 11 A2
Canterbury Pl SE17 ... 150 B3
Canterbury Rd NW6 ... 23 C3
Canterbury Terr NW6 ... 23 C3
Cantium Ret Pk SE1 ... 49 C4
Canton St E14 ... 33 C3
Cantrell Rd E3 ... 26 C1
Canute Ct SW16 ... 74 C1
Canute Gdns SE16 ... 40 C2
Canvey St SE1 ... 122 C2
Capel Ho **17** E9 ... 17 B1
Capel Lo **8** Richmond TW9 ... 44 B2
12 SW2 ... 74 B4
Capener's Cl SW1 ... 131 B3
Capern Rd SW18 ... 71 B3
Capital Interchange Way TW8 ... 36 C1
Capital Wharf E1 ... 125 C1
Capland Ho NW8 ... 89 C2
Caple Ho SW10 ... 157 A2
Caple Rd NW10 ... 21 B3
Capper St WC1 ... 93 A1
Capstan Ho **5** E14 ... 42 B2

Capstan Rd SE8 ... 41 B2
Capstan Sq E14 ... 42 B4
Capstan Way SE16 ... 33 A1
Capulet Mews **1** E16 ... 35 C1
Caradoc Cl W2 ... 31 C3
Caradoc St SE10 ... 43 A1
Caravel Cl E14 ... 41 C3
Caravel Mews **14** SE8 ... 51 C4
Caraway Hts E14 ... 34 B2
Carbery Ave W3 ... 36 B4
Carbis Rd E14 ... 33 B3
Carbroke Ho **10** E9 ... 25 B4
Carburton St W1 ... 92 B1
Cardale St **1** E14 ... 42 B3
Carden Rd SE15 ... 65 A4
Cardiff Ho **9** SE15 ... 49 C4
Cardigan Rd **8** E3 ... 26 B3
SW13 ... 46 C1
Richmond TW10 ... 54 A1
Cardigan St SE11 ... 149 B2
Cardigan Wlk **12** N1 ... 15 B1
Cardinal Bourne St SE1 ... 137 C1
Cardinal Cap Alley SE1 ... 122 C2
Cardinal Hinsley RC High Sch (Boys) NW10 ... 21 C4
Cardinal Pl SW15 ... 57 C3
Cardinal Pole Sch (Lower) **17** E9 ... 17 C1
Cardinal Pole Sch (Upper) E9 ... 18 A3
Cardinal Vaughan Memorial Sch W14 ... 126 A4
Cardinals Way N19 ... 4 C3
Cardine Mews SE15 ... 50 A3
Cardington St NW1 ... 93 A3
Cardozo Rd N7 ... 14 A3
Cardross St W6 ... 39 A3
Cardwell Rd N7 ... 14 A4
Career Ct **11** SE16 ... 40 C4
Carew Cl N7 ... 5 B2
Carew Ct **19** SE14 ... 50 C4
Carew Ho SW16 ... 74 C1
Carew St SE5 ... 48 B1
Carey Ct **22** SE5 ... 48 B3
Carey Gdns SW8 ... 171 B3
Carey La EC2 ... 108 C2
Carey Pl SW1 ... 147 B3
Carey St WC2 ... 107 A1
Carfax Pl SW4 ... 61 C3
Carfree Cl **3** N1 ... 14 C1
Cargill Rd SW18 ... 71 B3
Carisbrook Ct **1** SW16 ... 74 B1
Carisbrooke Ct **3** W3 ... 37 B4
Carisbrooke Gdns SE15 ... 49 B3
Carisbrooke Ho TW10 ... 54 C2
Carleton Gdns N19 ... 13 B3
Carleton Rd N7 ... 13 C4
Carlile Cl E3 ... 26 B3
Carlile Ho SE1 ... 137 C1
Carlingford Rd NW3 ... 11 C4
Carlisle Ave EC3 ... 110 C1
W3 ... 29 A3
Carlisle La SE1 ... 135 A2
Carlisle Pl SW1 ... 132 C1
Carlisle Rd N4 ... 5 C4
NW6 ... 23 A4

Carlisle St W1 ... 105 B1
Carlisle Wlk **8** E8 ... 16 B2
Carlos Pl W1 ... 118 A3
Carlow St NW1 ... 82 C2
Carlton Cl NW3 ... 1 C2
Carlton Ct NW6 ... 78 B2
NW2 ... 9 B2
SW9 ... 48 A2
Carlton Dr SW15 ... 58 A2
Carlton Gdns SW1 ... 119 B1
Carlton Gr SE15 ... 50 A2
5 SE15 ... 50 A3
Carlton Hill NW8 ... 78 C2
Carlton Ho **11** NW6 ... 103 B2
8 NW6 ... 23 B3
NW6 ... 23 C3
Carlton House SW1 ... 103 C2
Carlton House Terr SW1 ... 119 C2
Carlton Lo N4 ... 5 C4
Carlton Mans W9 ... 88 B4
W14 ... 126 B4
N16 ... 7 B3
7 NW6 ... 10 C1
SW9 ... 62 C3
Carlton Prim Sch NW5 ... 12 C3
Carlton Rd N4 ... 5 C4
W4 ... 37 C4
SW14 ... 55 B3
Carlton Sq E1 ... 25 C1
Carlton St SW1 ... 119 B3
Carlton Tower Pl SW1 ... 131 A2
Carlton Vale NW6 ... 23 C3
Carlton Vale Inf Sch NW6 ... 23 B2
Carltons The **5** SW15 ... 58 A2
Carlyle Cl NW10 ... 20 C4
Carlyle Ct SW6 ... 166 B3
Carlyle Ho **6** SE5 ... 157 C4
12 N16 ... 7 A1
4 SE5 ... 48 B3
Carlyle Mans SW3 ... 158 A3
Carlyle Pl SW15 ... 57 C3
Carlyle Sq SW3 ... 143 C1
Carlyle's Ho SW3 ... 158 A3
Carmalt Gdns SW15 ... 57 B3
Carmarthen Ho **6** SW15 ... 69 B4
Carmarthen Pl SE1 ... 138 A4
Carmel Ct W8 ... 128 A4
Carmelite St EC4 ... 121 C4
Carmen St E14 ... 34 A3
Carmichael Ct **5** SW13 ... 46 B1
Carmichael Ho **6** E14 ... 34 B2
Carmichael Mews SW18 ... 71 C4
Carminia Rd SW17 ... 73 A2
Carnaby St* W1 ... 104 C1
Carnac St SE21,SE27 ... 75 C1
Carnegie Ho NW3 ... 2 C1
Carnegie Pl SW19 ... 69 C1
Carnegie St N1 ... 85 A3
Carnicot Ho **9** SE15 ... 50 A2
Carnoustie Dr N1 ... 84 C4
N1 ... 14 B1
Carnwath Ho SW6 ... 59 A4
Carnwath Rd SW6 ... 59 A4

Carol St NW1 ... 82 C4
Caroline Cl W2 ... 114 B3
N16 ... 7 A4
SW16 ... 74 B1
Caroline Gdns **2** E2 ... 98 B4
Caroline Ho **2** W2 ... 114 B3
20 W6 ... 39 B1
Caroline Martyn Ho **8** N19 ... 4 C4
Caroline Pl **2** W2 ... 114 B3
SW11 ... 169 C1
Caroline Pl Mews W2 ... 114 B3
Caroline St E1 ... 32 C3
Caroline Terr SW1 ... 145 B3
Caroline Wlk W6 ... 154 A3
Caronia Ct **4** SE16 ... 41 A2
Carpenter Ho **11** N19 ... 13 C4
10 E14 ... 33 C4
Carpenter St W1 ... 118 A3
Carpenter's Pl SW4 ... 61 C3
Carpenter's Rd E15 ... 19 A1
Carpenters Bsns Pk E15 ... 19 A1
Carpenters Ct NW1 ... 82 C4
Carpenters Prim Sch E15 ... 27 B4
Carr St **14** E14 ... 33 A4
Carrara Wharf SW6 ... 58 A4
Carrara Wlk **10** SW9 ... 63 A3
Carriage Dr E SW11 ... 159 C2
Carriage Dr N SW11 ... 158 C2
SW11 ... 159 A3
Carriage Dr S SW11 ... 169 B4
Carriage Dr W SW11 ... 158 C1
Carrick Ho SE11 ... 150 A2
N7 ... 14 B2
Carrick Mews SE8 ... 51 C4
Carrington Ho W1 ... 118 A1
Carrington Lo **9** TW10 ... 54 A2
Carrington Rd TW10 ... 54 C3
Carrington St W1 ... 118 A1
Carrol Cl NW5 ... 13 A4
Carron Cl E14 ... 34 A3
Carroun Rd SW8 ... 162 C2
Carslake Rd SW15 ... 57 B1
Carson Rd E16 ... 35 C4
E21 ... 75 C2
Carter Ct EC4 ... 108 B1
Carter Ho E1 ... 110 C3
Carter La EC4 ... 108 B1
Carter Pl SE17 ... 151 A1
Carter St SE17 ... 150 C1
Carter's Yd SW18 ... 58 C2
Carteret Ho **8** W12 ... 30 A2
Carteret St SW1 ... 133 B3
Carteret Way SE8 ... 41 A2
Carters Cl **3** NW5 ... 13 C2
Carthew Rd W6 ... 39 A3
Carthew Villas W6 ... 39 A3
Carthusian St EC1 ... 108 C4
Cartier Circ E14 ... 34 B1
Carting La WC2 ... 120 B3
Cartmel NW1 ... 92 C4
Cartoon Mus The **7** WC1 ... 106 A3
Carton Ho **12** W11 ... 30 C2
Cartwright Gdns WC1 ... 94 A3
Cartwright Ho SE1 ... 137 A1

Cartwright St E1 ... 125 A3
Cartwright Way SW13 ... 47 A3
Carvel Ho E14 ... 42 B1
Carver Rd SE24 ... 63 B1
Carville Cres TW8 ... 36 A2
Caryl Ho **6** SW19 ... 70 A3
Carysfort Rd N16 ... 15 C4
Casby Ho SE16 ... 139 B2
Casella Rd SE14 ... 50 C3
Casino Ave SE24 ... 63 C2
Caspian Ho **7** E1 ... 32 C4
Caspian St SE5 ... 48 C3
Cass Ho **23** E9 ... 17 C2
Cassandra Ct NW2 ... 9 B2
Cassell Ho SW9 ... 172 B2
Casserley Ho W4 ... 37 C3
Cassidy Rd SW6 ... 155 B1
Cassinghurst SE24 ... 63 C2
Cassland Rd E9 ... 17 C2
Casson Ho **1** E1 ... 111 A4
Casson St E1 ... 111 A3
Castalia Sq **6** E14 ... 42 B4
Castell Ho **11** SE8 ... 51 C3
Castellain Mans W9 ... 88 A2
Castellain Rd W9 ... 88 B2
Castellan Rd W9 ... 88 C1
Castello Ave SW15 ... 57 B2
Castelnau SW13 ... 47 A3
Castlebridge NW6 ... 78 B4
3 W11 ... 31 C3
Casterton St E8 ... 17 A2
Castle Baynard St EC4 ... 122 C4
Castle Cl E9 ... 18 A3
SW19 ... 69 C1
Castle Ct EC3 ... 109 C1
Castle Ho SE1 ... 150 C4
SW8 ... 162 B2
Castle Ind Est SE17 ... 150 C4
Castle La SW1 ... 132 C2
Castle Mead SE5 ... 48 B3
Castle Mews NW1 ... 13 A2
Castle Pl **8** W4 ... 38 A2
Castle Rd NW1 ... 13 A2
Castle Way SW19 ... 69 C1
Castle Yd SE1 ... 122 B2
N6 ... 3 C4
Castleacre W2 ... 102 A1
Castlebrook Cl SE11 ... 150 A4
Castlecombe Dr SW19 ... 69 C4
Castleden Ho NW6 ... 11 C1
Castleford Ct NW8 ... 89 C2
Castlefrank Ho N1 ... 98 B4
Castlegate TW9 ... 54 B4
Castlehaven Rd NW1 ... 13 A1
Castlemaine SW11 ... 169 A2
Castlemaine Gdns SW13 ... 47 A4
Castlemaine Mans SW13 ... 47 A4
Castlemaine Row SW13 ... 47 A4
Castlereagh St W1 ... 102 C2
Castleton Ho **2** E14 ... 42 B2
Castletown Rd W14 ... 140 B1
Castleview Cl N4 ... 6 B2
Castor La E14 ... 34 A2
Caterham Rd SE13 ... 67 C4
Catesby Ho **25** E9 ... 17 B1
Catesby St SE17 ... 151 C3

Cathay Ho SE16 ....40 A4
Cathay St **9** SE16 .....40 A4
Catcart Hill N19 ....4 B1
Cathcart Rd SW10 ...156 C4
Cathcart St NW5 ....13 A2
Cathedral Pl EC4 ....108 C2
Cathedral Sch of St
  Saviour & St Mary
  Overie Prim Sch
SE1 ....137 A4
Cathedral St SE1 ....123 B2
Catherall Rd N5,N16 ...6 B1
Catherine Baird Ct **12**
SW12 ....73 A4
Catherine Dr TW9 ....54 A3
Catherine Gr SE10 ....52 A2
Catherine Griffiths Ct
EC1 ....95 C2
Catherine Ho **16** N1 ..24 A4
Catherine Pl SW1 ...132 C2
Catherine St WC2 ...120 C4
Catherine Wheel Alley
E1 ....110 B3
Catherine Wheel Yd
SW1 ....118 C1
Catherwood Ct N1 ...87 B1
Cathles Rd SW12 .....61 A1
Cathnor Rd W12 ......39 A4
Catinthia St **5** SE8 ...41 A2
Catlin St SE16 ....40 A1
Catman Ho N4 ....5 B3
Cato Rd SW4 ....61 C3
Cato St W1 ....102 B2
Cator St SE15 ....49 B3
SE15 ....49 B3
Catton St WC1 ......106 C3
Caughley Ho SE11 ..135 B1
Caulfield Ct **12** NW1 ..13 B1
Caulfield Rd SE15 ....50 A1
Causeway The
SW18 ....59 A2
Causton Cotts **3**
E14 ....33 A3
Causton Rd N6 ....4 A4
Causton St SW1 ....147 C2
Cautley Ave SW4 .....61 B2
Cavan Ho **7** E3 ....26 B4
Cavaye Ho SW10 ....157 A4
Cavaye Pl SW10 ......143 A1
Cavell Ho **8** N1 ....24 A4
Cavell St E1 ....32 A4
Cavendish Ave NW8 ..79 C1
Cavendish Cl NW8 ...89 C4
NW6 ....10 B2
3 SW15 ....58 A2
Cavendish Ct EC2 ..110 B2
Cavendish Gdns
SW4 ....61 B1
Cavendish Ho NW8 ..79 C1
SW8 ....172 A4
Cavendish Jun & Inf Sch
W4 ....46 A3
Cavendish Mans
EC1 ....95 B1
3 NW6 ....10 C3
E5 ....17 B3
3 SW12 ....60 C1
Cavendish Mews N
W1 ....104 B4
Cavendish Mews S
W1 ....104 B3
Cavendish Par
SW12 ....61 A1
Cavendish Pl W1 ....104 B2

Cavendish Rd NW6 ...10 B1
W4 ....45 B2
SW12 ....73 B3
Cavendish Sch The
NW1 ....82 B4
Cavendish Sq W1 ...104 B2
Cavendish St N1 .....87 B1
Cavendish Terr **10**
E3 ....26 B2
Cavendish The NW11 ..2 A4
Caversham Ho **7**
N15 ....7 C3
Caversham Rd NW5 ..13 B2
Caversham St
SW3 ....158 C4
Caverswall St W12 ...30 B3
Cavour Ho SE17 .....150 B2
Caxton Gr E3 ....26 C2
Caxton Hall SW1 ....133 B2
Caxton Rd W12 ......39 C4
Caxton St SW1 ......133 B2
Caxton St N E16 .....35 B3
Cayford Ho **3** NW3 ..12 B3
Cayley Sch E14 ....33 A3
Cayton Pl EC1 ....97 B3
Cayton St EC1 ....97 B3
Cazenove Mans **1**
N16 ....7 C2
Cazenove Rd N16 .....7 C2
Cecil Ct WC2 ....120 A3
SW10 ....156 C4
NW6 ....11 A1
Cecil Mans **2** SW17 ..72 C2
Cecil Rd NW10 ....21 A4
W3 ....28 B4
Cecil Rhodes Ho
NW1 ....83 B2
Cecil Rd E8 ....16 C3
Cedar Cl SE21 ....75 B2
Cedar Ct W1 ....102 B2
N1 ....15 B1
SW14 ....55 B3
SW19 ....69 C1
Cedar Gr W5 ....36 A3
Cedar Ho **4** W8 ....128 A2
16 SE16 ....40 C4
6 E14 ....42 B4
SE14 ....50 C2
Cedar Hts NW2 ......10 B2
Cedar Lo SW6 ....47 C2
Cedar Rd NW2 ....9 B4
Cedar Terr TW9 ......54 A3
Cedar Tree Ct SE5 ...48 B3
Cedar Way NW1 ....83 B4
Cedarne Rd SW6 ....156 A1
Cedars Cl SE13 ....67 C4
Cedars Ct SW15 ......56 C1
Cedars Mews SW4 ..61 A3
Cedars Rd W4 ....38 A1
4 E15 ....19 C3
Cedars The E9 ....17 C1
Cedra Ct N16 ....7 C3
Cedric Chambers
NW8 ....89 B2
Celandine Cl E3,E14 ..33 C4
Celandine Dr E8 .....16 B1
Celbridge Mews
W2 ....100 B2
Celestial Gdns SE13 ..67 C3
Celia Ct **1** TW9 ......44 A2
Celia Ho **16** N1 ......24 A4
Celia Rd N19 ....13 B4
Celtic St E14 ....34 A4
Cenacle Cl NW3 ....1 C1
Cenotaph * SW1 ....134 A4

Centaur Ct **3** TW8 ...36 A1
Centaur St SE1 .....135 A2
Central Ave SW11 ..159 A1
Central Bsns Ctr
NW10 ....8 A3
Central Criminal Court
  (Old Bailey)*
EC4 ....108 B2
Central Foundation
  Lower Sch E3 ......26 A2
Central Foundation Sch
EC2 ....97 C2
Central Foundation
  Upper Sch E3 ......26 C2
Central Middlesex Hospl
NW10 ....20 B2
Central Par W3 ......37 A4
Central Sch of Ballet
EC1 ....95 C1
Central Sch of Speech &
  Drama The NW3 ..11 C1
Central St EC1 ....96 C3
Central St Martin's
  Coll of Art & Design
W1 ....105 C1
Central St Martin's Coll
  of Art & Design (The
  London Institute)
WC1 ....106 C3
Centre Ave NW10 ...20 B2
W3 ....28 C1
Centre Bldg SE17 ...151 A4
Centre Hts **5** NW3 ..11 C1
Centre Point SE1 ...105 C2
SE1 ....153 B2
Centre St E2 ....25 A3
Centurion Cl N7 .....14 B1
Centurion La E3 ......26 B3
Century Ho SE13 ....52 A1
Cephas Ave E1 ....25 B1
Cephas Ho **8** E1 ...25 B1
Cephas St E1 ....25 B1
Cerise Rd SE15 ......49 C2
Cerney Mews W2 ..115 B4
Cervantes Ct W2 ...100 B1
Ceylon Rd W14 .....126 A1
6 W14 ....39 C3
Chadbourn St E14 ..34 A4
Chaddacre Ho **10**
SW9 ....63 A3
Chadston Ho **11** N1 ..15 A1
Chadswell WC1 ......94 B3
Chadwell St EC1 .....95 C4
Chadwick Rd NW10 ..21 B4
SE15 ....49 B1
Chadwick St SW1 ..133 B1
Chadworth Ho EC1 ..96 C3
N4 ....6 B3
Chagford Ho NW1 ...90 C1
16 E3 ....27 A2
Chagford St NW1 ....91 A1
Chalbury Ho **8**
SW9 ....62 B3
Chalbury Wlk N1 .....85 B2
Chalcot Cres NW1 ...81 A4
Chalcot Gdns NW3 ..12 B2
Chalcot Mews
SW16 ....74 A1
Chalcot Rd NW1 .....81 B4
Chalcot Sq NW1 .....12 C1
Chaldon Rd SW6 ...154 B2
Chale Rd SW2 ....62 A1
Chalfont Ct NW1 .....91 A1

Chalfont Ho **2**
SE16 ....40 A3
Chalfont Ct **18**
SW15 ....57 C1
Chalford Rd SE21 ...75 C1
Chalgrove Rd E8,E9 ..17 C2
Chalk Farm Rd NW1 ..82 B4
Chalk Farm Sta
NW3 ....12 C1
Chalk Hill Rd W6 .....39 C2
Chalkers Cnr TW9 ...55 A4
Chalkwell Ho **9** E1 ..32 C3
Challenger Ho **7**
E14 ....33 A2
Challice Way SW2 ...74 B3
Challoner Cres
W14 ....140 C1
Challoner Mans
W14 ....140 C1
Challoner St W14 ...140 C1
Chalmer's Wlk **14**
SE17 ....48 A4
Chalmers Ho **18**
SW11 ....59 B4
Chalner Ho SW2 .....74 C3
Chaloner Ct SE1 ....137 B4
Chalsey Rd SE4 ......66 B3
Chalton St NW1 ......83 B1
Chamber St E1 ......125 A4
Chamberlain Cotts
SE5 ....48 C2
Chamberlain Ho
NW1 ....93 C4
5 E1 ....32 B2
Chamberlain St **7**
NW1 ....12 B1
Chamberlayne Mans **3**
NW10 ....22 C2
Chamberlayne Rd
NW10 ....22 B4
Chambers La NW10 ..9 B1
Chambers Rd N7 ....14 A4
Chambers St SE16 .139 C3
Chamberson Pl W6 ..38 C2
Chambord Ho **21** E2 ..99 A3
Chambord St E2 .....99 A3
Champion Gr SE5 ....63 C4
Champion Hill SE5 ...63 C4
Champion Pk SE5 ....48 C1
Champlain Ho **26**
W12 ....30 A2
Chance St E2 ....98 C2
Chancel Ct W1 ......119 B4
Chancel St SE1 .....122 A1
Chancellor Gr SE21 ..75 B1
Chancellor Ho
SW7 ....129 A2
26 E1 ....32 A1
Chancellor Pas E14 ..33 C1
Chancellor's Rd W6 ..39 B1
Chancellor's St W6 ..39 B1
Chancellors Wharf **21**
W6 ....39 B1
Chancellors' Ct
WC1 ....106 C4
Chancery Bldgs **13**
E1 ....32 B2
Chancery La EC4 ...107 B2
Chancery Lane Sta
WC1 ....107 B3
Chandler Ave E14 ...33 B4
Chandler St E1 ......32 A1
Chandler Way SE15 ..49 B3
Chandlers Mews
E14 ....41 C4

Chandlers Way **11**
SE24 ....74 C4
Chandos Pl WC2 ...120 A3
Chandos Rd NW2 .....9 B3
E15 ....19 C3
NW10 ....21 A1
Chandos St W1 .....104 B3
Chandos Way N11 ....2 A3
Change Alley EC3 ..109 C1
Channel Ho E14 ......33 A4
Channelsea Rd E15 ..27 C4
Channing Sch N6 .....4 A3
Chant Sq E15 ....19 C1
Chant St E15 ....19 C1
Chantrey Rd SW9 ...62 B4
Chantry Cl W9 ....23 B1
Chantry St SW6 ......58 A4
Chantry Sq W8 .....128 A1
Chantry St N1 ....86 B3
Chapel Ct EC2 ......109 B2
SE1 ....137 B4
Chapel House St
E14 ....42 A2
Chapel Market N1 ...85 B2
Chapel Pl N1 ....85 C2
EC2 ....98 A3
W1 ....104 A1
Chapel Side W2 ....114 A3
Chapel St NW1 .....102 A3
SW1 ....131 C3
Chapleton Ho SW2 ..62 C2
Chaplin Cl SE1 ......136 A4
Chaplin Ho **6** SW9 ..62 C3
Chaplin Rd NW2 ....8 C2
Chapman Ho **29** E1 ..32 A3
2 SE27 ....75 A1
Chapman Rd E9 .....18 B2
Chapman St E1 ....32 A2
Chapmans Park Ind Est
NW10 ....8 B2
Chapone Pl W1 .....105 B1
Chapter Cl **15** W4 ...37 B3
Chapter House Ct
EC4 ....108 C1
Chapter Rd SE17 ...150 B1
NW2 ....9 A3
SE17 ....150 B2
Chapter St SW1 ....147 B3
Chara Pl W4 ....45 C4
Charcot Ho **9**
SW15 ....56 B1
Charcroft Ct **11**
W14 ....39 C4
Chard Ho **7** N7 ......5 B2
Chardin Ho SW9 ...173 C4
Chardin Rd **11** W4 ..38 A2
Chardmore Rd N16 ...7 C3
Charecroft Way
W12 ....39 C4
Charfield Ct W9 ......88 B1
Charford Rd E16 .....35 C4
Chargrove Cl **24**
SE16 ....40 C4
Charing Cross
SW1 ....120 A2
Charing Cross Hospl
W6 ....39 C1
Charing Cross Rd
WC2 ....105 C2
Charing Cross Sta
SW1 ....120 B2
Charing Ho SE1 ....135 C4
Charlbert Ct NW8 ...80 A2

Charlbert St NW8 .....80 A2

Charles Allen Ho
EC1 ....95 B4

Charles Auffray Ho 26
E1 ....32 B4

Charles Barry Ct
SW4 ....61 B4

Charles Burton Ct
E5 ....18 A4

Charles Coveney Way 4
SE15 ....49 B2

Charles Darwin Ho 8
E2 ....25 A2

Charles Dickens Ho
E2 ....99 C4
1 E2 ....25 A2

Charles Dickens Prim
Sch SE1 ....136 C3

Charles Edward Brooke
Girls Sch (Lower)
SE5 ....48 A2

Charles Edward Brooke
Girls Sch (Upper)
SW9 ....48 A2

Charles Flemmell Mews
8 E16 ....35 C1

Charles Hobson Ho
W3 ....37 B4

Charles Hocking Ho 8
W3 ....37 B4

Charles II Pl SW3 ...144 C1
Charles II St SW1 ...119 B2
Charles La NW8 .....80 A2

Charles Lamb Prim Sch
N1 ....86 C4

Charles Mackenzie Ho
SE16 ....153 C4

Charles Pl NW1 .....93 A3

Charles Rowan Ho
EC1 ....95 B3

Charles Sq N1 ......97 C3
Charles St W1 ......118 A2
SW13 ....46 A1

Charles Townsend Ho
EC1 ....96 A2

Charleston St
SE17 ....151 A3

Charlesworth Ho 2
E14 ....33 C3

Charleville Ct SW5 ..140 C1

Charleville Mans
W14 ....140 B1

Charleville Rd
W14 ....140 C1

Charlotte Despard Ave
SW11 ....169 C3
SW11 ....170 A3

Charlotte Ho 12 W6 .39 B1

Charlotte Mews
W1 ....105 A4
W14 ....140 A4
W10 ....30 C3

Charlotte Pl W1 ....105 A3
SW1 ....146 B3

Charlotte Rd
EC2 .....24 A1 98 A2
SW13 ....46 B2

Charlotte Row SW4 ..61 B4

Charlotte Sharman Prim
Sch SE11 ....136 A1

Charlotte Sq 5
TW10 ....54 B1

Charlotte St W1 ....105 A4

Charlotte Terr N1 ...85 A3
Charlow Cl SW6 ....166 C1
Charlton Ct 17 N7 ...13 C3
25 E2 ....24 B4
Charlton Ho NW1 ...93 B4
5 Brentford TW8 ...44 A4

Charlton King's Rd
NW5 ....13 C3
Charlton Ho N1 ....86 A2
Charlton Ho NW10 ..21 A4
SE3 ....53 C3

Charlton Way SE10,
SE3 ....53 A2

Charlwood Ho
 SW1 ....147 B3
6 SW2 ....74 B3
Charlwood Pl SW1 ..147 A3
Charlwood Rd
SW15 ....57 C3
Charlwood St SW1 ..147 A2
SW15 ....57 C3
Charlwood Terr 5
SW15 ....57 C3

Charman Ho 162 A2
 Charman Ho 4 N1 ..24 A3
Charmouth Ct TW10 .54 B2
Charmouth Ho
SW8 ....162 C2

Charnock Ho 22
W12 ....30 A2

Charnwood Gdns
E14 ....41 C2
Charrington St NW1 .83 B2
Chart St N1 ....97 C4
Charter Ct W1 ......102 B3
N4 ....5 C3
Charter Ho WC2 ....106 B1

Charter Nightingale
Hospl The NW1 ....102 B4
Charterhouse Bldgs
EC1 ....96 C1
Charterhouse Mews
EC1 ....108 B4
Charterhouse Sq
EC1 ....108 B4

Charterhouse St
EC1 ....108 A4
Charteris Rd N4 ....5 C3
NW6 ....23 B4
Chartes Ho SE1 ....138 B2
Chartfield Ave
SW15 ....57 B2
Chartfield Sch
SW15 ....57 A2
Chartfield Sq SW15 .57 C2
Chartham Ct 13
SW9 ....62 C4
Chartham Gr SE27 ..75 A1
Chartham Ho SE1 ..137 C2
Chartridge SE17 ....48 C4
Chartwell 25 SW19 .69 C3
Chase Ct SW3 ......130 C1

Chase Ctr The
NW10 ....20 C2
Chase Rd NW10 ....20 C1

Chase Road Trad Est
NW10 ....20 C1
Chase The SW4 ....61 A4
Chaseley Ct W4 ....37 A1
Chaseley St E14 ....33 A3
Chasemore Ho
SW6 ....154 B2
Chater Ho 6 E2 ....25 C2
Chatfield Rd SW11 ..59 B4
Chatham Ct SW11 ..60 A1
Chatham Ho 7 SE5 .49 A1
Chatham Pl E9 .....17 B2

Chatham Rd SW11 ..60 B2
Chatham St SE17 ...151 C4
Chatsworth Ct 48 W8 .141 B4
E5 ....17 C4
Chatsworth Est E5 ..17 C4
Chatsworth Gdns
W3 ....28 A1
Chatsworth Lo 1
W4 ....37 C1
Chatsworth Rd NW2 .9 C2
E5 ....17 C4
W4 ....45 B4
Chatsworth Way
SE27 ....75 B1

Chattenden Ho 8
N4 ....6 C4
Chatterton Ct TW9 ..44 B1
Chatterton Rd N4 ..6 A1
Chatto Rd SW11 ....60 B2
Chaucer Ave TW9 ..44 C1
Chaucer Ct 7 N16 ..16 A4
Chaucer Dr SE1 ....153 A3
Chaucer Ho SW1 ...146 C1
Chaucer Rd SW11 ..59 C4
SE24 ....63 A2
Chaulden Ho EC1 ..97 C3
Cheadle Ct NW8 ...89 C2
Cheadle Ho 11 E14 .33 B3
Cheam St 4 SE15 ..65 A4
Cheapside EC2 .....109 A1
Chearsley SE17 ....151 A4

Cheddington Ho 8
E2 ....24 C4
Chedworth Cl E16 ..35 B1
Chedworth Ho 2 E5 .7 C2
Chelmsford Ho 5
N7 ....14 B4
Chelmsford Sq
NW10 ....22 B4

Chelsea & Westminster
Hospl SW10 ....157 A3
Chelsea Barracks
SW1 ....145 C1
Chelsea Bridge
SW1 ....160 A4
Chelsea Bridge Rd
SW1 ....145 C2
Chelsea Cl NW10 ...20 C4
Chelsea Cloisters
SW3 ....144 B3

Chelsea Coll of Art &
Design
SW3 ....144 A1
SW6 ....166 C2
SW6 ....59 A4
Chelsea Cres
SW10 ....167 A3
Chelsea Ct SW3 ....159 B4
Chelsea Emb SW3 ..158 C3
Chelsea Est SW3 ...158 C3
Chelsea Farm Ho
SW10 ....157 C3
Chelsea Gate SW1 ..145 C1
Chelsea Gdns SW1 ..145 C1
Chelsea Harbour Design
Ctr SW10 ....167 A4
Chelsea Harbour Dr
SW10 ....167 A4
Chelsea Harbour Pier
SW10 ....167 B3

Chelsea Hospl for
Women SW3 ....144 A2
Chelsea Lo SW3 ....159 A4
SW6 ....166 A4
Chelsea Manor Ct
SW3 ....158 B4
Chelsea Manor Gdns
SW3 ....144 B1
Chelsea Manor St
SW3 ....144 B1
Chelsea Manor Studios
SW3 ....144 B1
Chelsea Park Gdns
SW3 ....157 B4
Chelsea Physic Gdn *
SW1 ....158 C4
Chelsea Reach Twr
SW10 ....157 B2
Chelsea Sq SW3 ...143 C1
Chelsea Twrs SW3 ..158 B4
Chelsfield Ho
SE17 ....152 A3
Chelsfield Point 3
E9 ....17 C1
Chelsham Ho 1
SW4 ....61 C4
Chelsham Rd SW4 ..61 C4
Cheltenham Pl 1
W3 ....37 A4
Cheltenham Rd
SE15 ....65 B2
Cheltenham Terr
SW3 ....145 A2
Chelverton Ct SW15 .57 C3
Chelverton Rd
SW15 ....57 C3
Chelwood Ho 5 ....12 C3
Chelwood Ct
SW11 ....167 C4
Chelwood Gdns
TW9 ....44 C1
Chelwood Ho W2 ..101 C1
Cheney Rd N1 ......84 A1
Chenies Ho W2 ....114 A4
Chenies Mews WC1 .93 B1
Chenies St WC1 ....105 B4
Chenies The NW1 ..83 C2
Cheniston Gdns
W8 ....128 A2
Chepstow Ct SW15 .58 A2
Chepstow Cres
W11 ....31 C2 113 B4
Chepstow Cnr W11 .113 B4
Chepstow Pl
W2 ....31 C2 113 C4
Chepstow Rd W2 ..31 C3
Chepstow Villas
W11 ....31 C2 113 B4
Chepstow Way SE15 .49 B2
Chequer Ct E1 .....97 A1
Chequers Ho NW8 ..90 A2
Cherbury Ct N1 ....87 C1
Cherbury St N1 ....87 C1
Cheriton Ho 9 E5 ..17 A3
Cheriton Sq SW17 ..72 C2
Cherry Cl 7 SW2 ..74 C4
Cherry Ct W3 ....29 A1
Cherry Garden Specl
Sch SE16 ....153 C4
Cherry Garden St
SE16 ....40 A4
Cherry Laurel Wlk
SW2 ....62 B1

Cherry Tree Dr
SW16 ....74 A1
Cherry Tree Ho
SE14 ....51 B1
Cherry Tree Terr
SE1 ....138 B4
Cherry Tree Wlk
EC1 ....97 A1
Cherrytree Ho 8
W10 ....22 C2
Cherrywood Cl E26 .26 A2
Cherrywood Dr
SW15 ....57 C2
Chertsey Ct SW14 ..55 A4
Chertsey Ho E2 ....98 C3
Cherwell Ho NW8 ..89 C1
Cheryls Cl SW6 ....166 B4
Chesham Cl SW1 ...131 B1
Chesham Ct SW18 ..71 C4
Chesham Flats W1 ..117 C4
Chesham Mews
SW1 ....131 B2
Chesham Pl SW1 ...131 B1
Chesham St SW1 ...131 B1
Cheshire St
E2 ....24 C1 99 B2
Chesholm Rd N16 ..7 A1
Cheshunt Ho NW6 ..78 A3
Chesil Ct SW3 .....158 B4
18 E2 ....25 B3
Cheson Rd SW14 ..155 A4
Chester Ave TW10 ..54 B1
Chester Cl SW1 ....132 A3
1 Richmond TW10 ..54 B1
SW13 ....57 A4
Chester Close N
NW1 ....92 B4
Chester Close S
NW1 ....92 B3
Chester Cres E8 ....16 B3
Chester Ct NW1 ....92 B4
NW5 ....12 C4
SE8 ....40 C1
4 SE5 ....48 C3
Chester Gate NW1 ..92 B3
Chester Ho N19 ....4 C2
1 SE8 ....51 B4
Chester Mews
SW1 ....132 A2
Chester Pl NW1 ....92 A4
Chester Rd NW1 ...91 C4
N19 ....4 A2
Chester Row SW1 ..145 C4
Chester Sq SW1 ...146 A4
Chester Sq Mews
SW1 ....132 A1
Chester St E2 .24 C1 99 C2
SW1 ....131 C2
E2 ....24 C1
Chester Terr NW1 ..92 A4
Chester Way SE11 ..149 C3
Chesterfield Gdns
W1 ....118 A2
SE10 ....52 C3
Chesterfield Gr
SE22 ....64 B2
Chesterfield Hill
W1 ....118 A2
Chesterfield Ho
W1 ....117 C2

Chesterfield Rd W4 .45 B4
Chesterfield St
W1 . . . . .118 A2
Chesterfield Way
SE15 . . . . .50 B3
Chesterford Gdns
NW3 . . . . .11 A4
Chesterman Ct W4 .46 A3
Chesterton Cl SW18 58 C2
Chesterton Ho
3 W10 . . . . .31 A4
21 SW11 . . . . .59 C4
Chesterton Prim Sch
SW11 . . . . .169 B3
Chesterton Rd W10 .31 A4
Chesterton Sq W8 .141 B3
Chestnut Alley
SW6 . . . . .155 A3
Chestnut Ave **11**
SW14 . . . . .55 C4
Chestnut Cl **1** N16 . .6 C2
SE14 . . . . .51 B2
Chestnut Ct SW6 . .155 A4
Chestnut Gr SW12 . .72 C3
Chestnut Grove Sch
SW12 . . . . .72 C3
Chestnut Ho
7 NW3 . . . . .12 B2
1 W4 . . . . .46 B4
SE27 . . . . .75 B1
Chestnut Rd SE21,
SE27 . . . . .75 B1
Chestnuts The **1**
N5 . . . . .15 A4
Chettle Cl SE1 . . . .137 B2
Chetwode Ho NW8 .90 A2
Chetwode Rd SW17 .72 B1
Chetwynd Rd NW5 . .4 A1
Cheval Ct SW15 . . . .57 A3
Cheval Pl SW7 . . . .130 B2
Cheval St E14 . . . . . .41 C3
Chevening Rd NW6 .23 A4
SE10 . . . . .43 B1
Cheverell Ho **2** E2 .24 C3
Cheverton Rd N19 . . .4 C3
Chevet St E9 . . . . . . .18 A3
Chevington NW2 . . .10 B2
Cheviot Ct **16** SE14 .50 B3
Cheviot Gate NW2 . . .1 A2
Cheviot Gdns NW2 . .1 A2
Cheviot Ho N16 . . . . .7 B3
Chevron Cl E16 . . . .35 C3
Cheylesmore Ho
SW1 . . . . .146 A2
Cheyne Ct SW3 . . . .158 C4
Cheyne Gdns SW3 . .158 B3
Cheyne Mews SW3 .158 B3
Cheyne Row SW3 . .158 A3
Cheyne Wlk SW10 .157 B2
Cheyney Ho **8** E9 . .17 C2
Chichele Rd NW2 . . . .9 C3
Chicheley St SE1 . . .135 A1
Chichester Ho NW6 .23 C3
Chichester Rd W2 .100 B4
NW6 . . . . .23 C3
Chichester Rents
WC2 . . . . .107 B2
Chichester St SW1 .147 A1
Chichester Way E14 .42 C2
Chicksand Ho E1 . . .111 A4
Chicksand St E1 . . . .111 A3
Chiddingstone SE13 .67 B2
Chiddingstone St
SW6 . . . . .165 C2
Chigwell Hill E1 . . . .32 A2

Chilam Ho **5** SE15 . .50 B4
Chilcombe Ho **6**
SW15 . . . . .68 C4
Chilcot Cl **13** E14 . .34 A3
Child's Pl SW5 . . . .141 C3
Child's St SW5 . . . .141 C3
Child's Wlk SW5 . . .141 C3
Childebert Rd SW17 .73 A2
Childeric Prim Sch
SE14 . . . . .51 A3
Childeric Rd SE14 . .51 A3
Childerley St SW6 .164 A4
Childers St SE8 . . . .51 B4
Childs Hill Prim Sch
NW2 . . . . .1 A1
Chilham Ho **14** SE15 .62 C4
Chilham Ho SE1 . . .137 C2
Chillingworth Rd
N7 . . . . .14 C3
Chiltern Ct NW1 . . . .91 A1
12 SE14 . . . . .50 B3
Chiltern Ho N16 . . . . .7 B3
18 W10 . . . . .31 A4
SE17 . . . . .48 C4
Chiltern Rd E3 . . . . .26 C1
Chiltern St W1 . . . .103 B4
Chilton Gr SE8 . . . . .41 A2
Chilton Rd TW9 . . . .54 C4
Chilton St **24** E1 .99 A2
Chilver St SE10 . . . . .43 B1
Chilworth Ct **5**
SW19 . . . . .69 C3
Chilworth Mews
W2 . . . . .101 B1
Chilworth St W2 . . .101 A1
Chimney Ct **22** E1 . .32 A1
China Ct **10** E1 . . . .32 A2
Chindit Ho **10** N16 . .15 C4
Chinnocks Wharf
E14 . . . . .33 A2
Chip St SW4 . . . . . . .61 C3
Chipka St E14 . . . . . .42 B4
Chipley St SE14 . . . .51 A4
Chippendale Ho
SW1 . . . . .146 B1
Chippendale Gdns
SW1 . . . . .23 C2
Chippenham Mews
W9 . . . . .23 C1
Chippenham Rd W9 .23 C1
Chipstead Ho **4**
SW2 . . . . .74 A3
Chipstead St SW6 .165 C2
Chisenhale JMI Sch
E3 . . . . .26 A3
Chisenhale Rd E3 . . .26 A3
Chisholm Ct W6 . . . .38 C1
Chisholm Rd **1**
TW10 . . . . .54 B1
Chisledon Wlk E9 . . .18 B2
Chislehurst Rd
TW10 . . . . .54 A2
Chislet **5** NW5 . . . .12 C2
Chiswell St EC1 . . . .109 B4
Chiswick Comm Sch
W4 . . . . .45 C3
Chiswick Common Rd
W4 . . . . .37 C2
Chiswick High Rd
W4 . . . . .38 A2
Chiswick High Road
(North Circular Rd)
W4 . . . . .36 C1
Chiswick House ⋆
W4 . . . . .45 C4
Chiswick La W4 . . . .38 A1

Chiswick La S W4 . . .46 A4
Chiswick Mall W4 . . .38 B1
Chiswick Maternity
Hospl W4 . . . . .38 B1
Chiswick Park Sta
W4 . . . . .37 B2
Chiswick Pier W4 . . .46 B3
Chiswick Plaza W4 . .45 B4
Chiswick Quay W4 . .45 B2
Chiswick Rd W4 . . . .37 B2
Chiswick Rdbt W4 . .36 C1
Chiswick Sq W4 . . . .46 A4
Chiswick Sta W4 . . . .45 B3
Chiswick Staithe
W4 . . . . .45 B2
Chiswick Terr **6**
W4 . . . . .37 B2
Chiswick Village
W4 . . . . .45 A4
Chiswick Wharf W4 .46 B4
Chitty St W1 . . . . . .105 A4
Chivalry Rd SW11 . . .60 A2
Chobham Gdns
SW19 . . . . .69 C2
Chobham Rd E15 . . .19 C3
Cholmeley Cres N6 . .4 A4
Cholmeley Lo N6 . . . .4 A3
Cholmeley Pk N6 . . . .4 A4
Cholmley Gdns
NW6 . . . . .10 C3
Cholmondeley Ave
NW10 . . . . .21 C3
Chopin's Ct **15** E14 . .41 C2
Chopwell Cl E15 . . . .19 C1
Choumert Gr SE15 . .49 C1
Choumert Rd SE15 . .49 B1
Choumert Sq **2**
SE15 . . . . .49 C1
Chow Sq **2** E8 . . . .16 B3
Chrisp Ho SE10 . . . . .53 A4
Chrisp St E14 . . . . . .34 A3
Christ Church Bentinck
CE Prim Sch NW1 **102** B4
Christ Church CE JMI
Sch SE10 . . . . .43 C1
Christ Church CE Prim
Sch
NW1 . . . . .92 B4
SW9 . . . . .173 C4
E1 . . . . .111 C4
SW2 . . . . .74 B3
Christ Church Ct
NW10 . . . . .10 A1
NW6 . . . . .21 A4
Christ Church JMI Sch
E1 . . . . .111 A3
Christ Church Prim Sch
SW11 . . . . .60 A1
Christ Church Sq **6**
E9 . . . . .25 B4
Christ the King Coll
SE13 . . . . .67 C4
Christ the King RC Prim
Sch N4 . . . . .5 B2
Christ's Coll SE3 . . . .53 C2
Christ's Sch (East Side)
TW10 . . . . .54 C4
Christ's Sch (West Side)
TW10 . . . . .54 B2
Christchurch Ave
NW6 . . . . .10 A1
Christchurch Hill
NW3 . . . . .11 C4
Christchurch Ho **2**
SW2 . . . . .74 A3

Christchurch Pas
NW3 . . . . .11 B4
Christchurch Prim Sch
SW3 . . . . .158 C4
NW6 . . . . .10 B1
Christchurch Rd
SW14 . . . . .55 B2
SE27 . . . . .74 C1
Christchurch St
SW3 . . . . .158 C4
Christchurch Terr
SW3 . . . . .158 C4
Christchurch Way
SE10 . . . . .43 A1
Christian Ct SE16 . . .33 B1
Christian St E1 . . . .111 C1
Christie Ct **1** N19 . . .5 A2
NW3 . . . . .12 A3
Christie Ho **2** SE10 .43 B1
Christie Rd E9 . . . . . .18 A2
Christina Sq N4 . . . . .6 A3
Christina St EC2 . . . .98 A2
Christopher Boone's
Almshouses **2** SE13 .67 C3
Christopher Cl SE16 .40 C4
Christopher Lo **2** N6 .4 C4
Christopher Pl NW1 .93 C3
Christopher St EC2 . .97 C1
Chryssell Rd SW9 . .163 C1
Chubworthy St
SE14 . . . . .51 A4
Chudleigh Rd NW6 . . .9 C1
SE4 . . . . .66 C2
Chudleigh St E1 . . . .32 C3
Chumleigh Gdns
SE5 . . . . .49 A4
Chumleigh St SE5 . .49 A4
Church Almshouses **7**
TW9 . . . . .54 B3
Church App SE21 . . .75 C1
Church Ave NW1 . . . .13 A2
SW14 . . . . .55 C4
Church Cl W8 . . . . .128 A4
Church Cres E9 . . . . .17 C1
Church Ct EC4 . . . . .107 C1
Church Entry EC4 . .108 B1
Church Garth **3** N19 .4 C2
Church Gate SW6 . . .58 A4
Church Gn SW9 . . . .173 C2
Church Gr SE13 . . . . .67 A2
Church Green Ho **1**
W4 . . . . .37 B2
Church Mead SE5 . . .48 B3
Church Path W4 . . . .37 B3
Church Pl SW1 . . . .119 A3
Church Rd NW10 . . . .8 A1
W3 . . . . .37 B4
SW13 . . . . .46 C2
Richmond TW10,TW9 .54 A2
W4 . . . . .37 B3
Church Row NW3 . . .11 B4
Church St NW8 . . . . .90 A1
W4 . . . . .46 B4
Church Wlk NW2 . . . .1 B1
N16 . . . . .15 C4
Churchcroft Cl
SW12 . . . . .72 C4
Churchdale Ct **1**
W4 . . . . .45 A4
Churchfield Ho NW8 .89 B1
Churchfield Mans
SW6 . . . . .165 A1
Churchfield Rd W3 . .28 B1
Churchfields SE10 . . .52 B4
Churchill Ct N4 . . . . .5 B4

Churchill Gardens Prim
Sch SW1 . . . . .147 A1
Churchill Gdns
SW1 . . . . .160 C4
Churchill Gdns Rd
SW1 . . . . .160 C4
Churchill Pl E14 . . . .34 A1
Churchill Rd NW2 . . . .9 A2
NW5 . . . . .13 A4
Churchill Wlk E9 . . . .17 B3
Churchmead Rd
NW10 . . . . .8 C2
Churchward Ho
SW5 . . . . .141 A1
SE17 . . . . .48 A4
Churchway NW1 . . . .93 C4
Churchyard Row
SE11 . . . . .150 B4
Churnfield **2** N4 . . . .5 C2
Churston Cl **2** SW2 .74 C3
Churston Mans
WC1 . . . . .95 A1
Churton Pl SW1 . . .147 A3
Churton St SW1 . . .147 A3
Chute Ho SW9 . . . . .173 B1
Chuter Ede Ho
SW6 . . . . .155 A3
Cicada Rd SW18 . . . .59 B2
Cicely Ho NW8 . . . . .79 C1
Cicely Rd SE15 . . . . .49 C2
Cinnamon Row **3**
SW11 . . . . .59 B4
Cinnamon St E1 . . . .32 A1
Cinnamon Wharf
SE1 . . . . .139 A4
Circle Ho **3** E14 . . . .34 C3
Circle The SE1 . . . . .139 A4
Circus Mews W1 . . .102 C4
Circus Pl EC2 . . . . . .109 C3
Circus Rd NW8 . . . . .79 B1
Circus St SE10 . . . . .52 B3
Cirencester St W2 . .100 A4
Cissbury Ho **6**
SE26 . . . . .76 C1
Citizen Ho N7 . . . . . .14 C4
Citizen Rd N7 . . . . . .14 C4
Citron Terr **3** SE15 .65 A4
Citrus Ho **14** SE8 . . .41 B1
City & Guilds of London
Art Sch The SE11 . .149 C1
City & Islington Coll
N1 . . . . .87 B4
EC1 . . . . .97 A3
N7 . . . . .14 B4
N4 . . . . .6 A2
N7 . . . . .14 B4
City Airport Pier
E16 . . . . .35 B1
City Banking Coll
SE1 . . . . .138 A4
City Bsns Ctr **16**
SE16 . . . . .40 B4
City Central Est EC1 .96 C3
City Forum EC1 . . . . .96 C4
City Garden Row
N1 . . . . .86 B1
City Gate E1 . . . . . . .25 B1
City Institute The
WC2 . . . . .106 C1
City Literature Inst The
WC2 . . . . .106 B2

City of London Sch EC4 ....122 C4
City of London Sch for Girls EC2 ....109 A4
City of Westminster Coll W10 ....23 A2
City of Westminster Coll W2 ....101 B4
NW1 ....102 B4
W9 ....23 C2
City Rd EC1 ....97 A4
City Thameslink Sta EC4 ....108 A1
City Univ The EC1 ....96 A3
City Univerity The EC1 ....96 A4
Civil Service Coll SW1 ....146 C3
Clabon Mews SW1 ....144 C4
Clack St SE16 ....40 B4
Claire Ct NW2 ....10 A2
Claire Pl E14 ....41 C3
Clancarty Rd SW6 ....165 C1
Clandon Cl W3 ....37 A4
Clandon St SE8 ....51 C1
Clanfield Ho 12 SW15 ....68 C3
Clanfield Way 12 SE15 ....49 A3
Clanricarde Gdns W2 ....31 C2 113 C3
Clapham Common* SW4 ....61 B3
Clapham Common North Side SW4 ....60 C3
Clapham Common South Side SW4 ....61 B2
Clapham Common Sta SW4 ....61 B3
Clapham Common West Side SW4,SW11 ....60 B3
SW4 ....60 C2
Clapham Court Terr 2 SW4 ....62 A2
Clapham Cres SW4 ....61 C3
Clapham Ct 3 SW4 ....62 A2
Clapham High St SW4 ....61 C3
Clapham High Street Sta SW4 ....61 C4
Clapham Junction Est SW11 ....60 B4
Clapham Junction Sta SW11 ....60 A4
Clapham Manor Ct 1 SW4 ....61 B4
Clapham Manor Prim Sch SW4 ....61 B4
Clapham Manor St SW4 ....61 C4
Clapham Mans SW4 ....61 A1
Clapham North Sta SW4 ....62 A4
Clapham Park Rd SW4 ....61 C3
Clapham Park Sch SW4 ....62 A2
Clapham Park Terr 5 SW2 ....62 A2
Clapham Rd SW9 ....173 A4
Clapham South Sta SW4 ....61 A1

Clapton Comm E5 ....7 C4
Clapton Girls Sch E5 ....17 B4
Clapton Pas E5 ....17 B3
Clapton Sq E5 ....17 B3
Clapton Terr E5 ....7 C1
Clapton Way E5 ....7 C1
Clara Grant JMI Sch E3 ....26 C1
Clare Ct WC1 ....94 B3
Clare Gdns W11 ....31 A3
Clare Grant Ho 3 E3 ....41 C3
Clare Ho SE1 ....153 A2
E3 ....26 B4
Clare La N1 ....15 B1
Clare Lawn Ave SW14 ....55 C2
Clare Mews SW6 ....156 A1
Clare Mkt WC2 ....107 A1
Clare Rd NW10 ....8 C1
SE14 ....51 B2
Clare St E2 ....25 A3
Claredale Ho 3 E2 ....25 A3
Claredale Ct E2 ....24 C3
Claremont 1 SW15 ....58 A2
Claremont Cl N1 ....85 C1
4 SW2 ....74 B3
Claremont Ct 1 W9 ....23 B3
Claremont Gr W4 ....46 A3
Claremont Rd N6 ....4 A4
W9 ....23 B3
Claremont Sq N1 ....85 B1
Claremont St SE10 ....52 A4
Clarence Ave SW4 ....61 C1
Clarence Ct 10 W6 ....39 A2
Clarence Gate Gdns NW1 ....91 A1
Clarence Gdns NW1 ....92 B3
Clarence Ho* SW1 ....119 A1
SE17 ....48 B4
Clarence La SW15 ....56 B1
Clarence Mews E5 ....17 A3
1 SE16 ....32 C1
SW12 ....73 A4
Clarence Pas NW1 ....84 A1
Clarence Pl 22 E5 ....17 A3
Clarence Rd NW6 ....10 B1
E5 ....17 A4
W4 ....36 C1
Richmond TW9 ....44 C2
Clarence St 1 TW9 ....54 A3
Clarence Terr NW1 ....91 A2
Clarence Way NW1 ....13 A1
Clarence Wlk SW4 ....172 A2
Clarendon Cl W2 ....116 A4
Clarendon Cross W11 ....112 B3
Clarendon Gr NW1 ....89 A2
1 Richmond TW9 ....44 C2
Clarendon Ho SW15 ....57 B3
Clarendon Flats W1 ....103 C1
Clarendon Gdns W9 ....89 A1
Clarendon Gr NW1 ....93 B4
Clarendon Ho NW1 ....83 A1
Clarendon Mews W2 ....116 A4
Clarendon Pl W2 ....116 A4
Clarendon Rd W11 ....31 A1 112 B3
Clarendon Rise SE13 ....67 B3

Clarendon St SW1 ....146 B2
Clarendon Terr W9 ....89 A2
Clarendon Wlk 10 W11 ....31 A3
Clareville St SW7 ....143 A3
Clareville Gr SW7 ....143 A3
Clareville Grove Mews SW7 ....143 A3
Clareville St SW7 ....143 A3
Clarewood Ct W1 ....102 C3
Clarewood Wlk SW9 ....62 C3
Clarges Ho W1 ....118 B2
Clarges Mews W1 ....118 A2
Clarges St W1 ....118 B2
Claribel Rd SW9 ....48 A1
Claridge Ct SW6 ....164 C3
Clarissa Ho 7 E14 ....34 A3
Clarissa St E8 ....24 B4
Clark Lawrence Ct 11 SW11 ....59 C4
Clark St E1 ....32 B4
Clark's Pl EC2 ....110 A2
Clarke Ho 8 SW4 ....61 B4
Clarke Path N16 ....7 C3
Clarkes Mews W1 ....103 C4
Clarkson Ho SW11 ....59 C3
Clarkson Rd E16 ....35 B1
Clarkson Row NW1 ....82 C1
Clarkson St E2 ....25 A2
Classic Mans 88 E9 ....17 B1
Classinghall Ho 8 SW15 ....57 C1
Claude Rd SE15 ....50 A1
Claude St E14 ....41 C2
Claudia Jones Way SW2 ....62 A1
Claudia Pl SW19 ....70 A3
Clave St E1 ....32 B1
Clavell St 7 SE10 ....52 B4
Claverdale Rd SW2 ....74 C4
Clavering Ave SW13 ....47 A4
Clavering Ho SW13 ....67 C3
Claverton St SW1 ....147 A1
Claxton Gr SE16 ....139 C1
Clay St W1 ....103 A3
Claybank Gr SE13 ....67 A4
Claybrook Rd W6 ....47 C4
Claydon SE17 ....150 C4
Clayhall Ct 10 E3 ....26 B3
Claylands Pl SW8 ....163 B2
Claylands Rd SW8 ....163 A3
Claypole Rd E15 ....27 B3
Claypoands Ave Terr 38 E4 ....36 A2
Clays Ct N16 ....7 B3
Clays La E15 ....19 A4
Clays Lane Cl E15 ....19 A3
Clayton Cr N16 ....7 C4
Clayton Ho 22 E9 ....17 B1
Clayton Mews SE10 ....52 C2
Clayton Rd SE15 ....49 C2
Clayton St SE11 ....163 B4
Clearbrook Way 13 E1 ....32 B3
Clearwater Ho 6 TW10 ....54 A2
Clearwater Terr 4 W11 ....39 C4
Clearwell Dr W9 ....88 B1
Cleaver Ho 6 NW3 ....12 B1
Cleaver Sq SE11 ....149 C1
Cleaver St SE11 ....149 C2

Cleeve Ho 98 B3
Cleeve Workshops E2 ....98 B3
Clegg St 10 E1 ....32 A1
Cleland Ho 20 E2 ....25 B3
Clem Attlee Ct SW6 ....155 A3
Clematis St W12 ....29 C2
Clemence St E14 ....33 B4
Clement Attlee Ho NW10 ....8 B1
Clement Ave SW4 ....61 C3
Clement Cl NW6 ....9 C1
W4 ....37 C2
Clement Ho 30 84
SE8 ....41 A2
Clement's La EC2, EC4 ....123 C4
Clement's Rd SE16 ....40 A3
Clements Ave 1 E16 ....35 C2
Clements Inn WC2 ....107 A1
Clements Inn Pas WC2 ....107 A1
Clemson Ho 9 E8 ....24 B4
Clenham St SE1 ....137 A4
Clenston Mews W1 ....102 C2
Cleon Ho 4 ....7 B3
Cleopatra's Needle* WC2 ....120 C3
Clephane Rd 5 N1 ....15 C2
Clephane Rd N N1 ....15 B2
Clephane Rd S N1 ....15 C2
Clere Pl EC2 ....97 C2
Clere St EC2 ....97 C2
Clerkenwell Cl EC1 ....95 C1
Clerkenwell Rd EC1 ....96 A1
Clerkenwell Parochial CE Prim Sch EC1 ....95 B4
Clerkenwell Rd EC1 ....96 A1
Clermont Rd E9 ....25 B4
Cleve Ho NW6 ....11 A1
Cleve Rd NW6 ....11 A1
Clevedon Ct SW11 ....168 A4
Clevedon Mans NW5 ....12 C4
Cleveland Ave W4 ....38 B2
Cleveland Gdns W2 ....100 C1
SW13 ....46 B1
Cleveland Gr 33 E1 ....25 B1
Cleveland Mans SW9 ....163 B1
4 NW6 ....10 B1
NW2 ....23 C1
Cleveland Mews W1 ....104 C4
Cleveland Pl SW1 ....119 A2
Cleveland Rd N1 ....15 C1
14 W4 ....37 B3
SW13 ....46 B1
Cleveland Row SW1 ....119 A1
Cleveland Sq W2 ....100 C1
Cleveland St W1 ....92 C1
Cleveland Terr W2 ....101 A2
Cleveland Way E1 ....25 B1
Clevendon Cl N16 ....7 B1
Cleverly Cotts W12 ....29 B1
Cleverly Est W12 ....29 C2
Cley Ho SE8 ....51 C4
Clichy Ho 25 E1 ....32 B4
Clifden Rd E5 ....17 C3
Cliff Ct 5 NW1 ....13 C2

Cliff Rd NW1 ....13 C2
Cliff Terr SE8 ....51 C1
Cliff Villas NW1 ....13 C2
Cliff Wlk E16 ....35 B2
Cliffe Ho 4 SE10 ....43 B1
Clifford Ave SW14, TW10,TW9 ....45 B1
Clifford Ct W2 ....100 A3
NW10 ....8 A4
SW18 ....71 C4
Clifford Dr SW9 ....63 A3
Clifford Gdns NW10 ....22 B3
Clifford Haigh Ho SW6 ....47 C3
Clifford Ho W14 ....140 C3
Clifford St W1 ....118 C3
Clifford Way NW10 ....8 B4
Clifford's Inn Pas EC4 ....107 B1
Cliffsend Ho 173 SW9 ....173 C3
Cliffview Rd SE13 ....66 C4
Clifton Ave W12 ....29 B1
Clifton Cres SE15 ....50 A3
Clifton Ct NW8 ....89 B2
N4 ....5 C2
SE15 ....50 A3
SW15 ....57 C2
Clifton Gate SW10 ....156 C4
Clifton Gdns W9 ....88 C1
W4 ....37 C2
Clifton Gr E8 ....16 C2
Clifton Hill NW8 ....78 C3
Clifton Ho E2 ....98 C2
Clifton Mans 4 SW9 ....62 C3
Clifton Pl W2 ....101 C1
SE16 ....40 B4
Clifton Rise SE14 ....51 A3
Clifton St EC2 ....24 A1 98 A1
Clifton Terr N4 ....5 C2
Clifton Villas W9 ....100 C4
Clifton Way SE15 ....50 B3
Clinch Ct 10 E16 ....35 C4
Cline Ho SW15 ....56 C2
Clinger Ct N1 ....24 A4
Clink St SE1 ....123 B2
Clinton Rd E3 ....26 A2
Clipper Cl 3 SE16 ....40 C4
Clipper Ho E14 ....42 B1
Clipper Way SE13 ....67 B3
Clipstone Ho 10 SW15 ....56 C2
Clipstone Mews W1 ....104 C4
Clipstone St W1 ....104 C4
Clissold Cres N16 ....15 C4
Clissold Ct N4 ....6 B2
Clissold Ho 4 N16 ....6 C2
Clissold Rd N16 ....6 C1
Clitheroe Rd SW9 ....172 B1
Clive Ct W9 ....89 A2
Clive Ho SW8 ....171 B2
SE10 ....52 B4
Clive Rd SE21,SE27 ....75 C1
Cliveden Pl SW1 ....145 B4
Cloak La EC4 ....123 A4
Clochar Ct NW10 ....21 B4
Clock Ho N16 ....7 C4
Clock Tower Mews N1 ....87 A3
Clock Tower Pl N7 ....14 A2

Clockhouse Cl
SW19 ....69 B2
Clockhouse Pl
SW15 ....58 A1
Clockhouse The
SW19 ....69 B1
Cloister Rd NW2 ......1 B2
W3 ....28 B4
Cloisters Ct N6 ......4 A3
Cloisters The SW9 ..173 C3
Clonbrock Rd N16 ...16 A4
Cloncurry St SW6 ...47 C1
Clone Ct ❹ W12 .....38 A3
Clonmel Rd SW6 ....165 A4
Clonmore St SW18 ...70 B3
Clorane Gdns NW3 ...1 C1
Close The TN9 ....55 A4
Cloth Ct EC1 ....108 B3
Cloth Fair EC1 ......108 B3
Cloth St EC1 ....108 C4
Clothier St EC3 ....110 B2
Cloudesdale Rd
SW17 ....73 A2
Cloudesley Mans
N1 ....85 C3
Cloudesley Pl N1 ...85 C3
Cloudesley Rd N1 ...85 B3
Cloudesley Sq N1 ...85 C3
Cloudesley St N1 ...85 C3
Clove Cres E14 ....34 C2
Clovelly Ct NW2 ......9 B3
Clovelly Ho W2 .....100 C2
Clovelly Rd W4 ......37 C4
Clovelly Way E1 .....32 B3
Clover Mews SW3 ..159 A4
Clowes Ho ❸ SW4 ..62 A3
Cloysters Gn E1 ....125 B2
Club Row E2 ....24 B1 98 C2
Clunbury St N1 ......87 C1
Clunie Ho SW1 .....131 A2
Cluny Mews SW5 ...141 B3
Cluny Pl SE1 ....138 A2
Cluse Ct N1 ....86 C2
Clutton St E14 ....34 A4
Clyde Ct NW1 ....83 C2
Clyde Flats SW6 ....154 C2
Clyde St SE8 ....51 B4
Clydesdale Gdns
TW10 ....55 A3
Clydesdale Ho ❹
W11 ....31 B3
Clydesdale Rd W11 ..31 B3
Clynes Ho ❸ E2 .....25 C2
Clyro Ct N4 ....5 B3
Clyston St SW8 .....171 A2
Coach & Horses Yd
W1 ....118 C4
Coach House La N5 ..15 A4
SW19 ....69 C1
Coach House Yd
NW3 ....11 C4
Coal Wharf Rd W12 .30 C1
Coalbrook Mans ❸
SW12 ....73 A3
Coaldale Wlk SE21 ..75 B4
Coalecroft Rd SW15 .57 B2
Coalport Ho SE11 ..149 B4
Coate St E2 ....24 C3
Coates Ct E3 ....12 A3
Coates Wlk TW8 ....36 A1
Cobb St E1 ....110 C3
Cobb's Ct EC4 ......108 A1
Cobb's Hall ❶ SW6 .47 C4
Cobbett St SW8 ....163 A1
Cobble La N1 ....15 A1
Cobble Mews N4,N5 ..6 B1

Cobbold Ct SW1 ...147 B4
Cobbold Mews W12 .38 B4
Cobbold Rd NW10 ...8 B2
W12 ....38 B4
Cobden Bldgs WC1 ..94 C4
Cobden Ho NW1 .....82 C2
E2 ....99 C4
Cobham Mews ❸
NW1 ....13 C1
Coborn Rd E3 ....26 B2
Coborn St E3 ....26 B2
Cobourg Jun & Inf Sch
SE5 ....49 B4
Cobourg Rd SE5 .....49 B4
Cobourg St NW1 ...93 A3
Coburg Cl SW1 .....147 A4
Coburg Cres SW2 ...74 C3
Coburg Dwellings ❿
E1 ....32 B2
Cochrane Cl NW8 ...79 C1
Cochrane Mews
NW8 ....79 C1
Cochrane St NW8 ...79 C1
Coci Ho W14 ....141 A3
Cock Hill E1 ....110 B3
Cock La EC1 ....108 B3
Cockburn Ho SW1 .147 C1
Cockpit Yd WC1 ...107 A4
Cockspur Ct SW1 ..119 C2
Cockspur St SW1 ..119 C2
Coda Ctr The SW6 .164 B4
Code St E1 ....24 B1 99 A1
Codicote Ho ❷❷ SE8 .40 C2
Codicote Terr N4 ....6 B2
Codling Cl E1 ....125 C2
Codrington Ct SE16 .33 A1
Codrington Ho ❼
E1 ....25 A1
Codrington Mews
W11 ....31 A3
Cody Rd E16 ....27 C1
Cohen Lo E5 ....17 A3
Coin St SE1 ....121 B2
Coity Rd NW5 ....12 C2
Coke St E1 ....111 C2
Cokers La SE21 ....75 C3
Colas Mews ❼ NW6 .23 C4
Colbeck Mews
SW5 ....142 B3
Colberg Pl N16 ......7 B4
Colbert ❸ SE5 ......48 B2
Colborne Ho ❼ E14 .33 C2
Colchester Ho
SW8 ....171 B2
Colchester St E1 ...111 A2
Coldbath Sq EC1 ...95 B2
Coldbath St SE13 ...52 A1
Coldblow La SE14 ..50 C4
Coldharbour E14 ....34 B1
Coldharbour Ind Est
SE5 ....48 B1
Coldharbour La
SW9 ....163 C3
Coldharbour Pl SE5 48 C1
Coldstream Gdns
SW18 ....58 B1
Cole Ho SE1 ....135 C3
Cole St SE1 ....137 A3
Colebert Ave E1 .....25 B1
Colebert Ho ❷❶ E1 ..25 B1
Colebrook Cl SW19 .69 C4
Colebrook Ct SW3 .144 B3

Colebrook Ho ❶
E14 ....34 A3
Colebrooke Pl N1 ...86 B3
Colebrooke Row
N1 ....86 B2
Colebrooke Sch N1 .86 B2
Coleby Path ❷❻ SE5 .48 C3
Colechurch Ho
SE1 ....153 B1
Coleford Rd SW18 ..59 B2
Colegrave Prim Sch
E15 ....19 C3
Colegrave Rd E15 ...19 C3
Colegrove Rd SE15 .49 B4
Coleherne Ct
SW10 ....142 B1
Coleherne Mans
SW5 ....142 B2
Coleherne Mews
SW10 ....142 A1
Coleherne Rd
SW10 ....142 A1
Colehill Gdns SW6 .164 A3
Colehill La SW6 ....164 B3
Coleman Ct SW18 ...70 C4
Coleman Fields N1 ..87 A4
Coleman Mans N8 ...5 A4
Coleman Rd SE5 ....49 A3
Coleman St EC2 ...109 B2
Coleman St Bldgs
EC2 ....109 B2
Colenso Rd E5 ......17 B4
Coleraine Rd SE3 ..53 B4
Coleridge Cl SW8 ..170 B1
Coleridge Ct W14 ...39 C3
Coleridge Gdns
NW6 ....11 B1
Coleridge Ho SW1 .147 A1
SE17 ....151 A2
Coleridge Prim Sch
N8 ....4 C4
Coleridge Rd N4,N7 ..5 C2
Coles Ct SW11 .....167 C3
Colesbourne Ct SE9 49 A3
Coleshill Flats
SW1 ....145 C3
Colestown St
SW11 ....168 B2
Colet Gdns W14 ....39 C2
Colet Ho SE17 .....150 B1
Colette Ct ❸ SE16 ..40 C4
Coley St WC1 ....95 A1
Colfe & Hatchcliffe's
Glebe SE13 ....67 A2
Colgate Ho SE13 ...52 A1
Colin Blanchard Ho
SE4 ....51 C1
Colin Ct SW16 ......73 C2
Colin Rd NW10 ....8 C2
Colin Winter Ho ❸❼
E1 ....25 B1
Colinette Rd SW15 ..57 B3
Colinsdale N1 ....86 A3
Coliston Pass SW18 ..70 C4
Coliston Rd SW18 ..70 C4
Coll of NW London
(Willesden Centre) Ho
NW10 ....8 B3
Coll Sharp Ct E2 ...98 C3
Coll's Rd SE15 ......50 B2
Collamore Ave
SW18 ....72 A3
Collard Pl NW1 ....13 A1
College App SE10 ...52 B4
College Ct ❶
SW3 ....11 C3

College Cross N1 ...14 C1
College Ct SW3 ....145 A1
N3 ....39 B1
W6 ....39 B1
College Gdns SW17 .72 A2
SE21 ....76 A3
College Hill EC4 ....123 A4
College Hill Ct EC4 123 A4
College Mans ❺ NW6 .23 A4
College La NW5 .....13 A4
College Park Cl
SE13 ....67 C3
College Park Sch
W2 ....100 A1
College Pl NW1 ......83 A3
SW10 ....156 C2
College Rd NW10 ...22 B3
SE19,SE21 ....76 A2
College Terr E3 .....26 B2
College St EC4 .....123 A4
Collent Ho ❶❷ E9 ...17 B2
Collent St E9 ....17 B2
Collerston Ho SE10 .43 B1
Collett Rd SE16 ....139 C2
Collette Ho N16 .....7 B3
Colley Ho ❶❼ N7 ...13 C3
Collier St N1 ....84 C1
Collingbourne Rd
W12 ....30 A1
Collingham Gdns
SW5 ....142 B3
Collingham Pl
SW5 ....142 B4
Collingham Rd
SW5 ....142 B3
Collington St ❶
SE10 ....42 C1
Collingwood Ho ❷❼
E1 ....25 A1
Collingwood St E1 ..25 A1
Collins Ct E8 ....16 C2
Collins Ho ❹ E14 ...34 B2
SE10 ....43 B1
Collins Sq SE3 ......53 B1
Collins St SE3 ......53 A1
Collins Yd N1 ....86 A3
Collinson Ct SE1 ..136 C3
Collinson Ho ❶❺
SE15 ....49 C3
Collinson St SE1 ..136 C3
Collinson Wlk SE1 136 C3
Collyer Pl SE15 ....49 C2
Colmans Wharf ❹
E14 ....34 A4
Colmar Cl ❸ E1 ....25 C1
Colmore Mews SE15 .50 A2
Colne Ho NW8 .....101 C4
Colne Rd E5 ....18 A4
Cologne Rd SW11 ..59 C3
Colomb St SE10 ....43 A1
Colombo St SE1 ....122 A1
Colonades The ❹
SW5 ....48 C2
Colonial Dr W4 .....37 B2
Colonnade WC1 ....94 B1
Colonnades The ❸
E8 ....17 A2
Colstead Ho ❷❶ E1 .32 A3
Colston Rd SW14 ...55 B3
Colthurst Cres N4 ...6 B2
Coltman Ho ❶ E14 .33 A3
SE10 ....52 B4
Columba Ho SE14 ..51 B2
Columbia Ho ❶❻ E3 25 C3
Columbia JMI Sch
E2 ....99 A4

Columbia Point ❼
SE16 ....40 B3
Columbia Rd E2 ....98 C4
E2 ....24 B2 99 B4
Colverson Ho ❶❶ E1 .32 B4
Colvestone Cres E8 .16 B3
Colvestone JMI Sch
E8 ....16 B3
Colville Gdns W11 .31 B3
Colville Ho ❷ E2 ...25 B4
W11 ....31 B3
Colville Mews W11 .31 B3
Colville Pl W1 .....105 A3
Colville Prim Sch
W11 ....31 B3
Colville Rd W11 ....31 B3
W3 ....37 A3
Colville Sq W11 ....31 B3
Colville Sq Mews ❻
W11 ....31 B3
Colville Terr W11 ...31 B3
Colwall Ho SW9 ...173 A1
Colwell Rd SE22 ...64 B2
Colwick Cl N6 ....4 C4
Colwith Rd W6 .....47 B4
Colworth Gr SE17 .151 A3
Colwyn Ho SE1 ....135 B1
Colyton Rd SE22 ...65 A2
Com Coll Sixth Form Ctr
The E9 ....17 C2
Combe Ave SE3 .....53 B3
Combe Ho ❷❻ W2 ..31 C4
SW14 ....45 B1
Combe Mews ❹
SE3 ....53 B3
Combe The NW1 ...92 B3
Combedale Rd SE10 .43 C1
Combemartin Rd
SW18 ....70 A3
Comber Gr SE5 .....48 B3
Comber Grove Jun & Inf
Sch SE5 ....48 B3
Combermere Rd
SW9 ....62 B4
Comeragh Mews
W14 ....140 B1
Comeragh Rd W14 140 B1
Comerford Rd SE4 .66 B3
Comet Pl SE8 ....51 C3
Comet St SE8 ....51 C3
Comins Ho SW4 ....61 B2
Commercial Rd E1 .111 C2
E14 ....110 C4
Commercial St E1 ..110 C4
Commercial Way
NW10 ....20 A3
SE15 ....49 C3
Commerell Pl SE10 .43 B1
Commerell St SE10 .43 A1
Commodore Ct SE8 .51 C2
Commodore Ho ❼
E14 ....34 B2
Commodore St E1 .26 A1
Common Rd SW13 .56 C4
Common View
SW15 ....57 B4
Commonwealth Ave ❷
W12 ....30 A2
Community Coll The
E9 ....17 C3
E9 ....25 C2

Community Rd E15 ...19 C3
Compania Bldg 12
E1 ....32 C2
Compass Cl E1 ....124 C1
Compass Ho W2 ...100 A1
SE8 ....52 A1
Compass Point 9
E14 ....33 C2
Companye Gdns
NW6 ....11 A1
Compton Ave N6 ......3 A4
N1 ....15 A2
Compton Cl NW1 .....92 B3
Compton Cres W4 ...45 B4
Compton Ho SW11 168 A4
Compton Pas EC1 ...96 B2
Compton Pl WC1 .....94 A2
Compton Rd N1 ....15 A2
NW10 ....22 C2
Compton St EC1 ......96 B2
Compton Terr N1 ....15 A2
Comus Ho E3 ....27 B2
Comus Pl SE17 ......152 A3
Comyn Rd SW11 .....60 A3
Comyns Cl E16 ....35 B2
Conant Ho SE11 .....48 A4
Conant Mews E1 ...125 C4
Concanon Rd SW2,
SW4 ....62 B3
Concert Hall App
SE1 ....121 A1
Concord Bsns Ctr
W3 ....28 A4
Concord Ctr W12 .....39 C4
Concord Rd W3 ....20 A1
Concordia Wharf
E14 ....34 B1
Condell Rd SW8 .....171 A3
Condor St E14 ....33 A3
Condray Pl SW11 ...158 A1
Conduit Ct WC2 .....120 A4
Conduit Ho SE10 .....52 C2
Conduit Mews W2 ...101 B1
Conduit Pl W2 ....101 B1
Conduit Pas W2 .....101 B1
Conduit St W1 ....118 C4
Conewood St N5 ......6 A1
Coney Acres SE21 ...75 B3
Coney Way SW8 .....163 A3
Congers Ho SE8 .....51 C3
Congreve Ho 10
N16 ....16 A3
Congreve St SE17 ..152 A3
Conifer Ct 28 SW19 ..69 C3
Conifer Gdns SW16 ..74 B1
Conifer Ho SE4 ....66 B3
Coniger Rd SW6 ....165 B2
Coningham Ct
SW10 ....157 A2
Coningham Mews
W12 ....29 C1
Coningham Rd W12 ..39 A4
Coningsby Rd N4 ......6 A4
Conington Rd SE13 ..52 B1
Conisbrough NW1 ....82 C3
Coniston NW1 ....92 C4
Coniston Cl W4 ....45 B3
SW13 ....46 B3
Coniston Ct W2 .....102 B1
6 SE16 ....40 C4
10 Coniston Ho 15 E3 ..26 B2
18 SE5 ....48 B3
Coniston Wlk E9 .....17 B3

Conistone Way N7 ...14 A1
Conlan St W10 ....23 A1
Conley Rd NW10 ......8 A2
Conley St SE10 ....43 A1
Connaught Ave
SW14 ....55 B3
Connaught Cl W2 ...102 B1
Connaught Ho W1 ..118 A3
NW10 ....22 A2
Connaught Lo N4 .....5 C4
Connaught Mans
SW6 ....164 A4
SW11 ....168 B3
15 N16 ....15 C4
3 SW9 ....62 C3
Connaught Pl W2 ...102 C1
Connaught Rd N4 .....5 C4
NW10 ....21 A3
5 Richmond TW10 ....54 B2
Connaught Sq W2 ...102 C1
Connaught St W2 ...102 B1
Connell Ct 6 SE14 ..50 C4
Connett Ho 5 E2 .....25 A3
Connor Ct SW11 ....170 A3
Connor St E9 ....25 C4
Conrad Ho SW8 .....162 A2
8 N16 ....16 A3
8 SE16 ....33 A2
Cons St SE1 ....135 C4
Consort Ho W2 ......114 B3
Consort Lo NW8 .....80 C3
Consort Rd SE15 .....50 A1
Constable Ct 11
SE16 ....40 A1
Constable Ho NW3 ..12 B1
Constable Wlk SE21 ..76 A1
Constant Ho 21 E14 ..34 A2
Constantine Ho
SW2 ....75 A3
Constantine Rd
NW3 ....12 A4
Constitution Hill
SW1,W1 ....132 B4
Consul Ho 3 E3 ......26 C1
Content St SE17 ....151 B3
Convent of Jesus &
Mary CE Inf Sch
NW2 ....9 B2
Convent of Jesus &
Mary Language Coll for
Girls The NW10 ...... 21 B4
Convent of the Sacred
Heart Digby-Stuart
Coll SW15 ....56 B2
Conway Gr W3 ....28 C4
Conway Ho 5 E14 ....42 A2
6 SW3 ....74 A3
Conway Mews W1 ...92 C1
Conway St W1 ....92 C1
Conybeare NW3 ......12 A1
Conyer St 19 E3 ......26 A3
Cook's Rd E15 ....27 A3
SE17 ....48 A4
Cookham Cres SE16 40 C4
Cookham Ho E2 ....98 C2
Coomassie Rd W9 ...23 B1
Coombe Ho 13 N7 ...13 C3
Coomber Ho SW6 ....59 A4
Coombs St N1 ....86 B1
Coomer Mews
SW6 ....155 A3
Cooper Pl SW8 ......155 A3
Cooper Cl SE1 ....135 C3
Cooper Ct E15 ....76 B3
Cooper Ho NW8 ......89 B1

Cooper Rd NW10 ......8 C3
Cooper St 10 E16 ....35 B2
Cooper's Rd SE1 ....153 A2
Cooper's Row
EC3 ....124 C4
Cooperage The
E1 ....124 C1
Coopers Cl E1 ....25 B1
Coopers La NW1 .....83 C1
Coopers Rd E9 ....17 C3
Cope Ho EC1 ....97 A3
Cope Pl W8 ....127 B1
Cope St SE16 ....40 C2
Cope Yd E1 ....125 C2
Copeland Dr E14 .....41 C2
Copeland Ho SE11 ..135 A1
Copeland Rd SE15 ...50 A1
Copenhagen Ct W4 ...37 C4
Copenhagen Ho N1 ..85 B3
Copenhagen Pl E14 ..33 B3
Copenhagen Prim Sch
..............................84 C3
Copenhagen St N1 ..84 C3
Copford Wlk N1 ....86 C4
Copleston Rd SE15 ..64 B4
Copley Cl 19 SE17 ....48 A4
Copnor Way 14
SE15 ....49 A3
Coppedhall 1 SE7 ....75 C2
Copper Beech N6 .....3 C4
Copperas St SE8 .....52 A4
Copperfield Ho
SE1 ....139 B3
Copperfield Rd E3 ...33 A4
Copperfield St
SE1 ....136 C4
Copperfields Ct W3 ..36 C4
Coppice Dr SW15 .....57 A1
Coppin Ho SW2 ....75 A3
Coppock Cl SW11 ...168 A1
Copse Ct SW15 ....58 A2
Copthall Ave EC2 ...109 C2
Copthall Bldgs
EC2 ....109 C2
Copthall Ct EC2 .....109 B2
Copthorne Ave
SW12 ....73 C4
Coptic St WC1 ....106 A3
Copton Cl E3 ....33 C4
Coral Ho 6 E1 ....26 A1
Coral St SE1 ....135 C3
Coram Ho WC1 ....94 A2
4 W4 ....38 A1
Coram St WC1 ....94 A1
Corbet Ct EC3 ....109 C1
Corbet Ho N1 ....85 B3
Corbet Pl E1 ....110 C4
Corbett Ho SW10 ...156 C4
Corbett's La SE16 ...40 B2
Corbiere Ho 5 N1 ...24 A4
Corbin Ho 7 E3 ....27 A2
Corbridge Cres E2 ...25 A3
Corby Rd NW10 ......20 C3
Corby Way E3 ....26 C1
Corbyn St N4,N19 ....5 A3
Cord Way 7 E14 .....41 C3
Cordelia Cl SE24 .....63 A3
Cordelia Ho 26 N1 ...24 A3
Cordelia St E14 ....34 A3
Cording St E14 ....34 A4
Cordova Rd E3 ....26 A2
Cordwainers Coll
..............................17 A1
Cordwainers Ct 18
E9 ....17 B1
Corfe Ho SW8 ....162 C2

Corfe Lo SE21 ....75 C2
Corfe Twr 6 W3 ....37 B4
Corfield St E2 ....25 A2
Coriander Ave E14 ...34 C3
Corinne Rd N19 ....13 B4
Cork Sq E1 ....32 A1
Cork St W1 ....118 C3
Cork St Mews W1 ..118 C3
Corlett St NW1 ....102 A4
Cormont Rd SE5 ......48 A2
Cormorant Ct
24 SE8 ....51 B4
6 SE21 ....75 C2
Cornbury Ho 5 SE8 ..51 B4
Cornelia St N7 ....14 B2
Corner Fielde SW2 ..74 B3
Corner Gn SE3 ....53 C1
Corner House St
WC2 ....120 A2
Cornerways SW5 .....56 C3
Corney Rd W4 ....46 A4
Corney Reach Way
W4 ....46 A3
Cornflower Terr
SE22 ....65 A1
Cornford Gr SW12 ...73 A2
Cornhill EC3 ....109 C1
Cornick Ho 6 SE16 ..40 A3
Cornish Ho
Brentford TW8 ....36 B1
7 SE17 ....48 A4
Cornmill La SE13 .....67 B4
Cornmow Dr NW10 ...8 C3
Cornwall Ave E2 .....25 B2
Cornwall Cres
W11 ....112 A4
1 ....31 A3
Cornwall Gdns
SW7 ....128 B1
NW10 ....9 A2
Cornwall Gdns Wlk
SW7 ....128 B1
Cornwall Gr W4 ....38 A1
3 SW15 ....69 B4
Cornwall Mans
NW1 ....91 A1
SW10 ....157 A2
Cornwall Mews S
SW7 ....128 C1
Cornwall Mews W
SW7 ....128 B1
Cornwall Rd SE1 ....135 C4
N4 ....5 C4
Cornwall Terr NW1 ..91 A1
Cornwall Terr Mews
NW1 ....91 A1
Cornwallis Ct 8 172 A4
Cornwallis Ho 24
W12 ....30 A2
Cornwallis Rd N19 ...5 A2
Cornwallis Sq N19 ...5 A2
Cornwood Dr E1 ......32 B3
Coronation Ave 1
N16 ....16 B4
Coronation Ct W10 ..30 B4
Coronet St N1 ....98 A3
Corporation Row
EC1 ....95 C2
Corporation St N7 ...14 A3
Corpus Christi RC Prim
Sch SW2 ....62 B2
Corrance Rd SW2,
SW4 ....62 A3
Corringham Ct NW11 1 C4

Corringham Ho 10
E1 ....32 C3
Corringham Rd
NW11 ....1 C4
Corringway NW11 .....2 A4
Corry Ho 2 E14 ....34 A2
Corseley Way E9 .....18 B2
Corsham St N1 ....97 C3
Corsica St N5 ....15 A2
Cortis Rd SW15 ....57 A1
Cortis Terr SW15 .....57 A1
Corunna Rd SW8 ....171 A4
Corunna Terr SW8 ..170 C4
Corvette Sq 9 SE10 ..52 C4
Coryton Path W9 .....23 B1
Cosbycote Ave SE24 ..63 B2
Cosgrove Ho 11 E2 ..24 C4
Cosmo Pl WC1 ....106 B4
Cosmur Cl W12 ....38 B3
Cossall Wlk SE15 ....50 A2
Cosser St SE1 ....135 B2
Costa St SE15 ....49 C1
Coston Wlk 4 SE4 ...65 C3
Cosway Mans NW1 ..102 B4
Cosway St NW1 ......102 B4
Cotall St E14 ....33 C4
Cotes Ho NW8 ....90 A1
Cotham St SE17 .....151 A3
Cotherstone Rd
SW2 ....74 B3
Cotleigh Rd NW6 ....10 C1
Cotman Cl SW15 ......57 C2
Cotman Ho NW8 ......80 A2
Cotswold Ct EC1 ......96 C2
Cotswold Gate NW2 ..1 A3
Cotswold Ho N16 .....7 B3
Cotswold Mews
SW11 ....167 C3
Cottage Gn SE5 ....48 C3
Cottage Gr SW9 ......62 A4
Cottage Pl SW3 ......130 A1
Cottage St E14 ....34 A2
Cottage Wlk 2 N16 ...7 B1
SE15 ....49 B2
Cottenham Ho 4
N19 ....5 A2
Cottesbrook St 9
SE14 ....51 A3
Cottesloe Ho NW8 ...90 A2
Cottesloe Mews
SE1 ....135 C2
Cottesmore Ct 8 128 B2
Cottesmore Gdns
W8 ....128 B2
Cottingham Rd
SW8 ....163 A2
Cottington St SE11 ..150 A2
Cotton Ave W3 ....28 C3
Cotton Ho W12 ....38 B4
18 SW2 ....74 A4
Cotton Row SW11 ...59 C4
Cotton St E14 ....34 B2
Cotton's Gdns E2 .....98 B4
Cottons La SE1 ......123 C2
Couchman Ho 2
SW4 ....61 B1
Coulgate St SE4 ......66 A4
Coulson Ho 9
SW2 ....74 A3
Coulter Rd W6 ....39 A3
Coults Cres NW5 ....3 C1
Councillor St SE5 ....48 B3
Counter St SE1 ....124 A4
Counters Ct W14 ....126 B2
Countess Rd NW5 ...13 B3

Countisbury Ho
SE26 ....76 C1
County Gr SE5 ....48 B2
County Ho SW9 ....173 B4
County St SE1 ....137 A1
Courier Ho 17 SW2 ....74 C4
Courland Gr SW8 .....171 C3
Courland St SW8 ......171 C3
Court Gdns N7 ....14 C2
Court La SE21 ....76 B4
Court Lane Gdns
SE21 ....78 A4
Court Mans 8 W6 .....38 C2
Court Royal SW15 ......58 A2
Court St E1 ....32 A4
Court Way W3 ....28 B4
Courtauld Ho 11 E2 ...24 C3
Courtauld Inst of Art★
W1 ....103 A2
WC2 ....120 C4
Courtauld Rd N19 ......5 A3
Courtenay Ave N6 ......3 A4
Courtenay Sq SE11 ..149 B1
Courtenay St SE11 ...149 B2
Courtfield Gdns
SW5 ....142 B3
Courtfield Ho EC1 ....107 B4
Courtfield Mews
SW7 ....142 B3
Courtfield Rd SW7 ...142 C3
Courthill Rd SE13 .....67 B3
Courthope Ho
SW8 ....162 A1
  14 SE16 ....40 B3
Courthope Rd NW3 ...12 B4
Courtlands TW10 ......54 C2
Courtlands Ave
TW9 ....45 A1
Courtmead Ct SE24 ..63 B1
Courtnell St W2 ....31 C3
Courtney Ct N7 ....14 C3
Courtney Rd N7 ....14 C3
Courtrai Rd SE23 ......66 A1
Courtville Ho 11
W10 ....23 A2
Courtyard The
SW6 ....164 A3
  1 N1 ....14 B1
  13 SE1 ....59 C3
Cousin La EC4 ....123 B3
Couzens Ho 9 E3 .....33 B4
Coval Gdns SW14 .....55 A3
Coval La SW14 ....55 A3
Coval Rd SW14 ....55 B3
Covent Garden Sta
WC2 ....120 B4
Covent Gdn WC2 .....120 B4
Coventry Cl NW6 ......23 C4
Coventry Rd E1 ....25 A1
Coventry St W1 ....119 B3
Coverdale Pl NW6 ......9 C1
Coverdale Rd NW2 ...10 A2
W12 ....39 A4
Coverham Ho 5
SE4 ....65 C3
Coverley Cl E1 ....111 C4
Coverley Point
SE11 ....148 C3
Cowcross St EC1 .....108 A4
Cowdenbeath Path
N1 ....84 C4
Cowdray Hall Coll of
  Nursing★ W1 ....104 A2
Cowdray Ho 23
SE22 ....64 A4
Cowdry Rd E9 ....18 B2

Cowley Rd SW9 ......173 C4
W3 ....29 B1
SW14 ....56 A4
Cowley St SW1 ....134 A1
Cowling Cl W11 ....112 A2
Cowper Ho SW1 ......147 C1
SE17 ....151 A2
Cowper Rd N16 ....16 A4
W3 ....28 C1
Cowper St EC1,EC2 ...97 C2
Cowper Terr W10 ......30 C4
Cowper's Ct EC3 .....109 C1
Cowthorpe Rd
SW8 ....171 C4
Cox Ho W6 ....154 A4
Cox's Ct E1 ....110 C3
Coxson Way SE1 .....138 C3
Coysh Ct 5 SW15 .....58 A2
Crabtree Cl E2 ....24 B3
Crabtree Ct E15 ....19 A3
Crabtree Hall SW6 ....47 B3
Crabtree La SW6 ......47 C3
Craddock St NW5 .....12 C2
Craig's Ct SW1 ....120 A2
Craigie Ho SE1 ....153 A3
Craigleith SW15 ....57 C1
Craignair Rd SW2 .....74 C4
Craik Ct NW6 ....23 B3
Crail Row SE17 ....151 C3
Cramer St W1 ....103 C3
Crammond Cl W6 ....154 A3
Crampton Jun & Inf Sch
SE17 ....150 B2
Crampton St SE17 ...150 C2
Cranbourn Alley
WC2 ....119 C4
Cranbourn Ho 4
SE16 ....40 A4
Cranbourn St WC2 ..119 C4
Cranbourne Ct
SW11 ....158 B2
Cranbourne Rd E15 ...76 B4
Cranbrook Ho 5
E5 ....17 A3
Cranbrook Rd W4 .....38 A1
SE8 ....51 C2
Cranbrook St E2 ....25 C3
Cranbury Rd SW6 ...166 B1
Crandale Ho 8 E5 .....17 A3
Crandley Ct SE8 ....41 A2
Crane Ave W3 ....28 B2
Crane Ct EC4 ....107 C1
  7 W12 ....30 A1
Crane Gr N7 ....14 C2
Crane Ho 22 E3 ....26 A3
  9 SE15 ....49 B2
Crane Mead SE16 .....40 C2
Crane St 5 SE15 ....49 B2
Cranfield Ct NW1 ....102 B3
Cranfield Rd SE4 ......66 B4
Cranford Cotts
E1 ....32 C2
Cranford Lo SW19 ....69 C2
Cranford St E1 ....32 C2
Cranhurst Rd NW2 ...9 B3
Cranleigh W11 ....112 C3
Cranleigh Ct 4 E11 ...4 A2
  Richmond TW9 ....54 C4
Cranleigh Hos NW1 ..83 A1
Cranleigh Mews
SW11 ....168 B1
Cranleigh St NW1 .....83 A1
Cranley Gdns SW7 ..143 B2
Cranley Mews
SW7 ....143 A2

Cranley Pl SW7 ......143 B3
Cranmer Ct SW3 .....144 B3
Cranmer Ho SW11 ..168 A4
Cranmer Rd SW9 ....163 C2
Cranswick Rd SE16 ..40 A1
Cranwell Cl E3 ....27 A1
Cranwich Rd N16 ......7 A4
Cranwood Ct EC1 .....97 C3
Cranwood St EC1 .....97 C3
Cranworth Gdns
SW9 ....173 B4
Cranworth Ho 6
N7 ....14 B4
Craster Rd SW2 ....74 B4
Craston Ho 2 SE5 ....49 A1
Craven Cl N16 ....7 C4
Craven Cottage (Fulham
  FC) SW6 ....47 C2
Craven Ct NW10 ......21 A4
Craven Hill W2 ....115 A4
Craven Hill Gdns
W2 ....115 A4
Craven Hill Mews
W2 ....115 A4
Craven Lo 9 SW2 .....74 C4
Craven Lo W2 ....115 A4
Craven Mews 5
SW11 ....60 C4
Craven Park Mews
NW10 ....21 A4
Craven Pas WC2 .....120 A2
Craven Pk NW10 ......21 A4
Craven Rd NW10 ......21 A4
  W2 ....101 A1
  W5 ....36 A4
Craven St WC2 ....120 A2
Craven Terr W2 ......115 A4
Craven Wlk E5,N16 ....7 C4
Craven Bldgs
WC2 ....102 B3
Crawford Jun & Inf Sch
SE5 ....48 B2
Crawford Mews
W1 ....102 C3
Crawford Pas EC1 .....95 C1
Crawford Pl W1 ......102 B3
Crawford Place
  Dwellings W1 ....102 B3
Crawford Point 4
E16 ....35 B1
Crawford Rd SE5 .....48 B1
Crawford St W1 ......102 C3
Crawshay Ct SW9 ...173 C4
Crawshay Ho 7
N16 ....6 C1
Crawthew Gr SE22 ...64 B3
Crayford Ho SE1 .....137 C3
N7 ....14 A4
Crayford Rd N7 ....14 A4
Crayle Ho EC1 ....96 B2
Crealock St SW18 .....59 A1
Creasy Est SE1 ....138 A1
Crebor St SE22 ....64 C1
Credenhill Ho 2
SE15 ....50 A3
Crediton Hill NW6 ....11 A3
Crediton Rd NW10 ...22 C4
NW6 ....10 C1
Credon Rd SE16 ....40 A1
Creechurch La
EC3 ....110 B1
Creechurch Pl EC3 ..110 B1
Creed Ho SE15 ....65 A4
Creed La EC4 ....108 B1

Creek Ho W14 ....126 B2
Creek Rd SE10,SE8 ...52 A4
Creekside SE8 ....52 A3
Crefeld Cl W6 ....154 A3
Creighton Rd W3 .....29 C2
Creighton Rd NW6 ...22 C3
Cremer Bsns Ctr 8
E2 ....24 B3
Cremer Ho 9 SE8 .....51 C3
Cremer St E2 ....24 B3
Cremorne Rd
SW10 ....157 B2
Creon Ct SW9 ....173 B4
Crescent EC3 ....124 C4
Crescent Ct SW4 ......61 C2
Crescent Gdns
SW19 ....70 C1
Crescent Gr SW4 .....61 B3
Crescent Ho SE13 ...52 A1
Crescent La SW4 ......61 C2
Crescent Mans
W11 ....112 B4
N5 ....15 A3
Crescent Pl SW3 ....144 B4
Crescent Row EC1 ....96 C1
Crescent St N1 ....14 B1
Crescent Stables
SW15 ....58 A2
Crescent The 3 W3 ...29 A3
SW13 ....46 C1
SW19 ....70 C1
Crescent Way SE4 ....66 C4
Crescent Wood Rd
SE21,SE26 ....76 C1
Cressage Ho 9
TW8 ....44 A4
Cressall Ho 8 E14 ....41 C3
Cresset Ho 8 E9 ......17 B2
Cresset Rd E9 ....17 B2
Cresset St SW4 ....61 C4
Cressfield Cl NW5 ....12 C3
Cressida Rd N19 ....4 C3
Cressingham Rd
SE13 ....67 B4
Cressington Cl 4
N16 ....16 A3
Cresswell Gdns
SW5 ....142 C2
Cresswell Pl SW10 ..143 A2
Cressy Ct SW6 ....33 A4
W6 ....39 A3
Cressy Ho SW13 ......57 A4
Cressy Hos 7 E1 ......32 B4
Cressy Pl E1 ....32 B4
Cressy Rd NW3 ....12 B4
Cresta Ho NW6 ....11 C1
  7 E3 ....26 C1
Crestfield St N1,
WC1 ....94 B4
Crestview NW5 ....4 A1
Crestway SW15 ....57 A1
Creswick Ct W3 ......28 A2
Creswick Rd W3 ......28 A2
Creswick Wlk 6 E3 ..26 C2
Crewdson Rd SW9 ..163 B1
Crewe Pl NW10 ....21 B2
Crewkerne Ct
SW11 ....167 C4
Crews St E14 ....41 C2
Crewys Rd NW2 ....1 B1
SE15 ....50 A1
Crichton St SW8 .....170 C2

Cricketers Mews 4
SW18 ....59 A2
Cricketfield Rd E5 ....17 A4
Cricklade Ave SW2 ...74 B2
Cricklewood Broadway
NW2 ....9 C4
Cricklewood La NW2 .1 C1
Cricklewood Sta
NW2 ....9 C4
Crieff Rd SW18 ....59 B1
Criffel Ave SW2 ....73 C3
Crimscott St SE1 ....138 B1
Crimsworth Rd
SW8 ....161 C1
Crinan St N1 ....84 B2
Cringle St SW8 ......160 C2
Cripplegate St
EC1 ....109 A4
Crisp Rd W6 ....39 B1
Crispe Ho N1 ....85 A3
Crispian Cl NW10 ......8 A4
Crispin Ct SE17 ......152 A3
Crispin St E1 ....110 C3
Cristowe Rd SW6 ...165 A1
Criterion Mews N19 ..4 C2
Crockerton Rd
SW17 ....72 B2
Croft Ho 5 W10 ....23 A2
SW15 ....58 A1
Croft St SE8 ....41 A2
Croft The NW10 ......21 B3
Crofters Ct 9 SE8 ....41 A2
Crofters Way NW1 ...83 B4
Crofton Ave W4 ....45 C3
Crofton Gate Way
SE4 ....66 A2
Crofton L Ctr SE4 ....66 C1
Crofton Park Rd
SE4 ....66 B1
Crofton Park Sta
SE4 ....66 B2
Crofton Rd SE5 ....49 A1
Crofton Sch SE4 .....66 C1
Crofton Terr E5 ....18 A3
  Richmond TW9 ....54 B3
Crofts Ho 10 E2 ....24 C3
Crofts St E1 ....125 B3
Crogsland Rd NW1 ...12 C1
Cromartie Rd N19 .....4 C4
Cromarty Ho 8 E1 ....33 A4
Crombie Mews
SW11 ....168 B2
Cromdale Ct N16 ......7 B4
Cromer Ct SW13 .....58 B1
SW16 ....74 A1
Cromer St WC1 ....94 B3
Cromer Terr E8 ....16 C3
Cromer Villas Rd
SW18 ....58 B1
Cromford Path 1
E5 ....17 C4
Cromford Rd SW18 ..58 C2
Crompton Ct SW3 ...144 A4
Crompton Ho W2 .....89 B1
SE1 ....137 A1
SW8 ....171 A3
Crompton St W2 ......89 B1
Cromwell Ave N6 ......4 A3
W6 ....39 A2
Cromwell Cl W3 ....28 B1
  2 W6 ....37 A1

Cromwell Cres
SW5 ....**141** B4
Cromwell Ctr NW10 .20 C2
Cromwell Gdns
SW7 ....**129** C1
Cromwell Gr W6 ....**39** B3
Cromwell Ho
SW11 ....**169** C3
SW15 ....56 C3
Cromwell Hospl
SW5 ....**142** A4
Cromwell Lo **38** E1 .25 B1
Cromwell Mans
SW5 ....**141** C4
Cromwell Mews
SW7 ....**143** C4
Cromwell PI SW7 .**143** C4
Cromwell Rd
SW5,SW7 ....**142** B4
SW9 ....48 A2
Cromwell Twr EC2 **109** A4
Crondace Rd SW6 .**165** C3
Crondall Ct **7** N1 ..24 A3
Crondall Ho N5 .....68 C3
Crondall PI **15** N1 ..24 A3
Crondall St **1** N1 ..**87** C1
N1 ....24 A3
Crone Ct **8** NW6 ..23 B3
Cronin St SE15 .....49 B3
Crooke Rd SE8 .....41 A1
Crooked Billet Yd
E2 ....**98** B4
Crookham Rd SW6 **164** C3
Croom's Hill SE10 ..52 C3
Croom's Hill Gr
SE10 ....52 B3
Cropley Ct N1 ......**87** B2
Cropley St N1 ......**87** B2
Cropthorne Ct W9 .**89** A3
Crosby Ct SE1 .....**137** B4
Crosby Ho **4** E14 .42 B3
Crosby Row SE1 ..**137** B4
Crosby Sq EC3 ...**110** A2
Crosby Wlk **8** E8 .16 B2
SE24 ....74 C4
Crosfield Ct **3** W10 .30 C3
Crosfield Ho W11 .**112** A3
Crosland PI **5**
SW11 ....60 C4
Cross CI SE15 ......50 A1
Cross La EC3 .....**124** A3
Cross Rd SE5 ......49 A1
Cross St N1 ....**86** B4
SW13 ....54 A4
Crossbow Ho **15** N1 .24 A4
Crossfield Rd NW3 .11 C2
Crossfield St SE8 ..51 C3
Crossford St SW9 .**172** C1
Crossharbour & London
Arena E14 ....42 A3
Crossleigh Ct **3**
SE14 ....51 B3
Crosslet St SE17 ..**151** C4
Crosslet Vale SE10 .52 A2
Crossley St N7 .....14 C2
Crossman Hos **5**
SW12 ....74 A4
Crossmount Ho **13**
SE5 ....48 B3

Crossthwaite Ave
SE5,SE24 ....63 C3
Crosswall EC3 ....**124** C4
Crossway E8,N16 ..16 A3
Crossway Ct SE4 ..51 A1
Croston St E8 ......24 C4
Crouch End Hill N8 .4 C4
Crouch Hall Ct N19 .5 A3
Crouch Hall Rd N19 .5 A3
Crouchmans Ct
SE21,SE26 ....76 C1
Crowder St E1 ......32 A2
Crowfield Ho N5 ...15 B4
Crowfoot Cl E9 .....18 B3
Crowhurst Ct SW9 **173** C2
Crowhurst Ho
SW9 ....**173** A1
Crowland Ho NW8 .**78** C3
Crowland Terr N1 ..15 C1
Crowline Wlk **1** N1 .15 B2
Crown Cl E3 ....**26** C4
E3 ....26 C4
Crown Cl NW8 .....**90** B3
WC2 ....**106** B1
E14 ....**109** A1
4 SW15 ....57 C3
Crown Lo SW3 ....**144** B3
Crown Office Row
EC4 ....**121** B4
Crown Pas SW1 ..**119** A1
Crown Pl NW5 .....13 A2
Crown Reach SW1 **147** C1
Crown St W3 ....28 A1
SE5 ....48 B3
Crown Terr TW9 ...54 B3
Crowndale Ct NW1 .**83** B2
Crowndale Rd NW1 .**83** A2
Crownfield Rd E15 .19 C4
Crownhill Rd NW10 .21 B4
Crownleigh Ct SW2 .62 C2
Crownstone Ct **1**
SW2 ....62 C2
Crownstone Rd
SW2 ....62 C2
Crows Rd E15 ......27 C2
Crowther Ave TW8 .36 A2
Crowthorne Cl
SW18 ....70 B3
Crowthorne Rd
W10 ....30 C3
Croxley Rd W9 .....23 B2
Croxted Cl SE21 ...75 B4
Croxted Mews SE24 .63 B1
Croxteth Ho SW8 .**171** B2
Croydon Ho SE1 ..**135** C4
Crozier Ho SW8 ..**162** C1
Crozier Terr E9 ....17 C3
Crucifix La SE1 ...**138** A4
Cruden Ho **22** E3 .26 B3
1 SE17 ....48 A4
Cruden St N1 ......**86** B3
Cruikshank St
WC1 ....**95** A4
Cruikshank Ho NW8 **80** B2
Crusoe House Sch
N1 ....**97** B4
Crusoe Mews N16 ..6 C2
Crutched Friars
EC3 ....**124** A4
Crystal Palace Rd
SE22 ....64 C2
Cuba St E14 ....41 C4
Cubitt Ho **4** SW4 .61 B1

Cubitt St WC1 .....**95** A3
Cubitt Terr SW4 ...61 B4
Cubitt Town Jun & Inf
Sch E14 ....42 B3
Cuddington SE17 .**151** A4
Cudworth Ho SW8 **171** A3
Cudworth St E1 ...25 A1
Cuff Pt E2 ....**98** C4
Cuffley Ho W10 ...30 B4
Culand Ho SE17 ..**152** A3
Culford Gdns SW3 **145** A3
Culford Gr N1 ......16 A2
Culford Mans SW3 **145** A3
Culford Mews N1 ..16 A2
Culford Rd N1 .....16 A2
N1 ....24 A4
Culham Ho E2 .....**98** C3
22 W2 ....31 C4
Cullen Ho W9 ......23 B3
Cullen Way NW10 .20 B1
Culling Rd SE16 ...40 B3
Cullingworth Rd
NW10 ....9 A3
Culloden Cl SE16 .**153** C1
Culloden JMI Sch
E14 ....34 B3
Cullum St EC3 ....**124** A4
Culmore Rd SE15 .50 B3
Culmstock Rd SW11 .60 C2
Culpepper Ct SE11 **149** B4
Culpepper Ho **5**
E14 ....33 A3
Culpin Ho E2 ......**99** B3
Culross Bldgs NW1 **84** A2
Culross St W1 .....**117** B3
Culvert Ct SW18 ..59 A1
Culverden Rd SW12 .73 B2
Culverhouse WC1 .**106** C3
Culverhouse Gdns
SW16 ....74 B1
Culvert Ct SW11 ..**169** B2
Culvert Pl SW11 ..**169** B1
Culvert Rd SW11 .**169** A2
Culworth Ho NW8 .**80** A2
Culworth St NW8 ..**80** A1
Cumber Ho SW18 .70 C3
Cumberland Ave
NW10 ....20 A2
Cumberland Bsns Ctr
NW10 ....20 A2
Cumberland Cl E8 .16 B2
Cumberland Comp Sch
E16 ....35 C4
Cumberland Cres
W14 ....**140** B4
Cumberland Ct
W1 ....**103** A1
Cumberland Gate
W1 ....**117** A4
Cumberland Gdns
WC1 ....**95** B4
Cumberland Ho **1**
SW15 ....69 B4
Cumberland Mans
W1 ....**102** C2
7 NW6 ....10 C3
Cumberland Market
NW1 ....**92** B4
Cumberland Mills Sq
E14 ....42 C1
Cumberland Park Ind
Est NW10 ....22 C2
Cumberland Pk W3 .28 B2
Cumberland Pl
NW1 ....**92** A4
Cumberland Rd W3 .28 B2

Cumberland Rd continued
Richmond TW9 ....44 C3
SW13 ....46 C2
Cumberland St
E16 ....35 B2
Cumberland St
SW1 ....**146** B2
Cumberland Terr
NW1 ....**82** A1
Cumberland Terrace
Mews NW1 ....**82** A1
Cumberland Villas
W3 ....28 B2
Cumbria Ho **2**
SW15 ....57 B3
Cumbrian Gdns NW2 .1 A2
Cumming St N1 ...**85** A1
Cumnor Cl SW9 ..**173** A2
Cunard Pl EC3 ....**110** B1
Cunard Rd NW10 .20 C2
Cunard Wlk **3** SE16 .41 A2
Cundy St SW1 .....**145** C3
Cunningham Ct W2 **89** B1
Cunningham Ho **16**
SE5 ....48 C3
Cunningham Pl
NW8 ....**89** B2
Cunnington St W4 .37 B2
Cupar Rd SW11 ..**169** C4
Cureton St SW1 ..**147** C3
Curlew Ho **6** SE15 .**49** B2
SE4 ....66 A3
Curlew St SE1 ....**139** A4
Curran Ho SW3 ..**144** A3
Curricle St W3 ....29 A1
Currie Ho **13** SW12 .73 C4
Cursitor St EC4 ..**107** B2
Curtain Rd EC2 ...**98** B2
Curtain Rd
EC2 ....24 A1,**98** B2
Curtis Dr W3 ......28 C3
Curtis Ho SE17 ...**151** B2
Curtis St SE1 .....**152** C4
Curtis Way SE1 ..**152** C4
Curve The W12 ...29 C2
Curwen Rd W12 ..38 C4
Curzon Cres SW6 **166** B3
Curzon Gate W1 .**117** C1
Curzon Pl W1 .....**117** C1
Curzon St W1 .....**118** A2
Custance Ho N1 ..**87** B1
Custance St N1 ..**97** B4
Custom House
SE16 ....41 B3
Cut The SE1 ......**135** C4
Cutbush Ho N7 ...13 C3
Cutcombe Mans **22**
SE5 ....48 B1
Cutcombe Rd SE5 .48 B1
Cuthbert Harrowing Ho
EC1 ....**96** C1
Cuthbert Ho W2 ..**101** B4
Cuthbert St W2 ...**89** B1
Cuthill Wlk **3** SE5 .48 C2
Cutler Ho SW11 ..**167** A4
Cutlers Gdns EC2 **110** B2
Cutlers Sq E14 ...41 C2
Cutty Sark * SE10 .52 B4
Cutty Sark Sta SE10 .52 B4
Cuxton Ho SE17 ..**152** B2
Cyclops Mews **9**
E14 ....41 C2
Cygnet St E1 ......**99** A2

Cygnus Bsns Ctr
NW10 ....8 B2
Cynthia St N1 .....**85** A1
Cypress Cl **5** E11 .19 C4
Cypress Gdns SE4 .66 A2
Cypress Ho SE14 .50 C2
Cyprus Pl **7** W1 ..**93** A1
11 E2 ....25 B3
Cyprus St E2 ......25 B3
Cyrena Rd SE22 ..64 B2
Cyril Jackson JMI Sch
E14 ....33 B2
Cyril Mans SW11 .**169** A3
Cyril Thatcher Ho
SW6 ....**165** C3
Cyrus Ho EC1 .....**96** B2
Cyrus St EC1 ......**96** B2
Czar St SE8 ....51 C4

D

D'arblay St W1 ...**105** A1
D'eynsford Rd SE5 .48 C2
D'Oyley St SW1 ..**145** B4
Da Palma Ct SW6 **155** B3
Da Vinci Ct **15** SE16 .40 A1
Dabb's La EC1 ....**95** C1
Dabin Cres SE10 ..52 B2
Dacca St SE8 ......51 B4
Dace Rd E3 ....26 C4
Dacre Ho SW3 ....**157** C3
Dacre St SW1 .....**133** B2
Daffodil St W12 ...29 B2
Dafforne Rd SW17 .72 C1
Dagmar Ct E14 ...42 B3
Dagmar Gdns NW10 .22 C3
Dagmar Pas N1 ...**86** B4
Dagmar Rd N4 .....5 C4
SE5 ....49 A2
Dagmar Terr N1 ..**86** B4
Dagnall St SW11 .**169** B3
Dagnan Rd SW12 .73 B4
Dagobert Ho **22** E1 .32 B4
Daimler Ho **8** E3 ..26 C1
Dainton Ho **22** W2 .31 C4
Daintry Way E9 ...18 B2
Dairyman Cl NW2 ...1 A1
Daisy Dormer Ct **11**
SW9 ....62 B3
Daisy La SW6 .....58 C4
Dalberg Rd SW2 ..62 C2
Dalbury Ho **6** SW9 .62 B3
Dalby Rd SW18 ...59 B3
Dalby St NW5 .....13 A2
Dale Croft N4 ......6 B1
Dale Ho NW8 .....**78** C4
SE4 ....66 A3
Dale Rd NW5 .....12 C3
SE17 ....48 A4
Dale Row W11 ....31 A3
Dale St W4 ....38 A1
Dalebury Rd SW17 .72 B2
Daleham Gdns NW3 .11 C2
Daleham Mews
NW3 ....11 C2
Dalehead NW1 ...**82** C1
Dalemain Ho **18** SW8 .**171** C2
Dalemain Mews **3**
E16 ....35 C1
Daley Ho W12 .....30 A3
Daley St E9 ....17 C2
Daley Thompson Way **1**
SW8 ....**61** A4
Dalgarno Gdns W10 .30 B4

Dalgarno Way W10 ...22 B1
Daling Way E3 ...26 A3
Dalkeith Ct SW1 ...147 C3
Dalkeith Ho 8 SW9 ...48 A2
Dalkeith Rd SE21 ...75 B4
Dalling Rd W6 ...39 A2
Dallington St EC1 ...96 B2
Dallington St EC1 ...96 B2
Dalmeny Ave N7 ...13 C4
Dalmeny Ct 5 SW4 ...172 A2
Dalmeny Rd N7 ...13 C4
Dalmeyer Rd NW10 ...8 B2
Dalmore Rd SE21 ...75 B2
Dalrymple Rd SE4 ...66 A3
Dalston Jct E8 ...16 B2
Dalston Kingsland Sta
  E8 ...16 B3
Dalston La E8 ...16 C3
Dalton Ho 6 E3 ...26 A3
  15 SE14 ...50 C4
  7 SW12 ...73 A4
Dalton St SE27 ...75 A1
Dalwood St SE5 ...49 A2
Daly Ct E15 ...76 B3
Dalyell Rd SW9 ...62 B4
Damascene Wlk
  SE21 ...75 B3
Dame St N1 ...86 C2
Damer Ho 9 TW10 ...54 B1
Damer Terr SW10 ...157 A1
Damien Ct 20 E1 ...32 A3
Damien St E1 ...32 A3
Damory Ho 1 SE16 ...40 B2
Dan Bryant Ho 5
  SW12 ...73 B4
Dan Leno Wlk
  SW6 ...156 A1
Danbury Ct N1 ...86 B2
Danby Ho 23 E9 ...17 B1
  8 W10 ...23 B2
Danby St SE15 ...64 B4
Dancer Rd SW6 ...164 C3
  Mortlake TW9 ...54 C4
Dandridge Cl SE10 ...43 B1
Dandridge Ho E1 ...110 C4
Dane Ho 15 SE5 ...48 B1
Dane Pl E3 ...26 B3
Dane St WC1 ...106 C3
Danebury W11 ...30 C2
Danebury Ave SW15 ...56 B1
Danebury Prim Sch
  SW15 ...68 B4
Danecroft Rd SE24 ...63 C2
Danehurst St SW6 ...164 A4
Danemere St SW15 ...57 B4
Danes Ct NW8 ...80 C3
Danes Ho 10 W10 ...30 B4
Danesdale Rd E9 ...18 A2
Danesfield SE5 ...49 A4
Daneville Rd SE5 ...48 C2
Daniel Bolt Cl E14 ...34 A4
Daniel Ct W3 ...29 A2
Daniel Gdns SE15 ...49 B3
Daniel's Rd SE15 ...65 B4
Daniell Ho N1 ...87 C2
Dansey Pl W1 ...119 B4
Dante Rd SE11 ...150 A4
Danube Ct 12 SE15 ...49 B3
Danube St SW3 ...144 B2
Danver Ho E1 ...111 C1
Danvers St SW3 ...157 C3
Daphne St SW18 ...59 B1
Daplyn St E1 ...111 B4
Darcy Ho E8 ...25 A4
Darell Prim Sch
  TW9 ...54 C4

Darell Rd TW9 ...54 C4
Daren Ct 7 N7 ...14 A4
Darent Ho NW8 ...101 C4
Darenth Rd N16 ...7 B3
Darfield NW1 ...82 C3
Darfield Rd SE4 ...66 B2
Darfield Way W10 ...30 C3
Darfur St 3 SW15 ...57 C4
Darien Ho 8 E1 ...32 C4
  7 SW11 ...59 C4
Darien Rd SW11 ...59 C4
Daring Ho 23 E3 ...26 A3
Darlan Rd SW6 ...155 A1
Darland Ct SW15 ...58 B1
Darley Ho SE11 ...148 C1
Darley Rd SW11 ...60 B1
Darling Rd SE4 ...66 C4
Darling Row E1 ...25 A1
Darlington Ho
  SW8 ...161 C1
Darnay Ho 6 SE16 ...139 B2
Darnell Ho 4 SE10 ...52 B2
Darnley Ho 9 E14 ...33 A3
Darnley Rd E9 ...17 B2
Darnley Terr 12
  W11 ...30 C1
Darrell Rd SE22 ...64 C2
Darren Cl N4 ...5 B4
Darsley Dr SW8 ...172 A4
Dart St W10 ...23 B2
Dartford Ho SE1 ...153 A4
Dartford St SE17 ...48 B4
Dartmouth Cl W11 ...31 C3
Dartmouth Ct SE10 ...52 B2
Dartmouth Gr SE10 ...52 B2
Dartmouth Hill
  SE10 ...52 B2
Dartmouth Ho N19 ...4 A2
  Dartmouth Pk NW5 ...4 A1
Dartmouth Park Ave
  NW5 ...4 A1
Dartmouth Park Hill
  N19 ...4 A2
Dartmouth Park Rd
  NW5 ...4 A1
Dartmouth Pl W4 ...46 A4
Dartmouth Rd NW2 ...9 C2
Dartmouth Row
  SE10 ...52 B2
Dartmouth St SW1 ...133 C3
Dartmouth Terr
  SE10 ...52 C2
Darton Ct W3 ...28 B1
Dartrey Twr SW10 ...157 B2
Dartrey Wlk SW10 ...157 A2
Darul Ammah Private
  Sch E1 ...32 A3
Darville Rd N16 ...7 B1
Darwin Ct NW1 ...81 C4
Darwin St SE17 ...151 C4
Daryngton Ho
  SW8 ...162 A1
Dashwood Ho SE21 ...76 B1
Data Point Bsns Ctr
  E16 ...27 C1
Datchelor Pl 15 SE5 ...48 C2
Datchet Ho NW1 ...92 B4
Datchett Ho 2 E2 ...98 C3
Datchwood Ct N4 ...6 B1

Datchworth Ho 8
  N1 ...15 A1
Date St SE17 ...151 B1
Daubeney JMI Sch
  E5 ...18 A4
Daubeney Rd E5 ...18 A4
Daubeney Twr 2
  SE8 ...41 B1
Dault Rd SW18 ...59 B1
Dauney Ho SE1 ...136 A3
Dave Adams Ho 7
  E3 ...26 B3
Dave Porter Hts
  SW19 ...70 A4
Davenant Ho E1 ...111 C4
Davenant Rd N19 ...4 C2
Davenant St E1 ...111 C3
Davenport Ho
  SE11 ...135 B1
Davenport Rd SE6 ...67 B1
Daventry St NW1 ...102 A4
Daver Ct SW3 ...144 B1
Davern Cl SE10 ...43 B2
Davey Cl N7 ...14 B2
Davey Lo 2 N1 ...14 C1
Davey Rd E9 ...18 C1
Davey St SE15 ...49 B4
Davey's Ct WC2 ...120 A4
David Devine Ho 7
  E8 ...16 C3
David Ho SW8 ...162 A2
  3 E14 ...34 A4
  SW15 ...56 C2
David Mews W1 ...103 C4
David St E15 ...19 C3
Davidge Ho SE1 ...135 C3
Davidge St SE1 ...136 B3
Davidson Gdns
  SW8 ...162 A2
Davidson Ho 7 N19 ...13 B4
Davies Mews W1 ...118 A4
Davies St W1 ...104 A1
Davis Ho W12 ...30 A2
Davis Rd W3 ...38 B4
Davisville Rd W12 ...38 C4
Dawes Ho SE17 ...151 B3
Dawes St SE17 ...151 C2
Dawlish Ave SW18 ...71 A2
Dawlish Rd NW2 ...9 C2
Dawn Cres E15 ...27 C4
Dawnay Gdns SW18 ...71 C2
Dawnay Rd 3 E9 ...25 B4
Dawnay Rd SW17,
  SW18 ...71 C2
Daws Ho 33 W12 ...30 A2
Dawson Ho 2 E2 ...25 B2
  5 SE5 ...49 A2
Dawson Pl
  W2 ...31 C2 113 C4
Dawson Rd NW2 ...9 B4
Dawson St E2 ...24 B3
Day Ho 5 SE5 ...48 B3
  5 SE5 ...48 B3
Daylesford Ave
  SW15 ...54 C3
Daynor Ho 4 NW6 ...23 C4
Daysbrook Rd SW2 ...74 B3
Dayton Gr SE15 ...50 B2
De Barowe Mews
  N5 ...15 A3
De Beauvoir Cres
  N1 ...24 A4
De Beauvoir Ct N1 ...15 C1

De Beauvoir JMI Sch
  N1 ...16 A2
De Beauvoir Pl 5
  N1 ...16 A2
De Beauvoir Rd N1 ...16 A1
De Beauvoir Sq N1 ...16 A1
De Crespigny Pk
  SE5 ...48 C1
De Gama Pl E14 ...41 C1
De Laune St SE17 ...150 A1
De Montfort Par 1
  SW16 ...74 A1
De Montfort Rd
  SW16 ...74 A2
De Morgan Rd SW6 ...59 A4
De Quincey Mews 3
  E16 ...35 C1
De Vere Cotts W8 ...128 C2
De Vere Gdns W8 ...128 C3
De Vere Mews W8 ...128 C2
De Walden Ho NW8 ...80 A2
De Walden St W1 ...103 C3
Deacon Ho SE11 ...149 A3
Deacon Mews N1 ...15 C1
Deacon Rd NW2 ...8 C2
Deacon Way SE17 ...151 A4
Deal Ho SE17 ...152 B2
  SE15 ...50 C4
Deal Porters Way
  SE16 ...40 C3
Deal St E1 ...111 B4
Deal Wlk SW9 ...163 C1
Dealtry Rd SW15 ...57 B3
Dean Bradley St
  SW1 ...134 A1
Dean Cl E9 ...17 B3
  SE16 ...32 C1
Dean Ct SW8 ...162 A2
Dean Farrar St
  SW1 ...133 C2
Dean Ho N4 ...6 B4
  N16 ...7 B3
  E1 ...32 B3
  SE14 ...51 B3
Dean Ryle St SW1 ...148 A4
Dean St W1 ...105 B1
Dean Stanley St
  SW1 ...134 A1
Dean Trench St
  SW1 ...134 A1
Dean's Bldgs
  SE17 ...151 C3
Dean's Ct EC4 ...108 B1
Dean's Mews W1 ...104 B2
Dean's Yd SW1 ...133 C2
Deancross St E1 ...32 B3
Deanery Mews W1 ...117 C2
Deanery St W1 ...117 C2
Deanhill Ct 2
  SW14 ...55 A3
Deanhill Rd SW14 ...55 A3
Deans Cl W4 ...45 A4
Deanshanger Ho 21
  SE8 ...40 C2
Dearmer Ho 6
  SW2 ...74 C4
Deason St E15 ...27 B4
Deauville Ct 4
  SE4 ...40 C4
  SW4 ...61 B1
Deauville Mans 3
  SW4 ...61 B1
Debdale Ho 11 E2 ...24 C4
Debenham Ct E8 ...24 C4
Debnams Rd SE16 ...40 B2
Decima St SE1 ...138 A2

Deck Cl SE16 ...32 C1
Dee Rd TW9 ...54 B3
Dee St E14 ...34 B3
Deeley Rd SW8 ...171 B4
Deepdale N4 ...5 A4
Deepdene Gdns
  SW2 ...74 B4
Deepdene Ho N16 ...6 C3
Deepdene Lo 5
  SW2 ...74 B4
Deepdene Mans
  SW6 ...164 C4
Deepdene Rd SE5,
  SE24 ...63 C3
Deer Lo SW6 ...58 A4
Deerbrook Rd SE24,
  SW2 ...75 A3
Deerdale Rd SE24 ...63 B3
Deerhurst Ho 6
  SE15 ...49 C4
Deerhurst Rd NW2 ...9 C2
Deeside Rd SW17 ...71 C1
Defoe Ave TW9 ...44 C3
Defoe Ho EC2 ...108 C4
  8 N16 ...7 A1
Defoe Pl EC2 ...108 C4
Defoe Rd N16 ...7 A1
  SE16 ...41 B4
Dekker Ho 16 SE5 ...48 C3
Dekker Rd SE21 ...64 A1
Delafield Ho E1 ...111 C1
Delaford Rd SE16 ...40 A1
Delaford St SW6 ...154 B3
Delamare Ho N4 ...6 C4
Delamere Rd W5 ...36 A4
Delamere St W2 ...100 C3
Delamere Terr W2 ...100 B4
Delancey Pas NW1 ...82 B3
Delancey St NW1 ...82 B3
Delancey Studios
  NW1 ...82 B3
Delany Ho SE10 ...52 B4
Delarch Ho SE1 ...136 A3
Delaware Rd W9 ...88 A2
Delawyk Cres SE24 ...63 C1
Delft Way 2 SE22 ...64 A2
Delhi St N1 ...84 B3
Delia St SW18 ...71 A4
Delius Gr E15 ...27 B3
Dell Cl E15 ...27 C4
Dell's Mews SW1 ...147 A3
Dellafield N4 ...5 C2
Dellow Ho 6 E1 ...32 A2
Dellow St E1 ...32 A2
Delmaine Ho 4 E14 ...33 A3
Delorean Ho 5 SE8 ...51 C2
Deloraine St SE8 ...51 C2
Delorme St W6 ...47 C4
Delta Bldg 4 E14 ...34 B3
Delta Pk SW18 ...59 A3
Delta St E2 ...99 B4
Delverton Ho SE17 ...150 B2
Delverton Rd SE17 ...150 B2
Delvino Rd SW6 ...165 C3
Dempster Rd SW18 ...59 B2
Denbigh Cl
  W11 ...31 B2 113 A4
NW10 ...8 A1
Denbigh Gdns TW10 ...54 B2
Denbigh Ho W11 ...113 A4
  SW1 ...131 A2
  7 W11 ...31 B3

Denbigh Mews
SW1 . . . . **146** C3
Denbigh Pl SW1 . . **146** C2
Denbigh Rd
W11 . . . . 31 B2 **113** A4
Denbigh St SW1 . . **147** A2
Denbigh Terr
W11 . . . . 31 B2 **113** A4
Denbury Ho **10** E3 . . 27 A2
Denby Cl SE1 . . . . **149** A4
Dence Ho E2 . . . . . . **99** B3
Denchworth Ho
SW9 . . . . **173** B1
Dendy St SW12 . . . . 73 A3
Dene Cl SE4 . . . . . . 66 A3
Dene Mans **11** NW6 . 10 C2
Denehurst Gdns
W3 . . . . 28 A1
  Mortlake TW10 . . . . 54 C3
Denesmead SE24 . . 63 B2
Denewood Rd N6 . . 3 B4
Dengie Wlk (off Maldon
Cl) N1 . . . . **86** C4
Denham Ho **23** W12 30 A2
Denham St SE10 . . **43** C1
Denholme Rd W9 . . 23 B2
Denland Ho SW8 . . **163** A1
Denman Ho N16 . . . . 7 A2
Denman Rd SE15 . . 49 B1
Denman St W1 . . . . **119** B3
Denmark Gr N1 . . . **85** B2
Denmark Hill SE5 . . 48 C1
Denmark Hill Sta
SE5 . . . . 48 B1
Denmark Mans **14**
SE5 . . . . 48 B1
Denmark Pl WC2 . . **105** C2
Denmark Rd NW6 . . 23 B3
SE5 . . . . 48 B1
Denmark St WC2 . . **105** C2
Denmead Ho **8**
SW15 . . . . 56 B1
Denmead Way SE15 49 B3
Denne Terr E8 . . . . 24 B4
Dennett's Gr SE14 . 50 C1
Dennett's Rd SE14 . 50 B2
Denning Cl NW8 . . **89** A3
Denning Point E1 . . **111** A2
Denning Rd NW3 . . 11 C4
Dennington Park Rd
NW6 . . . . 10 C2
Dennis Ho **8** E3 . . . 26 B3
Dennis Way SW4 . . 61 C4
Dennison Ho **8** E14 33 C3
Dennison Point E15 19 B1
Denny Cres SE11 . . **149** C2
Denny St SE11 . . . . **149** C2
Densham Ho NW8 . . **79** C1
Denstone Ho **5**
SE15 . . . . 49 C4
Dent Ho SE17 . . . . **152** A3
Denton NW1 . . . . . **12** C2
Denton Ho N1 . . . . . 15 A1
Denton St SW18 . . . 59 A1
Dents Rd SW11 . . . . 60 B1
Denver Rd N16 . . . . 7 A4
Denyer Ho **1** NW5 . 13 A4
Denyer St SW3 . . . . **144** B4
Denys Ho EC1 . . . . **107** B4
Denzil Rd NW10 . . . . 8 B3
Deodar Rd SW15 . . 58 A3
Depot App NW2 . . . . 9 C4
Depot Rd W12 . . . . 30 B2

Depot St SE5 . . . . . . 48 C4
Dept of Transport &
Environment
SW1 . . . . **133** C1
Deptford Bridge
SE8 . . . . 51 C2
Deptford Bridge Sta
SE8 . . . . 51 C2
Deptford Broadway
SE8,SE14 . . . . 51 C2
Deptford Church St
SE8 . . . . 51 C3
Deptford Ferry Rd **12**
E14 . . . . 41 C2
Deptford Gn SE8 . . . 51 C3
Deptford Green Sch
SE14 . . . . 51 A3
Deptford Green Sch
(Annexe) SE8 . . . . 51 A3
Deptford High St
SE8 . . . . 51 C3
Deptford Park Prim
Schs SE8 . . . . 41 A1
Deptford Sta SE8 . . 51 C3
Deptford Trad Est
SE8 . . . . 51 A4
Deptford Wharf SE8 41 B2
Derby Cl **8** E5 . . . . 17 C4
Derby Gate SW1 . . **134** A4
Derby Ho SE11 . . . . **149** B4
Derby Rd E9 . . . . . . 25 C4
SW14 . . . . 55 A3
Derby St W1 . . . . . **117** C1
Derbyshire St
E2 . . . . 24 C2 **99** C3
Dereham Ho **7** SE4 65 C3
Dereham Pl EC2 . . . **98** B2
EC2 . . . . **98** B3
Derek Walcott Cl
SE24 . . . . 63 A2
Dericote St E8 . . . . 25 A4
Dering St W1 . . . . **104** B1
Dermody Gdns
SE13 . . . . 67 C2
Dermody Rd SE13 . . 67 C2
Deronda Rd SE24,
SW2 . . . . 75 A3
Derrick Ho **13** SW2 74 C3
Derry St W8 . . . . . **128** A3
Derrycombe Ho
W11 . . . . 31 B4
W2 . . . . 31 C4
Dersingham Rd NW2 1 A1
Derwent NW1 . . . . . **92** C3
Derwent Ct **2** W6 . 38 C2
8 SE16 . . . . 40 C4
Derwent Gr SE22 . . **64** B3
Derwent Ho SW7 . . **143** A4
E3 . . . . 26 B1
Derwent St SE10 . . 43 A1
Derwentwater Mans **3**
W3 . . . . 28 B1
Derwentwater Prim Sch
W3 . . . . 28 B1
Derwentwater Rd
W3 . . . . 28 B1
Desborough Cl
W2 . . . . **100** B4
Desborough Ho
W14 . . . . **155** A4
Desenfans Rd SE21 64 A1
Desmond St SE14 . . 51 A4
Despard Ho SW2 . . 74 C2
Despard Rd N19 . . . 4 B3

Dethick Ct E3 . . . . . 26 A4
Detling Ho SE17 . . . **152** A3
Devas St E3 . . . . . . 27 A1
Deventer Cres **8**
SE22 . . . . 64 A2
Deverell St SE1 . . . **137** B1
Devereux Ct WC2 . . **107** B1
Devereux Ho **7**
SW15 . . . . 56 C2
Devereux La SW13 . 47 A3
Devereux Rd SW11 . 60 B1
Devitt Ho **4** E14 . . 34 A2
Devizes St N1 . . . . . **87** C3
Devon Mans SE1 . . **138** B4
SE1 . . . . **138** C3
SE1 . . . . **139** A3
Devon St SE15 . . . . 50 A4
Devonhurst Pl **7**
W4 . . . . 37 C1
Devonia Rd N1 . . . . **86** B2
Devonport W2 . . . **102** A2
Devonport Ho **25**
SE10 . . . . 52 B4
Devonport Rd W12 . 39 A4
Devonport St E1 . . . 32 C3
Devons Rd E3 . . . . . 27 A1
Devons Road Sta
E3 . . . . 27 A1
Devonshire Cl W1 . **104** A4
Devonshire Ct **6**
TW9 . . . . 44 B2
Devonshire Dr SE10 52 A3
Devonshire Gdns
W4 . . . . 45 B3
Devonshire Gr SE15 50 A4
Devonshire Hall **14**
E9 . . . . 17 B2
Devonshire Ho
W2 . . . . **101** C4
SE1 . . . . **136** C2
SW1 . . . . **147** C2
NW6 . . . . 10 B2
2 SW15 . . . . 69 B4
18 SW17 . . . . . . 73 A4
Devonshire Hospl
W1 . . . . **103** C4
Devonshire Mews **2**
W4 . . . . 38 A1
Devonshire Mews N
W1 . . . . **104** A4
Devonshire Mews S
W1 . . . . **104** A4
Devonshire Mews W
NW1 . . . . **104** A4
Devonshire Pl W1 . **103** C4
W8 . . . . **128** A1
W4 . . . . 1 C1
Devonshire Place Mews
W1 . . . . **103** C4
Devonshire Rd W4 . 38 A1
SE23 . . . . 65 C1
Devonshire Row
EC2 . . . . **110** B3
Devonshire Row Mews
W1 . . . . **92** B1
Devonshire Sq
EC2 . . . . **110** B2
Devonshire St W1 . **104** A4
W4 . . . . 38 A1
Devonshire Terr
W2 . . . . **101** A1
Dewar St SE15 . . . . 64 C4
Dewberry St E14 . . 34 B4
Dewey Rd N1 . . . . . **85** B2
Dewhurst Rd W14 . 39 C3
Dewsbury Ct **5** W4 37 B2

Dewsbury Rd NW10 . 8 C3
Dewsbury Terr NW1 **82** B4
Dhonau Ho SE1 . . . **153** A4
Diadem Ct W1 . . . . **105** B2
Dial Wlk The W8 . . **128** B4
Diamond Est SE17 . 72 A1
Diamond Ho **20** E3 . 26 A3
Diamond St SE15 . . 49 A3
Diamond Terr SE10 . 52 B2
Diana Ho **8** SW2 . . 62 B2
Diana Pl NW1 . . . . . **92** B2
Diana, Princess of
Wales Memorial Walk
W2 . . . . **114** C1
Dibden Ho **16** SE5 . 49 A3
Dibden St N1 . . . . . **86** C4
Dibdin Ho W9 . . . . . **78** A1
Dicey Ave NW2 . . . . 9 B3
Dick Sheppard Sch
SE24 . . . . 74 C4
Dickens Ho NW8 . . **89** C2
NW8 . . . . **94** A2
SE17 . . . . **150** B1
NW6 . . . . 23 C2
Dickens House Mus ★
WC1 . . . . **95** A1
Dickens Sq SE1 . . . **137** A2
Dickens St SW8 . . . **170** B2
Dickenson Rd N8 . . . 5 A4
Dickinson Ho **2** E2 . 99 B3
Dicksee Ho NW8 . . **89** B1
Dickson Ho **1** E1 . . 32 A3
Didbin Ho N7 . . . . . . 5 B2
Digby Bsns Ctr E9 . . 17 C2
Digby Cres N4 . . . . . 6 B2
Digby Mans W6 . . . 39 B1
Digby Rd E9 . . . . . . 17 C2
Digby St E2 . . . . . . 25 B2
Diggon St SE1 . . . . **32** C4
Dighton Ct SE17 . . . 48 B4
Dighton Rd SW18 . . 59 B3
Dignum St N1 . . . . . **85** B2
Digswell St N7 . . . . 14 C2
Dilke St SW3 . . . . . **159** A4
Dilston Gr SE16 . . . 40 B2
Dilton Gdns SW15 . 69 A3
Dimes Pl **9** W6 . . . 39 A2
Dimson Cres E3 . . . 26 C1
Dinerman Ct NW8 . . **79** A4
Dingle Gdns E14 . . 33 C2
Dingley La SW16 . . 73 C2
Dingley Pl EC1 . . . . **97** A3
Dingley Rd EC1 . . . **96** C3
Dingwall Rd SW18 . 71 B4
Dinmont Ho **28** E2 . 24 C3
Dinmont St **1** E2 . . 25 A3
Dinmore Ho **9** E9 . . 25 B4
Dinnington Ho **17**
E1 . . . . 25 A1
Dinsdale Rd SE3 . . . 53 B4
Dinsmore Rd SW12 73 A4
Dinton Ho NW8 . . . **90** A2
Dinwiddy Ho N1 . . . **84** C1
Dionis Ho SW6 . . . **165** B2
Disbrowe Rd W6 . . **154** B3
Discovery Bsns Pk
SE16 . . . . **139** C1
Discovery Ho **1**
E14 . . . . 34 B2
Disney Pl SE1 . . . . **137** A4
Disney St SE1 . . . . **137** A4
Disraeli Cl W4 . . . . 37 C2
Disraeli Gdns SW15 58 B3
Disraeli Rd NW10 . . 20 C3
SW15 . . . . 58 A3
Diss St E2 . . . . **98** C4

Distaff La EC4 . . . . **122** C4
Distillery La W6 . . . 39 B1
Distillery Rd W6 . . . 39 B1
Distillery Wlk **14**
TW8 . . . . 44 A3
Distin St SE11 . . . . **149** B3
Ditchburn St E14 . . 34 B2
Ditton Ho **10** E5 . . 17 A3
Divis Way SW15 . . . 57 A1
Dixon Clark Ct N1 . . 15 A2
Dixon Ho **1** NW10 . 30 C3
Dobree Ave NW10 . . 9 A1
Dobson Cl NW6 . . . 11 C1
Dobson Ho SE5 . . . 48 C3
10 SE14 . . . . 50 C4
Doby Ct EC4 . . . . . **123** A4
Dock Hill Ave SE16 . 40 C4
Dock Offices **17**
SE16 . . . . 40 B3
Dock Rd E16 . . . . . 35 B2
Dock St E1 . . . . . . **125** B4
Dockers Tanner Rd **13**
E14 . . . . 41 C2
Dockhead SE1 . . . . **139** A3
Dockhead Wharf
SE1 . . . . **139** A4
Docklands Heritage Mus
SE16 . . . . 33 B1
Dockley Rd SE16 . . **139** B1
Dockley Road Ind Est
SE16 . . . . **139** B1
Doctor Spurstowe
Almshos **13** E8 . . 17 A2
Docura Ho N7 . . . . . 5 B2
Docwra's Bldgs N1 . 16 A2
Dod St E14 . . . . . . 33 C3
Dodbrooke Rd SE27 75 A1
Dodd Ho **18** SE16 . 40 A2
Doddington Gr
SE17 . . . . **150** B1
Doddington Pl **4**
SE17 . . . . 48 A4
Dodson St SE1 . . . **135** C3
Dog Kennel Hill
SE5 . . . . 64 A4
Dog Kennel Hill Jun &
Inf Sch SE22 . . . . 64 A4
Dog La NW10 . . . . . 8 A4
Doggett Rd SE6 . . . 66 C1
Dolben Ct SE8 . . . . 41 B2
Dolben St SE1 . . . . **122** B1
Dolby Rd SW6 . . . . **164** C1
Dolland Ho SE11 . . **149** A1
Dolland St SE11 . . . **149** A1
Dollar Bay E14 . . . . 42 B4
Dollis Hill Sta NW2 . 8 C3
Dolman Rd W4 . . . . 37 C2
Dolman St SW4 . . . 62 B3
Dolphin Cl **3** SE16 . 40 C4
Dolphin Ct N7 . . . . 13 C4
Dolphin La E14 . . . 34 A2
Dolphin Sq SW1 . . **147** A1
Dolphin Twr **21** SE8 51 B4
Dolphin Yd NW1 . . **83** B3
4 N1 . . . . 30 C1
Dombey St WC1 . . . **106** C4
Domelton Ho SW18 59 A1
Domett Cl SE5 . . . . 63 C3
Domfe Pl E5 . . . . . 17 B4
Domingo St EC1 . . . **96** C1
Dominion St EC2 . . **109** C4
Don Phelan Cl SE5 . 48 C2
Donaghue Cotts **13**
E14 . . . . 33 A4
Donaldson Rd NW6 . 23 B4
Donegal Ho **2** E1 . 25 B1

Donegal St N1 ....85 A1
Doneraile Ho SW1 .146 A1
Doneraile St SW6 .164 A3
SW6 ....47 C2
Donkey Alley SE6 .64 C1
Donkin Ho 15 SE16 .40 A2
Donne Ct SE24 .63 B1
Donne Ho 11 N16 .15 C4
7 E14 .33 C3
SE14 .50 C4
Donne Pl SW3 .144 B4
Donnelly Ct SW6 .154 B2
Donnington Ct NW10 .9 A1
11 NW1 .13 A1
Donnington Ho
SW8 .171 B2
Donnington Prim Sch
NW10 .22 A4
Donnington Rd
NW10 .22 A4
Donovan Ct SW7 .143 B1
Donovan Ho 3 E1 .32 B2
Doon St SE1 .121 B2
Dora Ho 9 W11 .30 C2
7 E14 .33 B3
Dora St E14 .33 B3
Doradus Ct 20
SW19 .69 C3
Doran Wlk E15 .76 B1
Dorando Cl W12 .30 A2
Dorcas Ct 9 SW18 .59 C3
Dorchester Ct
SW1 .131 A1
1 N1 .16 A1
5 SE24 .63 B2
6 SW16 .74 A2
Dorchester Dr SE24 .63 B2
Dorchester Gr W4 .38 B1
Dordrecht Rd W3 .29 A1
Doria Rd SW6 .165 A2
Doric Ho 7 E2 .25 C3
Doric Way NW1 .93 B4
Doris Emmerton Ct
SW18 .70 A4
Dorking Cl SE8 .51 B4
Dorking Ho 3 SE1 .137 C2
Dorlcote Rd SW18 .72 A4
Dorleston Ct N1 .87 C3
Dorman Way NW8 .79 B4
Dormay St SW18 .59 A2
Dormstone Ho
SE17 .152 A3
Dornan Wlk E15 .27 B4
Dornberg Cl SE3 .53 C3
Dorncliffe Rd SW6 .164 B2
Dorney NW3 .12 A1
Dorney Ho SW6 .58 A4
Dornfell St NW6 .10 B3
Dornoch Ho 25 E3 .26 B3
Dornton Rd SW12,
SW17 .73 B2
Dorothy Charrington Ho
8 SE22 .64 C2
Dorothy Rd SW11 .60 B4
Dorrien Wlk SW16 .73 C2
Dorrington Point 20
E3 .27 A2
Dorrington St EC1 .107 B4
Dorrit Ho 9 W11 .30 C1
Dorrit St SE1 .137 A4
Dorset Bldgs EC4 .108 A1
Dorset Cl NW1 .102 C4
Dorset Ct 3 N1 .16 A1
Dorset Mans 2 W6 .47 C4
Dorset Mews SW1 .132 A2
Dorset Pl E15 .19 C2

Dorset Rd SW8 .162 C2
Dorset Rise EC4 .108 A1
Dorset Sq NW1 .90 C1
Dorset St W1 .103 A3
Dorville Cres W6 .39 A3
Doughty Ct 11 E1 .32 A1
Doughty Mews WC1 .94 C1
Doughty St WC1 .94 C1
Douglas Bldgs SE1 .137 A4
Douglas Ct 5 NW6 .10 C1
Douglas Gracey Ho
SW18 .70 A4
Douglas Johnstone Ho
SW6 .154 C3
Douglas Mews NW2 .1 A1
Douglas Rd N1 .15 B1
8 E16 .35 C4
Douglas Rd N N1 .15 B2
Douglas Rd S N1 .15 B2
Douglas St SW1 .147 B3
Douglas Waite Ho
NW6 .11 A1
Douglas Way SE8 .51 B3
Doulton Ho SE11 .149 A4
Doulton Mews 4
NW6 .11 A2
Dounesforth Gdns
SW18 .71 A3
Douro Pl W8 .128 B2
Douro St E3 .26 C3
Dove Ct EC2 .109 B1
Dove Mews SW7 .143 A2
Dove Rd N1 .15 C2
Dove Row E2 .24 C4
Dove Wlk SW1 .145 B2
Dovecote Gdns 3
SW14 .55 C4
Dovedale Cotts
SW11 .168 C2
Dovedale Ho N15 .6 A4
Dovedale Rd SE22 .65 A1
Dovehouse St
SW3 .144 A1
Dover Ct SE10 .52 A2
Dover Flats SE1 .152 B3
Dover Ho 5 SE15 .50 B4
7 SE15 .50 B4
Dover House Rd
SW15 .57 A2
Dover Mans 17 SW9 .62 C4
Dover Park Dr
SW15 .57 A1
Dover St W1 .118 C2
Dover Terr TW9 .44 C1
Dover Yd W1 .118 C2
Dovercourt Rd SE22 .64 B1
Doverfield Rd SW2 .74 A4
Doves Yd N1 .85 B3
Doveton Ho 6 E1 .25 B1
Doveton St 8 E1 .25 B1
Dowdeswell Cl
SW15 .56 A3
Dowding Ho N6 .3 C4
Dowell Ho SE21 .76 B1
Dowes Ho 15 SW16 .74 A1
Dowgate Hill EC4 .123 B4
Dowlas St SE5 .49 A3
Down Pl W6 .39 A1
Down St W1 .118 A1
W1 .118 A1
Downbarton Ho
SW9 .173 B4

Downbury Mews 13
SW18 .58 C2
Downend Ct 8
SE15 .49 A4
Downer's Cotts SW4 .61 B3
Downey Ho 6 E1 .25 C1
Downfield Cl W9 .88 A1
Downham Ct 1 N1 .15 C1
Downham Rd N1 .15 C1
Downing Ho
5 W10 .30 C3
6 SW15 .56 C2
Downing St* SW1 .134 A4
Drayton Park Prim Sch
N5 .14 C3
Drayton Pk N5,N7 .14 C4
Drayton Rd NW10 .21 B4
Dreadnought St
SE10 .43 A3
Dresden Cl NW6 .11 A2
Dresden Ho SE11 .149 A4
2 SW11 .169 B2
Dresden Rd N19 .4 C3
Dressington Ave
SE4 .66 C1
Drew Ho 12 SW16 .74 A1
Drewett Ho 1 E1 .111 C1
Drewstead Rd
SW16 .73 C2
Driffield Rd E3 .26 A3
Driftway Ho 13 E3 .26 B3
Drinkwater Ho 11
SE5 .48 C3
Drive Mans SW6 .164 B2
Drive The NW11 .1 A4
N7 .14 B2
NW10 .21 B4
W3 .28 B3
Droitwich Cl SE26 .76 C1
Dromore Rd SW15 .58 A1
Dron Ho 11 E1 .32 B4
Droop St W10 .23 A1
Drovers Ct 4 SE13 .67 B4
Drovers Pl SE15 .50 A3
Druce Rd SE21 .64 A1
Druid St SE1 .138 C3
Drum St E1 .111 A2
Drummer Lo N7 .5 B1
Drummond Cres
NW1 .93 B4
Drummond Gate
SW1 .147 C2
Drummond Ho 12
E2 .24 C3
Drummond Rd SE16 .40 A3
Drummond Sch NW1 .92 C2
Drummonds Pl TW9 .54 A3
Drury Ho SW8 .170 C4
Drury La WC2 .106 B1
Dryad St SW15 .57 C4
Dryburgh Ho SW1 .146 B2
Dryburgh Mans
SW15 .57 B4
Dryburgh Rd SW15 .57 B4
Dryden Ct SE11 .149 C3
Dryden Ho 8 N16 .7 A1
6 SE5 .49 A2
Dryden St WC2 .106 B1
Dryer's Bldgs EC1 .107 B3
Dryfield Wlk 8 SE8 .51 C4
Drysdale Flats 3
E8 .16 B3
Drysdale Ho 12 E2 .24 B3
Drysdale Pl N1 .98 B4
Drysdale St N1 .98 B4
Du Cane Ct SW12 .72 C3
Du Cane Rd W12 .29 C3
Du Cros Rd W3 .29 A1
Du Maurier Ho 2
NW3 .12 B3
Dublin Ave E8 .24 C4
Ducal St E2 .99 A3
Ducane Cl W12 .30 B3
Ducavel Ho SW2 .74 B3

Drayton Gdns
SW10 .143 A1
Drayton Ho 14 SE5 .48 C3
Drayton Park Sta
N5 .14 C3
Dreadnought St
Duchess Mews W1 .104 B3
Duchess of Bedford Ho
W8 .127 B4
Duchess of Bedford's
Wlk W8 .127 B3
Duchess St W1 .104 B3
Duchy St SE1 .121 C2
Ducie Ho 2 SE15 .57 B2
Ducie St SW4 .62 B3
Duck La W1 .105 B1
Duckett St E1 .33 A4
Dudden Hill La NW10 .8 B3
Dudley Ct W1 .102 C1
WC2 .106 A2
Dudley Ho W2 .101 B3
SW9 .173 B2
Dudley Mews NW6 .23 B3
Richmond TW9
Dudley St W2 .101 B3
Dudmaston Mews
SW3 .143 C2
Duff St E14 .34 A3
Duffell Ho SE11 .149 A1
Dufferin Ave EC1 .97 B1
Dufferin Ct EC1 .97 B1
Dufferin St EC1 .97 A1
Dufour's Pl W1 .105 A1
Dugard Ho N4 .6 B4
Dugdale Ho 10 N7 .13 C3
Duke Humphrey Rd
SE3 .53 A1
Duke of Wellington Pl
SW1,W1 .131 C4
Duke of York St
SW1 .119 A2
Duke Rd W4 .37 C1
Duke Shore Wharf
E14 .33 B2
Duke St St James's
SW1 .119 A2
Duke's Ave W4 .37 C1
Duke's Ho SW1 .147 C4
Duke's Mews W1 .103 C2
Duke Pl EC3 .110 B1
Duke's Rd WC1 .93 C3
Duke's Yd W1 .117 C4
Dukes Ct SE13 .52 B1
SE22 .65 A2
Dukes Gate 4 W4 .37 B2
Dukes Head Yd N6 .4 A3
Dukes La W8 .128 A4
Dukes Point N6 .4 A3
Dulas St N4 .5 B3
Dulford St
W11 .31 A2 112 A4
Dulka Rd SW11 .60 B2
Dulverton NW1 .83 A3
Dulverton Mans
WC1 .95 A1
Dulwich Coll (Endowed)
SE21 .76 A2
Dulwich Coll Picture
Gall SE21 .76 A2
Dulwich Coll Prep Sch
SE21 .76 A1
Dulwich Comm
SE21 .76 A1
Dulwich Hamlet Jun &
Inf Sch SE21 .63 C1

Dulwich High Sch for
Boys SE24 ....63 C2
Dulwich Hospl SE22 .....64 A3
Dulwich Mead SE8 ....63 B1
Dulwich Mews 1
SE22 ....64 B3
Dulwich Oaks The
SE21 ....76 B1
Dulwich Rd SE24 ....63 A1
Dulwich Village
SE21 ....64 A1
Dulwich Village CE Inf
Sch SE21 ....64 A1
Dumain Ct SE11 ....150 A3
Dumbarton Ct 16
SW2 ....74 A4
Dumbarton Rd SW2 .....62 A1
Dumont Rd N16 ....7 A1
Dumphreys Ho 5
SW4 ....73 C4
Dumpton Pl NW1 ....12 C1
Dunbar St SE27 ....75 B1
Dunboyne Rd NW3 ....12 B4
Dunbridge Ho 7
SW15 ....56 B1
Dunbridge St E2 ....25 A1
E2 ....99 B2
Duncan Gr W3 ....29 A3
Duncan Ho 3 NW3 .....12 B1
Duncan Rd E8 ....25 A4
Richmond TW9 ....54 A3
Duncan St N1 ....86 A2
Duncan Terr N1 ....86 A2
Duncannon Ho
SW1 ....147 C1
Duncannon St
WC2 ....120 A3
Dunch St **30** E1 ....32 A3
Duncombe Ho 3 ....69 C3
Duncombe Prim Sch
N19 .... 5 A3
Duncombe Rd N19 ....4 C3
Duncrievie Rd SE13 ....67 C1
Dundalk Ho 2 E1 ....32 B3
Dundalk Rd SE4 ....66 A4
Dundas Ho 12 E2 ....25 B3
Dundas Rd SE15 ....50 B1
Dundee Ct 11 E1 ....32 A1
Dundee Ho W9 ....88 C4
Dundee St E1 ....32 A1
Dundee Wharf E14 ....33 B2
Dundonald Rd
NW10 ....22 C4
Dundry Ho 8 SE26 .....76 C1
Dunelm Gr SE27 ....75 B1
Dunelm St E1 ....32 C3
Dunford Rd N7 ....14 B4
Dungarvan Ave
SW15 ....56 C3
Dungeness Ho
SW18 ....59 B3
Dunhill Point 12
SW15 ....69 A3
Dunkeld Ho **13** E14 .....34 C3
Dunlace Rd E5 ....17 C4
Dunlin Ct 11 SE21 .....75 C2
Dunlin Ho 13 SE16 .....40 C2
Dunloe Ct 7 E2 ....24 B3
Dunloe St E2 ....24 B3
Dunlop Pl SE16 ....139 A1
Dunmore Pt 6 E2 ......98 C4
Dunmore Rd NW6 ....23 A4

Dunmow Ho SE11 ......149 A2
Dunmow Rd E15 ....19 C4
Dunmow Wlk N1 ....86 C4
Dunn St E8 ....16 B3
Dunn's Pas WC1 ....106 B2
Dunnage Cres SE16 .....41 A2
Dunnet Ho **12** E3 ....26 B3
Dunnico Ho E17 ....152 A2
Dunnock Ct **10** SE21 ...75 C2
Dunollie Pl NW5 ....13 B3
Dunollie Rd NW5 ....13 B3
Dunoon Ho N1 ....84 C3
Dunraven Ho 3
TW9 ....44 B2
Dunraven Lower Sch
SW16 ....74 A1
Dunraven Rd W12 ....29 C1
Dunraven St W1 ....117 A4
Dunraven Upper Sch
SW16 ....74 B1
Dunrobin Ct NW3 ....11 A3
Dunsany Rd W14 ....39 C3
Dunsfold Ho 6
SW2 ....74 C3
Dunsford Way
SW15 ....57 A1
Dunsmure Rd N16 ....7 A3
Dunstable Ct 3
SE3 ....53 C3
Dunstable Mews
W1 ....103 C4
Dunstable Rd TW10,
TW9 ....54 A3
Dunstall Ho 9 SE15 ...49 C2
Dunstan Ho SE4 ....51 B1
Dunstan Hos E1 **11** 32 B4
Dunstan Rd NW11 ....1 C3
Dunstan's Gr SE22 .....65 A1
Dunstan's Rd SE22 ......64 C1
Dunster Ct EC3 ....124 B4
Dunster Gdns NW6 .....10 B1
Dunsterville Way
SE1 ....137 C3
Dunston Rd SW11 ...169 C1
E8 ....24 B4
Dunston St E8 ....24 B4
Dunton Ho **14** SW16 ...74 A1
Dunton Rd SE1 ....152 C3
Duntshill Rd SW18 ....71 A3
Dunworth Mews
W11 ....31 B3
Duplex Ride SW1 .....131 A3
Dupont St E14 ....33 A3
Durand Gdns SW9 .....173 A3
Durand Prim Sch
SW9 ....173 A3
Durant St E2 ..24 C2,99 B4
Durban Ho 26 W12 ....30 A2
Durbans Ho **11** NW1 ...13 B1
Durfey Ho SE5 ....48 C3
Durford Cres SW15 .....69 A3
Durham Ct 3 NW6 .....23 C3
Durham House St
WC2 ....120 B3
Durham Pl SW3 ....144 C1
Durham Rd E12 ....110 A4
Durham Row E1 ....33 A4
Durham St SE11 ....162 C4
Durham Terr W2 ......100 A2
Durley Rd N16 ....7 A4
Durlock Ho SW9 ....173 B4
Durlston Rd E5 ....7 C2
Durnford St 3 SE10 ...52 B4
Dursnford Ave
SW18,SW19 ....70 C1

Durnsford Rd SW18,
SW19 ....70 C1
Durrell Rd SW6 ....164 C3
Durrels Ho W14 ....141 A4
Durrington Rd E5 ....18 A4
Durrington Twr
SW8 ....171 A2
Durrisdeer Ho **2** NW2 ..10 B4
Dursley Cl SE3 ....53 D1
Dursley Gr SE3 ....49 A3
Durston NW5 ....12 C3
Durward St E1 ....32 A4
Durweston Mews
W1 ....103 A4
Durweston St W1 ......103 A3
Dutch Yd SW18 ....58 C2
Dutton Ho SW2 ....75 A3
Dutton St SE10 ....52 B2
Dwight Ct SW6 ....164 B2
Dycer Ho **19** E9 ....17 C2
Dye House La E3 ....26 C4
Dyer's Bldgs EC1 ....107 B3
Dyer's La SW15 ....57 A3
Dykes Ct **11** SW2 ....74 B3
Dylan Rd **2** SE24 ....63 A3
Dylways SE5 ....63 C3
Dymchurch Ho **12**
E5 ....17 A3
Dymes Path SW19 .....69 C2
Dymock St 3 SW15 .....69 B3
Dymock St SW6 ....59 A4
Dyne Rd NW6 ....10 B1
Dynevor Rd N16 ....7 B1
Richmond TW10 ....54 A2
Dynham Rd NW6 ....10 C1
Dyott St **3** 105 C2
WC1,WC2 ....106 A2
Dysart St EC2 ..24 A1,98 A1
Dyson Ho **3** SE10 ......43 B1

E

Eade Rd N4 ....6 B4
Eagle Cl SE16 ....40 B1
Eagle Ct EC1 ....108 A4
13 EC2 ....75 C2
Eagle Dwellings
EC1 ....97 A4
Eagle Ho **22** E1 ....25 A1
Eagle Hts **10** SW11 ....60 A4
Eagle Lo NW11 ....1 B4
Eagle Mans N16 ....16 B3
Eagle Pl SW1 ....119 A3
SW7 ....143 A2
Eagle St WC1 ....106 C3
Eagle Wharf E14 ......34 A2
Eagle Wharf Rd N1 .....87 A2
Ealing Tertiary Coll
W3 ....28 A1
Eamann Casey Ho
SW9 ....173 C3
Eamont Ct NW8 ....80 B2
Eamont St NW8 ....80 B2
Eardley Cres SW5 ......141 C1
Earl Ho NW1 ....90 B1
Earl Rd SW14 ....55 B3
Earl St EC2 ....110 A4
Earl's Court Ave ★
SW5 ....141 B1
Earl's Court Gdns
SW5 ....142 A3
Earl's Court Rd
SW5,W8 ....141 C4
Earl's Court Sq
SW5 ....142 A2
Earl's Court Sta
SW5 ....141 C3

Earldom Rd SW15 ......57 B3
Earlham St WC2 ....106 A1
Earlom Ho WC1 ....95 B3
Earls Terr W8 ....127 A1
Earls Wlk W8 ....127 B1
Earlsferry Way N1 ......14 A1
Earlsfield Prim Sch
SW18 ....71 B2
Earlsfield Rd SW18 .....71 B4
Earlsfield Sta SW18 ....71 B3
Earlsmead Rd NW10 ..22 B2
Earlsthorpe Mews
SW12 ....60 C1
Earlstoke St EC1 ....96 A4
Earlston Gr E9 ....25 A4
Earlswood Cl 10
SE10 ....43 A1
Earlswood Ho **2**
SW2 ....74 B3
Earlswood St SE10 ......43 A1
Early Mews NW1 ....82 B4
Earnshaw St WC1,
WC2 ....105 C2
Earsby St W14 ....140 B4
Eashing Point **5**
SW15 ....69 A3
Easley's Mews W1 ......103 C2
East Acton Arc W3 ......29 B2
East Acton La W3 ....29 A2
East Acton La W3 ....29 A1
East Acton Prim Sch
W3 ....29 A2
East Acton Sta W12 ....29 B3
East Arbour St E1 ....32 C3
East Bank N16 ....7 A4
East Block 5 E1 ....125 B2
East Churchfield Rd
W3 ....28 C1
East Cross Ctr E15 ....18 C2
East Cross Route
E9 ....18 B3
E3 ....26 C4
East Dulwich Gr
SE22 ....64 A2
East Dulwich Rd
SE15,SE22 ....64 B3
East Dulwich Sta
SE22 ....64 A3
East Ferry Rd E14 ....42 A2
East Harding St
EC4 ....107 C2
East Heath Rd NW3 ......2 C1
East Hill SW18 ....59 B2
East India Bldgs 8
E14 ....33 C2
East India Dock Basin
E14 ....35 A2
East India Dock Rd
E14 ....34 A2
East India Dock Road
Tunnel E14 ....34 C2
East India Dock Wall Rd
E14 ....34 C2
East La **12** SE16 ....139 B3
East London Coll &
Toynbee Theatre
E1 ....111 A3
East London Stadium
E3 ....33 B4
East Mount St E1 ....32 A4
East Pas EC1 ....108 C4
East Point SE1 ....153 B2
East Poultry Ave
EC1 ....108 A3

East Putney Sta
SW15 ....58 A2
East Rd N1 ....97 C4
East Row W10 ....23 A1
East Sheen Ave
SW14 ....55 C3
East Sheen Prim Sch
SW14 ....56 A3
East Smithfield E1 .....125 A3
East St SE17 ....151 B2
East Surrey Gr SE15 ...49 B3
East Tenter St E1 ....111 A1
East View NW3 ....2 C2
Eastbourne Ave W3 ....28 C3
Eastbourne Gdns
SW14 ....55 B4
Eastbourne Mews
W2 ....101 A2
Eastbourne Rd W4 .....45 B4
Eastbourne Terr
W2 ....101 A2
Eastbury Gr W4 ....38 A1
Eastbury Terr E1 ....25 C1
Eastcastle St W1 ....105 A2
Eastcheap EC3 ....124 A4
Eastcote St SW9 ....172 C1
Eastdown Ho E8 ....16 C4
Eastdown Pk SE13 .....67 C3
Eastern Rd SE4 ....66 C3
Eastfields Rd W3 ....28 B4
Eastlake Ho NW8 ....89 C1
Eastlake Rd SE5 ....48 B1
Eastlands Cres SE21 ...64 B1
Eastman Dental Hospl
WC1 ....94 C2
Eastman Rd W3 ....37 C4
Easton Ho **4** SE27 ......75 A1
Easton St WC1 ....95 B2
Eastry Ho SW8 ....162 A1
Eastvale W3 ....29 B1
Eastway E9,E10 ....18 C4
E3,E9 ....26 A4
Eastway Pk E9 ....18 B2
Eastwell Ho SE1 ....137 C2
Eastwick Ct 2
SW19 ....69 C3
Eaton Cl SW1 ....145 B3
Eaton Dr SW9 ....63 A3
Eaton Gate SW1 ....145 B4
Eaton Ho SW11 ....167 C3
Eaton House The Manor
Sch SW4 ....61 A3
Eaton La SW1 ....132 B1
Eaton Mans SW1 ....145 B3
Eaton Mews N
SW1 ....131 C1
Eaton Mews S
SW1 ....132 A1
Eaton Mews W
SW1 ....145 C4
Eaton Pl SW1 ....131 C1
Eaton Row SW1 ....132 A1
Eaton Sq SW1 ....131 C1
Eaton Terr SW1 ....145 C4
E3 ....26 A3
Eaton Terr Mews
SW1 ....145 B4
Eatonville Rd SW17 ...72 B2
Eatonville Villas
SW17 ....72 B2

Ebbisham Dr SW8 ... **162** C3
Ebbsfleet Rd NW2 ... 10 A4
Ebenezer Ho SE11 ... **150** A3
Ebenezer Mussel Ho **5**
E2 ... 25 B3
Ebenezer St N1 ... **97** B4
Ebley Cl SE15 ... 49 B4
Ebner St SW18 ... 59 A2
Ebony Ho **10** NW3 ... 11 A2
Ebor Cotts SW15 ... 68 A1
Ebor St E1,E2 ... **98** C2
Eburne Rd N7 ... 5 A1
Ebury Bridge Rd
SW1 ... **145** C1
Ebury Mews SW1 ... **146** A4
Ebury Mews E
SW1 ... **132** A1
Ebury Sq SW1 ... **145** C3
Ebury St SW1 ... **146** A4
Eccles Rd SW11 ... 60 B3
Ecclesbourne Prim Sch
N1 ... 15 C1
Ecclesbourne Rd
N1 ... 15 B1
Eccleston Ho **1**
SW2 ... 62 C1
Eccleston Mews
SW1 ... **131** C1
Eccleston Pl SW1 ... **146** A4
Eccleston Sq SW1 ... **146** B3
Eccleston Sq Mews
SW1 ... **146** C3
Eccleston St SW1 ... **146** A4
Eckersley St E1 ... 99 B1
Eckford St N1 ... 85 B2
Eckstein Rd SW11 ... 60 A3
Edans Ct W12 ... 38 B4
Edbrooke Rd W9 ... 23 C1
Eddisbury Ho **7**
SE26 ... 76 C1
Eddiscombe Rd
SW6 ... **165** A2
Eddystone Rd SE4 ... 66 A2
Eddystone Twr SE8 ... 41 A1
Eden Cl W8 ... **127** C2
NW3 ... 1 C2
Eden Gr N7 ... 14 B3
Eden Ho NW8 ... **90** A1
15 SW11 ... 60 A4
Eden Mews SW17 ... 71 B1
Edenbridge Cl **8**
SE16 ... 40 A1
Edenbridge Rd E9 ... 17 C1
Edendale ... 28 A2
Edenham Way W10 ... 31 B4
Edenhurst Ave SW6 ... 58 B4
Edensor Gdns W4 ... 46 A3
Edensor Rd W4 ... 46 A3
Edenvale St SW6 ... **166** C1
Edgar Ho SW9 ... **162** A2
E9 ... 18 A3
Edgar Kail Way ... 64 A3
Edgar Rd E3 ... 27 A2
Edgarley Terr SW6 ... 164 A3
Edgcott Ho W10 ... 30 B4
Edge St W8 ... 31 C1 **113** C2
Edgecombe Ho
4 SE5 ... 49 A1
SW19 ... 70 A4
Edgecote Cl **7** W3 ... 28 B1
Edgehill Ho **7** SW9 ... 48 A1
Edgel St SW18 ... 59 A3
Edgeley La SW4 ... 61 C4
Edgeley Rd SW4 ... 61 C4

Edgeworth Ho NW8 ... **78** C4
Edgson Ho N1 ... **146** A2
Edgware Rd W1,
W2,NW1,NW8 ... **102** A3
Edgware Road Sta
(Bakerloo) NW1 ... **102** A3
Edgware Rd Sta
(Ham,Distr,Circle)
NW1 ... **102** B3
Edinburgh Cl **7** E2 ... 25 B3
Edinburgh Ct N1
SE16 ... 32 C1
Edinburgh Ho W9 ... 88 B4
5 W3 ... 28 C3
Edington **20** NW5 ... 12 C2
Edis St NW1 ... 81 C4
Edison Ho SE1 ... **151** B4
Edith Gr SW10 ... **157** A2
Edith Ho **6** W6 ... 39 B1
Edith Neville Cotts
NW1 ... **83** B1
Edith Ramsay Ho **2**
E1 ... 33 A4
Edith Rd W14 ... **140** B3
E15 ... 19 C3
Edith Row SW6 ... **166** B4
Edith St E2 ... 24 C3
Edith Summerskill Ho
SW6 ... **154** C2
Edith Terr SW10 ... **156** C2
Edith Villas W14 ... **140** C2
Edith Yd SW10 ... **157** A2
Editha Mans SW10 ... **156** C3
Edithna St SW9 ... 62 A4
Edmeston Cl E9 ... 18 A2
Edmond Ct SE14 ... 50 B2
Edmonton Ct **5**
SE16 ... 40 B3
Edmund Ho SE17 ... **150** B1
SE14 ... 51 B2
Edmund St SE5 ... 48 C3
Edmund Waller Jun &
Inf Schs SE14 ... 50 C2
Edna St SW11 ... **168** A3
Ednam Ho SE15 ... 49 C4
Edred Ho E9 ... 18 A4
Edric Ho SW1 ... **147** C4
Edric Rd SE14 ... 50 C3
Edrich Ho SW4 ... **172** A3
Edridge Ho **6** SE27 ... 75 A1
Edward Alleyn Ho
SE21 ... 76 A4
Edward Ct **2** E16 ... 35 C4
Edward Dodd Ct N1 ... **97** C4
Edward Edward's Ho **1**
SE1 ... **122** A1
Edward Friend Ho **6**
N16 ... 7 A1
Edward Ho W2 ... 89 B1
SE11 ... **149** A2
Edward Kennedy Ho **18**
W10 ... 23 A1
Edward Mann Cl **1**
E1 ... 32 C3
Edward Mews NW1 ... **82** B1
Edward Pl SE8 ... 51 B4
Edward Robinson Ho **3**
SE14 ... 50 C3
Edward Sq N1 ... **84** C3
SE16 ... 33 A1
Edward St SE14 ... 51 B3
Edward VII Mans
NW10 ... 22 C2
Edward Wilson Prim Sch
W2 ... **100** A4

Edward's Cotts **11**
N1 ... 15 A1
Edward's La N16 ... 7 A2
Edwardes Sq W8 ... **127** A1
Edwards Mews
N1 ... **103** B1
N1 ... 14 C1
Edwin Ho SE15 ... 49 C3
Edwin St E1 ... 25 B1
E16 ... 35 C4
Edwin's Mead E9 ... 18 A4
Edwy Ho E9 ... 18 B4
Effie Ho SW4 ... **171** C1
Effie Pl SW6 ... **155** C1
Effie Rd SW6 ... **155** C1
Effingham Ho SW8 ... **171** B1
Effra Ct SW2 ... 62 B2
Effra Mans SW2 ... 62 C2
Effra Par SW2 ... 62 C2
Effra Rd SW2 ... 62 C2
Effra Road Ret Pk
SW2 ... 62 C2
Egbert Ho E9 ... 18 A3
Egbert St NW1 ... 81 B4
Egbury Ho SW15 ... 56 B1
Egerton Cres SW3 ... **144** B4
Egerton Ct **1** ... 29 C1
Egerton Dr SE10 ... 52 A2
Egerton Gdns SW3 ... **130** A1
NW10 ... 22 B4
Egerton Gdns Mews
SW3 ... **130** B1
Egerton Ho W4 ... 45 B4
Egerton Pl SW3 ... **130** B1
Egerton Rd N16 ... 7 B4
Egerton Terr SW3 ... **130** B1
Egham Cl SW19 ... 70 A2
Eglantine Rd SW18 ... 59 B2
Eglington Ct SE17 ... 48 B4
Egliston Mews
SW15 ... 57 B4
Egliston Rd SW15 ... 57 B4
Egmont St SE14 ... 50 C3
Egremont Ho SE13 ... 52 A1
Egremont Rd SE27 ... 74 C1
Egret Ho **10** SE16 ... 40 C2
Ekarra Ho SW8 ... **172** B4
Elaine Ct **19** NW3 ... 12 B2
Elaine Gr NW5 ... 12 C3
Elam Cl SE5 ... 48 A1
Elam St SE5 ... 48 A1
Eland Rd SW11 ... 60 B4
Elba Pl SE17 ... **151** A4
Elbe St SW6 ... **166** C2
Elborough St SW18 ... 70 C3
Elbury Dr E16 ... 35 C3
Elcho St SW11 ... **158** B1
Elcot Ave SE15 ... 50 A3
Elder Ct SE20 ... 51 B4
Elder St E1 ... 24 B1 **98** C1
Elder Wlk N1 ... **86** B4
Elderberry Rd W5 ... 36 A4
Elderfield Ho **8**
E14 ... 33 C2
Elderfield Rd E5 ... 17 B4
Eldon Ct NW6 ... 23 C4
Eldon Gr NW3 ... 11 C3
Eldon Ho SW9 ... 63 A4
Eldon Rd W8 ... **128** B1
Eldon St EC2 ... **109** C3
Eldon Way NW10 ... 20 A3
Eldridge Ct SE16 ... **139** B1
Eleanor Cl SE16 ... 40 C4
Eleanor Ct **13** E2 ... 24 C4

Eleanor Gr SW13 ... 56 A4
Eleanor Ho **1** NW5 ... 13 B3
18 W6 ... 39 B1
Eleanor Palmer Prim
Sch NW5 ... 13 B4
Eleanor Rathbone Ho **6**
N6 ... 4 C4
Eleanor Rd E8 ... 17 A1
E8 ... 17 A2
Electric Ave SW9 ... 62 C3
Electric Ho **12** E3 ... 26 C2
Electric La **2** SW9 ... 62 C3
Electric Mans **1**
SW9 ... 62 C3
Elephant & Castle
SE1 ... **136** B1
SE1 ... **150** B4
Elephant & Castle Sta
SE1 ... **136** B1
SE17 ... **136** B1
Elephant La SE16 ... 40 B4
Elephant Rd SE17 ... **150** C4
Elf Row E1 ... 32 B2
Elfindale Rd SE24 ... 63 B2
Elfort Rd N5 ... 14 C4
Elgar Ave SW9 ... 36 A4
Elgar Cl SE8 ... 51 C3
Elgar Ct W14 ... **126** A1
Elgar Ho SW1 ... **146** B1
NW6 ... 11 B1
Elgar St SE16 ... 41 A3
Elgin Ave W9 ... 88 B4
W12 ... 39 A3
Elgin Cres
W11 ... 31 A2 **112** B4
Elgin Ct W9 ... 88 A2
Elgin Ho **8** E14 ... 34 A3
Elgin Mans W9 ... 88 B4
Elgin Mews W11 ... 31 A3
Elgin Mews N W9 ... 88 B4
Elgin Mews S W9 ... 88 B4
Elgood Ho NW8 ... **79** C1
Elham Ho **15** E5 ... 17 A3
Elia Mews N1 ... **86** A1
Elia St N1 ... **86** A1
Elias Pl SW8 ... **163** B3
Elim Est SE1 ... **138** A2
Elim St SE1 ... **138** A2
Eliot Gdns SW15 ... 56 C3
Eliot Hill SE13 ... 52 B1
Eliot Ho **10** TW10 ... 54 B1
Eliot Mews NW8 ... **78** C1
Eliot Pk SE13 ... 52 B1
Eliot Pl SE3 ... 53 A1
Eliot Vale SE3 ... 52 C1
Elizabeth Ave N1 ... **87** A4
Elizabeth Barnes Ct **1**
SW6 ... **166** B2
Elizabeth Cl W9 ... **89** A1
12 E14 ... 34 A3
Elizabeth Cotts **3**
TW9 ... 44 C2
Elizabeth Ct SW1 ... **133** C1
SW10 ... **157** C3
SE22 ... 64 C3
Elizabeth Finn Ho
W12 ... 39 A3
Elizabeth Garrett
Anderson Hospl
NW1 ... **93** C3
Elizabeth Garrett
Anderson Sch N1 ... **85** A2
Elizabeth Gdns W3 ... 29 B1
Elizabeth Ho SE11 ... **149** C3

Elizabeth Ho continued
46 E3 ... 27 A2
8 W6 ... 39 B1
Elizabeth Ind Est
SE14 ... 50 C4
Elizabeth Kenny Ho
N1 ... 15 B2
Elizabeth Mews
NW3 ... 12 B2
Elizabeth Selby Inf Sch
E2 ... 24 C2 **99** C4
Elizabeth Sq **3**
SE16 ... 33 A2
Elizabeth St SW1 ... **145** C4
Elkington Point
SE11 ... **149** B3
Elkstone Ct **1** SE15 ... 49 A4
Elkstone Rd W10 ... 31 B4
Ella Mews NW3 ... 12 B4
Ella Rd N4,N8 ... 5 A4
Ellacombe Ho **1**
SW2 ... 74 C4
Ellaline Rd W6 ... 47 C4
Elland Ho **10** E14 ... 33 B3
Elland Rd SE15 ... 65 B3
Ellen St E1 ... **111** C1
Ellen Wilkinson Ho
SW6 ... **155** A3
7 E2 ... 25 C2
Ellenborough Ho **5**
W12 ... 30 A3
Ellenborough Pl
SW15 ... 56 C3
Ellerby St SW6 ... **164** A3
SW6 ... 47 C2
Ellerdale Rd NW3 ... 11 B3
Ellerdale St SE13 ... 67 A4
Ellerker Gdns TW10 ... 54 A1
Ellerslie Gdns
NW10 ... 21 C4
Ellerslie Ind Est
SE2 ... 62 A2
Ellerslie Rd W12 ... 30 A1
Ellerton Ct W3 ... 37 A4
Ellerton Rd SW13 ... 46 C2
SW17,SW18 ... 71 C3
Ellery Ho SE17 ... **151** C3
Ellery St SE15 ... 50 A1
Ellesmere Ct W4 ... 45 C4
Ellesmere Rd NW10 ... 8 C3
E3 ... 26 A3
Ellesmere Rd (Great
West Rd) W4 ... 45 C4
Ellesmere St E14 ... 34 A3
Ellingfort Rd E8 ... 17 A1
Ellingham Rd E15 ... 19 C4
W12 ... 38 C4
Ellington Ho SE1 ... **137** A1
Ellington St N7 ... 14 C2
Elliot Ho SW9 ... 48 A3
Elliott Rd W4 ... 38 A2
SW9 ... 48 A2
Elliott Sch SW15 ... 57 B1
Elliott's Pl N1 ... **86** B3
Elliott's Row SE11 ... **150** B4
Ellis Franklin Ct
NW8 ... **78** C2
Ellis Ho SE17 ... **151** B2
Ellis St SW1 ... **145** B4
Ellisfield Dr SW15 ... 68 C4
Ellison Ho **1** SE13 ... 52 B1
Ellison Rd SW13 ... 46 B1

Ellsworth St E2 . . . . . 25 A2
Ellwood Ct W9 . . . . . . **88** B1
Elm Bank Gdns
SW13 . . . . 46 A1
Elm Bank Mans
SW13 . . . . 46 A1
Elm Cl N19 . . . . 4 C2
Elm Court SE27 **75** B2
Elm Cres W5 . . . . 36 A4
Elm Ct EC4 . . . . **121** B4
SW9 . . . . **173** B4
SE13 . . . . 67 C4
Elm Friars Wlk
NW1 . . . . 13 C1
Elm Gn W3 . . . . 29 A3
Elm Gr NW2 . . . . 9 C3
SE15 . . . . 49 C1
Elm Grove Rd W5 . . 36 A4
SW13 . . . . 46 C1
Elm Ho 4 E14 . . . . . . 42 B4
Elm Lo SW6 . . . . 47 C2
Elm Park Gdns
SW10 . . . . **143** B1
Elm Park Ho SW10 **143** B1
Elm Park La SW3 . . . **143** B1
Elm Park Mans
SW10 . . . . **157** A4
Elm Park Rd SW3 . . **157** B4
Elm Pk SW7 . . . . 74 A2
Elm Pl SW7 . . . . **143** B2
Elm Quay SW8 . . . . . **161** B3
Elm Rd SW14 . . . . 55 B3
Elm Row NW3 . . . . 2 B1
Elm St WC1 . . . . **95** A1
Elm Terr NW2 . . . . 1 C1
Elm Tree Cl NW8 . . . **89** B4
Elm Tree Ct NW8 . . . **89** B4
5 SE5 . . . . 48 B2
Elm Tree Rd NW8 . . **89** B4
Elm Way NW10 . . . . . . 8 A4
Elm Wlk NW3 . . . . 1 C2
Elm Wood Prim Sch
SE27 . . . . **75** B2
Elmar Ct SW6 . . . . . . **164** B2
Elmbourne Rd
SW17 . . . . 73 A2
Elmbridge Wlk E8 . . 16 C1
Elmcourt Rd SE21,
SE27 . . . . 75 A2
Elmcroft N6 . . . . 4 B4
Elmcroft Ave NW11 . . 1 B4
Elmcroft Cres NW11 . 1 A4
Elmcroft St E5 . . . . . . 17 B4
Elmer Ho NW1 . . . . . **102** A4
Elmfield Ho 6 N5 . . 15 B3
W9 . . . . 23 C1
Elmfield Mans 5
SW17 . . . . 72 C2
Elmfield Rd SW17 . . 72 C2
Elmfield Way W9 . . 31 C4
Elmhurst Mans
SW4 . . . . 61 C4
Elmhurst St SW4 . . . 61 C4
Elmhurst Villas
SE15 . . . . 65 B3
Elmington Rd SE5 . . 48 C3
Elmira St SE13 . . . . . 67 A4
Elmore Ho SW9 . . . . 48 A1
Elmore St N1 . . . . . . 15 C1
Elms Cres SW4 . . . . . 61 C1
Elms Mews W2 . . . . . **115** B4
Elms Rd SW4 . . . . 61 B2
Elms The NW11 . . . . . 21 A3

Elms The continued
SW13 . . . . 56 B4
Elmshaw Rd SW15 . . 56 C2
Elmslie Point 2 E3 . . 33 C4
Elmstone Rd SW6 . . **165** B4
Elmton Ct NW8 . . . . . **89** B2
Elmton Way E5 . . . . . . 7 C1
Elmwood Ct SW11 . . **170** A4
Elmwood Ho NW10 . . 21 C4
NW10 . . . . 22 A3
Elmwood Rd W4 . . . . 45 B4
SE24 . . . . 63 C2
Elmworth Gr SE21 . . 75 C2
Elnathan Mews W9 **88** B1
Elphinstone St N5 . . 15 A4
Elrington Rd E8 . . . . 16 C2
Elsa St E1 . . . . 33 A4
Elsdale St E9 . . . . 17 B1
Elsden Mews E2 . . . . 25 B3
Elsenham St SW18,
SW19 . . . . 70 B2
Elsfield NW5 . . . . 13 A3
Elsham Rd W14 . . . . **126** A3
Elsham Terr W14 . . . **126** A3
Elsie Lane Ct W2 . . **100** A3
Elsiemaud Rd SE4 . . 66 B2
Elsinore Gdns NW2 . . 1 A1
Elsinore Ho N1 . . . . . 16 A3
Elsinore Ho SE1 . . . **122** C2
15 SE5 . . . . 48 B1
Elsinore Way TW9 . . 55 A4
Elsley Rd SW11 . . . . 60 C4
Elsley Rd SW11 . . . . 60 C4
Elspeth Rd SW11 . . . 60 B3
Elstead Ho 9 SW2 . . 74 B4
Elsted St SE17 . . . . . **151** C3
Elstow Grange NW6 . 9 C1
Elswick Rd SE13 . . . . 52 A1
Elswick St SW6 . . . . **166** C2
SW6 . . . . **166** C2
Elsworthy Rd NW3 . . **80** A4
Elsworthy Rise NW3 12 A1
Elsworthy Terr NW3 12 A1
Elsynge Rd SW18 . . 59 C2
Elsynge Road Mans
SW18 . . . . 59 C2
Elthiron Rd SW6 . . . **165** C3
Elthorne Rd N19 . . . . . 4 C2
Elthruda Rd SE13 . . . 67 C1
Elton Ho 3 E3 . . . . . 26 B4
Elton Pl N16 . . . . 16 A3
Elton St 11 N16 . . . . 16 A3
Eltringham St SW18 59 B3
Elvaston Mews
SW7 . . . . **129** A2
Elvaston Pl SW7 . . . **129** A1
Elveden Ho 10 SW9 . 63 A3
Elver Gdns E2 . . . . . . 25 A2
Elverson Rd SE8 . . . . 52 A1
Elverson Rd Sta
SE8 . . . . 52 A1
Elverton St SW1 . . . **147** B4
Elvin Ho 8 E9 . . . . . 17 B2
Elvis Rd NW2 . . . . 9 B2
Elwin St E2 . . 24 C2 **99** B4
Elwood Ho N5 . . . . 6 A1
Elwood St N4,N5 . . . . 6 A1
Elworth Ho SW8 . . . **163** A1
Ely Cottages SW8 **163** A1
Ely Court Flats
SW6 . . . . **164** A3
Ely Ho 22 SE15 . . . . 49 C3
Ely Pl EC1 . . . . **107** C3
Elysium Gate SW6 . **164** C1
Elysium St SW6 . . . **164** C1

Elystan Pl SW3 . . . . **144** C2
Elystan St SW3 . . . . **144** B3
Elystan Wlk N1 . . . . . **85** B3
Elyston Ct SW15 . . . . 57 A2
Emanuel Ave W3 . . . 28 B3
Emanuel Ho SW1 . . **133** B2
Emanuel Sch SW11 . 60 A2
Emba St SE16 . . . . . . **139** C3
Embankment SW15 47 C1
Embankment Gdns
SW3 . . . . **159** A4
Embankment Pier
WC2 . . . . **120** B2
Embankment Pl
WC2 . . . . **120** B2
Embankment Sta
WC2 . . . . **120** B2
Embassy Ct Mews
NW6 . . . . 79 C1
Embassy Ho 2 NW6 . 10 C1
Ember Ct 2 W12 . . . 38 A3
Emberton SE5 . . . . . . 49 A4
Emberton Ct EC1 . . **96** A3
Embleton Rd SE13 . . 67 A3
Embley Point 2 E5 . . 17 A4
Emden St SW6 . . . . . **166** B4
Emerald Rd NW10 . . 20 C4
Emerald St WC1 . . . **106** C4
Emerson Ho N16 . . . 16 A3
Emerson St SE1 . . . **122** C2
Emery Hill St SW1 . . **133** A1
Emery St SE1 . . . . . **135** C2
Emily Pl N7 . . . . 14 C4
Emily St 2 E16 . . . . 35 B1
Emlyn Gdns 3 W12 38 B3
Emlyn Rd W12 . . . . . 38 B3
Emma St E2 . . . . 25 A3
Emmanuel CE Prim Sch
NW6 . . . . 10 C3
Emmanuel Ho
SE11 . . . . **149** B3
Emmanuel Rd SW12 73 C3
Emminster NW6 . . . **78** A4
Emmott Cl E1 . . . . . . 26 A1
Emperor's Gate
SW7 . . . . **142** C4
Empingham Ho 20
SE8 . . . . 40 C2
Empire Ho SW3 . . . **130** A1
Empire Wharf E3 . . . 26 A4
Empire Wharf Rd
E14 . . . . 42 C2
Empress Pl SW5 . . . **141** B1
Empress St SE17 . . . 48 B4
Empson St 3 E3 . . . 27 A1
Emsworth St SW2 . . 74 B2
Emu Rd SW8 . . . . . . **170** A1
Enard Ho 27 E3 . . . . 26 B3
Enbrook St W10 . . . . 23 A2
Endeavour Way
SW18 . . . . 71 A1
Endell St WC2 . . . . . **106** A1
Enderby St SE10 . . . 43 A1
Endlesham Ct 2
SW12 . . . . 72 C4
Endlesham Rd
SW12 . . . . 72 C4
Endsleigh Gdns
WC1 . . . . **93** B2
Endsleigh Mans 4
SW16 . . . . 74 A1
Endsleigh Pl WC1 . . **93** C2
Endsleigh St WC1 . . **93** C2
Endwell Rd SE4 . . . . 51 A1
Endymion Rd N4 . . . . 6 A4
SW2 . . . . 62 B1

Energen Cl NW10 . . . . 8 A1
Enfield Cloisters
N1 . . . . **98** A4
Enfield Ho 27 SW9 **172** B2
Enfield Rd E8,N1 . . . 16 A1
W3 . . . . 37 A4
Enford St W1 . . . . . . **102** C4
Engadine St SW18 . . 70 C3
Engate St SE13 . . . . 67 B3
England's La NW3 . . 12 B2
Englefield NW1 . . . . **92** C3
Englefield Rd N1 . . . 16 A1
Englewood Rd
SW12 . . . . 61 B1
English Grounds
SE1 . . . . **124** A1
English Martyrs JMI
Sch SE17 . . . . **151** C3
English Martyrs RC Sec
Sch SE17 . . . . **151** C3
English St E3 . . . . 26 B1
Enid St SE16 . . . . . . **139** A2
Enid Stacy Ho 11
N19 . . . . 4 C4
Enmore Ct SW14 . . . 55 C2
Enmore Gdns SW14 55 C2
Enmore Rd SW15 . . 57 B2
Ennerdale Ho 3 N4 . 6 C4
Ennerdale Rd TW9 . . 44 B1
Ennersdale Prim Sch
SE13 . . . . 67 C2
Ennersdale Rd SE13 67 C2
Ennis Ho 10 E14 . . . 34 A3
Ennis Rd N4 . . . . 5 C3
Ennismore Ave W4 38 B2
Ennismore Gdns
SW7 . . . . **130** A3
Ennismore Gdns Mews
SW7 . . . . **130** A2
Ennismore Mews
SW7 . . . . **130** A2
Ennismore St SW7 . **130** A2
Ensbury Ho SW8 . . . **162** C2
Ensign Ind Ctr E1 . . **125** B3
Ensign St E1 . . . . . . **125** B4
Ensor Mews SW7 . . **143** B2
Enterprise Way
NW10 . . . . 21 C2
SW18 . . . . 58 C3
Enterprize Way SE8 . 41 B2
Epirus Mews SW6 . . **155** B2
Epirus Rd SW6 . . . . **155** A2
Epping Cl E14 . . . . . 41 C2
Epping Ho 5 E5 . . . . . 7 C2
Epple Rd SW6 . . . . . **165** A4
Epworth St EC2 . . . . **97** C1
Equity Sq E2 . . . . . . **99** A3
Erasmus St SW1 . . . **147** C3
Erconwald St W12 . . 29 B3
Eresby Ho SW7 . . . . **130** B3
Eresby Pl NW6 . . . . . 10 C1
Eric Fletcher Ct 7
N1 . . . . 15 B1
Eric Macdonald Ho
SW6 . . . . **165** C3
Eric Rd NW10 . . . . 8 B2
Eric Rd W3 . . . . 28 B3
Eric Wilkins Ho
SE1 . . . . **153** B1
Erica Ct SW4 . . . . . . **172** B3
Erica Ho SE4 . . . . . . 66 B4
Erica St W12 . . . . . . 29 C2
Ericcson Cl SW18 . . 58 C2

Ericson Ho N16 . . . . . . 7 B3
SE13 . . . . 67 C3
Eridge Ho SE22 . . . . 64 B4
Eridge Rd W4 . . . . . . 37 C3
Erlanger Rd SE14 . . 50 C1
Ermine Rd SE13 . . . . 67 A3
Ernest Bevin Sch
SW17 . . . . 72 A1
Ernest Gdns W4 . . . 45 A4
Ernest Simmonds Ho
SE14 . . . . 50 B1
Ernest St E1 . . . . 25 C1
Ernshaw Pl SW15 . . 58 A2
Eros (Shaftesbury
Meml)* W1 . . . . . . **119** B3
Erpingham Rd
SW15 . . . . 57 B4
Errington Rd W9 . . . 23 B1
Errol St EC1 . . . . **97** A1
Erskine Ho SW1 . . . **146** C1
Erskine Rd NW3 . . . 12 B1
Esher Ho SW8 . . . . . **171** C2
Esher Gdns SW19 . . 69 C2
Esk Ho E3 . . . . 26 B1
Eskdale NW1 . . . . **82** C1
Esme Ho SW15 . . . . 56 B3
Esmeralda Rd SE1 . **153** C3
Esmond Ct W8 . . . . **128** B2
Esmond Gdns W4 . . 37 C2
Esmond Rd NW6 . . . 23 B4
W4 . . . . 37 C2
Esmond St SW15 . . . 58 A3
Esparto St SW18 . . . 71 A4
Essendine Mans
W9 . . . . 23 C2
Essendine Prim Sch
W9 . . . . 23 C2
Essendine Rd W9 . . 23 C2
Essex Ct EC4 . . . . . . **107** B1
W6 . . . . 39 B3
SW13 . . . . 46 B1
Essex Ho 2 E14 . . . . 34 A3
Essex Park Mews
W3 . . . . 29 A1
Essex Pl W4 . . . . 37 B2
Essex Place Sq W4 37 C2
Essex Rd N1 . . . . 86 B4
W3 . . . . 8 A1
W4 . . . . 37 C2
Essex Road Sta N1 . 15 B1
Essex St WC2 . . . . . **121** B4
Essex Villas W8 . . . **127** B3
Essian St E1 . . . . 33 A4
Essington SW15 . . . 58 A1
Estcourt Rd SW6 . . **154** C2
Este Rd SW11 . . . . . 60 A4
Estella Ho W11 . . . . 30 C2
Estelle Rd NW3 . . . . 12 B4
Esterbrooke St
SW1 . . . . **147** B3
Estoria Cl 22 SW2 . . 74 C4
Etal Ho N1 . . . . 15 A1
Etchingham Rd E15 . 76 B4
Ethel Rankin Ct
SW6 . . . . **164** C2
Ethel St SE17 . . . . . **151** A3
Ethelbert Ho E9 . . . 18 A4
Ethelbert St SW12 . . 73 A3
Ethelburga Prim Sch
SW11 . . . . **168** B4
Ethelburga St
SW11 . . . . **168** B4
Ethelburga Tower
SW11 . . . . **168** B4

Ethelden Rd W12 .....30 A1
Ethelworth Ct 4
 SW2 .....74 C3
Etherow St SE22 .....76 C1
Ethnard Rd SE15 .....50 A4
Eton Ave NW3 .....12 A1
Eton Cl SW18 .....71 A4
Eton College Rd
 NW3 .....12 B2
Eton Ct NW3 .....11 C1
Eton Garages 11
 NW3 .....12 A2
Eton Hall NW3 .....12 B2
Eton Ho N5 .....15 A4
Eton Pl NW1 .....12 C1
Eton Rd NW3 .....12 B2
Eton Rise NW3 .....12 B2
Eton St SW10 .....54 A2
Eton Villas NW3 .....12 B2
Etta St SE8 .....51 A4
Ettrick St E14 .....34 B3
Eugene Cotter Ho
 SE17 .....151 C3
Eugenia Rd SE16 .....40 B2
Euro Cl NW10 .....8 C2
Eurolink Bsns Ctr
 SW2 .....62 C2
Europa Pl EC1 .....96 C3
Eustace Ho SE11 .....148 C4
Eustace Rd SW6 .....155 B2
Euston Rd NW1 .....93 A2
Euston Sq NW1 .....93 B3
Euston Square Sta
 WC1 .....93 A2
Euston St NW1 .....93 A3
Euston Sta NW1 .....93 A3
Euston Underpass
 NW1 .....92 C2
Evandale Rd SW9 .....173 C2
Evangelist Rd NW5 .....13 A4
Evans Cl E8 .....16 B2
Evans Ho SW8 .....161 C1
34 W12 .....30 A2
Evelina Mans 6
 SE5 .....48 C3
Evelina Rd SE15 .....50 B1
Eveline Lowe Prim Sch
 SE1 .....153 C1
Evelyn Ct N1 .....87 B1
 W1 .....102 C1
 E8 .....16 C4
Evelyn Denington Ct 2
 N1 .....15 A1
Evelyn Fox Ct W10 .....30 B4
Evelyn Gdns SW7 .....143 B1
 Richmond TW9 .....54 A3
Evelyn Ho W12 .....38 B4
 3 SW2 .....62 A2
 Richmond TW9 .....54 A3
Evelyn Rd W4 .....37 C3
 Richmond TW9 .....54 A4
Evelyn St SE8 .....41 A1
Evelyn Terr TW9 .....54 A4
Evelyn Wlk N1 .....87 B1
Evelyn Yd W1 .....105 B2
Evenwood Cl SW15 .....58 A2
Everard Ho 1 E1 .....111 C1
Everatt Cl SW18 .....58 B2
Everdon Rd SW13 .....46 C4
Everest Pl E14 .....34 B4
Everett Ho SE17 .....151 C2
 7 N7 .....14 C4
Everilda St N1 .....85 A3
Evering Rd E5,N16 .....7 C1
Everington St W6 .....47 C4
Everitt Rd NW10 .....20 C1
Everleigh St N4 .....5 B3

Eversfield Rd TW9 .....44 B1
Evershed Ho E1 .....111 A2
Evershed Wlk 5 W4 .....37 C2
Evershot Rd N4 .....5 B3
Eversleigh Rd
 SW11 .....169 B1
Eversley Ho E2 .....99 B3
Everthorpe Rd SE15 .....64 B4
Everton Bldgs NW1 .....92 C3
Evesham Ho NW8 .....78 C3
 2 SW1 .....146 B2
 1 E2 .....25 B3
Evesham St W11 .....30 C2
Evesham Way SW11 .....60 C4
Evesham Wlk 3
 SE5 .....48 C1
Ewald Rd SW6 .....164 C1
Ewart Pl 18 E3 .....26 B3
Ewe Cl N7 .....14 A2
Ewen Cres SW2 .....74 C4
Ewen Ho N1 .....84 C3
Ewer St SE1 .....122 C1
Ewhurst 13 SW15 .....57 C1
Ewhurst Cl E1 .....32 B4
Ewhurst Rd SE4 .....66 B1
Exbury Ho 5 E9 .....17 B2
 8 SW9 .....62 B3
Excel Ct WC2 .....119 C3
Excelsior Gdns SE13 .....52 B1
Excelsior Ind Est
 SE16 .....50 B4
Exchange Arc EC2 .....110 B4
Exchange Ct WC2 .....120 B3
Exchange Mans 2
 NW11 .....1 B4
Exchange Pl EC2 .....110 A4
Exeter Ct NW6 .....23 C3
Exeter Ho W2 .....100 C2
 11 SE15 .....49 C4
 SW15 .....57 B1
Exeter Mans NW2 .....10 A2
Exeter Mews NW6 .....155 B2
Exeter Rd NW2 .....10 A2
 E16 .....35 C4
Exeter St WC2 .....120 C4
Exeter Way 2 SE14 .....51 B3
Exford Ct SW11 .....167 C4
Exhibition Cl W12 .....30 B2
Exhibition Rd SW7 .....129 C2
Exmoor Ho 23 E3 .....26 A3
Exmoor St W10 .....30 C4
Exmouth Ho 6 E14 .....42 A2
Exmouth Market
 EC1 .....95 C2
Exmouth Mews
 NW1 .....93 A3
Exmouth Pl E8 .....17 A1
Exmouth St E1 .....32 B3
Exon St SE17 .....152 A3
Exonbury NW8 .....78 B3
Exton St SE1 .....121 B1
Eynella Rd SE21 .....76 B4
Eynham Rd W12 .....30 B3
Eynsford Ho SE1 .....137 B4
 12 SE15 .....50 B4
Eyot Gdns W6 .....38 B1
Eyot Gn W4 .....38 B1
Eyre Ct NW8 .....79 B2
Eyre St Hill EC1 .....95 B1
Eythorne Rd SW9 .....173 C3
Ezra St E2 .....99 A4

Fabian Rd SW6 .....155 A2

Fabyn Ho TW9 .....44 C3
Fair St SE1 .....138 C4
Fairacres SW15 .....56 C3
Fairbairn Gn 1
 SW9 .....48 A2
Fairbridge Rd N19 .....4 C2
Fairburn Ct SW15 .....58 A2
Fairburn Ho SW5 .....141 A1
 7 N16 .....7 A3
Fairby Ho SE1 .....153 A4
Faircharm Trad Est
 SE8 .....52 A3
Fairchild Cl SW11 .....167 C1
Fairchild Ho N1 .....98 A4
 SW1 .....147 A3
 12 E9 .....17 B1
Fairchild Pl EC2 .....98 B1
Fairchild St EC2 .....98 B1
Fairclough St E1 .....111 C1
Faircourt 14 NW3 .....12 B2
Faircroft N22 .....81 C4
Fairdale Gdns SW15 .....57 A3
Fairdene Ct N7 .....14 A3
Fairfax Ho SW9 .....173 C1
 6 SW15 .....56 C2
Fairfax Mews SW15 .....57 B3
Fairfax Pl NW6 .....11 B1
 W14 .....126 A1
Fairfax Rd NW6 .....11 B1
 W4 .....38 A3
Fairfield NW1 .....82 C3
 3 E1 .....32 B4
Fairfield Ct NW10 .....21 C4
 1 SW18 .....59 A2
Fairfield Dr SW18 .....59 A2
Fairfield Rd E3 .....26 C3
Fairfield St SW18 .....59 A2
Fairfoot Rd E3 .....26 C1
Fairford Ho SE11 .....149 C3
Fairhazel Gdns
 NW6 .....11 B1
Fairheathe SW15 .....57 C1
Fairholme Rd W14 .....140 B1
Fairholt Cl N16 .....7 A3
Fairholt Rd N16 .....6 C3
Fairholt St SW7 .....130 B2
Fairhurst 4 NW6 .....11 A3
Fairlawn Ave W4 .....37 B2
Fairlawn Ct 3 W4 .....37 B2
Fairlawn Gr W4 .....37 B2
Fairlawn Mans SE14 .....50 C2
Fairlawns SW15 .....57 C2
Fairlie Ct 1 N7 .....13 C4
 22 E3 .....27 A2
Fairlight Ave NW10 .....21 A3
Fairlight Ct NW10 .....21 A3
Fairlop Pl NW8 .....89 C3
Fairmead Ho E9 .....18 A4
Fairmead Rd N7,N19 .....5 A1
Fairmont Ho 3 E3 .....26 C1
Fairmount Rd SW2 .....62 B1
Fairstead Wlk N1 .....86 C4
Fairthorn Rd SE7,
 SE10 .....43 C1
Fairview Ho 2 SW2 .....74 B4
Fairview Pl SW2 .....74 B4
Fairwall Ho 9 SE5 .....49 A2
Fairway Cl NW11 .....2 A4
Fairway Ct 13 SE16 .....40 C4
Fairway The W3 .....29 A3
Fairweather Ho N7 .....14 A4
Faith Ct NW2 .....9 A2
Faithfull Ho N5 .....15 B3
Fakruddin St
 E1 .....24 C1 99 C1
Falcon Cl SE1 .....122 B2
 W4 .....45 B4

Falcon Ct N1 .....86 B1
 2 EC4 .....107 B1
 8 SE21 .....75 C2
Falcon Gr SW11 .....60 A4
Falcon Ho 10 SE15 .....49 B2
Falcon La SW11 .....60 A4
Falcon Lo NW3 .....11 A4
 1 W9 .....31 C4
Falcon Point SE1 .....122 B3
Falcon Rd SW11 .....60 A4
Falcon Terr SW11 .....60 A4
Falcon Way E14 .....42 A2
Falconberg Ct W1 .....105 C2
Falconberg Mews
 W1 .....105 C2
Falconbrook Prim Sch
 SW11 .....59 C4
Falconer Wlk 12 N7 .....5 B2
Falconwood Ct SE3 .....53 B1
Falkener Ct SW11 .....169 C3
Falkirk Ct 11 SE16 .....32 C1
Falkirk Ho W9 .....88 B4
Falkirk St N1 .....24 A3
Falkland Ho W8 .....128 A1
 W14 .....140 C2
Falkland Pl 2 NW5 .....13 B3
Falkland Rd NW5 .....13 B3
Falladon Ho W11 .....31 B4
Fallodon Ho SW8 .....171 C2
Fallow Ct SE16 .....153 C1
Fallowfield N4 .....5 B2
Falmouth Ho 4
 W2 .....116 A4
 SE11 .....149 C2
Falmouth Rd SE1 .....137 A1
Falmouth St E15 .....19 C3
Falstaff Ct SE11 .....150 A3
Falstaff Ho 18 N1 .....24 A3
Fane Ho 3 E2 .....25 B4
Fane St W14 .....155 A4
Fann St EC1 .....97 A1
Fanshaw St N1 .....98 A4
Fanthorpe St SW15 .....57 B4
Faraday Cl N7 .....14 B2
Faraday Ho 6 NW5 .....13 A4
 W10 .....31 A4
 6 E14 .....33 B2
 SW12 .....73 A4
Faraday Rd W3 .....28 B2
 W10 .....31 A4
Fareham Ho 13
 SW15 .....68 C3
Fareham St W1 .....105 B2
Farjeon Ho NW6 .....11 C1
Farleigh Pl N16 .....16 B4
Farleigh Rd N16 .....16 B4
Farley Ct NW1 .....91 B1
 W14 .....126 C2
Farley Rd SE13 .....67 B1
Farlington Pl SW15 .....69 A4
Farlow Rd SW15 .....57 C4
Farlton Rd SW18 .....71 A4
Farm Ave NW2 .....1 B1
Farm Cl SW6 .....155 C2
Farm La SW6 .....155 C2
Farm Lane Trad Ctr
 SW6 .....155 C3
Farm Pl W8 .....31 C1
Farm St W1 .....118 A3
Farmdale Rd SE10 .....43 C1
Farmer Ho 4 SE16 .....40 A3
Farmer Rd SW8 .....113 B2
Farmers Rd SE5 .....48 A3
Farmleigh Ho SW9 .....63 A2
Farnaby Ho 2 W10 .....23 B2
Farnborough Ho 1
 SW15 .....68 C3

Farnborough Way 10
 SE15 .....49 A3
Farncombe St
 SE16 .....139 C3
Farndale Ho NW6 .....78 A4
Farnell Mews SW5 .....142 A2
Farnell Point 5 .....16 C4
Farnham Ct 2 N16 .....7 A3
Farnham Ho NW1 .....90 B1
 SE1 .....122 C1
Farnham Pl SE1 .....122 B1
Farnham Royal
 SE11 .....149 A1
Farnhurst Ho
 SW11 .....169 B2
Farningham Ho 9
 N4 .....6 C4
Farnley Ho SW8 .....171 B2
Farnworth Ho 5
 E14 .....42 C2
Faroe Rd W14 .....39 C3
Farquhar Rd SW19 .....70 C1
Farrance St E14 .....33 C3
Farrant Ho 19 SW11 .....59 C4
Farrell Ho E1 .....32 B3
Farrer Ho SE8 .....51 C3
Farrier St NW1 .....13 B1
Farrier Wlk SW10 .....156 C4
Farringdon La EC1 .....95 C1
Farringdon Rd EC1 .....95 C1
Farringdon St EC4 .....108 A2
Farringdon Sta
 EC1 .....108 A4
Farrins Rents SE16 .....33 A1
Farrow La SE14 .....50 B3
Farrow Pl SE16 .....41 A3
Farthing Alley SE1 .....139 B3
Farthing Fields 8
 E1 .....32 A1
Fashion St E1 .....111 A3
Fassett Rd E8 .....16 C2
Fassett Sq E8 .....16 C2
Fauconberg Ct W4 .....45 B4
Fauconberg Rd W4 .....45 B4
Faulkner Ho SW15 .....47 B1
Faulkner St SE14 .....50 B2
Faulkner's Alley
 EC1 .....108 A4
Faunce Ho 1 SE17 .....48 A4
Faunce St SE17 .....150 A1
Favart Rd SW6 .....165 C4
Faversham Ho NW1 .....83 A3
 SE17 .....152 A1
Fawcett Cl SW11 .....167 C1
Fawcett Est E5 .....7 C3
Fawcett Ho SW9 .....172 B2
Fawcett Rd NW10 .....8 B1
Fawcett St SW10 .....156 C4
Fawe Park Rd SW15 .....58 B3
Fawe St E14 .....34 A4
Fawkham Ho SE1 .....153 A3
Fawley Lo 2 E14 .....42 C2
Fawley Rd NW6 .....11 A3
Fawnbrake Ave
 SE24 .....63 B2
Faygate Rd SW2 .....74 B2
Fearnley Ho SE5 .....49 A1
Fearon St SE10 .....43 C1
Feathers Pl SE10 .....52 C4

Featherstone St
EC1 ....97 B2
Featley Rd SW9 ....63 A4
Felbridge Ho **22**
SE22 ....76 A2
Felday Rd SE13 ....67 A1
Felden St SW6 ....164 C3
Feldman Cl N16 ....7 C3
Felgate Mews **4**
W6 ....39 A2
Felix St **19** E2 ....25 A3
Felixstowe Rd
NW10 ....22 A2
Fellbrigg Rd SE22 ....64 B2
Fellbrigg St **21** E1 ....25 A1
Fellows Ct E2 ....24 B3
Fellows Rd NW3 ....12 A1
Fells Haugh **6** W3 ....28 B3
Felltram Way SE7 ....43 C1
Felmersham Cl **2**
SW4 ....61 C3
Felsberg Rd SW2 ....74 A4
Felsham Ho SW15 ....57 C4
Felsham Rd SW15 ....57 C4
Felstead St E9 ....18 B2
Felstead Wharf E14 ....42 B1
Felton Ho N1 ....87 C3
Felton St N1 ....87 C3
Fen Ct EC3 ....124 A4
Fen St E16 ....35 B2
Fenchurch **34** N1 ....24 A4
Fenchurch Ave
EC3 ....110 A1
Fenchurch Bldgs
EC3 ....110 B1
Fenchurch Pl EC3 ....124 B4
Fenchurch St EC3 ....124 B4
Fenchurch Street Sta
EC3 ....124 B4
Fendall St SE1 ....138 B1
Fender Ct SW4 ....172 A2
Fendt Cl **6** E16 ....35 B1
Fenelon Pl W14 ....141 A3
Fenham Rd SE15 ....50 A3
Fenner Cl SE16 ....40 A2
Fenner Ho **25** E1 ....32 A1
Fenner Sq **10** SW11 ....59 C4
Fenning St SE1 ....138 A4
Fenstanton Prim Sch
SW2 ....74 C3
Fentiman Rd SW8 ....162 C2
Fenton Cl SW9 ....172 C1
E8 ....16 B2
Fenton Ho SE14 ....51 A3
Fenton St E1 ....32 A3
Fentons SE3 ....53 B3
Fenwick Gr SE15 ....64 C4
Fenwick Pl SW9 ....62 A4
Fenwick Rd SE15 ....64 C4
Ferdinand Ho **1**
NW1 ....13 A1
Ferdinand Pl NW1 ....12 C1
Ferdinand St NW1 ....12 C1
Fergus Rd N5 ....15 A3
Ferguson Dr W3 ....28 C3
Ferguson Ho SE10 ....52 B2
Ferguson's Cl E14 ....41 C2
Fermain Ct E **7** N1 ....24 A4
Fermain Ct N **1** N1 ....24 A4
Fermain Ct W N1 ....24 A4
Fermoy Rd W9 ....23 B1
Fern Cl **3** N1 ....24 A3

Fern Ct SE14 ....50 C1
Fern St E3 ....26 C1
Fern Wlk SE16 ....153 C1
Fernbank Mews
SW12 ....61 B1
Ferncliff Rd E8 ....16 C3
Ferncroft Ave NW3 ....10 C4
Ferndale Ct **3** SE3 ....53 B3
Ferndale Ho N16 ....6 C3
Ferndale Rd SW4,
SW9 ....62 B3
Ferndene Rd SE24 ....63 B3
Fernhead Rd W9 ....23 B2
Fernhill Ho E5 ....7 C2
Fernholme Rd SE15 ....65 C2
Fernhurst Rd SW6 ....164 B4
Fernie Ho SE22 ....64 B4
Fernlea Rd SW12 ....73 A3
Fernsbury St WC1 ....95 B3
Fernshaw Mans
SW10 ....156 C3
Fernshaw Rd
SW10 ....156 C3
Fernside Rd SW12 ....72 C4
Ferntower Rd N5 ....15 C3
Fernwood SW19 ....70 B3
Ferriby Cl N1 ....14 C1
Ferrier Ind Est
SW18 ....59 A3
Ferrier Point **6**
E16 ....35 C4
Ferrier St SW18 ....59 A3
Ferrings SE21 ....76 A1
Ferris Rd SE22 ....64 C3
Ferry La
  Brentford TW8 ....44 A4
  Richmond TW9 ....44 B4
SW13 ....46 B4
Ferry Rd SW13 ....46 C2
Ferry Sq **1** TW8 ....44 A4
Ferry St E14 ....42 B1
Ferrybridge Ho
SE11 ....135 A1
Festing Rd SW15 ....57 C4
Festival Pier SE1 ....120 C2
Festival Pleasure Gdns
SW11 ....158 C1
Fetter La EC4 ....107 C2
Fettes Ho NW8 ....79 C1
Finch St SE8 ....51 C3
Field Ct WC1 ....107 A3
NW3 ....11 B3
N7 ....14 A3
SW19 ....70 C1
Field Rd W6 ....154 A4
Fieldgate Mans **1** E1 ....111 C3
Fieldgate St E1 ....111 C3
Fieldhouse Rd
SW12 ....73 B3
Fielding Ho NW8 ....78 C4
3 NW6 ....23 C2
W4 ....46 A4
Fielding Mews
SW13 ....47 A4
Fielding Rd W14 ....38 A3
W14 ....39 C3
Fielding St SE17 ....48 B4
Fields Est E8 ....16 C1
Fieldsway Ho N5 ....14 C3
Fieldview SW17,
SW18 ....71 C3
Fieldview Ct N5 ....15 A3
Fieldway Cres N5,
N7 ....14 C3
Fieldwick Ho **14** E9 ....17 C2

Fife Rd E16 ....35 C4
SW14 ....55 B2
Fife Terr N1 ....85 A2
Fifth Ave W10 ....23 A2
Fig Tree Cl NW10 ....21 A4
Filey Ave N16 ....7 C3
Filey Ho SW18 ....59 B3
Filigree Ct SE16 ....33 B1
Filmer Ho SW6 ....164 B4
Filmer Rd SW6 ....154 C1
Filmer Road Studios
SW6 ....164 B4
Filton Ct **14** SE14 ....50 B3
Finborough Ho
SW10 ....156 C4
Finborough Rd
SW10 ....156 C4
Finch Ho **1** SE8 ....52 A3
Finch La EC2,EC3 ....109 C1
Finch Lo **19** W9 ....31 C4
Finch Mews **3** SE15 ....49 B2
Finch's Ct **9** E14 ....34 A2
Finchdean Ho SW15 ....68 B4
Finchley Pl NW8 ....79 B2
Finchley Rd NW8 ....79 B2
Finchley Road & Frognal
Sta NW3 ....11 B3
Finchley Road Sta
NW3 ....11 B2
Findhorn St E14 ....34 B3
Findon Cl SW18 ....58 C1
Findon Rd W12 ....38 C4
Fineran Ct **1** SW11 ....59 C3
Fingal St SE10 ....43 B1
Fingest Ho NW8 ....90 A2
Finland Rd SE4 ....66 A4
Finland St SE16 ....41 A3
Finlay St SW6 ....47 C2
Finley Ct **21** SE5 ....48 B3
Finmere Ho **4** N4 ....6 B4
Finn Ho N1 ....97 C4
Finnemore Ho N1 ....86 C4
Finnis St E2 ....25 A2
Finsbury Ave EC2 ....109 C3
Finsbury Cir EC2 ....109 C3
Finsbury Ct EC2 ....109 B4
Finsbury Market
EC2 ....110 A4
Finsbury Mkt EC2 ....98 A1
Finsbury Park N4,
N5 ....6 A2
Finsbury Park Sta
N4 ....5 C2
Finsbury Pavement
EC2 ....109 C4
Finsbury Sq EC2 ....109 C4
Finsbury St EC2 ....109 B4
Finsen Rd SE5 ....63 B4
Finstock Rd W10 ....30 C3
Finton House Sch
SW17 ....72 B2
Fincuane Ct TW9 ....54 B4
Finwhale Ho E14 ....42 A3
Fiona Ct **8** NW6 ....23 B3
Fir Lo SW15 ....57 A3
Fir Tree Ho **11** SE14 ....50 B3
Fir Trees Cl SE16 ....33 A1
Firbank Rd SE15 ....50 A1
Fircroft N1 ....86 B4
Fircroft Prim Sch
SW17 ....72 B1
Fircroft Rd SW17 ....72 B1
Fire Brigade Pier
SE1 ....148 B4
Firecrest Dr NW3 ....2 A1

Firle Ho W10 ....30 B4
Firmston Ho **9**
SW14 ....55 C4
Firs Ave SW14 ....55 B3
Firsby Rd N16 ....7 C3
First Ave W10 ....23 B1
W3 ....29 B1
SW14 ....56 A4
First St SW3 ....144 B4
Firth Gdns SW6 ....164 A3
Fish St Hill EC3 ....123 C3
Fisher Ho N1 ....85 B3
2 N19 ....4 B1
8 E1 ....32 B2
Fisher St WC1 ....106 C3
E16 ....35 C4
Fisher's La W4 ....37 C2
Fisherman's Wlk
E14 ....33 C1
Fishermans Dr SE16 ....40 C4
Fishers Ct SE14 ....50 C2
Fisherton St NW8 ....89 C2
Fisherton Street Est
NW8 ....89 C1
Fishlock Ct SW4 ....172 A2
Fishponds Rd SW17 ....72 A1
Fisons Rd E16 ....35 C1
Fitch Ct SW2 ....62 C2
Fitz-George Ave
W14 ....140 A3
Fitzalan St SE11 ....149 B4
Fitzgerald Ave
SW14 ....56 A4
Fitzgerald Ho **9** SW9 ....173 B1
14 E14 ....34 A3
Fitzgerald Rd SW14 ....55 C4
Fitzhardinge Ho
W1 ....103 B2
Fitzhardinge St
W1 ....103 B2
Fitzherbert Ho **11**
TW10 ....54 B1
Fitzhugh Gr SW18 ....59 C1
Fitzjames Ave
W14 ....140 B3
Fitzjohn's Ave NW3 ....11 C3
Fitzjohns Prim Sch
NW3 ....11 C3
Fitzmaurice Ho **17**
SE16 ....40 A2
Fitzmaurice Pl W1 ....118 B2
Fitzneal St W12 ....29 B3
Fitzroy Cl N6 ....3 B3
Fitzroy Cres W4 ....45 C3
Fitzroy Ct W1 ....93 A1
Fitzroy Ho SE1 ....153 A2
14 E14 ....33 B3
Fitzroy Mews W1 ....92 C1
Fitzroy Pk N6 ....3 B3
Fitzroy Rd NW1 ....81 B4
Fitzroy Sq W1 ....92 C1
Fitzroy St W1 ....92 C1
Fitzroy Yd NW1 ....81 B4
Fitzsimmons Ct **1**
NW10 ....20 C4
Fitzwarren Gdns N19 ....4 B3
Fitzwilliam Ave
TW9 ....44 B1
Fitzwilliam Mews
E16 ....35 C1
Fitzwilliam Rd SW4 ....61 B4
Fives Ct SE11 ....136 A1
Fiveways Rd SW9 ....173 C1

Flamborough Ho **11**
SE15 ....49 C2
Flamborough St
E14 ....33 A3
Flamingo Ct **2** SE8 ....51 C3
Flamsteed House
SE10 ....52 C3
Flanchford Rd W12 ....38 B3
Flanders Mans **1**
W4 ....38 B2
Flanders Rd W4 ....38 A2
Flanders Way E9 ....17 C2
Flank St E1 ....125 B4
Flansham Ho **2**
E14 ....33 B3
Flask Wlk NW3 ....11 C4
Flavell Mews SE10 ....43 A1
Flaxman Ct W1 ....105 B1
Flaxman Ho SE1 ....136 B2
10 W4 ....38 A1
Flaxman Rd SE5 ....48 A1
Flaxman Terr WC1 ....93 C3
Flecker Ho **6** SE5 ....48 C3
Fleece Wlk N7 ....14 A2
Fleet Ct **1** W12 ....38 A3
Fleet Ho **2** E14 ....33 A2
6 SW2 ....62 C2
Fleet Pl EC4 ....108 A2
Fleet Prim Sch NW3 ....12 B3
Fleet Rd NW3 ....12 B3
Fleet Sq WC1 ....95 A3
Fleet St EC4 ....107 C1
Fleet Street Hill E1 ....99 B1
Fleetfield WC1 ....94 B4
Fleetway WC1 ....94 B4
Fleetwood Rd NW10 ....8 C3
Fleetwood St N16 ....7 A2
Fleming Ct W2 ....101 B4
Fleming Ho SE16 ....139 B3
N4 ....6 B3
Fleming Rd SE17 ....48 A4
Fletcher Bldgs
WC2 ....106 B1
Fletcher Ct **3** NW5 ....13 A4
Fletcher Ho **10** N16 ....16 A4
22 N1 ....24 A4
Fletcher Path **7**
SE8 ....51 C3
Fletcher Rd W4 ....37 B3
Fletcher St E1 ....125 C4
Fleur Gates **7**
SW19 ....69 C4
Flinders Ho **28** E1 ....32 A1
Flint St SE17 ....151 C3
Flinton St SE17 ....152 B2
Flitcroft St WC2 ....105 C1
Flitton Ho **8** N1 ....15 A1
Flock Mill Pl SW18 ....71 A3
Flockton St SE16 ....139 B3
SE16 ....139 B4
Flodden Rd SE5 ....48 B2
Flood St SW3 ....158 B4
Flood Wlk SW3 ....158 B4
Flora Cl E14 ....34 A3
Flora Gardens Prim Sch
W6 ....39 A2
Flora Gdns **2** W6 ....39 A2
Floral St WC2 ....120 A4
Florence Ct W9 ....89 A3
4 E5 ....7 C1
Florence Gdns W4 ....45 B4
Florence Ho
10 W11 ....30 C2
20 SE16 ....40 A1
7 SW18 ....59 C3
2 SW2 ....62 B2

Florence Mans
SW6 . . . .**164** C4
Florence Nightingale Ho
11 N1 . . . . .15 B3
Florence Nightingale
Mus SE1 . . . .**135** A3
Florence Rd N4 . . . . . .5 C4
W4 . . . . .37 C3
SE14 . . . . .51 B2
Florence St N1 . . . . . . .15 A1
Florence Terr SE14 . .51 B2
SW15 . . . . .68 A1
Florence Way SW12 .72 B3
Flores Ho **16** E1 . . . . .32 C4
Florfield Rd E8 . . . . . .17 A2
Florian SE5 . . . . .49 A2
Florian Rd SW15 . . . .58 A3
Florida St E2 . .24,**99** C3
Florys Ct **7** SW19 . . .70 A3
Floss St SW15 . . . . . . .47 B1
Flower & Dean Wlk
E1 . . . .**111** A3
Flower Wlk The
SW7 . . . .**129** A4
Flowers Mews **1**
N19 . . . . .4 B2
Flowersmead SW17 .72 C2
Fluer De Lis St E1 . . .**98** C1
Flynn Ct **12** E14 . . . . .33 C2
Foley Ho **19** E1 . . . . . .32 B3
Foley St W1 . . . .**104** C3
Folgate St E1 . . . . . .**110** C4
Foliot Ho N1 . . . .**84** C2
Foliot St W12 . . . . . . .29 B3
Follett Ho SW10 . . . .**157** B2
Follett St E14 . . . . . . .34 B3
Folly Wall E14 . . . . . .42 B4
Fontarabia Rd
SW11 . . . . .60 C3
Fontenelle SE5 . . . . . .49 A2
Fontenoy Ho SE11 . .**150** A3
Fontenoy Rd SW12,
SW17 . . . . .73 B2
Fonthill Ho SW1 . . .**146** B2
Fonthill Mews N4 . . . .5 B2
Fonthill Rd N4 . . . . . . .5 C2
Fontley Way SW15 . .68 C4
Footpath The SW15 . .56 C2
Forber Ho **25** E2 . . . . .25 B2
Forbes Ho **2** W4 . . . . .36 C1
Forbes St E1 . . . .**111** C1
Forburg Rd N16 . . . . . .7 C3
Ford Cl **17** E3 . . . . . . .26 A3
Ford Rd E3 . . . . .26 A4
Ford Sq E1 . . . . .32 A4
Ford St E3 . . . . .26 A4
E16 . . . . .35 B1
Fordcombe **13** NW5 .12 C2
Fordham St E1 . . . . .**111** C2
Fordingley Rd W9 . . .23 B2
Fords Park Rd E16 . .35 C3
Fordwych Ct NW2 . . .10 A2
Fordwych Rd NW2 . .10 A3
Fordyce Rd SE13 . . . .67 B2
Fore St EC2 . . . .**109** B3
Fore St Ave EC2 . . . .**109** B3
Foreign, Commonwealth
& Home Offices
SW1 . . . .**134** A4
Foreland Ho W11 . . .**112** A4
Foreshore SE8 . . . . . .41 B2
Forest Gr E8 . . . . .16 B2
Forest Hill Rd SE22 . .65 A1
Forest Rd E8 . . . . .16 B2
Richmond TW9 . . . . . .44 C3
Forest Way **6** N19 . . .4 B2

Forester Rd SE15 . . . .65 A4
Forfar Rd SW11 . . . .**169** C4
Forge Pl NW1 . . . . . . .12 C2
Forman Ho SE4 . . . . .65 C3
Forman Pl N16 . . . . . .16 B4
Formby Ct **9** N7 . . . . .14 C3
Formosa Ho **1** E1 . . .26 A1
Formosa St W9 . . . . . .**88** B1
Forrest Ct E16 . . . . . . .35 B2
Forrest Ct N7 . . . . . . .14 C2
Forrest Ho SW15 . . . .47 B1
Forset Ct W1 . . . .**102** B2
Forset St W1 . . . .**102** B2
Forster Rd SW2 . . . . .74 A4
Forstic Wlk E1 . . . . . .**111** A3
Forston St N1 . . . .**87** A2
Forsyth Gdns SE17 . .48 A4
Forsyth Ho SW1 . . . .**147** A3
E9 . . . . .17 B1
Forsythia Ho SE4 . . . .66 A4
Fort Rd SE1 . . . .**153** A3
Fort St E1 . . . .**110** B3
Fortescue Ave **1**
E8 . . . . .17 A1
Fortess Gr NW5 . . . . .13 B3
Fortess Rd NW5 . . . . .13 B4
Fortess Wlk NW5 . . . .13 A3
Fortethie Ho **20** E3 . . .26 B3
Forthbridge Rd
SW11 . . . . .60 C3
Forties The **9** NW5 . .13 B3
Fortior Ct N6 . . . . .4 B4
Fortnam Rd N19 . . . . . .4 C2
Fortrose Gdns
SW12,SW2 . . . . .74 A3
Fortuna Cl N7 . . . . . . .14 B2
Fortune Gate Rd
NW10 . . . . .21 A4
Fortune Green Rd
NW6 . . . . .10 C4
Fortune Ho EC1 . . . . .**97** A1
SE11 . . . .**149** B3
Fortune St EC1 . . . . .**97** A1
Fortune Way NW10 . .21 C2
Forty Acre La E16 . . .35 C4
Forward Bsns Ctr The
E16 . . . . .27 C1
Fosbroke Ho SW8 . .**162** A1
Fosbury Ho **7** SW9 . .62 B3
Fosbury Mews W2 . .**114** B3
Foscote Mews W9 . . .31 C4
Foskett Rd SW6 . . . .**165** A1
Fossil Rd SE13 . . . . . .66 C4
Foster Ct **4** NW1 . . . .13 B1
E16 . . . . .35 B2
Foster Ho SE14 . . . . .51 B2
Foster La EC2 . . . . . .**108** C2
Foster Rd W3 . . . . . . .29 A2
W4 . . . . .37 C1
Foubert's Pl W1 . . . .**104** C1
Foulden Rd N16 . . . . .16 B4
Foulden Terr N16 . . .16 B4
Foulis Terr SW7 . . . .**143** C2
Foulser Rd SW17 . . . .72 C1
Foundary Ho **7** E14 .34 A4
Founders Ct EC2 . . . .**109** B2
Founders Ho **1**
SW1 . . . .**147** B2
Foundling Ct WC1 . . .**94** A2
Foundry Cl SE16 . . . .33 A1
Foundry Mews NW1 .**93** A2
Fount St SW8 . . . . . .**161** C1
Fountain Ct EC4 . . . .**121** B4
SW1 . . . .**146** A3
Fountain Green Sq
SE16 . . . .**139** C3
Fountain Ho W1 . . . .**117** B2

Fountain Ho continued
SE16 . . . .**139** C2
NW6 . . . . .10 A1
Fountain Mews
NW3 . . . . .12 B2
1 N5 . . . . .15 B4
Fountain Pl SW9 . . . .**173** C3
Fountayne Rd N16 . . . .7 C2
Fournier St E1 . . . . . .**111** A4
Fourth Ave W10 . . . . .23 A2
Fovant Ct SW8 . . . . .**170** C1
Fowey Cl E1 . . . . .32 A1
Fowey Ho SE11 . . . . .**149** C2
Fowler Cl SW11 . . . . .59 C4
Fowler Ho N1 . . . .**86** B4
SW8 . . . .**171** C3
3 SE5 . . . . .49 A1
Fowler Rd N1 . . . .**86** B4
Fox and Knot St EC1 **108** B4
Fox Cl E1 . . . . .25 B1
E16 . . . . .35 C4
Fox Ho **2** SW11 . . . . .59 C3
Fox Prim Sch
W8 . . . . .31 C1 **113** B1
Fox Rd E16 . . . . .35 B2
Fox's Yd E2 . . . .**99** A2
Foxberry Ct SE4 . . . . .66 B3
Foxberry Rd SE4 . . . .66 A4
Foxborough Gdns
SE4 . . . . .66 C2
Foxbourne Rd
SW17 . . . . .72 C2
Foxcombe Rd **6**
SW15 . . . . .68 C3
Foxcote SE5 . . . .**152** B1
Foxcroft N1 . . . .**85** A1
Foxglove St W12 . . . .29 B2
Foxham Rd N19 . . . . . .4 C1
Foxley Cl E8 . . . . .16 C3
Foxley Ho **4** E3 . . . . .27 A2
Foxley Rd SW9 . . . . . .48 A3
Foxley Sq **3** SW9 . . .48 A2
Foxmore St SW11 . . .**168** C3
Foxwell Mews SE4 . .66 A4
Foxwell St SE4 . . . . . .66 A4
Foyle Rd SE3 . . . . . . .53 B4
Fradel La N16 . . . . .6 C3
Framfield Rd N5 . . . . .15 A3
Frampton NW1 . . . . . .13 C1
Frampton Ct **3** W3 . .37 B4
Frampton Ho NW8 . . .**89** C1
Frampton Park Rd
E9 . . . . .17 B1
Frampton St NW8 . . .**89** C1
Francemary Rd SE4 . .66 C2
Frances Grey Ho **13**
E1 . . . . .32 C4
Franche Court Rd
SW17 . . . . .71 B1
Francis Chichester Way
SW11 . . . .**169** C3
Francis Cl **6** E14 . . . .42 C2
Francis Ct **5** SE14 . .50 C4
Francis Ho NW10 . . . .21 A4
11 N1 . . . . .24 A4
Francis Holland Sch
for Girls SW1 . . . .**90** C2
Francis Holland Sch
SW1 . . . .**145** C3
Francis Snary Lo **6**
SW18 . . . . .58 C2
Francis St SW1 . . . . .**147** A4
Francis Terr N19 . . . . . .4 B1
Francis Wlk N1 . . . . . .**84** C4
Franconia Rd SW4 . . .61 C2

Frank Barnes Prim Sch
for Deaf Children
11 C1
Frank Beswick Ho
SW6 . . . .**155** A3
Frank Dixon Cl
SE21 . . . . .76 A3
Frank Dixon Way
SE21 . . . . .76 A3
Frank Douglas Ct
W6 . . . . .38 C2
Frank Ho SW8 . . . . . .**162** A2
Frank Soskice Ho
SW6 . . . .**155** A3
Frankfort Rd SE24 . . .63 B2
Frankham Ho **3**
SE8 . . . . .51 C3
Frankham St SE8 . . . .51 C3
Frankland Cl SE16 . . .40 A2
Frankland Ho **4**
SW12 . . . . .73 A4
Frankland Rd SW7 . .**129** B1
Franklin Cl SE13 . . . .52 A2
SE27 . . . . .75 A1
Franklin Ho **20** E1 . . .32 A1
Franklin Sq SW5 . . .**141** A1
Franklin St **13** E3 . . .27 A2
Franklin's Row
SW3 . . . .**145** A2
Franklyn Rd NW10 . . .8 B2
Frans Hals Ct E14 . . .42 C3
Fraser Ct SW11 . . . .**168** A4
Fraser Ho SW8 . . . . .**171** B1
Brentford TW8 . . . . . .36 B1
Fraser Regnart Ct **12**
NW5 . . . . .12 B3
Fraser St W4 . . . . .38 A1
Fraserburgh Ho **20**
E3 . . . . .26 B3
Frazier St SE1 . . . . . .**135** B3
Frean St SE16 . . . . . .**139** B2
Frearson Ho WC1 . . .**95** A4
Freda Corbett Cl **9**
SE15 . . . . .49 C3
Frederic Mews
SW1 . . . .**131** B3
Frederica St **4** N7 . .14 B1
Frederica Rd E4 . . . . .33 B1
Frederick Charrington
Ho **1** E1 . . . . .25 B1
Frederick Cl W2 . . . .**102** C1
W2 . . . .**116** C4
Frederick Cres SW9 .48 A3
Frederick Rd SE17 . .**150** B1
Frederick Sq **11**
SE16 . . . . .33 A2
Frederick Terr E8 . . . .16 B1
Frederick's Pl
EC2 . . . .**109** B1
Frederick's Row
EC1 . . . .**96** A4
Freedom St SW11 . .**169** A2
Freegrove Rd N7 . . . .14 A3
Freeling Ho NW8 . . . .**79** B4
Freeling St **7** N1 . . .14 B1
Freeman Ho **13**
SW2 . . . . .74 A4
Freemantle St
SE17 . . . .**152** A2
Freemens Hos **1**
SW9 . . . . .62 B3
Freke Rd SW11 . . . . . .60 C4
Fremantle Ho **14** E1 .25 A1

Fremont St E9 . . . . . . .25 B4
French Ordinary Ct
EC3 . . . .**124** B4
French Pl E1 . . . .**98** B2
Frendsbury Rd SE4 . .66 A3
Frensham Ct N5 . . . . .15 B3
Frensham Dr SW15 . .68 C2
Frensham St SE15 . . .49 C4
Frere St **11** SW11 . . .**168** B2
Freshfield Ave E8 . . .16 B1
Freshfield Cl SE13 . . .67 C3
Freshford St SW17,
SW18 . . . . .71 B1
Freston Rd W10,
W11 . . . . .30 C2
Freud Mus The **11** B2
Frewell Ho EC1 . . . . .**107** B4
Friar Mews SE27 . . . .75 A1
Friar St EC4 . . . .**108** B1
Friars Ave SW15 . . . .68 B1
Friars Cl SE1 . . . .**122** B1
Friars Gdns W3 . . . . .28 C3
Friars Mead E14 . . . .42 B3
Friars Place La W3 . .28 C2
Friars Prim Sch
SE1 . . . .**136** B3
Friars Stile Pl **9**
TW10 . . . . .54 A1
Friars Stile Rd
TW10 . . . . .54 A1
Friary Way W3 . . . . . .28 B3
Friary Park Ct **3**
W3 . . . . .28 B3
SE15 . . . . .49 C3
Friday St EC4 . . . . . .**122** C4
Frideswide Pl NW5 . .13 B3
Friend Rd SE5 . . . . . .**96** A4
Friendly Pl SE13 . . . .52 A2
Friendly St SE8 . . . . .51 C2
Friendly Street Mews
SE8 . . . . .51 C1
Frien Rd SE22 . . . . . . .64 C1
Friern Sch (Lower)
SE22 . . . . .65 A2
Frigate Ho **6** E14 . . .42 B2
Frigate Mews SE8 . . .51 C4
Frimley Cl SW19 . . . .70 A2
Frimley Way E1 . . . . .25 C1
Frinstead Ho **1**
W10 . . . . .30 C2
Friston St SW6 . . . . .**166** A1
Frith Ho NW8 . . . .**89** C1
E2 . . . . .24 C2 **99** B3
Frith Rd E11 . . . . .19 C4
Frith St W1 . . . .**105** B1
Frithville Ct W12 . . . .30 B1
Frithville Gdns W12 .30 B1
Frobisher Ct **3**
W12 . . . . .39 B4
Frobisher Ho **27** E1 .32 A1
Frobisher Pas E14 . .33 C1
Frobisher Sq **1**
SE10 . . . . .52 C4
Frobisher St SE10 . . .53 A4
Frogley Rd SE22 . . . .64 B3
Frogmore SW18 . . . . .58 C2
Frogmore Est NW10 .20 B2
Frogmore Ind Est
N5 . . . . .15 B4
Frognal NW3 . . . . . . .11 B3

Frognal Cl NW3 . . . . .11 B3
Frognal Ct NW3 . . . . .11 B2
Frognal Gdns NW3 . . . . . .11 B4
Frognal La NW3 . . . . .11 A3
Frognal Par NW3 . . . . .11 B2
Frognal Rise NW3 . . . . . . .11 B4
Frognal Way NW3 . . . . . .11 B4
Frome Ho SE15 . . . . .65 B3
Frome St N1 . . . . .86 C2
Frontenac NW10 . . . . .9 A1
Froude St SW8 . . . . .170 B1
Fry Rd NW10 . . . . .21 B4
Frye Ct E2 . . . . .26 B2
Frying Pan Alley
E1 . . . . .110 C3
Fulbeck Ho N7 . . . . .14 B2
Fulbourne St E1 . . . . .32 A4
Fulbrook Rd N19 . . . . . . .13 B4
Fulcher Ho **10** N1 . . . . . . .24 A4
13 SE8 . . . . .41 B1
Fulford Mans N19 . . . . . . .5 A1
Fulford St SE16 . . . . .40 A4
Fulham Broadway
SW6 . . . . .155 C1
Fulham Broadway Sta
SW6 . . . . .155 C2
Fulham Cross Sch
SW6 . . . . .154 A2
Fulham Ct SW6 . . . . .165 B4
Fulham High St
SW6 . . . . .164 B1
Fulham Palace ★
SW6 . . . . .164 A1
Fulham Palace Rd
SW6 . . . . .164 A3
Fulham Park Gdns
SW6 . . . . .164 C2
Fulham Park Rd
SW6 . . . . .164 C2
Fulham Prep Sch The
SW6 . . . . .155 B3
Fulham Prim Sch
SW6 . . . . .155 B3
Fulham Rd SW10 . . . . . . .157 A4
Fuller Cl E2 . . . . .99 B2
Fullers Ho **6** SW18 . . . . . .58 C2
Fullerton Rd SW18 . . . . . .59 B2
Fullwood's Mews
N1 . . . . .97 C4
Fulmar Ct **5** SE21 . . . . . . .75 C2
Fulmar Ho NW8 . . . . .90 B1
Fulmead St SW6 . . . . . . .166 B3
Fulneck **1** E1 . . . . .32 B4
Fulthorp Rd SE3 . . . . .53 C1
Fulton Mews W2 . . . . . . .114 C4
Fulwood Pl WC1 . . . . . . .107 A3
Fulwood Wlk SW19 . . . . . .70 A3
Furber St W6 . . . . .39 A3
Furley Ho **2** SE15 . . . . . . .49 C3
Furley Rd SE15 . . . . .49 C3
Furlong Rd N7 . . . . .14 C2
Furmage St SW18 . . . . . . .71 A4
Furness Ho SW1 . . . . . . .146 A2
Furness Lo **4** SW14 . . . . . .55 A3
Furness Rd NW10 . . . . . . .21 C3
NW10 . . . . .21 C3
Furnival St EC4 . . . . .107 B2
Furrow La E9 . . . . .17 B3
Fursecroft W1 . . . . .102 C2
Furze St E3 . . . . .33 C4
Fyfield N4 . . . . .5 C2

Fyfield Rd **6** SW9 . . . . . . .62 C4
Fynes St SW1 . . . . .147 B4

G

Gable Ho **12** W4 . . . . .38 A2
Gables Cl SE5 . . . . .49 A2
Gables The NW3 . . . . .2 C1
Gabriel Ho **5** SE11 . . . . . .148 C4
Gabriel's Wharf
SE1 . . . . .121 B2
Gabrielle Ct NW3 . . . . . . .11 C2
Gaddesden Ho EC1 . . . . . .97 C3
Gadsden Ho **8** W10 . . . . . .23 A1
7 E9 . . . . .17 B1
Gagarin Ho SW11 . . . . . . .59 C4
Gage Rd E16 . . . . .35 A4
Gage St WC1 . . . . .106 B4
Gainford Ho **10** E2 . . . . . . .25 A2
Gainford St N1 . . . . .85 B4
Gainsborough Ct
W12 . . . . .39 B4
8 SE16 . . . . .40 A1
2 SE21 . . . . .76 A2
Gainsborough Gdns
NW11 . . . . .1 B4
2 NW3 . . . . .2 C1
Gainsborough Ho
Gage Rd E16 . . . . .147 C3
N4 . . . . .5 B3
8 E14 . . . . .41 C3
Gainsborough Prim Sch
E9 . . . . .18 C2
SE22 . . . . .64 A4
Gainsborough Rd
W4 . . . . .38 B2
Richmond TW9 . . . . .54 B4
Gainsborough Sch E2 . .139 A4
Gairloch Ho **6**
NW1 . . . . .13 C1
Gairloch Rd SE5 . . . . .49 A1
Gaisford St NW5 . . . . .13 B2
Gaitskell Ct SW11 . . . . . .168 A2
Gaitskell Rd SE9 . . . . .97 C4
Galata Rd SW13 . . . . .46 C3
Galatea Sq SE15 . . . . .65 A4
Galbraith St E14 . . . . .42 B3
Gale Ho **5** SW2 . . . . .62 B2
Gale St E3 . . . . .33 C4
Galen Pl WC1 . . . . .106 B3
Galena Ho **6** W6 . . . . .39 A2
Galena Rd W6 . . . . .39 A2
Gales Gdns E2 . . . . .25 A2
Galesbury Rd SW18 . . . . . .59 B1
Galgate Cl **4** SW19 . . . . . .70 A3
Galleon Cl SE16 . . . . .40 C4
Galleon Ho **2** E14 . . . . . . .42 B2
Gallery Rd SE21 . . . . .75 C3
Galleywall Prim Sch
SE16 . . . . .40 A2
Galleywall Rd SE16 . . . . . .40 A2
Galleywall Road Trad
Est **13** SE16 . . . . .40 A2
Galleywood Ho W10 . . . . .30 B4
Gallia Rd N5 . . . . .15 A3
Gallions Rd SE7 . . . . .43 C2
Galloway Rd W12 . . . . . . .29 C1
Galsworthy Ho **4**
W11 . . . . .31 A3
Galsworthy Rd NW2 . . . . .10 A4
Galton St W10 . . . . .23 A2
Galveston Ho **2** E1 . . . . . . .26 A1
Galveston Rd SW15 . . . . . .58 B2
Galway Cl **28** SE16 . . . . . . .40 A1

Galway Ho EC1 . . . . .97 A3
11 E1 . . . . .32 C4
Galway St EC1 . . . . .97 A3
Gambetta St SW8 . . . . . .170 B1
Gambia St SE1 . . . . .122 B1
Gambier Ho EC1 . . . . .97 A3
Gamlen Rd SW15 . . . . . . .57 C3
Ganley Ct **10** SW11 . . . . . .59 C4
Gannet Ct **21** SE21 . . . . . . .75 C2
Gannet Ho SE15 . . . . .49 B2
Ganton St W1 . . . . .105 A1
Garbett Ho **2** SE17 . . . . . .48 A4
Garbutt Pl W1 . . . . .103 C3
Gard St EC1 . . . . .96 B4
Garden Cl SW15 . . . . .69 A4
Garden Ct NW8 . . . . .89 B4
EC4 . . . . .121 B4
7 W4 . . . . .37 B1
4 Richmond TW9 . . . . . .44 C2
Garden Flats SW16 . . . . . .74 A1
Garden Ho **5** SW9 . . . . . .172 B2
Garden La SW2 . . . . .74 B3
Garden Mews W2 . . . . . .113 C3
Garden Rd NW8 . . . . .89 A4
Mortlake TW9 . . . . .54 C4
Garden Row SE1 . . . . . . .136 A2
Garden Royal 18
SW15 . . . . .57 C1
Garden Terr SW1 . . . . . . .147 B2
SW7 . . . . .130 B3
Garden Wlk
EC2 . . . . .24 A2 98 A2
Gardens The N16 . . . . .7 B4
SE22 . . . . .64 C3
Gardiner Ave NW2 . . . . . . .9 B3
Gardiner Ct NW10 . . . . . . .20 C4
Gardiner Ho SW11 . . . . . .168 A4
Gardner Ct N5 . . . . .15 B4
Gardners La EC4 . . . . . . .122 C4
Gardnor Mans 10
NW3 . . . . .11 B4
Gardnor Rd NW3 . . . . .11 C4
Gareth Ct SW16 . . . . .73 C1
Garfield Rd SW11 . . . . . . .60 C4
Garford St E14 . . . . .33 C2
Garland Ho N16 . . . . .6 C1
Garlick Hill EC4 . . . . .123 A4
Garlinge Ho SW9 . . . . . . .173 B4
Garlinge Rd NW2 . . . . . . .10 B2
Garnault Mews EC1 . . . . .95 C3
Garnault Pl EC1 . . . . .95 C3
Garner St E2 . . . . .24 C3
Garnet Rd NW10 . . . . .8 A2
Garnet St E1 . . . . .32 B2
Garnett Ho **3** NW3 . . . . . .12 B3
Garnett Rd NW3 . . . . .12 B3
Garnham St **1** N16 . . . . . . .7 B2
Garnham St **1** N16 . . . . . . .7 B2
Garnies Cl SE15 . . . . .49 B3
Garrad's Rd SW16 . . . . . . .73 C1
Garrard Wlk NW10 . . . . . . .8 A2
Garratt Ho **6** N16 . . . . .7 A3
Garratt La SW18 . . . . .71 A3
Garratt Park Sec Sch
SW18 . . . . .71 B1
Garraway Ct SW13 . . . . . .47 B3
Garraway Ho SE21 . . . . . . .76 B1
Garrett Cl W3 . . . . .28 C4
Garrett Ho W12 . . . . .30 A3
Garrett St EC1 . . . . .97 A2
Garrick Cl SW18 . . . . .59 B3
Garrick Ho W1 . . . . .118 A1
W4 . . . . .46 A4
Garrick Rd TW9 . . . . .44 C1
Garrick St WC2 . . . . .120 A4

Garrick Yd WC2 . . . . .120 A4
Garsington Mews
SE4 . . . . .66 B4
Garson Ho W2 . . . . .115 B4
Garston Ho **5** N1 . . . . .15 A1
Garter Way SE16 . . . . .40 C4
Garth Ct W4 . . . . .45 C4
Garth Ho NW2 . . . . .1 B2
Garth Rd NW2 . . . . .1 B2
8 W4 . . . . .37 C1
Gartmoor Gdns
SW19 . . . . .70 B3
Garton Ho **6** N6 . . . . .4 C4
Garton Pl SW18 . . . . .59 B1
Gartons Way SW11 . . . . . .59 B4
Garway Rd W2 . . . . .100 A1
W2 . . . . .114 A4
Gascoigne Pl E2 . . . . .98 C3
Gascony Ave NW6 . . . . . . .10 C1
Gascoyne Ho **2** E9 . . . . . . .17 C1
Gascoyne Rd E9 . . . . .17 C1
Gaselee St E14 . . . . .34 B2
Gasholder Pl SE11 . . . . . .149 A1
Gaskarth Rd SW12 . . . . . .61 A1
Gaskell St SW4 . . . . .172 A2
Gaskin Ho N16 . . . . .6 C1
Gaskin St N1 . . . . .86 A4
Gaspar Cl SW7 . . . . .142 B4
Gaspar Mews SW5 . . . . . .142 B4
Gasson Ho **2** SE14 . . . . . .50 C4
Gastein Rd W6 . . . . .154 A4
W6 . . . . .47 C4
Gastigny Ho EC1 . . . . .97 A3
Gaston Bell Cl TW9 . . . . . .54 B4
Gaston Gate SW8 . . . . . .172 C4
Gataker Ho **5** SE16 . . . . . .40 A3
Gataker St **6** SE16 . . . . . .40 A3
Gatcombe Ho **20**
SE22 . . . . .64 A4
3 E16 . . . . .35 C1
Gate Hill Ct W11 . . . . . . .113 A2
Gate Mews SW7 . . . . . . .130 B3
Gate St WC2 . . . . .106 C2
Gatebeck Ho **21**
SE22 . . . . .64 A4
Gatefield Ct SE15 . . . . . . .64 C4
Gateforth St NW8 . . . . . . .90 A1
Gatehouse Sch E2 . . . . . .25 C3
Gatehouse Sq SE1 . . . . . .123 A2
Gateley Ho **6** SE4 . . . . . . .65 C3
Gateley Rd SW9 . . . . .62 B4
Gates Ct SE17 . . . . .150 C2
Gatesborough St 9
EC2 . . . . .98 A2
Gatesden WC1 . . . . .94 B3
Gateside Rd SW17 . . . . . . .72 B1
Gateway SE17 . . . . .48 B4
Gateway Mews 4
E8 . . . . .16 B3
Gateway Prim Sch
NW8 . . . . .89 C2
Gateway Trad Est
NW10 . . . . .21 B2
Gateways The
SW3 . . . . .144 B3
Gathorne St **19** E2 . . . . . . .25 C3
Gatliff Rd SW1 . . . . .146 A1
Gatwick Ho **6** E14 . . . . . . .33 B3
Gatwick Rd SW18 . . . . . . .70 B4
Gauden Cl SW4 . . . . .61 C4
Gauden Rd SW4 . . . . .61 C4
Gaugin Ct **13** SE16 . . . . . . .40 A1
Gaunt St SE1 . . . . .136 C2
Gautrey Rd SE15 . . . . .50 B1

Gavel St SE17 . . . . .151 C4
Gaviller Pl **4** E5 . . . . .17 A4
Gavrelle Ho EC1 . . . . .97 B1
Gawber St E2 . . . . .25 B2
Gawthorne Ct E3 . . . . .26 C3
Gay Cl NW2 . . . . .9 A3
Gay Ho N16 . . . . .16 A3
Gay Rd E15 . . . . .27 C3
Gayfere St SW1 . . . . .134 A1
Gayford Rd W12 . . . . .38 B4
Gayhurst SE17 . . . . .48 C4
Gayhurst Ho NW8 . . . . . . .90 B2
Gayhurst JMI Sch
E8 . . . . .16 C1
Gayhurst Rd E8 . . . . .16 C1
Gaymead NW8 . . . . .78 B3
Gaysley Ho SE11 . . . . . . .149 B3
Gayton Cres NW3 . . . . . . .11 C4
Gayton Ho E3 . . . . .26 C1
Gayton Rd NW3 . . . . .11 C4
Gayville Rd SW11 . . . . . . .60 B1
Gaywood Cl SW2 . . . . . . .74 C3
Gaywood St SE1 . . . . . . .136 B1
Gaza St SE17 . . . . .150 A1
Gaze Ho **10** E14 . . . . .34 C3
Gean Ct **3** E11 . . . . .19 C4
Geary Ho N7 . . . . .14 B3
Geary Rd NW10 . . . . .8 C3
Geary St N7 . . . . .14 B3
Gedling Ho SE22 . . . . .64 B4
Gedling Pl SE1 . . . . .139 A2
Gee St EC1 . . . . .96 C2
Gees Ct W1 . . . . .103 C1
Geffrye Ct N1 . . . . .24 A3
Geffrye Mus ★ E2 . . . . . . .24 B3
Geffrye St E2 . . . . .24 B3
Geldart Rd SE15 . . . . .50 A3
Geldeston Rd E5 . . . . .7 C2
Gellatly Rd SE14 . . . . .50 C1
Gemini Bsns Ctr
E16 . . . . .27 C1
Gemini Ho SE15 . . . . .48 B1
General Hospl NW1 . . . . . .82 B4
General Wolfe Rd
SE10 . . . . .52 C2
Geneva Ct N16 . . . . .6 C3
1 SW15 . . . . .57 C2
Geneva Dr SW9 . . . . .62 C3
Genoa Ave SW15 . . . . . . .57 B2
Genoa Ho **19** E1 . . . . .25 C1
Geoffrey Chaucer Sch
SE1 . . . . .137 B1
Geoffrey Cl SE5 . . . . .48 B1
Geoffrey Ct SE4 . . . . .66 B4
Geoffrey Ho SE1 . . . . . . .137 C2
Geoffrey Jones Ct
NW10 . . . . .21 C4
Geoffrey Rd SE4 . . . . .66 B4
Geological Mus
SW7 . . . . .129 C1
George Beard Rd **10**
SE8 . . . . .41 B2
George Beare Lo **9**
SW4 . . . . .61 B2
George Belt Ho **8**
E2 . . . . .25 C2
George Ct WC2 . . . . .120 B3
George Downing Est
N16 . . . . .7 B2
George Eliot Ho
SW1 . . . . .147 A3
George Eliot Jun & Inf
Sch NW8 . . . . .79 B4

George Elliot Ho
SE17 ....150 C2

George Elliston Ho
SE1 ....153 B1

George Eyre Ho
NW8 ....79 C1

George Green's Sec Sch
E14 ....42 B1

George Inn Yd SE1 .123 B1

George La SE13 ......67 B1

George Lansbury Ho
NW10 ....8 A1
7 E3 ....26 B2

George Lashwood Ct **12**
SW9 ....62 B3

George Leybourne Ho
E1 ....125 C4

George Lindgren Ho
SW6 ....155 A2

George Loveless Ho
E2 ....99 A4

George Orwell Sch
N4 ....21 A2

George Row SE16 ...139 B3
George St W1 ....103 A2
6 E16 ....35 B1

George Tingle Ho
SE1 ....139 A2

George Vale Ho **32**
E2 ....24 C3

George Walter Ho **7**
SE16 ....40 B2

George Wyver Cl
SW18 ....70 A4

George Yd EC3 .....109 C1
W1 ....117 C4

George's Rd N7 .....14 B3
George's Sq SW6 ..155 A4
Georgette Pl SE10 ...52 B3
Georgian Ct **19** E9 ..25 B4
Georgiana St NW1 ..83 A4
Georgina Gdns E2 ..99 A4
Gerald Mews SW1 .145 C4
Gerald Rd SW1 ....145 C4
Geraldine Rd W4 ...45 C4
SW18 ....59 B2
Geraldine St SE11 .136 A1
Gerard Ct NW2 ....9 C3
Gerard Rd SW13 ....46 B2
Gerards Cl SE16 .....40 B4
Gernigan Ho SW18 ..59 C1
Gernon Rd E3 ....26 A3
Gerrard Ho **5** SE14 .50 C3
Gerrard Pl W1 .....119 C4
Gerrard Rd N1 ......86 B2
Gerrard St W1 .....119 C4
Gerridge Ct SE1 ....135 C2
Gerridge St SE1 ....135 C2
Gertrude St SW10 ..157 A4
Gervase St SE15 ....50 A3
Ghent Way E8 ....16 B2
Giant Arches Rd
SE24 ....63 B1
Gibbings Ho SE1 ...136 B3
Gibbins Rd E15 ......76 B1
Gibbon Ho NW8 .....89 C1
Gibbon Rd W3 ......29 A2
SE15 ....50 B1
Gibbon Wlk SW15 ..56 C3
Gibbon's Rents
SE1 ....124 A1
Gibbons Rd NW10 ...8 A2
Gibbs Gn W14 .....141 A2
Gibbs Green Sch
W14 ....141 A2

Gibbs Ho **6** SW12 ..73 A4
Gibraltar Ho NW10 ..21 A3
Gibraltar Wlk E2 ....99 A3
Gibson Cl E1 ....25 B1
Gibson Gdns N16 .....7 B2
Gibson Rd SE11 ....149 A3
Gibson Sq N1 ....85 C4
Gibson St SE10 .....43 A1
Gideon Rd SW11 ....60 C4
Giesbach Rd N19 ....4 C2
Giffen Square Mkt
SE8 ....51 C3
Giffin St SE8 ....51 C3
Gifford Ho SE10 ....42 C1
5 SW4 ....61 C3
Gifford St N1 ....14 A1
Gilbert Ho EC2 .....109 A3
SW1 ....146 B1
SW8 ....162 A2
5 E2 ....25 C2
SE8 ....51 C4
Gilbert Pl WC1 .....106 A3
Gilbert Rd SE11 ....149 C4
Gilbert Sheldon Ho
W2 ....101 C4
Gilbert St W1 ......103 C1
Gilbertson Ho **1**
E14 ....41 C3
Gilbeys Yd NW1 ....12 C1
Gilby Ho **5** E9 .....17 C2
Gilda Cres N16 ......7 C3
Gilda St W1 ....108 B3
Gilden Cres NW5 ...12 C3
Giles Ho SE16 ......139 B2
W11 ....31 C3
Gilesmead SE5 .....48 C2
Gilkes Cres SE21 ...64 A1
Gilkes Pl SE21 ......64 A1
Gill Ave E16 ....35 C3
Gill St E14 ....33 B2
Gillam Ho **8** SE16 ..40 B2
Gillender St E3 ......27 B1
Gillespie Prim Sch
N5 ....5 C1
Gillespie Rd N4,N5 ...6 A1
Gillet Ho **2** 99 B3
Gillett Pl **7** E8 .....16 A3
Gillett St E8,N16 ...16 A3
Gillfoot NW1 ....82 C1
Gillian St SE13 .....67 A2
Gillies Ho NW6 .....11 C1
Gilling Ct **5** NW3 ..12 A2
Gillingham Mews
SW1 ....146 C4
Gillingham Rd NW2 ..1 A1
Gillingham Row
SW1 ....146 C4
Gillingham St SW1 146 C4
Gillison Wlk SE16 .139 C2
Gillman Ho **22** E2 ..24 C3
Gillray Ho SW10 ...157 B3
Gilmore Ho SW4 ...60 B3
Gilmore Rd SE13 ...67 C3
Gilpin Ave SW14 ...55 C3
Gilpin Rd E5 ....18 A4
Gilray Ho W2 ....115 B4
Gilstead Rd SW6 ...166 B2
Gilston Rd SW10 ..143 A1
Giltspur St EC1 ....108 B2
Gilwell Ct **5** E5 ....17 A4
Gipsy Corner W3 ...28 C4
Gipsy La SW15 .....57 A4
Gipsy Moth IV SE10 .52 B4
Giraud St E14 ....34 A3
Girdlers Rd W14 ...39 C2
Girdlestone Wlk N19 ..4 B2

Girdwood Rd SW18,
SW19 ....70 A4
Girling Ho **6** N1 ...24 A4
Gironde Rd SW6 ...155 A1
Girton Villas **6** W10 .30 C3
Girton Villas **6**
W10 ....30 C3
Gissing Wlk N1 .....14 C1
Gladiator St SE23 ...66 A1
Glading Terr N16 ....7 B1
Gladsmuir Rd N19 ...4 B3
Gladstone Ct SW1 147 C3
1 SW8 ....172 A4
E14 ....33 C3
Gladstone Park Prim
Sch NW10 ....9 A3
Gladstone St SE1 .136 A2
Gladstone Terr
SW8 ....170 B4
Gladwin Ho NW1 ...83 A1
Gladwyn Rd SW15 .57 C4
Gladys Rd NW6 .....10 C1
Glaisher St SE10 ...52 B3
Glamis Ct W3 ....37 A4
Glamis Est **3** E1 ...32 C2
Glamis Pl E1 ....32 B2
Glamis Rd E1 ....32 B2
Glanville Ho **4**
SW12 ....73 B4
Glanville Rd SW2 ..62 A2
Glasbury Ho **5** SW9 62 B3
Glaserton Rd N16 ...7 A4
Glasgow Ho W9 .....78 B1
Glasgow Terr SW1 .146 C1
Glass St **2** E2 .....25 A1
Glasshill St SE1 ....136 B4
Glasshouse Fields
E1 ....32 C2
Glasshouse St W1 .119 A3
Glasshouse Wlk
SE11 ....148 C2
Glasshouse Yd EC1 .96 C1
Glastonbury Ct **2**
SE14 ....50 B3
Glastonbury Ho
SW1 ....146 A2
Glastonbury St NW6 10 B3
Glaucus St E3 ....34 A4
Glazbury Rd W14 ..140 B2
Glazebrook Cl SE21 .75 C2
Glebe Cl **1** W4 .....38 A1
Glebe Ho **5** SE16 ..40 A3
Glebe Pl SW3 ......158 A4
Glebe Rd NW10 .....8 B2
E8 ....16 B1
SW13 ....47 A1
Glebe St W4 ....38 A1
Glebe Terr **1** E3 ....27 A2
Gledhow Gdns
SW5 ....142 C3
Gledstanes Rd
W14 ....140 B1
Glegg Pl **3** SW15 ...57 C3
Glen Albyn Rd
SW19 ....69 C2
Glen Ho **1** E16 ....35 C1
Glenaffric Ave E14 ..42 C2
Glenalmond Ho **2**
SW15 ....57 C1
Glenarm Rd E5 .....17 C4
Glenbrook Rd NW6 .10 C3

Glenburnie Rd
SW17 ....72 B1
Glencoe Mans
SW9 ....163 B1
Glendall St SW9 ....62 B3
Glendarvon St
SW15 ....57 C4
Glendower Gdns **10**
SW14 ....55 C4
Glendower Pl SW7 143 B4
Glendown Ho **2** E8 16 C3
Glendun Ct W3 .....29 A2
Glendun Rd W3 ....29 A2
Gleneagles Cl **21**
SE16 ....40 A1
Glenfield Rd SW12 .73 B3
Glenfinlas Way SE5 .48 A3
Glenforth St SE10 ..43 B1
Glengall Gr E14 ....42 B3
Glengall Pass **2**
NW6 ....23 C4
Glengall Rd NW6 ...23 B4
SE15 ....49 B4
Glengall Terr SE15 .49 B4
Glengarnock Ave
E14 ....42 B2
Glengarry Rd SE22 .64 B2
Glenhurst Ave NW5 .12 C4
Glenilla Rd NW3 ...12 A2
Glenister Rd SE10 ..43 B1
Glenloch Ct **2** NW3 12 A2
Glenloch Rd NW3 ..12 A3
Glenluce Rd SE3 ...53 C4
Glenmore Ho **6** *
TW10 ....54 A1
Glenmore Rd NW3 .12 A2
Glennie Ct SE21 ....76 C3
Glennie Ho SE10 ...52 B2
Glennie Rd SE27,
SW16 ....74 C1
Glenridding NW1 ...83 A1
Glenrosa St SW6 ..166 C2
Glenroy St W12 .....30 B3
Glensdale Rd SE4 ..66 B4
Glenshaw Mans
SW9 ....163 B1
Glentanner Way
SW17 ....71 C1
Glentham Gdns
SW13 ....47 A4
Glentham Rd SW13 47 A4
Glenthorne Mews
W6 ....39 A2
Glenthorne Rd W6 .39 A2
Glenthorpe SW15 ..56 C3
Glentworth St NW1 .91 A1
Glenville Gr SE8 ...51 B3
Glenville Mews
SW18 ....70 C4
Glenworth Ave E14 .42 C2
Gliddon Rd W14 ...140 A2
Glifford Ho SW1 ...146 C1
Globe JMI Sch E2 ...25 B2
Globe Pond Rd
SE16 ....33 A1
Globe Rd E1,E2 .....25 B1
Globe St SE1 ....137 B3
Globe Terr **1** E2 ....25 B2
Globe Theatre The *
SE1 ....122 C3
Globe Yd W1 ....104 A1

Gloucester Ave
NW1 ....81 C4
Gloucester Cir SE10 52 B3
Gloucester Cres
SE1 ....124 B3
W1 ....82 A4
Gloucester Ct EC3 .124 B3
SE1 ....137 A2
Richmond TW9 ......44 C3
Gloucester Dr N4 ...6 A2
Gloucester Gate
NW1 ....82 A2
Gloucester Gate Mews
NW1 ....82 A2
Gloucester Gdns
W2 ....100 C2
NW11 ....1 B4
Richmond TW10 ....54 C2
Gloucester Mews
W2 ....101 A1
Gloucester Mews W
W2 ....101 A1
Gloucester Pk
SW7 ....142 C4
Gloucester Pl W1 ..103 A4
Gloucester Pl Mews
W1 ....103 A3
Gloucester Prim Sch
SE15 ....49 A3
Gloucester Rd
SW7 ....142 C4
W3 ....37 B4
Richmond TW9 ......44 C3
Gloucester Road Sta
SW7 ....142 C4
Gloucester Sq W2 .101 C1
6 E2 ....24 C4
Gloucester St SW1 146 C2
Gloucester Terr
W2 ....101 A1
Gloucester Way
EC1 ....95 C3
Gloucester Wlk
W8 ....127 C4
Glover Ho **2** NW6 ..11 B1
SE15 ....65 A3
Glycena Rd SW11 ..60 B4
Glyn Ct SE27 ....74 C1
Glyn Mans W14 ...140 B4
Glyn Rd E5 ....17 C4
Glyn St SE11 ......148 C1
Glynde Mews SW3 130 B1
Glynde Reach WC1 .94 B3
Glynde St SE4 ......66 B1
Glynfield Rd NW10 ..8 A1
Goat Wharf TW8 ...44 A4
Goater's Alley
SW6 ....155 A1
Godalming Rd E14 .34 A4
Godbold Rd E15 ....76 C4
Goddard Pl N19 .....4 B1
Godfrey Ho EC1 .....97 B3
Godfrey St SW3 ...144 B2
E15 ....76 B3
Goding St SE11 ....148 B1
Godley Rd SW18 ...71 C3
Godliman St EC4 ..122 C4
Godman Rd SE15 ...50 A1
Godolphin & Latymer
Sch W6 ....39 A2
Godolphin Ho NW3 .12 A1
2 SW2 ....74 C3

Godolphin Pl W3 . . . .28 C2
Godolphin Rd W12 . . . .39 A4
Godson St N1 . . . . .85 B2
Godstone Ct **1** N16 . .7 A3
Godstone Ho SE1 . .137 C2
Godwin Cl N1 . . . . .87 A2
Godwin Cl NW1 . . . . . .83 A2
Godwin Ho NW6 . . . . .78 A2
2 E2 . . . . .24 B3
Goffers Ho SE3 . . . . . .53 A1
Goffers Rd SE3,SE13 . .53 A1
Goffton Ho SW9 . . . .173 A1
Golborne Gdns
 5 W10 . . . . .23 A1
 W10 . . . . .23 A1
Golborne Mews **9**
 W10 . . . . .31 A4
Golborne Rd W10 . . . .31 A4
Golden Hind Pl **4**
 SE8 . . . . .41 B2
Golden La EC1 . . . . . . .97 A1
Golden Plover Cl
 E16 . . . . .35 C3
Golden Sq W1 . . . . . .119 A4
Golders Ct NW11 . . . . .1 B4
Golders Gdns NW11 . . .1 B4
Golders Green Cres
 NW11 . . . . .1 C4
Golders Green Rd
 NW11 . . . . .1 A4
Golders Green Sta
 NW11 . . . . .1 C3
Golders Hill Sch
 NW11 . . . . .1 C4
Golders Park Cl
 NW11 . . . . .1 C3
Goldhawk Ind Est The
 W6 . . . . .39 A3
Goldhawk Mews **2**
 W12 . . . . .39 A4
Goldhawk Rd W12 . . .38 C4
Goldhawk Road Sta
 W12 . . . . .39 B4
Goldhurst Terr NW6 . .11 B1
Goldie Ho N19 . . . . . . .4 C4
Golding St E1 . . . . . . .111 C1
Golding Terr E1 . . . . .111 C2
Goldington Cres
 NW1 . . . . .83 B2
Goldington Ct NW1 . . .83 B3
Goldington St NW1 . . .83 B2
Goldman Cl
 E2 . . . . .24 C1 99 B2
Goldney Rd W9 . . . . . .23 C1
Goldsboro Rd SW8 . .161 C1
Goldsborough Ho
 SW8 . . . . .171 C2
Goldsmith Ave W3 . . .28 C2
Goldsmith Ho W3 . . . .28 C2
Goldsmith Rd SE15 . .49 C2
Goldsmith St EC2 . . .109 A2
Goldsmith's Pl
 NW6 . . . . .78 A3
Goldsmith's Row **2** E2 . .24 C3
Goldsmith's Sq **1**
 E2 . . . . .24 C3
Goldsmiths Bldgs
 W3 . . . . .28 C1
Goldsmiths Coll
 SE14 . . . . .51 A2
Goldsworthy Gdns
 SE16 . . . . .40 B1

Goldthorpe NW1 . . . . .82 C3
Goldwell Ho SE22 . . . .64 A4
Goldwin Cl SE14 . . . . .50 B2
Goldwing Cl E16 . . . . .35 C3
Gomm Rd SE16 . . . . . .40 B3
Gondar Gdns NW6 . . .10 B3
Gondar Mans NW6 . . .10 B3
Gonson St SE8 . . . . . . .52 A4
Gonston Cl SW19 . . . .70 A2
Gonville Ho **3**
 SW15 . . . . .57 C1
Gonville St SW6 . . . . .58 A4
Gooch Ho EC1 . . . . . .107 B4
Good Hart Pl E14 . . . .33 A2
Goodall Ho **10** SE4 . . .65 C3
Goodfaith Ho **10**
 E14 . . . . .34 A2
Goodge Pl W1 . . . . . .105 A3
Goodge St W1 . . . . . .105 A3
Goodge Street Sta
 W1 . . . . .105 A4
Goodhall St NW10 . . .21 B2
Goodhope Ho **13**
 E14 . . . . .34 A2
Goodinge Cl N7 . . . . .14 A2
Goodinge Rd N7 . . . . .14 A2
Goodman Cres SW2 . .73 C2
Goodman's Stile
 E1 . . . . .111 B2
Goodman's Yd E1,
 EC3 . . . . .124 C4
Goodrich Ct **11** W10 . .30 C3
Goodrich Ho N16 . . . . .7 A4
 11 E2 . . . . .25 B3
Goodrich Prim Sch
 SE22 . . . . .64 C1
Goodrich Rd SE22 . . .64 C1
Goodson Rd NW10 . . .8 A1
Goodspeed Ho **11**
 E14 . . . . .34 A2
Goodsway NW1 . . . . . .84 A2
Goodway Gdns E14 . .34 C3
Goodwill Ho **12** E14 . .34 A2
Goodwin Cl SE16 . . .139 A1
Goodwin Ho **2**
 SE15 . . . . .65 A4
Goodwin Rd W12 . . . .38 C4
Goodwin St N4 . . . . . .5 C2
Goodwins Ct WC2 . . .120 A4
Goodwood Ho **4**
 W4 . . . . .38 B1
Goodwood Mans **4**
 SW9 . . . . .62 C4
Goodwood Rd SE14 . .51 A3
Goosander Ct **33**
 SE8 . . . . .51 B4
Goose Green Trad Est
 SE22 . . . . .64 C3
Gophir La EC4 . . . . . .123 B4
Gopsall St N1 . . . . . . .87 C3
Gordon Ave SW14 . . .56 A3
Gordon Ct W12 . . . . . .30 B3
Gordon Gr SE5 . . . . . .48 A1
Gordon Ho E1 . . . . . . .32 B2
 1 SE10 . . . . .52 C4
Gordon Hospl The
 SW1 . . . . .147 B3
Gordon House Rd
 NW5 . . . . .12 C4
Gordon Lo N16 . . . . . .6 C3
Gordon Mans W14 . .127 C4
Gordon Rd
 Richmond TW9 . . . . .44 B1
 W4 . . . . .45 A4
 SE15 . . . . .50 A1
 E15 . . . . .76 B4
Gordon Sq WC1 . . . . .93 C2

Gordon St WC1 . . . . . .93 B2
Gordonbrock Jun & Inf
 Sch SE4 . . . . .66 C2
Gordonbrock Rd
 SE4 . . . . .66 C2
Gordondale Rd
 SW18,SW19 . . . . .70 C2
Gore Rd E9 . . . . .25 B4
Gore St SW7 . . . . . . .129 A2
Gorefield Ho NW6 . . .23 C3
Gorefield Pl NW6 . . . .23 C3
Gorham Ho **12** SW4 . .61 B1
Gorham Pl W11 . . . . .112 A3
Goring St EC3 . . . . . .110 B2
Gorleston St W14 . . .140 B4
Gorse Cl E16 . . . . .35 C3
Gorsefield Ho **5**
 E14 . . . . .33 C2
Gorst Rd NW10 . . . . . .20 C1
 SW11 . . . . .60 B1
Gorsuch Pl **12** E2 . . . .98 C4
Gorsuch St E2 . . . . . . .98 C4
Gosberton Rd SW12 .72 C3
Gosfield St W1 . . . . . .104 C3
Gosford Ho **19** E3 . . . .26 B3
Goslett Yd WC2 . . . .105 C2
Gosling Ho **1** E1 . . . . .32 B2
Gosling Way SW9 . . .173 B4
Gospel Oak Prim Sch
 NW5 . . . . .12 C4
Gospel Oak Sta
 NW5 . . . . .12 C4
Gosport Ho **9**
 SW15 . . . . .68 C3
Gosport Way **5**
 SE15 . . . . .49 B3
Gosset St E2 . . .24 C2 99 B4
Gosterwood St SE8 . .51 A4
Goswell Pl EC1 . . . . . .96 B3
Goswell Rd EC1 . . . . . .96 B3
Gothic Ct **15** SE5 . . . .48 B3
Gottfried Mews
 NW5 . . . . .13 B4
Gough Ho N1 . . . . . . .86 B4
Gough Sq EC4 . . . . . .107 C2
Gough St WC1 . . . . . . .95 A1
Gough Wlk **7** E14 . . . .33 C3
Gould Terr **23** E8 . . . .17 A3
Goulden Ho SW11 . .168 A2
Goulman Ho **21** E1 . . .25 B1
Goulston St E1 . . . . . .110 C2
Goulton Rd E5 . . . . . . .17 A4
Govan St E2 . . . . .24 C4
Gover Ct SW4 . . . . . . .172 B2
Gowan Ave SW6 . . . .164 A4
Gowan Ho **2** E2 . . . . .99 A3
Gowan Rd NW10 . . . . .9 A2
Gower Cl SW4 . . . . . .61 B1
Gower Ct WC1 . . . . . . .93 B2
Gower Ho SE17 . . . . .151 A2
Gower Mews WC1 . . .105 C4
Gower Pl NW1,WC1 . .93 B2
Gower St WC1 . . . . . . .93 B1
Gower's Wlk E1 . . . . .111 B1
Gowlett Rd SE15 . . . .64 C4
Gowrie Rd SW11 . . . .60 C4
Grace Ho SE11 . . . . .163 A4
Grace Jones Cl E8 . . .16 C2
Grace Pl E3 . . . . .27 A2
Grace St E3 . . . . .27 A2
Grace's Mews SE5 . . .49 A1
Grace's Rd SE5 . . . . . .49 A1
Gracechurch St
 EC3 . . . . .109 C1
Gracefield Gdns
 SW16 . . . . .74 A1

Gracehill **2** E1 . . . . . .32 B4
Graces Alley E1 . . . . .125 B4
Graces Mews NW8 . . .79 A1
Graemesdyke Ave
 SW14 . . . . .55 A3
Grafton Cres NW1 . . . .13 A2
Grafton Ct **10** E8 . . . .16 C3
Grafton Ho **1** E3 . . . .26 C2
 12 SE8 . . . . .41 B1
Grafton Mews W1 . . .92 C1
Grafton Pl NW1 . . . . . .93 C3
Grafton Prim Sch N7 . .5 A1
Grafton Rd NW5 . . . . .12 C3
 W3 . . . . .28 B2
Grafton Sq SW4 . . . . .61 B4
Grafton St W1 . . . . . .118 B3
Grafton Terr NW5 . . . .12 C3
Grafton Way W1 . . . . .93 A1
Grafton Yd NW5 . . . . .13 A2
Graham Ct **5** SE14 . . .50 C4
Graham Ho **5** SW19 . .69 C3
 21 SW12 . . . . .73 A4
Graham Mans **2** E8 .17 A2
Graham Rd **8** E8 . . . . .16 C2
 W4 . . . . .37 C3
Graham St N1 . . . . . . .86 B1
Graham Terr SW1 . . .145 C3
Grainger Ct **22** SE5 . .48 B3
Grampian Gdns NW2 . .1 A3
Grampians The **19**
 W14 . . . . .39 C4
Granard Ave SW15 . . .57 A2
Granard Ho **10** E9 . . . .17 C2
Granard Prim Sch
 SW15 . . . . .57 A1
Granard Rd SW11,
 SW12 . . . . .59 C3
Granary Rd E1 . . . . . . .25 A1
Granary St NW1 . . . . .83 B3
Granby Pl SE1 . . . . . .135 B3
Granby St E2 . . . . .99 A2
 E2 . . . . .24 C1 99 B3
Granby Terr NW1 . . . .82 C1
Grand Ave EC1 . . . . .108 B4
Grand Junction Wharf
 N1 . . . . .86 C1
Grand Par SW14 . . . . .55 B3
Grand Union Cl W9 . .31 B4
Grand Union Cres
 E8 . . . . .24 C4
Grand Union Ind Est
 NW10 . . . . .20 A3
Grand Vitesse Ind Est
 SE1 . . . . .122 B1
Grandfield Ct W4 . . . .45 C4
Grandison Rd SW11 . .60 B2
Granfield St SW11 . . .167 C3
Grange Ct WC2 . . . . .107 A1
 SE15 . . . . .49 B1
Grange Gdns NW3 . . . .2 A1
Grange Gr N1 . . . . .15 B2
Grange Ho NW10 . . . .21 C4
 SE1 . . . . .138 C1
Grange La SE21 . . . . . .76 B2
Grange Mills SW12 . . .73 B3
Grange Mus of
 Community History The
 NW10 . . . . .10 C1
Grange Prim Sch
 SE1 . . . . .138 A1
Grange Rd SE1 . . . . .138 C1
 NW10 . . . . .9 A2
 W4 . . . . .37 A1
 SW13 . . . . .46 C2
Grange St N1 . . . . .87 C3

Grange The SE1 . . . .138 C1
 W14 . . . . .140 C3
 10 NW3 . . . . .12 B2
 7 W4 . . . . .37 A1
 W3 . . . . .37 A4
 W12 . . . . .39 A3
Grange Wlk SE1 . . . .138 C1
Grange Yd SE1 . . . . .138 C1
Grangecourt Rd N16 .7 A3
Grangefield NW1 . . . . .14 A1
Grangemill **1** NW5 . .13 A4
Grangeway NW6 . . . . .10 C1
Gransden Ave E8 . . . .17 A1
Gransden Ho **5** SE8 . .41 B1
Gransden Rd W12 . . . .38 B4
Grant Ho SW8 . . . . . .171 B1
Grant Rd SW11 . . . . . .60 A4
Grant St N1 . . . . .85 B2
Grantbridge St N1 . . . .86 B2
Grantham Ct **5**
 SE16 . . . . .40 C4
Grantham Ho **12**
 SE15 . . . . .49 C4
Grantham Pl W1 . . . .118 A1
Grantham Rd SW9 . .172 B1
 W4 . . . . .46 A3
Grantley Ho
 2 SE14 . . . . .50 C4
 5 SW19 . . . . .69 C3
Grantley St E1 . . . . . . .25 C1
Grantully Rd W9 . . . . .88 A3
Granville Ct N1 . . . . . .87 C4
 4 SE14 . . . . .51 A3
Granville Gr SE13 . . . .67 B4
Granville Ho **13** E14 .33 C3
Granville Mans **8**
 W12 . . . . .39 B4
Granville Pk SE13 . . . .67 C4
Granville Pl **1** W1 . . .103 B1
 SW6 . . . . .156 A1
Granville Point NW2 . .1 B2
Granville Rd NW2 . . . . .1 B2
 NW6 . . . . .23 C3
 SW18 . . . . .70 B4
Granville Sq **1** 95 A3
 SE15 . . . . .49 A3
Granville St WC1 . . . . .95 A3
Grape St WC2 . . . . . .106 A2
Grasmere NW1 . . . . . .92 B3
Grasmere Ave W3 . . . .28 C2
Grasmere Ct SW13 . .46 C4
Grasmere Ho **16**
 N16 . . . . .15 C4
Grasmere JMI Sch
 SE15 . . . . .50 B3
Grasmere Point **2**
 SE15 . . . . .50 B3
Grately Ho **10** SW15 . .69 A3
Gratton Rd W14 . . . .126 A1
Gravel La E1 . . . . . . .110 C2
Graveley Ho **7** SE8 . .41 B2
Gravesend Rd W12 . .29 C2
Gray Ho SE17 . . . . . .151 A2
Gray's Inn* WC1 . . . .107 A3
Gray's Inn Pl WC1 . . .107 A3
Gray's Inn Rd WC1 . . .95 A2
Gray's Inn Sq
 WC1 . . . . .107 B4
Gray's Yd W1 . . . . . . .103 C2
Grayfriars Pas EC1 . .108 B2
Grayling Rd N16 . . . . . .6 C2
Grayling Sq
 E2 . . . . .24 C2 99 C4
Grayshott Rd SW11 . .60 C4
Grayson Ho EC1 . . . . .97 A3

Grayswood Point 14 SW15 68 C3
Grazebrook JMI Sch N16 7 A2
Grazebrook Rd N16 6 C2
Great Arthur Ho EC1 96 C1
Great Bell Alley EC2 109 B2
Great Brownings E15 76 B1
Great Castle St W1 104 C2
Great Central St NW1 102 C4
Great Chapel St W1 105 B2
Great Chertsey Rd SW14,W4 45 C2
Great Church La W6 39 C1
Great College St SW1 134 A2
Great Croft WC1 94 B3
Great Cumberland Mews W1 102 C1
Great Cumberland Pl W1 103 A1
Great Dover St SE1 137 B2
Great Eastern Bldgs 10 E8 17 A2
Great Eastern Ent Ctr E14 42 A4
Great Eastern Pier E14 41 C1
Great Eastern Rd E15 19 C2
Great Eastern St EC2 24 A1 98 A2
Great Eastern Wharf SW11 158 B1
Great Field 7 NW5 13 B3
Great George St SW1 134 A3
Great Guildford Bsns Sq SE1 122 C1
Great Guildford St SE1 122 C1
Great James St WC1 106 C4
Great Marlborough St W1 104 C1
Great Mathers Rd SE11 150 A4
Great Maze Pond SE1 137 C4
Great New St EC4 107 C2
Great Newport St WC2 120 A4
Great Ormond St WC1 94 C1
Great Ormond St Hospl for Children WC1 94 C1
Great Percy St WC1 95 B4
Great Peter St SW1 133 C1
Great Portland St W1 104 B4
Great Portland Street Sta W1 92 B1
Great Pulteney St W1 119 A4
Great Queen St WC2 106 B2
Great Russell St WC1 106 A3
Great Scotland Yd SW1,WC2 120 A2
Great Smith St SW1 133 C2
Great Spilmans SE22 64 A2
Great St Helen's EC3 110 A2
Great St Thomas Apostle EC4 123 A4
Great Suffolk St SE1 122 B1
Great Sutton St EC1 96 B1
Great Swan Alley EC2 109 B2
Great Titchfield St W1 104 C3
Great Tower St EC3 124 A4
Great Trinity La EC4 123 A4
Great Turnstile WC2 107 A3
Great West Rd W4, W6 45 C4
Great West Road Cedars Rd W4 45 B4
Great West Road Hogarth La W4 46 A4
Great Western Rd W2,W9 31 B4
Great Winchester St EC2 109 C2
Great Windmill St W1 119 B4
Great Yd SE1 138 B4
Greatfield Cl 4 N19 13 B4
SE4 66 C3
Greatham Wlk 8 SW15 68 C3
Greatorex Ho E1 111 B4
Greatorex St E1 111 B4
Greaves Cotts 12 E14 33 A4
Greaves Twr SW10 157 A2
Grebe Ct 11 E14 42 B4
38 SE8 51 B4
Greek Ct W1 105 C1
Greek St W1 105 C1
Green Arbour Ct EC1 108 A2
Green Bank E1 32 A1
Green Cl NW11 2 B4
Green Dale SE22 64 A2
Green Dragon Ct SE1 123 B1
Green Dragon Jun & Inf Sch TW8 44 A4
Green Dragon La TW8 36 B1
Green Dragon Yd E1 111 B3
Green Ho The 5 SW19 70 A3
Green Hundred Rd SE15 49 C4
Green Lanes N4,N8, N15 6 A4
Green Park SW1, W1 132 B4
Green Park Sta W1 118 C2
Green St W1 117 B4
Green Terr EC1 95 C3
Green The W3 29 A3
Green Wlk SE1 138 A1
Green Wood NW5 13 B3
Green Yd WC1 95 A2
Green's Ct W11 112 C1
Greenacre Ct E8 16 C3
Greenacre Sq 26 SE16 40 C4
Greenaway Gdns NW3 11 A4
Greenaway Ho NW8 78 C4
WC1 95 B3
Greenberry St NW8 80 A1
Greencoat Pl SW1 147 A4
Greencoat Row SW1 133 A1
Greencroft Gdns NW6 11 B1
Greene Ct 20 SE14 50 C4
Greene Ho SE1 137 B1
Greenend Rd W4 38 A4
Greener Ho 3 SW4 61 C4
Greenfield Gdns NW2 1 A1
Greenfield Ho 28 SW19 69 C3
Greenfield Rd E1 111 C2
Greenham Cl SE1 135 B3
Greenham Ho 6 E9 25 B4
Greenheath Bsns Ctr 3 E2 25 A1
Greenhill NW3 11 C4
Greenhill Pk NW10 21 A4
Greenhill Rd NW10 21 A4
Greenhill's Rents EC1 108 A4
Greenhills Terr 16 N1 15 C2
Greenland Ho 4 E1 26 A1
SE8 40 C1
Greenland Mews SE8 40 C1
Greenland Pl NW1 82 B4
Greenland Quay SE16 40 C2
Greenland Rd NW1 82 C4
Greenland St NW1 82 B4
Greenleaf Cl 8 SW2 74 C4
Greenman St N1 86 C4
Greenmead Sch SW15 57 A2
Greenock Rd 11 W3 37 B3
Greens Ct W1 119 B4
Greenside Prim Sch W12 38 C4
Greenside Rd W12 38 C4
Greenstead Gdns SW15 57 A2
Greenstreet Hill SE4 65 C4
Greenway Cl N4 6 B2
Greenwell St W1 92 B1
Greenwich Bsns Ctr SE10 52 A3
Greenwich Bsns Pk SE10 52 A3
Greenwich Church St SE10 52 B4
Greenwich Ct 18 E1 32 A3
Greenwich District Hospl SE10 43 B1
Greenwich High Rd SE10 52 A3
Greenwich Ind Est SE10 52 A3
Greenwich Mkt 1 SE10 52 B4
Greenwich Park SE10 53 A3
Greenwich Park Sch SE10 52 B3
Greenwich Park St SE10 52 C4
Greenwich South St SE10 52 B2
Greenwich Sta SE10 52 A3
Greenwich View E14 42 A3
Greenwood 8 SW19 69 C4
Greenwood Ho WC1 95 B3
8 SE4 65 C3
Greenwood Pl NW5 13 A3
Greenwood Rd E8 16 C2
Greenwood Terr NW10 20 C3
Greet Ho SE1 135 C3
Greet St SE1 121 C1
Gregor Mews SE3 53 C3
Gregory Pl W8 128 A4
Greig Terr SE17 48 A4
Grena Gdns TW9 54 B3
Grena Rd TW10,TW9 54 B3
Grenada Ho 18 E14 33 B2
Grenade St E14 33 B2
Grendon Ho N1 84 C1
29 E9 17 B1
Grendon St NW8 90 A2
Grenfell Ho SE5 48 B3
Grenfell Rd W11 30 C2
Grenfell Sch E1 32 A3
Grenfell Twr 5 W11 30 C2
Grenfell Wlk 4 W11 30 C2
Grenville Ho 24 E3 26 A3
4 SE8 51 C4
Grenville Lo N6 4 B4
Grenville Mews SW7 143 A3
Grenville Pl SW7 142 C4
Grenville Rd N19 5 A3
Grenville St WC1 94 B1
Gresham Almshouses 3 SW9 62 B3
Gresham Coll EC1 107 C3
Gresham Rd SW9 62 C4
Gresham St EC2 109 A2
Gresham Way SW19 70 C1
Gresham Way Est SW19 71 A1
Gresley Ho SW8 171 C4
Gresley Rd N19 4 B4
Gresse St W1 105 B2
Gressenhall Rd SW18 70 B4
Greswell St SW6 47 C2
Gretton Ho 2 E2 25 B2
Greville Hall NW6 78 B2
Greville Ho SW1 131 B2
SW15 57 C4
Greville Lo W2 100 A2
Greville Mews NW6 78 A3
Greville Pl NW6, NW8 78 B3
Greville Rd NW6 78 A2
NW6 78 B2
Richmond TW10 54 B1
Greville St EC1 107 C4
Grey Coat Hospital CE Sch The SW1 133 B1
Grey Coat Hospital St Michaels The SW1 147 B3
Grey Eagle St E1 24 B1 99 A1
Grey Ho 27 W12 30 A2
Grey Turner Ho W12 29 C3
Greycoat Pl SW1 133 B1
Greycoat St SW1 133 B1
Greyfriars 16 SE26 76 C1
Greyfriars Ho SE3 53 B4
Greyhound Ct WC2 121 B4
Greyhound Rd W6 154 A4
NW10 22 A2
Greyladies Gdns SE10 52 B1
Greystoke Ho SE15 49 C4
Greystoke Pl EC4 107 C2
Grice Ct N1 15 B2
Grierson Rd SE23 65 C1
Griffin Cl NW10 9 A3
Griffin Ct W12 30 A1
W4 38 B1
8 Brentford TW8 44 A4
Griffin Gate SW15 57 C4
Grifton Ho 3 SW11 60 A4
Grigg's Pl SE1 138 B1
Grimaldi Ho N1 84 C2
Grimsby St E2 99 A2
Grimsel Path SE5 48 A3
Grimshaw Cl N6 3 C4
Grimston Rd SW6 164 C1
Grimthorpe Ho EC1 96 A2
Grimwade Cl SE15 65 B4
Grindal St SE1 135 B3
Grindall Ho 26 E1 25 A1
Grindley Ho 3 E3 33 B4
Grinling Gibbons Prim Sch SE8 51 B4
Grinling Pl SE8 51 C4
Grinstead Rd SE8 41 A1
Grisedale NW1 92 C4
Grittleton Rd W9 23 C1
Grocers' Hall Ct EC2 109 B1
Groom Cres SW18 71 C4
Groom Pl SW1 131 C2
Groombridge Rd E9 17 C1
Groome Ho SE11 149 A3
Grosse Way SW15 57 A1
Grosvenor Ave N5 15 B3
Richmond TW10 54 A2
SW14 56 A4
Grosvenor Bridge SW1 160 B4
Grosvenor Cotts SW1 145 B4
Grosvenor Cres SW1 131 C3
Grosvenor Cres Mews SW1 131 B3
Grosvenor Ct NW6 22 C4
W4 37 A1
2 Richmond TW10 54 B1
SW15 58 A2
Grosvenor Ct Mans W2 102 C1
Grosvenor Gdns SW1 132 B1
NW2 9 B3
SW14 56 A4

Grosvenor Gdns Mews E
SW1 ....**132** B2
Grosvenor Gdns Mews N
SW1 ....**132** A1
Grosvenor Gdns Mews S
SW1 ....**132** B1
Grosvenor Hill W1 .**118** A4
Grosvenor Hill Ct
W1 ....**118** A4
Grosvenor Ho E5 ....**7** C3
Grosvenor Park SE5 **48** B3
Grosvenor Pier
SW1 ....**161** B4
Grosvenor Ho PL SE5 .**48** A3
Grosvenor PI SW1 ...**132** A3
Grosvenor Rd SW1 ..**161** A4
W4 ....**37** B1
Richmond TW10 ....**54** A2
Grosvenor Residences
8 W14 ....**39** C2
Grosvenor Sq W1 ...**117** C4
Grosvenor St W1 ...**118** A4
Grosvenor Terr SE5 .**48** B4
Grosvenor The NW11 .**2** A4
Grosvenor Wharf Rd
E14 ....**42** C2
Grote's Bldgs SE3 ..**53** A1
Grote's PI SE3 .....**53** A1
Groton Rd SW18 ....**71** A2
Grotto Ct SE1 ....**136** C4
Grotto Pas W1 ....**103** C4
Grove Crescent Rd
E15 ....**19** C2
Grove Ct NW8 ......**89** B4
SW10 ....**143** A4
SE5 ....**49** A1
SW4 ....**61** B4
Grove Dwellings E1 .**32** B4
Grove End NW5 ....**13** A4
Grove End Gdns
NW8 ....**79** A1
Grove End Ho NW8 ..**89** B3
Grove End Rd NW8 ..**89** B3
Grove Gdns NW8 ....**90** B3
Grove Hall Ct NW8 ..**89** A4
Grove Hill Rd SE5 ..**64** A4
Grove Ho SW3 .....**158** B4
SE3 ....**53** B1
Grove House Froebel Ed
Inst SW15 ....**56** B1
Grove House Prim Sch
SE27 ....**75** A1
Grove Jun & Inf Sch
W4 ....**45** B4
Grove La SE5 ......**64** A4
Grove Lane Terr
SE5 ....**48** C1
Grove Lo SW4 ......**61** B3
Grove Mans **8** SE8 ..**16** C4
2 W6 ....**39** B4
SW6 ....**60** B3
Grove Mews W6 ....**39** B3
Grove Park Bridge
W4 ....**45** B3
Grove Park Gdns
W4 ....**45** B3
Grove Park Terr
W4 ....**45** A4
Grove Pk SE5 ......**49** A1
Grove PI NW3 ......**2** C1
W3 ....**28** B1
SW12 ....**61** A1

Grove Rd NW2 ......**9** B2
E3 ....**26** A3
W3 ....**28** B1
SW13 ....**46** B1
Richmond TW10 ....**54** B1
Grove St SE8 ....**41** B1
Grove Terr NW5 ....**13** A4
Grove The NW11 ....**1** A4
N6 ....**3** C4
N4 ....**5** B4
SE21 ....**76** C3
Grove Vale SE22 ....**64** B3
Grove Vale Prim Sch
SE22 ....
Grovedale Rd N19 ...**4** C2
Groveland Ct EC4 ..**109** A1
Grovelands CI SE5 ..**49** A1
Groveley Ho N4 .....**6** B4
Grover Ct SE13 .....**52** A1
Grover Ho SE11 ...**149** A1
SW4 ....**61** B2
Groveside Ct
SW11 ....**167** B2
Groveway SW9 .....**173** A3
Grovewood **1** TW9 ..**44** C2
Grummant Rd SE15 .**49** B2
Grundy St E14 ......**34** A3
Guardian Angels RC JMI
Sch E3 ....**26** A2
Guards Mus The
SW1 ....**133** A3
Gubyon Ave SE24 ...**63** A2
Guerin Sq E3 ....**26** B2
Guernsey Gr SE24 ..**75** B4
Guernsey Ho **9** N1 ..**15** B2
Guernsey Rd **8** N1 ..**15** B2
*Guild Hall*** EC2 ....**109** A2
Guildford Gr SE10 ..**52** A2
Guildford Ho **2** SE5 .**48** B1
Guildford Rd SW8 ..**172** B4
Guildford St WC1 ...**94** B1
Guildhall Bldgs
EC2 ....**109** B2
Guildhall Sch Music &
Drama EC2 ....**109** A4
Guildhall Yd EC2 ..**109** A2
Guildhouse St
SW1 ....**146** C3
Guilford PI WC1 ....**94** C1
Guillemot Ct 8 SE8 .**51** B4
Guilsborough CI
NW10 ....**8** A1
Guinness CI E9 .....**18** A1
Guinness Ct NW8 ...**80** B3
EC1 ....**97** A3
E1 ....**111** A1
SW3 ....**144** C3
Guinness Sq SE1 ..**152** A4
Guinness Trust Bldgs
SE11 ....**138** A4
SW3 ....**144** C3
SE11 ....**150** A2
7 E2 ....**24** C3
W6 ....**39** B1
Guion Rd SW6 .....**165** A1
Gujarat Ho **1** N16 ...**7** A1
Gulland Wlk **20** N1 .**15** B2
Gullane Ho **22** E3 ...**26** B3
Gulliver St SE16 ....**41** B3
Gulston Wlk SW3 ..**145** A3
Gun St E1 ....**110** C3
Gun Wharf E1 ......**26** A4
E1 ....**32** B1
Gunmakers La E3 ...**26** A4
Gunners Rd SW18 ..**71** C2

Gunnersbury Avenue
(North Circular Rd)
W3 ....**36** C3
Gunnersbury CI 8
W4 ....**37** A1
Gunnersbury Cres
W3 ....**36** C3
Gunnersbury Ct 8
W3 ....**37** A4
Gunnersbury Dr W5 .**36** B4
Gunnersbury Gdns
W3 ....**36** C4
Gunnersbury La W3 .**36** C4
Gunnersbury Mews 6
W4 ....**37** A1
Gunnersbury Park
W3 ....**36** C3
Gunnersbury Park Mus
W3 ....**36** C3
Gunnersbury Sta
W4 ....**37** A1
Gunpowder Sq
EC4 ....**107** C2
Gunstor Rd N16 ....**16** A4
Gunter Gr SW6 ....**156** C2
Gunterstone Rd
W14 ....**140** B2
Gunthorpe St E1 ...**111** A2
Gunwhale CI SE16 ...**32** C1
Gurdon Ho 8 E14 ...**33** C3
Gurdon Rd SE7 .....**43** C1
Gurney Ho W2 .....**100** A2
14 E2 ....**24** C3
Guthrie Ct SE1 ....**135** C3
Guthrie St SW3 ...**144** A2
Gutter La EC2 .....**108** C2
Guy St SE1 ....**137** C4
Guy's Evelina Hospl
SE1 ....**123** C1
Guy's Hospl SE1 ...**123** C1
Guyscliff Rd SE13 ..**67** B2
Gwalior Rd SW15 ..**57** C4
Gwendolen Ave
SW15 ....**57** C2
Gwendolen CI SW15 **57** C2
Gwendwr Rd W14 ..**140** B2
Gwent Ct 36 SE16 ...**32** C1
Gwilym Maries Ho **1**
E2 ....**25** A2
Gwyn CI SW6 ......**156** C1
Gwynne Ho WC1 ....**46** B4
Gwynne Ho WC1 ....**95** B3
5 SE2 ....**74** B1
Gwynne PI WC1 ...**167** C2
Gye Ho **2** SW4 ....**62** A3
Gylcote CI SE5 .....**63** C3

H

Haarlem Rd 17 W14 .**39** C3
Haber Dasher PI N1 .**98** A4
Haberdasher St N1 .**97** C4
Haberdashers' Aske's
Hatcham Coll SE14 **51** A2
Haberdashers' Aske's
Hatcham Coll (Boys)
SE4 ....**51** A1
Habington Ho 9
SE5 ....**48** C3
Hackett CI SE8 .....**41** B2
Hackford Rd SW9 ..**173** B4
Hackford Wlk SW9 .**173** B3
Hackney Central Sta
E8 ....**17** A2

Hackney Coll (Poplar
Centre) E3 ....**27** A1
Hackney Com Coll
N1 ....**98** B4
N4 ....**6** C2
Hackney Downs Sch
E5,E8 ....**16** C3
Hackney Downs Sta
E8 ....**17** A3
Hackney Free &
Parochial CE Sch
(Secondary) E9 ....**17** B2
Hackney Gr E8 .....**17** A2
Hackney Grove E9 .**18** A3
Hackney Hospl E9 ..**18** C3
Hackney Rd E2 ....**24** C3
Hackney Wick E9 ...**18** B2
Hackney Wick Sta
E9 ....**18** C2
Hackworth Point **24**
E3 ....**27** A2
Haddington Ct **4**
SE10 ....
Haddo Ho NW5 .....**13** A4
SE10 ....**52** A4
Haddo St SE10 .....**52** B4
Haddon Ct W3 .....**29** B2
Haden Ct N4 ....**5** C2
Hadfield Ho EL **111** C1
Hadleigh CI **8** E1 ..**25** B1
Hadleigh Ho 8 E1 ..**25** B1
Hadleigh St E2 .....**25** B2
Hadley Ct N16 ......**7** C3
Hadley Gdns W4 ...**37** C1
Hadley St NW1 .....**13** A2
Hadlow Ho SE17 ...**152** B2
Hadrian CI SE4 .....**66** C4
Hadrian Est 39 E2 ..**24** C3
Hadrian St SE10 ...**43** A1
Hadstock Ho NW1 ..**93** C4
Hadyn Park Ct **13**
W12 ....**38** C4
Hadyn Park Rd W12 **38** C4
Hafer Rd SW11 .....**60** B3
Haggerston Rd E8 ..**24** B4
Haggerston Sch E2 .**24** B3
Hague JMI Sch E2 ..**25** A1
Hague St E2 ....**99** C3
Haig Ho **4** E2 ......**24** C3
Hailsham Ave SW2 .**74** B2
Hailsham Ho NW8 ..**90** A1
Hainford CI SE4 ....**65** C3
Haining CI **8** W4 ...**36** C1
Hainthorpe Rd SE27 **75** A1
Hainton CI E1 ......**32** A3
Halcomb St N1 .....**24** A4
Halcrow St E1 ......**32** A4
Haldane PI SW18 ...**71** A3
Haldane Rd SW6 ..**155** A3
Haldon Rd SW18 ...**58** B1
Hale Ho SW1 ......**147** C2
Hale St E14 ....**34** A2
Hales Ho **83** SW12 ..**73** A4
Hales Prior N1 .....**84** C1
Hales St SE8 ....**51** C3
Halesworth Rd
SE13 ....**67** A4
Half Moon Ct EC1 .**108** C3
Half Moon La SE24 .**63** B1
Half Moon St W1 ..**118** B1
Halfmoon Pas E1 ..**111** A1
Halford Ho **9** SW15 **57** C4
Halford Rd SW6 ...**155** B3
Richmond TW10 ....**54** A2
Haliday Ho N1 .....**15** C2
Haliday Wlk **4** N1 ..**15** C2
Halidon CI E9 ......**17** B3

Haliwell Ho NW6 ...**78** A3
Halkett Ho 1 E2 ...**25** B4
Halkin Arc SW1 ...**131** A2
Halkin Mews SW1 .**131** B2
Halkin PI SW1 .....**131** B2
Halkin St SW1 ....**131** C3
Hall *see* **Hall**
Hall Gate NW8 .....**89** A4
Hall Sch The
NW3 ....**11** C2
Hall Oak Wlk NW6 .**10** B2
Hall PI W2 ....**89** B1
Hall Rd NW8 ......**89** A4
E15 ....**19** C4
Hall Sch Wimbledon
SW15 ....**68** C1
Hall St EC1 ....**96** B4
Hall Twr W2 ....**101** C4
Hallam Ct W1 .....**104** B4
Hallam Ho N1 .....**147** A1
SW9 ....**173** B4
Hallam Mews W1 ..**104** B4
Hallam Rd SW13 ...**57** A4
Hallam St W1 ......**104** B4
Halley Gdns SE13 ..**67** C3
Halley Ho 15 E2 ...**24** C3
8 SE10 ....**43** B1
Halley Prim Sch
E14 ....**33** A4
Halley St E14 ......**33** A4
Hallfield Ho W2 ...**100** C1
Hallfield Jun & Inf Sch
W2 ....**100** B1
Halliday Ho E1 ....**111** C1
Halliford St N1 .....**15** C1
Halling Ho SE1 ....**137** C3
Halliwell Ct SE22 ..**64** C2
Halliwell Rd SW2 ..**62** B1
Hallsville Prim Sch
E16 ....**35** C3
Hallsville Rd E16 ...**35** C3
Halpin PI SE17 ....**151** C3
Halsbury Ho 7 N7 .**14** B4
Halsbury Rd W12 ..**30** A1
Halsey St SW3 ....**144** C4
Halsmere Rd SE5 ..**48** A2
Halstead Ct N1 ....**87** C1
Halston CI SW11 ...**60** B1
Halstow 12 NW5 ...**12** C2
Halstow Prim Sch
SE10 ....
Halstow Rd NW10 ..**22** C2
SE3,SE10 ....**43** C1
Halton Cross St N1 .**86** B4
Halton Ho **22** N1 ...**15** A1
Halton Mans N1 ...**15** A1
Halton PI N1 ....**86** C4
Halton Rd N1 ......**86** B4
Haltone Ho SW4 ..**171** C1
Halyard Ho E14 ....**42** B3
Ham Yd W1 ....**119** B4
Hambalt Rd SW4 ...**61** B2
Hamble St SW6 ....**59** A4
Hambledon SE17 ...**48** C4
Hambledon Chase
N4 ....**5** A4
Hambledon Ho SE21 **76** B3
Hambledon Rd
SW18 ....**70** B4
Hambley Ho 5
SE16 ....**40** A2
Hamblyn Ct N16 ...**7** B4
Hambridge Way
SW2 ....**74** C4

Hambrook Ct 12
NW5 . . . . .13 A4
Hanbury Ho SW8 .162 B3
Hamers Ho 19 SW2 .74 C4
Hamilton Cl NW8 . . . .89 B3
SE16 . . . . .41 A4
Hamilton Gdns NW8 .88 C4
Hamilton Gdns
NW8 . . . . .89 A4
Hamilton Hall NW8 .78 C1
Hamilton Ho NW8 .89 B4
W8 . . . . .128 A4
19 E3 . . . . .26 B2
1 E14 . . . . .33 B2
16 Richmond TW9 . .44 C2
W4 . . . . .46 A4
SW15 . . . . .56 C2
Hamilton La N5 . . . . .15 A4
Hamilton Lo 32 E1 . .25 B1
Hamilton Mews
W1 . . . . .132 A4
Hamilton Pk N5 . . . . .15 A4
Hamilton Pk W N5 .15 A4
Hamilton Pl W1 . . . .117 C1
Hamilton Rd NW11 . .1 A4
NW10 . . . . .8 C3
W4 . . . . .38 A4
Hamilton Sq SE1 .137 C4
Hamilton St SE8 . . . .51 C4
Hamilton Terr NW8 .89 A4
Hamlet (Day) Hospl The
TW9 . . . . .54 A4
Hamlet Ct SE11 . . .150 A2
1 W6 . . . . .38 C2
Hamlet Gdns W6 . . .38 C2
Hamlet Ind Est E9 . .18 C1
Hamlet Sq NW2 . . . . .1 A1
Hamlet The SE5 . . . . .63 C4
Hamlet Way SE1 . . .137 C4
Hamlets Way E3 . . . .26 B1
Hammelton Gn 2
SW9 . . . . .48 A2
Hammersley Ho 8
SE14 . . . . .50 B3
Hammersmith & West
London Coll
W14 . . . . .140 A2
W12 . . . . .39 A4
Hammersmith & West
London Coll Olympia
Annexe W14 . . . .140 B4
Hammersmith Bridge Rd
W6,SW13 . . . . .39 B1
Hammersmith Broadway
W14 . . . . .140 A2
W6 . . . . .39 B1
Hammersmith Flyover
W14 . . . . .140 A2
W6 . . . . .39 B1
Hammersmith Gr
W6 . . . . .39 B3
Hammersmith Hospl
W12 . . . . .30 A3
Hammersmith Rd
W14 . . . . .140 B4
W6 . . . . .39 C2
Hammersmith Sta
W6 . . . . .39 B2
Hammersmith Terr
W6 . . . . .38 C1
Hammett St EC3 . . . .124 C4
Hammond Ho E14 . .42 A3
10 SE14 . . . . .50 C4
Hammond Lo 6
W9 . . . . .31 C4
Hammond St NW5 . .13 B2
Hamond Sq N1 . . . . .24 A3

Hampden Cl NW1 . . . .83 C2
Hampden Gurney CE
Prim Sch W1 . . . .102 B2
Hampden Gurney St
W1 . . . . .102 C1
Hampden Ho SW9 .173 C1
Hampden Rd N19 . . .4 C2
Hampshire Ct 6
SW13 . . . . .46 B1
Hampshire Hog La 11
W6 . . . . .39 A2
Hampshire St NW1 . .13 C2
Hampson Way
SW8 . . . . .172 C4
Hampstead Gate
NW3 . . . . .11 B3
Hampstead Gn NW3 .12 A3
Hampstead Gr NW3 . .2 B1
Hampstead Heath*
NW3 . . . . .2 C2
Hampstead Heath Sta
NW3 . . . . .12 A4
Hampstead High St
NW3 . . . . .11 C3
Hampstead Hill Gdns
NW3 . . . . .12 A3
Hampstead Hill Sch
NW3 . . . . .12 A3
Hampstead La N6 . . . .3 A4
Hampstead Parochial CE
Sch NW3 . . . . .11 B4
Hampstead Rd NW1 .92 C4
Hampstead Sch
NW2 . . . . .1 B2
Hampstead Sq NW3 . .2 B1
Hampstead Sta
NW3 . . . . .11 B4
Hampstead West 4
NW6 . . . . .10 C2
Hampstead Wlk 7
E3 . . . . .26 B4
Hampton Cl NW6 . . .23 C2
Hampton Ct N1 . . . . .15 A2
19 SE16 . . . . .32 C1
Hampton St SE1 . . .150 B3
Hanameel St 6 E16 .35 C1
Hanbury Ho E1 . . . .111 B4
Hanbury Rd W3 . . . . .37 A4
Hanbury St E1 . . . . .111 A4
Hancock Nunn Ho 1
NW3 . . . . .12 B1
Hancock Rd E3 . . . . .27 B2
Hand Ct WC1 . . . . . .107 A3
Handa Wlk 3 N1 . . . .15 B2
Handforth Rd SW9 .163 B2
Handley Rd E9 . . . . . .25 B4
Hands Wlk E16 . . . . .35 C3
Hanford Cl SW18 . . .70 C3
Hanley Pl SE1 . . . . .137 C3
Hanley Gdns N4 . . . . .5 B3
Hanley Rd N4,N19 . . . .5 A3
Hanmer Wlk N7 . . . . .5 B2
Hannah Mary Way
SE1 . . . . .153 C3
Hannay La N8 . . . . . . .4 C4
Hannay Wlk SW16 . .73 C2
Hannell Rd SW6 . .154 B2
Hannen Ho SE5 . . . . .63 C4
Hannen Rd SE27 . . . .75 A1
Hannibal Rd E1 . . . . .32 B4
Hannington Rd
SW4 . . . . .61 A4
Hanover Ave E16 . . . .35 C1
Hanover Cl TW9 . . . . .44 C3

Hanover Ct N16 . . . . . .7 B4
W12 . . . . .29 C1
Hanover Gate Mans
NW1 . . . . .90 B2
Hanover Gdns
SE11 . . . . .163 B3
Hanover Ho NW8 . . .80 A1
Hanover Mans 5
SW2 . . . . .62 C2
Hanover Pk SE15 . . . .49 C2
Hanover Pl WC2 . . .106 B1
Hanover Rd NW10 . .22 B4
Hanover Sch N1 . . . . .86 C2
Hanover Sq W1 . . . .104 B1
Hanover Steps W2 .102 B1
Hanover Terr NW1 . .90 C3
Hanover Terr Mews
NW1 . . . . .90 B3
Hanover Yd N1 . . . . .86 C2
Hans Cres SW1 . . . .130 C2
Hans Pl SW1 . . . . . .130 C2
Hans Rd SW3 . . . . . .130 C2
Hans St SW1 . . . . . .131 A1
Hansard Mews W14 .39 C4
Hansler Rd SE22 . . . .64 B2
Hanson Cl SW14 . . . .55 B4
SW12 . . . . .73 A4
Hanson St W1 . . . . .104 C4
Hanway Ho SW9 . . .173 C4
Hanway Pl W1 . . . . .105 B2
Hanway St W1 . . . . .105 B2
Hanwell Ho 24 W2 . .31 C4
Hanworth Ho SE5 . . .48 A3
Harben Rd NW6 . . . .11 B1
Harberson Rd SW12 .73 A3
Harberton Rd N19 . . .4 B3
Harbet Rd W2 . . . . .101 C3
Harbin Ho 3 SW2 . . .74 C3
Harbinger JMI Sch
E14 . . . . .42 A2
Harbinger Rd E14 . . .42 A2
Harbledown Ho
SE1 . . . . .137 B3
Harbledown Rd
SW6 . . . . .165 B4
Harbord Cl SE5 . . . . .48 C1
Harbord Ho 5 SE16 .40 C2
Harbord St SW6 . . .47 C2
Harborough Sch N19 . .4 C2
Harbour Ave SW10 .167 A3
Harbour Exchange Sq
E14 . . . . .42 A4
Harbour Rd SE5 . . . .63 B4
SW15 . . . . .68 C4
Harbut Rd SW11 . . . .59 C3
Harcombe Rd N16 . . .7 A1
Harcourt Ho W1 . . .104 A2
1 W6 . . . . .171 B2
Harcourt Rd SE4 . . . .66 B4
Harcourt St W1 . . . .102 B3
Harcourt Terr
SW10 . . . . .142 C1
Hardcastle Ho 8
SE15 . . . . .49 C2
Hardel Rise SW2 . . . .75 A3
Hardel Wlk SE24,
SW2 . . . . .74 C4
Harden Ho SE5 . . . . .49 A1
Harders Rd SE15 . . . .50 A1
Hardess St SE24 . . . .63 B4

Hardham Ho 5
SW2 . . . . .62 C1
Harding Cl SE17 . . . .48 B4
Harding Ho SW13 . . .47 A4
Harding Rd NW10 . . .22 B4
Hardinge St E1 . . . . .32 B3
Hardington 2 NW1 . .12 C1
Hardwick Ho NW8 . .90 B2
SW8 . . . . .171 B2
Hardwick St EC1 . . . .95 C3
Hardwick's Way
SW18 . . . . .58 C2
Hardwicke Ho 14
E3 . . . . .27 A2
Hardwicke Mews
WC1 . . . . .95 A3
Hardwicke Rd W4 . . .37 C2
Hardwidge St SE1 .138 A4
Hardy Ave 4 E16 . . . .35 C1
Hardy Cl SE16 . . . . . .40 C4
Hardy Cotts 2 SE10 .52 C4
Hardy Rd SE3 . . . . . .53 B4
Hare & Billet Rd
SE3 . . . . .52 C1
Hare Ct EC4 . . . . . . .107 B1
Hare Marsh
E2 . . . . .24 C1 99 B2
Hare Pl EC4 . . . . . . .107 C1
Hare Row E2 . . . . . . .25 A3
Hare Wlk N1 . . . . .24 A3
Harecourt Rd N1 . . . .15 B2
Haredale Ho 26 SE16 .139 B3
Haredale Rd SE24 . . .63 B3
Harefield Mews SE4 .66 B4
Harefield Rd SE4 . . . .66 B4
Harewood Ave NW1 .90 B1
Harewood Pl W1 . . .104 B1
Harewood Row
NW1 . . . . .102 B4
Harfield Gdns 1
SE5 . . . . .64 A4
Harfleur Ct SE11 . . .150 A3
Harford Ho W11 . . . .31 B4
SE5 . . . . .48 B4
Harford St E1 . . . . . . .26 A1
Hargrave Mans 2
N19 . . . . .4 C2
Hargrave Park Prim Sch
N19 . . . . .4 B2
Hargrave Pk N19 . . . .4 B2
Hargrave Pl N7 . . . . .13 C3
Hargrave Rd N19 . . . .4 B2
Hargraves Ho 14
W12 . . . . .30 A2
Hargwyne St SW9 . . .62 B4
Harkness Ho E1 . . . .111 C1
Harlech Twr 5 W3 . . .37 B4
Harlescott Rd SE15 .65 C3
Harlesden Gdns
NW10 . . . . .21 B4
Harlesden Prim Sch
NW10 . . . . .21 A3
Harlesden Rd NW10 .21 C4
Harlesden Sta
NW10 . . . . .20 C3
Harley Gdns SW10 .143 A1
Harley Gr E3 . . . . . . .26 B2
Harley Ho NW1 . . . . .91 C1
Harley Pl W1 . . . . . .104 A3
Harley Rd NW3 . . . . .11 C1
NW10 . . . . .21 A3
Harley St W1 . . . . . .104 A3
Harley Villas NW10 .21 A3
Harleyford Ct SW8 .162 C4

Ham – Har 213

Harleyford Manor 8
W3 . . . . .28 B1
Harleyford Rd
SE11 . . . . .162 C4
Harleyford St SE11 .163 B3
Harling Ct SW11 . . .168 C2
Harlow Ho 18 SE8 . .51 B4
Harlynwood 21 SE5 .48 B3
Harman Cl E1 . . . . . .153 B1
NW2 . . . . .1 A1
Harman Dr NW2 . . . .10 A4
Harmon Ho 6 SE8 . .41 B2
Harmood Gr NW1 . . .13 A1
Harmood Ho 2
NW1 . . . . .13 A1
Harmood St NW1 . . .13 A1
Harmsworth St
SE17 . . . . .150 A1
Harold Ct 14 SE16 . .40 C4
Harold Est SE1 . . . . .138 B1
Harold Ho 16 E2 . . . .25 C3
Harold Laski Ho
EC1 . . . . .96 B3
Harold Maddison Ho
SE17 . . . . .150 B2
Harold Pl SE11 . . . .149 B1
Harold Rd NW10 . . . .20 C2
Harold Wilson Ho
SW6 . . . . .155 A3
Harp Alley EC4 . . . .108 A2
Harp La EC3 . . . . . . .124 A3
Harpenden Rd SE27,
SW16 . . . . .75 A2
Harpenmead Point
NW2 . . . . .1 B2
Harper Ho 8 SW9 . . .63 A4
Harper Rd SE1 . . . . .137 A2
Harpley Sch E1 . . . . .25 C1
Harpley Sq E1 . . . . . .25 C1
Harpsden St SW11 .169 B3
Harpur Mews WC1 .106 C4
Harpur St WC1 . . . .106 C4
Harrier Ho 9 SW11 .60 A4
Harriet Cl E8 . . . . . . .24 C4
Harriet Ho SW6 . . . .156 B1
Harriet St SW1 . . . .131 A3
Harriet Tubman Cl 21
SW2 . . . . .74 C4
Harriet Wlk SW1 . . .131 A3
Harrington Ct
SW7 . . . . .143 C4
Harrington Gdns
SW7 . . . . .142 C3
Harrington Ho NW1 .92 C4
SW1 . . . . .147 C2
Harrington Rd
SW7 . . . . .143 B4
Harrington Sq NW1 .82 C1
Harrington St NW1 . .92 C3
Harriott Cl SE10 . . . .43 B2
Harriott Ho 11 E1 . . .32 B3
Harris Ho 19 E3 . . . .26 C2
8 SW9 . . . . .62 C4
Harris St SE5 . . . . . . .48 C3
Harrison Ho SE17 . .151 B2
Harrison St WC1 . . . .94 B3
Harrisons Ct 1
SE14 . . . . .50 C4
Harrodian Sch
SW13 . . . . .46 B3
Harrogate Ct 2
SE26 . . . . .76 C1

Harrold Ho **1** NW3 ....11 B1
Harrow La E14 ....34 B2
Harrow Pl E1 ....110 B2
Harrow Rd W2 ....101 B3
  W2,W9 ....23 C1
Harrow St NW1 ....102 A4
Harroway Rd
  SW11 ....167 C2
Harrowby St W1 ....102 B2
Harrowgate Ho **22**
  E9 ....117 C2
Harrowgate Rd E9 ...18 A1
Harry Gosling JMI Sch
  E1 ....111 C1
Harry Hinkins Ho
  SE17 ....151 A1
Harry Lambourn Ho **10**
  SE15 ....50 A3
Hart Ho SW2 ....74 C3
Hart St EC3 ....124 B4
Hart's La SE14 ....51 A2
Hartfield Terr E3 ......26 C3
Hartham Cl N7 ....14 A3
Hartham Rd N7 ....14 A3
Hartington Ct SW8 172 A4
  W4 ....45 A3
Hartington Rd
  SW8 ....162 A1
  W4 ....45 B2
Hartismere Rd
  SW6 ....155 A2
Hartlake Rd E9 ....18 A2
Hartland NW1 ....83 A3
Hartland Rd NW1 .....13 A1
  NW6 ....23 B4
Hartley Ho SE1 ....153 A4
  SW15 ....57 C2
Hartley St E2 ....25 B2
Hartnoll Ho **4** N7 ....14 C3
Hartnoll St N7 ....14 B3
Harton Lo **2** SE8 .....51 C2
Harton St SE8 ....51 C2
Hartopp Ct N16 ....7 A1
Hartopp Point
  SW6 ....154 B2
Hartshorn Alley
  EC3 ....110 B1
Hartswood Ho **10**
  SW2 ....74 A3
Hartswood Rd W12 ...38 B3
Hartwell St E8 ....16 B2
Harvard Ct NW6 ....11 A3
Harvard Hill W4 ....45 A4
Harvard Ho **3** SE17 ..48 A4
  SW15 ....57 C1
Harvard Mans **18**
  SW11 ....59 C3
Harvard Rd W4 ....37 A1
  11 W4 ....37 B1
  SE13 ....67 B2
Harvey Ct SW11 .....168 B4
Harvey Ho N1 ....87 C3
  SW1 ....147 C1
  10 E1 ....25 A1
  Brentford TW8 ....36 A1
Harvey Lo **8** W1 ....35 C2
Harvey Point **7** E16 35 C4
Harvey Rd **13** SE5 ....48 C2
Harvey St N1 ....87 C3
Harvington Wlk E8 ..16 C1
Harvist Rd NW6 ....23 A3
Harwood Ct N1 ....87 C3
  SW15 ....57 B3

Harwood Rd SW6 .....156 A1
Harwood Terr
  SW6 ....166 A4
Hascombe Ho **11**
  SW15 ....69 A3

Haselrigge Prim Sch
  SE5 ....48 C1
Haselrigge Rd SW4 ..61 C3
Haseltine Rd SE26 ....91 A4
Hasker Ho NW10 ....20 C4
Hasker St SW3 ....144 B4
Haslam Cl N1 ....14 C1
Haslam Ho **1** N1 .....15 B1
Haslam St SE15 ....49 B2
Haslemere Ave
  SW18 ....71 A2
Haslemere **5** N16 ...7 A3
Haslemere Ind Est
  SW18 ....71 A2
Haslemere Rd N8 ....5 A4
Hassard St E2 ....24 B3
Hassett Rd E9 ....18 A2
Hassop Rd NW2 ....9 C4
Hastings Cl **3** SE15 49 C3
Hastings Ho **8** W12 30 A2
Hastings Hos WC1 ....94 A3
Hastings St WC1 ....94 A3
Hat & Mitre Ct EC1 ...96 B1

Hatcham Mews Bsns Ctr
  SE14 ....50 C2
Hatcham Park Mews
  SE14 ....50 C2
Hatcham Park Rd
  SE14 ....50 B2

Hatcham Wood Sch
  SE4 ....51 A1
Hatchard Rd N19 ....5 A2
Hatcliffe Almshouses **8**
  SE10 ....43 B1
Hatcliffe St SE10 ......43 B1
Hatfield Cl SE14 ....50 C3
Hatfield Ct SE3 ....53 C3
Hatfield Ho EC1 ....96 C1
Hatfield Rd W4 ....37 C4
Hatfields SE1 ....121 C2
Hathaway Ho N1 ....98 A4
Hatherley Gr W2 .....100 A2
Hatherley Gr W2 .....100 A2
Hatherley Rd TW9 ....44 B2
Hatherley St SW1 ...147 A3
Hathersage Ct N1 .....15 C3
Hathersley Ho **3**
  SW2 ....50 A1
Hathway Ho **3**
  SE15 ....50 B1
Hathway St **3** SE15 50 B1
Hatley Rd N4,N7 ....5 B2
Hatteraick St **8**
  SE16 ....40 B4
Hatton Gdn EC1 ......107 C4
Hatton Ho **1** E1 .....125 C4
Hatton Pl EC1 ....107 C4
Hatton Row NW8 .....89 C1
Hatton St NW8 ....89 C1
Hatton Wall EC1 ......107 C4
Haunch of Venison Yd
  W1 ....104 A1
Hauteville Court Gdns **2**
  W6 ....38 B3
Havana Rd SW18, ...
  SW19 ....70 C2
Havannah St E14 ....41 C4

Havant Way **8** SE15 49 B3
Havelock Cl **13** W12 30 A2
Havelock St N1 ....84 B4
Havelock Terr
  SW8 ....160 B1
Haven Cl SW19 ....69 C1
Haven St **17** NW1 ...13 A1
Haven The TW9 ....54 C4
Havenpool Ho **8** 78 B3
Havercourt **8** NW3 ..12 A2
Haverfield Gdns
  TW9 ....44 C3
Haverfield Rd E3 ......26 A2
Haverhill Rd SW12 ..73 B3
Havering **8** NW1 .....13 A1
Havering Ho N4 ....6 B4
Haversham Lo NW2 ...9 C2
Haversham Pl N6 ....3 B2
Haverstock Hill
  NW3 ....12 B2
Haverstock Rd NW5 ..13 A3

Haverstock Sch
  NW3 ....12 B3

Haverstock St N1 ......86 B1
Havil St SE5 ....49 A2
Havisham Ho SE16 .139 B3
Hawarden Gr SE24 ...75 B4
Hawberry Ho N7 ....14 A2
Hawes St N1 ....15 A1
Hawgood St **3** E3 ...33 C4
Hawk Ho **7** SW11 ..60 A4
Hawke Ho **3** E1 .....25 C1
Hawke Pl **22** SE16 ..40 C4
Hawke Twr **4** SE14 ..51 A4
Hawkesbury Rd
  SW15 ....57 A2
Hawkesworth Ho **5**
  SW4 ....61 B1
Hawkins Ho **3** SE8 ..51 C4
Hawkley Gdns SE27 ..75 A2
Hawkridge Ho NW5 ..12 C2
Hawks Mews **10**
  SE10 ....52 B3
Hawkshead **4** NW1 ..92 C4
Hawkshead Rd NW10 ..8 B1
  W4 ....38 A4
Hawkslade Rd SE15 ..65 C2
Hawksley Rd N16 ....7 A1
Hawksmoor Ho
  E14 ....33 A4
Hawksmoor Mews
  E1 ....32 A2
Hawksmoor St **5**
  W6 ....47 C4
Hawkstone Rd SE16 40 B2
Hawkwell Wlk (off
  Maldon Cl) N1 ....87 A4
Hawley Cres NW1 ....13 A1

Hawley Inf Sch
  NW1 ....13 A1

Hawley Mews **4**
  NW1 ....13 A1
Hawley Rd **3** NW1 ..13 A1
Hawley St NW1 ....13 A1
Haworth Ct E15 ....76 B3
Haworth Ho **7** SW2 62 C1
Hawstead Rd SE6 ....67 A1
Hawthorn Ct
  Richmond TW9 ....45 A2
  SW15 ....57 A4
Hawthorn Rd NW10 ...8 C1
Hawthorn Wlk W10 ..23 A1
Hawthorne Cl N1 .....16 A2
Hawthorne Ho
  SW1 ....147 A1

Hawtrey Rd NW3 ......12 A1
Hay Currie St E14 .....34 A3
Hay Hill W1 ....118 B3
Hay St E2 ....24 C4

Hay's Galleria *
  SE1 ....124 A2
Hay's La SE1 ....124 A2
Hay's Mews W1 ......118 A2
Haycroft Gdns
  NW10 ....22 A4
Haycroft Mans
  NW10 ....21 C4
Haycroft Rd SW2 .....62 A2
Hayday Rd E16 ....35 C4
Hayden's Pl W11 ......31 B3
Haydon St EC3,E3 ...124 C4
Haydon Way SW11 ..59 C3
Haydon Wlk E1 ....111 A1
Hayes Ct **22** SE5 ....48 B3
  SW12 ....74 A3
Hayes Pl NW1 ....90 B1
Hayfield Rd **30** E1 ..25 B1
Hayfield Pas E1 ....25 B1
Hayles Bldgs SE11 ..150 B4
Hayles St SE11 ....150 A4
Hayling Cl **30** N16 ...16 A3
Haymans Point
  SE11 ....148 C2
Haymarket SW1 ......119 B3
Haymerle Ho **6**
  SE15 ....49 C3
Haymerle Sch SE15 ..49 C4
Hayne Ho W11 ....112 A2
Hayne St EC1 ....108 B4
Haynes Ho **3** E9 ....18 A2
Hayter Ho W12 ....29 C2
Hayter Rd SW2 ....62 B2
Haythorn Ho SW11 ..167 C3
Hayward Ct SW4 .....172 B2

Hayward Gallery *
  SE1 ....121 A2

Hayward Gdns
  SW15 ....57 B1
Hayward Ho N1 ....85 B2
Hayward's Pl EC1 .....96 A2
Haywood Lo **20** N7 .13 C3
Hazel Ho NW3 ....12 B2
  SE15 ....49 C1
Hazel Ho **12** NW10 ..22 B2
  SE4 ....66 B4
Hazel Rd NW10 ....22 B2
Hazel Way SE1 ....152 C4
Hazelbourne Rd
  SW12 ....61 A1
Hazeldon Rd SE4 ......66 A2
Hazellville Rd N19 .....4 C3
Hazelmere Ct **10**
  SW2 ....74 B3
Hazelmere Rd NW6 ..23 B4
Hazelwood Cl W5 .....36 A4
Hazelwood Ho **1**
  SE8 ....41 A2
Hazelwood Mans
  SW6 ....164 C4
Hazlebury Rd SW6 ..166 B2
Hazledene Rd W4 ......45 B4
Hazlewell Rd SW15 ..57 B2
Hazlewood Cres
  W10 ....23 A1
Hazlewood Twr
  W10 ....23 B1
Hazlitt Mews W14 ..126 A1
Hazlitt Rd W14 ....126 A1
Head St E1 ....32 C3

Headbourne Ho
  SE1 ....137 C2
Headcorn **10** NW5 ..12 C2
Headfort Pl SW1 .....131 C3

Headington Rd
  SW18 ....71 B2
Headlam Rd SW4 .....73 C4
Headlam St E1 ....25 A1
Headley Ct SE26 ....91 C3
Heald St SE8,SE14 ...51 C2
Healey Ho SW9 ....163 C1
  2 E3 ....26 C1
Healey St NW1 ....13 A2
Heanor Ct **4** E5 ......17 C4
Hearn St EC2   24 A1 98 B1
Hearn's Bldgs
  SE17 ....151 C3
Hearne Rd W4 ....44 C4
Hearnshaw Ho **9**
  E14 ....33 A4

Hearnville Prim Sch
  SW12 ....72 C3
Hearnville Rd SW12 72 C3
Heath Brow NW3 ....2 B1
Heath Cl NW11 ....2 A4
Heath Ct N16 ....6 C3
  2 NW3 ....11 B2
Heath Hurst Rd
  NW3 ....12 A4
Heath La SE3 ....52 C1
Heath Mans NW3 ....2 B1
  SW9 ....69 C1

Heath Park Gdns
  NW3 ....2 A1
Heath Rd SW8 ....170 B1
Heath Rise SW15 ......57 C1
Heath Royal SW15 ....57 C1
Heath St NW3 ....2 B1
Heath View NW5 ....12 C4

Heathbrook Prim Sch
  SW4 ....170 C1
Heathcote St WC1 .....94 C3
Heathcroft NW11 ....2 A3
Heather Cl SW8 ....61 A4
  SE13 ....67 C1
Heather Ct SW4 ......172 B3
Heather Ho **7** E14 ..34 B3
Heather Lo N16 ....7 A3
Heather Wlk W10 ......23 A1
Heatherley St N16 ......7 C1
Heatherley Sch of Fine
  Art SW10 ....157 A1
Heathfield Ave
  SW18 ....71 C4
Heathfield Ct
  5 W4 ....37 C1
  SW18 ....71 C4
Heathfield Gdns
  W4 ....37 B1
  SW18 ....59 C1
Heathfield Ho SE3 ...53 A1
Heathfield Pk NW2 ....9 B2
Heathfield Rd W3 .....37 A4
  SW18 ....59 C1
Heathfield Sq SW18 ..71 C4
Heathfield Terr W4 ...37 B1
Heathland Rd N16 ......7 A3

Heathlands Sch
  SW19 ....69 B1

Heathman's Rd
  SW6 ....165 A3

Heathmere Prim Sch
  SW15 ....68 C3
Heathpool Ct **8** E1 ..25 A1
Heathshot **8** TW10 .54 A1

Heathside NW3 ...11 C4
Heathside Prep Sch
 NW3 ...11 C4
Heathstan Rd W12 ...29 C3
Heathview Ct SW19 ...69 C2
Heathview Gdns
 SW15 ...69 B4
Heathville Rd N4,N19 ...5 A4
Heathwall St SW11 ...60 B4
Heathway **6** SE3 ...53 B3
 SE3 ...53 C3
Heathway Ct NW11 ...1 C3
Heathwood Ct
 SW12 ...73 B3
 6 SE15 ...50 A1
Heaton Ho SW10 ...157 A4
 6 SE15 ...50 A1
Heaton Rd SE15 ...50 A1
Heaver Rd **24** SW11 ...59 C4
Hebden Ct **22** E2 ...24 B4
Hebdon Rd SW17 ...72 A1

Heber Prim Sch
 SE22 ...64 B1
Heber Rd NW2 ...9 C4
 SE22 ...64 B1
Hebron Rd W6 ...39 A3
Heckfield Pl SW6 ...155 B2
Heckford St E1 ...32 C2
Hector Ct SW9 ...173 B4
 SW15 ...57 C2
Hector Ho **2** E2 ...25 A3
Heddington Gr N7 ...14 B3
Heddon St W1 ...118 C4
Hedger St SE11 ...150 A4
Hedger's Gr E9 ...18 B2
Hedingham Cl **6**
 N1 ...15 B1
Hedley St SW15 ...57 C1
Hedley Ho E14 ...42 B3
Hedley Row N5,N16 ...15 C3
Hedsor Ho **2** ...98 C2
Heidegger Cres
 SW13 ...47 A3
Heighgate Pl NW3 ...12 B4
Heights The NW3 ...11 B4
Heiron St SE17 ...48 A4
Helby Rd SW4 ...61 C1
Heldar Ct SE1 ...137 C3
Helen Gladstone Ho
 SE1 ...136 A4
Helen Ho **9** E2 ...25 A3
Helen Mackay Ho **9**
 E14 ...34 C3
Helen Peele Cotts **10**
 SE16 ...40 B3
Helen Taylor Ho
 SE16 ...153 B4
Helen's Pl E2 ...25 B2
Helena Rd NW10 ...9 A3
Helena Sq **12** SE16 ...33 A2
Helenslea Ave NW11 ...1 C3
Heliport Est The
 SW11 ...167 B1
Helix Gdns SW2 ...62 B1
Helix Rd SW2 ...62 B1
Hellenic Coll of London
 SW1 ...130 C1
Hellings St E1 ...125 C1
Helmet Row EC1 ...97 A2
Helmsdale Ho NW6 ...78 A1
Helmsley Pl E8 ...17 A1
Helmsley St **7** E8 ...17 A1
Helsby Ct NW8 ...89 B2
Helsinki Sq SE16 ...41 A3
Helston NW1 ...83 A2
Helston Ho SE11 ...149 C2
Hemans Est SW8 ...161 C1

Hemans St SW8 ...161 C1
Hemberton Rd SW9 ...62 A4
Hemingford Rd N1 ...85 A4
Hemlington Ho **11**
 E14 ...33 A3
Hemlock Rd W12 ...29 B2
Hemming St
 E1 ...24 C1 99 C1
Hemp Wlk SE17 ...151 C4
Hemstal Rd NW6 ...10 C1
Hemsworth Ct N1 ...24 A3
Hemsworth St N1 ...24 A3
Hemus Pl SW3 ...144 B1
Henchman St W12 ...29 B3
Henderson Ct NW3 ...11 C3
 8 SE14 ...50 C4
Henderson Dr NW8 ...89 B2
Henderson Rd
 SW18 ...72 A4
Hendham Rd SW17 ...72 B2
Hendre Ho SE1 ...152 B3
Hendre Rd SE1 ...152 B3
Hendrick Ave SW12 ...72 B4
Heneage La EC3 ...110 B1
Heneage Pl EC3 ...110 B1
Heneage St E1 ...111 A4
Henfield Cl N19 ...4 B3
Hengrave Rd SE23 ...65 B1
Henley Cl SE16 ...40 B4
Henley Ct NW2 ...9 C2
 SE15 ...64 C4
Henley Dr SE1 ...153 A4
Henley Ho E2 ...99 A2
Henley Prior N1 ...84 C1
Henley Rd NW10 ...22 B4
Henley St SW11 ...169 C2
Henniker Mews
 SW3 ...157 B4
Henniker Rd E15 ...19 C3
Henning St SW11 ...168 A3
Henrietta Cl SE8 ...51 C4
Henrietta Ho **11** W6 ...39 B1
Henrietta Mews
 WC1 ...94 B2
Henrietta Pl W1 ...104 A2
Henrietta St WC2 ...120 B4
 E15 ...76 B3
Henriques St E1 ...111 C1
Henry Cavendish Prim
 Sch SW12 ...73 B3
Henry Compton Sec Sch
 SW6 ...164 A4
Henry Dickens Ct
 W11 ...112 A2
Henry Fawcett Prim Sch
 SE11 ...163 B4
Henry Ho NW8 ...80 A2
 SE1 ...121 C1
 SW8 ...162 A2
Henry Jackson Ho
 SW15 ...57 C4
Henry Jackson Rd
 SW15 ...57 C4
Henry Rd N4 ...6 B3
Henry Wise Ho
 SW1 ...147 A3
Henryson Rd SE4 ...66 C2
Henshall Point **11**
 E3 ...27 A2
Henshall St N1 ...15 C2
Henshaw St SE17 ...151 B4
Henslow Ho **11**
 SE15 ...49 C3
Henslowe Rd SE22 ...64 C2
Henson Ave NW2 ...9 B3
Henson Ct **3** N5 ...15 B4

Henstridge Pl NW8 ...80 A2
Henty Cl SW11 ...168 B4
Henty Wlk SW15 ...57 A2
Hepburn Mews
 SW11 ...60 B2
Hepplestone Cl
 SW15 ...57 A1
Hepscott Rd E9 ...18 C1
Hera Ct **7** E14 ...41 C2
Herald St **5** E2 ...25 A1
Heralds Pl SE11 ...150 A4
Herbal Hill EC1 ...95 C1
Herbert Chapman Ct
 N5 ...5 A4
Herbert Cres SW1 ...131 A2
Herbert Gdns NW10 ...22 A3
 W4 ...45 A4
Herbert Ho E1 ...110 C2
Herbert Morrison Ho
 SW6 ...154 C3
Herbert Morrison Prim
 Sch SW8 ...162 B1
Herbert St NW5 ...12 C2
Herbrand Est WC1 ...94 A2
Herbrand St WC1 ...94 A2
Hercules Pl N7 ...5 A1
Hercules Rd SE1 ...135 A1
Hercules St N7 ...5 A1
Hercules Twr SE14 ...51 A4
Hereford Bldgs
 SW3 ...157 C4
Hereford Ho SW3 ...130 B2
 SW10 ...156 B2
 28 SE5 ...48 B1
 5 SW2 ...62 C3
Hereford Mans **10**
 W2 ...31 C3
Hereford Mews
 W2 ...31 C3
Hereford Pl SE14 ...51 B3
Hereford Rd
 W2 ...31 C4 113 C4
 W3 ...28 B2
Hereford Retreat **5**
 SE15 ...49 C3
Hereford Sq SW7 ...143 A3
Hereford St
 E2 ...24 C1 99 B2
Heritage Cl SW9 ...63 A4
Heritage Ct SE8 ...40 C1
Heritage Ho **22**
 SW19 ...69 C3
Herm Ho **10** N1 ...15 B2
Hermes Cl SW9 ...173 B2
Hermes St N1 ...85 B1
Hermit Pl NW6 ...78 A3
Hermit St EC1 ...96 A4
Hermitage Ct E1 ...125 C1
 2 NW2 ...1 C1
Hermitage Gdns
 NW2 ...1 C1
Hermitage JMI Sch
 E1 ...125 C2
Hermitage Row **9**
 E8 ...16 C3
Hermitage St W2 ...101 B3
Hermitage The **13**
 SW13 ...46 B2
 Richmond TW10 ...54 A2
Hermitage Wall
 E1 ...125 C1
Herndon Rd SW18 ...59 B2
Herne Hill SE24 ...63 B2
Herne Hill Ho SE24 ...63 A1

Herne Hill Mans
 SE24 ...63 B1
Herne Hill Rd SE24 ...63 B3
Herne Hill Sta SE24 ...63 A1
Herne Hill Stadium
 SE24 ...63 C1
Herne Pl SE24 ...63 A2
Heron Ct NW10 ...4 A2
Heron Ct **14** E14 ...42 B3
 10 SE12 ...75 C2
Heron Dr N4 ...6 B2
Heron Ho NW8 ...80 A1
 SW11 ...168 B4
 SE15 ...49 B4
Heron Ind Est E15 ...27 A3
Heron Pl W1 ...103 C2
 SE16 ...33 A1
Heron Quays E14 ...33 C1
Heron Quays Sta
 E14 ...33 C1
Heron Trad Est W3 ...28 A4
Herondale Ave
 SW18 ...72 A3
Herongate N1 ...87 A4
Herrick Ho **5** N16 ...16 A3
 18 SE5 ...48 C3
Herrick Rd N5 ...6 B1
Herrick St SW1 ...147 C3
Herries St W10 ...23 A3
Hersant Cl NW10 ...21 C4
Herschell's Mews
 SE5 ...63 B4
Hersham Cl SW15 ...68 C4
Hershell Ct **1**
 SW14 ...55 A3
Hertford Ave SW14 ...56 A3
Hertford Ct **18**
 SW11 ...60 A4
Hertford Lo **10**
 SW19 ...70 A3
Hertford Pl W1 ...93 A1
Hertford Rd N1 ...24 A4
Hertford St W1 ...118 A1
Hertmitage The **4**
 SE13 ...52 B1
Hertslet Rd N7 ...5 B1
Hertsmere Rd E14 ...33 C2
Hesewall Cl SW4 ...171 A1
Hesketh Pl W11 ...112 A3
Heslop Ct **1** SW12 ...72 C3
Heslop Rd SW12 ...72 B3
Hesper Mews SW5 ...142 A3
Hesperus Cres E14 ...42 A2
Hessel St E1 ...32 A3
Hester Rd SW11 ...158 B1
Hester Terr TW9 ...54 C4
Hestercombe Ave
 SW6 ...164 B3
Heston Ho W4 ...37 A1
 6 SE8 ...51 C2
Heston St SE14 ...51 C2
Hetherington Rd
 SW2,SW4 ...62 A3
Hethpool Ho W2 ...89 B1
Hetley Rd W12 ...39 A4
Hevelius Cl SE10 ...43 B1
Hever Ho SE15 ...50 C4
Heversham Ho SE15 ...50 B4
Hewer Ho **6** SW4 ...61 B2
Hewer St W10 ...30 C4
Hewett St EC2 ...24 A1 98 B1
Hewison St E3 ...26 B3
Hewlett Rd E3 ...26 A3
Hewling Ho **11** N16 ...16 A3

Hewitt Ho SW15 ...47 B1
Hexagon The N6 ...3 B3
Hexham Rd SE27 ...75 B2
Hey Bridge **9** NW1 ...13 A2
Heydon Ho **5** SE14 ...50 B2
Heyford Ave SW8 ...162 B2
Heygate St SE17 ...151 A4
Heylyn Sq **2** E3 ...26 B2
Heysham La NW3 ...2 A1
Heythorp St SW18 ...70 B2
Heywood Ho
 11 SE14 ...50 C4
 6 SW2 ...62 C1
Heyworth Rd E5 ...17 A4
Hibbert St SW11 ...59 C4
Hichisson Rd SE15 ...65 B2
Hickes Ho **6** NW6 ...11 C1
Hickey's Almshouses **7**
 TW9 ...54 B3
Hickin St **2** E14 ...42 B3
Hickleton NW1 ...83 A3
Hickling Ho **10** SE16 ...40 A3
Hickmore Wlk SW4 ...61 B4
Hicks Cl SW11 ...60 A4
Hicks St SE8 ...41 A1
Hide Pl SW1 ...147 B3
Hide Twr SW1 ...147 B3
Hieover SE21 ...75 B2
Higgins Ho **7** N1 ...24 A4
Higginson Ho **2**
 NW3 ...12 B1
Higgs Ind Est **5**
 SE24 ...63 A4
High Holborn WC1 ...106 C3
High London **5** N6 ...4 C4
High Par The SW16 ...74 A1
High Park Ave TW9 ...44 C2
High Park Rd TW9 ...44 C2
High Point N6 ...3 C4
High Rd NW10 ...8 C2
High St E15 ...27 B4
 W3 ...28 A1
 Brentford TW8 ...44 A4
High Street Harlesden
 NW10 ...21 B3
High Street Kensington
 Sta W8 ...128 A3
High The SW16 ...74 A1
High Timber St
 EC4 ...122 C4
High Trees SW2 ...74 C3
High View Prim Sch
 SW11 ...59 C3
Highbridge Ct **13**
 SE14 ...50 B3
Highbury & Islington Sta
 N1 ...15 A2
Highbury (Arsenal FC)
 N5 ...6 A1
Highbury Cnr N5 ...15 A2
Highbury Corner
 N5 ...15 A2
Highbury Cres N5 ...14 C3
Highbury Fields Sch
 N5 ...15 A3
Highbury Gr N5 ...15 A3
Highbury Grange
 N5 ...15 A4
Highbury Grove Ct
 N5 ...15 A2
Highbury Grove Sch
 N5 ...15 A3
Highbury Hill N5 ...15 A4

Highbury New Pk
N5 ....15 B4
Highbury Pk N5 ....15 A4
Highbury Pl N5 ....15 A4
Highbury Quadrant
N5 ....6 B1
Highbury Quadrant Prim
Sch N5 ....15 B4
Highbury Station Rd
N1 ....14 C2
Highbury Terr N5 ...15 A3
Highbury Terrace Mews
N5 ....15 A3
Highcliffe Dr SW15 .56 B1
Highcroft Rd N19 ....5 A4
Highcross Way 4
SW15 ....68 C3
Highdown Rd SW15 .57 A1
Highenden Ho NW8 .90 A2
Highfield Ave NW11 ..1 A4
Highfield Cl SE13 ...67 C1
Highfield Gr N6 ....3 B3
Highfield Rd W3 ....28 B4
Highfield Sch SE18 .72 A4
Highfield Archway
N6 ....4 B3
Highgate Ave N6 .....4 A4
Highgate Cemetery*
N19 ....4 A2
Highgate Cl N6 ....3 C4
Highgate High St N6 .4 A3
Highgate Hill N19 ....4 C3
Highgate Ho 11
SE26 ....76 C1
Highgate Jun Sch N6 .3 B4
Highgate Sch N6 ....3 C4
Highgate West Hill
N6 ....3 C2
Highgrove Point 2
NW3 ....11 B4
Highlands Ave W3 ..28 B2
Highlands Cl N4 ......5 A4
Highlands Heath
SW15 ....69 B4
Highlever Rd W10 ...30 B4
Highmore Rd SE3 ...53 A3
Highshore Rd SE15 .49 B2
Highshore Sch SE15 .49 B2
Highstone Mans 15
NW1 ....13 B1
Hightrees Ho SW12 .60 C1
Highview N6 ....4 A4
Highview Ct 2
SW19 ....70 A3
Highway Bsns Pk The 7
E1 ....32 B2
Highway The E1 ....32 B2
Highway Trad Ctr The 8
E1 ....32 C2
Highwood Rd N19 ....5 A1
Highway Wall N102 .84 B3
Hilary Cl SW6 ......156 A2
Hilary Rd W12 ......29 B2
Hilborough Ct 1
E8 ....24 B4
Hilborough Rd 1
E8 ....16 B1
Hilda Terr SW9 ....173 C2
Hilditch Ho 7
TW10 ....54 B1
Hildred Ho SW1 ...146 A4
Hildreth St SW12 ...73 A3

Hildreth Street Mews 2
SW12 ....73 A3
Hildyard Rd SW6 ..155 C4
Hiley Rd NW10 ......22 B2
Hilgrove Rd NW6 ...11 B1
Hill Burgess Mews ...10 C4
Hill Ct NW3 ....12 A4
SW15 ....57 C2
Hill Farm Rd W10 ..30 C4
Hill House Int Jun Sch
SW1 ....131 A1
Hill Lo SW11 ....59 C3
Hill Rd NW8 ....79 A1
Hill Rise TW10 ......54 A1
Hill St W1 ....118 A2
Hill Wood Ho NW1 ..83 B1
Hilary Ho E14 ....34 B4
Hilbeck Ct SE13 ....50 B4
SE15 ....50 B4
Hillbrook Rd SW17 .72 B1
Hillbrow 7 TW10 ...54 A1
Hillbury Rd SW17 ...73 A1
Hillcourt Rd SE22 ...65 A1
Hillcrest W11 ....112 C3
N6 ....3 C4
SE24 ....63 C3
Hillcrest Ct NW2 ...10 A3
Hillcrest Rd W3 .....28 A1
Hilldrop Cres N7 ...13 C3
Hilldrop Est 4 N7 .13 C4
Hilldrop La N7 ......13 C3
Hilldrop Rd N7 .....13 C3
Hillersdon Ave
SW13 ....46 C1
Hillersdon Ho
SW1 ....146 A2
Hillery Cl SE17 .....151 C3
Hillfield Ct NW3 ....12 A3
Hillfield Ho N5 ....15 B3
Hillfield Mans NW3 .12 A3
Hillfield Rd NW6 ....10 C3
Hillgate Pl
W8 ....31 C1 113 B2
SW12 ....73 A4
Hillgate St W8 .....113 B2
Hilliard Ho 11 E1 ...32 A1
Hilliard's Ct E1 .....32 B1
Hillier Ho 11 NW1 ..13 C1
Hillier Rd SW11 ....60 B1
Hillingdon St SE17 .48 A4
Hilman St E8 ....17 A2
Hillmarton Rd N7 ..14 A3
Hillmead Dr SW9 ...63 A3
Hillmead Prim Sch
SW9 ....63 A3
Hillmore Ct SE13 ..67 C4
Hillrise Mans N19 ...5 A4
Hillrise Rd N19 ....5 A4
Hills Pl W1 ....104 C1
Hillsboro Rd SE22 ..64 A2
Hillsborough Ct 5
NW6 ....78 A3
Hillside NW10 ......20 C4
Hillside Cl NW8 ....78 B2
Hillside Ct NW3 ....11 A3
Hillside Gdns SW2 ..74 C2
Hillside Rd SW2 ....74 C2
Hillsleigh Rd
W14 ....31 B1 113 A2
Hillstone Ct 3 E3 ..27 A1
Hilltop Ct NW8 .....11 C1
15 SW18 ....59 C3
Hilltop Ho 6 N6 .....4 C4
Hilltop Rd NW6 .....10 C1
Hillway N6 ....3 C2
Hillworth Rd SW2 ..74 C4

Hilly Fields Cres
SE4 ....66 C4
Hillyard St SW9 ...173 B3
Hilsea Point 7
SW15 ....69 A3
Hilsea St E5 ....17 B4
Hilton Ho N7 ....14 A4
9 SE4 ....65 C3
Hilversum Cres 10
SE22 ....64 A2
Hinckley Rd SE15 ..64 C3
Hind Ct EC4 ....107 C1
Hind Gr E14 ....33 C3
13 SE14 ....50 C4
Hinde Mews W1 ...103 C2
Hinde St W1 ....103 C2
Hindhead Point 6
SW15 ....69 A3
Hindle Ho E8 ....16 B3
Hindley Ho N7 ....5 B1
Hindlip Ho SW8 ...171 B3
Hindmans Rd SE22 .64 C2
Hindmarsh Cl E1 ..125 C4
Hindrey Rd E5 ......17 A3
Hinstock NW6 ....78 A4
Hinton Rd SE24 ....63 A4
Hippodrome Mews
W11 ....112 A3
Hippodrome Pl
W11 ....112 B3
Hitchin Sq E3 ....26 A3
Hither Green Hospl
SE13 ....67 C1
Hither Green La
SE13 ....67 C1
Hither Green Prim Sch
SW2 ....74 C2
Hitherfield Rd
SW16,SW27 ....74 C1
Hitherlands SW12 ..73 A2
HM Prison Wormwood
Scrubs W12 ....29 C3
HMS Belfast* SE1 ..124 B2
Hoadly Rd SW16 ...73 C2
Hobart Pl SW1 .....132 A2
9 SW10 ....54 B1
Hobb's Ct SE1 .....139 A4
Hobbes Wlk SW15 ..57 A2
Hobb's Pl N1 ....24 A4
Hobday St E14 ......34 A3
Hobsons Pl E1 .....111 B4
Hobury St SW10 ...157 B3
Hocker St E2 ....24 B2
Hockley Ho 4 E9 ...17 B2
Hockliffe Ho W10 ..30 B4
Hockney Ct 1 SE16 .40 A1
Hockworth Ho 7
N16 ....7 A3
Hocroft Ave NW2 ....1 B1
Hocroft Ct NW2 ......1 B1
Hocroft Rd NW2 ......1 B1
Hocroft Wlk NW2 ....1 B1
Hodford Rd NW11 ....1 B3
Hodister Cl 28 SE5 .48 B3
Hodnet Grove SE16 .40 B2
Hofland Rd W14 ...126 A2
Hogan Mews W2 ..101 B4
Hogan Way E5 ....7 C2
Hogarth Bsns Pk
W4 ....46 A4
Hogarth Ct E1 .....111 C1
EC3 ....124 B4
6 NW1 ....13 B1

Hogarth Ho SW1 ..147 C3
Hogarth Ind Est
NW10 ....21 C1
Hogarth La W4 ......46 A4
Hogarth Pl SW5 ...142 A3
Hogarth Prim Sch
W4 ....38 A1
Hogarth Rd SW5 ..142 A3
Hogarth Roundabout
W4 ....46 A4
Holbeach Mews 1
SW12 ....73 A3
Holbeck Row SE15 .49 C3
Holbein Ho SW1 ...145 B2
Holbein Mews
SW1 ....145 B2
Holbein Pl SW1 ....145 B3
Holberton Gdns
NW10 ....22 A2
Holborn EC1 ....107 C3
Holborn Cir EC1 ...107 C3
Holborn Coll W14 .154 B4
Holborn Pl WC1 ...106 C3
Holborn Sta WC1 ..106 C3
Holbrook Cl N19 ....4 A3
Holbrook Ho W3 ...28 C4
5 SW2 ....74 B3
Holbrooke Ct N7 ...14 A4
Holburn 33 N1 ......24 A4
Holborn Viaduct
EC1 ....108 A3
Holcombe Ho SW9 .62 A4
Holcombe St W6 ...39 A2
Holcroft Ct W1 ....104 C4
Holcroft Ho SE10 ..52 B2
SW11 ....59 C4
Holcroft Rd E9 ......17 B1
Holden Ho N1 ....86 C3
SE8 ....51 C3
Holden St SW11 ...169 B1
Holdenby Rd SE4 ..66 A2
Holderness Ho SE5 .64 A4
Holdernesse Rd 6
SW17 ....72 C1
Holdsworth Ho 5
SW2 ....74 C4
Holford Ho W1 ......95 B4
6 SE16 ....40 A2
Holford Pl WC1 .....95 A4
Holford Rd NW3 ...11 B4
Holford St WC1 .....95 B4
Holgate Ave SW11 .59 C4
Holland Gdns W14 126 B2
Holland Gr SW9 ...163 C1
Holland Park
W11 ....31 B1 112 C1
Holland Park Ave
W11 ....31 B1 112 C1
Holland Park Ct
W14 ....126 B4
Holland Park Gdns
W14 ....126 A4
Holland Park Mews
W11 ....31 B1 112 C1
Holland Park Rd
W14 ....127 A1
Holland Park Rdbt
W12 ....39 C4
Holland Park Sch
W8 ....127 A4
Holland Park Sta
W11 ....31 B1 112 C1
Holland Pl W8 ......128 A4
Holland Rd W14 ....126 B2
NW10 ....22 A3

Holland Rise Ho
SW9 ....163 A1
Holland St SE1 ......122 B2
W8 ....127 C4
Holland Villas Rd
W14 ....126 A3
Holland Wlk W14 ..127 C3
N19 ....4 C3
Hollar Rd N16 ....7 B1
Hollen St W1 ....105 B2
Holles Ho SW9 ....173 B2
Holles St W1 ....104 B2
Holley Rd W3 ....38 A4
Holliday Sq 7
SW11 ....59 C4
Hollies Way 1
SW12 ....72 C4
Hollingbourne Rd
SE24 ....63 B2
Hollins Ho N7 ....14 A4
Hollisfield WC1 .....94 B3
Holloway Rd N19 ...5 A2
N7 ....14 B3
Holloway Road Sta
N7 ....14 B3
Holloways Sch N7 .13 C3
Holly Berry La 6
NW3 ....11 B4
Holly Bush Vale 9
NW3 ....11 B4
Holly Bush Wlk
SW9 ....63 A3
Holly Cl NW10 ....8 A1
Holly Dale Prim Sch
SE15 ....50 B1
Holly Gr SE15 ....49 C1
Holly Hedge Terr
SE13 ....67 C2
Holly Hill NW3 .....11 B4
Holly Lo SE13 ......67 A4
Holly Lodge Gdns N6 .3 C2
Holly Lodge Mans
N6 ....3 C2
Holly Mews SW10 .143 A1
Holly Mount NW3 ..11 B4
Holly Park Est N4 ..5 B4
Holly Pk N4 ....5 B4
Holly St W8 ....4 C1
Holly St E8 ....16 B1
Holly Terr N6 ....3 C2
Holly Tree Ho SE4 ..66 B4
Holly Village N6 .....4 A2
Holly Wlk NW3 .....11 B4
Hollybush Gdns E2 .25 A2
Hollybush Ho 22 E2 .25 A2
Hollybush Pl E2 .....25 A2
Hollycroft Ave NW3 ..1 C1
Hollydale Rd SE15 .50 B1
Hollydene 5 SE15 .50 A2
SE13 ....67 C4
Hollymount Ct 9
SE10 ....52 B2
Holmtree Ct SE19 .69 C3
Hollywell Row
EC2 ....24 A1 98 A1
Hollywood Mews
SW10 ....156 C4
Hollywood Rd
SW10 ....156 C4
Holm Oak Cl SW15 .58 B1
Holm Wlk SE3 ......53 C1
Holman Ho 2 E2 ...25 C2
Holman Hunt Ho
W14 ....140 A1
Holman Rd SW11 ..167 B1
Holmbury Ct SW17 .72 B1

Holmbury Ho SW9 ...63 A2
Holmbush Rd SW15 ..58 A1
Holmcote Gdns N5 ..15 B3
Holmdale Rd NW6 ...10 C3
Holmdene Ave SE24 .63 B2
Holmead Rd SW6 ..156 B1
Holmefield Ho W10 .23 A1
Holmes Ct SW4 ....172 A2
7 W4 ....37 B3
Holmes Pl SW10 ...157 A4
Holmes Rd NW5 ....13 A3
Holmes Terr SE1 ..135 B4
Holmesdale Ave
  SW14 ....55 A3
Holmesdale Ho **2**
  NW6 ....23 C4
Holmesdale Rd N6 ...4 A4
  Richmond TW9 .....44 B2
Holmesley Rd SE23 .66 A1
Holmewood Gdns
  SW2 ....74 B4
Holmewood Rd
  SW2 ....74 B4
Holmfield Ct **4**
  NW3 ....12 A2
Holmhurst SE13 ....67 C1
Holmleigh JMI Sch
  N16 ....7 A3
Holmleigh Rd N16 ...7 A3
Holmsbury Ho **6**
  N7 ....13 C3
Holmsdale Ho **8**
  E14 ....34 A2
Holmside Ct SW12 ..60 C1
Holmside Rd SW12 ..60 C1
Holmsley Ho SW15 ..68 B4
Holmwood Ct **8** N1 .24 A4
Holroyd Rd SW15 ...57 B2
Holsgrove Ct W3 ...29 A1
Holst Mans SW13 ...47 B4
Holsworthy Ho **19**
  E3 ....27 A2
Holsworthy Sq WC1 .95 A1
Holt Ct E15 ....76 B3
Holt Ho SW2 ....62 C1
Holton St E1 ....25 C1
Holwood Pl **7** SW4 .61 C3
Holy Cross RC Prim Sch
  SW6 ....165 B4
Holy Family RC JMI Sch
  E14 ....33 C2
Holy Ghost & St Stephen
  RC Prim Sch The
  W12 ....38 B4
Holy Ghost RC Prim Sch
  SW12 ....72 C4
Holy Trinity CE Inf Sch
  SW17 ....72 C2
Holy Trinity CE Jun Sch
  TW10 ....54 C3
Holy Trinity CE Prim Sch
  SW1 ....145 B4
  SW1 ....145 B4
  NW3 ....11 B2
  NW1 ....13 A1
  SW2 ....74 B4
Holy Trinity Dalston CE
  JMI Sch E8 ....16 B2
Holyburne Ave
  SW15 ....68 C4
Holyhead Cl E3 ....26 C2
Holyoak Rd SE11 ..150 B3
Holyoake Ct SE16 ..41 B4
Holyport Rd SW6 ...47 C3
Holyrood Ho N4 .....6 A3

Holyrood Mews **11**
  E16 ....35 C1
Holyrood St SE1 ..124 A1
Holywell Cl **11** SE16 .40 A1
Holywell La EC2 ...98 B2
Holywell Row EC2 ..97 C1
Home Office SW1 ..133 C3
Home Park Rd
  SW19 ....70 B1
Home Rd SW11 ....168 A2
Homefield Rd W4 ...38 B1
Homefield St **3** N1 .24 A3
Homeleigh Ct **8**
  SW16 ....74 A1
Homeleigh Rd SE15 .65 C2
Homemead SW12 ...73 A2
Homer Dr E14 ......41 C2
Homer Rd E9 ....18 A2
Homer Row W1 ....102 B3
Homer St W1 ......102 B3
Homerton Coll of
  Technology E9 ....17 B3
Homerton Gr E9 ...17 C3
Homerton High St
  E9 ....17 C3
Homerton Hospl E9 .17 C3
Homerton Rd E9 ....18 B3
Homerton Row E9 ..17 B3
Homerton Terr E9 ..17 C2
Homestall Rd SE22 .65 B2
Homestead Rd
  SW6 ....155 A1
Homewoods **2**
  SW12 ....73 B4
Homildon Ho **10**
  SE26 ....76 C1
Honduras St EC1 ...96 C2
Honey La EC2 .....109 A1
Honeybourne Rd
  NW6 ....11 A3
Honeybrook Rd
  SW12,SW4 ....73 B4
Honeyfield N4 ......5 C2
Honeyman Cl NW6 ...9 C1
Honeywell Jun & Inf
  Schs SW11 ....60 B1
Honeywell Rd SW11 .60 B1
Honeywood Ho **5**
  SE15 ....49 C2
Honeywood Rd
  NW10 ....21 B3
Honiton Gdns **1**
  SE15 ....50 B1
Honiton Ho **5** SE5 .48 B1
Honiton Rd NW6 ...23 B3
Honor Oak Park Sta
  SE23 ....65 C1
Honor Oak Pk SE23 .65 C1
Honor Oak Rise
  SE23 ....65 B1
Honwell Ho W2 ....31 C4
Hood Ave SW14 ....55 B2
Hood Ct N7 ....5 B1
Hood Ho **15** SE5 ...48 C3
Hooke Ct SE10 .....52 B2
Hooke Ho **30** E3 ...26 A3
Hookham Ct SW8 ..171 B4
Hooks Cl SE15 .....50 A2
Hoop La NW11 ......1 C4
Hooper Ho **2** SW18 .58 C2
Hooper Rd E16 .....35 C3
Hooper St E1 .....111 B1
Hooper's Ct SW1 ..130 C3

Hooper's Mews **4**
  W3 ....28 B1
Hop Gdns WC2 ....120 A3
Hope Ct **4** SE1 ...138 B2
9 Brentford TW8 ..36 A1
Hope St SW11 ......59 C4
Hopefield Ave NW6 .23 A3
Hopetown St E1 ...111 A3
Hopewell St SE5 ...48 C3
Hopgood St W12 ...30 B1
Hopkins Ho **7** E14 .33 C3
Hopkins St W1 ....105 B1
Hopkinson Ho **7**
  SW11 ....169 B2
Hopkinson's Pl
  NW1 ....81 B4
Hopping La N1 .....15 A2
Hopton Ho **2** SW9 .48 A1
Hopton St SE1 ....122 B2
Hopton's Gdns
  SE1 ....122 B2
Hopwood Cl SW17 ..71 B1
Hopwood Rd SE17 ..48 C4
Hopwood Wlk E8 ...16 C1
Horatio Ho **4** E2 ..24 B4
Horatio Pl E14 ....34 B1
Horatio St **1** E2 ..24 B3
Horbury Cres
  W11 ....31 C2 113 B3
Horbury Mews
  W11 ....31 C2 113 A3
Horder Rd SW6 ...164 B3
Hordle Promenade E **14**
  SE15 ....49 B3
Hordle Promenade N **6**
  SE15 ....49 B3
Hordle Promenade S **9**
  SE15 ....49 B3
Hordle Promenade W **8**
  SE15 ....49 A3
Horizon Sch N16 ...16 A4
Horle Wlk SE5 .....48 A1
Hormead Rd W9 ....23 B1
Horn La W3 ....28 B3
  SE10 ....43 C2
Hornbeam Cl SE11 .149 B4
Hornbeam Ho **2**
  NW3 ....12 B2
Hornbeam Sq **7** E3 .26 B4
  SE16 ....41 A2
Hornby Cl NW3 ....11 C3
Hornby Ho **2** SE11 .163 C4
Horndean Cl **3**
  SW15 ....68 C3
Horne Way SW15 ...47 B1
Horner Hos **16** N1 ..24 A4
Hornsey La N6 ......4 B4
Hornsey Lane Gdns
  N6 ....4 B4
Hornsey Rd N7,N19 .5 A2
Hornsey Rise N19 ...5 A4
Hornsey Rise Gdns
  N19 ....5 A4
Hornshay St SE15 ..50 B4
Hornton Ct W8 ....127 C3
Hornton Pl W8 ....127 C3
Hornton St W8 ....127 C4
Horrocks Ho SW15 .57 A2
Horse & Dolphin Yd
  W1 ....119 C4
Horse Guards Par ✱
  SW1 ....119 C1
Horse Guards Rd
  SW1 ....133 C4
Horse Shoe Yd W1 .118 B4
Horse Yd N1 ....86 B4

Horseferry Pl SE10 .52 B4
Horseferry Rd
  SW1 ....147 C4
  SE1 ....33 A2
Horseferry Road Est
  SW1 ....133 B1
Horseguards Ave
  SW1 ....120 A1
Horsell Rd N5 .....14 C3
Horselydown La
  SE1 ....124 C1
Horselydown Mans
  SE1 ....138 C4
Horsendon Ho **11**
  N7 ....13 C3
Horseshoe Cl E14 ..42 B1
Horsfield Ho **1** N1 .15 B1
Horsford Rd SW2 ...62 B2
Horsley Ho **10** SE4 .65 C3
Horsley St **5** SE17 .48 C4
Horsman St SE5 ....48 B4
Horsmonden Rd
  SE4 ....66 B1
Horston Ho N4 ......6 B4
Hortensia Ho
  SW10 ....156 C2
Hortensia Rd
  SW10 ....156 C2
Horticultural Pl **1**
  W4 ....37 C1
Horton Ave NW2 ...10 A4
Horton Ho **5** W14 .140 A1
  SW8 ....163 C2
  21 SE15 ....50 B4
Horton Rd E8 ......17 A2
Horton St SE13 ....67 A4
Horwood Ho NW8 ..90 B2
  24 E2 ....25 A2
Hosack Rd SW12,
  SW17 ....72 C2
Hosier La EC1 ....108 B3
Hoskins St SE10 ...42 C1
Hospital Way SE13 .67 C1
Hospl for Tropical
  Diseases NW1 .....83 B3
Hospl of St John and St
  Elizabeth NW8 ....79 B1
Hotham Prim Sch
  SW15 ....57 C3
Hotham Rd SW15 ...57 B4
Hothfield Pl SE16 ..40 B3
Hotspur St SE11 ..149 B2
Houblon Rd TW10 ..54 A2
Houghton Cl **11** E8 .16 B2
Houghton St WC2 ..107 A1
Houndsditch EC3 ..110 B2
Houses of Parliament ✱
  SW1 ....134 B2
Housman Way **20**
  SE5 ....48 C3
Hoveden Rd NW2 ...10 A3
How's St E2 ....24 B3
Howard Cl NW2 ....10 A4
  W3 ....28 A3
Howard Ct SE15 ...64 C4
Howard Ho **6** W1 ..92 B1
  14 SE8 ....51 B4
  9 SW9 ....62 C4
Howard Rd NW2 ....9 C4
Howard's La SW15 .57 B3
Howbury Rd SE15 ..65 B4
Howcroft Ho **3** E3 .26 B2
Howden St SE15 ...64 C4
Howell Ho **5** N7 ...13 C3

Howell Wlk SE1 ...150 B3
Howgate Rd SW14 .55 C4
Howick Pl SW1 ...133 A1
Howie St SW11 ....158 A1
Howitt Cl **6** NW3 ..12 A2
Howitt Rd NW3 ....12 A2
Howland Ho **7**
  SW16 ....74 A1
Howland Mews E
  W1 ....105 A4
Howland St W1 ...105 A4
Howland Way SE16 .41 A4
Howletts Rd SE24 ..63 B1
Howley Pl W2 .....101 A4
Howsman Rd SW13 .46 C4
Howson Rd SE4 ....66 A3
Howson Terr TW10 .54 A1
Hoxton Mkt N1 .....98 A3
Hoxton Sq N1 ......98 A3
Hoxton St N1 ......98 B4
  N1 ....24 A3
Hoy St E16 ....35 B1
Hoylake Rd W3 ....29 A3
Hoyland Cl **4** SE15 .50 A3
Hubbard St E15 ....27 C4
Hubert Gr SW9 ....62 A4
Hubert Ho NW8 ....90 A1
Hucknall Ct NW8 ...89 B2
Huddart St **1** E3 ..33 B4
Huddleston Cl E2 ..25 B3
Huddleston Rd N7 ..13 B4
Huddlestone Rd NW2 .9 A2
Hudson Cl **15** W12 .30 A2
Hudson Ho SW10 ..156 C2
  16 W11 ....31 A3
Hudsons Ho N1 ....97 C3
Huggin Ct EC4 ....123 A4
Huggin Hill EC4 ..123 A4
Huggins Ho **6** E3 ..26 C2
Huggins Pl SW2 ...74 B3
Hugh Astor Ct SE1 .136 B2
Hugh Gaitskell Cl
  SW6 ....154 C3
Hugh Gaitskell Ho
  N16 ....7 B2
Hugh Mews SW1 ..146 B3
Hugh Morgan Ho **1**
  SW4 ....61 C4
Hugh Platt Ho **3**
  E2 ....25 A3
Hugh St SW1 .....146 B3
Hughan Rd E15 ....19 C3
Hughendon Terr
  E15 ....76 B4
Hughes Fields Prim Sch
  SE8 ....51 C4
Hughes Ho SE17 ..150 B3
  2 E2 ....25 B2
  6 SE8 ....51 C4
Hughes Mans
  E1 ....24 C1 99 C1
Hughes Terr **1** E16 .35 B2
Hugo Ho SW1 .....131 A2
Hugo Rd N19 ......13 B4
Hugon Rd SW6 ....59 A4
Huguenot Pl SW18 .59 B2
Huguenot Sq SE15 .65 A4
Hull Cl SE16 ....32 C1

Hull Ct SE5 . . . . .48 C1
Hull St EC1 . . . . .96 C3
Hullbridge Mews
N1 . . . . .87 B4
Hulme Pl SE1 . . . . .137 B3
Humber Dr W10 . . . . . . .22 C1
Humber Rd SE3 . . . . . . .53 B4
Humberton Cl E9 . . . . . .18 A3
Humbolt Rd W6 . . . . . .154 A3
Hume Ct N1 . . . . .15 A1
Hume Ho E2 . . . . .99 B3
14 W11 . . . . .30 C1
Humphrey Ct
SW11 . . . . .167 C3
Humphrey St SE1 . . . .152 C2
Humphry Ho **19**
SW15 . . . . .57 C2
Hungerford Bridge
WC2 . . . . .120 C2
Hungerford Ho
SW1 . . . . .161 A4
Hungerford Inf Sch
N7 . . . . .14 A2
Hungerford Jun & Inf
Schs N7 . . . . .13 C2
Hungerford La
WC2 . . . . .120 B2
Hungerford Prim Sch
N7 . . . . .14 A2
Hungerford Rd
4 N7 . . . . .13 C2
N7 . . . . .14 A2
Hungerford St **24**
E1 . . . . .32 A3
Hunsdon Rd SE14 . . . . .50 C3
Hunslett St **22** E2 . . . . .25 B3
Hunstanton Ho
NW1 . . . . .102 B4
Hunt St W11 . . . . .30 C1
Hunt's Ct WC2 . . . . . . .119 C3
Hunt's La E15 . . . . .27 B3
Hunter Cl SE1 . . . . .137 C1
SW12 . . . . .72 C3
Hunter Ct **8** SE5 . . . . . .63 C3
Hunter Ho WC1 . . . . . . .94 B2
SE1 . . . . .136 B3
SW5 . . . . .141 C1
SW8 . . . . .161 C1
1 N19 . . . . .4 B1
Hunter Lo **9** W9 . . . . . .31 C4
Hunter St WC1 . . . . .94 B2
Huntingdon Ct
SW14 . . . . .55 B4
Huntingdon Gdns
W4 . . . . .45 B3
Huntingdon St
SW5 . . . . .141 C4
Huntingdon St N1 . . . . .14 B1
E16 . . . . .35 B1
Huntingfield Rd
SW15 . . . . .56 C2
Huntingford Ho
SW15 . . . . .47 B1
Huntley St WC1 . . . . . . .93 B1
Hunton St E1 . . . . .111 B4
Hunts Cl SE3 . . . . .53 C1
Hunts Slip Rd SE21 . . . .76 A2
Huntshaw Ho **9** E3 . . . .27 A2
Huntsman St SE17 . . . .152 A3
Huntspill St SW17 . . . . .71 B1
Huntsworth Mews
NW1 . . . . .90 C1
Hurdwick Ho NW1 . .82 C2

Hurleston Ho **11**
E14 . . . . .87 B4
Hurley Cres SE16 . . . . . .40 C4
Hurley Ho E2 . . . . .98 C3
SE11 . . . . .149 C3
Hurley Lo SE22 . . . . .65 B1
Hurlingham &
Chelsea
Sch SW6 . . . . .58 C4
Hurlingham Bsns Pk
SW6 . . . . .58 C4
Hurlingham Court Mans
SW6 . . . . .165 B1
Hurlingham Ct SW6 . . .58 B4
Hurlingham Gdns
SW6 . . . . .58 B4
Hurlingham Rd
SW6 . . . . .165 A1
Hurlingham Sq
SW6 . . . . .59 A4
Hurlock Ho N5 . . . . .6 A1
Hurlock St N5 . . . . .6 A1
Huron Rd SW17 . . . . . . .72 C1
Hurst Ho N1 . . . . .85 A1
Hurst St SE24 . . . . .63 A1
Hurstbourne Ho **2**
SW15 . . . . .56 B1
Hurstdene Gdns N15 . .7 A4
Hurstway Wlk **2**
W11 . . . . .30 C2
Husbourne Ho **8**
SE8 . . . . .41 A2
Huson Cl NW3 . . . . .12 A1
Hutching's St E14 . . . . .41 C4
Hutchins Cl E15 . . . . . . .76 B1
Hutchins Ho **9**
SW4 . . . . .73 C4
Hutchinson Ho **9**
SE14 . . . . .50 B3
Hutton Ct **3** N4 . . . . . . .5 B3
Hutton Ho E2 . . . . .99 B3
Hutton St EC4 . . . . . . .107 C1
Huxbear St SE4 . . . . . . .66 B2
Huxley Ho NW8 . . . . . . .89 C1
SW9 . . . . .172 C2
Huxley St W10 . . . . .23 A2
Hyacinth Rd SW15 . . . .68 C3
Hyde Farm Sch
SW12 . . . . .73 C3
Hyde La SW11 . . . . . . .168 A4
Hyde Park★ W2 . . . . . .116 C2
Hyde Park Cnr
SW1 . . . . .131 C4
Hyde Park Corner Sta
SW1 . . . . .131 C4
Hyde Park Cres
W2 . . . . .102 A1
Hyde Park Gate
SW7 . . . . .129 A3
Hyde Park Gate Mews
SW7 . . . . .129 A3
Hyde Park Gdns
W2 . . . . .115 C4
Hyde Park Gdns Mews
W2 . . . . .116 A4
Hyde Park Mans
NW1 . . . . .102 A3
Hyde Park Pl W2 . . . . .116 B4
Hyde Park Sq W2 . . . . .102 A1
Hyde Park Sq Mews
W2 . . . . .102 A1
Hyde Park St W2 . . . . .102 A1
Hyde Park Twrs
W2 . . . . .114 C3
Hyde Rd N1 . . . . .24 A4
Richmond TW10 . . . . . .54 B2
Hyde St SE8 . . . . .51 C4

Hyde Vale SE10 . . . . . . .52 B3
Hyde's Pl **17** N1 . . . . . . .15 A1
Hydethorpe Rd
SW12 . . . . .73 B3
Hylda Ct NW5 . . . . .3 C1
Hyndman Ho **5**
N19 . . . . .13 C4
Hyndman St SE15 . . . . .50 A4
Hyperion Ho **23** E3 . . . .26 A3
SW2 . . . . .74 B4
Hyson Rd SE16 . . . . .40 A1
Hythe Ho **16** SE16 . . . . .40 B4
Hythe Rd NW10 . . . . . . .21 C1
Hythe Road Ind Est
NW10 . . . . .21 C1

I

Ibberton Ho SW8 . . . .162 C2
Ibbotson Ave E16 . . . . .35 B1
Ibbott St **22** E1 . . . . . . .25 B1
Iberia Ho **17** N19 . . . . . . .4 C4
Ibis Ct **18** SE8 . . . . .51 B4
Ibis La W4 . . . . .45 B2
Ibsley Gdns SW15 . . . . .68 C3
Ibstock Place Sch
SW15 . . . . .56 A1
Icarus Ho **18** E3 . . . . . . .26 B2
Iceland Rd E3 . . . . .26 C4
Ida St E14 . . . . .34 B3
Idmiston Rd SE21,
SE27 . . . . .75 B2
Idol La EC3 . . . . .124 A3
Idonia St SE8 . . . . .51 C3
Iffley Ho E2 . . . . .98 C3
Iffley Rd W6 . . . . .39 A3
Ifield Ho SE17 . . . . . . .152 B2
Ifield Rd SW10 . . . . . . .156 B4
Ifor Evans Pl E1 . . . . . . .25 C1
Ightham Ho SE17 . . . . .152 A3
Ilbert St W10 . . . . .22 C2
Ilchester Gdns W2 . . . .114 A4
Ilchester Mans **48**
W8 . . . . .127 B2
Ilchester Pl W14 . . . . . .127 A2
Ildersly Gr SE21 . . . . . . .75 C2
Ilderton Jun & Inf Sch
SE16 . . . . .40 B1
Ilderton Rd SE15,
SE16 . . . . .50 B3
Ilex Rd NW10 . . . . .8 B2
Ilford Ho **14** N1 . . . . . . .15 C2
Iliffe St SE17 . . . . .150 B2
Iliffe Yd SE17 . . . . .150 B2
Ilkeston Ct **7** E5 . . . . . .17 C4
Ilminster Gdns
SW11 . . . . .60 A3
Ilsley Ct SW8 . . . . .170 C1
Imber St N1 . . . . .87 B3
Imperial Ave **5** N16 . .16 A4
Imperial Coll of Science
& Technology
SW7 . . . . .129 B2
Imperial College Rd
SW7 . . . . .129 B2
Imperial Ct NW8 . . . . . .80 B2
Imperial Ho **2** E3 . . . . .26 A2
2 E14 . . . . .33 B2
Imperial Rd SW6 . . . . .166 B3
Imperial Sq SW6 . . . . .166 B4
Imperial St E3 . . . . .27 B2
Imperial Twrs **3**
NW3 . . . . .11 B4
Imperial War Mus★
SE1,SE11 . . . . .135 C1
Independant Pl E8 . . . .16 B3
Indescon Ct E14 . . . . . . .42 A4

India St EC3 . . . . .110 C1
Indigo Mews N16 . . . . . . .6 C1
Indus Ct **13** SE15 . . . . . .49 B3
Ingate Pl SW8 . . . . .170 B3
Ingelow Ho **8** 128 A4
Ingelow St SW8 . . . . . .170 B3
Ingersoll Rd W12 . . . . . .30 A1
Ingestre Pl W1 . . . . . . .105 A1
Ingestre Rd NW5 . . . . . .13 A4
Ingham Rd NW6 . . . . . . .10 C4
Ingle Ho **8** SW12 . . . . . .73 C3
Inglebert St EC1 . . . . . . .95 B4
Ingleborough St
SW9 . . . . .173 B2
Ingleby Rd N7 . . . . .5 A1
Inglefield Sq **12** E1 . . . .32 A1
Ingleshaw Wlk E9 . . . . .18 B2
Ingleside Gr SE3 . . . . . . .53 B4
Inglethorpe Ho **6** E5 . .7 C2
Inglethorpe St SW6 . . .47 C2
Ingleton St SW9 . . . . . .173 B2
Inglewood Cl E14 . . . . .41 C2
Inglewood Mans **11**
NW6 . . . . .10 C3
Inglewood Rd NW6 . . . .10 C3
Inglis Ho **1** SW15 . . . . .57 B2
Inglis St SE5 . . . . .48 A2
Ingram Ave NW11 . . . . . .2 B4
Ingram Cl SE11 . . . . . . .149 A4
Ingram Ho **2** E3 . . . . . . .26 A4
Ingrave St SW11 . . . . . .60 A4
Ingrebourne Ho
NW8 . . . . .101 C4
Ingress St **4** W4 . . . . . .38 A1
Inigo Pl WC2 . . . . .120 A4
Inkerman Rd NW5 . . . . .13 A2
Inkerman Terr **38** 127 C1
Inkster Ho **9** SW11 . . . .60 A4
Inman Rd NW10 . . . . . . .21 A4
SW18 . . . . .71 B4
Inner Circ NW1 . . . . .91 B3
Inner Park Rd SW19 . . .69 C2
Inner Temple EC4 . . . . .121 B4
Inner Temple La
EC4 . . . . .107 B1
Innes Gdns SW15 . . . . .57 A1
Innis Ho SE17 . . . . .152 A2
Insley Ho **18** E3 . . . . . . .27 A2
Inst for Child Health
WC1 . . . . .94 C1
Institute Pl E8 . . . . .17 A3
Interchange The
NW5 . . . . .13 A3
International Sch of
London W3 . . . . .36 C2
Inveagh Cl E9 . . . . .25 C4
Inver Ct W2 . . . . .100 B1
Inverforth Cl NW3 . . . . . .2 B2
Inverforth House Hospl
NW3 . . . . .2 B2
Invergarry Ho NW6 . . .78 A1
Inverness Gdns
W8 . . . . .114 A1
Inverness Mews
W2 . . . . .114 B4
Inverness Pl W2 . . . . . .114 B4
Inverness St NW1 . . . . .82 B4
Inverness Terr W2 . . . .114 B4
Invicta Plaza SE1 . . . . .122 A2
Invicta Prim Sch
SE3 . . . . .53 C3
Invicta Rd SE3,SE7 . . . .53 C4
Inville Rd SE17 . . . . . . .151 C1

Inwen Ct SE8 . . . . .41 A1
Inwood Ho **16** NW1 . . .13 B1
Inwood Ho **5** SE22 . . . .64 A4
Inworth St SW11 . . . . .168 B2
Inworth Wlk N1 . . . . . . .86 C4
Ion Sq **8** E2 . . . . .24 C3
Ionian Ho **22** E1 . . . . . . .25 C1
Ipsden Bldgs SE1 . . . . .135 C4
Ipswich Ho SE4 . . . . . . .65 C2
Irby Ho SW2 . . . . .62 C1
Ireland Yd EC4 . . . . . . .108 B1
Irene Rd SW6 . . . . .165 C3
Ireton Ho SW9 . . . . . . .173 C1
Ireton St **12** E3 . . . . . . .26 C1
Iroko Ho **9** NW3 . . . . . . .11 A2
Iron Bridge Cl NW10 . . .8 A3
Iron Bridge Ho NW3 . .12 B1
Iron Mill Pl SW18 . . . . .59 A1
Iron Mill Rd SW18 . . . . .59 A1
Ironmonger La
EC2 . . . . .109 B1
Ironmonger Pas
EC1 . . . . .97 A3
Ironmonger Row
EC1 . . . . .97 A3
Ironmonger's Pl **8**
E14 . . . . .41 C2
Ironside Cl SE16 . . . . . . .40 C4
Ironside Ho E9 . . . . .18 A4
Irvine Ct W1 . . . . .93 A1
Irvine Ho N7 . . . . .14 B2
2 E14 . . . . .34 A4
Irving Gr SW9 . . . . .172 C1
Irving Ho SE17 . . . . . . .150 A1
Irving Mews N1 . . . . . . .15 B2
Irving Rd W14 . . . . .39 C3
Irving St WC2 . . . . .119 C3
Irwell Est **5** SE16 . . . . .40 B4
Irwin Gdns NW10 . . . . .22 A4
Isaac Newton Ctr
N1 . . . . .31 A3
Isabel St SW9 . . . . .173 A3
Isabella Ct **8** TW10 . . . .54 B1
Isabella Ho **10** 150 A2
13 W6 . . . . .39 B1
Isabella Rd E9 . . . . .17 B3
Isabella St SE1 . . . . . . .122 A1
Isambard Mews E14 . . .42 B3
Isambard Pl SE16 . . . . . .32 B1
Isel Way **4** SE22 . . . . . .64 A2
Iseldon Ct N7 . . . . .14 A4
Isis Cl SW15 . . . . .57 B3
Isis Ct W4 . . . . .45 A3
Isis Ho NW8 . . . . .89 C1
Isis St SW18 . . . . .71 B2
Islamia Sch Ctr
N1 . . . . .31 B2
Islamic Coll for
Advanced Studies
NW10 . . . . .9 A2
Island Gardens Sta
E14 . . . . .42 B1
Island Row E14 . . . . . . .33 B3
Isledon Ho N1 . . . . .86 C4
Isledon Rd N4,N7 . . . . . .5 C1
Islington Est N1 . . . . . . .86 C4
Islington Gn N1 . . . . . . .86 A3
Islington Green Sch
N1 . . . . .86 C2
Islington High St
N1 . . . . .86 A2
Islington Park Mews **1**
N1 . . . . .15 A1
Islington Park St
N1 . . . . .15 A1

Islington Sixth Form Ctr
N7 .....14 C4
Islip St NW5 .....13 B3
Isokon Flats **8**
NW3 .....12 B3
Ivanhoe Ho **32** E3 .....26 A3
11 SW12 .....73 A4
Ivanhoe Rd SE5 .....64 B4
Ivatt Pl W14 .....141 A1
Iveagh Ct EC3 .....110 C1
Iveagh Ho SW10 .....157 A2
2 SW9 .....48 A1
Ivebury Ct W10 .....30 B3
Iveley Rd SW4 .....170 C1
Iver Ct N1 .....15 B2
Iverna Ct W8 .....127 C2
Iverna Gdns W8 .....127 C2
Iverson Rd NW6 .....10 C2
Ives Rd E16 .....35 A4
Ives St SW3 .....144 B4
Ivimey St E2 .....24 C2 99 C4
Ivinghoe Ho **7** N7 .....13 C3
Ivor Ct NW1 .....90 C2
Ivor Pl NW1 .....90 C1
Ivor St NW1 .....13 B1
Ivories The N1 .....15 B1
Ivory Ho E1 .....125 A2
9 SW11 .....59 B4
Ivy Church La SE1,
SE17 .....152 C2
Ivy Cres W4 .....37 B2
Ivy Ct SE16 .....153 C1
SE13 .....66 C2
Ivy Lodge W8 .....113 B2
Ivy Rd NW2 .....9 B4
E16 .....35 C3
SE4 .....66 C3
Ivy St N1 .....24 A3
Ivybridge Ho **18**
SE22 .....64 A4
Ivybridge La WC2 .....120 B3
Ivydale Jun & Inf Sch
SE15 .....65 C3
Ivydale Rd SE15 .....65 C3
Ivyday Gr SW16 .....74 B1
Ivymount Rd SE27 .....74 C1
Ixworth Pl SW3 .....144 A3

J

Jack Taylor Sch
NW8 .....78 C4
Jack Tizard Sch
SW6 .....47 C2
Jack Walker Ct N5 .....15 A4
Jackman Ho **2** E1 .....32 A1
Jackman St E8 .....25 A4
Jackson Cl E9 .....17 C1
Jackson Ho **16**
SW11 .....59 C4
Jackson Rd N7 .....14 B4
Jackson's La N6 .....4 A4
Jacob Mans **1** E1 .....32 A3
Jacob St SE1 .....139 A4
SE1 .....139 B4
Jacob's Well Mews
W1 .....103 C2
Jacobin Lo N7 .....14 A3
Jacobson Ct SW11 .....168 B3
Jacobson Ho E1 .....110 C2
Jacotts Ho W10 .....22 B1
Jaggard Way SW12 .....72 B4
Jagger Ho SW11 .....168 C4
Jamahirya Sch
SW3 .....158 A4

Jamaica Rd
SE1,SE16 .....139 B2
Jamaica Rd 40 A3
James Allen's Girls' Sch
SE22 .....64 A2
James Allen's Prep Sch
SE21 .....63 C1
James Anderson Ct **7**
E2 .....24 A3
James Ave NW2 .....9 B3
James Brine Ho **2** E2 .....99 A4
James Campbell Ho **2**
E2 .....25 B3
James Collins Cl
W9 .....23 B1
James Docherty Ho **4**
E2 .....25 B3
James Hammett Ho **6**
E2 .....24 B3
James Ho E1 .....26 A1
3 SE16 .....40 C4
James Joyes Wlk **7**
SE24 .....63 A3
James Leicester Hall of
Residence N7 .....14 A2
James Lind Ho **6**
SE8 .....41 B2
James Middleton Ho **20**
E2 .....25 A2
James St W1 .....103 C1
WC2 .....120 B4
James Stewart Ho
NW6 .....10 B1
James Stroud Ho
SE17 .....151 A1
James Wolfe Jun & Inf
Sch SE10 .....52 B3
Jameson Ct **6** E2 .....25 B3
Jameson Ho **3** SE11 .....148 C2
Jameson St W8 .....113 C2
Jamestown Rd NW1 .....82 A4
Jamestown Way
E14 .....34 C2
Jane St E1 .....32 A3
Janet St E14 .....41 C3
Janeway Pl **2** SE16 .....40 A4
Janeway St SE16 .....139 C3
Japan Cres N4 .....5 B3
Jardine Rd E1 .....32 C2
Jarman Ho **13** E1 .....32 B4
SE16 .....40 C2
Jarrett Cl SW2 .....75 A3
Jarrow Rd SE16 .....40 B1
Jarrow Way E9 .....18 A4
Jarvis Ct **3** SE10 .....52 B2
Jarvis Ho **3** SE15 .....49 C2
Jarvis Rd SE22 .....64 A3
Jasmin 125 A1
Jasmin Ho SE14 .....66 B4
Jasmin Lo **17** SE16 .....40 A1
Jason Ct W1 .....103 C2
Jasper Wlk N1 .....97 B4
Java Wharf SE1 .....139 A4
Jay Ho SW15 .....47 B1
Jay Mews SW7 .....129 A3
Jean Darling Ho
SW10 .....157 B3
Jean Pardies Ho **8**
E1 .....32 B4
Jebb Ave SW2 .....62 A1
Jebb St E3 .....26 C3
Jedburgh St SW11 .....60 C3

Jeddo Mews W12 .....38 B4
Jeddo Rd W12 .....38 B4
Jeffrey's Ct **4** SW4 .....172 A2
Jeffrey's Pl NW1 .....13 B1
Jeffrey's Rd SW4 .....172 A2
Jeffrey's St NW1 .....13 B1
Jeger Ave E2 .....24 B4
Jelf Rd SW2 .....62 C2
Jellicoe Ho **5** E2 .....24 C3
9 SW15 .....57 C2
Jemotts Ct **9** SE14 .....50 C4
Jenkins Ho **9** SW8 .....171 B4
Jenkinson Ho **19** E2 .....25 C2
Jenner Ave W3 .....28 C4
Jenner Ho SE3 .....53 A4
Jenner Pl SW13 .....47 A4
Jenner Rd N16 .....7 B1
Jennifer Ho SE11 .....149 C3
Jennings Ho SE10 .....42 C1
Jennings Rd SE22 .....64 B1
Jensen Ho **10** E3 .....26 C1
Jephson Ho **6** 48 A4
Jephson St SE5 .....48 C2
Jephtha Rd SW18 .....58 C1
Jepson Ho SW6 .....166 B3
Jerdan Pl SW6 .....155 B2
Jeremiah St **1** E14 .....34 A3
Jeremy Bentham Ho
E2 .....99 C3
Jermyn St SW1 .....119 A2
Jerningham Ct
SE14 .....51 A2
Jerningham Rd
SE14 .....51 A2
Jerome Cres NW8 .....90 A2
Jerome Ho NW1 .....102 B4
8 E14 .....33 A3
Jerome St E1 .....24 B1 98 C1
Jerome Twr **5** W3 .....37 A4
Jerrard St SE13 .....67 A4
Jerrold Lo SW15 .....57 B4
Jerrold St **21** N1 .....24 A3
Jersey Ho **12** N1 .....15 B2
Jersey Rd E16 .....35 C3
Jersey St E2 .....25 A2
Jerusalem Pas EC1 .....96 A1
Jervis Bay Ho **8**
E14 .....34 C3
Jervis Ct W1 .....104 B1
Jessel Ho WC1 .....94 A3
SW1 .....147 C4
Jessica Rd SW18 .....59 B2
Jessie Blythe La **2**
N19 .....5 A4
Jesson Ho SE17 .....151 B3
Jessop Ct N1 .....86 B1
Jessop Prim Sch
SE24 .....63 B3
Jessop Sq E14 .....33 C1
Jeston Ho **10** SE27 .....75 A1
Jethou Ho **19** N1 .....15 B2
Jevons Ho **9** NW8 .....11 C1
Jewell Ho **6** SW12 .....73 A4
Jewry St EC3 .....110 C1
Jews Free Sch NW1 .....13 C2
Jews Row SW18 .....59 B3
Jeymer Ave NW2 .....9 B3
Jeypore Rd SW18 .....59 B1
Jim Griffiths Ho
SW6 .....155 A3
Joan St SE1 .....122 A1
Joanna Ho **7** W6 .....39 B1
Jocelin Ho N1 .....85 A3
Jocelyn Rd TW9 .....54 A4
Jocelyn St SE15 .....49 C2

Jockey's Fields
WC1 .....107 A4
Jodane Rd SE8 .....41 B2
Jodrell Rd E3 .....18 B1
Johanna Prim Sch
SE1 .....135 B3
Johanna St SE1 .....135 B3
John Adam St
WC2 .....120 B3
John Aird Ct W2 .....101 A4
John Archer Way
SW18 .....59 C1
John Ashby Cl SW2 .....62 A1
John Ball Prim Sch
SE3 .....53 A1
John Barker Ct
NW6 .....10 A1
John Betts' Ho W12 .....38 C3
John Bond Ho **2**
E3 .....26 B3
John Brent Ho **8**
SE8 .....40 C2
John Buck Ho
NW10 .....21 B4
John Burns Prim Sch
SW11 .....169 C1
John Carpenter St
EC4 .....122 A4
John Cartwright Ho **7**
E2 .....25 A2
John Dee Ho **3**
SW14 .....55 C4
John Donne Jun & Inf
Sch SE15 .....50 A2
John Dwight Ho
SW6 .....59 A4
John F. Kennedy Sch
E15 .....27 C4
John Felton Rd
SE16 .....139 B3
John Fielden Ho **16**
E2 .....25 A2
John Fisher St E1 .....125 B4
John Glynes Ct
SW15 .....57 A3
John Harris Ho
SE11 .....64 C4
John Islip St SW1 .....148 A3
John Keall Ho
SW15 .....57 C4
John Keats Sec & Prim
Sch NW8 .....11 C1
John Keble CE Prim Sch
NW10 .....21 B4
John Kennedy Ct **1**
N1 .....15 C2
John Kennedy Ho **2**
SE16 .....40 C2
John Kennedy Lo **2**
N1 .....15 C2
John King Ct **4** N19 .....4 C2
John Kirk Ho
SW11 .....59 C4
6 SW16 .....74 A1
John Knight Lo
SW6 .....155 C2
John Maurice Cl
SE17 .....151 B4
John McDonald Ho **3**
E14 .....42 B3
John McKenna Wlk
SE16 .....139 C2
John Milton Prim Sch
SW8 .....160 C1

John Nettleford Ho **14**
E2 .....25 A2
John Orwell Sports Ctr
E1 .....32 A1
John Parker Sq **1**
SW11 .....59 C4
John Parry Ct **28**
N1 .....24 A3
John Paul II RC Sec Sch
SW15 .....57 C4
John Penn St SE13 .....52 A2
John Perryn Prim Sch
W3 .....29 A3
John Prince's St
W1 .....104 B2
John Pritchard Ho
E1 .....99 C1
John Ratcliffe Ho **5**
NW6 .....23 C2
John Rennie Wlk **1**
E1 .....32 B1
John Roan Sec Sch
(Lower) The SE3 .....53 B3
John Roan Sec Sch
(Upper) The SE3 .....53 A3
John Roll Way
SE16 .....139 C2
John Ruskin Jun & Inf
Sch SE5 .....48 B4
John Ruskin St SE5 .....48 B4
John Scurr Ho **6**
E14 .....33 A3
John Scurr JMI Sch
E1 .....25 B1
John Silkin La SE8 .....40 C1
John Smith Ave
SW6 .....154 C2
John Spencer Sq
N1 .....15 A2
John St WC1 .....95 A1
John Steiner Jun Sch
SE4 .....66 A4
John Strachey Ho
SW6 .....155 A3
John Trundle Ct
EC2 .....108 C4
John Tucker Ho **2**
E14 .....41 C3
John Wesley's House &
Mus* EC1 .....97 C2
John Wheatley Ho
SW6 .....155 A3
1 N19 .....4 C4
John Williams Cl
SE14 .....50 C4
John's Mews WC1 .....95 A1
John's Pl E1 .....32 A3
Johnson Cl E8 .....24 C4
Johnson Ct **10**
SW18 .....59 C3
Johnson Ho NW1 .....83 A1
E2 .....99 C3
SW1 .....145 C3
SW8 .....161 C1
Johnson Lo **19** W9 .....31 C4
Johnson St E1 .....32 B3
Johnson's Pl
SW1 .....146 C1
Johnsons Ct EC4 .....107 C1
Johnsons Way
NW10 .....20 A1
Johnston Cl SW9 .....173 A3
Johnstone Ho SE13 .....67 C4

Johsen Ho **5** SW15 ....56 C2
Joiner St SE1 ....**123** C1
Joiners Arms Yd **1**
SE5 ....48 C2
Jolles Ho **3** E3 ....27 A2
Jonathan Ct **9** W4 ..38 A2
Jonathan St SE11 ...**148** C2
Jones Ho N16 ....7 A3
4 E14 ....30 A3
Jones St W1 ....**118** A3
Jones Wlk **6** TW10 ..54 B1
Jonson Ho **137** C1
16 N16 ....15 C4
Jordan Ct SW15 ....57 C3
Jordan ho N1 ....**87** C3
12 SE4 ....65 C2
Jordans Ho NW8 ......90 A1
Joscoyne Ho **4** E1 ..32 A3
Joseph Ave W3 ....28 C3
Joseph Conrad Ho
SW1 ....**147** A3
Joseph Ct N16 ....7 A4
Joseph Irwin Ho **11**
E14 ....33 B2
Joseph Lancaster Jun &
Inf Sch SE1 ......**137** B1
Joseph Powell Cl **1**
SW12 ....61 B1
Joseph Priestley Ho **12**
E2 ....25 A2
Joseph St E3 ....26 B1
Joseph Tritton Prim Sch
SW18 ....71 A2
Joseph Trotter Cl
EC1 ....95 C3
Josephine Ave SW2 ..62 B2
Joshua St E14 ....34 B3
Josseline Ct **8** E3 ...26 B3
Joubert Mans SW3 ..144 B2
Joubert St SW11 ....**169** A2
Jowett Ho SW9 .....**172** B1
Jowett St SE15 ....49 B3
Jubet Ho **3** N16 .....15 C4
Jubilee Bldgs NW8 ..79 B2
Jubilee Cres E14 .....42 B3
Jubilee Mans **10** E1 .32 B3
Jubilee JMI Sch N16 ..7 C2
Jubilee Mkt WC2 ...**120** B4
Jubilee Pl SW3 ......**144** B2
Jubilee The **2** SE10 .52 A3
Jubilee Yd SE1 ......**138** C4
Judd St WC1 ....94 A3
Jude St E16 ....35 B3
Judges' Wlk NW3 ......2 B1
Juer St SW11 ....**158** B1
Julia St NW5 ....12 C3
Julian Ave W3 ....28 A2
Julian Pl E14 ....42 A1
Juliet Ho **11** N1 ......24 A3
Julius Ct TW8 ....44 A3
Junction App SE13 ....67 B4
Junction Mews
W2 ....**102** A2
Junction Pl W2 ......**101** C2
Junction Rd N19 ......4 B1
Juniper Cres NW1 .....12 C1
Juniper Ct N16 ....6 C2
Juniper St **15** E1 ....32 B2
Juno Ct SW9 ....**163** B1
Juno Way SE14 ....50 C4

Juno Way Ind Est
SE14 ....50 C4
Jupiter Ct SW9 .....**163** B1
Jupiter Way N7 ....14 B2
Jupp Rd E15 ....19 C1
Jupp Rd W E15 ....27 C4
Jura Ho SE16 ....41 A2
Jurston Ct SE1 ......**135** C3
Justice Wlk SW3 ....**158** A3
Jutland Cl N19 ....5 A3
Jutland Ho **4** SE5 ...48 B1
Juxon St SE11 ....**149** A4

K

Kambala Rd SW11 ....59 C4
Karen Ct **2** SE5 ......64 A4
Karen Ho **7** N16 .....15 C4
Kasmin Ct NW10 ....8 C1
Kassala Rd SW11 ...**169** A3
Katherine Cl **3**
SE16 ....32 C1
Katherine Ho **19**
W10 ....23 A1
Katherine Sq SW11 .**132** A2
Katherine's Wlk **1**
SW1 ....30 C1
Kathleen Ave W3 .....28 B4
Kathleen Rd SW11 ...60 B4
Kay Rd SW9 ....**172** C1
Kay St E15 ....19 C1
2 E2 ....24 C3
Kean Ho **5** SE17 ....48 A4
Kean St WC2 ....**106** C1
Keates Est N16 ....7 B2
Keats Cl SE1 ....**152** C3
NW3 ....12 A4
Keats Gr NW3 ....12 A4
Keats Ho **6** SW1 ....**161** A4
2 E2 ....25 B2
3 SE5 ....48 B3
Keats Pl EC2 ....**109** B3
Keble Ho **4** SW15 ...57 C1
Keble Pl SW13 ....47 A4
Kedge Ho **10** E14 ...41 C3
Kedleston Ct E5 ....18 A4
Kedleston Wlk **21**
E2 ....25 A2
Keel Cl SE16 ....32 C1
Keeley St WC2 ......**106** C1
Keen's Yd N1 ....15 A2
Keep The SE3 ....53 C1
Keeper Wharf E1 .....32 C2
Keeton's Rd SE16 ....40 A3
Keevil Dr SW19 ....70 A4
Keighley Cl N7 ....14 A4
Keildon Rd SW11 .....60 B3
Keir Hardie Ho
............................4 C4
N19 ....4 C4
NW10 ....8 B1
W6 ....47 C4
Keith Connor Cl **5**
............................49 A4
Keith Gr W12 ....29 C1
Keith Ho NW6 ....78 A1
Kelby Ho N7 ....14 B2
Kelfield Ct **1** W10 ..30 C3
Kelfield Gdns W10 ...30 C3
Kellett Ho N1 ....87 C3
Kellett Rd SW2 ....62 C3
Kellow Ho SE1 ......**137** B4
Kelly Ct **13** E14 .....33 C2
Kelly St NW1 ....13 A2
Kelman Cl SW4 .....**171** C1
Kelmore Gr SE22 .....64 C3

Kelmscott Gdns
W12 ....38 C2
Kelmscott Rd SW11 .60 B2
Kelross Rd N5 ....15 B4
Kelsey St **24** E2 ....99 B2
Kelshall Ct N4 ....6 B2
Kelso Pl W8 ....**128** B2
Kelson Ho E14 ....42 B3
Kelvedon Ho SW8 ...**172** B4
Kelvedon Rd SW6 ...**155** A1
Kelvin Ct W11 ....**113** B3
W4 ....45 B3
Kelvin Rd N5 ....15 B4
Kelvington Rd SE15 ..65 C2
Kelway Ho **2** SW14 .74 C4
Kember St N1 ....14 B1
Kemble Ho SW9 ......63 A4
Kemble St WC2 .....**106** C1
Kemerton Rd SE5 ....63 B4
Kemey's St **9** E9 ....18 A3
Kemp Ct SW8 ....**162** A1
Kemp Ho **1** E2 .....25 C3
3 W1 ....**105** B1
Kempe Ho SE1 ......**137** C1
Kempe Rd NW6 ....22 C3
Kempis Way **5**
SE22 ....64 A2
Kemplay Rd NW3 ....11 C4
Kemps Dr E14 ....33 C2
Kempsford Gdns
............................**141** C1
SW5 ....**141** C1
Kempsford Rd
............................**149** C3
SE11 ....**149** C3
Kempson Rd SW6 ...**155** C1
Kempthorne Rd SE8 .41 B2
Kempton Ct **1** E1 ...32 A4
Kempton Ho **13** N1 .24 A4
Kemsford Rd SE11 ..**150** A3
Kemsing Rd SE10 ....43 C1
Kemsley SE13 ....67 A2
Ken Wilson Ho **17**
E2 ....24 C3
Kenbrook Ho W14 ..**127** A1
5 NW5 ....13 B3
Kenbury Gdns **10**
SE5 ....48 B1
Kenbury Mans **8**
SE5 ....48 B1
Kenbury St SE5 ....48 B1
Kenchester Cl
SW8 ....**162** B1
Kendal NW1 ....92 B4
Kendal Ave W3 ....28 A4
Kendal Cl SE5 ....48 A3
Kendal Ct NW2 ....10 A3
Kendal Ho N1 ....85 A2
2 E9 ....17 B1
Kendal Pl SW15 ......58 B2
Kendal Rd NW10 ....8 C4
Kendal St W2 ....**102** B1
Kendal Steps W2 ...**102** B1
Kendall Ct **3** SE22 .64 C2
Kendall Pl W1 ....**103** B3
Kender Prim Sch
............................50 B2
SE14 ....50 B2
Kender St SE14 ....50 B2
Kendoa Rd **1** SW4 .61 C3
Kendrick Mews
SW7 ....**143** B3
Kendrick Pl SW7 ....**143** B3
Kenilford Rd SW12 ..73 A4
Kenilworth Ct SW6 ..58 A4
Kenilworth Rd NW6 ..23 B4
E3 ....26 A3

Kenley Wlk W11 .....**112** A3
Kenmare Mans
NW6 ....10 B3
Kenmont Gdns
NW10 ....22 A2
Kenmont Prim Sch
NW10 ....22 A2
Kenmore Cl TW9 .....44 C3
Kenmore Ct NW6 ....10 C1
Kenmure Rd E8 ....17 A3
Kenmure Yd E8 ....17 A3
Kennacraig Cl **7**
E16 ....35 C1
Kennard Ho SW11 .**169** C3
Kennard Rd E15 ......19 C1
Kennard St SW11 ..**169** B3
Kennedy Cox Ho **9**
E16 ....35 B4
Kennedy Ho SE11 ..**148** C2
Kennedy Wlk SE17 **151** C3
Kennet Cl SW11 ......59 C3
Kennet Ho NW8 ....89 C1
Kennet Rd W9 ....23 B1
Kennet St E1 ....**125** C2
Kennet Wharf La
EC4 ....**123** A4
Kenneth Campbell Ho
NW8 ....89 C2
Kenneth Cres NW2 ...9 A3
Kenneth Ct SE11 ...**149** C4
Kenneth Younger Ho
SW6 ....**155** A3
Kenning Ho **6** N1 ..24 A4
Kenning St **16** SE16 40 B4
Kennings Way
SE11 ....**149** C2
Kennington Gr
SE11 ....**163** A4
Kennington La
SE11 ....**149** B1
Kennington Oval
SE11 ....**163** A3
Kennington Palace Ct
SE11 ....**149** B2
Kennington Park Gdns
SE17 ....48 A4
Kennington Park Ho
SE11 ....**149** B2
Kennington Park Pl
SE11 ....48 A4
Kennington Park Rd
SE11 ....**150** A2
Kennington Rd
............................**149** B4
SE11 ....**149** B4
Kennington Sta
SE17 ....**150** A2
Kennoldes SE21 ......75 C2
Kenrick Pl W1 ....**103** B3
Kensal Green Cemetery
(All Souls)* NW10 22 B2
Kensal Green Sta
NW10 ....22 B2
Kensal Rise Prim Sch
NW6 ....22 C2
Kensal Rise Sta
NW6 ....22 C2
Kensington & Chelsea
Coll
SW10 ....**156** C2
W10 ....31 A4
Kensington Church Ct
W8 ....**128** A3

Kensington Church St
W8 ....**31** C1 **113** C1
Kensington Church Wlk
W8 ....**128** A3
Kensington Court Mans
W8 ....**128** B3
Kensington Court Mews
W8 ....**128** B3
Kensington Court Pl
W8 ....**128** B2
Kensington Ct **8** W8 **128** B3
Kensington Ct Gdns
W8 ....**128** B2
Kensington Gardens
............................**115** A1
Kensington Gardens Sq
W2 ....**100** A1
Kensington Gate
W8 ....**128** C2
Kensington Gate Sq
W2 ....**114** A4
Kensington Gore
SW7 ....**129** B3
Kensington Hall Gdns
W14 ....**140** C2
Kensington High St
W8 ....**127** C2
Kensington Ho **3**
NW5 ....13 B3
Kensington Hts
W8 ....**113** B1
Kensington Mall
W8 ....**113** C2
Kensington Olympia Sta
W14 ....**126** A2
Kensington Palace*
W8 ....**114** B1
Kensington Palace Gdns
W11 ....**31** B2 **113** A3
Kensington Park Gdns
W11 ....31 B3
Kensington Park Mews
W11 ....31 B3
Kensington Park Rd
W11 ....**31** B2 **113** A4
Kensington Pl
W8 ....**31** C1 **113** C2
Kensington Prep Sch
SW6 ....**165** A4
Kensington Rd
SW7 ....**129** A3
W8 ....**128** C2
W14 ....**112** A4
Kensington Sq **4** W8 **128** A3
Kensington Village
W14 ....**141** A3
Kensington W
W14 ....**140** A4
Kensworth Ho EC1 ...**97** C3
Kent Cl **3** E2 ....24 B3
Kent Ho SW1 ....**147** B1
SE1 ....**153** A1
3 W4 ....38 A1
Richmond TW10 ....54 C2
Kent Lo **3** SW19 ...69 C3
Kent Pas NW1 ....90 C2
Kent Rd W4 ....37 B3
2 E9 ....17 C2
Richmond TW9 ....44 C3
Kent St E2 ....24 B3
Kent Terr NW1 ....90 B3
Kent Wlk SW9 ....63 A3
Kent Yard SW7 .....**130** B3
Kentish Bldgs SE1 .**123** B1

Kentish Town CE Prim
Sch NW5 . . . . .13 B3
Kentish Town Rd
NW1 . . . . .82 B4
NW1 . . . . .13 A2
Kentish Town Sta
NW5 . . . . .13 A2
Kentish Town West Sta
NW5 . . . . .13 A2
Kentmere Ho SE15 . .50 B4
Kenton Ct W14 . . . .126 C1
Kenton Ho N5 . . . . . . .5 C1
21 E1 . . . . .25 B1
Kenton Rd E9 . . . . . .17 C2
Kenton St WC1 . . . . .94 A2
Kentwell Cl SE4 . . . .66 A3
Kentwode An SW13 .46 C3
Kenway Rd SW5 . . .142 A3
Kenwood Cl NW3 . . . .2 C3
Kenwood Ho* NW3 . .3 A3
15 SE26 . . . . .41 B1
Kenworthy Rd E9 . . .18 A2
Kenwrick Ho N1 . . . .85 A3
Kenwyn Rd SW4 . . . .61 C3
Kenyon Ho **10** SE5 . .48 B3
Kenyon St SW6 . . . . .47 C2
Kepler Ho **3** SE10 . .43 B1
Kepler Rd SW2,SW4 .62 A3
Keppel Ho **3** SW3 .144 A3
8 SE8 . . . . .41 B1
Keppel Row SE1 . . .122 C1
Keppel St WC1 . . . .105 C4
Kerbela St E2 . . . . . .99 B2
Kerbey St E14 . . . . . .34 A3
Kerfield Cres SE5 . . .48 C2
Kerfield Pl SE5 . . . . .48 C2
Kerridge Ct N1 . . . . .16 A2
Kerrier Ho SW10 . . .157 A1
Kerrin Point SE11 . .149 B2
Kerrington Ct **7**
W12 . . . . .39 B4
Kerrison Rd E15 . . . .27 C4
SW11 . . . . .60 A4
Kerry N7 . . . . .14 A2
Kerry Ho **5** E1 . . . . .32 B3
Kerry Path SE8 . . . . .51 B4
Kerry Rd SE8 . . . . . . .51 B4
Kerscott Ho **20** E3 . .27 A2
Kersfield Ho SW15 . .57 C1
Kersfield Rd SW15 . .57 C1
Kershaw Cl SW18 . . .59 C1
Kershaw Ho **7**
SE27 . . . . .75 A1
Kersley Mews
SW11 . . . . .168 C3
Kersley Rd N16 . . . . . .7 A1
Kersley St SW11 . . .168 C2
Kerwick Cl **1** N7 . . .14 B1
Keslake Mans
NW10 . . . . .22 C3
Keslake Rd NW6 . . . .22 C3
Keston Ho **2** SE17 . .152 B2
Keston Rd SE15 . . . . .64 C4
Kestral Ho E5 . . . . . . .7 C3
Kestrel Ave SE24 . . . .63 B2
Kestrel Ct **27** SE8 . . .51 B4
Kestrel Ho **4** SW11 .60 A4
Kestrel Pl SE14 . . . . .51 A4
Keswick Ct **2** SE22 .64 C2
Keswick Ho **5** SE5 . .48 B2
Keswick Ho **8**
SW15 . . . . .57 C1
Keswick Lo E8 . . . . . .16 B2
Keswick Rd SW15 . . .58 A2
Ketley Ho SE15 . . . . .49 C2
Kett Gdns SW2 . . . . .62 B2

Kettleby Ho SW9 . . . .63 A4
Ketton Ho W10 . . . . .22 B1
Kevan Ho SE5 . . . . . .48 B3
Kew Bridge TW8 . . . .36 B3
Kew Bridge Ct **8**
W4 . . . . .36 C1
Kew Bridge Rd TW8 .36 B3
Kew Bridge Sta
TW8 . . . . .36 B3
Kew Bridge Steam Mus
TW8 . . . . .36 B3
Kew Foot Rd TW9 . . .54 A4
Kew Gardens Rd
TW9 . . . . .44 C2
Kew Gardens Sta
TW9 . . . . .44 C2
Kew Gardens(Royal
Botanic)* TW9 . . . . .44 A2
Kew Gn TW9 . . . . . . .44 B4
Kew Green TW9 . . . . .44 C3
Kew Lo **1** TW9 . . . . .44 A2
Kew Palace TW9 . . . .44 A3
Kew Pier TW9 . . . . . .44 C4
Kew Ret Pk TW9 . . . .45 A2
Key Cl E1 . . . . .25 A1
Key Ho SE11 . . . . . . .163 B4
Keyes Ct SE22 . . . . . .64 C2
Keyes Rd NW2 . . . . . . .9 C3
Keyham Ho **31** W2 . .31 C4
Keymer Rd SW2 . . . . .74 B2
Keynsham Ho **2** N4 . .6 B4
Keyse Rd SE1 . . . . . .138 C1
Keystone Cres N1 . . .84 B1
Keyworth Cl E5 . . . . .18 A4
Keyworth Pl SE1 . . .136 B2
Keyworth St SE1 . . .136 B2
Kezia St SE8 . . . . .41 A1
Khyber Rd SW11 . . .168 A1
Kibworth St SW8 . . .162 C1
Kidbrooke Gdns
SE3 . . . . .53 C2
Kidbrooke Gr SE3 . . .53 C2
Kidbrooke Park Rd
SE3 . . . . .53 C2
Kidderpore Ave
NW3 . . . . .10 C4
Kidderpore Gdns
NW3 . . . . .10 C4
Kidron Way **18** E9 . .25 B4
Kiffen St EC2 . . . . . . .97 C2
Kilbrennan Ho **5**
E14 . . . . .34 B3
Kilburn Bridge **14**
NW6 . . . . .23 C4
Kilburn Gate NW6 . . .78 A2
Kilburn High Rd
NW6 . . . . .78 A3
Kilburn High Road Sta
NW6 . . . . .78 A3
Kilburn Ho **9** W9 . . .23 B2
Kilburn La W10 . . . . .23 A2
Kilburn Park Jun Sch
NW6 . . . . .23 B3
Kilburn Park Rd
NW6 . . . . .23 C2
Kilburn Park Sta
NW6 . . . . .23 C3
Kilburn Pl NW6 . . . . .23 C4
Kilburn Priory NW6 . .78 A3
Kilburn Sq NW6 . . . . .23 C4
Kilburn Sta NW2 . . . .10 B2
Kilburn Vale NW6 . . .78 A3

Kilburn Vale Est **13**
NW6 . . . . .78 A3
Kildare Ct W2 . . . . . . .31 C3
Kildare Gdns W2 . . . .31 C3
Kildare Rd E16 . . . . . .35 C4
Kildare Terr W2 . . . . .31 C3
Kildare Wlk E14 . . . . .33 C3
Kildoran Rd SW2 . . . .62 A2
Kilgour Rd SE23 . . . . .66 A1
Kilkie St SW6 . . . . . .166 C1
Killarney Rd SW18 . .59 B1
Killick St N1 . . . . .84 C1
Killieser Ave SW2 . . .74 A2
Killip Cl E16 . . . . .35 B1
Killowen Rd E9 . . . . .17 C2
Killyon Rd SW8 . . . .171 B1
Kilmaine Rd SW6 . .154 B1
Kilmarsh Rd W6 . . . .39 B2
Kilmington Rd
SW13 . . . . .46 C4
Kilmore Ho **17** E14 .34 A3
Kilmuir Ho SW1 . . . .145 C3
Kiln Ct E14 . . . . .33 B2
Kiln Pl NW5 . . . . .12 C3
Kilner Ho SE11 . . . .163 B4
Kilner St E14 . . . . . . .33 C4
Kiloh Ct **3** SW11 . . .60 A4
Kilpatrick Ct N16 . . . .7 B3
Kilpeck Ho **9** N4 . . . .6 B4
Kilravock St W10 . . . .23 A2
Kilronan **3** W3 . . . . .28 C3
Kimbell Gdns SW6 .164 A3
Kimber Ctr The
SW18 . . . . .70 C4
Kimber Rd SW18 . . . .71 A4
Kimberley Ave SE15 .65 B4
Kimberley Ho **7**
E14 . . . . .42 B3
Kimberley Rd NW6 . .23 A4
SW9 . . . . .62 A4
1 N7 . . . . .14 B2
Kimble Ho NW8 . . . . .90 B2
1 SE10 . . . . .52 B4
Kimbolton Row
SW3 . . . . .144 A3
Kimpton Ct **12** SE5 .48 C2
Kimpton Ho SW15 . . .68 C4
Kimpton Rd SE5 . . . .48 C2
Kinburn St SE16 . . . .40 C4
Kincaid Rd SE15 . . . .50 A3
Kincardine Gdns
W9 . . . . .23 C1
Kindell Ho **4** SW14 .55 C4
Kinder Ho N1 . . . . . . .87 C2
Kinder St **9** E1 . . . . .32 A3
Kindersley Ho **1** E1 .111 C1
Kinefold Ho N7 . . . . .14 A2
Kinfauns Rd SW2 . . .74 C2
King & Queen St
SE17 . . . . .151 A2
King Alfred Sch
NW11 . . . . .2 A3
King Arthur Ct SW11 .60 A4
King Charles Ho
SW6 . . . . .156 B2
King Charles St
SW1 . . . . .134 A4
King Charles Wlk **6**
SW19 . . . . .70 A3
King David La E1 . . . .32 B2
King Edward Mans **6**
E8 . . . . .25 A4
King Edward Mews
SW13 . . . . .46 C2
King Edward St
EC1 . . . . .108 C2

King Edward The Third
Mews **6** SE16 . . . . .40 A4
King Edward Wlk
SE1 . . . . .135 C2
King Edward's Rd
E9 . . . . .25 B4
King Edwards Mans
SW6 . . . . .155 B1
King Fahed Acad The
W3 . . . . .29 B2
King Frederick IX Ct
SE16 . . . . .41 B3
King George Sq
TW10 . . . . .54 B1
King George St
SE10 . . . . .52 B3
King Henry St N16 . . .16 A3
King Henry's Rd
NW3 . . . . .12 A1
King Henry's Yd **5**
N1 . . . . .16 A3
King Ho W12 . . . . .30 A3
King James St SE1 .136 B3
King John Ct EC2 . . . .98 B2
King John St E1 . . . . .32 C4
King St EC2 . . . . .109 A1
SW1 . . . . .119 A2
WC2 . . . . .120 A4
W3 . . . . .28 B1
W6 . . . . .38 C2
King Stairs Cl SE16 . .40 A4
King Street Cloisters **6**
W6 . . . . .39 A2
King William La **3**
SE10 . . . . .43 A1
King William St
EC4 . . . . .123 C4
King William Wlk
SE10 . . . . .52 B4
King's Arms Ct
E1 . . . . .111 B3
King's Arms Yd
EC2 . . . . .109 B2
King's Bench St
SE1 . . . . .136 B4
King's Bench Wlk
EC4 . . . . .107 C1
King's Coll SE1 . . . . .63 C1
King's Coll WC2 . . . .121 A4
King's College Hospl
SE5 . . . . .48 C1
King's College London
NW3 . . . . .10 C4
King's Court S
SW3 . . . . .144 A1
King's Cres N4,N5 . . .6 B1
King's Cross WC1 . . .94 B4
King's Cross (Midland
City) Sta WC1 . . . . . .94 B4
King's Cross (Thames
Link) Sta WC1 . . . . . .94 B4
King's Cross Bridge
WC1 . . . . .94 B4
King's Cross Rd
WC1 . . . . .95 A3
King's Cross Sta
N1 . . . . .84 B1
King's Cross, St
Pancras Sta WC1 . . .94 A4
King's Gdns **6** NW6 .10 C1
King's Gr SE15 . . . . . .50 A3

King's Gr continued
SE15 . . . . .50 A3
King's Head Yd
SE1 . . . . .123 B1
King's House Jun Sch
TW10 . . . . .54 B2
King's House Sch
TW10 . . . . .54 B2
King's Keep **6**
SW15 . . . . .57 C2
King's Mansions
SW3 . . . . .158 A3
King's Mead Way
E5,E9 . . . . .18 A4
King's Mews **1**
SW4 . . . . .62 A2
King's Mews WC1 . . .95 A1
King's Par NW10 . . . .22 B4
W12 . . . . .38 C3
King's Pl SE1 . . . . . .136 C3
King's Quay
SW10 . . . . .167 A4
King's Rd SW14 . . . . .55 C4
King's Rd SW3 . . . . .144 A1
SW10 . . . . .156 B1
King's Scholars' Pas
SW1 . . . . .146 C4
King's Terr NW1 . . . . .82 C3
Kingdon Ho **6** E14 . .42 B3
Kingdon Rd NW6 . . . .10 C2
Kingfield St E14 . . . . .42 B2
Kingfisher Ct
E1 . . . . .42 B4
11 SW18 . . . . .60 A4
9 SW19 . . . . .70 A2
Kingfisher Ho
W14 . . . . .126 C2
SE15 . . . . .49 B2
Kingfisher Mews
SE13 . . . . .67 A2
Kingfisher Sq **10**
SE8 . . . . .51 B4
Kingham Cl **3** W11 .39 C4
SW18 . . . . .71 B4
Kinghorn St EC1 . . .108 C3
Kinglake St SE17 . . .152 B2
Kingley St W1 . . . . .104 C1
Kingly Ct W1 . . . . . .119 A4
Kingly St W1 . . . . . .118 C4
Kings Acre Prim Sch
SW4 . . . . .62 A1
Kings Ave SW4 . . . . .62 A1
Kings Coll Chelsea
Campus (Univ of
London) SW10 . . . .156 B2
Kings Coll London
(Chelsea Campus)
SW3 . . . . .144 A1
Kings College Ct
NW3 . . . . .12 A1
Kings Coll London
W6 . . . . .127 B4
Kings Ct **1** NW8 . . . .80 C3
6 N7 . . . . .14 B1
W6 . . . . .38 C3
SE22 . . . . .64 C3
10 SW15 . . . . .68 C4
Kings Farm Ave
TW10 . . . . .54 C2
Kings Hall Mews
SE13 . . . . .67 B4
Kings Ho SW8 . . . . .162 B2
Kings Mall W6 . . . . . .39 B2

Kings Pl W4 . . . . .37 B2
Kings Rd NW10 . . . . .9 A1
  Richmond TW10,TW9 . .54 B2
Kings Ride Gate
  TW10 . . . . .54 C3
Kings Wood Ct 4
  NW6 .10 C3
Kingsbridge N16 . . . . .6 C3
Kingsbridge Ave
  W3 . . . . .36 B4
Kingsbridge Ct E14 .41 C2
Kingsbridge Rd
  W10 .30 B3
Kingsbury Rd N1 . . . . .16 A2
Kingsbury Terr N1 . . . . .16 A2
Kingsclere Cl SW15 .68 C4
Kingscliffe Gdns
  SW19 . . . . .70 B3
Kingscote NW11 . . . . .1 B3
Kingscote Rd W4 . . .37 C3
Kingscote St EC4 . .122 C4
Kingscourt Rd
  SW16 . . . . .74 A1
Kingscroft SW4 . . . . .62 A1
Kingscroft Rd NW2 .10 B2
Kingsdale Gdns
  W11 .30 C1
Kingsdale Sch SW11 .76 A1
Kingsdown Ave W3 .29 A2
Kingsdown Cl W10 .30 C3
  11 W11 . . . . .31 A3
  20 SE16 . . . . .40 A1
Kingsdown Ct SW11 60 A1
Kingsdown Ho 1
  E8 . . . . .16 C3
Kingsdown Rd 3
  N19 . . . . .5 A2
Kingsfield Ho 10 N16 .7 A1
Kingsford St NW5 . . .12 B3
Kingsgate Est N1 . . .16 A2
Kingsgate Ho SW9 173 C4
Kingsgate Jun & Inf Sch
  NW6 .10 C1
Kingsgate Pl NW6 . .10 C1
Kingsgate Rd NW6 . .10 C1
Kingshill SE17 . . . . . .151 A4
Kingshold Rd E9 . . . .17 B1
Kingsland NW8 . . . . . .80 B3
Kingsland Gn 1 E8,
  N1 . . . . .16 B3
Kingsland High St
  E8 . . . . .16 B3
Kingsland Pas 2
  E8 . . . . .16 A2
Kingsland Rd E2 . . . .24 A3
  Kingsland Sch E8 . . . .16 B3
  Kingsland Sh Ctr E8 16 B2
Kingslawn Cl SW15 .57 A2
Kingsley Cl N2 . . . . .9 A2
Kingsley Flats SE1 .152 B4
Kingsley Ho 3
  SW4 .171 C2
Kingsley Mews
  W8 . . . . .128 B1
Kingsley Pl N6 . . . . . . .3 C4
Kingsley Rd NW6 . . .23 B4
Kingsley St SW11 . . .60 B4
Kingsmead TW10 . . .54 B1
Kingsmead Ct N6 . . . .4 C4
Kingsmead Ho
  E9 . . . . .18 A4
  Kingsmead JMI Sch
  E9 . . . . .18 A4
Kingsmead Rd SW2 .74 C2

Kingsmere Cl SW15 .57 C4
Kingsmere Pl N16 . . .6 C3
Kingsmere Rd
  SW19 . . . . .69 C2
Kingsmill NW8 . . . . . .79 C2
Kingsmill Terr NW8 .79 C2
Kingsnorth Ho 12
  W10 .30 C3
Kingsridge SW19 . . .70 A2
Kingston Ho 7
  NW6 .10 A1
Kingston Ho E
  SW7 .130 A3
Kingston Ho N
  SW7 .130 A3
Kingston Ho S
  SW7 .130 A3
Kingston Univ
  Roehampton Vale Ctr
  SW15 . . . . .68 A1
Kingston Vale SW15 .68 A1
Kingstown St 1 NW1 .81 B4
Kingswater Pl
  SW11 . . . . .158 A1
Kingsway WC2 . . . . . .106 C2
Kingsway Coll WC1 . . .94 C4
  WC1 .95 A4
  NW5 .13 A2
Kingswear Rd NW5 . . .4 A1
Kingswood 2 E2 . . . . .25 B3
Kingswood Ave
  NW6 .23 A3
Kingswood Cl SW8 162 B1
Kingswood Ct 7
  TW10 . . . . .54 B2
Kingswood Rd W4 . . .37 B3
  SW2 .74 A4
Kingswood Terr W4 .37 B3
Kington Ho NW6 . . . .78 B3
Kingward Ho E1 . . . .111 B4
Kingwood Rd SW6 154 A1
Kinloch St N7 . . . . .5 B1
Kinnaird Ave W4 . . . .45 B3
Kinnear Rd W12 . . . .38 B4
Kinnerton Pl N
  SW1 .131 A3
Kinnerton Pl S
  SW1 .131 B3
Kinnerton St SW1 . .131 B3
Kinnerton Yd SW1 .131 B3
Kinnoul Rd W6 . . . .154 A4
Kinnoull Mans 10
  E5 . . . . .17 A4
Kinross Ho N1 . . . . . .84 C4
Kinsale Rd SE15 . . . .64 C4
Kinsham Ho E2 . . . . .99 B2
Kintore Way SE1 . . .152 C4
Kintyre Ct 17 SW2 . .74 A4
Kinver Ho N4 . . . . .6 C4
Kipling Ho 20 SE5 . . .48 B3
Kipling St SE1 . . . . . .137 C4
Kipling Twr 8 W3 . . .37 B3
Kirby Est SE16 . . . . . .40 A3
Kirby Gr SE1 . . . . .138 A4
Kirby St EC1 . . . . .107 C4
Kirk's Pl E3 . . . . .33 B4
Kirkeby Ho EC1 . . . .107 B4
Kirkland Wlk 4 E8 . .16 B2
Kirkley Ho N16 . . . . . .7 A3
Kirkman Pl W1 . . . . .105 B3
Kirkmichael Rd E14 .34 B3
Kirkside Rd SE3 . . . . .53 C4
Kirkstall Gdns SW2 .74 A3

Kirkstall Ho SW1 . . .146 A2
Kirkstall Rd SW2 . . .74 A3
Kirkstead Ct E5 . . . . .18 A4
Kirkstone NW1 . . . . . .92 C4
Kirkstone NW1 . . . . . .92 C4
Kirkstone Wlk 3
  NW5 .12 C2
Kirkwall Pl E2 . . . . . . .25 B2
Kirkwood Rd SE15 . .50 A1
Kirtley Ho SW8 . . . .171 A4
Kirtling St SW8 . . . .160 C2
Kirton Cl W4 . . . . .37 C2
Kirton Gdns E2 . . . . .99 A3
Kirwin Way SE5 . . . . .48 A3
Kitcat Terr E3 . . . . . . .26 C2
Kite Ho 5 SW11 . . . . .60 A4
Kite Pl E2 . . . . .99 C4
Kitson Rd SW13 . . . .46 C2
  SE5 . . . . .48 B3
Kittiwake Ct 2 SE8 .51 B4
Kitto Rd SE14 . . . . . . .50 C1
Kiver Rd N19 . . . . .5 A2
Klea Ave SW4 . . . . . . .61 C1
Kleffens Ct 2 SE3 . .53 B3
Knapp Cl NW10 . . . . .8 A2
Knapp Rd E3 . . . . .26 C1
Knaresborough Dr
  SW18 . . . . .71 A3
Knaresborough Ho
  N4 . . . . .6 B4
Knaresborough Pl
  SW5 .142 A4
Knatchbull Rd
  NW10 . . . . .20 C4
  SE5 . . . . .48 A2
Knebworth Ho
  SW8 .171 C3
  2 N16 . . . . .16 A4
Knebworth Rd 3
  N16 . . . . .16 A4
Kneller Ho SW8 . . . .171 C2
Kneller Rd SE4 . . . . . .66 B3
Knight Ho SE17 . . . . .152 A3
Knight's Ave W5 . . . .36 A4
Knight's Ho SW10 . .156 C2
  SE11 .150 A3
Knighten St E1 . . . . . .32 A1
Knighthead Point
  E14 . . . . .41 C4
Knightleas Ct NW2 . . .9 B2
Knightrider Ct EC4 122 C4
Knightrider St EC4 122 B4
Knights Arc SW1 . . .130 C3
Knights Cl E9 . . . . . . .17 B3
Knights Ho SW5 . . . .141 C4
  SW8 .162 B1
Knights Rd E16 . . . . . .43 C4
Knightsbridge
  SW1,SW7 . . . . .130 C3
Knightsbridge Ct
  SW1 .131 A3
Knightsbridge Gn
  SW1 .130 C3
  SW1 .131 A3
Knightsbridge Sta
  SW1 .131 A3
Knightswood Ct N6 . .4 C4
Knivett Rd SW6 . . . .155 B3
Knobs Hill Rd E15 . .27 A4
Knoll Ho NW8 . . . . . . .78 C2
Knoll Rd SW18 . . . . . .59 B2
Knolly's Cl SE27,
  SW16 . . . . .74 C1
Knolly's Rd SE27,
  SW16 . . . . .74 C1
Knot Ho SE1 . . . . .124 C1

Knottisford St E2 . . .25 B2
Knowden Ho 4 E1 . .32 B2
Knowle Cl SW9 . . . . .62 C4
Knowles Hill Cres
  SE13 .67 C2
Knowles Ho NW10 . .21 C4
  SW18 . . . . .59 A1
Knowles Wlk SW4 . .61 B4
Knowlton Ho SW9 .173 C4
Knowsley Rd
  SW11 . . . . .168 C1
Knox Ct SW4 . . . . . . .172 B2
Knox Ho SW15 . . . . . .47 B1
Knox St W1 . . . . .102 C4
Knoyle St SE14 . . . . . .51 A4
Kobi Nazrul Prim Sch
  E1 . . . . .111 C2
Kossuth St SE10 . . . .43 A1
Kramer Mews
  SW5 .142 A1
Kreedman Wlk 8
  E8 . . . . .16 C3
Kreisel Wlk TW9 . . . .44 B4
Kylemore Ct 4
  W12 .38 C4
Kylemore Rd NW6 . .10 C1
Kylestrome Ho
  SW1 .145 C3
Kynance Mews
  SW7 .128 B1
Kynance Pl SW7 . . . .128 C1
Kynaston Ho 7
  SW2 .74 B3
Kynaston Rd N16 . . . .7 A1
Kyrle Rd SW11 . . . . . .60 C1
Kyverdale Rd N16 . . .7 B3

L

L'Ecole des Petits Sch
  SW6 .166 B2
La Retraite RC Girls Sch
  SW12 . . . . .73 B4
La Saint Union Convent
  Sch NW5 . . . . .3 C1
Laburnum Cl 5
  SE15 .50 B3
Laburnum Ho SE4 . . .51 B1
Laburnum Ho 4
  N16 . . . . .6 C4
  Laburnum JMI Sch
  E2 . . . . .24 B4
Laburnum St E2 . . . .24 B4
Lacey Ho 6 SE13 . . .52 B1
Lacey Wlk E3 . . . . . . .26 C3
Lacine Ct 12 SE16 . . .40 C4
Lackington St EC2 .109 C4
Lackland Ho SE1 . . .153 A2
Lacland Ho SW10 . .157 B2
Lacon Rd SE22 . . . . . .64 C3
Lacy Rd SW15 . . . . . .57 C3
Ladbroke Cres W11 .31 A3
Ladbroke Gdns
  W11 . . . . .31 B2 112 C4
Ladbroke Gr
  W11 . . . . .31 B2 112 C4
  W10 .31 A4
Ladbroke Grove Ho
  W11 .112 C4
Ladbroke Grove Sta
  W10 .31 A4
Ladbroke Mews
  W11 .112 B1
Ladbroke Rd
  W11 . . . . .31 B1 112 C4

Ladbroke Sq
  W11 . . . . .31 B2 113 A3
Ladbroke Terr
  W11 . . . . .31 B1 113 A3
Ladbroke Wlk
  W11 . . . . .31 B1 113 A3
Ladlands SE22 . . . . . .76 C4
Lady Elizabeth Ho
  SW14 . . . . .55 B4
Lady Margaret Rd
  NW5 .13 B3
  Lady Margaret Sch
  SW6 .165 B3
Lady Somerset Rd
  NW5 .13 A4
Ladybower Ct 6 E5 .17 C4
Ladycroft Rd SE13 . .67 A4
Ladywell Cl SE4 . . . .66 C3
Ladywell Hts SE4 . . .66 B1
Ladywell Rd SE13 . .67 A2
  Ladywell Sta SE13 . .67 A2
Lafitte Ho 22 N19 . . .4 C4
Lafone Ho 11 SW2 . .74 A4
Lafone St SE1 . . . . . .138 C4
Lagado Mews SE16 .32 C1
Lagan Ho 1 SE15 . . .49 C3
  SE15 .49 C2
Lagonda Ho 11 E3 . .26 C1
Lagonier Rd EC1 . . . .97 A3
Laindon Ho 6 N16 . .7 B3
Laing Ho SE5 . . . . . . .48 B3
Lainson St SW18 . . .70 C4
Laird Ho SE5 . . . . .48 B3
Lairdale Cl SE21 . . . .75 B4
Lairs Cl N7 . . . . .14 A2
Laitwood Rd SW12 . .73 A3
Lakanal 14 SE5 . . . . .49 A2
Lake Ho SE1 . . . . . . .136 C3
Lake View Ct SW1 . .132 B2
Laker Ct SW4 . . . . . .172 B2
Laker Pl SW15 . . . . . .58 A1
Lakeside Ct N4 . . . . . .6 B3
Lakeside Rd W14 . . .39 C3
Lakeview 23 E3 . . . . .25 C3
Lakis Cl NW3 . . . . . . .11 B4
Laleham Ho E2 . . . . .98 C2
Lalor St SW6 . . . . . . .164 B2
Lamb Ho 20 SE5 . . . .48 B3
  11 SE5 . . . . .48 C2
  SE10 .52 B4
Lamb La E8 . . . . .17 A1
Lamb St E1 . . . . .110 C4
Lamb Wlk SE1 . . . . . .138 A3
Lamb's Bldgs EC1 . . .97 B1
Lamb's Conduit Pas
  WC1 .106 C4
Lamb's Conduit St
  WC1 . . . . .94 C1
Lamb's Mews N1 . . . .86 A3
Lamb's Pas EC1 . . . . .97 B1
Lamberhurst Ho 14
  SE15 .50 B4
Lambert Ave TW9 . . .55 A4
Lambert Ho SW9 . . .173 B1
  10 N19 . . . . .4 C4
Lambert Rd SW2 . . . .62 B2
Lambert St N1 . . . . . .14 C1
Lambert Way N2 . . . . .9 C1
Lambeth Coll (Clapham
  Ctr) SW4 . . . . .61 B2
Lambeth Coll (Tower
  Bridge Ctr) SE1 . . . .124 B1
Lambeth Coll (Vauxhall
  Ctr) SW8 . . . . .171 B4
Lambeth Ct 8
  SW18 . . . . .58 C2

Lambeth High St
SE1 . . . . 148 C4
Lambeth Hill EC4 . . . . 122 C4
Lambeth Inst Strand Ctr
SW2 . . . . 74 B4
Lambeth North Sta
SE1 . . . . 135 B2
Lambeth Palace ★
SE1 . . . . 134 C1
Lambeth Palace Rd
SE1 . . . . 134 C2
Lambeth Pier SE1 . . . . 134 B1
Lambeth Rd SE1 . . . . . 135 B1
Lambeth Twrs
SE11 . . . . 135 B1
Lambeth Wlk SE11 . . . 149 A4
Lambfold Ho N7 . . . . . 14 A2
Lamble St NW5 . . . . . 12 C4
Lambolle Pl NW3 . . . . . 12 A2
Lambolle Rd NW3 . . . . 12 A2
Lambourn Cl 9
NW5 . . . . 13 B4
Lambourn Rd SW4 . . . . 61 A4
Lambourne Ho
NW8 . . . . 101 C4
SE16 . . . . 40 C2
Lambrook Ho 12
SE15 . . . . 49 C2
Lambrook Terr
SW6 . . . . 164 A4
Lambton Ct 2 N19 . . . . 5 A3
Lambton Pl W11 . . . . 113 A4
Lambton Rd N19 . . . . . 5 A3
Lamerton Lo 10
TW9 . . . . 44 B2
Lamerton St 9 SE8 . . . 51 C4
Lamington St 3
W6 . . . . 39 A2
Lamlash St SE11 . . . . 150 A4
Lamley Ho SE1 . . . . . . 52 A3
Lammas Rd E9 . . . . . . 17 C1
Lammermoor Rd
SW12 . . . . 73 A4
Lamont Rd SW10 . . . . 157 B3
Lamont Rd Pas
SW10 . . . . 157 B3
Lampard Gr N16 . . . . . 7 B3
Lampern Sq 2 E2 . . . . 99 C4
Lampeter Sq W6 . . . . 154 A3
Lamplighter Cl 1
E1 . . . . 25 B1
Lamps Ct 11 SE5 . . . . 48 B3
Lampson Ho 6 N19 . . . 13 B4
Lanark Ho SE1 . . . . . 153 B1
Lanark Mans W9 . . . . . 89 A2
9 W12 . . . . 39 B4
Lanark Pl W9 . . . . 89 A2
Lanark Rd W9 . . . . 88 C3
Lanark Sq E14 . . . . . . 42 A3
Lanbury Rd SE15 . . . . . 65 C3
Lancashire Ct W1 . . . . 118 B4
Lancaster Ave SE21,
SE27 . . . . 75 B2
Lancaster Cl W2 . . . . 114 A3
9 N1 . . . . 16 A2
Lancaster Cotts 1
TW10 . . . . 54 A1
Lancaster Ct W2 . . . . 115 A4
SW6 . . . . 155 A1
SE27 . . . . 75 A1
Lancaster Dr NW3 . . . . 12 A2
E14 . . . . 34 B1
Lancaster Gate
W2 . . . . 115 A3
Lancaster Gate Sta
W2 . . . . 115 B4

Lancaster Gr NW3 . . . . 12 A2
Lancaster Ho SW1 . . . 132 C4
SW15 . . . . 47 B1
SW18 . . . . 71 A4
Lancaster Lo 2
W11 . . . . 31 A3
Lancaster Mews
W2 . . . . 115 A4
2 Richmond TW10 . . . . 54 A1
8 SW18 . . . . 59 A2
Lancaster Pk TW10 . . . 54 A2
Lancaster Pl WC2 . . . . 120 C3
Lancaster Rd N4 . . . . . 5 C4
NW10 . . . . 8 C3
W11 . . . . 31 A3
Lancaster St SE1 . . . . 136 B3
Lancaster Stables 3
NW3 . . . . 12 A2
Lancaster Terr W2 . . . 115 B4
Lancaster Wlk W2 . . . 115 A2
Lancefield Ct 1
W10 . . . . 23 A3
Lancefield Ho SE15 . . . 65 A4
Lancefield St W10 . . . . 23 A2
Lancell St N16 . . . . . . 7 A2
Lancelot Pl SW7 . . . . 130 C3
Lancer Sq W8 . . . . . . 128 A4
Lanchester Ct W2 . . . . 102 C1
Lancing St NW1 . . . . . 93 B3
Lancresse Ct N1 . . . . . 24 A4
Landale Ho 5 SE16 . . . 40 B3
Landcroft Rd SE22 . . . . 64 B1
Landells Rd SE22 . . . . . 64 C1
Landford Rd SW15 . . . . 57 B4
Landin Ho 1 E14 . . . . 33 C3
Landleys Field 21
N7 . . . . 13 C3
Landmann Ho 16
SE16 . . . . 40 A2
Landmann Way
SE14 . . . . 40 C1
Landon Pl SW1 . . . . . 130 C2
Landon Wlk 14 E14 . . . 34 A2
Landons Cl E14 . . . . . 34 B1
Landor Ct N16 . . . . . . 16 A3
Landor Ho 7 SE5 . . . . 48 C3
Landor Rd SW9 . . . . . 62 A4
Landor Wlk 11 W12 . . . 38 C4
Landrake NW1 . . . . . . 83 A3
Landridge Rd SW6 . . . 164 C2
Landseer Ho NW8 . . . . 89 C2
SW1 . . . . 147 C3
SW11 . . . . 169 C3
Landseer Rd N19 . . . . . 5 A2
Landulph Ho SE11 . . . 149 C2
Landward Ct W1 . . . . . 102 B2
Lane Ct SW11 . . . . . . 72 B4
Lane The NW8 . . . . . . 78 C1
Lanercost Cl SW2 . . . . 74 C2
Lanercost Rd SW2 . . . . 74 C2
Laneway SW15 . . . . . . 57 A2
Laney Ho EC1 . . . . . . 107 B4
Lanfranc Rd E3 . . . . . 26 A3
Lanfrey Pl W14 . . . . . 140 C1
Lang Ho SW8 . . . . . . 162 A1
2 N19 . . . . 4 B1
Lang St E1 . . . . 25 B1
Langbourne Ave N6 . . . 3 C2
Langbourne Ho 6
SW2 . . . . 62 C2
Langbourne Mans
N6 . . . . 3 C2
Langbourne Prim Sch
SE21 . . . . 76 A1
Langdale NW1 . . . . . . 92 C4
Langdale Cl SE17 . . . . . 48 B4

Langdale Cl continued
SW14 . . . . 55 A3
Langdale Ho SW1 . . . . 146 C1
Langdale Rd SE10 . . . . 52 B3
Langdale St 3 E1 . . . . 32 A3
Langdon Ct EC1 . . . . . 86 B1
Langdon Ho 1 E14 . . . 34 B3
Langdon Park Rd N6 . . . 4 B4
Langdon Park Sec Sch
E14 . . . . 34 B3
Langdon Pl SW14 . . . . 55 B4
Langdon Way 3
SE1 . . . . 153 C3
Langford Cl NW8 . . . . . 79 A2
E8 . . . . 16 C3
Langford Ct NW8 . . . . . 79 A1
Langford Gn SE5 . . . . . 64 A4
Langford Ho 6 SE8 . . . 51 C4
Langford Pl NW8 . . . . . 79 A2
Langford Prim Sch
SW6 . . . . 166 B2
Langford Rd SW6 . . . . 166 B2
Langham Ct 4
SW15 . . . . 57 C2
Langham Ho SW4 . . . . 61 B2
Langham Mans
SW5 . . . . 142 A1
Langham Pl W1 . . . . . 104 B3
W4 . . . . 46 A4
Langham St W1 . . . . . 104 B3
Langholm Cl SW12 . . . 73 C4
Langhorne Ct 10
NW8 . . . . 11 C1
Langhurst Ho
SW11 . . . . 169 B2
Langland Gdns
NW3 . . . . 11 A3
Langland Ho 10 SE5 . . 48 C3
Langler Rd NW10 . . . . . 22 B3
Langley Ct WC2 . . . . . 120 A4
SW9 . . . . 172 A4
Langley Dr W3 . . . . . . 37 A4
Langley Ho 6 E5 . . . . 17 A3
4 W2 . . . . 100 A4
Langley La SW8 . . . . . 162 B4
Langley Mans SW8 . . . 162 B4
Langley St WC2 . . . . . 106 A1
Langmead Ho 34 E3 . . 27 A2
Langmore Ho 1 E1 . . . 111 C1
Langport Ho 1
SW9 . . . . 48 A1
Langridge 15 NW5 . . . . 12 C2
Langroyd Rd SW17 . . . . 72 B2
Langside Ave SW15 . . . 56 C3
Langston Hughes Cl 5
SE24 . . . . 63 A3
Langthorn Ct EC2 . . . . 109 C2
Langthorne St SW6 . . . 47 C3
Langton Cl WC1 . . . . . 95 A2
Langton Ho SE11 . . . . . 149 A4
Langton Pl SW18 . . . . . 70 C3
Langton Rd SW9 . . . . . 48 A3
Langton St SW10 . . . . 157 A3
Langton Way SE3 . . . . . 53 C3
Langtry Pl SW6 . . . . . 155 C4
Langtry Rd NW8 . . . . . 78 A3
Langtry Wlk NW8 . . . . . 78 C4
Lanhill Rd W9 . . . . . . 23 C1
Lanier Ho SE13 . . . . . 67 C1
Lanner Ho 2 SW11 . . . 60 A4
Lannoy Point SW6 . . . 154 B2
Lanrick Rd E14 . . . . . . 35 A3
Lansbury Gdns 1
E14 . . . . 34 C3
Lanscombe Wlk
SW8 . . . . 162 A1

Lansdown Ho 29
SE5 . . . . 48 B1
Lansdowne Cres
W11 . . . . 31 A2
Lansdowne Dr E8 . . . . . 16 C1
Lansdowne Gdns
SW8 . . . . 172 A4
Lansdowne Gr NW10 . . 8 A4
Lansdowne Hill
SE27 . . . . 75 A1
Lansdowne Ho
W11 . . . . 112 C3
Lansdowne Mews
W11 . . . . 31 B2
Lansdowne Pl SE1 . . . 137 C2
Lansdowne Rd
W11 . . . . 31 A2 112 B3
E8 . . . . 16 C2
Lansdowne Rise
W11 . . . . 31 A2 112 B3
Lansdowne Row
W1 . . . . 118 B2
Lansdowne Sch
SW2 . . . . 62 B4
Lansdowne Terr
WC1 . . . . 94 B1
Lansdowne Way
SW4,SW8 . . . . 172 B3
Lansdowne Wlk
W11 . . . . 31 A2
Lansdowne Wood Cl 1
SE27 . . . . 75 A1
Lant Ho SE1 . . . . 136 C3
Lant St SE1 . . . . 137 A3
Lantern Cl SW15 . . . . . 56 C3
Lantern Ho E14 . . . . . 41 C4
Lanterns Ct E14 . . . . . 41 C3
Lantry Ct 1 W3 . . . . . 28 A1
Lanvanor Rd SE15 . . . . 50 B1
Lanyard Ho 8 SE8 . . . . 41 B2
Lapford Cl W9 . . . . . . 23 B1
Lapsang SE1 . . . . 125 A1
Lapwing Twr 8 SE8 . . . 51 B4
Lapworth Ct W2 . . . . . 100 B4
Lara Cl SE13 . . . . 67 B1
Larch Ave W3 . . . . . . 29 A1
Larch Cl 7 N19 . . . . . . 4 B2
1 SE8 . . . . 51 B4
SW12 . . . . 73 A2
Larch Ct 11 W9 . . . . . 31 C4
Larch Ho 16 SE16 . . . . 40 B4
Larch Rd NW2 . . . . . . 9 B4
Larches Ave SW14 . . . . 55 C3
Larchfield Ho 2 N5 . . . 15 B3
Larchmore Ct N19 . . . . . 5 A2
Larden Rd W3 . . . . . . 38 A4
Larissa St SE17 . . . . . 151 C3
Lark Hall Inf Sch
SW4 . . . . 171 C1
SW4 . . . . 172 A1
Lark Row E2 . . . . 25 B4
Larkfield Rd TW9 . . . . . 54 A3
Larkhall La SW4 . . . . . 172 A3
Larkhall Rise SW4 . . . . 171 B1
Larmenier RC Inf Sch
W6 . . . . 39 C2
Larnaca Ho SE1 . . . . . 138 C2
Larnach Rd W6 . . . . . . 47 C4
Larpent Ave SW15 . . . . 57 B2
Lasborough Ct 6
SE15 . . . . 49 A3
Lascelles Ho NW1 . . . . 90 B1
Lassell St SE10 . . . . . 42 C1
Lasseter Pl SE3 . . . . . 53 B4

Latchmere Rd
SW11 . . . . 168 C1
Latchmere St
SW11 . . . . 168 C2
Latham Ho E1 . . . . . . 32 C3
Latimer SE17 . . . . 152 A1
Latimer Ho W11 . . . . . 113 A4
11 E9 . . . . 17 C2
Latimer Pl W10 . . . . . 30 B3
W4 . . . . 46 A4
Latimer Rd W10 . . . . . 30 B3
W6 . . . . 30 C2
Latimer Road Sta
W10 . . . . 30 C2
Latona Rd SE15 . . . . . 49 C4
Latymer Ct W6 . . . . . . 39 C2
Latymer Upper Sch
W6 . . . . 38 C1
Laud St SE11 . . . . 148 C2
Lauderdale Mans
W9 . . . . 88 B3
Lauderdale Rd W9 . . . . 88 C3
Lauderdale Twr
EC2 . . . . 108 C4
Laughton Ho 11
SW2 . . . . 62 C1
Launcelot St SE1 . . . . 135 B3
Launceston Pl W8 . . . 128 C1
Launch St E14 . . . . . . 42 B3
Laundress La N16 . . . . . 7 C1
Laundry Rd W6 . . . . . . 154 A3
Laura Pl E5 . . . . 17 B4
Laurel Bank Gdns
SW6 . . . . 165 A2
Laurel Cl 8 N19 . . . . . 4 B2
Laurel Ct 11 . . . . 16 B2
2 SW15 . . . . 57 C2
Laurel Ho 5 . . . . 11 A2
9 SE8 . . . . 51 B4
Laurel Rd SW13 . . . . . 46 C1
Laurel St E8 . . . . 16 B2
Laurence Mews 12
W12 . . . . 38 C4
Laurence Pountney Hill
EC4 . . . . 123 B4
Laurence Pountney La
EC4 . . . . 123 C4
Laurie Gr SE14 . . . . . . 51 A2
Laurie Ho SE1 . . . . . . 136 B1
Laurier House
W8 . . . . 31 C1 113 B1
Laurier Rd NW5 . . . . . . 4 A1
Lauriston Ho 9 . . . . . . 19 C1
9 E9 . . . . 25 C4
Lauriston Lo NW6 . . . . 10 C2
Lauriston Rd E9 . . . . . 17 C1
Lausanne Rd SE15 . . . . 50 B2
Lavell St N16 . . . . 15 C4
Lavender Cl SW3 . . . . . 157 C3
Lavender Ct SW4 . . . . 172 B3
Lavender Gdns
SW11 . . . . 60 B3
Lavender Gr E8 . . . . . . 16 C1
Lavender Hill 14
SW11 . . . . 60 C4
SE16 . . . . 32 C1
Lavender Rd SE16 . . . . 33 A1
SW11 . . . . 59 C4
Lavender Sweep
SW11 . . . . 60 B3
Lavender Terr 12
SW11 . . . . 60 A4
Lavender Wlk SW11 . . . 60 B3

Lavendon Ho NW8 . . . . . **90** B2
Lavengro Rd SE27 . . . **75** B2
Lavenham Rd SW18 . . .70 C3
Lavers Ct N16 . . . . .7 A1
W4 . . . .
Laverstoke Gdns
SW15 . . . . .68 C4
Laverton Mews
SW5 . . . . **142** B3
Laverton Pl SW5 . . . . **142** B3
Lavina Gr N1 . . . . .84 C4
Lavington St SE1 . . . **122** B1
Law St SE1 . . . .**137** C2
Lawdale Jun Sch
E2 . . . . .24 C2 **99** C4
Lawford Rd NW5 . . . . .13 B2
N1 . . . . .16 A1
W4 . . . . .45 B3
Lawless Ho **5** E14 . . .34 B2
Lawless St **11** E14 . . .34 A2
Lawley St E5 . . . . .17 B4
Lawman Ct **2** TW9 . . .44 B2
Lawn Cres TW9 . . . . .44 C1
Lawn House Cl E14 . . .42 B4
Lawn La SW8 . . . . . .**162** C4
Lawn Rd NW3 . . . . . . .12 B3
Lawnfield NW6 . . . . . . .9 C1
Lawns The N16 . . . . . .16 A3
Lawrence Cl **3** E3 . . . .26 C3
6 W12 . . . . .30 A2
Lawrence Ct N16 . . . . . .7 A1
4 W3 . . . . .37 B3
Lawrence Ho **11** SW1 . **147** C3
Lawrence La EC2 . . . .**109** A2
Lawrence Mans
SW3 . . . .**158** A3
Lawrence Pl N1 . . . . . .84 B4
Lawrence St SW3 . . .**158** A3
E16 . . . . .35 B2
Lawrence Trad Est
SE10 . . . . .43 A2
Lawrence's Bldgs **1**
N16 . . . . .7 B1
Lawson Cl SW19 . . . . .69 C1
Lawson Ct **1** N4 . . . . . .5 B3
Lawson Ho **17** W12 . . .30 A2
Lawton Rd E3 . . . . . . .26 A2
Laxfield Ct E8 . . . . . . .24 C4
Laxley Cl SE5 . . . . . . .48 A3
Laxton Path **1** SE4 . . .65 C3
Laxton **71** NW1 . . . . . .92 B2
Layard Rd SE16 . . . . . .40 A2
Layard Sq SE16 . . . . . .40 A2
Laycock Prim Sch
N1 . . . . .15 A2
Laycock St N1 . . . . . .14 C2
Layfield Ho **1** SE10 . . .43 C1
Laystall Ct EC1 . . . . . .95 B1
Laystall St EC1 . . . . . .95 B1
Layton Ho **5** E9 . . . . .25 B4
Layton Pl TW9 . . . . . . .44 C2
Layton Rd N1 . . . . .85 C2
Lazar Wlk **2** N7 . . . . . .5 B2
Le Moal Ho **22** E1 . . . .32 B4
Lea Ct **3** W12 . . . . . . .38 A4
Lea Ho NW8 . . . . .90 A1
Lea Int E9 . . . . .18 C3
Leabank Sq E9 . . . . . .18 C2
Leabourne Rd N16 . . . . .7 C4
Leacroft Ave SW12 . . .72 B4
Leadenhall Mkt
EC3 . . . .**110** A1
Leadenhall Pl EC3 . . .**110** A1
Leadenhall St EC3 . . .**110** A1

Leadenham Ct **11**
E3 . . . . .26 C1
Leake St SE1 . . . .**135** A4
Leamington Ct W3 . . .28 C4
4 SE26 . . . . .76 C1
Leamington Ho **3**
W11 . . . . .31 B4
Leamington Pk W3 . . .28 C4
Leamington Rd Villas
W11 . . . . .31 B4
Leamore St W6 . . . . . .39 B2
Leamouth Rd E14 . . . .34 C3
Leander Ct **27** E9 . . . . .17 B1
SE8 . . . . .51 C2
Leander Rd SW2 . . . . .62 C1
Leary Ho SE11 . . . . . .**149** A1
Leather La EC1 . . . . .**107** C4
Leatherdale St **29**
E1 . . . .**138** A3
Leatherhead Cl N16 . . .7 B3
Leathermarket Ct
SE1 . . . .**138** A3
Leathermarket St
SE1 . . . .**138** A3
Leathwaite Rd
SW11 . . . . .60 B2
Lebanon Gdns
SW18 . . . . .58 C1
Lebanon Rd SW18 . . .58 C2
Lebus Ho NW8 . . . . . .**80** A1
Lechmere Rd NW2 . . . .9 A2
Leckford Rd SW18 . . .71 B3
Leckhampton Pl **22**
SW2 . . . . .74 C4
Lecky St SW7 . . . . . .**143** B2
Leconfield Ave
SW13,SW15 . . . . .56 B4
Leconfield Ho SE5 . . .64 A4
Leconfield Rd N5 . . . .15 C4
Leda Ct SW9 . . . .**163** B1
Ledam Ho EC1 . . . . . .**107** B4
Ledbury Ho **22** SE22 . . .64 A4
Ledbury Mews N
W11 . . . .**113** C3
Ledbury Mews W
W11 . . . .**113** B4
Ledbury Rd W11 . . . . . .31 C3
Ledbury Road W11 . . .**113** B4
Ledbury St SE15 . . . . .49 C3
Ledo Ho **1** N16 . . . . . .15 C4
Ledbury Ho **13** SE22 . . .64 A4
Lee Conservancy Rd
E9 . . . . .18 B3
Lee High Rd SE13 . . . .67 C3
Lee Ho **5** N19 . . . . . . .13 C3
Lee Rd SE3 . . . . .53 B1
Lee St E8 . . . . .24 B4
Lee Valley Sp Ctr
E15 . . . . .19 C4
Leeke St WC1 . . . . . . .94 C4
Leeland Way NW10 . . .8 B4
Leerdam Dr E14 . . . . .42 B3
Lees Ct W1 . . . .**117** B4
Lees Ho SE17 . . . . . .**151** C1
Lees Pl W1 . . . .**117** B4
Leeson Rd **12** SE24 . . .62 C3
Lees Pl W1 . . . .**117** B4
Leeve Ho **7** W9 . . . . . .23 B2
Leeward Ct **1** E1 . . . .**125** C2
Leeway SE8 . . . . .41 B1
Lefevre Wlk E3 . . . . . .26 C4
Leff Ho **2** NW6 . . . . . .10 A1
Leffern Rd W12 . . . . . .38 C4
Lefroy Ho SE1 . . . . . .**136** C3
Lefroy Rd W12 . . . . . .38 B4
Legard Rd N5 . . . . .6 A1

Leggatt Rd E15 . . . . . .27 B3
Legge St SE13 . . . . . . .67 B2
Leghorn Rd NW10 . . . .21 C3
Legion Ct N1 . . . . .14 C1
Legion Cl **7** SE15 . . .**119** C4
Leicester Ho
4 SW9 . . . . .63 A4
2 SW15 . . . . .69 B4
Leicester Pl WC2 . . . .**119** C4
Leicester Sq WC2 . . .**119** C3
Leicester Square Sta
WC2 . . . .**119** C4
Leicester St WC2 . . . .**119** C4
Leigh Gdns NW10 . . . .22 B3
Leigh Ho **9** SW15 . . . .56 C2
Leigh Orchard Cl
SW16 . . . . .74 B1
Leigh Pl EC1 . . . .**107** B4
Leigh Rd N5 . . . . .15 A4
Leigh St WC1 . . . . .94 A3
Leigham Ave SW16 . . .74 A1
Leigham Hall **3**
SW16 . . . . .74 A1
Leigham Hall Par **2**
SW16 . . . . .74 A1
Leigham Vale SE27,
SW16,SW2 . . . . .74 C2
Leighfield Ho **5** N4 . . . .6 B4
Leighton Cres NW5 . . .13 B3
Leighton Gdns
NW10 . . . . .22 B3
Leighton Gr NW5 . . . .13 B3
Leighton House (Art
Gall & Mus) W14 . . .**127** A2
Leighton Pl NW5 . . . . .13 B3
Leighton Rd NW5 . . . .13 B3
Leinster Ave SW14 . . .55 B3
Leinster Ct NW6 . . . . .23 C2
Leinster Gdns W2 . . .**100** C1
W2 . . . .**114** C4
Leinster Mews W2 . . .**114** C4
Leinster Pl W2 . . . . . .**100** C1
Leinster Sq W2 . . . . .**100** A1
Leinster Terr W2 . . . .**114** C4
Leitch Ho **8** NW8 . . . .11 C1
Leith Ho **7** N7 . . . . . . .13 C3
13 SW2 . . . . .74 B4
Leith Mans W9 . . . . . .**88** A3
Leith Yd **3** NW6 . . . . .23 C4
Leithcote Path
SW16 . . . . .74 B1
Lelitia Cl E8 . . . . .24 C4
Leman St E1 . . . .**111** A1
Lemmon Rd SE10 . . . .53 A4
Lemsford Ct N4 . . . . . .6 B2
Len Freeman Pl
SW6 . . . .**154** C3
Len Williams Ct
NW6 . . . . .23 C3
Lena Cres N9 . . . .
Lena Gdns Prim Sch
W6 . . . . .39 B3
Lena Gdns W6 . . . . . .39 B3
Lendal Terr **7** SW4 . . .61 C4
Lenham **7** NW5 . . . . .12 C2
Lenham Ho SE1 . . . . .**137** C3
Lennon Rd NW2 . . . . . .9 B2
Lennox Gdns SW1 . . .**130** C1
NW10 . . . . .8 B4
Lennox Gdns Mews
SW1 . . . .**144** C4
Lennox Ho **10** E9 . . . .17 B2
Lennox Rd N4,N7 . . . . .5 C2
Lenthall Ho SW1 . . . .**147** A1
Lenthall Rd E8 . . . . . .16 C1
Lenthorp Rd SE10 . . . .43 B2

Lenton Rise TW9 . . . . .54 A4
Leo St SE15 . . . . .50 A3
Leo Yd EC1 . . . . .96 B1
Leonard Ct WC1 . . . . .94 A2
W8 . . . .**127** B2
Leonard Day Ho
NW5 . . . . .13 A2
Leonard Ct SE1 . . . . .16 A4
Leonard St EC2 . . . . .**97** C2
Leonora Ho W9 . . . . . .88 C2
Leontine Cl SE15 . . . . .49 C3
Leopards Ct EC1 . . . .**107** B4
Leopold Bldgs **2** **98** C4
Leopold Mews E9 . . . .25 B4
Leopold Prim Sch
NW10 . . . . .8 B1
Leopold Rd NW10 . . . . .8 A1
Leopold Wlk SE11 . . .**148** C1
Leppoc Rd SW4 . . . . . .61 C2
Leroy St SE1 . . . .**152** A4
Lerwick Ho SW18 . . . .59 B3
Leslie Rd E11 . . . . . . .19 C4
Lessar Ave SW4 . . . . .61 B1
Lessar Ct SW4 . . . . . .61 B1
Lessing St SE23 . . . . .66 A1
Lester Ct **5** E3 . . . . . .27 A2
Leswin Pl N16 . . . . .7 B1
Leswin Rd N16 . . . . . . .7 B1
Letchford Gdns
NW10 . . . . .21 C2
Letchford Mews
NW10 . . . . .21 C2
Letchmore Ho W10 . . .22 B1
Lethbridge Cl SE13 . . .52 B1
Lett Rd E15 . . . . .19 C1
Letterstone Rd
SW6 . . . .**154** C1
Lettice St SW6 . . . . . .**165** A3
Lettsom St SE5 . . . . . .49 A1
Letterstone Rd SW9 . . .70 A3
Levant Ho **8** E1 . . . . . .25 C1
Leven Rd E14 . . . . . . .34 C3
Lever Ct **15** E9 . . . . . .17 C2
Lever St EC1 . . . . .96 C3
Leverett St SW3 . . . .**144** B4
Leverington Pl N1 . . .**97** C3
SW9 . . . .
NW5 . . . .**144** B2
Leverton Pl NW5 . . . . .13 B3
Leverton St NW5 . . . . .13 B3
Levison Way **2** N19 . . .4 C3
Levita Ho NW1 . . . . . .93 C4
Levyne Ct EC1 . . . . . . .95 B2
Lewes Ho SE1 . . . . . .**138** B4
SE15 . . . . .49 C4
Lewesdon Cl **13**
SW19 . . . . .69 C3
Leweston Pl N16 . . . . . .7 B4
Lewey Ho E3 . . . . .26 B1
Lewin Rd SW14 . . . . . .55 C4
Lewis Ct **5** SE16 . . . . .40 A1
Lewis Gr SE13 . . . . . . .67 B4
Lewis Pl E8 . . . . .16 C3
Lewis Silkin Ho **2**
SE15 . . . . .50 B4
Lewis St NW1 . . . . .13 A2
Lewisham Bridge Prim
Sch SE13 . . . . .67 A4
Lewisham Bsns Ctr
SE14 . . . . .50 C4
Lewisham Coll SE4 . . .51 C1
Lewisham Ctr SE13 . . .67 B4

Lewisham High St
SE13 . . . . .67 A2
Lewisham Hill SE13 . . .52 B1
Lewisham Hospl
SE13 . . . . .67 A2
Lewisham Pk SE13 . . .67 B1
Lewisham Rd SE13 . . .52 B1
Lewisham St SW1 . . .**133** C3
Lewisham Way SE4,
SE14 . . . . .51 B2
Lexden Rd W3 . . . . . . .28 A1
Lexfield Ho N5 . . . . . . .15 B4
Lexham Gardens Mews
W8 . . . .**128** B1
Lexham Gdns W8 . . .**142** A4
Lexham Mews W8 . . .**141** C4
Lexham Wlk W8 . . . . .**128** B2
Lexington St W1 . . . .**105** A1
W1 . . . .**119** A4
Lexton Gdns SW12 . . .73 C3
Ley Ho SE1 . . . .**136** C3
Leyborne Pk TW9 . . . .44 C2
Leybourne Ho
3 E14 . . . . .33 B3
17 SE15 . . . . .50 B4
Leybourne Rd **10**
NW1 . . . . .13 A1
Leybourne St **5**
NW1 . . . . .13 A1
Leyden Mans **3** N19 . .5 A4
Leyden St E1 . . . .**110** C3
Leydon Cl SE16 . . . . . .32 C1
Leyland Ho **5** E14 . . . .34 A2
Leylands SW18 . . . . . .58 B1
Leylang Rd SE14 . . . . .50 C3
Leys Ct **3** SW9 . . . . .**173** B1
Leysdown **9** NW5 . . . .12 C2
Leysdown Ho SE17 . .**152** B2
Leysfield Rd W12 . . . .38 C4
Lichfield Ho **2** SE17 . .48 C4
Lichfield Rd NW2 . . . .10 A4
E3 . . . . .26 A2
Richmond TW9 . . . . . .44 B2
Lichfield Terr **1**
TW9 . . . . .54 A2
Lichport Ct N4 . . . . . . .6 A3
Lickey Ho W14 . . . . . .**155** A4
Lidcote Gdns SW9 . . .**173** A1
Liddell Gdns NW10 . . .22 B3
Liddell Rd NW6 . . . . . .10 C2
Lidfield Rd N16 . . . . . .15 C4
Lidgate Rd **21** SE15 . . .49 B3
Lidiard Rd SW18 . . . . .71 B2
Lidlington Pl NW1 . . . .83 A1
Lidyard Rd N19 . . . . . . .4 B3
Liffey Ct NW10 . . . . . . .8 C1
Lifford St SW15 . . . . . .57 C3
Lighter Cl **11** SE16 . . .41 A2
Lighterman Mews **13**
E1 . . . . .32 C3

Lighterman's Rd
E14 . . . . .42 A4
Lightermans Wlk
SW18 . . . . .58 C3
Ligonier St E2 . . . . . . .98 C2
Lilac Ho SE4 . . . . .66 B4
Lilac Pl SE11 . . . . . . .148 C3
Lilac St W12 . . . . .29 C2
Lilburn Ct SW15 . . . . .57 C4
Lilestone Est NW8 . . . .89 C1
Lilestone Ho NW8 . . . .89 C2
Lilestone St NW8 . . . . .90 A2
Liford Rd 21 SE5 . . . . .48 B1
Liford Rd SE5 . . . . . . .48 A1
Lilian Baylis Ho N1 . . .15 B2
Lilian Baylis Sch
SE11 . . . . .149 A3
Lilian Baylis Sec Sch
SE11 . . . . .149 A3
Lilley Cl E1 . . . . .125 C1
Lillian Ave W3 . . . . . . .36 C4
Lillian Cl 14 N16 . . . . . .7 A1
Lillian Rd SW13 . . . . . .47 A4
Lillie Ho N5 . . . . .14 C3
Lillie Rd SW6 . . . . . . .154 C3
Lillie Yd SW6 . . . . . . .155 B4
Lillieshall Rd SW4 . . . .61 B4
Lillingston Ho N7 . . . . .14 C4
Lily Cl W14 . . . . .39 C2
Lily Pl EC1 . . . . .107 C4
Lilyville Rd SW6 . . . . .164 C3
Limberg Ho SE8 . . . . . .41 B2
Limborough Ho 5
E14 . . . . .33 C4
Limburg Rd SW11 . . . .60 A3
Lime Cl E1 . . . . .125 C2
Lime Ct SW15 . . . . . . .57 A4
Lime Gr W12 . . . . .39 B4
Lime St EC3 . . . . .110 A1
Lime St Pas EC3 . . . .124 A1
Limeburner La
EC4 . . . . .108 A2
Limeharbour E14 . . . . .42 A4
Limehouse Cswy
E14 . . . . .33 B2
Limehouse Cut 5
E14 . . . . .34 A4
Limehouse Fields Est
E14 . . . . .33 A4
Limehouse Link
(Tunnel) E14 . . . . . . .33 B2
Limehouse Sta 23 E14 .33 A3
Limerick Cl SW12 . . . .73 B4
Limerick Ct 4
SW12 . . . . .73 B4
Limerston St
SW10 . . . . .157 A3
Limes Ave NW11 . . . . . .1 A4
Limes Ave SW13 . . . . .46 B1
Limes Ct NW6 . . . . .9 C1
Limes Field Rd
SW14 . . . . .56 A4
Limes Gdns SW18 . . . .58 C1
Limes Gr SE13 . . . . . . .67 B3
Limes The W2 . . . . . .113 C3
SE5 . . . . .64 A4
Limes Wlk SE15 . . . . . .65 B3
Limesford Rd SE15 . . . .65 C3
Limetree Cl SW2 . . . . .74 B3
Limpsfield Ave
SW19 . . . . .69 C2
Limscott Ho 33 E3 . . . .27 A2
Linacre Ct W6 . . . . . . .39 C1
Linacre Rd NW2 . . . . . . .9 A2
Linale Ho N1 . . . . .87 B1
Linberry Wlk 8 SE8 . . .41 B2

Lincoln Ave SW19 . . . .69 C1
Lincoln Ct N16 . . . . .6 C4
Lincoln Ho SW1 . . . . .130 C3
SW3 . . . . .58 A2
Lincoln Mews NW6 . . .23 B4
Lincoln St SW3 . . . . .144 C3
Lincoln's Inn *
WC2 . . . . .107 A2
Lincoln's Inn Fields
WC2 . . . . .107 A2
Lind St SE8 . . . . .52 A1
Lindal Rd SE4 . . . . . . .66 B2
Lindale SW19 . . . . . . .70 A2
Linden Ave NW10 . . . .22 C3
Linden Ct 1 W12 . . . . .30 B1
8 SW18 . . . . .59 C3
Linden Gdns
W2 . . . . .31 C2 113 C3
W4 . . . . .37 C1
Linden Gr SE15 . . . . . .65 B4
Linden Ho 10 SE8 . . . . .51 B4
8 SE15 . . . . .65 A4
Linden Lodge Sch
SW19 . . . . .70 A3
Linden Mews N1 . . . . . .6 A3
Linden Mews W2 . . . .113 C3
N1 . . . . .15 C3
Lindens The W4 . . . . . .45 B2
Linfield Gdns NW3 . . . .11 B3
Linfield Hts NW3 . . . . .11 B3
Linfield St E14 . . . . . . .33 C3
Lindisfarne Mead
E9 . . . . .18 A4
Lindley Ho 12 SE15 . . .49 C3
Lindley Pl TW9 . . . . . . .44 C2
Lindley St E1 . . . . .32 B4
Lindo St SE15 . . . . .50 B1
Lindore Rd SW11 . . . . .60 B3
Lindrop St SW6 . . . . .166 C2
Lindsay Ct SW11 . . . .167 C3
Lindsay Sq SW1 . . . . .147 C2
Lindsell St 6 SE10 . . . .52 B2
Lindsey Ho SW10 . . . .157 C2
Lindsey Mews 18
N1 . . . . .15 B1
Lindsey St EC1 . . . . . .108 B4
Linfield WC1 . . . . .94 C2
Linford Ho 2 E2 . . . . . .24 C4
Linford St SW8 . . . . . .170 C3
Ling Rd E16 . . . . .35 C4
Ling's Coppice SE21 . . .75 C2
Lingard Ho 9 E14 . . . . .42 B3
Lingards Rd SE13 . . . . .67 B3
Lingfield Ho 6 SE1 . . .136 B3
8 W4 . . . . .37 B1
Lingham St SW9 . . . . .172 C1
Lingwell Rd SW17 . . . .72 A1
Lingwood Rd E5 . . . . . . .7 C4
Linhope St NW1 . . . . . .90 C1
Link St E9 . . . . .17 B2
Link The W3 . . . . .28 A3
Linkenholt Mans 3
W6 . . . . .38 B2
Links Yd E1 . . . . .111 A4
Linkway N4 . . . . .6 B4
Linkwood Wlk NW1 . . .13 C1
Linnell Ho NW8 . . . . . .78 C4
E1 . . . . .110 C4
Linnell Rd SE5 . . . . . . .49 A1
Linnet Mews SW12 . . .72 C4
Linom Rd SW4 . . . . . . .62 A3
Linscott Rd E5 . . . . . . .17 B4
Linsey St SE16 . . . . . .139 C1
SE16 . . . . .153 B4
Linslade Ho NW8 . . . . .90 B2

Linslade Ho continued
10 E2 . . . . .24 C4
Linstead St 11 NW6 . . .10 C1
Linstead Way SW18 . . . . . .
SW19 . . . . .70 A4
Lintaine Cl W6 . . . . . .154 B3
Linthorpe Rd N16 . . . . .7 A4
Linton Ho 2 E3 . . . . . . .33 C4
Linton St N1 . . . . .87 A3
Linver Rd SW6 . . . . . .166 A2
Linwood Cl SE5 . . . . . .49 B1
Lion Gate Gdns
TW9 . . . . .54 B4
Lion Gate Mews 3
SW18 . . . . .70 C3
Lion Yd SW4 . . . . .61 C3
Lionel Ho 5 W10 . . . . .31 A4
Lionel Mans 14
W14 . . . . .39 C3
Lionel Mews 14
W10 . . . . .31 A4
Lionel Rd E3 . . . . .26 B1
Lipton Rd 8 E1 . . . . . . .32 C3
Lisburne Rd NW3 . . . . .12 B4
Lisford St SE15 . . . . . . .49 B2
Lisgar Terr W14 . . . . .140 C4
Liskeard Gdns SE3 . . . .53 C2
Liskeard Ho SE11 . . . .149 C2
Lisle Ct NW2 . . . . .1 A1
Lisle St WC2 . . . . .119 C4
Lismore Wlk 4 N1 . . . .15 B2
Lissenden Gdns
NW5 . . . . .12 C4
Lissenden Mans
NW5 . . . . .12 C4
Lisson Cotts NW1 . . . .102 B4
Lisson Gr NW1,NW8 . . .90 A2
Lisson Ho NW1 . . . . . .102 A4
Lisson St NW1 . . . . . .102 A4
Lister Cl W3 . . . . .28 C4
Lister Ct N16 . . . . .7 A2
Lister Ho SE3 . . . . . . .53 A4
SW1 . . . . .146 A1
Lister Hospl SW1 . . . .146 A1
Lister Mews N7 . . . . . .14 B4
Liston Rd SW4 . . . . . . .61 B4
Listowel Cl SW9 . . . . .163 C2
Listria Pk N16 . . . . .7 B2
Listria Pl N16 . . . . .7 B2
Litcham Ho 9 E1 . . . . .25 C2
Litchfield Gdns
NW10 . . . . .8 C2
Litchfield St WC2 . . . .119 C4
Lithos Rd NW3 . . . . . .11 B2
Little Albany St
NW1 . . . . .92 B2
Little Argyll St W1 . . .104 C1
Little Boltons The
SW10 . . . . .142 B1
Little Britain EC1 . . . .108 C3
Little Chelsea Ho
SW10 . . . . .157 A3
Little Chester St
SW1 . . . . .132 A2
Little College St
SW1 . . . . .134 A2
Little Combe Cl 13
SW15 . . . . .68 C4
Little Dimocks
SW12 . . . . .73 A2
Little Dorrit Ct
SE1 . . . . .137 A4
Little Essex St
WC2 . . . . .121 B4
Little George St
SW1 . . . . .134 A3

Little Green St NW5 . .13 A4
Little Marlborough St
W1 . . . . .104 C1
Little New St EC4 . . . .107 C2
Little Newport St
WC2 . . . . .119 C4
Little Portland St
W1 . . . . .104 C2
Little Road Mans
SW6 . . . . .154 B3
Little Russell St
WC1 . . . . .106 A3
Little Sanctuary
SW1 . . . . .134 A3
Little Smith St
SW1 . . . . .133 C2
Little Somerset St
E1 . . . . .110 C1
Little St James's St
SW1 . . . . .118 C1
Little St Leonards
SW14 . . . . .55 B4
Little Titchfield St
W1 . . . . .104 C3
Little Trinity La
EC4 . . . . .123 A4
Little Venice* W9 . . . .100 C4
Littlebury Rd SW4 . . . .61 C4
Littlecote Cl SW19 . . . .70 A4
Littlefield Cl N19 . . . . .13 B4
Littleton St SW18 . . . . .71 B2
Littlewood SE13 . . . . . .67 B1
Livermere Ct 8 E8 . . . .24 B4
Livermere Rd E8 . . . . .24 B4
Liverpool Gr SE17 . . . .151 B1
Liverpool Ho N7 . . . . . .14 C2
Liverpool Rd N1 . . . . . .85 C3
N1,N7 . . . . .14 C1
E16 . . . . .35 A4
Liverpool St EC2 . . . . .110 A3
Liverpool Street Sta
EC2 . . . . .110 A3
Livesey Mus SE15 . . . .50 A4
Livesey Pl SE15 . . . . . .49 C4
Livingstone Ho 16
SE5 . . . . .48 B3
Livingstone Lo 9
W9 . . . . .31 C4
Livingstone Pl E14 . . . .42 B1
Livingstone Rd E15 . . .27 B4
14 SW11 . . . . .59 C4
Livonia St W1 . . . . . . .105 A1
Lizard St EC1 . . . . .97 A3
Llandovery Ho 1
E14 . . . . .42 B4
Llanelly Rd NW2 . . . . . .1 B2
Llanvanor Rd NW2 . . . .1 B2
Llewellyn St SE16 . . .139 C3
Lloyd Baker St WC1 . . .95 B3
Lloyd Ct 14
SE27 . . . . .75 A1
Lloyd Ho N16 . . . . .6 C1
Lloyd Sq WC1 . . . . . . .95 B4
Lloyd St WC1 . . . . .95 B4
Lloyd Villas SE4 . . . . . .51 C1
Lloyd's Ave EC3 . . . . .110 B1
Lloyd's Bldg*
EC3 . . . . .110 A1
Lloyd's PI SE3 . . . . . . .53 A1
Lloyd's Row EC1 . . . . . .96 A3
Loampit Hill SE13 . . . . .52 A1
Loampit Vale SE13 . . . .67 B4
Loanda Cl 18 E8 . . . . .24 B4
Loats Rd SW2 . . . . .62 A1
Locarno Rd 6 W3 . . . . .28 B1

Lochaline St W6 . . . . . .47 B4
Lochbie 8 N4 . . . . .5 A4
Lochinvar St SW12 . . . .73 A4
Lochmore Ho SW1 . . .145 C3
Lochnagar St E14 . . . . .34 B4
Lock Ho N16 . . . . .7 B3
Lock View Ct 9
E14 . . . . .33 A2
Lockbridge Ct 3
W9 . . . . .31 C4
Locke Ho SW8 . . . . . .170 C4
Lockesfield Pl E14 . . . .42 A1
Lockgate Cl E9 . . . . . . .18 B3
Lockhart Cl N7 . . . . . . .14 B2
Lockhart St 3 . . . . . . .26 B1
Lockhurst St E5 . . . . . .17 C4
Lockington Rd
SW8 . . . . .170 B4
Lockmead Rd SE13 . . . .67 B4
Locksley St E14 . . . . . .33 B4
Lockwood Ho
SE11 . . . . .163 B3
Lockwood Sq SE16 . . . .40 A3
Lockyer Est SE1 . . . . .137 C3
Lockyer Ho SW8 . . . .162 A2
7 SE10 . . . . .43 B1
SW15 . . . . .57 C4
Lockyer St SE1 . . . . . .137 C3
Locton Gn 4 E3 . . . . . .26 B4
Loddiges Ho 5 E9 . . . .17 B1
Loddiges Rd E9 . . . . . .17 B1
Loddon Ho NW8 . . . . . .89 C1
Loder St SE15 . . . . .50 B3
Lodge Rd NW8 . . . . . . .90 A3
Lodore St E14 . . . . .34 B3
Lodsworth Ho
SW11 . . . . .169 B3
Loftie St SE16 . . . . . . .139 C3
Lofting Rd N1 . . . . .14 C1
Loftus Rd W12 . . . . . . .30 A1
Loftus Rd (Queens Park
Rangers FC) W12 . . .30 A1
Logan Mews W8 . . . . .141 B4
Logan Pl W8 . . . . .141 B4
Loggetts SE21 . . . . . . .76 A2
Lohmann Ho 1 SE11 . .163 B4
Lolesworth Cl E1 . . . .111 A3
Lollard St SE11 . . . . . .149 B3
Loman St SE1 . . . . . . .136 B4
Lomas St E1 . . . . .111 C4
Lombard Ct EC3 . . . . .123 C4
Lombard Ho 4
SE10 . . . . .52 B3
Lombard La EC4 . . . . .107 C1
Lombard Rd SW11 . . .167 B2
Lombard St EC3 . . . . .109 C1
Lombardy Pl W2 . . . . .114 B3
Lomley Ho 10 SW2 . . . .62 C1
Lomond Gr SE5 . . . . . .48 C3
Lomond Ho 10 SW8 . . .48 C2
Loncroft Rd SE5 . . . . . .49 A4
Londale Ct SE10 . . . . . .52 B2
Londesborough Ho 9
N16 . . . . .16 A4
Londesborough Rd
N16 . . . . .16 A4
London Acad The
SW4 . . . . .61 B4
London Aquarium*
SE1 . . . . .134 C3
London Arena E14 . . . .42 A3
London Bridge
EC4,SE1 . . . . .123 C3

London Bridge City Pier
SE1 .... 124 A2
London Bridge Hospl
SE1 .... 123 C2
London Bridge St
SE1 .... 123 C2
London Bridge Sta
SE1 .... 123 C2
London Business Sch
NW1 .... 90 C2
London Canal Mus★
N1 .... 84 B2
London Central
Mosque★ NW8 ... 90 B3
London Chest Hospl
E2 .... 25 B3
London Clinic NW1 .. 91 C1
London Coll of Fashion
EC2 .... 24 A1 98 B2
London Coll of Fashion
The W1 .... 103 C1
London Coll of Printing
SE1 .... 136 B1
London Coll of Tech
SE1 .... 137 C3
London Docklands
Visitor Ctr E14 ... 42 B4
London Dungeon The★
SE1 .... 123 C2
London Eye (Millennium
Wheel)★ SE1 ... 134 C4
London Fields East Side
E8 .... 17 A1
London Fields JMI Sch
E8 .... 25 A4
London Fields Sta
E8 .... 17 A1
London Fields West Side
E8 .... 16 C1
London Foot Hospl
W1 .... 92 C1
London Gas Mus The
E3,E16 .... 27 C1
London Guildhall Univ
EC2 .... 109 C3
E1 .... 110 C1
E1 .... 111 A2
E14 .... 33 C3
London Guildhall Univ
(Coll of Tech & Design)
E1 .... 111 B2
London Ho NW8 .... 80 B2
London Hospital Dental
Inst E1 .... 32 A4
London Hospital
Medical Coll E1 .. 32 A4
London Hospl (Mile
End) The E2 ...... 25 B2
London Hospl (St
Clements) The E3 . 26 B2
London Independent
Hospl The E1 .... 32 C4
London Inst The
EC1 .... 95 C1
EC1 .... 96 A1
W1 .... 104 A1
EC1 .... 108 A4
London La E8 ...... 17 A1
London Mews W2 .. 101 C2
London Nautical Sch
The SE1 .... 121 C2
London Oratory Sch The
SW6 .... 155 C3

London Peace Pagoda★
SW3 .... 159 A2
London Rd SE1 ... 136 B2
London Sch of
Economics and
Political Science
WC2 .... 107 A1
London St W2 .... 101 B1
EC3 .... 124 B4
London Stile 8 W4 . 36 C1
London Toy & Model
Mus w W2 .... 114 C4
London Transport Mus★
WC2 .... 120 B4
London Wall EC2 .. 109 A3
London Wharf 4
E2 .... 25 A4
London Zoo★ NW1 . 81 B2
Long Acre WC2 .... 106 B1
Long Dr W3 .... 29 A3
Long La EC1 ...... 108 B4
SE1 .... 137 C3
Long Meadow 20
N7 .... 13 C3
Long Pond Rd SE3 . 53 A2
Long Rd SW4 ...... 61 B3
Long St E2 .... 98 C4
Long Wlk SE1 ..... 138 B2
Long Yd WC1 ...... 94 C1
Long's Ct W1 ..... 119 C3
Longbeach Rd
SW11 .... 60 B4
Longberrys NW2 ... 1 B1
Longbow Ho 21 N1 . 24 A4
Longbridge Way
SE1 .... 153 A3
Longcliffe Ho SE1 . 59 A2
Longfellow Way
SE1 .... 153 A3
Longfield St SW18 . 70 C4
Longford Ct E5 .... 17 C4
  1 W12 .... 38 A4
Longford Ho 8 E1 . 32 B3
Longford St NW1 .. 92 B2
Longford Wlk 9
SW2 .... 74 C4
Longhedge St
SW11 .... 169 C2
Longhope Cl SE15 . 49 B4
Longhurst Ho 8
W9 .... 23 B2
Longland Ct SE1 .. 153 B2
Longleat Ho SW1 .. 147 B2
Longleigh Ho 8
SE5 .... 49 A2
Longlents Ho 3
NW10 .... 20 C4
Longley Ho 5 N19 . 13 B4
Longley St SE1 ... 153 B4
Longman Ho 10 E8 . 24 B4
  8 E2 .... 25 C3
Longmoor Point 14
SW15 .... 69 A3
Longmore St SW1 .. 146 C3
Longnor Rd E1 .... 25 C2
Longridge Ho SE1 . 137 A1
Longridge Rd SW5 . 141 C2
Longs Ct 3 TW9 . 54 B3
Longshore SE8 .... 41 B2
Longstaff Cres
SW18 .... 70 C4

Longstaff Rd SW18 . 58 C1
Longstone Ave
NW10 .... 21 B4
Longthorne Ho 20
E3 .... 26 B2
Longton Ave SE26 . 76 C1
Longville Rd SE11 . 150 B4
Longwood Dr SW15 . 56 C1
Lonsdale Ho 6 N4 . 6 B4
SW6 .... 58 C4
Lonsdale Mews
W11 .... 31 B3
  4 Richmond TW9 . 44 C2
Lonsdale Pl N1 ... 14 C1
Lonsdale Rd NW6 . 23 B4
W11 .... 31 B3
W4 .... 38 B2
SW13 .... 46 B3
Lonsdale Sq. N1 .. 85 C4
Lonsdell Ho 9 SW2 . 62 C1
Lopez Ho 9 SW9 . 62 A4
Loraine Rd N7 .... 14 B4
W4 .... 45 A4
Lord David Pitt Ho 8
SE24 .... 62 C3
Lord Hills Rd W2 .. 100 B4
Lord Holland La
SW9 .... 173 C2
Lord Napier Pl 6 w . 38 C1
Lord North St SW1 . 134 A1
Lord Roberts Mews
SW6 .... 156 A1
Lord's (MCC &
Middlesex County
Cricket Ground)★
NW8 .... 89 C3
Lord's Cricket Mus★
NW8 .... 89 C3
Lord's View NW8 .. 89 C3
Lords Cl SE21 ..... 75 B2
Lordship Gr N16 .. 6 C2
Lordship Ho 3 N16 . 6 C2
Lordship La SE22 . 64 B1
Lordship Park Mews
N16 .... 6 B2
Lordship Pk N16 .. 6 C2
Lordship Pl SW3 .. 158 A3
Lordship Rd N16 .. 6 C2
Lordship Terr N16 . 6 C2
Loreburn Ho 2 N7 . 14 B4
Lorenzo St N1,WC1 . 94 C4
Loris Rd W6 ...... 39 B3
Lorn Ct SW9 ...... 173 B2
Lorn Rd SW9 ..... 173 B2
Lorne Cl NW8 ..... 90 B3
Lorne Ct SW15 ... 57 C1
Lorne Gdns W11 .. 126 A4
  1 W11 .... 39 C4
Lorne Ho 7 E1 ... 33 A4
  4 Richmond TW10 . 54 B2
Lorraine Ct 11 NW1 . 13 A1
Lorrimore Rd SE17 . 48 A4
Lorrimore Sq SE17 . 48 A4
Lorton Ho 9 NW6 . 23 C4
Lostock Ho SW8 .. 171 B2
Lothair Rd S N4 .. 6 A4
Lothbury EC2 ..... 109 B2
Lothian Rd SW9 .. 48 A2
Lothrop St W10 ... 23 A2
Lots Rd SW10 .... 157 A1
Loudoun Rd NW8 . 79 A3
Lough Rd N7 ..... 14 B2

Loughborough Ct 7
SW9 .... 63 A4
Loughborough Jun & Inf
Schs SW9 .... 48 A1
Loughborough Junction
Sta SW9 .... 63 A4
Loughborough Pk
SW9 .... 63 A3
Loughborough Rd
SE5,SW9 .... 48 A1
Loughborough St
SE11 .... 149 A1
Louisa Gdns E1 ... 25 C1
Louisa Ho SW15 .. 56 B3
Louisa St E1 ..... 25 C1
Louise Bennett Cl 9
SE24 .... 63 A3
Louise De Marillac Ho
 10 E1 .... 32 B4
Louise White Ho 11
N19 .... 4 C3
Louisville Rd SW17 . 72 C1
Louvaine Rd SW11 . 59 C3
Lovat La EC3 ..... 124 A3
Lovatt Ct SW12 ... 73 A3
Lovatt La EC3 .... 109 A2
Love Wlk SE5 ..... 48 C1
Loveday Ho 2 SW2 . 74 C3
Lovegrove St SE1 . 49 C4
Lovegrove Wlk E14 . 34 B1
Lovelace Ho 19 E8 . 24 B4
Lovelace Rd SE21 . 75 B3
Lovelinch Cl SE15 . 50 B4
Lovell Ho E8 ..... 24 C4
Lovell Pl SE16 .... 41 A3
Lover's Wlk w1 ... 117 B1
Loveridge Mews
NW6 .... 10 B2
Loveridge Rd NW6 . 10 B2
Lovette Ho 3 E3 . 26 C2
Low Cross Wood La
SE21 .... 76 B1
Lowden Rd SE24 .. 63 B3
Lowder Ho 6 E1 . 32 A1
Lowe Ave E16 .... 35 C4
Lowell Ho 10 SE5 . 48 B3
Lowell St E14 .... 33 A3
Lower Addison Gdns
W14 .... 126 A3
Lower Belgrave St
SW1 .... 132 A1
Lower Clapton Rd
E5 .... 17 B4
Lower Comm S
SW15 .... 57 A4
Lower Grosvenor Pl
SW1 .... 132 B2
Lower Grove Rd
TW10 .... 54 B2
Lower James St
W1 .... 119 A4
Lower John St w1 . 119 A4
Lower Lea Crossing
E14,E16 .... 35 A1
Lower Mall W6 .... 39 A1
Lower Marsh SE1 . 135 B3
Lower Merton Rise
NW3 .... 12 A1
Lower Mortlake Rd
TW9 .... 54 B4
Lower Pace Bsns Ctr
NW10 .... 20 B3
Lower Rd SE1 .... 135 B4
SE16 .... 40 B4

Lower Richmond Rd
TW4,TW9 .... 55 A4
SW15 .... 57 B4
Lower Robert St
WC2 .... 120 B3
Lower Sloane St
SW1 .... 145 B2
Lower Terr NW3 ... 2 B1
Lower Thames St
EC3 .... 124 A3
Lowerwood Ct W11 . 31 A3
Loweswater Ho E3 . 26 B2
Lowfield Rd NW6 . 10 C1
W3 .... 28 B3
Lowlands SW6 .... 166 A2
NW3 .... 12 A2
Lowman Rd N7 ... 14 B4
Lowndes Cl SW1 . 131 C1
Lowndes Ct SW1 . 131 A2
Lowndes Pl SW1 . 131 B1
Lowndes Sq SW1 . 131 A3
Lowndes St SW1 . 131 B2
Lowood Ho 11 E1 . 32 B2
Lowood St E1 .... 32 A2
Lowry Ct 8 SE16 . 40 A1
Lowth Rd SE5 .... 48 B1
Lowther Ho SW1 . 147 A1
  11 E8 .... 24 B4
Lowther Jun & Inf Sch
SW13 .... 46 C4
Lowther Rd N7 ... 14 C3
SW13 .... 46 B2
Loxford Ho SW1 .. 145 C3
Loxham St WC1 ... 94 B3
Loxley Rd SW18 .. 71 C3
Lubbock Ho 16 E14 . 34 A2
Lubbock St SE14 . 50 B3
Lucan Ho N1 ..... 87 C3
Lucan Pl SW3 .... 144 B3
Lucas Ct SW11 ... 169 C3
Lucas Ho SW10 .. 156 C2
  4 SW8 .... 171 A2
Lucas St SE4,SE8 . 51 C2
Lucas Vale Prim Sch
SE8 .... 51 C2
Lucerne Mews W8 . 113 C2
Lucerne Rd N5 ... 15 A4
Lucey Rd SE16 ... 139 B1
Lucey Way SE16 . 153 C4
Lucien Rd SW18 .. 71 A2
Lucraft Ho 6 SW2 . 74 A4
Lucy Ashe Ho SE17 . 150 B3
Lucy Brown Ho
SE1 .... 123 A1
Ludgate Broadway
EC4 .... 108 B1
Ludgate Cir EC4 .. 108 A1
Ludgate Hill EC4 . 108 B1
Ludgate Sq EC4 .. 108 B1
Ludham NW5 ..... 12 B3
Ludlow Ct W3 .... 37 B4
Ludlow St EC1 .... 96 C2
Ludovick Wlk SW15 . 56 B3
Ludwick Mews
SE14 .... 51 A3
Lugard Ho W12 ... 30 A1
Lugard Rd SE15 .. 50 A2
Luke Ho 31 E1 .. 32 A3
Luke St EC2 .. 24 A1 98 A2
Lukin St E1 ...... 32 B3
Lullingstone Ho 20
SE15 .... 50 B4
Lullingstone La
SE13 .... 67 C1
Lulot Gdns N19 ... 4 A2
Lulworth SE17 ... 151 B2
NW1 .... 13 C1

Lulworth Ho SW8 .162 C1
Lulworth Rd SE15 ....50 A1
Lumley Ct WC2 ....120 B3
Lumley Flats SW1 .145 B2
Lumley St W1 ......103 C1
Lumsden NW8 ....78 B3
Lunan Ho E12 ....26 B3
Lund Point E15 ......27 B4
Lupin Cl SW2 ....75 A2
Lupin Point SE1 ...139 A3
Lupton St NW5 ......13 B4
Lupus St SW1 ......147 A1
Luralda Gdns E14 ...42 C1
Lurgan Ave W6 .....47 C4
Lurline Gdns
  SW11 ....169 C4
Luscombe Ho SW18 .58 B2
Luscombe Way
  SW8 ....162 A2
Lusher Ho SW15 ....57 C1
Lushington Rd
  NW10 ....22 A3
Lushington Terr ⑪
  E8 ....16 C3
Luton Pl SE10 ....52 B3
Luton St NW8 ....89 C1
Luttrell Ave SW15 ..57 A2
Lutyens Ho SW1 ...146 C1
Luxborough Ho
  W1 ....103 B4
Luxborough St W1 .103 B4
Luxborough Twr
  W1 ....103 B4
Luxemburg Gdns
  W6 ....39 C2
Luxford St SE16 .....40 C2
Luxmore St SE4 .....51 B2
Luxor St SE5 ....63 B4
Lyal Rd E3 ....26 A3
Lyall Ave SE21 ......76 A1
Lyall Mews SW1 ...131 B1
Lyall Mews W SW1 .131 B1
Lyall St SW1 ....131 B1
Lycee Francais Charles
  de Gaulle (French Univ
  Coll) SW7 ....143 C4
Lycett Ho ⑩ SW2 ..74 A4
Lycett Pl ⑧ W12 ....38 C4
Lydden Gr SW18 ....71 A4
Lydden Rd SW18 ....71 A4
Lydford NW1 ....83 A3
Lydford Cl 22 N16 ..16 A3
Lydford Rd NW2 .....9 C2
  W9 ....23 B1
Lydgate Ho 8 N16 ..16 A3
Lydhurst Ave SW2 ..74 B2
Lydney Cl SE15 .....49 A3
  SW19 ....70 A2
Lydon Rd SW4 .....61 B4
Lydwell Ho SW8 ...171 B1
Lyford Rd SW18 ....72 A3
Lygoe Ho 8 N6 ......4 C4
Lygon Ho E2 ....99 B4
Lygon Pl SW1 ......132 A1
Lyham Cl SW2 ......62 A1
Lyham Rd SW2 .....62 A1
Lyly Ho SE1 ....137 C1
Lyme Gr E9 ....17 B1
Lyme Grove Ho ②
  E9 ....17 B1
Lyme St NW1 ....82 C4
Lyminge Gdns
  SW17,SW18 ......72 A3
Lymington Lo E14 ..42 C3

Lymington Mans
  NW6 ....11 A2
Lymington Rd NW6 .11 A2
Lympstone Gdns
  SE15 ....49 C3
Lynbrook Cl SE15 ...49 A3
Lynch Cl SE3 ....53 B1
Lynch Wlk ② SE8 ..51 B4
Lyncott Cres SW4 ..61 A3
Lyncourt SE3 ....52 C1
Lyncroft Gdns NW6 ..1 C1
Lyncroft Mans 4
  NW6 ....10 C3
Lyndale NW2 ....1 B1
Lyndale Ave NW2 ....1 B1
Lyndale Cl SE3 .....53 B4
Lynde Ho ② SW4 ...61 C4
Lynden Gate SW15 .69 A3
Lyndhurst Gdns
  NW3 ....11 C3
Lyndhurst Gr SE5,
  SE15 ....49 B1
Lyndhurst Ho ②
  SW15 ....68 C4
Lyndhurst Lo ⑧
  SE5 ....48 C1
Lyndhurst Lo ⑧
  E14 ....42 C2
Lyndhurst Rd NW3 .11 C3
Lyndhurst Sq SE15 .49 B2
Lyndhurst Terr
  NW3 ....11 C3
Lyndhurst Way SE15 49 B1
Lyneham Wlk E5 ....18 A3
Lynette Ave SW4 ...61 B1
Lynford French Ho
  SE17 ....150 C2
Lynmouth Rd N16 ...7 B3
Lynn Ho SE15 ....49 C4
Lynn Rd SW12 ......73 A4
Lynne Ct NW6 ....11 A1
Lynne Way NW10 ....8 A2
Lynnett Ct E9 ......18 A2
Lynton Cl NW10 ....10 B3
Lynton Est ⑧ W3 ..28 B3
Lynton Est SE1 ....153 B3
Lynton Ho W2 .....100 B1
Lynton Lo N5 ....15 A3
Lynton Mans SE1 ..135 B2
Lynton Rd SE1 .....153 A3
  NW6 ....23 B3
  W3 ....28 A2
Lynton Terr 4 W3 ..28 B3
Lynwood Rd SW17 ..72 B1
Lyon Ho NW8 ....90 A1
Lyon St N1 ....14 B1
Lyons Pl NW8 ....89 B1
Lyons Wlk W14 ....140 A4
Lyric Rd SW13 ......46 B2
Lysander Gr N19 .....4 C3
Lysander Ho ⑩ E2 .25 A3
Lysia Ct SW6 ....47 C3
Lysias Rd SW12 ....61 A1
Lytcott Gr SE22 ....64 B2
Lytham St SE17 ....151 B1
Lytten Ct 6 W12 ...38 C4
Lyttelton Cl NW3 ...12 A1
Lyttleton Ho ⑩ E9 .17 B1
Lytton Ct WC1 .....106 B3
Lytton Gr SW15 .....58 A1

M

Mabel Thornton Ho ⑫
  N16 ....15 C4
Mableton Pl NW1,
  WC1 ....93 C3
Mablethorpe Rd
  SW6 ....154 A1
Mabley St E9 ....18 A3
Mac's Pl EC4 ......107 C2
MacArthur Ho 4
  SW2 ....74 A4
Macaulay CE Prim Sch
  SW4 ....61 A3
Macaulay Ct SW4 ..61 A4
Macaulay Ho ⑩ N16 .7 A1
  2 W10 ....31 A4
Macaulay Sq SW4 ..61 A3
Macbeth Ho 4 N1 ..24 A3
Macbeth St W6 .....39 A1
Macclesfield Ho
  EC1 ....96 C4
Macclesfield St
  W1 ....119 C4
Macdonald Ho ⑦
  SW11 ....169 B2
Macdonald Rd N19 ..4 B2
Macduff Rd SW11 .169 C4
Mace Cl E1 ....32 A1
Mace St E2 ....25 C3
Macey Ho SW11 ...168 A3
  2 SE10 ....52 B4
Macfarlane Rd W12 .30 B1
Macfarren Ho ⑨
  W10 ....23 A2
MacFarren Pl NW1 ..91 C1
MacGregor Ho ②
  SW12 ....73 C3
Machell Rd SE15 ....65 B4
Mackay Ho ⑩ W12 .30 A2
Mackay Rd SW4 ....61 A4
Mackennal St NW8 .80 B2
Mackenzie Cl ⑦
  W12 ....30 A2
Mackenzie Rd N7 ...14 B2
Mackenzie Wlk E14 .33 C1
Mackeson Rd NW3 .12 B4
Mackie Ho ⑤ SW2 .74 C4
Mackie Rd SW2 ....74 C4
Mackintosh La E9 ..17 C3
Macklin St WC2 ...106 B2
Mackonochie Ho
  EC1 ....107 B4
Mackrow Wlk E1 ...34 B2
  E14 ....34 B2
Macks Rd SE16 ....153 C4
Mackworth Ho NW1 .92 C4
Mackworth St NW1 .92 C4
Maclean Rd SE23 ..66 A1
Macleod St SE17 ..151 A1
Maclise Rd W14 ...126 A1
Macmillan Ho NW4 ..9 A4
Macnamara Ho
  SW10 ....157 B2
Maconochies Rd
  E14 ....42 A1
Macquarie Way E14 42 A2
Macready Ho W1 ..102 B3
Macready Pl ⑧ N7 ..14 A4
Macroom Ho W9 ...23 B2
Macroom Rd W9 ...23 B2
Madame Tussaud's &
  Planetarium *
  NW1 ....91 B1
Maddams St E3 ....27 A1

Maddock Way SE17 .48 A4
Maddocks Ho ⑧ E1 .32 A2
Maddox St W1 .....104 C1
  W1 ....118 C4
Madinah Rd E8 .....16 C3
Madison Cl ⑯ E8 ...27 A2
  E8 ....27 B2
Madras Pl N7 ....14 C2
Madrid Rd SW13 ...46 C3
Madron St SE17 ...152 B2
Mafeking Ave TW8 .44 A4
Magdala Ave N19 ...4 B2
Magdalen Pas E1 ..125 A4
Magdalen Rd SW18 .71 C3
Magdalen St SE1 ..124 A1
Magdalene Cl ⑦
  SE15 ....50 A1
Magdalene Ho ⑩
  SW15 ....57 C1
Magee St SE11 ....163 B4
Magellan Ho ⑯ E1 .25 C1
Magellan Pl ⑩ E14 41 C2
Magnin Cl ⑧ E8 ...24 C4
Magnolia Ct
  TW9 ....45 A2
  SW11 ....60 B1
Magnolia Ho ⑱ SE8 51 B4
Magnolia Pl SW4 ...62 A2
Magnolia Rd W4 ....45 A4
Magnolia Wharf
  W4 ....45 A4
Magpie Alley EC4 .107 C1
Magpie Cl ⑥ E7 ...24 B1
Maguire St SE1 ...139 A4
Mahatma Ganhi Ind Est
  ⑪ SE24 ....63 A3
Mahogany Cl SE16 .33 A1
Mahoney Ho SE14 .51 B2
Maida Ave W2 ....89 A1
Maida Vale W9 .....88 C3
Maida Vale Psychiatric
  Hospl W9 ....23 C2
Maida Vale Sta W9 .88 B4
Maiden La WC2 ...120 B4
  SE1 ....123 A2
  NW1 ....13 C1
Maidenstone Hill
  SE10 ....52 B2
Maidstone Bldgs
  SE1 ....123 B1
Maidstone Ho 4
  E14 ....34 A3
Mail Coach Yd E2 ..98 B4
Maismore St SE15 .49 C4
Maitland Cl ⑫ SE10 52 A3
Maitland Ct W2 ...115 B4
Maitland Ho SW1 .160 C4
  ⑰ E2 ....25 B3
Maitland Park Rd
  NW3 ....12 B2
Maitland Park Villas
  NW3 ....12 B2
Maitland Pl E5 .....17 A4
Majestic Ct N4 ......6 A3
Major Rd SE16 ....139 C2
  E15 ....19 C3
Makepeace Ave N6 ..3 C2
Makepeace Mans N6 3 C2
Makins St SW3 ....144 B3
Malabar Ct 22 W12 30 A2
Malabar St E14 .....41 C4
Malacca Ho E1 .....33 A4
Malam Ct SE11 ....149 B3
Malam Gdns 3 E14 34 A2
Malay Ho 2 E1 .....32 B1
Malbrook Rd SW15 .57 A3

Lul – Mal 227

Malcolm Ho ⑱ N1 ..24 A3
Malcolm Pl E2 .....25 B1
Malcolm Rd E1 .....25 B1
Malcolmson Ho
  SW1 ....147 C1
Malden Cres NW1 ..12 C2
Malden Pl NW5 ....12 C3
Malden Rd NW5 ....12 C2
Maldon Cl N1 ....87 A4
  E15 ....19 C3
  SE5 ....64 A4
Maldon Rd W3 .....28 B2
Malet Pl WC1 ....93 B1
Malet St WC1 .....105 C4
Maley Ave SE27 ....75 A2
Malfort Rd SE5 .....64 A4
Mall Studios 9
  NW3 ....12 B3
Mall The SW1 ......119 B1
  SW14 ....55 B2
Mallams Mews 8
  SW9 ....63 A4
Mallard Cl E9 ......18 B2
  NW6 ....23 C4
Mallard Ho NW8 ....80 A1
  7 SE15 ....49 B2
Mallard Point 5 E3 26 C2
Mallet Ho ⑪ SW15 56 C2
Mallet Rd SE13 .....67 C1
Malling SE13 ....67 A2
Mallinson Rd SW11 60 B2
Mallon Gdns E1 ...111 A3
Mallord St SW3 ...157 C4
Mallory Cl SE4 .....66 A3
Mallory Cl SE4 .....66 A3
Mallory Ho E14 ....34 B4
Mallory St NW8 ....90 B2
Mallow St EC1 ......97 B2
Malmesbury 31 E2 25 B3
Malmesbury Inf Sch
  E2 ....26 B2
Malmesbury Rd E3 26 B3
  E16 ....35 A4
Malmesbury Terr
  E16 ....35 B4
Malmsey Ho SE11 .149 A2
Malmsmead Ho E9 .18 A3
Malorees Jun & Inf Schs
  NW6 ....9 C1
Malpas Rd E8 ......17 A2
  SE4 ....51 B1
Malt Mill SE1 .....124 C1
Malt St SE1 ....49 C4
Malta St EC1 ....96 B2
Maltby St SE1 ....138 C2
Malthouse Dr W4 ..46 B4
Malthouse Pas
  SW13 ....46 A1
Malting Ho E14 ....33 B2
Maltings W9 ....31 C4
Maltings Cl SW13 ..46 A1
Maltings Lo W4 ....46 A3
Maltings Pl SW6 ..166 B3
  SE1 ....138 C2
Malton Mews 1
  W10 ....31 A3
Malton Rd W10 ....31 A3
Maltravers St WC2 121 B4
Malva Cl SW18 .....59 A2
Malvern Cl W10 ....31 B4
Malvern Ct SW7 ...143 C4
Malvern Gdns NW2 ..1 A2
Malvern Ho N16 ....7 B3

Malvern Mews NW6 23 C2
Malvern Pl NW6 ......23 B2
Malvern Rd N19 ......4 C3
E8 ....16 C1
NW6 ....23 C2
Malvern Terr N1 ......85 B4
Malwood Rd SE12 ...61 A1
Malyons Rd SE13 ...67 A2
Malyons Terr SE13 ...67 A2
Managers St E14 ...34 B1
Manaton Cl SE15 ...65 A4
Manbre Rd W6 ......47 B4
Manchester Dr W10 23 A1
Manchester Gr E14 42 B1
Manchester Ho
SE17 ....151 A2
Manchester Mans
N19 ....4 C4
Manchester Mews
W1 ....103 B3
Manchester Rd E14 42 B3
Manchester Sq
W1 ....103 C2
Manchester St W1 103 B3
Manchuria Rd
SW11 ....60 C1
Manciple St SE1 ...137 C2
Mandalay Ho 6
N16 ....15 C4
Mandalay Rd SW4 ...61 B2
Mandarin Ct 6 SE8 .51 C4
Mandela Cl 38 W12 .30 A2
Mandela Ho 98 C4
Mandela Rd E16 ...35 C3
Mandela St NW1 ...83 A4
SW9 ....163 B1
Mandela Way SE1 .152 B4
Mandeville Ho
SE1 ....153 A2
Mandeville Cl 5
SE3 ....53 B3
Mandeville Ctyd
SW11 ....169 B3
Mandeville Ho 8
SW4 ....61 B2
Mandeville Pl W1 .103 C2
Mandrake Rd SW17 72 B1
Mandrell Rd SW2 ...62 A2
Manette St W1 ...105 C1
Manfred Ct 6
SW15 ....58 B2
Manfred Rd SW15 ...58 B2
Manger Rd N7 ......14 A2
Manilla St E14 ......41 C4
Manitoba Ct 22
SE16 ....40 B4
Manley Ct N16 ......7 B1
Manley Ho SE11 ...149 B2
Manley St NW1 ......81 B4
Mannebury Prior
N1 ....85 A1
Manneby Ho 17 .25 B4
Mannering Ho 16
SW2 ....62 B2
Manning Ho 3
W11 ....31 A3
Manning Pl TW10 ...54 B1
Manningford Cl EC1 96 A4
Manningtree Cl
SW19 ....70 A3
Manningtree St E1 111 B2

Manny Shinwell Ho
SW6 ....155 A3
Manor Ave SE4 ......51 B1
Manor Circus TW9 .54 C4
Manor Ct SW6 ....166 B3
W3 ....36 C2
SE15 ....49 B2
7 SW2 ....62 B2
SW16 ....74 A1
Manor Gdns SW4 .171 A1
N7 ....5 A1
W3 ....36 C2
8 W4 ....38 A1
Richmond TW10,TW9 54 B3
Manor Gr SE15 ......50 B4
Richmond TW9 ......54 C4
Manor Gt SW15 ...58 A2
Manor House NW1 102 B4
Manor House Ct
W9 ....88 C1
Manor House Dr
NW6 ....9 C1
Manor Mans N7 ......5 A1
NW3 ....12 A2
Manor Mews NW6 .23 C3
SE4 ....51 B1
Manor Oak Mans
SE22 ....65 A1
Manor Par N16 ......7 B2
Manor Park Rd
NW10 ....21 B4
Manor Pk
Richmond TW9 ......54 B3
SE13 ....67 C2
Manor Pl SE17 ...150 C2
Richmond TW10,TW9 54 B3
Manor Rd N16 ......7 A3
Richmond TW10,TW9 54 B4
SW20 ....10 A1
W9 ....22 B4
Manor Street Est
SW3 ....158 B4
Manor The W1 ...118 A3
Manor Way W3 ......36 C2
Manorfield Cl 3
N19 ....13 B3
Manorfield JMI Sch
E14 ....34 A4
Manresa Rd SW3 .144 A1
Manse Rd N16 ......7 B1
Mansel Ct SW11 ...168 B3
Mansel St E1 ......111 A1
Mansell Ho SW8 .171 A4
Mansell Rd W3 ......37 B4
Mansfield Ct 37 E2 .24 B4
Mansfield Ho SW15 57 C1
Mansfield Mews
W1 ....104 A3
Mansfield Pl 11
NW3 ....11 B4
Mansfield Rd NW3 .12 B4
SW19 ....20 A1
Mansfield St W1 ...104 A3
Manson Ct 2 ......24 C3
Mansion Cl SW9 .173 C4
Mansion Gdns NW3 .2 A1
Mansion House *
EC4 ....109 B1
Mansion House Pl
EC3,EC4 ....109 B1
Mansion House St
EC2 ....109 B1
Mansion House Sta
EC4 ....123 A4
Mansions The NW6 .10 B3
Manson Mews
SW7 ....143 B3

Manson Pl SW7 ...143 B3
Manston NW1 ......13 B1
Manstone Rd NW2 .10 A3
Mantell Ho SW4 ...61 B2
Mantle Rd SE4 ......66 A4
Manton Ho N16 ......6 C1
Mantua St 28 SW11 .59 C4
Mantus Cl E1 ......25 B1
Mantus Rd E1 ......25 B1
Manville Gdns
SW17 ....73 A1
Manville Rd SW17 .73 A2
Manwood Rd SE4 ...66 B1
Many Gates SW12 .73 A2
Mape St E2 ......25 A1
Mapes Ho 5 NW6 .10 A1
Mapesbury Ct NW2 10 A3
Mapesbury Rd NW2 10 A2
Mapeshill Pl NW2 ...9 B2
Maple Ave W3 ......29 A1
Maple Ct NW2 ......9 C4
Maple Ho 11 NW3 .12 B2
6 SE8 ....51 B3
Maple Leaf Sq 7
SE16 ....40 C4
Maple Lo SW15 ...58 A1
Maple Mews NW6 .78 A2
Maple Pl W1 ......93 A1
Maple St W1 ......93 A1
Maple Wlk W10 ...22 C1
Maplebank E18 ...66 C1
Mapledene Rd E8 .16 C1
Maples Pl 21 E1 ...32 A4
Maplestead Rd SW2 74 B4
Mapleton Cres
SW18 ....59 A1
Mapleton Rd SW18 59 A1
Maplin St E3 ......26 B2
Marada Ho NW6 ...10 A1
Marais W6 ....45 B3
Maran Way NW10 .8 B2
Marban Rd W9 ......23 B2
Marble Arch W1 .103 A1
W1 ....117 A4
Marble Arch Sta
W1 ....103 A1
Marble Cl W3 ......28 A1
Marble Ho W9 ......23 B1
Marbleford Ct 4 N6 4 C4
March Ct SW15 ......57 A3
Marchant Ct SE1 .153 A2
Marchant Ho 19
SW2 ....62 B2
Marchbank Rd
W14 ....155 A4
Marchmont Rd
TW10 ....54 B2
Marchmont St WC1 .94 A2
Marchwood Cl 17
SE5 ....49 A3
Marcia Rd SE1 ...152 B3
Marcilly Rd SW18 .59 C2
Marco Rd W6 ......39 B3
Marcon Ct 23 E8 ...17 A3
Marcon Pl E8 ......17 A3
Marcus Ct TW8 ...44 A3
Marcus Garvey Mews
SE22 ....65 A2
Marcus Garvey Way 5
SE24 ....62 C3
Marcus Ho 13 SE15 .49 B2
Marcus St SW18 ...59 A1
Marcus Terr SW18 .59 A1
Marden Ho 6 E8 ...17 A3
Marden Sq SE16 ...40 A3
Mardyke Ho SE17 .151 C4

Mare St E8 ......17 A2
E8,E2 ....25 A4
Maresfield Gdns
NW3 ....11 B2
Margaret Bondfield Ho
22 N7 ....13 C3
4 E3 ....26 A3
Margaret Ct W1 ...104 C2
Margaret Herbison Ho
SW6 ....155 A3
Margaret Ho 16 W6 39 B1
Margaret Ingram Cl
SW6 ....154 C3
Margaret Mcmillan Ho
11 N19 ....4 C4
Margaret Rd N16 ...7 B3
Margaret St W1 ...104 C2
Margaret's Ct
SE1 ....123 B1
Margaretta Terr
SW3 ....158 B4
Margate Rd SW2 ...62 A2
Margery Fry Ct N7 ...5 A1
Margery St WC1 ...95 B3
Margravine Gdns
W14 ....140 A2
W6 ....39 C1
Margravine Rd
W6 ....154 A4
Marham Gdns SW17,
SW18 ....72 A3
Maria Cl SE1 ......153 C4
Maria Fidelis Convent
Sch
NW1 ....93 A3
NW1 ....93 B4
Maria Terr E1 ......25 C1
Marian Ct E9 ......17 B3
Marian Pl E2 ......25 A3
Marian Sq E2 ......25 A3
Marian St 2 E2 ...25 A3
Marian Way NW10 .8 B1
Maribor 13 SE10 ...52 B3
Marie Curie SE5 ...49 A2
Marie Lloyd Ct 13
SW9 ....173 B4
Marie Lloyd Gdns 11
N19 ....5 A4
Marie Lloyd Ho N1 .87 B1
Marigold St SE16 ...40 A4
Marina Ct 8 E3 ...26 C2
Marine St SE16 ...139 B2
Marine Twr 22 SE8 .51 B4
Marinefield Rd
SW6 ....166 B2
Mariners Mews E14 42 C2
Marion Richardson JMI
Sch E1 ....32 C3
Marischal Rd SE13 .67 C4
Maritime Ho 5
SW4 ....61 B4
Maritime St E3 ......26 B1
Marius Mans 3
SW17 ....72 C2
Marius Rd SW17 ...72 C2
Marjorie Gr SW11 .60 B3
Mark Ho 3 E2 ......25 C3
Mark La EC3 ......124 B4
Mark Mans W12 ...38 C4
Mark Sq EC2 ......98 A2
Mark St EC2 ......98 A2
Market Ct W1 ......104 C2
Market Mews W1 .118 A1
Market Pl W1 ......104 C2
3 W3 ....28 B1

Market Pl continued
1 SE16 ....40 A2
Market Rd N7 ......14 A2
Mortlake TW9 ......54 C4
Market Sq E14 ......34 A3
Market Way E14 ...34 A3
Markham Pl SW3 .144 C2
Markham Sq SW3 .144 C2
Markham St SW3 .144 B2
Markland Ho W10 .30 C2
Marksbury Ave TW9 54 C4
Markstone Ho 7 .136 A3
Markyate Ho W10 .22 B1
Marl Rd SW18 ......59 B3
Marland Ho NW1 .131 A2
Marlborough W9 ...88 C4
3 SW19 ....69 C3
Marlborough Ave 8
E8 ....24 C4
Marlborough Cl
SE17 ....150 B3
Marlborough Cres
W4 ....38 A3
Marlborough Ct
W8 ....141 B4
Marlborough Day Hospl
..........78 C2
Marlborough Flats
SW3 ....144 B4
Marlborough Gr
SE1 ....153 B1
Marlborough Hill
NW8 ....79 A3
Marlborough Ho
NW8 ....78 C1
N4 ....6 B3
Richmond TW10 ...54 C2
SW19 ....69 C1
Marlborough Hospl
SW1 ....119 A1
Marlborough Mans 5
NW6 ....10 C3
Marlborough Pl
NW8 ....79 A2
Marlborough Prim Sch
SW3 ....144 B3
Marlborough Rd
SW1 ....119 A1
N19 ....5 A2
W4 ....37 B1
Richmond TW10 ...54 B1
Marlborough St
SW3 ....144 B3
Marlborough Trad Est
TW9 ....45 A2
Marlborough Yd N19 4 C2
Marlbury NW8 ......78 B3
Marley Ho 14 W11 .30 C2
Marley Wlk NW2 ...9 B3
Marlin Ho SW15 ...58 A2
Marloes Rd W8 ...128 A1
Marlow Ct NW6 ......9 C1
Marlow Ho E2 ......24 C2 2
SE1 ....138 C2
2 W2 ....100 B1
Marlow Studio
Workshops 2 ......98 C3
Marlow Way SE16 .40 C4
Marlowe Bsns Ctr 3
SE14 ....51 A3
Marlowe Ct SW3 .144 B3
Marlowe Ho 15 N16 .16 A4
Marlowes The NW8 .79 B4
Marlston NW1 ......92 B3
Marlton St SE10 ...43 B1

Marmion Ho 13	
SW12	73 A4
Marmion Mews 4	
SW11	60 C4
Marmion Rd SW11	60 C3
Marmont Rd SE15	49 C3
Marmora Rd E1	33 A4
Marmora St SE22	65 B1
Marne St W10	23 A2
Marner Prim Sch	
E3	27 A1
Marney Rd SW11	60 C3
Marnfield Cres SW2	74 B3
Marnham Ave NW2	10 A4
Marnock Ho SE17	151 B2
Marnock Rd SE4	66 B2
Maroon Ho 11 E14	33 A4
Maroon St E14	33 A4
Marquess Rd N1	15 C2
Marquess Rd N N1	15 C2
Marquess Rd S 17	
N1	15 B2
Marquis Ct N4	5 B3
Marquis Rd N4	5 C3
NW1	13 C2
Marrick Cl SW15	56 C3
Marrick Ho NW6	78 B3
Marriott Rd N4	5 B3
Marryat Ct 12 W6	39 A2
Marryat Ho SW1	146 C1
Marryat St SW11	146 C1
Marsala Rd SE13	67 A3
Marsalis Ho 2 E3	26 C2
Marsden Rd SE15	64 B4
Marsden St NW5	12 C2
Marsh Ct E8	16 C2
Marsh Hill E9	18 A3
Marsh Rd SW1	147 C1
Marsh St E14	42 A2
Marsh Wall E14	42 A4
Marshall Cl SW18	59 B1
Marshall Ct SW4	172 B3
Marshall Ho N1	87 C2
N16	23 B3
Marshall St W1	105 A1
Marshall's Pl	
SE16	139 A3
Marshalsea Rd	
SE1	137 A4
Marsham Ct SW1	147 C4
19 SW19	69 C3
Marsham St SW1	147 C4
Marshfield St E14	42 B3
Marshgate Bsns Ctr	
E15	27 B3
Marshgate La E15	19 A1
Marshwood Ho 10	
NW6	23 C4
Marsland Cl SE17	150 B1
Marsom Ho N1	87 B1
Marston Cl NW6	11 B1
Marston Ho SW9	173 C1
Marsworth Ho 8	
E2	24 C4
Martaban Rd N16	7 B2
Martel Pl E8	16 B2
Martell Rd SE21	75 C1
Martello St E8	17 A1
Martello Terr E8	17 A1
Martha St E1	32 B3
Martin Ct 10 E14	42 B4
Martin Ho SW1	137 A1
SW8	162 A2

Martin La EC4	123 C4
Martindale SW14	55 B2
Martindale Ave 2	
E16	35 C2
Martindale Ho 20	
E14	34 A2
Martindale Rd	
SW12	73 A4
Martineau Ho SW1	146 C1
Martineau Mews	
N5	15 A4
Martineau Rd N5	15 A4
Martlett Ct WC2	106 B1
Martlett Lo NW3	11 A4
Martley Ho SW8	171 A4
Martock Ct 16 SE15	50 B1
Marton Rd 8 N16	7 A1
Marvel Ho 8 SE5	48 C3
Marville Rd SW6	59 C1
Marville Rd SW6	59 C1
Marwell Ct 16 SE3	52 C1
Marwood Cl 5	
SE3	53 C3
Mary Adelaide Cl	
SW15	68 A1
Mary Ann Bldgs	
SE8	51 C4
Mary Datchelor Cl	
SE5	48 C2
Mary Dine Ct SW8	163 A1
Mary Gn NW8	78 B4
Mary Ho SW9	172 C1
8 W6	39 B1
Mary James Ho 20	
E2	24 C3
Mary Jones Ho 19	
E14	33 B2
Mary Lawrenson Pl 1	
SE3	53 C3
Mary Macarthur Ho	
E2	25 C2
W14	154 A4
Mary McArthur Ho 12	
N19	4 C4
Mary Pl	
W11	31 A2 112 A4
Mary Secole Cl 21	
E8	24 B4
Mary St N1	87 A3
E16	35 B2
Mary Terr NW1	82 C3
Mary Wharrie Ho 4	
NW3	12 B1
Maryland Rd N4	19 C3
Maryland Rd N19	4 C3
W9	23 C1
Maryland Wlk N1	86 C4
Marylands Rd W9	88 A1
Marylebone Flyover	
NW1,W1	102 A3
Marylebone High St	
W1	103 C4
Marylebone La	
W1	103 C2
Marylebone Mews	
W1	104 A3
Marylebone Pas	
W1	105 A2
Marylebone Rd	
NW1	103 A4
Marylebone Sta	
NW1	90 C1
Marylee Way SE11	149 A3
Maryon Mews NW3	12 A4
Masbro' Rd W14	126 A2
Mascotte Rd 2	
SW15	57 C3

Masefield Ct N5	15 C3
Masefield Ho 1	
NW6	23 C2
Mashie Rd W3	29 A3
Maskall Cl SW2	74 C3
Maskell Rd SW17	71 B1
Maskelyne Cl	
SW11	168 B4
Mason Bradbear Ct 3	
N1	15 C2
Mason Ho SE1	153 C2
E16	35 C2
16 Mason St SE17	17 B1
Mason St SE17	151 C4
Mason's Arms Mews	
W1	104 B1
Mason's Ave EC2	109 B2
Mason's Pl EC1	96 C4
Mason's Yd SW1	119 A2
Massie Rd E8	16 C2
Massinger St SE1,	
SE17	152 A3
Massingham St E1	25 C1
Mast Ct 17 SE16	41 A2
Mast House Terr	
E14	41 C2
Master's St 14 E1	32 C4
Masterman Ho 5	
SE5	48 C3
Masters Dr SE16	40 A1
Masters Lo 12 E1	32 B3
Mastin Ho SW18	70 C3
Mastmaker Rd E14	41 C4
Matching Ct 13 E3	26 C2
Matham Gr SE22	64 B3
Matheson Lang Ho	
SE1	135 B3
Matheson Rd W14	140 C3
Mathieson Ct SE1	136 B3
Matilda Ho 1 E1	125 B2
Matilda St N1	85 A4
Matlock Cl SE24	63 B3
Matlock Ct SE5	63 C3
16 SE24	63 B3
Matlock St E14	33 A3
Maton Ho SW6	154 C2
Matson Ho 19 SE16	40 A3
9 E9	17 C2
Matthew Cl W10	22 C1
Matthew Parker St	
SW1	133 C3
Matthews Ct N5	15 B4
Matthews Ho 5	
E14	33 C4
Matthews St SW11	168 C2
Matthias Ho 2 N16	16 A3
Matthias Rd N16	16 A3
Mattingly Way 4	
SE15	49 B3
Maud St E16	35 B2
Maude Ho 8 E2	24 C3
Maude Rd SE5	49 A2
Maudlins Gn E1	125 B2
Maudslay Hospl The	
SE5	48 C1
Maugham Ct 10 W3	28 C3
Mauleverer Rd SW2	62 A2
Maundeby Wlk NW10	8 A2
Maunsel St SW1	147 B4

Mauretania Bldg 11	
E1	32 C2
Maurice Ho SW9	172 C4
Maurice St W12	30 A3
Mauritius Rd SE10	43 A2
Maury Rd N16	7 C1
Maverton Rd E3	26 C4
Mavor Ho N1	85 A3
Mawbey Ho SE1	153 A1
Mawbey Pl SE1	153 A1
Mawbey Rd SE1	153 A1
Mawbey St SW8	162 A1
Mawdley Ho SE1	135 C3
Mawson Ho EC1	107 B4
Mawson La W4	46 B4
Maxden Ct SE15	64 C4
Maxted Rd SE15	64 B4
Maxwell Ct SE21	76 C3
Maxwell Rd SW6	156 B1
May St W14	140 C1
	141 A1
May Tree Ho SE4	66 B4
May's Buildings Mews	
SE10	52 C3
Mayall Rd SE24	63 A2
Maybury Ct W1	103 C3
Maybury Gdns NW10	9 A2
Maybury Mews N6	4 B4
Maydew Ho SE16	40 B2
Maydwell Ho 6	
E14	33 C4
Mayfair Pl W1	118 B2
Mayfield Ave W4	38 A2
Mayfield Cl 15 E8	16 B1
SW4	61 C2
Mayfield Ho 16 N16	7 A4
30 E2	25 A3
Mayfield Mans	
SW15	58 B2
Mayfield Rd 6 E8	16 B1
W3	28 A2
W12	38 A4
Mayflower Cl SE16	40 C2
Mayflower JMI Sch	
E14	34 A4
Mayflower Rd SW9	62 A4
Mayflower St 8	
SE16	40 B4
Mayford NW1	83 A2
Mayford Cl SW12	72 B4
Mayford Rd SW12	72 B4
Maygood Ho N1	85 B2
Maygood St N1	85 B2
Maygrove Rd NW6	10 B2
Mayhew Ct 5 SE5	63 C3
Maylands Ho SW3	144 B3
Maynard Cl SW6	156 B1
Maynard Ho E1	26 A2
Maynards Quay E1	32 B2
Mayo Rd NW10	8 A2
Mayola Rd E5	17 B4
Mays Ct WC2	120 A3
Maysoule Rd SW11	59 C3
Mayston Mews 3	
SE10	43 C1
Maythorne Cotts	
SE13	67 C1
Mayton St N7	5 B1
Maytree Wlk SW2	74 C2
Mayward Ho 7 SE5	49 A2
Maze Hill SE10,SE3	53 A4
Maze Hill Ho 8	
SE10	52 C4
Maze Hill Sch SE10	53 A4

Maze Hill Specl Sch	
SE10	52 B3
Maze Hill Sta SE10	53 A4
Mazenod Ave NW6	10 C1
McAuley Cl SE1	135 B2
McBride Ho 8 E3	26 B3
McCall Cl SW4	172 A2
McCall Ho N7	14 A4
McCarthy Ct SW11	168 B3
McCoid Way SE1	136 C3
McConnell Ho	
SW8	171 B3
McCormick Ho 9	
SW2	74 C3
McCrone Mews 3	
NW3	11 C2
McCullum Rd E3	26 B4
McDermott Cl	
SW11	60 A4
McDermott Rd SE15	64 C4
McDougall Ct TW9	44 C1
McDougall Ho E2	25 B2
McDowall Cl E16	35 B2
McDowall Rd SE5	48 B2
McEwan Way E15	27 C4
McGlashon Ho 12	
E1	99 B1
McGregor Ct N1	98 B4
McGregor Rd W11	31 B4
McIndoe Ct N1	87 B4
McIntosh Ho 9	
SE16	40 B2
McIntyre Ct SW4	172 B3
McKay Trad Est	
W10	23 A1
McKenna Ho 8 E3	26 B3
McKerrell Rd SE15	49 C2
McKiernan Ct	
SW11	168 A2
McKinnon Wood Ho	
E2	99 B3
Mcleod Ct SE21	76 C3
McLeod's Mews	
SW7	142 B4
McManus Ho 5	
SW11	59 C4
McMillan Ho SE4	66 A4
McMillan St SE8	51 C4
Mcmorran Ho N7	14 A4
Mcneil Rd SE5	49 A1
McNicol Dr NW10	20 B3
Mead Cl 3 NW1	12 C1
Mead Ho W11	112 C3
Mead Lo W4	37 C4
Mead Pl E9	17 B2
Mead Row SE1	135 B2
Meadcroft Rd SE17	48 A4
Meade Cl W4	44 C4
Meadow Bank 7	
SE13	52 C3
Meadow Ct E9	18 B3
Meadow Mews	
SW8	162 C3
Meadow Pl SW8	162 B2
Meadow Rd SW8	162 C2
Meadow Row SE1	136 C1
Meadowbank NW3	12 B1
Meadowcroft Cl	
SW6	47 B3
Meadowcroft 9	
W4	36 C1

Meadowgate Sch
SE4 ....66 A4
Meadway The SE3 ....52 C1
Meakin Est E1 ....138 A2
Meakin Ho N7 ....14 B3
Meard St W1 ....105 B1
Meath Ho SE24 ....63 A1
Meath St SW11 ....170 A4
Mecklenburgh Pl
WC1 ....94 C2
Mecklenburgh Sq
WC1 ....94 C2
Medburn St NW1 ...83 B2
Medcroft Gdns
SW14 ....55 B3
Medfield St SW15 ....69 A4
Medhurst Cl 17 E3 ...26 A3
Median Rd E5 ....17 B3
Medical Coll of St
Bartholomew's Hospl
The EC1 ....96 B1
Medina Ct N7 ....5 C1
Medina Gr N7 ....5 C1
Medina Ho SE15 ....65 B3
Medina Rd N7 ....5 C1
Medlar St SE5 ....48 B2
Medley Rd NW6 ....10 C2
Medora Rd SW2 ....74 B4
Medresco Ho NW3 ..11 C3
Medusa Rd SE6,SE13 ..67 A1
Medway Bldgs E3 ....26 A3
Medway Ct W1 ....94 A3
Medway Ho NW8 ...102 A4
SE1 ....137 C3
N16 ....15 C4
Medway Rd E3 ....26 A3
Medway St SW1 ....133 C1
Medwin St SW4 ......62 B3
Meecham Ct SW11 ..168 A2
Meeson St E5 ....18 A4
Meeting House Alley 7
E1 ....32 A1
Meeting House La
SE15 ....50 A3
Mehetabel Rd E9 ....17 B3
Melais Mews 1
NW6 ....23 C2
Melba Ct E8 ....16 B3
Melbourne Ct W9 ...89 A2
E5 ....18 A3
Melbourne Gr SE22 ..64 B3
Melbourne Ho W8 ..113 B1
Melbourne Mews
SW9 ....173 B3
Melbourne Pl WC2 ..107 A1
Melbourne Sq
SW9 ....173 B3
Melbourne Ho 11
SE22 ....64 A4
Melbury Ct W8 ......127 A2
Melbury Dr SE5 ......49 A3
Melbury Ho SW8 ...162 C2
Melbury Rd W14 ....127 A2
Melchester 11 W11 ..31 B3
Melchester Ho 1
N19 ....4 C1
Melcombe Ct NW1 ..102 C4
Melcombe Ho
SW8 ....162 C1
Melcombe Pl NW1 ..102 C4
Melcombe Prim Sch
W6 ....47 C4
Melcombe St NW1 ..91 A1

Meldon Cl SW6 ......166 B4
Melford Ct SE22 ......76 C4
Melford Rd
SE21,SE22 ....76 C4
Melford Rd E5 ....76 C4
Melgund Rd N5 ......14 C3
Melina Ct NW8 ....89 B3
Melina Pl NW8 ....89 B3
Melina Rd W12 ....39 A4
Melior Pl SE1 ....138 A4
Melior St SE1 ....138 A4
Melisa Ct N6 ....4 C4
Mell St 6 SE10 ....43 A1
Mellington Ct 2 N16 ..7 C1
Mellish Ho 12 E1 ....32 A3
Mellish St E14 ....41 C3
Mellitus St W12 ......29 B3
Melody La N5 ....15 B3
Melody Rd SW18 ....59 B2
Melon Pl W8 ....127 C4
Melon Rd SE15 ....49 C2
Meretone Cl SE4 ....66 A3
Melrose Ave NW2 ....9 B3
SW19 ....70 C1
Melrose Gdns W6 ....39 B3
Melrose Ho SW1 ...146 B2
NW6 ....23 C2
Melrose Rd
1 SW13 ....46 B1
SW18 ....58 B1
Melrose Terr W6 .....39 B3
Melton Ct 4 SW7 ...143 C3
Melton Ho E5 ....7 C2
Melton St NW1 ....93 B3
Melville Court Flats
W12 ....39 A4
Melville Ct 4 W4 ....36 C1
SE8 ....41 A2
Melville Ho SE10 ...52 B2
Melville Pl 2 N1 ....15 B1
Melville Rd SW13 ...46 C2
Melville Villas Rd
W3 ....28 C1
Melvin Ct 11 TW9 ..44 C2
Melwood Ho 3 E1 ..32 A3
Melyn Cl N7 ....13 B4
Memel Ct EC1 ....96 C1
Memel St EC1 ....96 C1
Mendham Ho SE1 ..138 A2
Mendip Ct SE14 ....50 B4
12 SW11 ....59 B4
Mendip Dr NW2,
NW11 ....1 A2
Mendip Ho 2 N4 ....6 C4
Mendip Hos 2 E2 ...25 B2
Mendip Rd SW11 ....59 B4
Mendora Rd SW6 ..154 C2
Menelik Rd NW2 ....10 B4
Menorah Gram Sch
NW11 ....1 A4
Menorah Prim Sch
NW11 ....1 A4
Menotti St 2 E2 ......99 B2
Menteath Ho 6
E14 ....33 C3
Mentmore Terr E8 ..17 A1
Meon Rd W3 ....37 B4
Mepham St SE1 .....121 B1
Merbury Cl SE13 ....67 C2
Merbury Rd P E14 ..41 C1
Mercator Rd SE13 ..67 C3
Mercer St WC2 .....106 A1
Mercer's Cotts 3
E3 ....33 A3
Merceron Ho 3 E2 ..25 B2

Merceron St E1 ....25 A1
Mercers Cl SE10 ....43 B2
Mercers Pl W6 ....39 C2
Mercers Rd N19 ....4 C1
Merchant St E3 ....26 B2
Merchant Taylors Hall
EC2 ....109 C1
Merchon Ho N7 .....13 B4
Mercia Gr SE13 ......67 B3
Mercia Ho 3 SE5 ...48 B1
Mercie Rd SW15 ....58 A2
Mercury Ct SW9 ...173 B4
8 E14 ....41 C2
Mercury Way SE14 ..50 C4
Mere Cl SW15,SW19 ..69 C4
Meredith Ave NW2* ..2 A1
Meredith Ho 16 N16 ..16 A3
Meredith Mews SE4 ..66 B3
Meredith St EC1 .....96 A3
Meredyth Rd SW13 ..46 C1
Meretone Cl SE4 ...66 A3
Mereworth Ho 5
SE15 ....50 B4
Merganser Ct 8
SE8 ....51 B4
Meridan Ct SE13 ....67 C3
Meriden Ho 3 N1 ..24 A4
Meriden Ct SW3 ...144 A1
Meridian Building
SE10 ....52 C3
Meridian Ho SE10 ..43 A2
Meridian Pl E14 ......42 B4
Meridian Prim Sch
SE10 ....52 C4
Merivale Rd SW15 ..58 A3
Merlin Ho NW3 ....11 A4
7 W4 ....37 C1
Merlin St EC1 ....95 B3
Mermaid Ct SE1 .....137 B4
E14 ....34 B1
SE16 ....33 B1
Mermaid Ho 8 E14 ..34 B2
Mermaid Twr 22
SE8 ....51 B4
Meroe Ct N16 ....7 A2
Merredene St SW2 ..62 B1
Merrick Sq SE1 .....137 B2
Merricks Ct 6
SW14 ....55 A3
Merrington Rd
SW6 ....155 C4
Merritt Rd SE4 ....66 B2
Merrivale NW1 ....83 A3
Merrow St SE17 .....151 B1
Merrow Wlk SE17 ..151 C2
Merryfield SE3 ....53 B1
Mersey Ho 10 N7 ..14 C3
Merston Ho SW18 ..59 A1
Merthyr Terr SW13 ..47 A4
Merton Abbey Mills
SW18 ....71 A3
Merton Ave W4 ....38 B2
Merton Ho SW18 ....70 C3
Merton La N6 ....3 B2
Merton Rd SW18 ....70 C4
Merton Rise NW3 ....12 A1
Merton Road Ind Est
SW18 ....70 C4
Merttins Rd SE15 ...65 C2
Meru Cl NW5 ....12 C3
Mervan Rd SW2 .....62 C3
Messaline Ave W3 ..28 B3
Messina Ave NW6 ..10 C1
Messiter Ho N1 ......85 A3
Metcalfe Ho SW8 ..171 B2
Meteor St SW11 ....60 C3

Methley Ho 8 N7 .....5 B2
Methley St SE11 ...149 C1
Methodist Central Hall*
SW1 ....133 C3
Methwold Rd W10 ..30 C4
Metropolitan Benefit
Societies Almshouses
3 N1 ....16 A2
Mews St E1 ....125 B2
Mexborough NW1 ...82 C3
Mexfield Rd SW15 ..58 B2
Meyer Ho 11 SW12 ..73 A4
Meymott St SE1 ...122 A1
Meynell Cres E9 ......17 C1
Meynell Gdns E9 ....17 C1
Meynell Rd E9 ....17 C1
Meyrick Ho 8 E14 ..33 C4
Meyrick Rd NW10 ...8 C2
SW11 ....60 A4
Miah Terr 5 E1 .....125 C1
Micawber Ct N1 .....97 A4
Micawber Ho SE16 ..139 C3
Micawber St N1 .....97 A4
Michael Cliffe Ho
EC1 ....95 C3
Michael Faraday Ho
SE17 ....151 C1
Michael Faraday Prim
Sch SE17 ....151 C1
Michael Rd SW6 ...166 B4
Michel's Row 2
TW9 ....54 A3
Michelangelo Ct 14
SE16 ....40 A1
Michelle Ct W3 ......28 C2
Michels Almshouses
TW10 ....54 A2
Michelsdale Dr 3
TW9 ....54 A3
Michelson Ho
SE11 ....149 A3
Michigan Ho E14 ...41 C3
Mickledore NW1 ....83 A1
Micklethwaite Rd
SW6 ....155 C3
Mickleton Ho 30
W10 ....31 C4
Middle Row W10 ...23 A1
Middle Row Prim Sch
W10 ....23 A1
Middle St EC1 ....108 C4
Middle Temple
EC4 ....121 B4
Middle Temple La
EC4 ....121 B4
Middlefield NW8 ....79 B4
Middlesex Ct 4 W4 ..38 B2
Middlesex Hospl
W1 ....105 A3
Middlesex Hospl Annexe
W1 ....104 C4
Middlesex Pas EC1 ..108 B3
Middlesex Pl 19 E9 ..17 B2
Middlesex St E1 ....110 C3
Middleton Bldgs
W1 ....104 C3
Middleton Dr SE16 ..40 C4
Middleton Gr N7 ....14 A3
Middleton Ho SE1 ..137 B1
E8 ....16 B1
Middleton Mews
N7 ....14 A3
Middleton Rd NW11 ..1 C4
E8 ....16 B1
Middleton St E2 ....25 A2

Middleton Way
SE13 ....67 C3
Midford Pl W1 ....93 A1
Midhope Ho WC1 ...94 B3
Midhope St WC1 ...94 B3
Midhurst N8 ....5 A4
Midhurst Ho 6 E14 ..33 B3
Midland Pl E14 ....42 B1
Midland Terr NW10 ..21 A1
Midlothian Rd E3 ...26 B1
Midmoor Rd SW12 ..73 B3
Midship Cl SE16 ....32 C1
Midship Point E14 ..41 C4
Midstrath Rd NW10 ..8 A4
Midway Ho EC1 ......96 B4
Milborne Gr SW10 ..143 A1
Milborne Ho 19 E9 ..17 B2
Milborne St E9 ....17 B2
Milcote St SE1 ......136 B3
Mildmay Ave N1 ....15 C2
Mildmay Ct N1 ......15 C3
Mildmay Gr N1 ......15 C3
Mildmay Mission Hospl
E2 ....98 C3
Mildmay Pk N1 ......15 C3
Mildmay Rd N1 .....16 A3
Mildmay St N1 ......15 C2
Mildmay Ho 6
SW9 ....57 B2
Mildmay Coverdale Prim
Sch W12 ....39 B4
Miles Ct E1 ....32 A3
Miles Ho 5 SE10 ....43 A1
Miles Lo E15 ....19 C3
Miles Pl NW8 ......101 C4
Miles St SW8 ....162 B3
Milestone Green
SW14 ....55 C3
Milfoil St W12 ....29 C2
Milford Ct 8 N16 ....7 A3
Milford La WC2 .....121 B4
Milford Mews SW16 ..74 B1
Milk St EC2 ....109 A2
Milk Yd E1 ....32 B2
Milkwell Yd SE5 ....48 B2
Milkwood Rd SE24 ..63 A3
Mill Hill SW13 ....56 C4
Mill Hill Rd W3 ......37 A4
SW13 ....46 C1
Mill Hill Terr 9 W3 ..28 A1
Mill La NW6 ....10 B3
Mill Pl E14 ....33 A3
Mill Row N1 ....24 A4
Mill St SE1 ....139 A4
W1 ....118 C4
Mill Trad Est The
NW10 ....20 B2
Mill Yd E1 ....125 B4
Millais Rd E11 ....19 C4
Millard Cl 10 N16 ..16 A3
Millard Rd SE8 ....41 B1
Millbank SW1 ....148 A3
Millbank Prim Sch
SW1 ....147 C3
Millbrook Ho 4
SE15 ....49 C4
Millbrook Rd SW9 ..63 A4
Millbrooke Ct 7
SW15 ....58 A2
Millender Wlk SE16 ..40 B2

Millennium Bridge*
SE1,EC4 ...122 C3
Millennium Dome*
SE10 ...35 A1
Millennium Dr E14 ...42 C2
Millennium Pl 2
E2 ...25 A3
Millennium Sq
SE1 ...139 A4
Miller Ho 8 SW2 ...74 A4
Miller St NW1 ...83 A2
Miller Wlk SE1 ...121 C1
Miller's Ave E8,N16 ...16 B3
Miller's Ct 1 W4 ...38 B1
Miller's Terr 1 E8 ...16 B3
Miller's Way W6 ...39 B4
Millers Wharf Ho
E1 ...125 B1
Millfield N4 ...5 C2
Millfield La N6 ...3 B2
Millfield Pl N6 ...3 C2
Millfields JMI Sch
E5 ...17 B4
Millgrove St SW11 ...169 B2
Millharbour E14 ...42 A4
Milligan St E14 ...33 B2
Millington Ho N16 ...6 C1
Millman Ct WC1 ...94 C1
Millman Mews WC1 ...94 C1
Millman Pl WC1 ...95 A1
Millman St WC1 ...94 C1
Millmark Gr SE14 ...51 A1
Millner Ct SE14 ...51 B1
Millpond Est SE16 ...40 A4
Mills Ct EC2 ...98 A3
Mills Gr E14 ...34 B3
Mills Ho SW8 ...171 A4
Mills Row W4 ...37 C2
Millshot Cl SW6 ...47 B2
Millstream Rd SE1 ...138 C3
Millwall Dock Rd
E14 ...41 C3
Millwood St 10 W10 ...31 A4
Milman Rd NW6 ...23 A3
Milman's Ho
SW10 ...157 B3
Milman's St SW10 ...157 B3
Milner Ho 2 SW11 ...59 C4
Milner Pl N1 ...85 C4
Milner Sq N1 ...15 A1
Milner St SW3 ...144 C4
Milnthorpe Rd W4 ...45 C4
Milo Rd SE22 ...64 B1
Milrood Ho 4 E1 ...32 C4
Milroy Wlk SE1 ...122 A2
Milson Rd W14 ...126 A2
Milsted Ho 2 E5 ...17 A3
Milton Ave N6 ...4 B4
NW10 ...20 C4
Milton Cl SE1 ...152 C3
Milton Court Rd
SE14 ...51 A4
Milton Ct EC2 ...109 B4
SE14 ...51 A4
SW6 ...58 C2
9 SW18 ...58 C2
Milton Gr N16 ...16 A4
Milton Ho 10 E2 ...25 B2
2 SE5 ...48 C3
Milton House Mans
E8 ...16 B4
Milton Pk N6 ...4 B4
Milton Pl 8 N7 ...14 C3
Milton Rd N6 ...4 B4
W3 ...28 C1
SW14 ...55 C4

Milton Rd continued
SE24 ...63 A2
Milton St EC1,EC2 ...109 B4
Milverton NW5 ...12 C3
Milverton Rd NW6 ...9 B1
Milverton St SE11 ...149 C1
Milward St 1 E1 ...32 A4
Mimosa SW4 ...172 B3
Mimosa St SW6 ...165 A3
Mina Rd SE17 ...152 B2
Minchin Ho 6 E14 ...33 C3
Mincing La EC3 ...124 A4
Minera Mews SW1 ...145 C4
Minerva Cl SW9 ...163 C2
Minerva Rd NW10 ...20 C2
Minerva St E2 ...25 A3
Minet Ave NW10 ...21 A3
Minet Gdns NW10 ...21 A3
Minet Rd SE5,SW9 ...48 A1
Minford Gdns W14 ...39 C4
Ming St E14 ...33 C2
Mingard Wlk N7 ...5 B1
Minnow Wlk SE17 ...152 B3
Minories EC3 ...124 C4
Minshull St SW8 ...171 B3
Minson Rd E9 ...25 C4
Minstead Gdns
SW15 ...68 B4
Minster Rd NW2 ...10 A3
Mint Bsns Pk 1 E1
E16 ...35 C4
Mint St SE1 ...137 A4
Mintern St N1 ...87 C2
Minton Ho SE11 ...149 B4
Minton Mews 3
NW6 ...11 A2
Mirabel Rd SW6 ...155 A2
Miranda Cl 16 E1 ...32 B4
Miranda Ho 7 N1 ...24 A3
Miranda Rd N19 ...4 B3
Missenden SE17 ...151 C1
Missenden Ho NW8 ...90 A2
Mission Pl SE15 ...49 C2
Mission Sq 13 SW8 ...44 A4
Misterton Ct SW11 ...167 C4
Mistral SE5 ...49 A2
Mitali Pas 1 E1 ...111 B1
Mitcham Ho 9 SE5 ...48 B2
Mitchelldean Ct
SE14 ...49 A3
Mitchell Brook Prim Sch
W10 ...22 A1
Mitchell Ho 9 W12 ...30 A2
3 W1 ...... 37 A1
Mitchell St EC1 ...97 A2
Mitchison Rd N1 ...15 C2
Mitford Rd N19 ...5 A2
Mitre Bridge Ind Pk
W10 ...22 A1
Mitre Ct 2 SE1 ...135 C4
Mitre Sq EC3 ...110 B1
Mitre St EC3 ...110 B1
Mitre The 2 E14 ...33 B2
Mitre Way W10 ...30 A4
Moat Pl W3 ...28 A3
SW9 ...62 B4
Moatfield NW6 ...10 A1
Moberly Rd SW4 ...73 C4
Mobey Ct SW4 ...172 A3
Mocatta Ho 7 E1 ...25 A1
Modbury Gdns NW5 ...12 C2
Modder Pl SW15 ...57 C3
Model Cotts SW14 ...55 B4
Modling Ho 8 E2 ...25 C3

Moelwyn Hughes Ct
N7 ...13 C3
Moffat Ho 2 SE5 ...48 B3
Mohawk Ho 3 E3 ...26 A3
Moiety Rd E14 ...41 C4
Moira Ho 2 SW9 ...173 B4
Moira Rd SE17 ...72 C2
Moland Mead SE16 ...40 C1
Molasses Ho 1
SW11 ...59 B4
Molasses Row 2
SW11 ...59 B4
Mole Ct 2 W12 ...38 A4
Mole Ho NW8 ...89 C1
Molesey Ho E2 ...98 C2
Molesford Rd SW6 ...165 B3
Molesworth Ho 9
SE5 ...48 B3
Molesworth St SE13 ...67 B4
Molly Huggins Cl
SW12 ...73 B4
Molton Ho N1 ...85 A3
Molyneux St W1 ...102 B3
Mona Rd SE15 ...50 B1
Mona St E16 ...35 B2
Monck St SW1 ...133 C1
Monck's Row SW18 ...58 B1
Monclar Rd SE5 ...63 C3
Moncorvo Cl SW7 ...130 A3
Moncrieff St SE15 ...49 C1
Mondragon Ho
SW8 ...172 B4
Monet Ct 2 SE16 ...40 A1
Moneyer Ho N1 ...97 B4
Monica Shaw Ct
NW1 ...83 C1
Monier Rd E3 ...18 C1
Monk Ct W12 ...29 C1
Monk Dr E16 ...35 C2
Monkbretton Ho E2 ...99 B3
Monkridge 8 N8 ...4 C4
Monksfield N4 ...5 C2
Monkswell Ho 2 E2 ...99 B3
Monkton Ct W14 ...126 C2
Monkton Ho 22 E5 ...17 A3
2 SE16 ...40 C4
Monkton St SE11 ...149 C4
Monkwell Sq EC2 ...109 A3
Monmouth Cl W4 ...37 C3
Monmouth Gr TW8 ...36 A2
Monmouth Ho 2 NW5 ...13 A2
2 SW18 ...58 C1
Monmouth Pl W2 ...100 A1
Monmouth Rd W2 ...31 C3
Monmouth St WC2 ...106 A1
Monnery Rd N19 ...4 B1
Monro Ho 8 NW3 ...11 B4
SW15 ...57 A2
Monroe Dr SW14 ...55 A2
Monroe Ho 16 N19 ...4 C4
Monsal Ct E5 ...18 A4
Monsell Rd N4,N5 ...6 A1
Monson Rd NW10 ...22 A3
SE14 ...50 C3
Montagu Mans
W1 ...103 A3
Montagu Mews N
W1 ...103 A3
Montagu Mews S
W1 ...103 A3

Montagu Mews W
W1 ...103 A2
Montagu Pl W1 ...103 A3
Montagu Row W1 ...103 A3
Montagu Sq W1 ...103 A3
Montagu St W1 ...103 A2
Montague Ave SE4 ...66 C3
Montague Cl SE1 ...123 B2
Montague Pl WC1 ...105 C4
EC1 ...108 C3
Montague Rd E8 ...16 C3
Richmond TW10 ...54 A1
Montague Sq SE15 ...50 B3
Montague St WC1 ...106 A4
Montana Rd SW17 ...72 C1
Montcalm Ho E14 ...41 C3
Montclare St
E2 ...24 B1 98 C2
Monteagle Ct 27 N1 ...24 A3
Monteagle Way E5 ...7 C2
SE15 ...65 A4
Montefiore Ct 2 N16 ...7 B3
Montefiore St
SW8 ...170 B1
Montem Prim Sch
N7 ...5 B1
Montem St N4 ...5 B3
Montesquieu Terr 3
E16 ...35 B1
Montford Pl SE11 ...149 B1
Montfort Ho 4 E2 ...25 B2
E14 ...42 B3
Montfort Pl SW19 ...69 C3
Montgo Cl 10 SW2 ...62 C3
Montgomery Ct W4 ...45 B4
Montgomery Ho 5
SW14 ...55 C4
Montgomery Lo 34
E1 ...25 B1
Montgomery Rd W4 ...37 B2
Montholme Rd
SW11 ...60 B1
Monthorpe Rd E1 ...111 B3
Montolieu Gdns
SW15 ...57 A2
Montpelier Gr NW5 ...13 B3
Montpelier Mews
SW7 ...130 B2
Montpelier Pl SW7 ...130 B2
2 E1 ...32 B3
Montpelier Rise
NW11 ...1 A4
Montpelier Row
SE3 ...53 B1
Montpelier Sq
SW7 ...130 B3
Montpelier St
SW7 ...130 B2
Montpelier Terr
SW7 ...130 B3
Montpelier Vale
SE3 ...53 B1
Montpelier Way
NW11 ...1 A4
Montpelier Wlk
SW7 ...130 B2
Montreal Pl WC2 ...120 C4
Montrell Rd SW2 ...74 A3
Montrose Ave NW6 ...23 A3
Montrose Ct SW7 ...129 C3
Montrose Ho 8
SW1 ...131 C3
E14 ...41 C3
Montrose Pl SW1 ...131 C3
Montrose Villas W6 ...38 C1
Montserrat Rd
SW15 ...58 A3

Monument Gdns
SE13 ...67 B2
Monument St EC3 ...124 A3
Monument Sta
EC3 ...123 C4
Monza St E1 ...32 B2
Moodkee St SE16 ...40 B3
Moody St E1 ...25 C2
Moon St N1 ...86 A4
Moor La EC2 ...109 B4
Moor Pl EC2 ...109 B3
Moor St W1 ...105 C1
Moorcroft Rd SW16 ...74 A1
Moore Cl SW14 ...55 B4
Moore Ho 16 E2 ...25 B2
6 E1 ...32 B2
5 SE10 ...43 B1
SW1 ...71 C1
Moore Park Ct
SW6 ...156 B2
Moore Park Rd
SW6 ...156 A1
Moore St SW3 ...144 C4
Moorfields EC2 ...109 B3
Moorfields Eye Hospl
EC1 ...97 B3
Moorfields Highwalk
EC2 ...109 B3
Moorfields Prim Sch
EC1 ...97 B2
Moorgate EC2 ...109 B3
Moorgate Pl EC2 ...109 B2
Moorgate Sta EC2 ...109 B3
Moorgreen Ho EC1 ...96 A4
Moorhen Ct 15 SE8 ...51 B4
Moorhouse Rd W2 ...31 C3
Moorland Rd SW9 ...63 A3
Moorlands Est SW9 ...62 C3
Mora Rd NW2 ...9 B4
Mora St EC1 ...97 A3
Morant Ho SW9 ...172 C2
Morant St E14 ...33 C2
Morat St SW9 ...173 A4
Moravian Cl SW3 ...157 C3
Moravian Pl SW10 ...157 C3
Moravian St 6 E2 ...25 B2
Moray Ho 6 E1 ...26 A1
Moray Mews N4,N7 ...5 B2
Moray Rd N4,N7 ...5 B2
Mordaunt Ho SW8 ...171 B1
2 NW10 ...20 C4
Mordaunt Rd NW10 ...20 C4
Mordaunt St SW9 ...62 B4
Morden Hill SE13 ...52 B1
Morden La SE13 ...52 B2
Morden Mount Prim Sch
SE13 ...52 A1
Morden Rd SE3 ...53 C1
Morden Road Mews
SE3 ...53 C1
Morden St SE13 ...52 A2
Morden Wharf Rd
SE10 ...43 A3
Mordern Ho NW1 ...90 B1
More Cl W14 ...140 A3
E16 ...35 B1
More House Sch
SW1 ...131 A1
More's Gdn SW3 ...157 C3
Morecambe Cl 1
E1 ...32 C4

Morecambe St
SE17 . . . .**151** A2
Moredown Ho 3
E8 . . . . .16 C3
Moreland Ct 5 NW2 . .1 C1
Moreland Prim Sch
EC1 . . . . .96 B3
Moreland St EC1 . . . . .96 B4
Morell Ho SW9 . . . . .172 C1
Morella Rd
SW12 . . . . .72 B4
Moresby Wlk SW8 .170 B1
Moreton Ho SE16 . . . .40 A3
SW17 . . . . .71 C1
Moreton Pl SW1 . . . .147 A2
Moreton Rd SW1 . . .147 B2
Moreton Terr SW1 . .147 A2
Moreton Terr Mews N
SW1 . . . . .147 A2
Moreton Terr Mews S
SW1 . . . . .147 A2
Moreton Twr 3 W3 . .28 A1
Morgan Ct SW11 . . . .167 C2
Morgan Ho SW11 . . .147 A2
SW8 . . . . .171 A4
Morgan Rd N7 . . . . . .14 C3
W10 . . . . .31 B4
Morgan St E3 . . . . . . .26 A2
E16 . . . . .35 B2
Morgan's Wlk
SW11 . . . . .158 A1
Morgans La SE1 . . . .124 A1
Moriatry Cl N7 . . . . . .14 A4
Morie St SW18 . . . . . .59 A2
Morkyns Wlk SE21 . . .76 A1
Morland Cl NW11 . . . . .2 A3
Morland Ct W12 . . . . .39 A4
Morland Est E8 . . . . . .16 C1
Morland Ho NW1 . . . .83 A1
SW1 . . . . .148 A4
NW6 . . . . .23 C4
W11 . . . . .31 A3
Morland Mews N1 . . .14 C1
Morley Coll SE1 . . . .135 C2
Morley Ho N16 . . . . . . .7 C2
SW2 . . . . .74 A4
Morley Rd SE13 . . . . .67 B3
Morley St SE1 . . . . . .135 C3
Morna Rd SE5 . . . . . . .48 B1
Morning La E9 . . . . . .17 B2
Morningside JMI Sch
E9 . . . . .17 B2
Mornington Ave
W14 . . . . .140 C3
Mornington Avenue
Mans W14 . . . . .140 C3
Mornington Cres
NW1 . . . . .82 C2
Mornington Crescent
Sta NW1 . . . . .82 C2
Mornington Ct NW1 . .82 C2
Mornington Gr E3 . . . .26 C2
Mornington Mews 2
SE5 . . . . .48 B2
Mornington Pl NW1 . .82 C2
4 SE8 . . . . .51 B3
Mornington Rd
SE14,SE8 . . . . .51 B3
Mornington St NW1 . .82 B2
Mornington Terr
NW1 . . . . .82 B2
Morocco St SE1 . . . .138 A3
Morpeth Gr E9 . . . . . .25 C4

Morpeth Rd E9 . . . . . .25 C4
Morpeth Sec Sch
E2 . . . . .25 B2
Morpeth St E2 . . . . . . .25 C2
Morpeth Terr SW1 . .146 C4
Morrel Ct 2 E2 . . . . . .24 C3
Morris Blitz Ct 2
N16 . . . . .16 B4
Morris Ct 3 SE5 . . . . .63 C3
Morris Gdns SW18 . . .70 C4
Morris Ho NW8 . . . . . .90 A1
11 E2 . . . . .25 B2
3 N19 . . . . .13 C3
2 E14 . . . . .34 A2
Morris Pl N4 . . . . .5 C2
Morris St E1 . . . . .32 A3
E14 . . . . .34 A4
Morrish Rd SW2 . . . . .74 A4
Morrison Bldgs E1 . .111 B2
Morrison Ho SW2 . . . .74 C3
Morrison St SW11 . . . .60 C4
Morriss Ho 7 SE16 . . .40 A4
Morshead Mans W9 . .23 C2
Morshead Rd W9 . . . . .23 C2
Mortain Ho 9 SE16 . . .40 A2
Morten Cl SW4 . . . . . .61 C1
Mortham St E15 . . . . . .19 C1
Mortimer Cl NW2 . . . . .1 B1
SW16 . . . . .73 C2
Mortimer Cres NW6 . .78 B3
Mortimer Ct NW8 . . . .79 A1
Mortimer Est NW6 . . .78 B3
Mortimer Ho W14 . . .140 B3
7 W11 . . . . .30 C1
Mortimer Lo 7
SW19 . . . . .70 A3
Mortimer Market
WC1 . . . . .93 A1
Mortimer Pl NW6 . . . .78 A3
Mortimer Rd N1 . . . . .16 A1
NW10 . . . . .22 B2
Mortimer Sq W11 . . . .30 C2
Mortimer St W1 . . . . .105 A3
Mortimer Terr NW5 . .13 A4
Mortlake High St
SW14 . . . . .55 C4
Mortlake Rd SW14,
TW9 . . . . .44 C2
Mortlake Sta SW14 . . .55 B4
Mortlock Cl SE15 . . . . .50 A2
Mortlock St SE7 . . . . .48 A4
Morton Mews
SW5 . . . . .142 A3
Morton Pl SE1 . . . . . .135 B1
Morton Rd N1 . . . . . . .15 B1
Morval Rd SW2 . . . . . .62 C2
Morville St E3 . . . . . . .26 C3
Morwell St WC1 . . . . .105 C3
Moscow Pl W2 . . . . . .114 A4
Moscow Rd W2 . . . . .114 A4
Mosedale NW1 . . . . . .92 B3
Moss Cl E1 . . . . .111 C4
Mossbury Rd SW11 . . .60 A4
Mossford St E3 . . . . . .26 B1
Mossington Gdns
SE16 . . . . .40 B2
Mossop St SW3 . . . . .144 B4
Mostyn Gardens Prim
Sch SW9 . . . . .173 C3
Mostyn Gdns NW10 . .22 C3
Mostyn Gr E3 . . . . . . .26 C3
Mostyn Lo N5 . . . . . . .15 B4
Mostyn Rd SW9 . . . .173 C3
Motcomb St SW1 . . . .131 B2

Mothers Sq The 13
E5 . . . . .17 A4
Motley Ave EC2 . . . . . .98 A2
Motley St SW8 . . . . . .170 C2
Moules Ct SE5 . . . . . . .48 B3
Moulins Rd E9 . . . . . . .17 C1
Moulsford Ho
N7 . . . . .14 A3
2 W2 . . . . .31 C4
Mounsey Ho 10
W10 . . . . .23 A2
Mount Adon Pk
SE21,SE22 . . . . .76 C4
Mount Angelus Rd
SW15 . . . . .68 B4
Mount Ararat Rd
TW10 . . . . .54 A2
Mount Carmel RC Sec
Sch
N19 . . . . .4 C3
N7 . . . . .14 B3
Mount Ephraim La
SW16 . . . . .73 C1
Mount Ephraim Rd
SW16 . . . . .73 C1
Mount Ford St E1 . . .111 B2
Mount Mills EC1 . . . . .96 B3
Mount Nod Rd
SW16 . . . . .74 B1
Mount Pl 7 W3 . . . . . .28 A1
Mount Pleasant
WC1 . . . . .95 B1
Mount Pleasant Cres
N4 . . . . .5 B4
Mount Pleasant Rd
SE13 . . . . .67 B1
Mount Pleasant Villas
N4 . . . . .5 B4
Mount Rd SW18,
SW19 . . . . .71 A2
Mount Row W1 . . . . .118 A3
Mount Sq The NW3 . . .2 B1
Mount St W1 . . . . . . .117 C3
Mount Terr E1 . . . . . . .32 A4
Mount The W8 . . . . . .113 B1
NW3 . . . . .2 B1
Mount Tyndal NW3 . . . .2 C3
Mount Vernon NW3 . .11 B4
Mount Villas SE27 . . . .75 A1
Mountague Pl 3
E14 . . . . .34 B2
Mountain Ho SE11 . . .148 C2
Mountbatten Ho 3 N6 .3 C4
Mountbatten Mews
SW18 . . . . .71 B3
Mountearl Gdns
SW16,SW2 . . . . .74 B1
Mountfield NW2 . . . . . .1 B2
Mountfield Ct SE13 . . .67 C1
Mountfort Cres N1 . . .14 C1
Mountfort Terr 1
N1 . . . . .14 C1
Mountgrove Rd N5 . . . .6 B1
Mountjoy Ho EC2 . . .108 C3
Mounts Pond Rd
SE3,SE13 . . . . .52 C1
Mountview 3 SW16 . . .74 B1
Mourne Ho NW3 . . . . .11 B2
Mowatt Cl N19 . . . . .4 C3
Mowbray Rd NW6 . . . .10 A1
Mowlem JMI Sch
E2 . . . . .25 B3
Mowlem St E2 . . . . . . .25 A3
Mowll St SW9 . . . . . . .163 B1
Moxon St W1 . . . . . . .103 B3

Moye Cl 9 E2 . . . . . . .24 C3
Moylan Rd W6 . . . . . .154 B3
Moyle Ho SW1 . . . . . .161 A4
Moyne Ho 10 SW9 . . .63 A3
Mozart St W10 . . . . . .23 B2
Mudchute Sta E14 . . . .42 A2
Mudie Ho 3 SW2 . . . . .74 A4
Muir Rd E5 . . . . .7 C1
Muirdown Ave
SW14 . . . . .55 C3
Muirfield W3 . . . . .29 A3
Muirfield Cl 22
SE16 . . . . .40 A1
Muirfield Cres E14 . . . .42 A3
Mulberry Bsns Ctr
SE16 . . . . .40 C4
Mulberry Cl SW3 . . . .157 C3
NW3 . . . . .11 C4
SE22 . . . . .64 C1
1 E11 . . . . .19 C4
16 W9 . . . . .23 B2
6 SE8 . . . . .51 B4
Mulberry Mews
SE14 . . . . .51 B2
Mulberry Pl W6 . . . . . .38 C1
Mulberry Rd E8 . . . . . .16 B1
Mulberry Sch for Girls
E1 . . . . .32 A3
Mulberry Sec Sch
E1 . . . . .32 A3
Mulberry St 1 E1 . . .111 B2
Mulberry Wlk SW3 . . .157 C3
Mulgrave Rd W14 . . .154 C4
NW10 . . . . .8 B4
Mulkern Rd N19 . . . . . . .4 C3
Mull Ho 13 E3 . . . . . . .26 B3
Mull Wlk N1 . . . . .15 C2
Mullard Ho WC1 . . . .105 B4
Mullen Twr EC1 . . . . . .95 B1
Mullens Ho 8
SW15 . . . . .57 B2
Mullet Gdns E2 . . . . . .99 C4
Mulletsfield WC1 . . . . .94 B3
Mullins Path SW14 . . . .55 C4
Mulready St NW8 . . . . .90 A1
Mult Way W3 . . . . .38 A4
Multon Ho E9 . . . . . . .17 B1
Multon Rd SW18 . . . . .71 C4
Mulvaney Way SE1 . .137 C3
Mumford Ct EC2 . . . .109 A2
Mumford Rd SE24 . . . .63 A2
Muncaster Rd SW11 . .60 C2
Mund St W14 . . . . . . .141 A1
Mundania Ct SE22 . . . .65 A1
Mundania Rd SE22 . . . .65 B1
Munday Ho SE1 . . . . .137 B1
Munday Rd E16 . . . . . .35 C2
Munden Ho 5 E3 . . . . .27 A2
Munden St W14 . . . . .140 A4
Mundy Ho 8 W10 . . . .23 A2
Mundy St N1 . . . . .98 B4
Munro Ho SE1 . . . . . .135 B3
SE1 . . . . .137 C3
Munro Mews W10 . . . .31 A4
Munster Ct SW6 . . . .164 C2
Munster Rd SW6 . . . .154 B1
Munster Residences
SW6 . . . . .164 B4
Munster Sq NW1 . . . . .92 B2
Munster St SE1,
SE7 . . . . .151 A4
Murchison Ho 1
W10 . . . . .31 A4

Murdoch Ho 4
SE16 . . . . .40 B3
Murdock Cl E16 . . . . . .35 B1
Murdock St SE15 . . . . .50 A4
Murfett Cl SW19 . . . . .70 A2
Muriel St N1 . . . . .85 A2
Murillo Rd SE13 . . . . .67 C3
Murphy Ho SE1 . . . . .136 B2
Murphy St SE1 . . . . . .135 B3
Murray Gr N1 . . . . .87 B1
Murray Mews NW1 . . .13 C1
Murray St NW1 . . . . . .13 C1
Murray Terr NW3 . . . .11 C4
Mus of Garden History
SE1 . . . . .134 C1
Mus of London*
EC2 . . . . .108 C3
Mus of the Moving
Image SE1 . . . . .121 A2
Musard Rd W6 . . . . . .154 B4
Musbury St E1 . . . . . . .32 B3
Muscal W6 . . . . .154 A4
Muscatel Pl SE5 . . . . .49 A2
Muschamp Rd SE15 . . .64 B4
Muscott Ho 19 E2 . . . .24 C4
Muscovy St EC3 . . . . .124 B4
Museum Ho 8 E2 . . . . .25 B2
Museum St WC1 . . . . .106 A2
Musgrave Cres
SW6 . . . . .165 C4
Musgrave Ct SW11 . . .168 A4
Musgrove Ho 1 E9 . . .17 C2
Musgrove Rd SE14 . . .51 A2
Musical Mus The
SW6 . . . . .167 A1
Musjid Rd SW11 . . . .167 C1
Mustow Pl SW6 . . . . .165 A2
Mutrix Rd NW6 . . . . . .23 C4
Mutton Pl NW1 . . . . . .12 C2
Myatt Ct SE4 . . . . .51 B1
Myatt Garden Prim Sch
SE4 . . . . .51 B1
Myatt Ho SE5 . . . . . . .48 A1
Myatt Rd SW9 . . . . . . .48 A2
Myatts Field Ct SE5 . . .48 B2
Mycenae Rd SE3 . . . . .53 C3
Myddelton Pas EC1 . . .95 C4
Myddelton Sq EC1 . . . .95 C4
Myddelton St EC1 . . . .95 C3
Myddleton Ave N4 . . . . .6 B2
Myers Ho 6 SE5 . . . . .48 B3
Myers La SE14 . . . . . . .50 C4
Mylius Cl SE14 . . . . . . .50 B2
Mylne Cl W6 . . . . .38 C1
Mylne St EC1 . . . . .85 B1
Mynterne Ct 18
SW19 . . . . .69 C3
Myrdle Ct E1 . . . . .111 C2
Myrdle St E1 . . . . .111 C2
Myron Pl SE13 . . . . . . .67 B4
Myrtle Ho SE14 . . . . . .50 C2
Myrtle Rd W3 . . . . .28 B1
Myrtle Wlk 20 N1 . . . .24 A3
Mysore Rd SW11 . . . . .60 B3
Myton Rd SE21 . . . . . .75 C1
Mytton Ho SW8 . . . . .162 C1

N

Nags Head N7 . . . . . . .14 B4
Nags Head Ct EC1 . . . .97 A1
Nailsworth Ct SE5
SE15 . . . . .49 A4
Nainby Ho SE11 . . . . .149 B3
Nairn St E14 . . . . .34 B4
Nairne Gr SE5,SE24 . . .63 C3

Naish Ct N1 ....84 B4
Nalton Ho 4 NW6 ...11 B1
Nankin St E14 ....33 C3
Nansen Rd SW11 ....60 C4
Nant Ct NW2 ....1 B2
Nant Rd NW2 ....1 B2
Nant St E2 ....25 A2
Nantes Cl SW18 ......59 B3
Naoroji St WC1 ....95 B3
Napier Ave E14 ....41 C1
SW6 ....58 B4
Napier Cl W14 ....126 C2
SE14,SE8 ....51 B3
Napier Ct N1 ....87 B2
SW6 ....58 B4
Napier Gr N1 ....87 A2
Napier Pl W14 ......126 C1
Napier Rd W14 ......126 C1
NW10 ....22 A2
Napier Terr N1 ....15 A1
Narbonne Ave SW4 .61 B2
Narborough St
SW6 ....166 A1
Narcissus Rd NW6 ..10 C3
Narford Rd E5 ....7 C2
Narrow St 6 W3 ......28 A1
E14 ....33 A2
Nascot St W12 ....30 B3
Naseby Cl NW6 ....11 B1
Naseby Twr SE14 ....51 A3
Nash Ho SE1 ....66 A2
Nashe Ho SE1 ....137 B1
Nash Rd SE4 ....66 A2
Nasmyth St W6 ....39 A3
Nassau Rd SW13 ....46 B2
Nassau St W1 ....104 C3
Nassington Rd NW3 .12 B4
Nat West Tower★
EC2 ....110 A2
Nat West Twr★
EC2 ....110 A2
Nathan Ho SE11 ....149 C3
Nathaniel Cl E1 .....111 A3
National Army Mus★
SW3 ....159 A4
National Fan Mus
SE10 ....52 B3
National Film Theatre★
SE1 ....121 A2
National Gallery★
W1 ....119 C3
National Hospl The
WC1 ....94 B1
National Maritime
Mus★ SE10 ....52 C4
National Portrait
Gallery★ 119 C3
National Portrait Gallery
(Annexe)★ SW1 ..119 C2
National Postal Mus★
EC1 ....108 C2
National Theatre
SE1 ....121 A2
Natural History Mus★
SW7 ....129 B1
Naval Row E14 ....34 B2
Navarino Gr E8 ....16 C2
Navarino Mans E8 ..16 C2
Navarino Rd E8 ......16 C2
Navarre St E2 ....98 C2
Navenby Wlk 3 E3 ..26 C1
Navy St SW4 ....61 C4
Naylor Ho SE17 ....151 C2
SW8 ....171 B1
5 W10 ....23 B2
Naylor Rd SE15 ......50 A3

Nazareth Cl SE15 ....50 A1
Neal St WC2 ....106 A1
Neal's Yd WC2 ......106 A1
Nealden St SW9 .....62 B4
Neasden Cl NW10 ....8 A3
Neasden Junc NW10 .8 A4
Neasden La NW10 ....8 A3
Neasden Sta NW10 ...8 A3
Neathouse Pl SW1 .146 C4
Nebraska St SE1 ....137 B3
Neckinger SE16 ......139 A2
Neckinger Est
SE16 ....139 A2
Neckinger St SE1 ...139 A2
Nectarine Way SE13 52 A1
Nedahall Ct 4 NW11 1 B4
Needham Ho SE11 .149 B3
Needham Rd W11 ...31 C3
Needleman St SE16 40 C4
Needwood Ho N4 ......6 B4
Neil Wates Cres 18
SW2 ....74 C3
Neilson-Terry Ct 9
SW9 ....62 B3
Nelgarde Rd SE4 ....66 C1
Nell Gwynn Ho
SW3 ....144 B3
Nella Rd W6 ....47 C4
Nelldale Rd SE16 ....40 B2
Nelson Cl SE16 ....23 B1
Nelson Gdns
E2 ....24 C2 99 C4
Nelson Pas EC1 ....97 A4
Nelson Pl N1 ....86 B1
Nelson Rd SE10 ......52 B4
Nelson Sq SE1 ......136 A4
Nelson St E1 ....32 A3
E16 ....35 B2
Nelson Terr N1 ....86 B1
Nelson's Monument★
WC2 ....120 A2
Nemoure Rd W3 .....28 B2
Nepaul Rd 17 SW11 .60 A4
Nepean St SW15 ....68 C4
Neptune Ct 5 E14 ..41 C2
Neptune Ho 14 N16 16 A3
SE16 ....40 B3
Neptune St SE16 ....40 B3
Nesham Ho 14 N1 ..24 A4
Nesham St E1 ....125 B2
Ness St SE16 ....139 B2
Nestor Ho 8 E2 ......25 A3
Netheravon Rd W4 .38 B1
Netheravon Rd S
W4 ....38 B1
Netherby Ho SW8 .171 B1
Netherby Rd SE22 ..65 B1
Nethercombe Ho 1
SE3 ....53 C4
Nethercott Ho 27
E3 ....27 A2
Netherfield Rd
SW17 ....72 C1
Netherford Rd
SW4 ....171 A1
Netherhall Gdns
NW3 ....11 B3
Netherhall Way
NW3 ....11 B3
Netherleigh Cl N6 ....4 A3
Netherton Gr
SW10 ....157 A3

Netherwood Rd
W14 ....39 C4
Netherwood St
NW6 ....10 C2
Netley SE5 ....49 A2
Netley Prim Sch
N1 ....92 C3
Netley Rd TW8 ....44 A4
Netley St NW1 ....92 C3
Nettlecombe NW1 ..13 C1
Nettleden Ho SW3 .144 B3
Nettlefold Pl SE27 ..75 A1
Nettleton Rd SE14 ..50 C2
Nevada St SE10 ......52 B4
Nevena Ct 3 SW2 ..62 C2
Nevern Mans SW5 .141 B2
Nevern Pl SW5 .....141 C3
Nevern Rd SW5 ....141 B3
Nevern Sq SW5 ....141 C3
Nevil Ho 7 SW9 .....48 A1
Nevill Ct SW10 .....156 C2
Nevill Rd N16 ....7 A1
Neville Cl NW1 ....83 C1
NW6 ....23 B3
W3 ....37 B4
17 SE15 ....49 C3
Neville Ct 10
SW12 ....73 B4
Neville Gill Cl SW18 59 A1
Neville Rd NW6 ....23 C3
Neville St SW7 ......143 B2
Neville Terr SW7 ...143 B2
Nevinson Cl SW18 ..59 C1
Nevis Rd SW17 ......72 C2
Nevitt Ho N1 ....87 C1
New Bentham Ct 11
N1 ....15 B1
New Bond St W1 ....104 B1
W1 ....118 B4
New Bridge St
EC4 ....108 A1
New Broad St EC2 .110 A3
New Bsns Ctr The
NW10 ....21 B2
New Burlington Mews
W1 ....118 C4
New Burlington Pl
W1 ....118 C4
New Burlington St
W1 ....118 C4
New Butt La SE8 .....51 C3
New Caledonian Wharf
SE16 ....41 B3
New Campden Ct 7
NW3 ....11 B4
New Cavendish St
W1 ....104 A3
New Change EC4 ...108 C1
New Charles St EC1 .96 B4
New Church Rd
32 SE5 ....48 C3
SE5 ....48 C4
New College Ct 6
NW3 ....11 B2
New College Par 1
NW3 ....11 C1
New Compton St
WC2 ....106 A1
New Concordia Wharf
SE1 ....139 A4
New Covent Garden
Flower Market
SW8 ....162 A3

New Covent Garden
Fruit & Vegetable
Market Market
SW8 ....161 B1
New Cross Gate
SE14 ....51 B3
New Cross Gate
SE14 ....50 C2
New Cross Gate Sta
SE14 ....51 A3
New Cross Hospl
SE14 ....50 B3
New Cross Rd SE14 .51 A2
New Cross Sta SE14 51 B3
New Ct EC4 ....107 B1
N16 ....6 C3
13 NW3 ....11 B4
New Den The(Millwall
FC) SE16 ....40 B1
New End NW3 ....2 B1
New End Sq NW3 ....11 C4
New Fetter La EC4 ..107 C2
New Furness Prim Sch
The NW10 ....21 C3
New Globe Wlk
SE1 ....122 C2
New Goulston St
E1 ....110 C2
New Inn Broadway
EC2 ....98 B2
New Inn Pas WC2 ..107 A1
New Inn Sq EC2 ......98 B2
New Inn St EC2 ....98 B2
New Inn Yd
EC2 ....24 A1 98 B2
New James Ct SE15 .65 A4
New Kent Rd SE1 ..151 A4
New King St SE8 .....51 C4
New King's Rd
SW6 ....165 C3
New King's Rd
SW6 ....165 B2
New Kings Sch
SW6 ....164 C2
New London St
EC3 ....124 B4
New Mount St E15 ..19 C1
New North Pl EC2 ....98 A2
New North Rd N1 ....87 B3
New North St WC1 .106 C4
New Oxford St
WC1 ....106 A2
New Palace Yd
SW1 ....134 A3
New Park Ct 25
SW2 ....74 A4
New Park Par 14
SW2 ....74 A4
New Place Sq SE16 .40 A3
New Priory Ct 9
NW6 ....10 C1
New Quebec St
W1 ....103 A1
New Rd E1 ....32 A4
New Ride SW7 ......130 B4
New River Ct N5 .....15 C4
New River Way N4 ....6 C4
New Row WC2 ......120 A4
New Royal Horticultural
Society SW1 ....133 B1
New Scotland Yard★
SW1 ....133 B2
New Spring Gardens
Wlk SE11 ....148 B3

Nai – New   233

New Sq WC2 ....107 A2
New Sq Pas WC2 ...107 B2
New St EC2 ....110 B3
New St Sq EC4 .....107 C2
New Tower Bldgs 21
E1 ....32 B3
New Union Cl E14 ...42 B3
New Union St EC2 .109 B3
New Wharf Rd N1 ...84 B2
Newall Ho SE1 .....137 A2
Newark Cres NW10 .20 C2
Newark Ho 3 SW9 ..48 A1
Newark St E1 ....32 A4
Newbery Ho N1 ......15 B1
Newbold Cotts 4
E1 ....32 B3
Newbolt Ho SE17 ..151 B2
Newburgh Rd W3 ...28 B1
Newburgh St W1 ...105 A1
Newburn Ho SE11 .149 A2
Newburn St SE11 ..149 A2
Newbury Ct E5 ....18 A3
Newbury Ho W2 ....100 B1
SW9 ....173 C1
SW9 ....48 A1
Newbury Mews
NW5 ....12 C2
Newbury St EC1 ....108 C4
Newby 1 NW1 ....92 C4
Newby Pl E14 ....34 B2
Newby St SW8 ....61 A4
Newcastle Cl EC4 ..108 A2
Newcastle Ct EC4 ..123 A4
Newcastle Ho W1 ..103 B4
Newcastle Pl W2 ...101 C4
Newcastle Row EC1 .95 C1
Newcombe Ho N5 ...15 B3
Newcombe St W8 ..113 C2
Newcomen Ho 5
SW5 ....13 A4
Newcomen Rd
SW11 ....59 C4
Newcomen St SE1 .137 B4
Newcourt Ho 26 E2 .25 A2
Newcourt St NW8 ...80 A1
Newdigate Ho 5
E14 ....33 B3
Newell St E14 ....33 B3
Newent Cl SE15 .....49 A3
Newfield Prim Sch
NW10 ....8 B1
Newgate St EC1 ....108 B2
Newham Sch of Nursing
E3 ....27 A1
Newham's Row
SE1 ....138 B3
Newhaven La 3
E16 ....35 C4
Newington Barrow Way
N7 ....5 B1
Newington Butts
SE11,SE11 ....150 B3
Newington Cswy
SE1 ....136 C2
Newington Green Mans
N16 ....15 C3
Newington Green Prim
Sch N16 ....15 C3
Newington Green Rd
N1 ....15 C3
Newington Ind Est
SE17 ....150 C3
Newland Ct EC1 ......97 B2

Newland Ho **17**
Newlands NW1 ....**50** C4
Newlands Quay E1 ....**32** B2
Newlyn NW1 ....**83** A3
Newman Pas W1 ..**105** A3
Newman St W1 ......**105** A3
Newman's Ct EC3 ..**109** C1
Newman's Row
WC2 ....**107** A3
Newmill Ho E3 ....**27** B1
Newmount NW3 ....**11** C3
Newnes Path SW15 ..**57** C4
Newnham Ho **9**
SW15 ....**57** C1
Newnham Terr
SE1 ....**135** B2
Newton Cl N4 ....**6** C4
Newport Ave E14 ....**34** C2
Newport Ct WC2 ....**119** C4
Newport Ho E3 ....**26** A2
Newport Pl WC2 ....**119** C4
Newport Rd SW13 ..**46** C2
Newport St SE11 ....**149** A4
Newquay Ho SE11 ..**149** B2
Newton Ave W3 ......**37** B4
Newton Gr W4 ....**38** A2
Newton Ho NW8 ......**78** B4
1 E1 ....**32** A2
Newton Point **1**
E16 ....**35** B1
Newton Prep Sch
SW8 ....**170** B4
Newton Rd W2 ......**100** A1
E15 ....**19** C3
Newton St WC2 ....**106** B2
Newton's Yd **14**
SW18 ....**58** C2
Newtown Ct SW11 ..**170** A3
SW4 ....**61** A2
Newtown St SW11 ..**170** A3
Niagara Cl N1 ....**87** A2
Niagara Ct **6** SE16 ..**40** B3
Nicholas Ct W4 ....**46** A3
Nicholas Ho **2**
SW15 ....**56** C2
Nicholas La EC2,
EC4 ....**123** C4
Nicholas Pas EC3 ..**123** C4
Nicholas Rd E1 ....**25** B1
Nicholay Rd N19 ....**4** C3
Nicholl Ho N4 ....**6** B3
Nicholl St E2 ....**24** C4
Nichols Cl N4 ....**5** C3
Nicholson Ho SE17 ..**151** B2
Nicholson St SE1 ..**122** A1
Nickleby Ho SE1 ..**139** B3
7 W11 ....**30** C1
Nicoll Ct NW10 ....**21** A4
Nicoll Rd NW10 ....**21** A4
Nicosia Rd SW18 ......**72** A4
Nigel Ho EC1 ....**107** B4
Nigel Playfair Ave
W6 ....**39** A1
Nigel Rd SE15 ....**64** C4
Nightingale Cl W4 ....**45** B4
Nightingale Ct
SW6 ....**166** B3
N4 ....**5** B2
2 E14 ....**42** B3
Nightingale Gr SE13 ..**67** C2
Nightingale Ho E1 ..**125** B2

Nightingale Ho continued
21 E1 ....**24** A4
W12 ....**30** B3
Nightingale La
SW11,SW12 ....**60** C1
Nightingale Lo **3**
W9 ....**31** C4
Nightingale Rd
NW10 ....**21** B3
Nightingale Sq
SW12 ....**72** C4
Nightingale Wlk
SW8,SW4 ....**61** A1
Nile Cl N16 ....**7** B1
Nile Ho N1 ....**97** B4
Nile St N1 ....**97** B4
Nile Terr SE1,SE15 ..**153** A1
Nimegen Way **1**
SE22 ....**64** A2
Nimrod Pas **4** N1 ..**16** A2
Nine Elms La SW8 ..**161** B3
Nisbet Ho E9 ....**17** C3
Niton Rd TW9 ....**54** C4
Niton St SW6 ....**47** C3
Nobel Ho **8** SE5 ....**48** B1
Noble Ct **1** **125** C4
1 ....**32** A2
Noble St EC2 ....**108** C2
Noel Coward Ho
SW1 ....**147** A3
Noel Ho **3** NW3 ..**11** C1
Noel Rd N1 ....**86** B2
W3 ....**28** A3
Noel St W1 ....**105** A1
Nolan Way E5 ....**16** C4
Noll Ho N7 ....**5** B2
Norbiton Rd E14 ......**33** B3
Norbroke St W12 ....**29** B2
Norburn St W10 ......**31** A4
Norcombe Ho **2** N19 ..**4** C1
Norcott Rd N16 ....**7** C1
Norcroft Gdns SE22 ..**76** C4
Norden Ho **28** E2 ..**25** A2
Nore Ct NW10 ....**8** C1
Norfolk Cres W2 ..**102** B2
Norfolk Ho EC4 ....**122** C4
SW1 ....**147** C4
SE8 ....**16** B4
SE8 ....**51** C2
E3 ....**26** B4
Richmond TW10 ......**54** C2
3 SW5 ....**78** B4
Norfolk House Rd
SW16 ....**74** A1
Norfolk Mans
SW11 ....**169** A3
10 SW18 ....**58** C2
Norfolk Pl W2 ....**101** C2
Norfolk Rd NW8 ......**79** C3
NW10 ....**8** A1
Norfolk Row SE1,
SE11 ....**148** C4
Norfolk Sq W2 ......**101** C2
Norfolk Sq Mews
W2 ....**101** C1
Norgrove St SW12 ..**72** C4
Norland Ho **13** W11 ..**30** C1
Norland Pl
W11 ....**31** A1 **112** B1
Norland Rd W11 ......**30** C1
Norland Sq
W11 ....**31** A1 **112** B1
Norley Vale SW15 ....**68** C3

Norman Butler Ho **10**
W10 ....**23** A1
Norman Ct N4 ....**5** C4
NW10 ....**22** A3
SE2 ....**76** C4
Norman Gr E3 ....**26** A3
Norman Rd SE10 ....**52** A3
Norman St EC1 ......**97** A3
Norman Way W3 ......**28** A3
Normanby Cl SW15 ..**58** B2
Normanby Rd NW10 ..**8** B4
Normand Mews
W14 ....**154** B4
Normand Rd W14 ..**154** C4
Normandy Rd SW9 **173** B3
Normanhurst Rd
SW2 ....**74** B2
Normanton Ave
SW18,SW19 ....**70** C2
Normanton Ho **6**
SW4 ....**61** B1
Norris Ho **12** N1 ....**24** A4
22 E9 ....**25** B4
Norroy Rd SW15 ......**57** C3
Norse Ho **10** SE5 ..**48** B1
Norstead Pl SW15 ..**68** C2
North Acton Rd
NW10 ....**20** C2
North Acton Sta
W3 ....**28** C4
North Audley St
W1 ....**103** B1
1 ....**117** B4
North Ave **8** TW9 ..**44** C2
North Bank NW8 ......**90** A3
North Block **1** E1 ..**32** B2
North Branch Ave
NW10 ....**22** B2
North Church Ho **19**
E2 ....**24** C4
North Circular Rd
NW10 ....**8** A3
North Colonnade
E14 ....**33** C1
North Cres WC1 ....**105** B4
E16 ....**27** C1
North Cross Rd
SE22 ....**64** C2
North Ct SW1 ......**134** A1
North End NW3 ....**2** B2
North End Ave NW3 ..**2** B2
North End Cres
W14 ....**140** C3
North End Ho W14 ..**140** B3
North End Par
W14 ....**140** B3
North End Rd W14 ..**141** A1
NW11 ....**2** A3
North End Way NW3 ..**2** B2
North Eyot Gdns **5**
W6 ....**38** B1
North Flower Wlk
W2 ....**115** B3
North Gate NW8 ......**80** A1
North Gower St
NW1 ....**93** A3
North Gr N6 ....**3** C4

North Greenwich Sta
SE10 ....**43** A4
North Hill Ct N6 ....**3** C4
North Ho **3** SE8 ....**41** B1
North Lodge Cl
SW15 ....**57** C2
North London Boys Sch
N16 ....**7** C3
North Mews WC1 ....**95** A1
North Pas SW18 ......**58** C2
North Pole Rd W10 ..**30** B4
North Rd N6 ....**3** C4
N7 ....**14** A2
Brentford TW8 ....**44** A4
Richmond TW9 ....**44** C1
North Ride W2 ......**116** A3
North Rise W2 ......**102** B1
North Row W1 ......**103** B1
.............................**117** B4
North Sheen Sta
TW10 ....**54** C3
North Side Wandsworth
Comm SW18 ....**59** C2
North St SW4 ....**61** B4
North Tenter St
E1 ....**111** A1
North Terr SW3 ....**130** A1
North Verbena Gdns
W6 ....**38** C1
North Villas NW1 ....**13** C2
North Westminster Com
Sch
NW1 ....**102** A4
W2 ....**23** C1
North Westminster Com
Sch (Upper) **2** ..**101** B3
North Wharf Rd
W2 ....**101** B3
North Wlk W2 ......**114** C3
North Wood Lo
NW3 ....**11** A4
North Worple Way
SW14 ....**55** C4
Northampton Gr N1 **15** C3
Northampton Pk
N1 ....**15** C2
Northampton Rd
EC1 ....**95** C2
Northampton Sq
EC1 ....**96** A3
Northampton St N1 ..**15** B1
Northaw Ho W10 ....**22** B1
Northbourne Ho **7**
E5 ....**17** A3
Northbourne Rd
SW4 ....**61** C2
Northbrook Rd
SE13 ....**67** C2
Northburgh St EC1 ..**96** B2
Northchurch SE17 ..**151** C2
Northchurch Rd N1 ..**15** C1
Northchurch Terr
N1 ....**16** A1
Northcote Ho NW10 ..**8** A1
SW11 ....**60** B2
Northcourt W1 ......**105** A4
Northcroft Ct **8**
W12 ....**38** C4
Northdown St N1 ....**84** C1
Northern Hts N8 ......**4** C4
Northesk Ho **6** E1 ..**25** A1
Northey St E14 ......**33** A2
Northfield Hall N6 ....**3** C4
Northfield Ho **3**
SE15 ....**49** C4
Northfield Rd N16 ....**7** A4

Northfields SW18 ....**58** C3
Northfields Prospect
SW18 ....**58** C3
Northfields Rd W3 ..**28** B4
Northfleet Ho SE1 ..**137** B4
Northgate Ct **15**
SW9 ....**62** C4
Northiam WC1 ....**94** B3
Northiam St E9 ....**25** A4
Northington St WC1 ..**95** A1
Northlands St SE5 ..**48** B1
Northleach Ct **3**
SE5 ....**49** A4
Northleigh Ho **36**
E3 ....**27** A2
Northolme Rd N5 ....**15** B4
Northport St N1 ......**87** C3
Northstead Rd SW2 ..**74** C2
Northumberland Alley
EC3 ....**110** B1
Northumberland Ave
WC2 ....**120** A2
Northumberland Ho
NW5 ....**13** B2
Northumberland Mans
E5 ....**17** B4
Northumberland Pl
W2 ....**31** C3
Northumberland St
WC2 ....**120** A2
Northumbria St E14 **33** C3
Northview **1** N7 ......**5** A1
Northview Cres
NW10 ....**8** B4
Northview Prim Sch
NW10 ....**8** B3
Northway Rd SE5 ....**63** B4
Northways Par **2**
NW3 ....**11** C1
Northwest Pl N1 ....**85** C2
Northwick Cl NW8 ..**89** B2
Northwick Ho NW8 ..**89** A2
Northwick Terr
NW8 ....**89** B2
Northwold JMI Sch
E5 ....**7** C2
Northwold Rd E5,N16 ..**7** C2
Northwood Ho NW6 ..**4** A4
Norton Folgate E1 ..**110** B4
Norton Ho SW9 ....**173** A1
18 E2 ....**25** C3
13 E1 ....**32** A3
Norval Gn SW9 ....**173** C2
Norvic Ho **5** SE5 ..**48** B1
Norway Gate SE16 ..**41** A3
Norway Pl E14 ....**33** B3
Norway St SE10 ......**52** A4
Norwich Ho **8** E14 ..**34** A3
Norwich St EC4 ....**107** B2
Norwood High St
SE27 ....**75** A1
Norwood Ho **22** E14 ..**34** A2
Norwood Rd SE24,
SE27 ....**75** A3
Notley St SE5 ....**48** C3
Notre Dame RC Sec Sch
SE1 ....**136** A2
Notting Barn Rd
W10 ....**22** C1
Notting Hill Gate
W11 ....**31** C1 **113** B2
Notting Hill Gate Sta
W11 ....**31** C1 **113** B2
Nottingdale Sq
W11 ....**112** A2

Nottingham Ct
WC2 ....**106** A1
Nottingham Ho N4 ....**6** B3
34 SE5 ....**92** B4
Nottingham Pl W1 **103** B4
Nottingham Rd
SW17 ....**72** B3
Nottingham St W1 **103** B4
Nottingham Terr
NW1 ....**91** B1
Nottingwood Ho
W11 ....**112** A4
Novello Ho **5** W10 ..**23** B2
Novello St SW6 .....**165** B4
Nowell Rd SW13 .....**46** C4
Noyna Rd SW17 ....**72** B1
Nuding Cl SE13 ......**66** C4
Nuffield Lo N6 ......**31** C4
Nugent Terr NW8 ....**79** A1
Nugent Rd N19 ....**5** A3
Nun Ct EC2 ....**109** B2
Nunhead Cres SE15 ...**65** A4
Nunhead Gr SE15 ....**65** B4
Nunhead La SE15 ....**65** A4
Nunhead Sta SE15 ...**50** B1
Nursery Cl SE4 .....**51** B1
SW15 ....**57** C3
Nursery La E2 ......**24** B4
W10 ....**30** B4
Nursery Rd E9 ......**17** B2
SW9 ....**62** B3
Nutbourne St W10 ...**23** A2
Nutbrook St SE15 ...**64** C4
Nutcroft Rd SE15 ...**50** A3
Nutfield Rd SE22 ...**64** B3
E15 ....
Nutford Pl W1 .....**102** C2
Nuthurst Ave SW2 ...**74** B2
Nutley Terr NW3 ....**11** C2
Nutmeg La E14 ......**34** C3
Nutt St SE15 ....**49** B3
Nuttall St N1 ......**24** A3
NW London Jewish Day
Prim Sch NW6 ......**10** A1
Nye Bevan Ho
SW6 ....**154** C2
Nye's Wharf SE15 ...**49** C4
Nylands Ave TW9 ....**44** C1
Nynehead St SE14 ...**51** A3
Nyton Cl N19 ....**5** A3

0

O'Brian Ho **10** E1 ...**25** C2
O'Donnell Ct WC1 ...**94** B2
O'Driscoll Ho W12 ...
O'Gorman Ho
SW10 ....**157** A2
O'Leary Sq E1 ......**32** B4
O'Neill Ho NW8 .....**79** C1
O'Shea Gr E3 ....**26** B4
Oak Cres E16 ....**35** A4
Oak Gr NW2 ....**10** A4
Oak Hill Lo NW3 ...**11** A4
Oak Hill Park Mews
NW3 ....**11** B4
Oak Hill Pk NW3 ...**11** A4
Oak Hill Way NW3 ...**11** B4
Oak Ho N16 ....**6** C2
6 NW3 ....**12** B2
8 E14 ....**42** B4
Oak La E14 ....**33** B2
Oak Lodge Sch
SW12 ....**72** C4
Oak Park Gdns
SW19 ....**69** C3
Oak Park Mews N16 ..**7** B1
Oak Tree Ct W3 .....**28** A2
Oak Tree Ho W9 .....**88** A2
Oak Tree Rd NW8 ....**90** A3
Oak Village NW5 ....**12** C4
Oak Way W3 ....**29** A1
Oakbank Gr SE24 ....**63** B3
Oakbury Rd SW6 ....**166** B1
Oakcourt **16** SE15 ...**49** B3
Oakcroft Rd SE13 ...**52** C1
Oakdale Ct N19 ......**5** A2
Oakdale Rd SE15 ....**65** B4
Oakden St SE11 ....**149** C4
Oakdene **8** SE15 ....**50** A2
Oak Ct SW15 ....**58** A2
Oake Ct SW15 ....**58** A2
Oakend Ho **10** N4 ....**6** C4
Oakeshott Ave N6 ....**3** C2
Oakey La SE1 ....**135** B2
Oakfield Ct N8 ......**5** A4
SW4 ....**62** A1
Oakfield Rd N4 ......**5** C4
SW19 ....**69** C1
Oakfield St SW10 ..**156** C4
Oakford Rd NW5 ....**13** B4
Oakham Ho W10 .....**22** B1
Oakhill Ave NW3 ....**11** A4
Oakhill Ct SW15 ....**58** B2
SE23 ....**65** B1
Oakhill Pl SW15 ....**58** C2
Oakhill Rd SW15 ....**58** B2
Oakhurst Gr SE22 ...**64** C3
Oakington Rd W9 ...**23** C1
Oakington Way N8 ....**5** A4
Oaklands Cl SW11 ...
Oaklands Gr W12 ...**29** C1
Oaklands Ho SE4 ...**66** B4
Oaklands Mews NW2 ..**9** C4
Oaklands Pas NW2 ...**9** C4
Oaklands Pl **8** SW4 ..**61** C3
Oaklands Rd NW2 ....**9** C4
SW14 ....**55** C4
Oaklands Sec Sch
E2 ....**25** A2
Oakley Cres EC1 ....**86** B1
Oakley Dr SE13 .....**67** C1
Oakley Gdns SW3 ...**158** B4
Oakley Ho SW1 ....**145** A4
Oakley Pl SE1 .....**152** C1
Oakley Rd N1 ....**15** C1
Oakley Sq NW1 .....**83** A2
Oakley St SW3 .....**158** A4
Oakman Ho **20**
SW19 ....**69** C3
Oakmead Rd SW12 ...**73** A3
Oaks Sh Ctr The
W3 ....**28** B1
Oaks The NW10 ......**9** A1
NW6 ....
Oakshaw Rd SW18 ...**71** A4
Oakshott Ct NW1 ...**83** B1
Oakview Lo NW11 ....**1** B4
Oakwell Ho NW8 ...**171** B1
Oakwood Cl SE13 ...**67** C1
Oakwood La W14 ...**126** C2
Oakworth Rd W10 ...**30** C4
Oast Ct **8** E14 .....**33** B2
Oast Lo W4 ....**46** A3
Oat La EC2 ....**109** A2
Oatlands Ct **3**
SW19 ....**69** C3
Oatwell Ho SW3 ...**144** B3
Oban Ho E14 ....**34** C3
Oban St E14 ....**34** C3
Oberon Ho **5** N1 ....**24** A3
Oberstein Rd **12**
SW11 ....**59** C3
Oborne Cl SE24 ....**63** A2
Observatory Gdns
W8 ....**127** C4
Observatory Rd
SW14 ....**55** B3
Occupation Rd
SE17 ....**150** C2
Ocean St E1 ....**32** C4
Ockbrook **3** E1 ....**32** B4
Ockendon Rd N1 ....**15** C2
Ockley Rd SW16 ....**74** A1
Octagon Arc EC2 ...**110** A3
Octagon The NW3 ...**10** C4
Octavia Ho W10 ....**23** A1
Octavia St SW11 ..**168** B3
Octavius St SE8 ...**51** C3
Odeon Ct NW10 ....**21** A4
1 E16 ....**35** C4
Odessa Rd NW10 ...**21** C3
Odessa St SE16 ....**41** B3
Odette Duval Ho **24**
E1 ....**32** B4
Odgers St SW11 ...**169** A2
Odhams Wlk WC2 ..**106** B1
Odin Ho **5** SE5 ....**48** B1
Offa's Mead E9 .....**18** A4
Offenbach Ho **12** E2 ..**25** C3
Offerton Rd SW4 ...**61** B4
Offham Ho SE17 ...**152** A3
Offley Ho **16** E9 ...**17** C2
Offley Rd SW9 ....**163** B2
Offord Rd N1 ......**14** B1
Offord St N1 ....**14** B1
Oglander Rd SE15 ...**64** B4
Ogle St W1 ....**104** C4
Oil Mill La W6 .....**38** C1
Okehampton Rd
NW10 ....**22** C4
Okeover Manor
SW4 ....**61** A3
Olaf St W11 ....**30** C2
Old Bailey EC4 ...**108** B1
Old Barrack Yd
SW1 ....**131** B3
Old Bellgate Wharf
E14 ....**41** C3
Old Bethnal Green Rd
E2 ....**25** A2
Old Bldgs WC2 ....**107** B2
Old Bond St W1 ...**118** C3
Old Brewery Mews
NW3 ....**11** C4
Old Broad St EC2 ..**109** C2
Old Brompton Rd
SW7 ....**143** A3
SW5 ....**143** A3
Old Burlington St
W1 ....**118** C3
Old Castle St E1 ..**111** A2
Old Cavendish St
W1 ....**104** A1
Old Change Ct
EC4 ....**108** C1
Old Church Rd E1 ...**32** C3
Old Church St
SW3 ....**157** C4
Old Compton St
W1 ....**105** B1
Old County Hall
SE1 ....**134** C4
Old Court Ho W8 ..**128** A3
Old Court Pl W8 ..**128** A3
Old Covent Garden
WC2 ....**120** B2
Old Dairy Mews **4**
NW5 ....**13** A2
Old Deer Park Gdns
TW9 ....**54** A4
Old Devonshire Rd
SW12 ....**73** A4
Old Dock Cl TW9 ...**44** C4
Old Dover Rd SE3 ...**53** C3
Old Fish St Hill
EC4 ....**122** C4
Old Fleet La EC4 ..**108** A2
Old Ford Inf Sch E3 .**26** B3
Old Ford Jun Sch
E3 ....
Old Ford Rd E2,E3 ..**25** C3
Old Ford Trad Ctr
E3 ....**26** C4
Old Forge Mews
W12 ....**39** A4
Old Gloucester St
WC1 ....**106** B4
Old Hospital Cl
SW12,SW17 ....**72** B3
Old Jamaica Rd
SE16 ....**139** B2
Old James St SE15 ..**65** A4
Old Jewry EC2 ....**109** B1
Old Kent Rd SE1 ..**152** B2
SE15 ....**50** B3
Old Laundry The **14**
SW18 ....**59** C3
Old Manor Yd
SW5 ....**142** A3
Old Market Sq E2 ..**99** A4
Old Marylebone Rd
NW1 ....**102** B3
Old Mitre Ct EC4 ..**107** C1
Old Montague St
E1 ....**111** B3
Old Nichol St
E2 ....**24** B1 **98** C2
Old North St WC1 .**106** C4
Old Oak Common La
NW10 ....**21** A1
Old Oak La NW10 ..**21** B2
Old Oak Prim Sch
W12 ....**22** A2
Old Oak Rd W3 .....**29** B2
Old Orch The **3** NW3 .**12** B4
Old Palace Jun Sch
E3 ....**27** A2
Old Paradise St
SE11 ....**148** C4
Old Park Ave SW12 .**60** C1
Old Park La W1 ...**118** A1
Old Pye St SW1 ...**133** B2
Old Pye Street Est
SW1 ....**133** B1
Old Quebec St W1 .**103** A1
Old Queen St SW1 .**133** C3
Old Royal Free Pl
N1 ....**85** C3
Old Royal Free Sq
N1 ....**85** C3
Old Royal Horticultural
Society SW1 ......**147** B4
Old Royal Observatory
Greenwich (National
Maritime Mus
Annexe)* SE10 ....**52** C3
Old Seacoal La
EC4 ....**108** A1
Old South Lambeth Rd
SW8 ....**162** B2
Old Sq WC2 ....**107** B2
Old St EC1 ....**97** B2
EC1 ....**97** B3
Old Stable Mews N5 ..**6** B1
Old Street Sta EC1 ..**97** C2
Old Sun Wharf E14 ..**33** A2
Old Swan Wharf
SW11 ....**167** C4
Old Theatre Ct
SE1 ....**123** A2
Old Town SW4 .....**61** B4
Old Woolwich Rd
SE10 ....**42** C1
Old York Rd SW18 ..**59** A2
Oldbury Ct E9 .....**18** A3
Oldbury Pl W1 ....**103** C4
Oldfield Gr SE16 ...**40** C2
Oldfield Ho **10** W4 ..**38** A1
Oldfield Mews N6 ....**4** B4
Oldfield Rd N16 .....**7** A1
NW10 ....
W3 ....**38** B4
W3,W12 ....**38** B4
Oldham Terr W3 ....**28** B1
Oldhill St N16 ......**7** C3
Olding Ho **6** SW12 .**73** B4
Oldridge Rd SW12 ..**73** A4
Olga JMI Sch E3 ...**26** A3
Olga St **8** E3 .....**26** A3
Olgar St **5** SW10 ..**23** A2
Olive Blythe Ho **14**
W10 ....**23** A1
Olive Rd NW2 ....**9** B4
Olive Tree Ho **7**
SE15 ....**50** B4
Olive Waite Ho
NW6 ....
Oliver Cl W4 ....**11** A1
Oliver Ho SE16 ...**139** B3
SW8 ....**162** A2
Oliver's Yd EC1 ....**97** C2
Olivette St **1** SW15 .**57** C4
Ollerton Gn E3 ....**26** B4
Ollgar Cl W12 .....**29** B1
Olliffe St E14 .....**42** B3
Olmar St SE1 ......**49** C4
Olmar Wharf SE1 ...**49** C4
Olney Ho NW8 .....**90** B2
Olney Rd SE17 ....**48** B4
Olympia Ex Hall*
W14 ....**126** B1
Olympia Way W14 .**126** B1
Olympia Yd W2 ...**114** B3
Olympian Ct **1** E14 ..**41** C2
Olympic Ho W10 ...**30** B3
Olympus Sq E5 .....**7** C1
Oman Ave NW2 .....**9** B4
Oman Ct NW4 ....**9** A4
Ombersley Ho N4 ....**6** A4
Omeara St SE1 ....**123** A1
Omega Cl E14 .....**42** A3
Omega Ho SW10 ..**157** A2
Omega Pl N1 ......**84** B1
Omega St SE14 ....**51** C2
Ommaney Rd SE14 ..**51** A2
Ondine Rd SE15 ...**64** B3
One Tree Cl SE23 ..**65** B1
Onega Gate SE16 ...**41** A3
Ongar Ho **15** N1 ...**15** C2
Ongar Rd SW6 ....**155** C4
Onslow Ave TW10 ..**54** A2

Onslow Avenue Mans 10 TW10 .... 54 A2
Onslow Ct SW10 .... 143 A1
Onslow Gdns SW7 .... 143 A2
Onslow Ho 1 W10 .... 23 A2
Onslow Mews E SW7 .... 143 B3
Onslow Mews W SW7 .... 143 B3
Onslow Rd TW10 .... 54 A1
Onslow Sq SW7 .... 143 C3
Onslow St EC1 .... 95 C1
Ontario St SE1 .... 136 B2
Ontario Way E14 .... 33 C2
Opal St SE11 .... 150 A2
Open Air Theatre, Regent's Park NW1 .... 91 B3
Openview SW17, SW18 .... 71 C2
Operating Theatre Mus & Herb Garret SE1 .... 123 C1
Ophelia Gdns NW2 .... 1 A1
Opie Terr SE15 .... 49 C2
Opie Ho NW8 .... 80 B2
Oppenheim Rd SE13 .... 52 B1
Oppidans Rd NW3 .... 12 B1
Orange Pl SE16 .... 40 B3
Orange St WC2 .... 119 C3
Orange Yd WC2 .... 105 C1
Oratory La SW3 .... 143 C2
Oratory RC Prim Sch SW3 .... 144 A2
Oratory The SW7 .... 130 A1
Orb St SE17 .... 151 B3
Orbain Rd SW6 .... 154 B1
Orbel St SW11 .... 168 A3
Orchard Cl N1 .... 15 B1
W10 .... 31 A4
SE23 .... 65 B1
Orchard Ct W1 .... 103 B2
SW13 .... 56 B4
Orchard Dr SE3 .... 53 A1
Orchard Hill SE13 .... 52 A2
Orchard Ho W12 .... 29 C1
SE16 .... 40 B3
.... 48 B2
Orchard JMI Sch E9 .... 17 B1
Orchard Mead House NW11 .... 1 C4
Orchard Mews N1 .... 15 C1
Orchard Pl E14 .... 35 A1
Orchard Rd N6 .... 4 A4
Mortlake TW9 .... 55 A3
Orchard Rise TW10 .... 55 A3
Orchard Sq W14 .... 140 C1
Orchard St W1 .... 103 C2
Orchard The W4 .... 37 C2
SE3 .... 52 C1
Orchardson Ho 89 C1
Orchardson St NW8 .... 89 C1
Orchid St W12 .... 29 C2
Orde Hall St WC1 .... 106 C4
Orde Ho 10 N16 .... 15 C4
Ordell Ct 20 E3 .... 26 B3
Ordell Rd E3 .... 26 B3
Ordnance Cres SE10 .... 43 A4
Ordnance Hill NW8 .... 79 C3

Ordnance Mews NW8 .... 79 C2
Ordnance Rd E16 .... 35 B2
Oregano Dr E14 .... 34 C3
Orford Ct SE27 .... 75 A2
Oriel Ct NW3 .... 11 B4
Oriel Dr SW13 .... 47 B4
Oriel Rd E9 .... 17 C2
Orient St SE11 .... 150 A4
Orion Bsns Ctr SE14 .... 40 C1
Orion Ho 6 E1 .... 25 A1
Orkney Ho N1 .... 84 C4
Orkney St SW11 .... 169 B2
Orlando Rd SW4 .... 61 B4
Orleston Mews N7 .... 14 C2
Orleston Rd N7 .... 14 C2
Orme Ct W2 .... 114 A3
Orme Ct Mews W2 .... 114 A3
Orme Ho 8 E8 .... 24 B4
Orme La W2 .... 114 A3
Orme Sq W2 .... 114 A3
Ormeley Rd SW12 .... 73 A3
Ormiston Gr W12 .... 30 A1
Ormiston Rd SE10 .... 43 C1
Ormond Cl WC1 .... 106 B4
Ormond Ho 8 N16 .... 6 C2
Ormond Mews WC1 .... 94 B1
Ormond Rd N4,N19 .... 5 A3
Ormond Yd SW1 .... 119 A2
Ormonde Ct SW15 .... 57 B3
Ormonde Gate SW3 .... 145 A1
Ormonde Mans WC1 .... 145 C2
Ormonde Rd SW14 .... 55 B4
Ormonde Terr NW8 .... 80 C3
Ormrod Ct W11 .... 31 B3
Ormsby Lo 2 W4 .... 38 A3
Ormsby Pl N16 .... 7 B1
Ormsby St E2 .... 24 B3
Ormside St SE15 .... 50 B4
Ornan Rd NW3 .... 12 A3
Oronsay Wlk 15 N1 .... 15 B2
Orpheus Ho 25 N19 .... 4 C4
Orpheus St SE5 .... 48 C2
Orpheus Twr 6 SE14 .... 51 A3
Orsett Mews W2 .... 100 B2
Orsett St SE11 .... 149 A2
Orsett Terr W2 .... 100 C2
Orsman Rd N1 .... 24 A4
Orton St E1 .... 125 B1
Orville Rd SW11 .... 167 C2
Orwell Ct N5 .... 15 B4
Orwell Ho W12 .... 29 C2
Osbaldeston Rd N16 .... 7 C3
Osbert St SW1 .... 147 B3
Osborn Cl E8 .... 24 C4
Osborn St E1 .... 111 A3
Osborne Rd N4 .... 5 C3
NW2 .... 9 A2
E9 .... 18 B2
E7 .... 16 B1
Osbourne Ho TW10 .... 54 C2
Oscar Faber Pl 8 N1 .... 16 A1
Oscar St SE8 .... 51 C2
Oseney Cres NW5 .... 13 C2
Osier Ct E1 .... 25 C1
Osier Mews W4 .... 46 B4
Osier St E1 .... 25 B1
Osiers Rd SW18 .... 58 C3
Oslo Ct NW8 .... 80 A1

Oslo Ho 2 SE5 .... 48 B1
Oslo Sq SE16 .... 41 A3
Osman Rd W6 .... 39 B3
Osmani JMI Sch E1 .... 111 C4
Osmington Ho SW8 .... 163 A1
Osmund St W12 .... 29 B4
Osnaburgh St NW1 .... 92 B2
Osnaburgh Terr NW1 .... 92 B2
Osprey Ct NW3 .... 11 A3
Osprey Ho 8 E14 .... 33 A2
SE15 .... 49 B2
Ospringe Ho SE1 .... 121 C1
Ospringe Rd NW5 .... 13 B4
Osram Ct W6 .... 39 B3
Osric Path 8 N1 .... 24 A3
Ossian Rd N4 .... 5 B4
Ossington Bldgs W1 .... 103 B3
Ossington Cl W2 .... 113 C3
Ossington St W2 .... 114 A3
Ossory Rd SE1 .... 49 C4
Ossulston St NW1 .... 93 C4
Ostade Rd SW2 .... 74 B4
Osten Mews SW7 .... 128 B1
Osterley Ho 8 E14 .... 34 A3
Osterley Rd N16 .... 16 A4
Oswald's Mead E9 .... 18 A4
Osward Rd SW17 .... 72 B2
Oswell Ho 9 E1 .... 32 A1
Oswin St SE11 .... 150 B4
Oswyth Rd SE5 .... 49 A1
Otford Ho SE1 .... 137 C3
8 SE15 .... 50 B4
Otha Ho SW9 .... 172 B2
Othello Cl SE11 .... 150 A2
Otis St E3 .... 27 B2
Otley Ho N5 .... 6 A1
Ottaway Ct E5 .... 7 C1
Ottaway St E5 .... 7 C1
Otterburn Ho 12 SE5 .... 48 B3
Otto St SE17 .... 48 A4
Our Lady & St Joseph RC JMI Sch N1 .... 16 A2
Our Lady of Dolours RC Prim Sch W2 .... 100 A4
Our Lady of Lourdes Prim Sch NW10 .... 20 B4
Our Lady of Lourdes RC Prim Sch SE13 .... 67 C4
Our Lady of the Assumption RC Inf Sch E2 .... 25 B3
Our Lady of the Sacred Heart RC Prim Sch (Annexe) N7 .... 14 B2
Our Lady of the Sacred Heart RC Sch N7 .... 14 B3
Our Lady of Victories RC Prim Sch SW7 .... 143 A3
SW15 .... 57 C2
Our Lady Queen of Heaven RC Prim Sch SW19 .... 69 C4
Our Lady RC JMI Sch
Our Lady's Convent High Sch N15,N16 .... 7 A4
Ouseley Rd SW12 .... 72 B3
Outer Circ NW1 .... 80 B1

Outgate Rd NW10 .... 8 B1
Outram Pl N1 .... 84 B4
Outwich St EC3 .... 110 B2
Outwood Ho 3 SW2 .... 74 B4
Oval Mans SE11 .... 163 A4
Oval Pl SW8 .... 163 A2
Oval Rd NW1 .... 82 A4
Oval St SE11 .... 163 B3
Oval The E2 .... 25 A3
Oval The (Surrey Cnty Crkt Gd) SE11 .... 163 A4
Oval Way SE11 .... 149 A1
Overbury Ho 3 E5 .... 17 C4
Overbury St E5 .... 17 C4
Overcliff Rd SE13 .... 66 C4
Overhill Rd SE21, SE22 .... 76 C4
Overlea Rd E5 .... 7 C4
Oversley Ho 17 W2 .... 31 C4
Overstone Ho 17 E14 .... 33 C3
Overstone Rd W6 .... 39 B2
Overstrand Mans SW11 .... 169 B3
Overton Ho SW15 .... 68 B4
Overton Rd SW9 .... 173 C1
Overy Ho SE1 .... 136 A3
Ovex Cl E14 .... 42 B4
Ovington Ct SW3 .... 130 B1
Ovington Gdns SW3 .... 130 B1
Ovington Mews SW3 .... 130 B1
Ovington Sq SW3 .... 130 B1
Ovington St SW3 .... 144 B4
Owen Ho 11 N19 .... 13 B4
Owen St EC1 .... 86 A1
Owen's Ct EC1 .... 96 A4
Owen's Row EC1 .... 96 A4
Owgan Cl SE5 .... 48 C3
Oxberry Ave SW6 .... 164 B2
Oxbridge Ct 4 W4 .... 37 A1
Oxendon St SW1, W1 .... 119 B3
Oxenford St SE15 .... 64 B4
Oxenham Ho 11 SE8 .... 51 C4
Oxenholme NW1 .... 83 A1
Oxestalls Rd SE8 .... 41 A1
Oxford & Cambridge Mans NW1 .... 102 B3
Oxford Ave NW10 .... 22 A2
Oxford Cir W1 .... 104 C1
Oxford Circus Ave W1 .... 104 C1
Oxford Circus Sta W1 .... 104 C1
Oxford Ct EC4 .... 123 B4
.... 37 A1
Oxford Gardens Prim Sch W10 .... 30 C3
Oxford Gate W6 .... 39 C2
Oxford Gdns W10 .... 30 C3
W4 .... 44 C4
Oxford Rd N4 .... 5 C3
E15 .... 19 C2
NW6 .... 23 C3
SW15 .... 58 A3
Oxford Rd S W4 .... 37 A1
Oxford Rd W6 .... 39 A1
Oxford Sq W2 .... 102 B1
Oxford St W1 .... 104 B1
Oxley Cl SE1 .... 153 A2
Oxo Tower SE1 .... 121 C3
Oxo Tower Wharf SE1 .... 121 C3

Oxonian St SE22 .... 64 B3
Oxted Ct N16 .... 7 A3
Oyster Row E1 .... 32 B3
Ozolins Way E16 .... 35 C3

P

Pablo Neruda Cl 4 SE24 .... 63 A3
Pace Pl E1 .... 32 A3
Pacific Ho 15 E1 .... 25 C1
Pacific Rd E16 .... 35 C3
Packenham Ho 2 24 N19 .... 4 C4
Packington Ho SW9 .... 172 B2
Packington Sq N1 .... 86 C4
Packington St N1 .... 86 B3
Padbury SE17 .... 152 B1
Padbury Ct E2 .... 99 A3
Padbury Ho NW8 .... 90 B2
Paddenswick Ct W6 .... 38 C3
Paddenswick Rd W6 .... 38 C3
Paddington Com Hospl W9 .... 31 C4
Paddington Gn W2 .... 101 B4
Paddington Green Prim Sch NW8 .... 89 B1
Paddington St W1 .... 103 B4
Paddington Sta W2 .... 101 B2
Paddock Cl SE3 .... 53 C1
Paddock St SE15 .... 56 B3
Padfield Rd SE5 .... 63 B4
Padstow Ho 12 E14 .... 33 B2
Pagden St SW8 .... 170 B4
Page Ho SE10 .... 52 B4
Page St SW1 .... 147 C4
Page's Wlk SE1 .... 138 B1
Page's Yd W4 .... 46 A4
Pageant Cres SE16 .... 33 B1
Pageantmaster Ct EC4 .... 108 A1
Paget Ho 15 E2 .... 25 B3
Paget Rd N16 .... 6 C3
Paget St EC1 .... 96 A4
Pagham Ho W10 .... 22 B1
Pagnell St SE14 .... 51 B3
Pagoda Ave TW9 .... 54 B4
Pagoda Gdns SE3 .... 52 C1
Paine Ct SE3 .... 53 B4
Painsthorpe Rd 3 N16 .... 7 A1
Painswick Ct 1 SE15 .... 49 B3
Pakeman Ho 1 SE1 .... 136 C3
Pakeman Prim Sch N7 .... 5 B1
Pakeman St N7 .... 5 B1
Pakenham Cl SW12 .... 72 C3
Pakenham St WC1 .... 95 A2
Palace Ave W8 .... 128 B4
Palace Ct W2 .... 114 A3
NW3 .... 11 A3
SW2 .... 74 C2
Palace Garden Mews W8 .... 113 C2
Palace Gate W8 .... 128 C3
Palace Gdns Mews W8 .... 114 A3
Palace Gn W8 .... 114 A3
Palace Mans W14 .... 140 B4
Palace Mews SW1 .... 145 C3

Palace Mews *continued*
SE5 ....155 A2
Palace Pl SW1 ....132 C2
Palace Rd SE27,
SW16,SW2 ....74 C2
Palace St SW1 ....132 C2
Palamon Ct SE1 ....153 A2
Palatine Ave N16 ....16 A4
Palatine Rd N16 ....16 A4
Palermo Rd NW10 ....21 C3
Palewell Common Dr
SW14 ....55 C2
Palewell Pk SW14 ......55 C3
Palfrey Pl SW8 ....163 A2
Palgrave Ho
4 NW3 ....12 B3
7 SE5 ....48 B3
Palgrave Rd W12 ......38 B3
Palissy St E2 ....98 C3
Pall Mall SW1 ....119 B1
Pall Mall E SW1 ....119 C2
Pall Mall Pl SW1 ....119 C2
Pallant Ho SE1 ....137 C1
Palliser Ct W14 ....140 A1
Palliser Rd 21 E1 ....25 C1
3 SE10 ....52 B2
Palliser Rd W14 ....140 A1
Palm Ct N16 ....6 C2
17 SE15 ....49 B3
Palm Gr W5 ....36 A3
Palm Tree Ho 2
SE14 ....50 C3
Palmer Ct NW10 ......22 C4
Palmer Ho 5 N19 ......4 B1
4 NW5 ....13 B4
6 SE14 ....50 C3
Palmer Pl N7 ....14 C3
Palmer St SW1 ....133 B2
Palmers Rd E2 ....25 C3
SW14 ....55 B4
Palmerston Ct 22
E3 ....25 C3
Palmerston Ho
W8 ....113 B1
SW11 ....169 C3
Palmerston Rd NW6 10 B1
NW6 ....10 C1
W3 ....37 B3
SW14 ....55 B3
Palmerston Way
SW8 ....160 B1
Pamela Ct NW10 ....8 A1
Pamela Ho 14 E8 ......24 B4
Pamlion Ct N4 ....5 A4
Panama Ho 5 E1 ....32 C4
Pancras La EC2 ....109 B1
Pancras Rd NW1 ....83 C2
Pandora Rd NW6 ......10 C2
Pangbourne NW1 ......92 C3
Pangbourne Ave
W10 ....30 B4
Pangbourne Ho 4
N7 ....14 A3
Pankhurst Cl 7
SE14 ....50 C3
Pansy Gdns W12 ....29 C2
Panton St SW1 ....119 B3
Panyer Alley EC2 ......108 C2
Panyer Alley Steps
EC2 ....108 C2
Paper Mill Wharf
E14 ....33 A2
Papillons Wlk SE3 .....53 C1
Papworth Gdns N7 ....14 B3
Papworth Way SW2 ..74 C4

Parade Mans 19
SE5 ....48 B1
Parade Mews SE27,
SW2 ....75 A2
Parade The SW11 .....159 A2
Paradise Rd SW4 .....172 A2
Richmond TW10 ....54 A2
Paradise Row E2 ....25 A2
Paradise St SE16 ......40 A4
Paradise Wlk SW3 ....159 A4
Paragon Cl E16 ....35 C3
Paragon Mews
SE1 ....151 C4
Paragon Pl SE3 ....53 B1
Paragon Rd E9 ....17 B2
Paragon The SE3 ....53 C1
Paramount Bldg
EC1 ....96 A2
Paramount Ct WC1 ...93 A1
Parbury Rd SE23 ......66 A1
Pardon St EC1 ....96 B2
Pardoner St SE1 ......137 C2
Parfett St E1 ....111 C2
Parfitt Cl NW3 ....2 B3
Parfrey St W6 ....47 B4
Paris Gdns SE1 ....122 A2
Paris Ho 22 E2 ....25 A3
Park Ave NW11 ....2 A3
NW2 ....9 B2
SW14 ....55 C3
Park Ave N N10 ....1 A4
Park Ave N N10 ....9 A3
Park Cl SW11 ....170 A4
W14 ....127 A2
SW1 ....130 C3
20 E9 ....25 B4
Park Cres W1 ....92 A1
Park Cres Mews E
W1 ....92 B1
Park Cres Mews W
W1 ....92 A1
Park Ct SW11 ....170 A4
SW4 ....61 C2
SW12 ....72 C3
SE21 ....75 C1
Park Dr NW11 ....2 A3
W3 ....36 C3
SW14 ....55 C3
Park Dwellings 7
NW3 ....12 B3
Park End NW3 ....12 A4
Park Flats N6 ....3 A4
Park Hall Rd SE21 .....75 C1
Park Hall Road Trad Est
SE21 ....75 C1
Park Hill
Richmond TW10 ....54 B1
SW4 ....61 C2
Park Hill Ct SW17 .....72 B1
Park Hill Wlk 10
NW3 ....12 B3
Park Ho N4 ....5 A4
32 E9 ....17 B1
8 SE5 ....48 C2
Park La W1 ....117 B3
E15 ....27 C4
Park Lea Ct N16 ....7 A4
Park Lo NW2 ....9 A4
11 NW8 ....11 C1
10 E1 ....32 A1
Park Lorne NW8 ....90 B3
Park Mans NW8 ....80 A1
SW8 ....162 B4
SW6 ....164 B3

Park Mans *continued*
SW11 ....168 C3
W6 ....38 B3
Park Mews SW10 ....23 A3
Park Par NW10 ....21 A3
W3 ....36 C3
Park Pl SW1 ....118 C2
E14 ....33 C1
W3 ....36 C2
Park Place Dr W3 ......36 C3
Park Place Villas
W2 ....101 A4
Park Rd NW1,NW8 ....90 B2
NW10 ....21 A4
W4 ....45 C4
Richmond TW10 ....54 B1
Park Rd E W3 ....37 B4
Park Rd N W3 ....37 A4
W4 ....37 C1
Park Row SE10 ....52 C4
Park Royal Bsns Ctr
NW10 ....20 B1
Park Royal Metro Ctr
NW10 ....20 A1
Park Royal Rd
NW10,W3 ....20 B1
Park Sheen 3
SW14 ....55 A3
Park Side NW2 ....9 A4
Park Sq E NW1 ....92 B1
Park Sq Mews NW1 ..92 A1
Park Sq W NW1 ....92 A1
Park St W1 ....117 B3
SE1 ....123 A2
Park St James NW8 .80 C3
Park Steps 2 W2 ......116 B4
Park The NW11 ....2 A3
Park Twrs W1 ....118 A1
Park View N5 ....9 B4
SW6 ....15 B4
W3 ....28 B3
Park View Ct SW18 ...58 C1
Park View Ho SE24 ..63 A1
Park View Rd NW10 ..8 B4
Park Village E NW1 ..82 B1
Park Village W
NW1 ....82 A2
Park Vista SE10 ....52 C4
Park Walk Prim Sch
SW10 ....157 B3
Park Way W3 ....36 C2
Park West W2 ....102 B1
Park West Pl W1,
W2 ....102 B2
Park Wlk SW10 ....157 B4
Park Wood Ho SE8 ...51 B4
Parke Rd SW13 ....46 C2
Parker Ct N1 ....87 A4
SW4 ....172 A3
Parker Mews WC2 ...106 B2
Parker St WC2 ....106 B2
Parker's Row SE1 ....139 A3
Parkers Row SE16 ...139 B3
Parkfield Ave SW14 ..56 A3
Parkfield Ind Est
SW11 ....169 C2
Parkfield Rd NW10 ....9 A1
SE14 ....51 B2
Parkfield St N1 ....85 C2
Parkfields SW15 ....57 B3
Parkgate Gdns
SW14 ....55 C2
Parkgate Mews N6 ....4 B4
Parkgate Rd SW11 ..158 B1

Parkham St SW11 ....168 A3
Parkhill Rd NW3 ....12 B3
Parkholme Rd E8 ......16 C2
Parkhouse St SE5 ....48 C3
Parkhurst Ct N7 ....14 A4
Parkhurst Rd N7 ....14 A4
Parkinson Ct N1 ....97 C3
Parkinson Ho 6 E9 ..17 B1
Parkland Ct W14 .....126 A4
Parkland Gdns 12
SW19 ....69 C3
Parkland Wlk N4,N8 ..5 A4
Parkmead SW15 ....57 A1
SE22 ....65 A2
Parklands Cl SW14 ...55 B2
Parklands Rd SW16 ..73 B1
Parkmead SW15 ....57 A1
Parkshot TW9 ....54 A3
Parkside W3 ....29 A1
SE3 ....53 B3
SW19 ....69 C1
Parkside Cres N7 ....5 C1
Parkside Ct SW11 ...169 B3
Parkside Est E9 ....25 C4
Parkside St SW11 ...169 B3
Parkstead Rd SW15 .57 A2
Parkside Rd 3
SE15 ....49 C1
Parkthorne Rd
SW12 ....73 C4
Parkview Ct SW6 ....164 B1
Parkville Rd SW6 ....154 C1
Parkway NW1 ....82 A3
Parkwood Prim Sch
N4 ....6 A3
Parliament Ct NW3 ..12 A4
Parliament Hill
Mans NW5 ....12 C4
Parliament Hill
NW3 ....12 A4
Parliament Hill Sch
NW5 ....12 C4
Parliament Mews
SW14 ....45 B1
Parliament Sq
SW1 ....134 A3
Parliament St
SW1 ....134 A4
Parma Cres SW11 ....60 B3
Parminter Ind Est 28
E2 ....25 A3
Parmiter St E2 ....25 A3
Parmoor Ct EC1 ....96 C2
Parnell Cl W12 ....39 A3
Parnell Rd E3 ....26 B4
Parnham St E14 ....33 A3
Parolles Rd N19 ....4 B3
Parr Ct N1 ....87 B2
Parr St N1 ....87 B2
Parrington Ho 1
SW4 ....61 C1
Parry Ho 22 E1 ....32 A1
Parry Rd W10 ....23 A2
Parry St SW8 ....162 B4
Parsifal Coll NW3 .....10 C4
Parsifal Ho NW3 ....10 C4
Parsifal Rd NW6 ....10 C3
Parson Ct SE13 ....67 A4
Parsonage St E14 .....42 B2
Parsons Gn SW6 .....165 B3
Parsons Green La
SW6 ....165 B4
Parsons Green Sta
SW6 ....165 B3
Parsons Ho W2 ....89 B1
21 SW12 ....74 A4
Parsons Lo NW6 ....11 A1

Parthenia Rd SW6 ...165 C3
Partington Cl N19 ......4 C3
Partridge Cl E16 ....72 A2
Partridge Ho 8 E3 ....26 B3
Pascal St SW8 ....161 C2
Pascall Ho SE17 ....48 B4
Pascoe Rd SE13 ....67 C2
Pasley Cl SE17 ....150 C1
Passfield Dr E14 ....34 A4
Passfields W14 ....140 C1
Passing Alley EC1 .....96 B1
Passmore St SW1 ...145 B2
Pastor St SE1,SE11 .150 B4
Pat Shaw Ho 2 E1 ....25 C1
Patcham Terr SW8 ..170 B4
Patchway Ct 2
SE15 ....49 A4
Patent Ho E14 ....34 A4
Pater St W8 ....127 B1
Paternoster Row
EC2,EC4 ....108 C3
Paternoster Sq
EC4 ....108 B2
Paterson Ct EC1 ....97 B3
Patience Rd SW11 ..168 A1
Patio Cl SW4 ....61 C1
Patmore Ho 9 N16 ..16 A3
Patmore St SW8 .....171 A4
Paton Cl E3 ....26 C2
Paton Ho SW9 ....172 C2
Paton St EC1 ....96 C3
Patrick Coman Ho
EC1 ....96 A3
Patrick Connolly Gdns
11 E3 ....27 A2
Patriot Sq E2 ....25 A3
Patrol Pl SE6 ....67 A1
Patshull Pl NW5 ....13 B2
Patshull Rd NW5 ......13 B2
Patten Ho N4 ....6 B3
Patten Rd SW18 ....72 A4
Patterdale NW1 ....92 B3
Patterdale Rd SE15 ..50 B3
Pattina Wlk SE16 ......33 A1
Pattison Point 1
E16 ....35 C4
Pattison Ho SE1 ......137 A4
11 E1 ....32 C3
Pattison Rd NW2 ....1 C1
Paul Ho 10 W10 ....23 A1
Paul Julius Cl E14 ....34 C2
Paul Robeson Ho 3
SE7 ....43 C2
Paul St N1 ....97 C4
Paulet Rd SE5 ....48 A2
Pauline Ho 1 E1 ....111 C4
Paultons Ho SW3 ....157 C4
Paultons Sq SW3 ....157 C4
Paultons St SW3 .....157 C3
Pauntley Ho 6 N19 ....4 B3
Pauntley St 4 N19 .....4 B3
Pavan Ct 2 E2 ....25 B2
Paveley Dr SW11 ....158 A1
Paveley Ho N1 ....84 C1
Paveley St NW8 ....90 B2
Pavement The W5 .....36 A3
SW4 ....61 B3
Pavilion Ct 5 NW3 ...11 B4
NW6 ....11 C1
NW3 ....11 C3
Pavilion Mans 10
SW9 ....62 B3
Pavilion Rd SW1 .....131 A1
Pavilion St SW1 ......131 A1

Pavilion Terr W12 . . . . . .30 B3
Paxton Cl TW9 . . . . .44 B1
Paxton Ho SE17 . . . . . . .151 A2
Paxton Terr SW1 . . . . . .160 B4
Payens Wlk W6 . . . . .154 A3
Paymal Ho 28 E1 . . . . . . .32 B4
Payne Ho E3 . . . . .85 A3
Payne Rd E3 . . . . .27 A3
Payne St SE8 . . . . .51 B4
Paynesfield Ave
SW14 . . . . .55 C4
Peabody Ave SW1 . . . . .146 B1
Peabody Bldgs
SE17 . . . . .151 B3
6 SE5 . . . . .48 C2
Peabody Cl SW1 . . . . . . .160 B4
Peabody Ct EC1 . . . . .97 A1
8 SE5 . . . . .48 C2
Peabody Est EC1 . . . . . . .95 C1
EC1 . . . . .97 A1
WC2 . . . . .106 C1
SE1 . . . . .121 C1
SE1 . . . . .122 C1
E1 . . . . .125 B4
SW1 . . . . .147 A4
SW6 . . . . .155 A4
11 E2 . . . . .25 A3
W10 . . . . .30 B4
4 E1 . . . . .32 C2
17 W6 . . . . .39 B1
SE24 . . . . .63 A3
Peabody Hill SE21 . . . . . .75 B3
Peabody Sq SE1 . . . . . . .136 A3
Peabody Twr EC1 . . . . . . .97 A1
Peabody Yd N1 . . . . .86 C4
Peach Rd W10 . . . . .23 A2
Peachum Rd SE3 . . . . . . .53 B4
Peacock St SE17 . . . . . .150 B3
Peacock Yd SE17 . . . . . .150 B3
Peak Ho N4 . . . . .6 B3
Pear Cl SE14 . . . . .51 A3
Pear Ct 20 SE15 . . . . .49 B3
Pear Pl SE1 . . . . .135 B4
Pear Tree Cl 22 E2 . . . . . .24 B4
Pear Tree Ct EC1 . . . . . . .95 C1
SW15 . . . . .57 A3
Pear Tree Ho SE4 . . . . . . .66 B3
Pearce Ho N19 . . . . .4 B1
7 SW2 . . . . .74 A4
Peardon St SW8 . . . . . . .170 B1
Pearfield Ho 1 N5 . . . . . .15 B3
Pearl St E1 . . . . .32 A1
Pearman St SE1 . . . . . . .135 C3
Pearscroft Ct SW6 . . . . .166 B3
Pearscroft Rd SW6 . . . . .166 B3
Pearson Ho SE15 . . . . . . .47 B1
Pearson St E2 . . . . .24 B3
Pearson's Ave SE8,
SE14 . . . . .52 A3
Peartree Ave SW17 . . . . .71 B1
Peartree La E1 . . . . .32 B2
Peartree St EC1 . . . . .96 C2
Peary Pl E2 . . . . .25 C2
Peckarmans Wood
SE21,SE26 . . . . .76 C1
Peckett Sq 3 N5 . . . . . . .15 A4
Peckford Pl SW9 . . . . . . .173 C1
Peckham Gr SE15 . . . . . .49 A3
Peckham High St
SE15 . . . . .49 C2
Peckham Hill St
SE15 . . . . .49 C3

Peckham Park Prim
Sch SE15 . . . . .49 C3
Peckham Park Rd
SE15 . . . . .49 C3
Peckham Rd SE5 . . . . . . .49 A2
Peckham Rye SE22 . . . . . .64 C3
SE15,SE22 . . . . .65 A3
Peckham Rye Jun & Inf
Sch SE15 . . . . .65 A4
Peckham Rye Sta
SE15 . . . . .49 C1
Peckwater St NW5 . . . . . .13 B3
Pedlars Wlk N7 . . . . .14 A3
Pedley St E1 . . . . .24 C1 99 B1
Pedro St E5 . . . . .17 C4
Pedworth Gdns 4
SE16 . . . . .40 B2
Peel Gr E2 . . . . .25 B3
Peel Pass W8 . . . . .113 B1
Peel Prec NW6 . . . . .23 C3
Peel St W8 . . . . . .31 C1 113 B1
Peerless St EC1 . . . . .97 B3
Pegasus Ct NW10 . . . . . .22 A2
Brentford 1 . . . . .36 B1
Pegasus Ho 9 E1 . . . . . . .25 C1
Pegasus Pl SE11 . . . . . . .163 B4
Pegwell Ho 111 E5 . . . . . . .17 A3
Pekin Cl 113 E14 . . . . .33 C3
Pekoe SE1 . . . . .125 A1
Peldon Ct TW10 . . . . .54 B2
Pelham Cl SE5 . . . . .64 A4
Pelham Cres SW7 . . . . . .144 A3
Pelham Ct SW3 . . . . .144 A3
Pelham Ho W14 . . . . . . .140 C3
Pelham Pl SW7 . . . . .144 A3
Pelham St SW7 . . . . .143 C4
Pelican Ho 7 SE8 . . . . . . .41 B2
Pelican Wlk SW9 . . . . . . .63 A3
Pelier St SE17 . . . . .48 B4
Pella Ho SE11 . . . . .149 A2
Pellant Rd SW6 . . . . .154 B2
Pellatt Rd SE22 . . . . .64 B2
Pellerin Rd N16 . . . . .16 A3
Pellew Ho 3 E1 . . . . .25 A1
Pelling St E14 . . . . .33 C3
Pelter St E2 . . . . .98 C4
Pelton Rd SE10 . . . . .43 A1
Pember Rd NW10 . . . . . . .22 C2
Pemberton Ct 18
E1 . . . . .25 C2
Pemberton Gdns N19 . . . .4 B1
Pemberton Pl 2 E8 . . . . .17 A1
Pemberton Row
EC4 . . . . .107 C2
Pemberton Terr N19 . . . . .4 B1
Pembridge Cres
W11 . . . . .31 C2 113 B4
Pembridge Gdns
W2 . . . . .31 C2 113 C3
Pembridge Mews
W11 . . . . .31 C2 113 C4
Pembridge Pl
W11 . . . . .31 C2 113 C4
1 SW15 . . . . .58 C2
Pembridge Rd
W11 . . . . .113 C3
Pembridge Sq W2 . . . . .113 C3
Pembridge Villas
W11 . . . . .31 C2 113 C4
Pembroke Bldgs
NW10 . . . . .21 C2
Pembroke Cl SW1 . . . . . .131 C3
Pembroke Gdns
W8 . . . . .141 A4

Pembroke Gdns Cl
W8 . . . . .127 B1
SE16 . . . . .33 A1
Pembroke Ho W3 . . . . . . .37 B4
SW1 . . . . .56 C2
SW2 . . . . .100 B1
Pembroke Mews
W8 . . . . .127 B1
Pembroke Pl W8 . . . . . .127 B1
Pembroke Rd W8 . . . . . .141 B4
Pembroke Sq W8 . . . . . .127 B1
Pembroke St N1 . . . . .84 B4
Pembroke Studios
W8 . . . . .127 A1
Pembroke Terr
NW8 . . . . .79 B3
Pembroke Villas
W8 . . . . .141 B4
Pembroke Wlk W8 . . . . .141 B4
Pembrook Lo 2
SW16 . . . . .74 B1
Pembury Cl E5 . . . . .17 A3
Pembury Ho SE5 . . . . . . .49 A1
Pembury Pl 15 E5,
E8 . . . . .17 A3
Pembury Rd E5 . . . . .17 A3
Pemell Cl 27 E1 . . . . .25 B1
Pemell Ho 20 E1 . . . . . . .25 B1
Penally Pl N1 . . . . .87 C4
Penang St E1 . . . . .32 A1
Penarth St SE15 . . . . .50 B4
Pencombe Mews
W11 . . . . .113 A4
Pencraig Way SE15 . . . . .50 A4
Penda's Mead E9 . . . . . . .18 A4
Pendennis Ho 15
SE8 . . . . .41 A2
Penderyn Way N7 . . . . . .13 C4
Pendle Ho 15 SE26 . . . . . .76 C1
Pendley Ho 18 E2 . . . . . . .24 C4
Pendrell Ho WC2 . . . . . .105 C1
Pendrell Rd SE4 . . . . .51 A1
Penelope Ho SW9 . . . . .173 B3
Penfield Lo 9 W9 . . . . . .31 C4
Penfields Ho N7 . . . . .14 A2
Penfold Ct NW8 . . . . .89 C1
Penfold Pl NW1 . . . . .102 A4
Penfold St NW8 . . . . .89 C1
Penford St SE5 . . . . .48 A1
Penge Ho SW11 . . . . . . .167 C1
Penhurst Mans
SW6 . . . . .164 C4
Peninsula Ct E14 . . . . . . .42 A3
Peninsular Park Rd
SE7 . . . . .43 C2
Penmayne Rd
SE13 . . . . .149 C2
Penn Almshouse 1
SE10 . . . . .52 B2
Penn Ho NW8 . . . . .90 A1
Penn Rd N7 . . . . .14 A4
Penn St N1 . . . . .87 C3
Pennack Rd SE15 . . . . . . .49 B4
Pennant Mews
W8 . . . . .142 A4
Pennard Mans 5
W12 . . . . .39 B4
Pennard Rd W12 . . . . . . .39 B4
Penner Cl SW19 . . . . .70 A2
Pennethorne Cl E9 . . . . . .25 B4
Pennethorne Ho
SW11 . . . . .59 C4
Pennethorne Rd
SE15 . . . . .50 A3
Pennine La NW2 . . . . .1 A2
Pennine Mans NW2 . . . . . .1 A2
Pennine Par NW2 . . . . .1 A2

Pennington Ct E1 . . . . . .125 C3
SE16 . . . . .33 A1
Pennington St E1 . . . . . . .32 A2
Penny Ct SW10 . . . . .157 A4
Penny Mews SW12 . . . . .73 A4
Penny Rd NW10 . . . . .20 A2
Pennyfields E14 . . . . .33 C2
Pennyford Ct NW8 . . . . . .89 B2
Pennymore Wk W9 . . . . .23 B1
Penpoll Rd E8 . . . . .17 A2
Penrhyn Cres SW14 . . . . .55 B3
Penrith Cl SW15 . . . . .58 A2
Penrith Ho SE27 . . . . .75 A2
Penrose Gr SE17 . . . . . . .150 C1
Penrose Ho SE17 . . . . . .150 C1
Penrose St SE17 . . . . . . .150 C1
Penry St SE1 . . . . .152 B3
Penryn Ho SE11 . . . . . . .150 A2
Penryn St NW1 . . . . .83 B2
Pensbury Pl SW8 . . . . . .171 A2
Pensbury St SW8 . . . . . .171 A2
Pensford Ave TW9 . . . . . .44 C1
Penshurst 2 NW5 . . . . . .12 C2
Penshurst Ho 1
SE15 . . . . .50 B4
Penshurst Rd E9 . . . . .17 C1
Pentland Cl NW11 . . . . .1 A2
Pentland Ho 4 N16 . . . . . .7 B3
☆ W5 . . . . .12 C2
Pentland St SW18 . . . . . .59 B1
Pentlow St SW15 . . . . . . .57 B4
Pentney Rd SW12 . . . . . .73 B3
Penton Gr N1 . . . . .85 B1
Penton Ho N1 . . . . .85 B1
Penton Pl SE17 . . . . .150 B2
Penton Rise WC1 . . . . . . .95 A4
Penton St N1 . . . . .85 B1
Pentonville Rd N1 . . . . . . .85 A1
Pentridge St SE15 . . . . . .49 B3
Penwith Rd SW18 . . . . . .71 A2
Penwood Ho 4
SW15 . . . . .56 B1
Penywern Rd SW5 . . . . .141 C2
Penzance Ho SE11 . . . . .149 C2
Penzance Pl
W11 . . . . .31 A1 112 B2
Penzance St
W11 . . . . .31 A1 112 A2
Peony Gdns W12 . . . . . . .29 C2
Peperfield WC1 . . . . .94 C3
Pepler Ho 15 W10 . . . . . . .23 A1
Peploe Rd NW6 . . . . .22 C3
Pepper St 1 SE1 . . . . . . .136 C4
E14 . . . . .42 A3
Peppermead Sq
SE13 . . . . .66 C2
Peppie Cl N16 . . . . .7 A2
Pepsi Trocadero
W1 . . . . .119 C3
Pepys Cres 2 E16 . . . . . .35 C1
Pepys Ho 14 E2 . . . . .25 B2
Pepys Rd SW4 . . . . .61 C2
Pepys St EC3 . . . . .124 B4
Perceval Ave NW3 . . . . . .12 A3
Perch St E8 . . . . .16 B4
Percival Rd SW14 . . . . . . .55 B3
Percival St EC1 . . . . .96 B3
Percy Cir WC1 . . . . .95 A4
Percy Mews W1 . . . . . . .105 B3
Percy Pass W1 . . . . .105 B3
Percy Rd E16 . . . . .35 A4
W12 . . . . .38 C4
Percy St W1 . . . . .105 B3
Peregrine Ho 7 SE8 . . . . .51 C4
EC1 . . . . .96 B4

Peregrine Ho continued
6 SW11 . . . . .60 A4
Perham Rd W14 . . . . . . .140 B1
Perifield SE21 . . . . .75 B3
Perkins Ho 6 E14 . . . . . . .33 B4
Perkins Rents
SW1 . . . . .133 B1
Perkins Sq SE1 . . . . .123 A2
Perks Cl SE3 . . . . .53 A1
Perley Ho 10 E3 . . . . .33 B4
Perotti Ho SW6 . . . . .59 A4
Perran Rd SE24,SW2 . . . .75 A3
Perran Wlk STW 36 A1
Perren St NW5 . . . . .13 A2
Perrers Rd W6 . . . . .39 A2
Perrin's Ct 11 NW3 . . . . .11 B4
Perrin's La NW3 . . . . .11 B4
Perrin's Wlk NW3 . . . . . . .11 B4
Perring Est E3 . . . . .33 C4
Perronet Ho SE1 . . . . . . .136 B1
Perry Ave W3 . . . . .28 C3
Perry Ho 24 SW2 . . . . . . .74 A4
Perry's Pl W1 . . . . .105 B2
Perrymead St SW6 . . . . .166 A3
Perryn Ho W3 . . . . .29 A2
Perryn Rd W3 . . . . .28 C2
4 SE16 . . . . .40 A3
Perrywood Ho 17
E5 . . . . .17 A3
Perseverance Works
2 . . . . .98 B4
Perseverance Pl
SW9 . . . . .163 C1
Perth Ct 5 SE5 . . . . .63 C3
Perth Ho N1 . . . . .14 B1
Perth Rd N4 . . . . .5 C3
Peter Ave NW10 . . . . .9 A1
Peter Best Ho 6 E1 . . . . .32 A3
Peter Butler Ho
SE1 . . . . .139 B3
Peter Hills Ho
SE16 . . . . .153 B4
Peter Hills with St
Mary's & St Paul's CE
Prim Sch SE16 . . . . .32 C1
Peter Ho SW8 . . . . .162 A2
Peter St W1 . . . . .119 B4
Peter's Ct SW4 . . . . .62 A1
Peter's La EC1 . . . . .108 B4
Peterboat Cl SE10 . . . . . .43 A2
Peterborough Ct
EC4 . . . . .107 C1
Peterborough Mews
SW6 . . . . .165 B2
Peterborough Prim Sch
SW6 . . . . .58 C4
Peterborough Villas
SW6 . . . . .166 A4
Peterchurch Ho
SE15 . . . . .50 A4
Petergate SW11 . . . . .59 B3
Peterley Bsns Ctr 2
E2 . . . . .25 A3
Peters Ct W2 . . . . .100 B2
Petersfield Rd W3 . . . . . .37 B4
Petersfield Rise
SW15 . . . . .69 A3
Petersham Ho
SW7 . . . . .143 B4
Petersham La
SW7 . . . . .128 C2
Petersham Mews
SW7 . . . . .129 A1
Petersham Pl SW7 . . . . .129 A2

Petersham Rd TW10 ...54 A1
Peterstow Cl SW11 ...70 A2
Petherton Cl N10 ...22 C4
Petherton Ho N4 ...6 B3
Petherton Rd N5 ...15 B3
Petiver Cl 20 E9 ...17 B1
Petley Rd W6 ...47 C3
Peto Pl NW1 ...92 B2
Peto St N E16 ...35 B1
Petrel Ct 2 SE21 ...75 C2
Petrie Cl NW2 ...10 A2
Petros Gdns 1 NW3 ...11 B2
Petticoat Lane Mkt★ EC2 ...110 C3
Petticoat Sq E1 ...110 C2
Petticoat Twr E1 ...110 C2
Pettiward Cl SW15 ...57 B3
Petty France SW1 ...133 B2
Petworth Ho 16 SE22 ...64 A4
Petworth St SW11 ...168 B4
Petyt Pl SW3 ...158 A3
Petyward SW3 ...144 B3
Pevensey Ct 4 W3 ...37 A4
SW16 ...74 C1
Peveril Ho SE1 ...137 C1
Pewsham Ho N4 ...6 B3
Peyton Pl SE10 ...52 B3
Pharamond NW2 ...9 C2
Phelp St SE17 ...48 C4
Phelps Ho SW15 ...57 C4
Phene St SW3 ...158 B4
Phil Brown Pl 3 SW8 ...61 A4
Philadelphia Ct SW10 ...157 A1
Philbeach Gdns SW5 ...141 B2
Philchurch Pl E1 ...111 C1
Philia Ho 2 NW1 ...13 B1
Philip Ct W2 ...101 B4
Philip Ho 8 NW6 ...78 A3
Philip Rd SE15 ...64 C4
Philip Turner Est E9 ...17 B1
Philip Wlk SE15 ...65 A4
Phillimore Ct W8 ...127 C3
Phillimore Gardens Cl W8 ...127 B2
Phillimore Gdns W8 ...127 B3
NW10 ...22 B4
Phillimore Pl W8 ...127 B3
Phillimore Terr W8 ...127 C2
Phillimore Wlk W8 ...127 C2
Phillip Ho E1 ...111 A3
Phillipp St N1 ...24 A4
Philpot La EC3 ...124 A4
Philpot Sq SW6 ...59 A4
Philpot St E1 ...32 A3
Phipp St EC2 ...24 A1 98 A2
Phipps Ho 16 W12 ...30 A2
Phoebeth Rd SE4 ...66 C2
Phoenix Cl 18 E8 ...24 B4
Phoenix Ct 1 Brentford TW8 ...36 A1
4 E14 ...41 C2
2 SE14 ...51 A4
Phoenix High Sch W12 ...29 C2

Phoenix Lodge Mans 1 ...39 B2
Phoenix Pl WC1 ...95 A1
Phoenix Rd NW1 ...93 B4
Phoenix Sch 3 ...26 B2
Phoenix St WC2 ...105 C1
Phoenix Wharf Rd SE1 ...139 A3
Physic Pl SW3 ...158 C4
Piccadilly W1 ...118 C2
Piccadilly Arc SW1 ...118 C2
Piccadilly Cir W1 ...119 B3
Piccadilly Circus Sta SW1 ...119 B3
Piccadilly Pl W1 ...119 A3
Pickard St EC1 ...96 B4
Pickering Ho N4 ...6 C4
W2 ...100 B1
Pickering Pl SW1 ...119 A1
Pickering St N1 ...86 B4
Pickets St SW12 ...73 A4
Pickfords Wharf N1 ...86 C1
Pickwick Ho SE16 ...139 B3
Pickwick St SE1 ...136 C3
Pickworth Cl SW8 ...162 B1
Picton Ho 1 SW4 ...74 A4
Picton Pl W1 ...103 C1
Picton St SE5 ...48 C3
Pied Bull Ct WC1 ...106 B3
Pied Bull Yd WC1 ...106 B3
Pier Ho SW3 ...158 B3
Pier St E14 ...42 B2
Pier Terr SW18 ...59 B3
Pierhead Wharf 27 E1 ...32 A1
Piermont Rd SE22 ...65 A2
Pierrepoint Rd W3 ...28 A2
Piggott Ho 2 E2 ...25 C3
Pigott St E14 ...33 C3
Pilgrim Ho SE1 ...137 C1
Pilgrim St EC4 ...108 A1
Pilgrim's La NW3 ...11 C4
Pilgrimage St SE1 ...137 B3
Pilgrims Cloisters SE5 ...49 A3
Pilgrims Ct 3 SE3 ...53 C2
Pilgrims Mews 1 E14 ...34 C2
Pilgrims Way N19 ...4 C3
Pilgrims Way Prim Sch SE15 ...50 B4
Pilkington Rd 4 SE15 ...50 A1
Pilot Ind Ctr NW10 ...21 A1
Pilsden Cl SW19 ...69 C3
Pilton Pl SE17 ...151 A2
Pimlico Gdns SW1 ...145 C1
Pimlico Sch SW1 ...147 A1
Pimlico Sta SW1 ...147 B2
Pimlico Wlk N1 ...98 A4
Pinchin St E1 ...125 C4
Pincombe Ho SE17 ...151 B2
Pincott St E14 ...34 A3
Pindar St EC2 ...110 A4
Pindock Mews W9 ...88 B1
Pine Apple Ct SW1 ...132 C2
Pine Ave E15 ...19 C3
Pine Cl 1 N19 ...4 B2
Pine Ct E8 ...
Pine Gr N4,N19 ...5 B2
Pine Ho 15 SE16 ...40 B4
Pine Lo SW15 ...58 A1
Pine Rd NW2 ...9 C4

Pine St EC1 ...95 B2
Pine Tree Ho SE14 ...50 C3
Pinedene 2 SE15 ...50 A2
Pinefield Cl E14 ...33 C2
Pinehurst Ct 3 W11 ...31 B3
Pinelands 1 E2 ...25 B3
Pines Ct 14 SW19 ...69 C3
Pinewood Ct SW4 ...61 C1
Pinkham Mans W4 ...36 C1
Pinnacle Ho EC3 ...110 A1
Pinner Ho 13 SE5 ...48 B1
Pintail Ct 8 SE8 ...51 B4
Pinter Ho SW9 ...172 B1
Pioneer Cl W12 ...30 A3
Pioneer St SE15 ...49 C2
Pioneer Way W12 ...30 B3
Piper Cl N7 ...14 B2
Pippins Ct SW8 ...162 C4
Pirbright Rd SW18 ...70 C3
Pitcairn Ho 9 E9 ...17 B1
Pitfield Ho N5 ...15 B3
Pitfield St N1 ...98 A4
Pitman Ho 8 SE8 ...51 C2
Pitman St SE5 ...48 B3
Pitmaston Ho 2 SE13 ...52 B1
Pitsea Pl E1 ...32 C3
Pitsea St E1 ...32 C3
Pitt Ho 4 SW11 ...59 C3
Pitt St W8 ...127 C4
Pitt's Head Mews W1 ...117 C1
Pixley St E14 ...33 B3
Plane Tree Ho SE8 ...51 A4
Planetree Ct W6 ...39 C2
Plantain Pl SE1 ...137 B4
Plantation The SE3 ...53 C1
Platina St EC2 ...97 C2
Plato Pl SW6 ...165 A2
Plato Rd SW2 ...62 A3
Platt St NW1 ...83 B2
Platt's La NW3 ...1 C1
Plaxdale Ho SE17 ...152 A3
Playfair St W6 ...39 B1
Playfield Cres SE22 ...64 B2
Playford Rd N4 ...5 B2
Playhouse Yd EC4 ...108 A1
Pleasance Rd SW15 ...57 A2
Pleasance The SW15 ...57 A3
Pleasant Pl N1 ...15 A1
Pleasant Row NW1 ...82 B3
Plender Ct NW1 ...83 A3
Plender St NW1 ...83 A3
Pleshey Rd N7 ...13 C4
Plevna St E14 ...42 B3
Pleydell Ave W6 ...38 B2
Pleydell Ct EC4 ...107 C1
Pleydell St EC4 ...107 C1
Plimsoll Cl E14 ...34 A3
Plimsoll Rd N4 ...6 A2
Plough Ct EC3 ...123 C4
Plough Ho 24 SE17 ...48 A4
Plough Pl EC4 ...107 C2
Plough Rd SW11 ...59 C3
Plough St 1 E1 ...111 B2
Plough Terr SW11 ...59 C3
Plough Way SE16 ...41 A2
Plough Yd EC2 ...98 B1
Ploughmans Cl NW1 ...83 B4
Plover Ho 3 SW9 ...163 B2

Plover Way SE16 ...41 A3
Plowman Ho SW19 ...69 C2
Plumbers Row E1 ...111 C2
Plumbridge St 7 SE10 ...52 B2
Plume Ho SE10 ...52 A4
Plummer Ct SE13 ...67 A1
Plummer Rd SW4 ...73 C4
Plumtree Ct EC4 ...108 A2
Plymouth Rd E16 ...35 C4
Plymouth Wharf E14 ...42 C2
Plympton Ave NW6 ...10 B1
Plympton Pl NW1 ...90 A1
Plympton Rd NW6 ...10 B1
Plympton St NW8 ...90 A1
Pocklington Ct SW15 ...68 C3
Pocock St SE1 ...136 B4
Podmore Rd SW18 ...59 B3
Poet's Corner SW1 ...134 A2
Poet's Rd N5 ...15 C3
Point Cl SE10 ...52 B2
Point Hill SE10 ...52 B2
Point Pleasant SW18 ...58 C3
Pointer Sch The SE3 ...53 C3
Pointers Cl E14 ...42 A1
Poland St W1 ...105 A1
Polesworth Ho 16 W2 ...31 C4
Pollard Cl N7 ...14 B4
E16 ...35 C2
Pollard Ho N1 ...85 A1
Pollard Row E2 ...24 C2 99 C4
Pollard St E2 ...24 C2 99 C4
Pollen St W1 ...104 B1
Pollitt Dr NW8 ...89 C2
Pollock Ho W10 ...23 A1
Polperro Mans 3 NW6 ...10 C3
Polygon Rd NW1 ...83 B1
Polygon The NW8 ...79 C4
SW4 ...61 B3
Pomell Way E1 ...111 A2
Pomeroy Ct W11 ...31 A3
Pomeroy Ho 5 E2 ...25 C3
Pomeroy St SE14 ...50 B2
Pomfret Rd SE5 ...63 A4
Pomoja La N19 ...5 A2
Pomona Ho 10 SE8 ...41 A2
Pond Cl SE3 ...53 C1
Pond Cotts SE21 ...76 A3
Pond Ho SW3 ...144 A3
Pond Mead SE21 ...63 C1
Pond Pl SW3 ...144 A3
Pond Rd SE3 ...53 B1
Pond Sq N6 ...3 C3
Pond St NW3 ...12 A3
Ponder St 5 N7 ...14 B1
Pondfield Ho 4 N5 ...15 B3
Ponler St E1 ...32 A3
Ponsard Rd NW10 ...22 A2
Ponsford St E9 ...17 B2
Ponsonby Ho 13 E2 ...25 B3
Ponsonby Pl SW1 ...147 C2
Ponsonby Rd SW15 ...69 A4
Ponsonby Terr SW1 ...147 C2
Pont St Mews SW1 ...130 C1
Ponton Ho SW2 ...74 C3

Ponton Rd SW8 ...161 C3
Pontypool Pl SE1 ...136 A4
Pool Ho NW8 ...101 C4
Poole Ct N1 ...16 A1
Poole Ho SE11 ...135 A1
Poole Rd E9 ...17 C2
Poole St N1 ...87 B3
Pooles Bldgs EC1 ...95 B1
Pooles La SW10 ...156 C1
Pooles Park Prim Sch N4 ...5 B2
Pooles Pk N4 ...5 B2
Poolmans St SE16 ...40 C4
Poonah St E1 ...32 B3
Pope Ho 7 SE16 ...40 A2
3 SE5 ...48 C3
Pope John RC Prim Sch W12 ...30 A2
Pope St SE1 ...138 B3
Pope's Head Alley EC3 ...109 C1
Pope's La W5 ...36 A3
Pope's Rd SW9 ...62 C4
Popham Ct N16 ...7 A1
Popham Gdns TW9 ...55 A4
Popham Rd N1 ...86 C4
Popham St N1 ...86 B4
N1 ...86 B4
Poplar Bath St 10 E14 ...34 A2
Poplar Bsns Pk E14 ...34 B2
Poplar Cl E9 ...18 B3
Poplar Ct 4 SW16 ...74 B1
Poplar Gr W6 ...39 B3
Poplar High St E14 ...34 A2
Poplar Ho 16 SE16 ...40 C4
SE4 ...66 B3
Poplar Mews W12 ...30 B1
Poplar Pl W2 ...114 A4
SE24 ...63 B3
Poplar Sta E14 ...34 A2
Poplar Wlk SE24 ...63 B3
Poplars The NW5 ...13 B3
Poppins Ct EC4 ...108 A1
Porchester Ct W2 ...114 B4
Porchester Garden Mews W2 ...100 B1
Porchester Gate W2 ...114 B3
Porchester Gdns W2 ...114 B4
Porchester Mews W2 ...100 B2
Porchester Pl W2 ...102 B1
Porchester Rd W2 ...100 B2
Porchester Sq W2 ...100 B2
Porchester Terr W2 ...114 C4
Porchester Terrace N W2 ...100 B2
Porden Rd SW2 ...62 B3
Porlock Ho 5 SE26 ...76 C1
Porlock St SE1 ...137 C4
Port House The 6 E14 ...41 C1
Port Royal Pl 3 N16 ...16 A3
Portal Cl SE27 ...74 C1
Portbury Cl 16 SE15 ...49 C2
Portchester Cl SE5 ...63 C3
Portelet Ct 1 N1 ...24 A4
Portelet Rd E1 ...25 C2
Porten Hos W14 ...126 B1
Porten Rd W14 ...126 A1

Porter Sq N19 ...5 A3
Porter St W1 ...103 A4
...123 A2
Porteus Rd W2 ...101 A4
Portgate Cl W9 ...23 B1
Portia Way E13 ...26 B3
Porticos The SW3 ...157 B3
Portinscale Rd
SW15 ...58 B2
Portishead Ho 29
W2 ...31 C4
Portland Ave N16 ...7 B4
Portland Ct 7 N1 ...16 A1
1 SE14 ...51 A4
Portland Gr SW8 ...172 C4
Portland Ho 20 SW2 74 C3
Portland Hospl for
Women & Children The
...92 B1
Portland Mews
W1 ...105 A1
Portland Pl W1 ...104 B3
Portland Rd W11 ...112 A3
...31 A2
Portland Rise N4 ...6 B3
Portland Sq 4 E1 ...32 A1
Portland St SE17 ...151 B1
Portland Village
W6 ...39 B3
Portman Ave SW14 ...55 C4
Portman Cl W1 ...103 B2
Portman Gate NW1 ...90 B1
Portman Hts 3
NW3 ...1 C1
Portman Mews S
W1 ...103 B1
Portman Pl E2 ...25 B2
Portman Sq W1 ...103 B2
Portman St W1 ...103 B1
Portman Twrs W1 ...103 A2
Portnall Rd W9 ...23 B2
Portobello Ct Est
W11 ...31 B3
Portobello Mews
W11 ...113 B3
Portobello Rd
W11 ...31 A4 113 A4
Portobello Road Mkt*
W10 ...31 A4
Portpool La EC1 ...107 B4
Portree St E14 ...34 C3
Portsea Hall W2 ...102 B1
Portsea Ho 3
SW15 ...69 A3
Portsea Mews W2 ...102 B1
Portsea Pl W2 ...102 B1
Portslade Rd SW8 170 C2
Portsmouth Rd
SW15 ...69 B4
Portsmouth St
WC2 ...107 A1
Portsoken St E1,
EC3 ...124 C4
Portswood Pl 10
SW15 ...56 B1
Portugal St WC2 ...107 A1
Poseidon Ct 4 E14 .41 C2
Post Office Way
SW8 ...161 B2
Postern The EC2 ...109 A3
Potier St SE1 ...137 C1
Pott St E2 ...25 A2

Potterne Cl 5
SW19 ...69 C4
Potters Fields SE1 124 B1
Potters Lo E14 ...42 B1
Potters Rd SW6 ...166 C1
Pottery La
W11 ...31 A1 112 B2
Pottery Rd TW8 ...44 A4
Pottery St SE16 ...40 A4
Poullett Ho SW2 ...75 A3
Poulton Cl E8 ...17 A2
Poultry EC2 ...109 B1
Pound La NW10 ...8 C2
Pountney Rd SW11 .60 C4
Povey Ho SE17 ...152 A3
...62 C1
Powell's Wlk W4 ...46 B4
Power Ho 12 TW9 ...44 C2
Power Ho The W4 ...38 B2
Powergate Bsns Pk
NW10 ...20 B2
Powis Gdns NW11 ...1 B4
...31 B3
Powis Ho WC2 ...106 B2
Powis Mews W11 ...31 B3
Powis Pl WC1 ...94 B1
Powis Rd E3 ...27 A2
Powis Sq W11 ...31 B3
Powis Terr W11 ...31 B3
Powlett Ho NW1 ...13 A2
Powlett Pl NW1 ...13 A1
Pownall Rd E8 ...24 C4
Powrie Ho 7 SW11 167 C2
Poynder Ct 3 N7 ...14 A3
Poynders Ct 9 SW4 61 B1
Poynders Gdns
SW12 ...73 B4
Poynings Rd N19 ...4 B1
Poynter Ho NW8 ...89 B2
10 W11 ...30 C1
Poyntz Rd SW11 ...168 C1
Poyser St E2 ...25 A3
Praed Mews W2 ...101 C2
Praed St W2 ...101 C2
Prague Pl SW2 ...62 A2
Prah Rd N4 ...5 C2
Prairie St SW8 ...170 A1
Pratt Mews NW1 ...82 C3
Pratt St NW1 ...82 C4
Pratt Wlk SE1,SE11 149 A4
Prebend Gdns W4,
W6 ...38 B2
Prebend Mans 4
...38 B2
Prebend St N1 ...86 C4
Precinct The N1 ...86 C4
N5 ...15 A3
Preedy Ho N1 ...85 A2
Premier Park Rd
NW10 ...20 A3
Premier Pl E14 ...33 C2
Prendergast Ho 7
SW4 ...73 C4
Prendergast Sch
SE4 ...66 C3
Prescot St E1 ...125 A4
Prescott Ho 13
SE17 ...48 A4
Prescott Pl SW4 ...61 C3
Presentation Mews
SW2 ...74 B3
President Dr E1 ...32 A1
President Ho EC1 ...96 B3
President St EC1 ...96 C4

Prestage Way E14 ...34 B2
Prested Rd SW11 ...60 A3
Preston Cl SE1 ...152 A4
Preston Gdns NW10 8 A2
Preston Ho SE1 ...138 C2
SE1 ...152 A4
Preston Pl NW2 ...8 C2
Richmond TW10 ...54 A2
Preston's Rd E14 ...34 B1
Prestwich Terr SW4 .61 C2
Prestwood Ho 6
SE16 ...40 A3
Prestwood St N1 ...87 A1
Prian Ho E2 ...25 A3
Price Cl SW17 ...72 B1
Price Ho N1 ...86 C3
Price's St SE1 ...122 B2
Price's Yd N1 ...85 A3
Prichard Ct SW11 167 C3
N7 ...14 B3
Prideaux Ho WC1 ...95 A4
Prideaux Pl W3 ...28 C2
WC1 ...95 A4
Prideaux Rd SW9 ...62 A4
Priest's Ct EC2 ...108 C2
Priestley Cl N16 ...7 B4
Priestley Ho EC1 ...97 A2
2 NW5 ...13 A2
Priestman Point 23
E3 ...27 A2
Priests Bridge
SW14 ...56 A4
Prima Road SW9 ...163 B2
Primrose Cl E1 11
SW12 ...73 C4
Primrose Gdns
NW3 ...12 A2
Primrose Hill Ct
NW3 ...12 B1
Primrose Hill Prim Sch
NW3 ...12 B1
Primrose Hill Rd
NW1,NW3 ...80 C4
Primrose Hill Sta
NW3 ...12 C1
Primrose Hill Studios
NW1 ...81 B4
Primrose Ho 9
Richmond TW9 ...44 B2
1 SE15 ...49 C2
Primrose Mans
SW11 ...169 B4
Primrose Mews 9
NW1 ...12 B1
Primrose Sq E9 ...25 B4
Primrose St EC2 ...110 B4
Primula St W12 ...29 C3
Prince Albert Ct
NW8 ...80 C3
Prince Albert Rd
NW8 ...80 C3
NW1 ...90 C4
Prince Arthur Ct 19
NW3 ...11 B4
Prince Arthur Mews 20
NW3 ...11 B4
Prince Arthur Rd
NW3 ...11 B3
Prince Charles Rd
SE3 ...53 B2
Prince Consort Rd
SW7 ...129 C2
Prince Edward Mans
W2 ...113 C4
Prince Edward Rd
E9 ...18 B2

Prince George Rd
N16 ...16 A4
Prince of Orange La 8
SE10 ...52 B3
Prince of Wales Dr
SW11 ...169 B4
Prince of Wales Mans
SW11 ...169 C4
SW4 ...60 A1
Prince of Wales Pas
NW1 ...92 C3
Prince of Wales Rd
NW5 ...12 C2
SE3 ...53 B2
Prince of Wales Terr
W8 ...128 B3
W4 ...38 A1
Prince Regent Ct
SE16 ...33 A1
Prince Regent Mews
NW1 ...92 C3
Prince St SE8 ...51 B4
Prince's Ct SE16 ...41 A3
Prince's Gate
SW7 ...130 A3
Prince's Mews W6 ...39 A1
Prince's Mews
W2 ...114 A4
Prince's Rd SW14 ...55 C4
Prince's Sq W2 ...114 A4
Prince's St TW10,
TW9 ...54 A2
Prince's St EC2 ...109 B1
Princedale Rd
W11 ...31 A1 112 B2
Princelet St E1 ...111 A4
Princes Arc SW1 ...119 A2
Princes Ave W3 ...36 C3
Princes Cir WC2 ...106 A2
Princes Ct NW2 ...10 A3
NW3 ...11 C3
E1 ...32 A2
Princes Gate SW7 129 C3
Princes Gate Ct
SW7 ...129 C3
Princes Gate Mews
SW7 ...129 C2
Princes Gdns SW7 129 C2
Princes Ho W11 ...113 B3
Princes Pl
W11 ...31 A1 112 B2
Princes Rd
Richmond TW9 ...44 B2
Richmond TW10 ...54 A2
Princes Rise SE13 ...52 B1
Princes Riverside Rd 5
SE16 ...32 C1
Princes St W1 ...104 B1
Princes Way W3 ...36 C3
SW15,SW19 ...70 A4
Princes Yd W11 ...112 B1
Princess Alexandra
School of Nursing The
E1 ...32 A4
Princess Alice Ho
W10 ...22 B1
Princess Beatrice Ho
SW10 ...142 A1
Princess Christian Coll
WC1 ...106 B4
Princess Cres N4 ...6 A2
Princess Ct W1 ...102 C3
W2 ...114 B4
NW6 ...11 A1

Princess Frederica CE
Prim Sch NW10 ...22 B3
Princess Grace Hospl
The W1 ...91 B1
Princess Louise Hospl
W10 ...30 B4
Princess Mary Ho
SW1 ...147 C3
Princess May JMI Sch
N16 ...16 A4
Princess Mews
NW3 ...11 C2
Princess Rd NW1 ...81 C4
NW6 ...23 C3
Princess SE1 ...136 B1
Princethorpe Ho
W2 ...100 A4
Princeton Ct SW15 ...57 C4
Princeton Mans
WC1 ...106 C3
Princeton St WC1 ...106 C4
Print Village Ind Est
SE15 ...49 B1
Printer St EC4 ...107 C2
Printing House Yd 11
E2 ...98 B3
Printon Ho 12 E3 ...33 B4
Prior Bolton St N1 ...15 A2
Prior St SE10 ...52 B3
Prior Weston Prim Sch
EC1 ...97 A1
Prioress Ho 2 E3 ...27 A2
Prioress Rd SE27 ...75 A1
Prioress St SE1 ...137 C1
Priors Lo 4 TW10 ...54 A1
Priorty Ct SE15 ...49 B3
Priory Ave W4 ...38 A3
Priory Ct EC4 ...108 B1
SW8 ...171 C4
E9 ...17 B3
SW15 ...56 B3
Priory Gdns 6 W4 ...38 A2
SW13 ...56 B4
Priory Gn N1 ...84 C2
Priory Gr SW8 ...172 A3
Priory Ho EC1 ...96 A2
E1 ...110 C4
SW1 ...147 B2
Priory Hospl The
SW15 ...56 B3
Priory La SW15 ...56 B2
Priory Lo 7 W4 ...36 C1
Priory Mans SW10 143 A1
NW3 ...12 B2
Priory Park Rd NW6 23 B4
Priory Rd N8 ...5 A4
NW6 ...11 A1
W4 ...37 C3
Richmond TW9 ...44 C3
Priory St 18 E3 ...27 A2
Priory Terr NW6 ...78 A4
Priory The SE1 ...136 A3
Priory Wlk SW10 ...143 A1
Pritchard Ho 34 E2 ...24 C3
Pritchard's Rd E2 ...24 C4
Priter Rd SE16 ...139 C1
Priter Road Hostel
SE16 ...139 C1
Probert Rd SW2 ...62 C2
Probyn Ho SW1 ...147 C4
Probyn Rd SW2 ...75 A2
Procter Ho 15 SE5 ...48 C3
Procter St WC1 ...106 C3
Proctor Ho 1 ...153 B3

Prome Ho **3** N16 . . . . . .15 C4
Promenade Approach
Rd W4 . . . . .46 A2
Promenade The W4 . . . .46 A2
Prospect Cotts
SW18 . . . . .58 C3
Prospect Ho N1 . . . . . . .85 B1
SE1 . . . . .136 B1
1 E8 . . . . .16 B2
14 N10 . . . . .25 C3
Prospect Pl **4** NW2 . .1 B1
E1 . . . . .32 B2
2 W4 . . . . .37 C1
6 E8 . . . . .51 B4
Prospect Rd NW2 . . . . .1 C1
Prospect St SE16 . . . . .40 A4
Prospect Wharf E1 . . . .32 B2
Prospero Rd N19 . . . . . .4 C3
Prothero Rd SW6 . . . .154 C2
Prout Gr NW10 . . . . . . .8 B4
Provence St N1 . . . . . . .86 C2
Providence Ct W1 . . . .117 C4
Providence Ho E9 . . . . .25 C4
Providence Pl N1 . . . . .86 A3
Providence Row N1 . . .84 C1
Providence Sq SE1 . .139 B4
Providence Twr
SE16 . . . . .139 B4
Provost Ct NW3 . . . . . .12 B2
Provost Rd NW3 . . . . . .12 B1
Provost St N1 . . . . .97 B4
Prowse Pl NW1 . . . . . . .13 B1
Prudent Pas EC2 . . . .109 A3
Prusom St E1 . . . . .32 A1
Prusom's Island **8**
E1 . . . . .32 B1
Pryors The NW3 . . . . . .2 C1
Public Record Office
EC4,WC2 . . . . .107 B2
Richmond TW9 . . . . . .45 A3
Pudding La EC3 . . . . . .123 C4
Pudding Mill La
E15 . . . . .27 A4
Pudding Mill Lane Sta
E15 . . . . .27 A4
Puddle Dock EC4 . . . .122 B4
Pugin Ct N1 . . . . .14 C1
Pulborough Rd
SW18 . . . . .70 B4
Pulham Ho SW8 . . . . .162 C1
Pullman Ct SW2 . . . . . .74 B3
Pullman Gdns SW15 . .57 B1
Pulross Rd SW9 . . . . . .62 B4
Pulteney Cl **1** E3 . . . .26 B4
Pulteney Terr N1 . . . . . .85 A4
Pulton Ho SE4 . . . . .66 A3
Pulton Pl SW6 . . . . . . .155 B1
Puma Ct E1 . . . . .110 C4
Pump Ct EC4 . . . . .107 B1
Pump La SE14 . . . . .50 B3
Pumping Station Rd
W4 . . . . .46 A4
Punderson's Gdns
E2 . . . . .25 A2
Purbeck Ho SW8 . . . .162 C1
Purbeck Est SE1 . . . . .138 B3
Purbrook Ho **2**
SW15 . . . . .69 A3
Purbrook St SE1 . . . . .138 C2
Purcell Ho SW10 . . . . .157 B3
Purcell Mews NW10 . . .8 A1
Purcell St N1 . . . . .24 A3
Purchese St NW1 . . . . .83 C1
Purday Ho **4** W10 . . . .23 B2
Purdon Ho **10** SE15 . . .49 C2

Purdy St E3 . . . . .27 A1
Purley Ave NW2 . . . . . . .1 A2
Purley Pl N1 . . . . .15 A1
Purser Ho **2** SW2 . . . .62 C1
Pursers Cross Rd
SW6 . . . . .165 A4
Purves Rd NW10 . . . . . .22 B3
Pusey Ho **16** E14 . . . . .33 C3
Puteaux Ho **6** E2 . . . .25 C3
Putney Bridge App
SW6 . . . . .58 A4
Putney Bridge Rd
SW15 . . . . .58 A3
Putney Bridge Sta
SW6 . . . . .58 A3
Putney Comm SW15 . .57 B4
Putney Heath SW15 . .57 B1
Putney Heath La
SW15 . . . . .57 C1
Putney High Sch
SW15 . . . . .57 C2
Putney High St
SW15 . . . . .58 A3
Putney Hill SW15 . . . . .57 C2
Putney Hosp SW15 . . . .57 B4
Putney Park Ave
SW15 . . . . .56 C3
Putney Park La
SW15 . . . . .57 A2
Putney Pier SW15 . . . . .58 A4
Putney School of Art &
Design SW15 . . . . . . .58 A3
Putney Sta SW15 . . . . .58 A4
Pylon Road Est E16 . . .34 C4
Pym Ho SW9 . . . . .173 C1
Pymers Mead SE21 . . .75 B3
Pynfolds SE16 . . . . . . .40 A4
Pynnersmead SE24 . . .63 B2
Pyrford Ho **15** SW9 . .63 A3
Pyrland Rd N5 . . . . .15 C3
Richmond TW10 . . . . .54 B1
Pyrmont Gr SE27 . . . . .75 A1
Pyrmont Rd W4 . . . . . .44 C4
Pytchley Rd SE22 . . . . .64 A4

Q

Quadrangle Cl SE1 . . .152 A4
Quadrangle The
W2 . . . . .102 A2
SW6 . . . . .154 A1
SW10 . . . . .167 A4
W12 . . . . .30 B3
SE24 . . . . .63 B2
Quadrant Arc W1 . . . .119 A3
Quadrant Bsns Pk
NW6 . . . . .23 A4
Quadrant The
4 W10 . . . . .22 C2
Richmond TW9 . . . . . .54 A3
Quaker Ct EC1 . . . . . . .97 A2
Quaker St E1 . . .24 B1 98 C1
Quality Ct WC2 . . . . . .107 B2
Quantock Ho N16 . . . . .7 B3
Quarley Way **3**
SE15 . . . . .49 B3
Quarrendon St
SW6 . . . . .165 C1
Quarry Rd SW18 . . . . .59 B1
Quarterdeck The
E14 . . . . .41 C4
Quartermile La E10,
E15 . . . . .19 A4
Quayside Ct **3**
SE16 . . . . .32 C1
Quebec & Crown
Wharves E14 . . . . . . .33 B3

Quebec Mews W1 . . . .103 A1
Quebec Way SE16 . . . .41 A4
Quebeck Ind Est
SE16 . . . . .41 A3
Quedgeley Ct **3**
SE15 . . . . .49 B4
Queen Alexandra Mans
WC1 . . . . .94 A3
Queen Anne Mews
W1 . . . . .104 B3
Queen Anne Rd E9 . . .17 C2
Queen Anne St
W1 . . . . .104 A3
Queen Anne's Gate
SW1 . . . . .133 B3
Queen Anne's Gdns
W5 . . . . .36 A4
W4 . . . . .38 A3
Queen Anne's Gr
W5 . . . . .36 A4
W4 . . . . .38 A3
Queen Caroline St
W6 . . . . .39 B1
Queen Charlotte's
Maternity Hospl
W6 . . . . .38 C2
Queen Elizabeth Hall &
Purcell Room*
SE1 . . . . .121 A2
Queen Elizabeth
Hospital for Children
The E2 . . . . .24 C3
Queen Elizabeth II Con
Ctr SW1 . . . . .133 C3
Queen Elizabeth II Pier
SE10 . . . . .35 B1
Queen Elizabeth II Sch
W9 . . . . .23 B1
Queen Elizabeth St
SE1 . . . . .138 C4
Queen Elizabeth Wlk
SW13 . . . . .47 A2
Queen Elizabeth's Cl
N16 . . . . .6 C2
Queen Elizabeth's Coll
SE10 . . . . .52 B3
Queen Elizabeth's Wlk
N16 . . . . .6 C2
Queen Margaret Flats **22**
E2 . . . . .25 A2
Queen Margaret's Gr
N1 . . . . .16 A3
Queen Margarets Ct
N1 . . . . .16 A3
Queen Mary's Gdns
NW1 . . . . .91 B3
Queen Mary's Hospl
NW3 . . . . .1 C2
Queen Mary's Univ
Hospl SW15 . . . . .56 C1
Queen of Denmark Ct
SE16 . . . . .41 B3
Queen Sq WC1 . . . . . .106 B4
Queen Sq Pl WC1 . . . .106 B4
Queen St W1 . . . . .118 A2
EC4 . . . . .123 A4
Queen St Pl EC4 . . . . .123 A4
Queen Victoria Mon*
SW1 . . . . .132 C4
Queen Victoria St
EC4 . . . . .122 C4
Queen's CE Jun Mix Sch
The TW9 . . . . .44 C3
Queen's CE Jun Sch The
TW9 . . . . .44 C3
Queen's Cir SW11 . . .160 A1

Queen's Club Gdns
W14 . . . . .154 B4
Queen's Club The
W14 . . . . .140 B1
Queen's Coll W1 . . . .104 A3
3 Richmond TW10 . . .54 B1
Queen's Cres SW5 . . .12 C2
Queen's Head St N1 . . .86 B3
SW13 . . . . .56 C4
Queen's Ct W2 . . . . . .114 B3
Queen's Dr N4 . . . . .6 A2
Queen's Elm Sq
SW3 . . . . .143 C1
Queen's Gallery The*
SW1 . . . . .132 B3
Queen's Gate
SW7 . . . . .129 A3
Queen's Gate Gdns
SW7 . . . . .129 A1
Queen's Gate Mews
SW7 . . . . .129 A2
Queen's Gate Pl
SW7 . . . . .129 A2
Queen's Gate Pl Mews
SW7 . . . . .129 A1
Queen's Gate Terr
SW7 . . . . .129 A2
Queen's Head Yd
SE1 . . . . .123 B1
Queen's Head Yd
N1 . . . . .86 B3
Queen's House The
SE10 . . . . .52 C4
Queen's Mans
W6 . . . . .39 C2
Queen's Mews
W2 . . . . .114 A4
N10 . . . . .23 A1
Queen's Park Prim Sch
NW6 . . . . .23 B3
Queen's Park Sta
NW6 . . . . .23 B3
Queen's Quay
EC4 . . . . .123 A4
Queen's Rd
SE14,SE15 . . . . .50 B2
Richmond TW10 . . . . .54 B1
SW14 . . . . .55 C4
Queen's Ride SW13 . . .57 A4
Queen's Rise TW10 . . .54 B1
Queen's Road Sta
SE15 . . . . .50 B2
Queen's Row SE17 . . .48 C4
Queen's Wlk SW1 . . .118 C1
Queen's Yd W1 . . . . . . .93 A1
Queenhithe EC4 . . . . .123 A4
Queens Cres SW11 . . .54 B2
Queens Ct SW11 . . . .170 A4
4 E14 . . . . .33 C2
SE5 . . . . .49 A1
Queens Down Rd
E5 . . . . .17 A4
Queens Ho **1** SE17 . .48 C4
Queens Manor Prim Sch
SW6 . . . . .47 C3
Queens Mans NW6 . .11 A3
Queens Par NW2 . . . . . .9 B2
Queens Park Com Sch
NW6 . . . . .9 C2
Queens Park Ct **5**
W10 . . . . .22 C2
Queens Terr NW8 . . . . .79 B2
Queens Yd E9 . . . . .18 C2
Queensberry Mews W
SW7 . . . . .143 B4

Queensberry Pl
SW7 . . . . .143 B4
Queensberry Way
SW7 . . . . .143 B4
Queensborough Mews
W2 . . . . .114 C4
Queensborough Pas
W2 . . . . .114 C4
Queensborough Terr
W2 . . . . .114 B4
Queensbridge Ct **1**
E2 . . . . .24 B3
Queensbridge Inf Sch
E8 . . . . .16 B1
Queensbridge Rd
E8 . . . . .16 B1
E2,E8 . . . . .24 B4
Queensbury St N1 . . . .15 B1
Queensdale Cres
W11 . . . . .30 C1
Queensdale Pl
W11 . . . . .112 A1
Queensdale Rd
W11 . . . . .31 A1 112 A1
Queensdale Wlk
W11 . . . . .112 A1
Queensgate Gdns
SW15 . . . . .57 A3
Queensgate Ho **10**
NW6 . . . . .10 C1
Queensland Pl N7 . . . .14 C4
Queensland Rd N7 . . .14 C4
Queensmead NW8 . . . .79 C4
Queensmere
(Southlands Coll)
SW19 . . . . .69 C2
Queensmere Cl
SW19 . . . . .69 C2
Queensmere Ct
SW13 . . . . .46 C4
Queensmere Rd
SW19 . . . . .69 C2
Queensmill Rd SW6 . .47 C3
Queensmill Sch
SW6 . . . . .166 B1
Queenstown Rd
SW8 . . . . .160 A2
Queenstown Road Sta
SW8 . . . . .170 B4
Queensville Rd
SW12,SW4 . . . . .73 C4
Queensway W2 . . . . .100 B2
W2 . . . . .114 B3
Queenswood Ct **2**
SW4 . . . . .62 A2
Quelch Ho **2** N19 . . .13 C3
Quemerford Rd N7 . . .14 B3
Quendon Ho W10 . . . .22 B1
Quenington Ct **5**
SE15 . . . . .49 B4
Quennel Ho **7**
SW12 . . . . .73 B4
Quentington Mans
SW6 . . . . .166 C4
Querrin St SW6 . . . . .166 C1
Quested Ct **27** E8 . . . .17 A3
Quex Mews NW6 . . . . .23 C4
Quex Rd NW6 . . . . .23 C4
Quick Rd W4 . . . . .38 A1
Quick St N1 . . . . .86 B1
Quicks Rd SW19 . . . . .79 B4
Quickswood NW3 . . . .12 A1

Quill La SW15 ....57 C3
Quill St N4 ....5 C1
Quilp St SE1 ....136 C4
Quilter Ho 11 W9 .....89 C2
Quilter St E2 ...24 C2 99 B4
Quilting Ct 22 SE16 .40 C4
Quintin Ct W4 ....45 B3
Quintock Ho 2
   TW9 ....44 C2
Quinton Ho SW8 ....162 A2
Quinton Kynaston Sch
   NW8 ....79 B3
Quinton St SW18 .....71 B2
Quixley St E14 ....34 C2
Quorn Rd SE22 ....64 A4

R

Rabbit Row W8 .....113 C2
Raby St E14 ....33 A3
Rachel McMillon Coll
   (Annexe) SE1 ....137 A1
Rachel Point E5 .....16 C4
Racine SE5 ....49 A2
Racton Rd SW6 .....155 B3
Radbourne Cl 1 ....17 C4
Radbourne Rd
   SW12 ....73 C3
Radcliff Ho EC1 ....107 B4
Radcliffe Ave NW10 .21 C3
Radcliffe Ho 1
   SE16 ....40 A2
Radcliffe Path
   SW8 ....170 B1
Radcliffe Rd SE1 ...138 B2
Radcliffe Sq SW15 ...57 C1
Radcot St SE11 .....149 C1
Raddington Rd W10 .31 A4
Radford Ho N7 ....14 B3
   8 E14 ....34 A4
Radford Rd SE13 .....67 B1
Radipole Rd SW6 ...164 C4
Radland Rd E16 .....35 C3
Radlett Pl NW8 ......80 A4
Radley Ct 2 SE16 ...40 C4
Radley Ho NW1 ......90 C2
Radley Lo 29 SW19 ..69 C3
Radley Mews W8 ...127 C1
Radley Terr 1 E16 ...35 B2
Radnor Lo 2 ....101 C1
Radnor Mews W2 ...101 C1
Radnor Pl W2 ....102 A1
Radnor Rd NW6 .....23 A4
   SE15 ....49 C3
Radnor St EC1 ....97 A3
Radnor Terr W14 ...140 C4
Radnor Way NW10 ..20 A1
Radnor Wlk SW3 ...144 C1
   14 E14 ....41 C2
Radstock St SW11 ..158 A1
Radwell Ho SW2 .....62 C2
Raeburn Ct 6
   SW16 ....74 A1
Raeburn St SW2 .....62 A3
Ragate Ho E5 ....7 C1
Ragged School Mus The
   E3 ....33 A4
Raglan Ct SW9 ....62 C4
Raglan St NW5 ....13 A2
Ragley Cl W3 ....37 B4
Rahere Ho EC1 ....96 C4
Railey Mews NW5 ....13 B3
Railton Rd SE24 .....63 A2

Railway App SE1 ...123 C2
Railway Ave SE16 ...40 B4
Railway Cotts W6 ...39 B4
Railway Gr SE14 .....51 B3
Railway Rise SE22 ..64 A3
Railway Side SW13 ..56 A4
Railway St N1 ....84 B1
Railway Terr SE13 ...67 A2
Rainbow Ave E14 ....42 A1
Rainbow Ct 2 SE14 .51 A4
Rainbow Quay SE16 .41 A3
Rainbow St SE5 ......49 A3
Raine St E1 ....32 A1
Raine's Foundation Sch
   E2 ....25 A2
Raine's Foundation Sec
   Sch E2 ....17 B3
Rainford Ho 2 N7 .....5 B2
Rainham Cl SW11 ...60 A1
Rainham Ho NW1 ....83 A3
Rainham Rd NW10 ...22 B2
Rainhill Way E3 ......26 C2
Rainsborough Ave
   SE8 ....41 A2
Rainsford Ct NW10 ..20 A3
Rainsford Ho 10
   SW2 ....62 B2
Rainsford Rd NW10 .20 A3
Rainsford St W2 ....102 A2
Rainton Rd SE7 .....43 C1
Rainville Rd W6 .....47 B4
Raleigh Ct 5 SE16 ...32 C1
Raleigh Gdns SW2 ..62 B1
Raleigh Ho SW8 ....171 B2
Raleigh Mews N1 ....86 B3
Raleigh St N1 ....86 B3
Ralph Ct W2 ....100 B2
Ralston St SW3 .....144 C1
Ram St SW18 ....59 A2
Ramar Ho 1 ....111 B4
Ramilles Cl SW2 .....62 A1
Ramillies Pl W1 ....104 C1
Ramillies Rd W4 .....37 C3
Ramillies St W1 ....104 C1
Rampart St E1 ....32 A3
Rampayne St SW1 ..147 B2
Ramsay Ho NW8 ....80 A2
Ramsay Rd W3 ....37 B4
Ramsdean Ho 1
   SW15 ....69 A3
Ramsden Rd SW12 ..72 C4
Ramsey Ho SW9 ...163 C1
Ramsey St E2 ...24 C1 99 C2
Ramsey Wlk N1 ......15 C2
Ramsfort Ho 6
   SE16 ....40 A2
Ramsgate St E8 .....16 B2
Randal Cremer JMI Sch
   E2 ....24 B3
Randall Cl SW11 ...168 A4
Randall Pl SE10 .....52 B3
Randall Rd SE11 ...148 C3
Randall Row SE1 ...148 C3
Randell's Rd N1 .....84 A4
Randolf Ct NW6 .....78 A1
Randolph Ave W9 ...88 C3
Randolph Cres W9 ..88 C2
Randolph Gdns
   NW6 ....78 A1
Randolph Mews W9 .89 A1
Randolph Rd W9 ....89 A1
Randolph St NW1 ...13 B1
Ranelagh Ave SW13 .46 C1

Ranelagh Ave continued
   SW6 ....58 B4
Ranelagh Bridge
   W2 ....100 B3
Ranelagh Gardens (site
   of Chelsea Flower
   Show)* SW1 ....145 C1
Ranelagh Gardens Mans
   SW6 ....58 A4
Ranelagh Gdns
   3 W6 ....38 B3
   W4 ....45 B3
   SW6 ....58 B4
Ranelagh Gr SW1 ..145 C2
Ranelagh Ho SW3 ..144 C2
Ranelagh Mans
   SW6 ....165 A2
Ranelagh Rd 8
   NW10 ....21 B3
Rangdon St EC3 ....110 C1
Rangers Sq SE10 ....52 C2
Rangoon Ho 5 N16 .15 C4
Rankine Ho SE1 ....136 C1
Ranmere St SW12 ...73 A3
Rann House 1
   SW14 ....55 C4
Rannoch Rd W6 .....47 C4
Ranston St NW1 ....102 A4
Ranulf Rd NW2 ......10 B4
Ranwell Cl 11 E3 ....26 B4
Ranwell Ho 6 E3 ...26 B4
Raphael Ct 5 SE16 .40 A1
Raphael St SW7 ....130 C3
Rapley Ho 2 ....99 B3
Rashleigh Ho 6
   SW8 ....61 A4
Rashleigh Ho WC1 ..94 A3
Rastell Ave SW12 ...73 C3
Ratcliffe Cross St
   E1 ....32 C3
Ratcliffe Ho 12 E14 .33 A3
Ratcliffe La 18 E14 ..33 A3
Ratcliffe Orch 9
   E1 ....32 C2
Rathbone Ho NW6 ..23 C4
   5 E16 ....35 B1
Rathbone Mkt 7
   E16 ....35 B2
Rathbone Pl W1 ....105 B2
Rathbone Point E5 .16 C4
Rathbone St W1 ....105 A3
   E16 ....35 B2
Rathgar Rd SW9 ....63 A4
Rathmell Dr SW4 ....61 C1
Rattray Rd SW2 .....62 C2
Raul Rd SE15 ....49 C2
Rav Pinter Ct N16 ...7 A4
Raveley St NW5 .....13 B4
Raven Ho 10 SE16 ..40 C2
Raven Row E1 ....32 A4
Ravenet St SW11 ...170 A3
   SW4 ....170 A3
Ravenfield Rd SW17 .72 B1
Ravenna Rd SW15 ..57 C2
Ravensbourne Ho
   NW8 ....102 A4
Ravensbourne Pk
   SE4 ....66 B4
Ravensbourne Pl
   SE13 ....52 A1
Ravensbury Rd
   SW18 ....71 A2
Ravensbury Terr
   SW18 ....71 A2
Ravenscar NW1 .....82 C3

Ravenscourt 1 N16 ..7 C1
Ravenscourt Ave
   W6 ....38 C2
Ravenscourt Gdns
   W6 ....38 C2
Ravenscourt Park Mans
   W6 ....39 A2
Ravenscourt Park Prep
   Sch W6 ....39 A2
Ravenscourt Park Sta
   W6 ....39 A2
Ravenscourt Pk W6 .39 A2
Ravenscourt Pl W6 .39 A2
Ravenscourt Rd W6 .39 A2
Ravenscourt Sq W6 .38 C3
Ravenscroft
   Ave NW11 ....1 B4
Ravenscroft Cl 4
   E16 ....35 C4
Ravenscroft St NW11 .1 B4
Ravenscroft Rd E16 .35 C4
   W4 ....37 B2
Ravenscroft St E2 ..99 A4
Ravensdon St
   SE11 ....149 C1
Ravenshaw St NW6 .10 B3
Ravenslea Rd SW11,
   SW12 ....72 B4
Ravensmede Way
   W4 ....38 B2
Ravenstone SE17 ..152 B1
Ravenstone Jun & Inf
   Schs SW12 ....72 C2
Ravenstone St
   SW12 ....72 C3
Ravenswood Rd
   SW12 ....73 A4
Ravensworth Ct
   SW6 ....155 B1
Ravensworth Rd
   NW10 ....22 A2
Ravent Rd SE11 ....149 A4
Ravey St EC2 ...24 A1 98 A2
Rawlings St SW3 ...144 C4
Rawlinson Ho SE13 .67 C3
Rawlinson Point 8
   E16 ....35 B4
Rawreth Wlk (off Basire
   St) N1 ....87 A4
Rawson Ct SW11 ...169 C3
Rawson St SW11 ...170 A3
Rawstone Pl EC1 ....96 A4
Rawstorne St EC1 ...96 A4
Ray Ho 7 W10 ....30 C3
Ray St EC1 ....95 C1
Ray Wlk N7 ....5 B2
Rayburne Ct W14 ..126 A2
Raydon St N19 ....4 A2
Raymede Twr W10 ..30 C3
Raymouth Rd SE16 .40 A2
Raynald Ho 15
   SW16 ....74 A1
Rayne Ct SE1 ......138 C4
Rayne Ho 9 W9 .....88 A2
   1 SW12 ....60 C1
Rayner Ct 10 W12 ..39 B4
Rayner's Rd SW15 ..58 A2
Raynes Ct NW2 ......10 A4
Raynham W2 ....102 A2
Raynham Ho 1 E1 ..25 C1
Raynham Rd W6 ....39 A2
Raynor Pl N1 ....87 A4
Re Sassoon Ho
   SE15 ....50 B2
Reachview Cl 14
   NW1 ....13 B1

Read Ho SE11 ......163 B4
Reade Ct 6 W3 ......37 B3
Reade Ho 7 SE10 ...52 C4
Reade Wlk NW10 ....8 A1
Reading Ho W2 ....100 C1
   SE15 ....49 C4
Reading La E8 ....17 A2
Reapers Cl NW1 .....83 B4
Reardon Ho 5 E1 ...32 A1
Reardon Path 31 E1 .32 A1
Reardon St E1 ....32 A1
Reaston St SE14 ....50 C3
Reay Prim Sch
   SW9 ....163 A1
Reckitt Rd W4 ....38 A1
Record St SE16 .....51 B4
Rector St N1 ....86 C3
Rectory Gdns SW4 ..61 B4
Rectory Gr SW4 .....61 B4
Rectory Rd N16 ......7 B1
   SW13 ....46 C1
   1 W3 ....28 B1
Rectory Road Sta
   N16 ....7 B1
Rectory Sq E1 ....32 C4
Reculver Ho 2
   SE15 ....50 B4
Reculver Rd SE16 ...40 C1
Red Anchor Cl
   SW3 ....158 A3
Red Lion Cl 13 SE17 .48 C4
Red Lion Ct EC4 ...107 C1
Red Lion Row SE17 .48 C4
Red Lion Sq WC1 ...106 C3
Red Lion St WC1 ...106 C3
Red Lion Yd W1 ....117 C2
Red Pl W1 ....117 B4
Red Post Hill SE21,
   SE24 ....63 C2
Red Rover SW13 ....56 C4
Redan Pl W2 ....100 A1
Redan St W14 ....39 C3
Redan Terr SE5 .....48 A1
Redbourn Ho W10 ..22 B1
Redbourne Ho 7
   E14 ....33 B3
Redbridge Gdns
   SE5 ....49 A3
Redburn St SW3 ...158 C4
Redcar St SE5 ......48 B3
Redcastle Cl E1 .....32 B2
Redchurch St
   E2 ....24 B1 98 C2
Redcliffe Cl SW5 ...142 A1
Redcliffe Gdns
   SW10 ....156 B4
Redcliffe Mews
   SW10 ....142 A1
Redcliffe Missionary
   Training Coll W4 ..45 A3
Redcliffe Pl SW10 ..156 C3
Redcliffe Rd SW10 .157 A4
Redcliffe Sq SW10 .142 A1
Redcliffe St SW10 ..156 B4
Redclyf Ho 12 E1 ...25 B1
Redcroft 5 NW6 ....10 C2
Redcross Way SE1 .123 A1
Reddins Rd SE15 ...49 C4
Rede Pl W2 ...31 A2 113 C4
Redesdale St SW3 .158 C4
Redfern Rd NW10 ...8 A1
Redfield La SW5 ...142 A4
Redfield Mews
   SW5 ....141 C4
Rediff Est SE16 .....40 C4
Redford Wlk N1 .....86 C4

Redgate Terr SW15	.57 C1
Redgrave Rd SW15	.57 C4
Redhill Ct SW2	.74 C2
Redhill St NW1	.92 B4
Redington Gdns	
NW3	.11 A4
Redington Ho N1	.85 A2
Redington Rd NW3	.11 A4
Redlands JMI Sch	
E1	.32 B4
Redlands Way SW2	.74 B4
Redlynch Ct W14	.126 B3
Redlynch Ho SW9	.173 C4
Redman Ho EC1	.107 B4
SE1	.137 A3
Redman's Rd E1	.32 B4
Redmayne Ho	
SW9	.173 A2
Redmead La E1	.125 B1
Redmill Ho ② E1	.25 A1
Redmond Ho N1	.85 A3
Redmore Rd W6	.39 A2
Redriff Prim Sch	
SE16	.40 C3
Redriff Rd SE16	.41 A3
Redrup Ho ② SE14	.50 C4
Redruth Rd E9	.25 B4
Redstart Cl SE14	.13 A3
Redvers St E2	.98 B4
Redwood Cl SE16	.33 A1
Redwood Ct N19	.4 C4
NW6	.10 A1
Redwood Mews ②	
SW4	.61 A4
Redwoods SW15	.68 C3
Reece Mews SW7	.143 B4
Reed Cl E16	.35 C4
Reed Ho SW15	.56 C1
Reedham St N1	.113 B1
Reedham St SE15	.64 C4
Reedholm Villas	
N16	.15 C4
Reedworth St	
SE11	.149 C3
Reef Ho E14	.42 B3
Rees St N1	.87 A3
Reeves Ho W1	.117 B3
SE1	.135 B3
Reeves Mews W1	.117 C3
Reeves Rd E3	.27 A1
Reform St SW11	.169 A2
SW11	.169 A2
Regal Cl E1	.111 C4
Regal La NW1	.81 C3
Regal Pl SW6	.156 B1
⑧ E3	.26 B2
Regan Way N1	.24 A3
Regency Ct ⑦ E18	.26 C2
Regency Lo NW3	.11 C1
Regency Mews ①	
NW10	.8 C2
Regency St SW1	.147 C3
Regency Wlk ⑧	
TW10	.54 A2
Regent Ct NW8	.90 A3
① N16	.7 B4
Regent Ho W14	.140 A4
Regent Lo ⑨ SW2	.74 B3
Regent Pl W11	.119 A4
Regent Rd SE24	.63 A2
Regent Sq WC1	.94 B3
❷ E3	.27 A2
Regent St W1	.104 C1
W1	.118 C4
W4	.36 C1
Regent's Coll NW1	.91 B2

Regent's Park	
Regent's Park Barracks	
NW1	.82 B1
Regent's Park Rd	
NW1	.81 B3
Regent's Park Sta	
NW1	.92 A1
Regent's Park Terr	
NW1	.82 A4
Regent's Pl SE3	.53 C1
Regent's Row ⑧ E1	.24 C4
Regents Bridge Gdns	
SW8	.162 B2
Regents Canal Ho ②	
E14	.33 A3
Regents Ct E8	.24 C4
Regents Mews NW8	.79 A2
Regents Plaza NW6	.78 A2
Regents Wharf ⑧	
E2	.25 A4
Regina Point SE16	.40 B3
Regina Rd N4	.5 B3
Reginald Pl ⑥ SE8	.51 C3
Reginald Rd SE8	.51 C3
Reginald Sq SE8	.51 C3
Regis Ct NW1	.102 C4
Regis Rd NW5	.13 A3
Regnart Bldgs NW1	.93 A3
Reid Ct SW14	.45 B1
Reighton Rd E5	.7 C2
Relay Rd W12	.30 B1
Relf Rd SE15	.64 C4
Reiton Mews SW7	.130 B2
Rembrandt Cl E14	.42 C3
Rembrandt Ct ①	
SE16	.40 A1
Remington St N1	.86 B1
Remnant St WC2	.106 C2
Remsted Ho NW6	.78 A3
Remus Rd E3	.18 C1
Renbold Ho ⑤ SE10	.52 B2
Rendlesham Ho ⑧	
E5,N16	.7 C1
Rendlesham Rd E5	.7 C1
Renforth St SE16	.40 B4
Renfrew Ho NW6	.78 A1
Renfrew Rd SE11	.150 A3
Rennell Ho ⑩ E9	.17 C2
Rennell St SE13	.67 B4
Rennie Cotts ② E1	.25 B1
Rennie Ct SE1	.122 A2
Rennie Ho SE1	.136 C1
Rennie St SE1	.122 A2
Renoir Ct ⑦ SE16	.40 A1
Renton Cl SW2	.62 B1
Rephidim St SE1	.138 A1
Replingham Rd	
SW18	.70 C3
Reporton Rd SW6	.154 B1
Repton Ho SW1	.147 A3
❷ E14	.33 A3
Repton St E14	.33 A3
Reservoir Rd SE4	.51 A1
Restell Cl SE3	.53 A4
Reston Pl SW7	.128 C3
Retcar Pl N19	.4 A2
Retford St E2	.24 A3
Retreat Ho ⑤ E9	.17 B2
Retreat Pl E9	.17 B2
Retreat The SW14	.56 A4
Reunion Row E1	.32 A2
Reveley Sq SE16	.41 A4
Revelon Rd SE4	.66 A4
Revelstoke Rd	
SW18,SW19	.70 C2

Reverdy Rd SE1	.153 B3
Rewell St SW6	.156 C1
Rex PI W1	.117 C2
Reynard Cl SE4	.51 A1
Reynard Pl SE14	.51 A4
Reynolds Cl NW11	.2 A4
Reynolds Ho NW8	.79 C1
N4	.5 A3
⑩ E2	.25 B3
Reynolds Pl ⑫	
TW10	.54 B1
Reynolds Rd W4	.37 B3
SE15	.65 C3
Rheidol Mews N1	.86 C2
Rheidol Terr N1	.86 C3
Rhoda St E2	.24 A1 99 A2
Rhodes Ho N1	.97 B4
W12	.30 A1
Rhodes St N7	.14 B3
Rhodesia Rd SW9	.172 B1
Rhodeswell Rd E14	.33 A4
Rhondda Gr E3	.26 B2
Rhyl Prim Sch NW5	.12 C2
Rhyl St NW5	.12 C2
Ribblesdale Ho ⑪	
NW6	.23 C4
Ribbon Dance Mews	
SE5	.48 C2
Ribstone Ho ⑫ E9	.17 C2
Ricardo St E14	.34 A3
Riceyman Ho WC1	.95 B3
Rich La SW5	.142 A2
Rich St E14	.33 B2
Richard Anderson Ct ⑧	
SE14	.50 C3
Richard Atkins Prim Sch	
SW2	.74 A4
Richard Cloudesley Sch	
EC1	.96 C1
Richard Cobden Prim	
Sch NW1	.83 A3
Richard Fox Ho N4	.6 B1
Richard Ho ⑥ SE16	.40 B2
Richard Knight Ho	
SW6	.165 C4
Richard Neale Ho ②	
E1	.32 A2
Richard's Pl SW3	.144 B4
Richard's Pl SW5	.144 B4
Richardson Cl ⑧ E8	.24 B4
Richardson Ct	
SW4	.172 B2
Richardson's Mews	
W1	.92 C1
Richbell Pl WC1	.106 C4
Richborne Terr	
SW8	.163 A2
Richborough Ho	
⑭ E5	.17 A4
⑩ SE15	.50 B4
Richborough Rd	
NW2	.10 A3
Richford Gate W6	.39 B3
Richford St W6	.39 B3
Richland Ho ④	
SE15	.49 C2
Richman Ho ⑩ SE8	.41 B1
Richmond Adult Coll ⑦	
TW9	.54 A3
Richmond Ave N1	.85 A4
NW10	.9 B2
Richmond Bldgs	
W1	.105 B1
Richmond Circus	
TW9	.54 A3
Richmond Coll W8	.128 B2

Richmond Cres N1	.85 B4
Richmond St SW1	.131 A3
Richmond Gr N1	.15 A1
Richmond Hill	
TW10	.54 A1
Richmond Hill Ct ⑤	
TW10	.54 A1
Richmond Ho NW1	.82 B1
SE17	.151 B2
⑫ SE26	.76 C1
Richmond Mans	
SW5	.142 A2
SW15	.58 A4
Richmond Mews	
W1	.105 B1
Richmond Park Rd	
SW14	.55 C3
Richmond Rd E8	.16 C1
SW14	.56 A4
Richmond Sta TW9	.54 A3
Richmond Terr	
SW1	.134 A4
Richmond Way	
W12,W14	.39 C4
Rickard Cl SW2	.74 C3
Rickett St SW6	.155 C4
Rickman Ho ⑳ E2	.25 B1
Rickman St ⑳ E1	.25 B1
Rickthorne Rd ⑥	
N19	.5 A2
Riddell Ct SE1	.152 C2
Riddgale St E3	.27 A3
Ridge Hill NW11	.1 A3
Ridge Rd NW2	.1 B1
Ridgeway ⑪ TW10	.54 A1
Ridgeway Dr W3	.36 C3
Ridgeway Gdns N6	.4 B4
Ridgeway The ⑭	
W3	.36 C3
Ridgewell Cl N1	.87 A4
Ridgmount Gdns	
WC1	.105 B4
Ridgmount Pl WC1	.105 B4
Ridgmount Rd	
SW18	.59 A2
Ridgmount St WC1	.105 B4
Ridgway Rd SW9	.63 A4
Riding House St	
W1	.104 C3
Riding The NW11	.1 B4
Ridings Cl N6	.4 B4
Ridley Ho ⑭ SW11	.60 A4
Ridley Rd E8	.16 B3
NW10	.21 C3
Ridley Road Mkt E8	.16 B3
Riffel Rd NW2	.9 B3
Rifle Court SE11	.163 C4
Rifle Pl W11	.30 C1
Rifle St E14	.34 A4
Rigault Rd SW6	.164 B1
Rigden St E14	.34 A3
Rigeley Rd NW10	.21 C2
Rigg Ho ② SW4	.74 A4
Rigge Pl SW4	.61 C3
Rignold Ho ⑧ SE5	.49 A1
Rigo Ho ⑧ E1	.32 C4
Riley Ho SW10	.157 A2
⑨ E3	.26 C1
❶ SW4	.73 C4
Riley Rd SE1	.138 C2
Riley St SW10	.157 B2
Rill Ho ⑳ SE5	.49 A3
Rinaldo Rd SW12	.73 A4
Ring Cross Prim Sch	
N7	.14 B3
Ring Ho ⑭ E1	.32 B2

Ringcroft St N7	.14 C3
Ringford Ho SW18	.58 B2
Ringford Rd SW18	.58 C1
Ringmer Ave SW6	.164 B3
Ringmer Gdns ②	
N19	.5 A2
Ringmer Ho ⑮	
SE22	.64 A4
Ringsfield Ho	
SE17	.151 A1
Ringwood Gdns	
❶ E14	.41 C2
SW15	.68 C3
Ripley Gdns SW14	.55 C4
Ripley Ho SW1	.160 C4
Ripley House SW14	.56 A4
Riplington Ct SW15	.69 A4
Ripplevale Gr N1	.14 B1
Risborough SE17	.150 C4
Risborough Ho	
NW8	.90 B2
Risborough St SE1	.136 B4
Risdon Ho ⑳ SE16	.40 B4
Risdon St ⑳ SE16	.40 B4
Riseholme Ho ⑭	
SE22	.64 A4
Riseldine Rd SE23	.66 A1
Rising Sun Ct EC1	.108 B3
Risinghill St N1	.85 B2
Risley Ho ⑦ E9	.17 C2
Rita Rd SW8	.162 C2
Ritchie Ho N19	.4 C4
❷ E14	.34 C3
❶ SE16	.40 B3
Ritchie St N1	.85 C2
Ritherdon Rd SW17	.73 A2
Ritson Ho N1	.84 C3
Ritson Rd E8	.16 C2
Rivaz Pl E9	.17 B2
River Barge Cl E14	.42 B4
River Ct SE1	.122 A3
River Ho SW13	.46 A1
River Pl N1	.15 B1
River St EC1	.95 B4
River Terr W6	.39 B1
River Way SE10	.43 B3
Riverains The	
SW11	.167 B3
Rivercourt Rd W6	.39 A1
Riverdale Dr SW18	.71 A3
Riverfleet WC1	.94 B4
Riverford Ho ⑳ W2	.31 C4
Rivermead Ct SW6	.58 B4
Rivermead Ho E9	.18 A3
Riverside Prim Sch	
SE16	.139 C3
Riverside SW11	.158 B2
Riverside Bsns Ctr	
SW18	.71 A3
Riverside Ct SW8	.161 C4
Riverside Dr W4	.46 A2
Riverside Gdns W6	.39 A1
Riverside Ind Est	
SE10	.43 B3
Riverside Mans ④	
E1	.32 B1
Riverside Prim Sch	
SE16	.139 C3
Riverside Rd E15	.27 B3
SW17	.71 B1

Riverside Rd continued
SW17,SW19 ....71 B1

Riverside Workshops
SE1 ....123 A2
Riverton Cl W9 ....23 B2
Riverview Gdns
SW13 ....47 A4
Riverview Gr W4 ....45 A4
Riverview Rd W4 ...45 A4
Rivet Ho SE1 ......153 A2
Rivington Ct NW10 ..21 C4
Rivington Pl EC2 ....98 B3
Rivington St EC2 ....98 A3
Rivington Wlk
E8 ....24 C4
Rixon St N7 ....5 C1
Roach Rd E3 ....18 C1
Roach Works E3 .....18 C1
Roads Pl N19 ....5 A2
Roan St SE10 ....52 B4

Robert Adam St
W1 ....103 B2
Robert Bell Ho
SE16 ....153 B4
Robert Blair Prim Sch
N7 ....14 A2
Robert Browning Prim
Sch SE17 ....151 B2
Robert Cl W9 ....89 A1
Robert Dashwood Way
SE17 ....150 C3
Robert Gentry Ho
W14 ....140 B1
Robert Jones Ho
SE16 ....153 B4
Robert Keen Cl [17]
SE15 ....49 C2
Robert Lowe Cl
SE14 ....50 C3
Robert Owen Ho [2] ..99 A4
SW6 ....47 C2
Robert Owen Lo [3]
E5 ....17 A4
Robert St NW1 ......92 B3
WC2 ....120 B3
Robert Sutton Ho [20]
E1 ....32 B3
Robert's Pl EC1 ..24 95 C2
Roberta St
E2 ....24 C2 99 C3
Roberts Ct NW10 .....8 A2
Roberts Ho [5] SE27 ..75 A1
Roberts Mews
SW1 ....131 B1
Robertson Ho [11]
SE10 ....52 B2
Robertson Rd E15 ...27 B4
Robertson St SW8 ...170 B1
Robeson St E3 ......33 B4
Robin Ct SE16 ......153 B4
E14 ....42 B3
Robin Gr N6 ....3 C2
Robin Ho NW8 ....80 A1
Robin Hood SW15 ...68 A1
Robin Hood Gdns [12]
E14 ....34 B2
Robin Hood La E14 ..34 B2
SW15 ....68 A1
Robin's Ct SW4 .....62 A1
Robins Ct TW10 ....54 A1
Robinscroft Mews
SE10 ....52 A2

Robinsfield Inf Sch
NW8 ....80 A2
Robinson Ct N1 .....86 B4
[Fl] Richmond TW9 ...54 B3
Robinson Ho
[4] W10 ....30 C3
[11] E14 ....33 C4
Robinson Rd E2 .....25 B3
Robinson St SW3 ...158 C4
Robsart St SW9 ....173 B2
Robson Ave NW10 ....8 C1
Robson Rd SE21,
SE27 ....75 B1
Roby Ho EC1 ....96 C2
Rochdale Way [4]
SE8 ....51 C3
Roche Ho [15] E14 ...33 B2
Rochelle Cl SW11 ...59 C3
Rochelle Ct E1 .....32 B3
Rochelle St E2 .....98 C3
Rochemont Wlk [2]
E8 ....24 C4
Rochester Ct
[7] NW1 ....13 B1
[1] E2 ....25 A1
Rochester Ho SE1 ..137 C3
SE15 ....50 B4
Rochester Mews
NW1 ....13 B1
Rochester Pl NW1 ...13 B2
Rochester Rd NW1 ...13 B2
Rochester Row
SW1 ....147 A4
Rochester Sq NW1 ..13 B1
Rochester St SW1 ..133 B1
Rochester Terr
NW1 ....13 B2
Rochester Wlk
SE1 ....123 B2
Rochford Wlk [8] E8 16 C1
Rochfort Ho [4] SE8 ..41 B1
Rock Ave [13] SW14 ..55 C4
Rock Grove Way
SE16 ....153 C4
Rock St N4 ....5 C2
Rockell's Pl SE22 ...65 A1
Rockfield Ho SE10 ...52 B4
Rockhall Rd NW2 .....9 C4
Rockingham Cl
SW15 ....56 B3
Rockingham St
SE1 ....136 C1
Rockland Rd SW15 ..58 A3
Rockley Ct [9] SW14 ..39 C4
Rockley Rd W14 .....39 C4
Rocks La SW13 ......56 C4
Rockstraw Ho [5]
NW3 ....12 B1
Rockwood Ct N16 ....7 C4
Rocliffe St N1 ......86 B1
Rocque Ho SW6 ....154 C2
Rodborough Rd
NW11 ....1 C3
Roden St N7 ....5 B1
Rodenhurst Ct SW4 .61 C2
Rodenhurst Rd SW4 .61 C1
Roderick Ho [5]
SE16 ....40 B2
Roderick Rd NW3 ...12 B4
Rodgers Ho [4] SW4 .172 B2
Roding Ct [8] W12 ...38 A4
Roding Ho N1 ....85 B5
Roding Mews E1 ...125 C2
Roding Rd E5 ....18 A3
Rodmarton St W1 ...103 A3
Rodmell WC1 ....94 B3

Rodmere St SE10 ...43 A1
Rodmill La SW2 .....74 A4
Rodney Ct NW8 .....89 A2
Rodney Ho N1 ....85 A1
W11 ....113 B4
[1] E14 ....42 A2
Rodney Pl SE17 ....151 A4
Rodney Rd SE17 ...151 B3
Rodney St N1 ....85 A1
Rodway Rd SW15 ...68 C4
Rodwell Rd SE22 ....64 B1
Roebuck Ho SW1 ...132 C2
Roedean Cres SW15 .56 A2
Roehampton CE Prim
Sch SW15 ....69 A4
Roehampton Cl
SW15 ....56 C3
Roehampton Ct
SW15 ....56 C4
Roehampton Gate
SW15 ....55 B1
Roehampton Gate Cty
Prim Sch SW15 ...56 A1
Roehampton High St
SW15 ....69 A4
Roehampton La
SW15 ....68 C4
Roehampton Lane
SW15 ....69 A3
Roehampton Vale
SW15 ....68 B2
Roffey St E14 ....42 B4
Roger Dowley Ct [8]
E2 ....25 B3
Roger St WC1 ....95 A1
Roger's Almshouses [7]
SW9 ....62 B3
Rogers Est [28] E2 ..25 B2
Rogers Ho SW1 ....147 C4
Rogers Rd E16 ......35 B1
Rokeby Ho WC1 .....94 C1
[3] SW12 ....73 A4
Rokeby Rd SE4 .....51 B1
Rokeby Sch E15 ....19 C1
Rokeland Ho SE4 ....66 A3
Roland Gdns SW7 ..143 A2
Roland Mews E1 ...32 C4
Roland Way SW7 ...143 A2
SE17 ....151 C1
Rollins St SE15 .....50 B4
Rollit Ho N7 ....14 C3
Rollit St N7 ....14 C3
Rollo Ct SW11 .....170 A3
Rolls Bldgs EC4 ....107 C2
Rolls Pas EC4 ......107 B2
Rolls Rd SE1 ....147 C3
Rollscourt Ave SE24 .63 B2
Rolt St SE8 ....51 A4
Roma Read Cl
SW15 ....69 A4
Roman Cl W3 ....37 A4
Roman Rd E2,E3 ....25 C3
[4] W4 ....38 B2
Roman Square Mkt [8]
E3 ....26 B3
Roman Way N7 .....14 B2
[4] SE15 ....50 B3
Romanfield Rd SW2 .74 B4
Romayne Ho SW4 ...61 C4
Romberg Rd SW17 ..72 C1
Romborough Gdns
SE13 ....67 B2
Romborough Way
SE13 ....67 B2
Rodmell WC1 ....94 B3

Romer Ho [12] W10 ..23 B2
[1] SW2 ....62 B2
Romero Cl SW9 .....62 B4
Romney Mews W1 ..103 B4
Romeyn Rd SW16 ...74 B1
Romford Ho [3] N1 ..15 C2
Romford St E1 ......32 A4
Romilly Rd N4 ....6 A2
Romilly St W1 ......105 C1
W1 ....119 C4
Romily Ct SW6 .....164 B2
Romney Cl NW11 ....2 B3
[7] SE14 ....50 B3
Romney Ct [9] NW3 .12 A2
[9] W12 ....39 B4
Romney Ho SE12 ...52 C4
Romney St SW1 ....134 A1
Romola Rd SE24,
SW2 ....75 A3
Romsey Ho [5]
SW11 ....59 C3
Rona Rd NW3 ......12 C4
Rona Wlk [17] N1 ...15 C2
Ronald Ross Prim Sch
SW19 ....70 A4
Ronald St E1 ....32 B3
Ronalds Rd N5 .....15 A3
Ronaldshay N4 ......5 C3
Rondu Rd NW2 .....10 A3
Rood La EC3 ....124 A4
Rooke Way SE10 ...43 B1
Rookery Rd SW4 ...61 B3
Rookwood Rd N16 ...7 C4
Rootes Dr W10 ......30 C4
Rope St SE16 ....41 A3
Ropemaker Rd
SE16 ....41 A3
Ropemaker St EC2 .109 B4
Ropemaker's Fields [7]
E14 ....33 B2
Roper La SE1 ......138 B3
Roper's Orchard
SW3 ....158 A3
Ropers Wlk [3] SE24 .74 C4
Ropery St E3 ....26 B1
Ropewalk Gdns E1 .111 C2
Ropley St [7] E2 .....24 C3
Rosa Alba Mews N5 .15 B4
Rosa Parks Ho
SW9 ....172 C1
Rosalind Ho [20] N1 ..24 A3
Rosaline Rd SW6 ..154 B1
Rosaline Terr SW6 .154 B1
Rosary Gdns SW7 ..143 A3
Rosary RC Prim Sch
NW3 ....12 A3
Rosaville Rd SW6 ..154 C1
Rosbury SW15 ......58 A1
Roscoe St EC1 ......97 A1
Roscommon Ho [2]
NW3 ....11 C3
Rose & Crown Ct
EC2 ....108 C2
Rose & Crown Yd
SW1 ....119 A2
Rose Alley SE1 ....110 B3
SE1 ....123 A2
Rose Bruford Coll
SE8 ....51 C4
Rose Bush Ct NW3 .12 B3
Rose Ct E1 ....111 A3
Rose St WC2 ....120 A4
Rosebank [2] W3 ...28 C3
SW6 ....47 B2
Rosebank Gdns E3 ..26 B3
[1] W3 ....28 C3

Rosebank Way W3 ..28 C3
Rosebank Wlk NW1 .13 C1
Roseberry Pl E8 ....16 B2
Roseberry St SE16 ..40 A2
Rosebery Ave EC1 ..95 C3
EC1 ....95 B2
W1 ....118 A2
Rosebery Ho [22] E2 .25 B3
Rosebery Rd SW2 ..62 A1
Rosebery Sq EC1 ...95 B1
Rosebery Sq SW6 ..166 B1
Rosecroft Ave NW3 ..1 C1
Rosedale Ct N5 ....15 A4
Rosedale Ho N16 ....6 C3
Rosedale Rd TW9 ...54 A3
Rosedale Terr W6 ...39 A3
Rosedene W3 ......28 A1
Rosedene Ave
SW16 ....74 B1
Rosedew Rd W6 ....47 C4
Rosefield Gdns E14 .33 C2
Roseheart Mews [8]
W11 ....31 C3
Rosehill Rd SW18 ..59 B2
Roseland Ho SW6 ...58 A4
Roseleigh Ave N5 ..15 A4
Rosemary Dr [5]
E14 ....34 C3
Rosemary Gdns
SW14 ....55 B4
Rosemary Ho N1 ...87 C3
Rosemary La SW14 .55 B4
Rosemary Mews N1 .87 C4
Rosemary Rd SE15 ..49 B3
SW17 ....71 B1
Rosemary St N1 ...87 A4
EC1 ....96 A2
Rosemead Sch SE27 .75 B1
Rosemont Mans [11]
NW3 ....11 A2
Rosemont Rd NW3 ..11 B2
W3 ....28 A2
Richmond TW10 ....54 A1
Rosemoor St SW3 ..144 C3
Rosemount Ct [2]
W3 ....28 A1
Rosemount Lo W3 ..28 A2
Rosenau Cres
SW11 ....168 C3
Rosenau Rd SW11 .168 C4
Rosendale Inf Sch
SE21 ....75 B4
Rosendale Jun Sch
SE21 ....75 B4
Rosendale Rd SE21,
SE24 ....75 B3
Roseneath Rd SW11 60 C1
Rosenthal Rd SE6 ...67 B1
Rosenthorpe Rd
SE15 ....65 C2
Roserton St E14 ....42 B4
Rosethorn Cl SW12 .73 C4
Rosetta Cl SW8 ....162 B1
Roseway SE21 ....63 C1
Rosewood Ct [2]
E11 ....19 C4
Rosewood Ho [9]
NW3 ....11 A2
Rosewood Sq W12 ..29 C3
Rosher Cl E15 ....19 C1
Rosina St E9 ....17 C2
Roskell Rd SW15 ...57 C4
Roslin Ho [2] E1 ....32 C2
Roslin Rd W3 ....37 A3
Rosmead Rd
W11 ....31 A2 112 A2

Rosoman Pl EC1 .....95 C2
Ross Ct 4 SW15 ....69 C4
Ross Ho 18 E1 .....32 A1
Rossdale Rd SW15 ..57 B3
Rossendale Way
 NW1 ....83 A4
Rossetti Gdns Mans
 SW3 ....158 C4
Rossetti Ho SW1 ..147 C3
Rossetti Mews NW8 .79 C3
Rossetti Rd SE16 ...40 A1
Rossington St E5 ....7 C2
Rossiter Rd SW12 ..73 A3
Rosslyn Ave SW13 ..56 B4
Rosslyn Hill NW3 ...11 C3
Rosslyn Ho 19 TW9 .44 B2
Rosslyn Mans NW6 .10 C3
Rosslyn Park Mews
 NW3 ....11 C3
Rossmore Ct NW1 ..90 C2
Rossmore Rd NW1 ..90 B2
Rostrevor Mans
 SW6 ....164 C4
Rostrevor Rd SW6 .164 C4
Rotary St SE1 .....136 B2
Roth Wlk N7 ....5 B2
Rothay NW1 ....92 B4
Rothbury Rd E9 .....18 C1
Rother Ho SE15 ....65 A3
Rotherfield Ct N1 ...87 B4
Rotherfield Prim Sch
 N1 ....87 A4
Rotherfield St N1 ...87 A4
Rotherham Wlk
 SE1 ....122 A1
Rotherhithe SE16 ..33 B1
Rotherhithe Holiday Inn
 Pier(River Bus)
 SE16 ....33 B1
Rotherhithe New Rd
 SE16 ....40 A1
Rotherhithe Old Rd
 SE16 ....40 C2
Rotherhithe Prim Sch
 SE16 ....40 A4
Rotherhithe St
 10 SE16 ....40 A4
 SE16 ....40 B4
Rotherhithe Sta
 SE16 ....32 C1
Rotherhithe Tunnel
 SE16 ....32 C1
Rotherwick Rd NW11 .1 C4
Rotherwood Rd
 SW15 ....57 C4
Rothery St N1 .....86 B4
Rothesay Ave SW14,
 TW10 ....55 A3
Rothesay Ct SE11 .163 B3
Rothley Ct NW8 ....89 B2
Rothsay St SE1 ...138 A1
Rothsay Wlk 18 E14 .41 C2
Rothschild Rd W4 ..37 B3
Rothwell St NW1 ...81 A4
 10 NW1 ....12 B1
Rotten Row SW1 ..130 C4
Rotterdam Dr E14 ..42 B3
Rouel Rd SE16 ....139 B1
Roundacre SW19 ...69 C2
Roundel Cl SE4 ....66 B3
Roundwood Rd
 NW10 ....8 B1
Rounton Rd E3 .....26 C1
Roupell Rd SW2 ....74 B3

Roupell St SE1 ....121 C1
Rousden St NW1 ...13 B1
Routh Rd SW18 ....72 A4
Rover Ho 7 N1 .....24 A4
Rowallan Rd SW6 .154 A1
Rowan Cl W5 ....36 A4
Rowan Ct 18 SE15 .49 B3
 SW11 ....60 B1
Rowan Ho 5 NW3 ..12 B2
 NW10 ....21 A1
Rowan Rd W6 ......39 C2
Rowan Wlk N19 .....4 B2
 W10 ....23 A1
Rowberry Cl SW6 ..47 B3
Rowcross St SE1 ..153 A2
Rowditch La SW11 .169 B2
Rowdon Ave NW10 ..9 A1
Rowe La E9 ....17 B3
Rowena Cres
 SW11 ....168 B1
Rowfant Rd SW12,
 SW17 ....72 C2
Rowhill Mans 11 E5 .17 A4
Rowhill Rd E5 .....17 A4
Rowington Cl W2 ..100 A4
Rowland Hill Ho
 SE1 ....136 A4
Rowland Hill St
 NW3 ....12 A3
Rowley Gdns N4 ....6 B4
Rowley Ho SE8 ....51 C4
Rowley Ind Pk W3 .37 A3
Rowley Way NW8 ..78 C4
Rowntree Cl NW6 ..10 C2
Rowse Cl E15 ......27 B4
Rowstock 1 NW1 ...13 C1
Rowstock Gdns N7 .13 C3
Roxby Pl SW6 .....155 C4
Roxford Ho 8 E3 ...27 A1
Roxley Rd SE13 ...67 A1
Roxwell 10 NW1 ...13 A2
Roxwell Rd W12 ...38 C4
Roy Ho N1 ....87 C3
Roy Ridley Ho 6
 SW4 ....61 C4
Roy Sq E14 ....33 A2
Royal Acad of Arts*
 W1 ....118 C3
Royal Acad of Dancing
 The SW11 ......167 C3
Royal Acad of Music
 NW1 ....91 C1
Royal Albert Hall*
 SW7 ....129 B3
Royal Arc W1 .....118 C3
Royal Army Medical Coll
 SW1 ....148 A2
Royal Ave SW3 ...144 C2
Royal Avenue Ho
 SW3 ....144 C2
Royal Ballet Sch
 W14 ....140 A2
Royal Brompton & Nat
 Heart Hospl The
 SW3 ....144 A2
Royal Cir SE27 ....75 A1
Royal Cl N16 ....7 A3
Royal Coll of Art
 SW7 ....129 C3
Royal Coll of Art
 Sculpture Sch
 SW11 ....158 A1
Royal Coll of Midwives
 W1 ....104 A3

Royal Coll of Music
 SW7 ....129 B2
Royal Coll of
 Obstetricians &
 Gynaecologists
 NW1 ....90 C2
Royal Coll of Organists
 SW7 ....129 B3
Royal Coll of Physicians
 NW1 ....92 B2
Royal Coll of Science
 SW7 ....129 B2
Royal Coll of Surgeons
 WC2 ....107 A2
Royal College St
 NW1 ....83 A4
Royal Courts of Justice
 WC2 ....107 A2
Royal Cres
 W11 ....31 A1 112 A4
Royal Crescent Mews
 W11 ....30 C1
Royal Ct SE16 .....41 B3
Royal Duchess Mews
 SW12 ....73 A4
Royal Ear Hospl
 WC1 ....93 B1
Royal Exchange
 EC3 ....109 C1
Royal Exchange Ave
 EC3 ....109 C1
Royal Exchange Bldgs
 EC3 ....109 C1
Royal Festival Hall*
 SE1 ....121 A1
Royal Free Hospl
 NW3 ....12 A3
Royal Geographical
 Society SW7 ....129 C3
Royal Hill SE10 ....52 B3
Royal Hospital (Army
 Pensioners) SW1 .145 B1
Royal Hospital Rd
 SW3 ....145 A1
Royal Hospl SW15 .58 A1
Royal Langford
 NW6 ....78 A2
Royal London Est The
 NW10 ....20 C3
Royal London
 Homeopathic Hospl
 The WC1 ......106 B4
Royal London
 (Whitechapel) The
 E1 ....32 A4
Royal Marsden Hospl
 SW3 ....143 C2
Royal Masonic Hospl
 W6 ....38 C2
Royal Mews The*
 SW1 ....132 B2
Royal Mint Pl 11 E1 .125 B4
Royal Mint St E1 ..125 A4
Royal National
 Orthopaedic Hospl
 W1 ....92 B1
Royal National TNE
 Hospl The WC1 ...94 C4
Royal Naval Coll
 Buildings SE10 ...52 C4
Royal Naval Sch SE14 .51 B3
Royal Oak Ct N1 ...24 A3
Royal Oak Pl SE22 .65 A1
Royal Oak Rd 8 E8 .17 A2
Royal Oak Sta W2 .100 B3

Royal Opera Arc
 SW1 ....119 B2
Royal Opera House,
 Covent Garden*
 WC2 ....106 B1
Royal Orchard Cl
 SW18 ....70 A4
Royal Par 4 SW6 ..154 A2
Royal Pl 11 SE10 ...52 B3
Royal Rd SE17 .....48 A4
Royal Sch The W3 ..11 C4
Royal St SE1 .....135 A2
Royal United Services
 Mus SW1 ....120 A1
Royal Veterinary Coll
 NW1 ....83 B3
Royal Victor Pl E3 ..25 C3
Royal Victoria Sta
 E16 ....35 C2
Royalty Studios
 W11 ....31 A3
Roycroft Cl SW2 ...74 C3
Roydon Cl SW11 ..168 C2
Royston Ct 13 TW9 .44 B2
Royston Ho 15 SE15 .50 A4
Royston Rd TW10 ..54 A2
Royston St 22 E2 ...25 B3
Rozel Ct 3 N1 .....24 A4
Rozel Rd SW4 .....61 B4
Ruby St SE15 ......50 A4
Ruby Triangle SE15 .50 A4
Rucklidge Ave
 NW10 ....21 C3
Rudall Cres NW3 ...11 C4
Rudbeck Ho 10
 SE15 ....49 C3
Ruddington Cl E5 ..18 A4
Rudge Ho SE16 ...139 C2
Rudgwick Terr NW8 .80 B3
Rudhall Ho 4 SW2 .62 C1
Rudloe Rd SW12 ...73 B4
Rudolf Pl SW8 ....162 B3
Rudolph Rd NW6 ..23 C3
Rudstone Ho 10 E3 .27 A2
Rudyard Ct SE1 ...137 C3
Rufford St N1 ......84 B4
Rufford Twr 5 W3 ..28 A1
Rufus Bsns Ctr
 SW18 ....71 A2
Rufus Ho SE1 ....139 A2
Rufus St N1 ....98 A3
Rugby Mans W14 ..140 B4
Rugby Rd W4 ......38 A4
Rugby St WC1 .....94 C1
Rugg St E14 ....33 C2
Rugless Ho 7 E14 ..42 B4
Rugmere 8 NW1 ...12 C1
Rum Cl E1 ....32 B2
Rumball Ho 22 SE5 .49 A3
Rumbold Rd SW6 ..156 B1
Rumford Ho SE1 ..136 C1
Rumsey Rd SW9 ...62 B4
Runacres Ct SE17 .150 C1
Runcorn Pl W11 ...112 A4
Rundell Tower
 SW8 ....162 C1
Running Horse Yd 12
 TW8 ....44 A4
Runnymead Ho
 TW10 ....54 C2
Runnymede Ho E9 .18 A4
Rupack St 3 SE16 .40 B4
Rupert Ct W1 .....119 B4
Rupert Gdns SW9 .48 A1
Rupert Ho SE11 ...149 C3

Rupert Rd N19 .....4 C2
 NW6 ....23 B3
 W4 ....38 A3
Rupert St W1 .....119 B4
Ruscoe Rd E16 ....35 B3
Rush Hill Mews 3
 SW11 ....60 C4
Rush Hill Rd SW11 .60 C4
Rusham Rd SW12 .72 B4
Rushbrook Ho
 SW8 ....171 B2
Rushby Ct SW4 ...172 A3
Rushcroft Rd SW2,
 SW9 ....62 C3
Rushcutters Ct 18
 SE16 ....41 A2
Rushey Grn SE13 ..67 A1
Rushey Mead SE4 .66 B2
Rushford Rd SE4 ..66 B1
Rushlake Ho SW11 .60 B1
Rushmead 6 E2 ...25 A2
Rushmere Ho 2
 SW15 ....68 C3
Rushmore Cres 6
 E5 ....17 C4
Rushmore Ho 9 N7 .13 C3
 W14 ....126 B1
Rushmore JMI Sch
 E5 ....18 A4
Rushmore Rd SW15 .58 A1
 E5 ....17 C4
Rusholme Rd SW15 .58 A1
Rushton Ho SW8 ..171 B1
Rushton St N1 .....87 C2
Rushworth St SE1 .136 B3
Ruskin Ave TW9 ...44 C3
Ruskin Ct SE5 .....63 C4
Ruskin Ho SW1 ...147 C3
Ruskin Park Ho SE5 .63 C4
Ruskin Wlk SE24 ..63 B2
Rusper Ct SW9 ...172 B1
Russell Ct W4 .....46 B4
 SW11 ....60 A1
 5 SE15 ....50 A1
Russell Gdns W14 .126 A2
Russell Gdns Mews
 W14 ....126 A2
Russell Gr 5 SW9 .173 C4
Russell Ho SW1 ...146 C2
 18 E14 ....33 C3
Russell Kerr Cl W4 .45 B3
Russell Pickering Ho 2
 SW4 ....62 A4
Russell Pl 9 NW3 ..12 A3
 SE16 ....41 A3
Russell Rd W14 ...126 B1
Russell Sq WC1 ...94 A1
Russell Square Sta
 WC1 ....94 A1
Russell St 10 WC2 .120 B4
Russell Wlk 4
 TW10 ....54 B1
Russet Cres N7 ....14 B3
Russet Way SE13 ..52 A2
Russia Ct EC2 ....109 A2
Russia Dock Rd
 SE16 ....33 A1
Russia La E2 ......25 B3
Russia Row EC2 ..109 A1
Rust Sq SE5 ....48 C3
Rusthall Ave W4 ...37 C3
Rusthall Mans W4 .37 C2
Ruston Mews W11 .31 A3

Ruston St E3 .... 26 B4
Ruth Ct E14 E3 .... 26 A3
Ruth Ho W10 .... 23 A1
Rutherford Ho E2

E1 .... 25 A1
Rutherford St SW1 .107 B4
Ruthin Rd SE3 .... 53 C4
Ruthven St E9 .... 25 C4
Rutland Cl SW14 ...... 55 B4
Rutland Ct SW7 ..130 B3

SE5 .... 48 C3
Rutland Gate SW7 .130 B3
Rutland Gate Mews

SW7 .... 130 A3
Rutland Gdns SW7 .130 B3
Rutland Gdns Mews

SW7 .... 130 B3
Rutland Gr W6 .... 39 A1
Rutland Ho W8 ..128 A1
10 SW15 .... 69 B4
Rutland Mews E

SW7 .... 130 A3
Rutland Mews S

SW7 .... 130 A2
Rutland Mews W

SW7 .... 130 A2
Rutland Park Gdns

NW2 .... 9 B2
Rutland Park Mans

NW2 .... 9 B2
Rutland Pk NW2 .... 9 B2
Rutland Pl EC1 ..108 B4
Rutland Rd E9 .... 25 C4
Rutland St SW7 ..130 B2
Rutland Studios

NW10 .... 21 C2
Rutley Cl SE11 .... 48 A4
Rutt's Terr SE14 ...... 50 C2
Ruvigny Gdns SW15 .57 C4
Ruvigny Mans SW15 .57 C4
Rycott Path SE22 ...76 C4
Ryculff Sq SE3 .... 53 B1
Rydal Ho SE9 ..171 B1
Rydal Water SW11 ...92 C3
Ryde Ho 1 NW6 .... 23 C4
Ryde Vale Rd SW12 .73 B2
Ryder Ct SW1 ..119 A2
Ryder Dr SE16 .... 40 A1
Ryder Ho 14 E1 .... 25 B1
Ryder St SW1 ..119 A2
Ryder Yd SW1 ..119 A2
Ryder's Terr NW8 ...78 C2
Rydon St N1 .... 87 A4
Rydston Cl 2 N7 ...14 B1
Rye Hill Pk SE15 ...... 65 B3
Rye Ho 10 SE16 .... 40 B4
Rye La SE15 .... 49 C1
Rye Rd SE15 .... 65 C3
Rye Wlk SW15 .... 57 C2
Ryecotes Mead

SE21 .... 76 A3
Ryecroft Rd SE13 ....67 B2
Ryecroft St SW6 .....166 A3
Ryedale SE22 .... 77 A3
Ryefield Path 7

SW15 .... 68 C3
Ryegates 2 SE15 .....50 A1
Ryfold Rd SW19 ...... 70 C1
Ryland Rd NW5 .... 13 A2
Rylett Cres W12 ...... 38 B3
Rylett Rd W12 .... 38 B3
Rylston Rd SW6 .....154 C2
Rymer St SE24 .... 63 A1

S

Rysbrack St SW1 ..130 C2

Sabella Ct E3 .... 26 B3
Sabine Rd SW11 ......60 C4
Sable St N1 .... 15 A1
Sacketts Ho SW9 ...173 C4
Sackville Ho 16

SW16 .... 74 A1
Sackville St W1 ..119 A3
Sacred Heart High Sch

W6 .... 39 B2
Sacred Heart Jun Sch

W6 .... 39 C2
Sacred Heart Prim Sch

SW15 .... 56 C2
Sacred Heart RC Jun &
Inf Schs SW11 ..168 B1
Sacred Heart RC Sch

The SE5 .... 48 B2
Saddlers Mews

SW8 .... 172 B4
Sadler Ho EC1 .... 96 A4
17 E3 .... 27 A2
Saffron Ave E14 ....34 C2
Saffron Ct 16 N1 ...15 C2
Saffron Hill EC1 ..107 C4
Saffron St EC1 ..107 C4
Saffron Wharf SE1 .139 A4
Sage St E1 .... 32 B2
Sage Way WC1 ...94 C3
Sail St SE11 ..149 A4
Sailmakers Ct SW6 .59 B4
Sainfoin Rd SW17 ...72 C2
Salamanca Pl SE1 ..148 C3
Salamanca St SE1,

SE11 .... 148 C3
Salcombe Gdns

SW4 .... 61 A3
Salcombe Lo NW5 ...12 C4
Salcombe Rd 20

N16 .... 16 A3
Salcot N4 .... 5 B2
Salcott Rd SW11 ......60 B2
Sale Pl W2 ..102 A2
Sale St E2 ..24 C1 99 B2
Salehurst Rd SE4 ....66 B1
Salem Ho 3 E9 .... 17 C2
Salem Rd W2 ..114 B4
Salesian Coll

SW11 .... 168 A3
Salford Rd 4 E14 ....42 B2
Salford Rd SW12,

SW2 .... 73 C3
Salisbury Cl SE17 ..151 B4
Salisbury Ct EC4 ..108 A1

SE16 .... 139 C3
E9 .... 18 A3
W4 .... 38 B2
Salisbury Ho N1 ...86 A4

SW1 .... 147 C2
3 E14 .... 34 A3
SW9 .... 69 C1
Salisbury Mews

SW6 .... 154 C1
Salisbury Pl W1 ..102 C4
SW9 .... 48 A3
Salisbury Rd TW9 ...54 A3
Salisbury St NW8 ...90 A1

8 W3 .... 37 B4
Salisbury Terr SE15 .65 B4
Salisbury Wlk N19 ...4 B2
Salmon La E14 ....33 A3
Saltash St SE11 ..150 A2

Saltcoats Rd W4 ....38 A4
Saltdene N4 .... 5 B3
Salter Rd SE16 ....33 A1
Salter St NW10 .... 21 C2
10 E14 .... 33 C2
Salters Rd W10 ...22 C1
Salters' Hall Ct

EC4 .... 123 B4
Salterton Rd N7 .... 5 B1
Saltoun Rd SW2,

SW9 .... 62 C3
Saltram Cres W9 ......23 C2
Saltwell St E14 .... 33 C2
Saltwood Gr SE17 ..151 B1
Salusbury Prim Sch

NW6 .... 23 A4
Salusbury Rd NW6 ...23 A4
Salvin Rd SW15 ....57 C4
Salway Ho SW8 ..172 B4
Salway Rd E15 ....19 C2
Salween Ho 2 N16 .15 C4
Sam Manners Ho 8

SE10 .... 43 A1
Sam March Ho 5

E14 .... 34 C3
Samaritan Hospl for
Women NW1 ..102 C4
Sambrook Ho 10 E1 .32 B4
Samels Ct W6 .... 38 C1
Samford Ho N1 ...85 B3
Samford St NW8 ...90 A1
Sampson St E1 ..125 C1
Samuel Cl E8 ....24 B4
SE14 .... 50 C4
Samuel Ho 8 E8 .24 B4
Samuel Jones Ind Est 18

SE15 .... 49 A3
Samuel Lewis Bldgs

N1 .... 14 C2
Samuel Lewis Trust
Dwellings

W14 .... 140 B4
SW3 .... 144 A3
E8 .... 16 C3
6 SE5 .... 48 B2
Samuel Rhodes Sch

N1 .... 85 B4
Samuel Richardson Ho

W14 .... 140 C3
Samuel's Cl 2 W6 ...39 B2
Sancroft St SW11 ..168 B4
Sancroft St SE11 ..149 B2
Sanctuary St SE1 ..137 A4
Sanctuary The

SW1 .... 133 C2
6 E1 .... 32 A1
Sandale Cl N16 .... 6 C1
Sandall Ho 6 E3 ......26 A3
Sandall Rd NW5 ......13 B2
Sandalwood Cl 10

E1 .... 26 A1
Sandalwood Ho 6

NW3 .... 11 A2
Sandbourne NW8 ...78 B4
4 W11 .... 31 C3
Sandbourne Rd SE4 .51 A1
Sandbrook Rd N16 ...7 A1
Sandby Ho 6 NW6 .23 C4
11 SE5 .... 49 A2
Sandcroft Ho SE11 .149 A2
Sandell St SE1 ..135 B4
Sanderling Ct 20

SE8 .... 51 B4
Sanders Ho WC1 ...95 B4
Sanders Way 8 N19 .4 C3

Sanderson Cl NW5 ..13 A4
Sanderson Ho 7

SE8 .... 41 B1
Sanderstead Ave

NW2 .... 1 A2
Sanderstead Cl

SW12 .... 73 B4
Sandfield WC1 ...94 B3
Sandford Ct N16 ...... 7 A3
Sandford Row

SE17 .... 151 C2
Sandford St SW6 ...156 B1
Sandford Wlk 4 N16 .7 B2
SE14 .... 51 A4
Sandgate Ho 15 E5 .17 A4
Sandgate La SW17,

SW18 .... 72 A3
Sandgate St 18 SE15 .50 A4
Sandgate Trad Est

SE15 .... 50 A4
Sandham Ct SW4 ..172 B3
Sandhills The

SW10 .... 157 A4
Sandhurst Ct SW2 ...62 A3
Sandhurst Ho 10 E1 .32 B4
Sandilands Rd

SW6 .... 166 A3
Sandison St SE15 ....64 C4
Sandland St WC1 ..107 A3
Sandlings Cl SE15 ....50 A1
Sandmere Rd SW4 ..62 A3
Sandon Ho 5 SW2 ...74 A4
Sandown Ho 2 W4 .37 B1
Sandpiper Cl SE16 ..41 B4
Sandpiper Ct

11 E14 .... 42 B3
1 SE8 .... 51 C3
Sandridge Ct N4 ...... 6 B2
Sandridge St 3 N19 ..4 B2
Sandringham Cl 1

SW19 .... 69 C3
Sandringham Ct

W9 .... 89 A3
W1 .... 105 A1
18 SE16 .... 32 C1
SW15 .... 57 C1
Sandringham Flats

WC2 .... 119 C4
Sandringham Ho

W14 .... 140 A4
Richmond TW10 ...54 C2
Sandringham Rd

NW11 .... 1 A4
NW2 .... 9 A2
E8 .... 16 B3
Sandrock Rd SE13 ...66 C4
Sands End La SW6 .166 B4
Sandstone TW9 ....44 C3
Sandstone Pl N19 .... 4 A2
Sandways 6 TW9 ...44 C2
Sandwell Cres 2

NW6 .... 10 C2
Sandwell Mans 3

NW6 .... 10 C2
Sandwich Ho WC1 ...94 A3
16 SE16 .... 40 B4
Sandwich St WC1 ...94 A3
Sandy Lo N6 .... 4 A4
Sandy Rd NW3 .... 2 A2
Sandy's Row E1 ..110 B3
Sandycombe Rd

TW9 .... 44 C1
Sanford La 3 N16 ....7 B2
Sanford St SE14,SE8 .51 A4
Sanford Terr N16 .....7 B1

Sangora Rd 17

SW11 .... 59 C3
Sankey Ho 22 E2 ...25 B3
Sans Wlk EC1 ...96 A2
Sansom St SE5 ....48 C3
20 SE5 .... 48 C2
Santley Ho SE1 ..135 C3
Santley St SW4 .... 62 B3
Santos Rd SW18 ......58 C2
Sapcote Trad Ctr

NW10 .... 8 B2
Saperton Wlk

SE11 .... 149 A4
Sapperton Ct EC1 ...96 C2
Sapphire Ct 1 E1 ..125 B4
Sapphire Rd SE8 .....41 A2
Sara Lane Ct 8 N1 .24 A3
Saracen St E14 .... 33 C3
Sarah Ho 11 E1 .... 32 A3
SW15 .... 56 B3
Sarah House SW15 ...56 B3
Sarah Swift Ho

SE1 .... 137 C4
Saratoga Rd E5 ....17 B4
Sardinia St WC2 ..106 C2
Sarjant Path SW19 ...69 C2
Sark Ho 11 N1 ....15 B2
Sarnersfield Ho

SE15 .... 50 A4
Sarratt Ho W10 .... 30 B4
Sarre Rd NW2 .... 10 B3
Sarsden Bldgs W1 ..103 C1
Sarsfeld Rd SW12,

SW17 .... 72 B3
Sartor Rd SE15 .... 65 C3
Sarum Hall Sch

NW3 .... 12 A1
Sarum Ho W11 ..113 A3
Satchwell Rd E2 ......99 B3
Saul Ct 4 SE15 ......49 B4
Saunders Cl 14 E14 .33 B2
Saunders Ho

6 W11 .... 30 C1
11 SW2 .... 74 C4
Saunders Ness Rd

E14 .... 42 C2
Saunders St SE11 ..149 B4
Savage Gdns EC3 ..124 B4
Savana N1 .... 7 A2
Savernake Ho N4 ..... 6 C4
Savernake Rd NW3 .12 B4
Savill Ho 2 SW4 ...61 C1
Saville Rd W4 .... 37 C3
Saville Row W1 ..118 C4
Savona Ct SW8 ..160 C1
Savoy Bldgs WC2 ...29 B2
Savoy Circus W3 .....29 B2
Savoy Ct WC2 ..120 B3
SW5 .... 141 C4
Savoy Hill WC2 ..120 C3
Savoy Pier WC2 ..120 C3
Savoy Pl WC2 ..120 C3
Savoy Row WC2 ..120 C4
Savoy St WC2 ..120 C3
Savoy Steps WC2 ..120 C3
Savoy Way WC2 ..120 C3
Sawkins Cl SW19 ....70 A2
Sawley Rd W12 ....29 C1
Sawyer St 1 SE1 ..136 C4
Saxby Rd SW2 .... 74 A4
Saxon Dr W3 .... 28 A4
Saxon Hall W2 ..114 A3
Saxon Ho 4 SW4 ....61 C3
Saxon Rd E3 .... 26 B3
Saxonbury Ct 10 N7 .13 C3
2 N7 .... 14 A3
Saxonfield Cl SW2 ...74 B4

Saxton Cl SE13 .... 67 C4
Sayer Ho SE14 ...... 66 A3
Sayes Court St SE8 .. 51 B4
Sayes Ct SE8 .... 51 B4
Scafell NW1 .... 92 C4
Scala St W1 .... 105 A4
Scampston Mews **6**
W10 .... 30 C3
Scandrett St **30** E1 .. 32 A1
Scarba Wlk N1 ...... 15 C2
Scarborough Rd N4 .. 5 C3
Scarborough St
E1 .... 111 A1
Scarlette Manor Wlk **10**
SE24 .... 74 C4
Scarsbrook Ho **2**
SW2 .... 62 C1
Scarsdale Pl W8 .. 128 A2
Scarsdale Villas
W8 .... 127 C1
Scarth Rd SW13 .... 56 B4
Scawen Rd SE8 ..... 41 A1
Scawfell St E2 ...... 24 B3
Sceptre Ho **9** E1 .. 25 B1
Sceptre Rd E2 ...... 25 B2
Sch of Nursing
W1 .... 104 C4
Sch of Pharmacy
WC1 .... 94 B2
Schofield Wlk SE3 .. 53 C3
Scholars Rd SW12 .. 73 B3
Scholefield Rd N19 .. 4 C2
Scholey Ho SW11 .. 60 A4
Schomberg Ho
SW1 .... 147 C4
Schooner Cl
1 E16 .... 40 C4
E14 .... 42 C3
Schubert Rd SW15 .. 58 B2
Science Mus *
SW7 .... 129 B1
Sclater St **1** 99 A2
Scoles Cres SW2 .... 74 C3
Scoresby St SE1 ... 122 A1
Scorton Ho **2** N1 .. 24 A3
Scotch House
SW1 .... 130 C3
Scoter Ct **2** SE8 ... 51 B4
Scotia Bldg **10** E1 .. 32 C2
Scotia Ct **3** SE16 .. 40 B3
Scotia Rd **2** SW2 .. 74 C4
Scotland Pl SW1 ... 120 A1
Scotney Ho E9 ...... 17 B2
Scotson Ho SE11 .. 149 B3
Scotswood St EC1 .. 95 C2
Scott Ct SW11 ..... 170 B1
17 N16 .... 7 A1
W4 .... 37 C4
Scott Ellis Gdns
NW8 .... 89 B3
Scott Ho N1 .... 87 B4
NW8 .... 90 A1
N7 .... 14 B2

Scott Lidgett Cres
SE16 .... 139 C3
Scott St E1 .... 25 A1
Scott's Rd W12 .... 39 A4
Scott's Sufferance
Wharf SE1 .... 139 A3
Scott's Yd EC4 .... 123 B4
Scotts Ct **6** SE12 .. 39 A4
Scoulding Ho 6
E14 .... 41 C3
Scoulding Rd E16 .. 35 C3
Scouler St E14 ...... 34 C2
Scout App NW10 .... 8 A4
Scovell Cres SE1 .. 136 C3
Scovell Rd SE1 .... 136 C3
Scriven Ct **2** E8 .. 24 B4
Scriven St E8 ...... 24 B4
Scroope St SE6 .... 67 A1
Scrope Ho EC1 .... 107 B4
Scrubs La NW10,
W10,W12 .... 22 A2
Scrutton Cl SW12 .. 73 C4
Scrutton St
EC2 .... 24 A1 98 A1
Scutari Rd SE22 .... 65 B2
Scylla Rd SE15 .... 65 A4
Seabright St **2** 25 A2
Seacole Cl W3 ...... 29 A3
Seaford Ho **8** SE16 .. 40 B4
Seaford St WC1 .... 94 B3
Seaforth Cres N5 .. 15 B3
Seaforth Lo **2**
SW13 .... 46 B1
Seaforth Pl SW1 .. 133 A2
Seager Pl **3** E3 ... 33 B4
Seagrave Lodge
SW6 .... 155 C4
Seagrave Rd SW6 .. 155 C4
Seagrove Cl E1 .... 32 C4
Seal Ho SE1 .... 137 C2
Seal St E8 .... 16 B4
Searle Ct N4 .... 5 B3
Searle Ho **15** E1 .. 32 C4
Searles Cl SW11 .. 158 B1
Searles Rd SE1 .... 151 C4
Sears St SE5 .... 48 C3
Searson Ho SE17 .. 150 B3
Seasalter Ho SW9 .. 173 B4
Seaton Cl SE11 .... 149 A2
SW15 .... 69 A3
Seaton Point E5 .... 16 C4
Seavington Ho **3**
SE5 .... 48 C2
Sebastian Ho **22** N1 .. 24 A3
Sebastian St EC1 .. 96 B3
Sebbon St N1 ...... 15 A1
Sebright Ho **2** E2 .. 24 C3
Sebright JMI Sch
E2 .... 24 C3
Secker Ho SW9 .... 48 A1
Secker St SE1 .... 121 B1
Second Ave W10 .. 23 A1
W3 .... 29 B1
SW14 .... 56 A4
Sedan Way SE17 .. 152 A2
Sedding St SW1 .. 145 B4
Seddon Ho EC2 .. 108 C4
Seddon St WC1 .... 95 A3
Sedgeford Rd W12 .. 29 B1
Sedgewick Ho
SW19 .... 69 C2
Sedgley Ho N4 ...... 5 B2
Sedgmoor Pl SE5 .. 49 A3
Sedgwick St E9 .... 17 C3
Sedleigh Rd SW18 .. 58 B1

Sedlescombe Rd
SW6 .... 155 B4
Sedley Ho SE11 .. 149 A2
Sedley Pl W1 ..... 104 A1
Seething La EC3 .. 124 B4
Sefton St SW15 .... 57 B4
Sekforde St EC1 .... 96 A2
Selbie Ave NW10 .. 8 B3
Selborne **2** SW11 .. 60 C4
Selborne Ho SE1 .. 137 B3
Selborne Rd **5** SE5 .. 48 C1
Selby Ho **10** 22 B1
10 SW4 .... 61 B1
Selby St E1 ... 24 C1 99 C1
Selden Ho **2** SE15 .. 50 B1
Selden Rd SE15 .... 50 B1
Selden Wlk N7 ...... 5 B2
Seldon Ho SW1 .. 146 C1
SW8 .... 160 C1
Selfridges W1 .. 103 C1
Selhurst Cl SW19 .. 69 C3
Selina Ho NW8 ...... 89 C2
Selkirk Ho N1 ...... 84 C4
4 N16 .... 7 A1
Sellons Ave NW10 .. 21 B4
Selma Ho W12 ...... 30 A3
Selman Ho **8** E9 .. 18 A2
Selsdon Rd SE27 .. 75 A1
Selsea Pl N16 ...... 16 A3
Selsey St E14 ...... 33 C4
Selwood Ho **4** N4 .. 6 C4
Selwood Pl SW7 .. 143 B2
Selwood Terr SW7 .. 143 B2
Selworthy Ho
SW11 .... 167 C4
Selwyn Ave TW9 .. 54 B4
Selwyn Ct **3** TW10 .. 54 B2
Selwyn Ho **3** SW15 .. 57 C1
Selwyn Rd NW10 .. 8 A1
E3 .... 26 B3
Semley Ho SW1 .. 146 A3
Semley Pl SW1 .. 146 A3
Senate St SE15 .... 50 B1
Senators Lo **29** E3 .. 26 A3
Sendall Ct **13** SW11 .. 59 C4
Senior St W2 ..... 100 A4
Senrab St E1 ...... 32 C3
Seraph Ct EC1 ...... 96 C4
Sergeant Ind Est The
SW18 .... 59 A1
Serica Ct **14** SE10 .. 52 B3
Serjeants' Inn
EC4 .... 107 C1
Serlby Ct W14 .... 126 C2
Sermon La EC4 ... 108 C1
Serpentine Br 8
W2 .... 115 C3
Serpentine Ct 10
SE16 .... 40 C4
Serpentine Gallery *
W2 .... 129 C4
Serpentine Rd W2 .. 116 C1
Serpentine The *
W2 .... 116 B1
Service Route No 1
E15 .... 19 C1
Service Route No 2
E15 .... 19 C1
Service Route No 3
E15 .... 19 C1
Servite Ho SE13 .... 52 A2
Servite RC Prim Sch
SW10 .... 156 C4
Setchell Rd SE1 .. 152 C4
Setchell Way SE1 .. 152 C4

Seth St **18** SE16 .. 40 B4
Settles St E1 ..... 111 C2
Settrington Rd
SW6 .... 166 A1
Seven Dials WC2 .. 106 A1
Seven Mills JMI Sch
E14 .... 41 C4
Seven Sisters Rd N4,
N7,N15 .... 5 C2
Seven Stars Cnr
W12 .... 38 C3
Sevenoaks Rd SE4 .. 66 B1
Severn Ho **7** W10 .. 23 A2
Severn Way NW10 .. 8 B3
Severnake Cl E14 .. 41 C2
Severus Rd SW11 .. 60 A3
Seville Ho **9** E1 .. 125 C1
Seville Mews N1 .. 16 A1
Seville St SW1 ... 131 A3
Sevington St W9 .. 88 A1
Seward St EC1 ...... 96 C3
Sewardstone Rd E2 .. 25 B3
Sewell Ho **2** N16 .. 16 A3
Sextant Ave E14 .. 42 C2
Sexton's Ho **3** SE13 .. 52 B4
Seymour Ct N16 .... 7 C3
SW15 .... 57 B2
Seymour Gdns SE4 .. 66 A4
Seymour Ho NW1 .. 93 C3
WC1 .... 94 A2
SW8 .... 171 A2
Seymour Mews
W1 .... 103 B2
Seymour Pl W1 .. 102 C2
Seymour Rd W4 .... 37 B2
SW18 .... 58 B1
SW19 .... 69 C3
Seymour St W1 .. 103 A1
W2 .... 103 A1
Seymour Wlk
SW10 .... 156 C4
Seyssel St E14 ...... 42 B2
Shaa Rd W3 .... 28 C2
Shackleton Cl
4 W12 .... 39 A4
1 SE21 .... 75 C2
Shackleton Ho 5
E1 .... 32 B1
Shacklewell Ho 3
E8 .... 16 B4
Shacklewell JMI Sch
E8 .... 16 B3
Shacklewell La E8 .. 16 B3
Shacklewell Prim Sch
E8 .... 16 B4
Shacklewell Row
E8 .... 16 B4
Shacklewell St **21** .. 24 B2
Shad Thames SE1 .. 139 A4
Shadwell Gdns E1 .. 32 B2
Shadwell Pierhead
E1 .... 32 B2
Shadwell Sta E1 .. 32 A2
Shaftesbury Ave
WC2 .... 105 C1
W1 .... 119 C4
Shaftesbury Gdns
NW10 .... 21 A1
Shaftesbury Ho
W2 .... 114 B4
4 N16 .... 7 A3
Shaftesbury Lo 8
E14 .... 34 A3
Shaftesbury Mews
W8 .... 127 C1

Shaftesbury Park
Chambers 1
SW11 .... 60 C4
Shaftesbury Rd
N4,N19 .... 5 A3
Richmond TW9 .... 54 A4
Shaftesbury St N1 .. 87 B1
Shaftesbury Ct
SW17 .... 72 B1
Shafto Mews SW1 .. 131 A1
Shafton Rd E9 ...... 25 C4
Shafts Ct EC3 ..... 110 A1
Shaftsbury Ct SW6 .. 166 B3
Shaftsbury Mews 2
SW4 .... 61 B2
Shaftsbury Park Prim
Sch SW11 .... 169 B1
Shahjalal Ho **10** E2 .. 24 C3
Shakespeare Ave
NW10 .... 20 C4
Shakespeare Cres
NW10 .... 20 C4
Shakespeare Ho 3
E9 .... 17 B1
Shakespeare Rd
W3 .... 28 B1
SE24 .... 63 A3
Shakespeare Twr
EC2 .... 109 A4
Shakespeare's Globe
Theatre (site of) *
SE1 .... 123 A2
Shakspeare Mews 7
N16 .... 7 A1
Shakspeare Wlk
N16 .... 7 A1
Shalcomb St SW10 .. 157 A3
Shalden Ho **6**
SW15 .... 56 B1
Shalfleet Dr W10 .. 30 C2
Shalford NW10 .... 21 C4
Shalford Ct N1 .... 86 A2
Shalford Ho SE1 .. 137 C2
Shalimar Gdns W3 .. 28 B2
Shalimar Lo W3 .... 28 B2
Shalimar Rd W3 .... 28 B2
Shalstone Rd SW14,
TW9 .... 55 A4
Shamrock St SW4 .. 61 C4
Shand St SE1 ..... 138 B4
Shandon Rd SW4 .. 61 B1
Shandy St E1 ...... 25 C1
Shannon Ct N16 .... 7 A1
2 NW10 .... 8 C2
SE15 .... 49 B3
Shannon Gr SW9 .. 62 B3
Shannon Pl NW8 .. 80 B2
Shanti Ct SW18 .... 70 C3
Shapla JMI Sch E1 .. 125 B4
Shard's Sq SE15 .... 49 C4
Shardcroft Ave
SE24 .... 63 A2
Shardeloes Rd SE14 .. 51 B1
Sharebourne Ho
SW2 .... 62 C2
Sharnbrook Ho
W6 .... 155 B4
Sharon Gdns E9 .... 25 B4
Sharon Rd W4 ...... 37 C1
Sharp Ho SW8 ...... 61 A4
Sharples Hall St 8
NW1 .... 12 B1

Sharpness Ct 2
SE15 ....49 B3
Sharratt St SE15 .....50 B4
Sharstead St SE17 ..150 A1
Sharwell Ho SW18 ..59 A1
Sharwood WC1 ....85 A1
Shaver's Pl SW1 .....119 B3
Shaw Cr N19 ....5 A2
  6 W3 ....37 B3
  12 SW11 ....59 C2
Shaw Ho E16 ....33 A3
Shaw Rd SE22 ....64 A3
Shawbury Ct SE22 ..64 B2
Shawbury Rd SE22 ..64 B2
Shawfield St SW3 ..144 B1
Shawford Ct
  SW15 ....68 C4
Shearling Way N7 ..14 A2
Shearsmith Ho E1 ..125 C4
Shearwater Ct 24
  SE8 ....51 B4

Sheen Common Dr
  SW14,TW10 ....54 C2
Sheen Court Rd
  TW10 ....54 C3
Sheen Ct TW10 ....54 C3
Sheen Gate Gdns
  SW14 ....55 B3
Sheen Gr N1 ....85 B4
Sheen La SW14 ......55 B3
Sheen Mount JMI Sch
  SW14 ....55 A2
Sheen Pk TW10,TW9 54 A3
Sheen Rd TW10,TW9 54 A3
Sheen Wood SW14 ..55 B2
Sheendale Rd TW9 ..54 B3
Sheep La E8 ....25 A4
Sheepcote La
  SW11 ....169 A1
Sheffield Ho 10
  SE15 ....49 B2
Sheffield Sq 2 E3 ..26 B2
Sheffield St WC2 ..106 C1
Sheffield Terr
  W8 ....31 C1 113 C1
Shelbourne Ho 20
  N19 ....4 C4
Shelburne Ct SW5 ..57 C2
Shelburne Rd N7 ....14 B4
Shelburne Rd SE22 ..65 A2
Shelgrove Rd N16 ..16 A3
Shell Ctr SE1 ....121 A1
Shell Rd SE13 ....67 A4
Shelley Cl SE15 ....50 A1
Shelley Ct SW3 .....159 A4
  N4 ....5 B3
Shelley Ho SE17 ....151 A2
  SW1 ....160 C4
  6 N16 ....16 A4
  21 E2 ....25 B2
  Shelley Sch SE11 ..149 C3
Shellness Rd E5 ......17 A3
Shellwood Rd
  SW11 ....168 C1

Shelmerdine Cl E3 ..33 C4
Shelton St WC2 .....106 A1
Shene Ho EC1 ....107 B4
  Shene Sec Sch
  SW14 ....56 A3
Shenfield St N1 ....24 A3
Shenley Rd SE5 ....49 A2
Shepherd Cl W1 ....117 B4
Shepherd Ho N7 .....14 A2
  10 E14 ....34 A3
Shepherd Mkt W1 ..118 A1
Shepherd St W1 ....118 A1
Shepherd's Bush Gn
  W12 ....39 B4
Shepherd's Bush Market
  W12 ....39 B4
Shepherd's Bush Pl
  W12 ....39 B4
Shepherd's Bush Rd
  W6 ....39 B3
Shepherd's Bush Sta
  W12 ....30 B1
Shepherd's La E9 ....17 C2
Shepherd's Wlk
  NW3 ....2 C1
Shepherdess Pl N1 ..97 A4
Shepherdess Wlk
  N1 ....87 A1
Shepherds Ct 1
  W12 ....39 C4
Shepherds Pl W1 ..117 B4
Sheppard Dr SE16 ..40 A1
Sheppard Ho 28 E2 ..24 C3
  18 SW11 ....59 C4
  5 SW2 ....74 C3
Shepperton Rd N1 ..87 B4
Sheppey Ho 10 E5 ..17 A4
Sheppey Wlk N1 .....15 B1
Shepton Ct SW11 ..167 C4
Shepton Ho 11 E2 ..25 B2
Sherard Ct N19 ....4 A1
Sherard Ho 24 E9 ..17 B1
Sheraton Ho SW1 ..160 B4
Sheraton St W1 .....105 B1
Sherborne Ho
  SW1 ....146 B2
  SW8 ....162 C1
Sherborne La EC4 ..123 C4
Sherborne St N1 .....87 B4
Sherbrooke Ho 9
  E2 ....25 B3
Sherbrooke Rd
  SW6 ....154 B1
Sherbrooke Terr
  SW6 ....154 B1
Shere Ho SE1 ....137 B2
Sherfield Gdns
  SW15 ....56 B1
Sheridan Bldgs
  WC2 ....106 B1
Sheridan Ct NW6 .....11 B1
Sheridan Ho SE11 ..149 C3
  7 N16 ....7 A1
  16 E1 ....32 B3
Sheridan Pl SW13 ..56 B4
Sheridan St 2 E1 ....32 A3
Sheridon Ct SW5 ..142 A3
Sheringdale Prim Sch
  SW18 ....70 B2
Sheringham NW8 ....79 C4
Sheringham Ho
  NW1 ....102 B4
Sheringham Rd N7 ..14 B2
Sherlock Ct NW8 ....79 B2
Sherlock Holmes Mus ✱
  NW1 ....91 A1

Sherlock Mews
  W1 ....103 B4
Sherrick Green Rd
  NW10 ....9 A3
Sherriff Ct NW6 ....10 C2
Sherriff Rd NW6 .....10 C2
Sherrin Rd E10 ....19 A4
Sherston Ct WC1 ....95 B3
  SE1 ....150 B4
Sherwin Ho SE11 ..163 B4
Sherwin Rd SE14 ....50 C2
Sherwood NW6 ....10 A1
Sherwood Ct SW13 ..57 A4
Sherwood Ct W1 ....102 C3
  SE13 ....52 A1
  11 SW1 ....146 B1
Sherwood Gdns
  SE16 ....40 A1
  E14 ....41 C2
Sherwood Ho N4 .....6 B4
Sherwood St W1 ....119 B4
Shetland Rd E3 ....26 B3
Shillaker Ct W3 ....29 B1
Shillibeer Pl W1 ....102 B3
Shillingford Ho 40
  E3 ....27 A2
Shillingford St 26
  N1 ....15 A1
Shinfield St W12 .....30 B3
Ship and Mermaid Row
  SE1 ....138 A4
Ship La SW14 ....45 B1
Ship St SE8 ....51 C2
Ship Tavern Pas
  EC3 ....124 A4
Shipka Rd SW12 .....73 A3
Shiplake Ho E2 ....98 C3
Shipley Ho SW8 ....171 B1
Shipton Ho 7 NW5 ..12 C2
  1 E2 ....24 B3
Shipwright Rd SE16 ..41 A4
Shipwright Yd SE1 ..124 A1
Shirbutt St E14 ....34 A2
Shire Pl SW18 ....71 B4
Shirland Mews W9 ..23 B2
Shirland Rd W9 ....23 C1
Shirley Gr SW11 ......60 C4
Shirley Ho 13 SE5 ..48 C3
Shirley Rd W4 ....37 C4
Shirley St E16 ....35 B1
Shirlock Rd NW3 .....12 B4
Shoe La EC4 ....107 C2
Shoot-Up Hill NW2 ..10 A2
Shooters Hill Rd
  SE3,SE10 ....53 A1
Shore Bsns Ctr 51 ..
  ....17 B1
Shore Ho SW8 ....61 A4
Shore Mews E9 ......17 B1
Shore Pl E9 ....17 B1
Shore Rd E9 ....17 B1
Shoreditch Ct 6 E8 ..16 B1
Shoreditch High St
  E1 ....24 A1 98 B2
Shoreditch Sta
  E1 ....24 A1 99 A1
Shoreham Cl SW18 ..59 A2
Shorncliffe Rd
  SE1 ....152 C2
Shorrolds Rd SW6 ..155 A2
Short Rd E15 ....27 C4
  W4 ....46 A4
Silesia Bldgs E8 .....17 A1
Silex St SE1 ....136 B3
Silk Mills Path SE13 ..67 B4
Silk Mills Sq E9 ......18 B2
Silk St EC2 ....109 A4
Sillitoe Ho N1 ....87 C3

Shortlands W6 ....39 C2
Shorts Gdns WC2 ..106 A1
Shottendane Rd
  SW6 ....165 B4
Shottfield Ave
  SW14 ....56 A3
Shottsford 1 W11 ..31 C3
Shoulder of Mutton
  Alley 10 E14 ....33 A2
Shouldham St W1 ..102 B3
Shreveport Ho 20
  N19 ....4 C4
Shrewsbury Ave
  SW14 ....55 C3
Shrewsbury Cres
  NW10 ....8 A1
Shrewsbury Ho
  SW3 ....158 A3
  SW3 ....163 A3
Shrewsbury Mews 33
  W2 ....31 C4
Shrewsbury Rd W2 ..31 C3
Shrewsbury St W10 ..22 B1
Shropshire Pl WC1 ..93 A1
Shroton St NW1 ....102 B4
Shrubland Rd E8 .....24 C4
Shrubs Ho SW1 ......147 C3
Shubbery Cl N1 ......87 A3
Shurland Gdns SE15 ..49 B3
Shuters Sq W14 .....140 C1
Shuttle St E1 ..24 C1 99 B1
Shuttleworth Rd
  SW11 ....168 A2
Sibella Rd SW4 ......171 C1
Sicilian Ave WC1 ...106 B3
Sidbury St SW6 .....164 A4
Siddons Ct WC2 .....106 C1
Siddons Ho WC2 ....101 C3
  8 NW3 ....11 B2
Siddons La NW1 ....91 A1
Sidford Ho SE1 ......135 A1
Sidford Pl SE1 ....135 A1
Sidgwick Ho SW9 ..172 B1
Sidings Mews N7 ....14 C4
Sidlaw Ho N16 ....7 B3
Sidmouth Ho W1 ....102 B2
  18 SE15 ....49 C3
Sidmouth Par NW2 ..9 B1
Sidmouth Rd NW2 ....9 B1
Sidmouth St WC1 ....94 C3
Sidney Boyd Ct
  NW6 ....10 C1
Sidney Godley (VC) Ho
  E2 ....25 B2
Sidney Gr EC1 ....86 A1
Sidney Ho 4 E2 ....25 C3
Sidney Miller Ct 3
  W3 ....28 A1
Sidney Rd SW9 ......173 A1
Sidney Sq E1 ....32 B4
Sidney St E1 ....32 B4
Sidworth St 6 E8 .....17 A1
Siebert Rd SE3 ....53 C4
Siege Ho 4 E1 ....32 A3
Sigdon Rd E8 ....16 C3
Signmakers Yd
  NW1 ....82 B3
Silbury Ho 3 SE26 ..76 C1
Silbury St N1 ....97 B4
Silchester Rd W10 ..30 C3

Silsoe Ho NW1 ....82 B1
Silver Cl SE14 ....51 A3
Silver Cres W4 ....37 A2
Silver Ct N19 ....4 B1
Silver Pl W1 ....119 A4
Silver Rd W12 ....30 C2
Silver Wlk SE16 ....33 B1
Silverbirch Ct E8 .....16 B1
Silverbirch Wlk 1
  NW3 ....12 C2
Silverburn Ho 4
  SW9 ....48 A2
Silverdale NW1 ....92 C4
Silvermere Rd SE6 ..67 A1
Silverthorn NW8 .....78 B3
Silverthorne Rd
  SW8 ....170 A3
  SW8 ....170 B1
Silverton Rd W6 ....154 A3
Silvertown Way E16 ..35 C1
Silvester Ho 27 E2 ..25 B2
  2 W11 ....31 B3
  11 E1 ....32 A3
Silvester Rd SE22 ..64 B2
Silvester St SE1 .....137 B3
Silwood St SE16 .....40 B1
Simla Cl SE14 ....51 A4
Simla Ho SE1 ....137 C3
Simmons Ho E2 ....99 B3
  N7 ....13 C3
Simms Rd SE1 ....153 C3
Simon Cl
  W11 ....31 A2 113 A4
Simon Ct W9 ....23 C2
Simon Lo 11 SW19 ..69 C3
Simon Marks (Jewish)
  JMI Sch N16 ....7 B2
Simons Wlk E15 .....19 C3
Simpson Dr W3 ....28 C3
Simpson Ho NW8 ....90 A3
  SE11 ....148 C1
Simpson St SW11 ..168 A1
Simpson's Rd E14 ..34 A2
Sinclair Ct N5 ....15 A2
Sinclair Gdns W14 ..39 C4
Sinclair Ho 1
  SW12 ....73 C3
Sinclair Mans 13
  W12 ....39 C4
Sinclair Rd W14 ....126 A2
Sinclairs Ho 14 E3 ..26 B3
Singer St EC2 ....97 C3
Sion-Manning Sch for
  Girls W10 ....30 C4
Sion-Manning Sec Sch
  W10 ....31 A4
Sir Abraham Dawes
  Cotts SW15 ....58 A3
Sir Alexander Cl
  W3 ....29 B1
Sir Alexander Rd
  W3 ....29 B1
Sir Francis Drake Prim
  Sch SE8 ....41 A1
Sir James Barrie Prim
  Sch SW8 ....171 A3
Sir John Cass's
  Foundation & Redcoat
  CE Sec Sch E1 ....32 C4
Sir John Cass's
  Foundation CE Prim
  Sch EC3 ....110 B1
Sir John Lillie Prim Sch
  SW6 ....154 B3

Sir Oswald Stoll
Foundation The
SW6 . . . . **156** A2
Sir Thomas Abney JMI
Sch N16 . . . . .6 C3
Sir Thomas More Est
SW3 . . . . **157** C3
Sir William Burrough
JMI Sch E14 . . . . . . .33 A3
Sir William Powell's
Almshos SW6 . . . . .58 A4
Sirdar Rd
W11 . . . . .31 A2 **112** A3
Sirinham Point
SW8 . . . . **163** A3
Sirius Bldg 13 E1 . . .32 C2
Sise La EC4 . . . . . . **109** B1
Siskin Ho 12 SE16 . .40 C2
Sispara Gdns SW18 .58 B1
Sissinghurst Ho 17
SE15 . . . . .50 B4
Sister Mabel's Way 14
SE15 . . . . .49 C3
Sisters Ave SW11 . . .60 B3
Sistova Rd SW12 . . .73 A3
Sisulu Pl SW9 . . . . .62 C4
Site of the Changing of the
Guard* SW1 . . . . **132** C3
Sivill Ho E2 . . . . . . .99 A4
Siward Rd SW17 . . .71 B1
Six Bridges Ind Est
SE1 . . . . **153** C1
Sixth Ave W10 . . . . .23 A2
Skardu Rd NW2 . . . .10 A3
Skeena Hill SW18,
SW19 . . . . .70 A4
Skeggs Ho 9 E14 . . .42 B3
Skegness Ho 3 N7 . .14 B1
Skelbrook St SW18 .71 B2
Skelgill Rd SW15 . . .58 B3
Skelton 7 E8 . . . . . .16 B2
Skelton Ho N16 . . . .16 A3
Skelwith Rd W6 . . . .47 B4
Skenfrith Ho SE15 . .50 A4
Sketchley Gdns
SE16 . . . . .40 C1
Skiffington Cl SW2 . .74 C3
Skinner St EC1 . . . **145** B3
Skinner St 2
(Upper) N16 . . . . . . .6 C2
Skinners Company Sch
(Upper) N16 . . . . . . .6 C4
Skinners La EC4 . . **123** A4
Skipsea Ho SW18 . . .59 C1
Skipton Ho SE4 . . . .66 A3
Skipwith Ho EC1 . . **107** B4
Skipworth Rd E9 . . .25 B4
Skomer Wlk N1 . . . .15 B1
Skua Ct 25 SE8 . . . .51 B4
Skylines E14 . . . . . .42 B4
Slade Ct NW2 . . . . .10 A3
Slade Wlk SE17 . . . .48 B4
Sladen Pl 12 E5 . . . .17 A4
Slagrove Pl SE13 . . .67 A2
Slaidburn St SW10 **157** A3
Slaithwaite Rd SE13 .67 B3
Slaney Ct NW10 . . . .9 B1
Sleaford Ho 13 E3 . .26 C1
Sleaford Ind Est
SW8 . . . . **161** A1
Sleaford St SW8 . . **161** A1
Sleat Ho 9 E3 . . . . .26 B3
Slievemore Cl 8
SW4 . . . . .61 C4
Sligo Ho 8 E1 . . . . .25 C1
Slingsby Pl WC2 . . **120** A4
Slippers Pl SE16 . . .40 A3

Sloane Ave SW3 . . **144** B3
Sloane Avenue Mans
SW3 . . . . **144** C3
Sloane Ct E SW3 . . **145** B2
Sloane Ct W SW3 . . **145** B2
Sloane Gate Mans
SW1 . . . . **145** B4
Sloane Gdns SW1 . **145** B3
Sloane Ho 7 E9 . . . .17 B1
Sloane Sq SW1 . . . **145** A3
Sloane Square Sta
SW1 . . . . **145** B3
Sloane St SW1 . . . **131** A1
Sloane Terr SW1 . . **145** B4
Sloane Terr Mans
SW1 . . . . **145** B4
Slomon Ho 2 W10 . .23 A2
Sly St 17 E1 . . . . . . .32 A3
Smallbrook Mews
W2 . . . . **101** B1
Smalley Cl N16 . . . . .7 B1
Smart St E2 . . . . . . .25 C2
Smart's Pl WC1,
WC2 . . . . **106** B2
Smeaton Ct SE1 . . **136** C1
Smeaton Rd SW18 . .70 C4
Smeaton St E1 . . . . .32 A1
Smedley St SW4 . . **171** C2
Smeed Rd E3 . . . . . .18 C1
Smethwick Ho 13
E9 . . . . .25 B4
Smiles Pl SE13 . . . . .52 B1
Smith Cl SE16 . . . . .32 C1
Smith Sq SW1 . . . **134** A1
Smith St SW3 . . . . **144** C1
Smith Terr SW3 . . . **144** C1
Smith's Ct W1 . . . **119** B4
Smith's Yd SW18 . . .71 B2
Smithfield Mkt* . . . .
EC1 . . . . **108** B3
Smithfield St EC1 . **108** A3
Smithies Ct E15 . . . .76 B3
Smithwood Cl
SW19 . . . . .70 A2
Smithy JMI Sch E1 . .32 B4
Smithy St E1 . . . . . .32 B4
Smugglers Way
SW18 . . . . .59 A3
Smyrk's Rd SE17 . . **152** B1
Smyrna Mans 8
NW6 . . . . .10 C1
Smyrna Rd NW6 . . .10 C1
Smythe St E14 . . . . .34 A2
Snarsgate St W10 . .30 B4
Sneath Ave NW11 . . .1 B4
Sneyd Rd NW2 . . . . .9 B4
Snipe Ct 5 SE8 . . . .51 A4
Snow Hill EC1 . . . . **108** A3
Snow Ho SE27 . . . . .75 A1
Snowberry Cl E11 . . .19 C4
Snowbury Rd SW6 **166** B1
Snowden St
EC2 . . . . .24 A1 **98** A1
Snowman Ho NW6 . .78 A3
Snowsfield Prim Sch
SE1 . . . . **138** A4
Snowsfields SE1 . . **137** C4
Soames St SE15 . . . .64 B4
Soane Ct 8 NW1 . . .13 B1
Soane Ho SE17 . . . **151** C1
Soane Mus* SE2 . **106** C2
Soho Parish CE Prim
Sch W1 . . . . **119** B4
Soho Sq W1 . . . . . **105** B2
Soho St W1 . . . . . . **105** B2

Sojourner-Truth Cl 11
E8 . . . . .17 A2
Solander Gdns E1 . .32 A2
12 E1 . . . . .32 B2
Soldene Ct N7 . . . . **114** B2
Solebay St E1 . . . . .26 A1
Solent Ho 6 E1 . . . .33 A4
Solent Rd NW6 . . . .10 C3
Soley Mews WC1 . . **95** B4
Solna Ave SW15 . . . .57 B2
Solomon's Pas SE15 .65 A3
Solon New Rd SW4 .62 A3
Solon Rd SW2 . . . . .62 A3
Solway Ho 15 E1 . . .25 C1
Solway Rd SE22 . . . .64 C3
Somali Rd NW2 . . . .10 B3
Somborne Ho SW15 .68 C4
Sombrook Ho
SE11 . . . . **149** B3
Somer Ct SW6 . . . **155** B3
Somerfield Ho SE16 .40 C1
Somerfield Rd N4 . . .6 A2
Somerford Gr N16 . . .7 C1
Somerford Grove Est
N16 . . . . .7 C1
Somerford St E1 . . . .25 A1
Somerford Way
SE16 . . . . .41 A4
Somerleyton Rd
SW9 . . . . .62 C3
Somers Cl NW1 . . . **83** B2
Somers Cres W2 . . **102** A1
Somers Pl SW2 . . . .74 B4
Somers Rd SW2 . . . .62 B1
Somers Town Est
NW1 . . . . **83** A1
Somerset Gdns N6 . .3 C4
SE13 . . . . .52 A1
Somerset Ho W2 . . .31 C4
Somerset House
WC2 . . . . **121** A4
Somerset Lo SW15 .57 A3
Somerset Rd W4 . . .37 C3
SW19 . . . . .70 A1
Somerset Sq W14 . **126** C3
Somerton Ave TW9 .55 A4
Somerton Rd NW2 . .1 A1
SE15 . . . . .65 A3
Somerville Ho 10
SW15 . . . . .57 C1
Sonderburg Rd 10
N7 . . . . .5 B2
Sondes St SE17 . . . **48** C4
Sonia Gdns NW10 . . .4 B4
Sonning Ho 2 . . . .
SE16 . . . . .40 B4
Sophia Cl N7 . . . . . .14 B2
Sophia Ho 10 W6 . . .39 B1
Sophia Sq 16 SE16 . .33 A2
Sopwith Way
SW11 . . . . **160** A2
Sorrel La 16 E14 . . . .34 C3
Sorrell Cl SW9 . . . **173** C2
SE14 . . . . .51 A3
Sotheby Rd N5 . . . . .15 B4
Sotheran Cl E8 . . . .24 C4
Sotheron Pl SW6 . . **156** B1
Soudan Rd SW11 . . **168** C3
Souldern Rd 10
W14 . . . . .39 C3
South Acton Sta
W3,W4 . . . . .37 B3
South Africa Rd
W12 . . . . .30 A2
South Audley St
W1 . . . . **117** C2
South Ave TW9 . . . .44 C1

South Bank Bsns Ctr
SW8 . . . . **161** A3
South Bank Univ
SE1 . . . . **136** B2
South Bermondsey Sta
SE16 . . . . .40 B1
South Black Lion La
W6 . . . . .38 C1
South Block 19 E1 . .32 B2
South Bolton Gdns
SW10 . . . . **142** B2
South Building
SE10 . . . . **52** C3
South Camden Com Sch
NW1 . . . . **83** B1
South Carriage Dr
SW1,SW7 . . . . **130** C4
South Colonnade
E14 . . . . .33 C1
South Cres WC1 . . **105** B3
South Ct 11 SW15 . .57 C1
South Eaton Pl
SW1 . . . . **145** C4
South Edwardes Sq
W8 . . . . **127** B1
South End W8 . . . **128** B2
South End Cl NW3 . .12 A4
South End Gn NW3 .12 A4
South End Rd NW3 . .12 A4
South End Row
W8 . . . . **128** B2
South Gr N6 . . . . . . .3 C3
South Grove Ho N6 . .3 C3
South Hampstead High
Sch (Jun Dept)
NW3 . . . . .11 B2
South Hampstead High
Sch for Girls NW3 . .11 C2
South Hampstead Sta
NW8 . . . . .11 B1
South Hill Pk NW3 . .12 A4
South Hill Pk Gdns
NW3 . . . . .12 A4
South Island Pl
SW9 . . . . **163** B1
South Kensington Sta
SW7 . . . . **143** C4
South Lambeth Pl
SW8 . . . . **162** B4
South Lambeth Rd
SW8 . . . . **162** B2
South Lo NW8 . . . . **89** B4
South Molton La
W1 . . . . **104** A1
South Molton Rd
E16 . . . . .35 C3
South Molton St
W1 . . . . **104** A1
South Par W4 . . . . .37 C2
South Parade SW3 **143** C2
South Park Mews
SW6 . . . . .59 A4
South Pl EC2 . . . . **109** C3
South Pl Mews
EC2 . . . . **109** C3
South Quay Plaza
E14 . . . . .42 A4
South Quay Sta E14 .42 A4
South Rise W2 . . . **116** B4
South Row SE3 . . . .53 B1
South Sea St SE16 . .41 B3

South Side W6 . . . .38 B3
South Sq WC1 . . . **107** B3
South St W1 . . . . . **117** C2
South Tenter St
E1 . . . . **111** A1
South Terr SW7 . . **144** A4
South Thames Coll
SW15 . . . . .57 C2
SW18 . . . . .59 A2
South Thames Coll
(Roehampton Centre)
SW15 . . . . .56 C1
South Villas NW1 . . .13 C2
South West London Coll
SW16 . . . . .74 A1
South Western Hospl
SW9 . . . . .62 B4
South Wharf Rd
W2 . . . . **101** C2
South Worple Way
SW14 . . . . .55 C4
South Yd EC1 . . . . **109** B4
Southall St EC1 . . . **137** B3
Southam Ho 9
W10 . . . . .23 A1
Southampton Bldgs
WC2 . . . . **107** B3
Southampton Pl
WC1 . . . . **106** B3
Southampton Rd
NW5 . . . . .12 B3
Southampton Row
WC1 . . . . **106** B4
Southampton St
WC2 . . . . **120** B4
Southampton Way
SE5 . . . . .49 A3
Southborough Ho
SE17 . . . . **152** B2
Southborough Rd
E9 . . . . .25 C4
Southbury NW8 . . . .79 A4
Southcombe St
W14 . . . . **140** A4
Southcote Rd N19 . .13 B4
Southcott Ho W9 . . .89 A1
E3 . . . . .27 A2
Southdean Gdns
SW19 . . . . .70 A2
Southdown N7 . . . . .14 A2
Southern Gr E3 . . . .26 B1
Southern Row W10 . .23 A1
Southern St N1 . . . **84** C2
Southerngate Way
SE14 . . . . .51 A3
Southerton Rd W6 . .39 B2
Southey Ho SE17 . . **151** A2
Southey Rd SW9 . . **173** B4
Southfield Prim Sch
W4 . . . . .38 A4
Southfield Rd W4 . . .37 C4
Southfields Rd
SW18 . . . . .58 C1
Southfields Sch
SW18 . . . . .70 C3
Southgate Ct N1 . . .15 C1
Southgate Gr N1 . . .15 C1
Southgate Rd N1 . . **87** C4
Southill St E14 . . . . .34 A3

Southlands Coll
SW15 ....56 C2
Southlands Dr
SW19 ....69 C2
Southmead Jun & Inf
Sch SW19 ....70 A3
Southmead Rd
SW19 ....70 A3
Southmoor Way C9 .18 B3
Southolm St SW11 .170 B3
Southside N7 ....13 C4
Southside Ind Est
SW8 ....170 C4
Southside Quarter
SW11 ....168 C2
Southvale Rd SE3 ..53 A1
Southview Ave NW10 .8 B3
Southville SW8 ......171 C3
Southwark Bridge
SE1,EC4 ....123 A3
Southwark Bridge Office
Village SE1 ....123 A3
Southwark Bridge Rd
SE1 ....123 B2
Southwark Cath★
SE1 ....123 B2
Southwark Coll
SE1 ....136 A4
SE15 ....50 A3
SE15 ....50 B2
Southwark Coll
(Blackfriars Ctr)
SE1 ....122 A1
Southwark Coll
(Camberwell Centre)
SE5 ....49 A3
Southwark Coll (Grange
Ctr) SE1 ....138 B1
Southwark Coll (Surrey
Docks Ctr) SE16 ....40 A3
Southwark Park Est ⓳
SE16 ....40 A2
Southwark Park Prim
Sch SE16 ....40 A3
Southwark Park Rd
SE16 ....153 B4
SE16 ....153 B4
Southwark St SE1 ..122 C1
Southwater Cl ⓫
E14 ....33 B3
Southwell Gdns
SW7 ....142 C3
Southwell Ho
⓭ N16 ....16 A3
⓮ SE16 ....40 A2
Southwell Rd SE5 ...63 B4
Southwick Mews
W2 ....101 C2
Southwick Pl W2 ...102 A1
Southwick St W2 ....102 A1
Southwick Yd W2 ...102 A1
Southwold Mans
W9 ....23 C2
Southwood Ave N6 ..4 B4
Southwood Ct EC1 ...96 A3
Southwood Ho
W11 ....112 A4
Southwood Hospl
(Geriatric) N6 ....3 C4
Southwood Hts N6 ...4 A4
Southwood La N6 .....3 C4
Southwood Lawn Rd
N6 ....4 A4

Southwood Park N6 ..3 C4
Southwood Smith Ho ④
E2 ....25 A2
Southwood Smith St
N1 ....86 A3
Southwyck Ho SW9 ..62 C3
Sovereign Cl E1 ....32 A2
Sovereign Cres
SE16 ....32 A2
Sovereign Ct E1 ......32 A2
⑤ Richmond TW9 ...54 B3
Sovereign Ho ⓳ E1 ...25 C1
Sovereign Mews ⑧
E2 ....24 B3
Sovereign Pk NW10 .20 A1
Spa Ct SE16 ....139 B1
Spa Rd SE16 ....139 A1
Spa Sch SE1 ....153 B4
Spa View SW16 ......74 B1
Spade Wlk NW3 ......11 A3
Spafield St EC1 ....95 B2
Spalding Ho SE4 ......66 A2
Spanby Rd E3 ....26 C1
Spaniards Cl NW11 ...2 C3
Spaniards End NW3 ...2 C3
Spaniards Rd NW3 ....2 B3
Spanish Bilingual Sch
W10 ....21 A4
Spanish Pl W1 ....103 C2
Spanish Rd SW18 ...59 B2
Sparke Terr ② E16 ..35 B1
Sparkford Ho
SW11 ....167 C4
Sparks Cl W3 ....28 C3
Sparsholt Rd N19 ....5 B3
Sparta St SE10 ....52 B2
Speakers' Corner★
W1 ....117 A4
Speakman Ho SE4 ...66 A4
Spear Mews SW5 ...141 C3
Spears Rd N19 ....5 A3
Spectrum Ho NW5 ...12 C4
Spedan Cl NW3 ....2 B1
Speed Ho EC2 ....109 A4
Speedwell St ⑧
SE8 ....51 C3
Speedy Pl WC1 ....94 A3
Speldhurst Rd E9 ....17 C1
E7 ....37 C3
Spellbrook Wlk (off
Basire St) N1 ....87 A4
Spelman Ho ⓫ E1 ..111 B3
Spelman St E1 ....111 B3
E1 ....111 B4
Spence Cl SE16 ....41 B4
Spencer Gdns SW14 .55 B2
Spencer Ho SW8 ...171 B1
SW19 ....69 C1
SW19 ....69 C3
Spencer Mews W6 ..154 A4
Spencer Park Ct
SW18 ....59 C2
Spencer Pk SW18 ....59 C2
Spencer Pl SW1 .....133 A1
⓮ N1 ....15 A1
Spencer Rd W3 ....28 B1
W4 ....45 B3
SW18 ....59 C2
Spencer Rise NW5 ....4 A1
Spencer St EC1 ......96 A3
Spencer Wlk
⓮ NW3 ....11 B4
SW15 ....57 C3
Spenlow Ho SE16 ..139 C2
Spens Ho WC1 ....94 C1

Spenser Gr N16 ......16 A4
Spenser Mews SE21 .75 C3
Spenser Rd SE24 ....63 A2
Spenser St SW1 ....133 A2
Spensley Wlk N16 ....6 C1
Spert St E14 ....33 A2
Spey St E14 ....34 B4
Spezia Rd NW10 .....21 C3
Spice Ct E1 ....125 C2
⓾ SW11 ....59 B4
Spicer Cl SE5,SW9 ..48 A1
Spicer Ho ⑦ E2 ......99 B3
Spindrift Ave E14 ....42 A2
Spinnaker Ho E14 ...41 C4
Spinney The SW13 ..47 A4
SW16 ....73 C1
Spire Ho ⑳ W2 ....101 C4
Spire Ho W2 ....115 A4
Spirit Quay E1 ......125 C2
Spital Sq E1 ....110 B4
Spital St E1 ....99 B1
Spital Yd E1 ....110 B4
Spitalfields Mkt
E1 ....110 C4
Splendour Wlk
SE16 ....40 B1
Spode Ho SE11 ......135 B4
Sporle Ct ⑥ SW11 ..59 C4
Sprewell SW15 ....58 A1
Spriggs Ho ⓫ N1 .....15 A1
Sprimont Pl SW3 ...144 C2
Spring Cott ⑫ W12 ..38 C4
Spring Gdns SW1 ...120 A2
N5 ....15 B3
Spring Gr W4 ....44 C4
Spring Grove Rd
TW10 ....54 B2
Spring Hill E5 ....7 C4
Spring Ho WC1 ......95 B3
Spring Mews W1 ...103 A4
Spring Pl NW5 ....13 A3
Spring St W2 ....101 B1
Spring Terr TW10 ....54 A2
Spring Wlk E1 ....111 C4
Springall St ⑫ SE15 .50 A3
Springalls Wharf
SE16 ....139 B4
Springbank Wlk
NW1 ....13 C1
Springdale Rd N16 ..15 C4
Springett Ho ⑤
SW2 ....62 B2
Springfield Ct
SW4 ....171 C2
⑥ W3 ....12 A1
⑦ W3 ....28 B3
Springfield Ho W3 ...28 B1
⑧ SE5 ....49 A1
Springfield Hospl
SW17 ....72 A1
Springfield La NW6 ..78 A3
Springfield Rd NW8 ..79 A3
Springfield Sch
NW6 ....78 A3
Springhill Cl SE5 .....63 C4
Springpark Dr N4 .....6 B3
Springrice Rd SE13 ..67 C1
Springvale Ave TW8 .36 A1
Springvale Terr ⑤
W14 ....39 C3
Springwater WC1 ..106 C4
Springwell Ave
NW10 ....21 A4
Spruce Ct W5 ....36 A3
Spruce Ho ⓰ SE16 .40 C4

Sprules Rd SE4 ......51 A1
Spur Rd SE1 ....135 B4
Spurgeon St SE1 ...137 B2
Spurling Rd SE22 ....64 B3
Spurstowe Rd E8 ....17 A2
Spurstowe Terr E8 ..17 A3
Square Rigger Row ⑦
SW11 ....59 B4
Square The SW6 ....165 B3
W6 ....39 B1
Squarey St SW17 ....71 B1
Squire Gdns NW8 ...89 B3
Squire's Mount NW3 ..2 C1
Squires Ct SW4 .....172 B3
Squirrels The SE13 ..67 C4
Squirries St
E2 ....24 C2 99 C3
St Agnes Cl E9 ....25 B4
St Agnes Pl SE11 ....48 A4
St Agnes RC Prim Sch
W2 ....1 A1
St Agnes' RC JMI Sch
E3 ....27 A2
St Aidan's Prim Sch
N4 ....5 C4
St Aidan's Rd SE22 .65 A2
St Alban's Cl NW11 ...1 C3
St Alban's Gr W8 ...128 B2
St Alban's Pl N1 .....86 A3
St Alban's RC Prim Sch
SE15 ....49 B2
St Alban's Rd NW5 ...4 A1
NW10 ....21 A4
St Alban's St SW1 ..119 B3
St Albans Villas NW5 .3 C1
St Albans Ave W4 ...37 C3
St Albans La NW11 ...1 C3
St Albans Mans
W8 ....128 B2
St Albans Studios
W8 ....128 B2
St Albans Terr W6 ..154 A4
St Alfege Pas SE10 ..52 B4
St Alfege with St Peter's
CE Prim Sch SE10 .52 B4
St Aloysius' R C Jun &
Inf Sch NW1 ....93 B4
St Aloysius' RC Coll
N6 ....4 A4
St Alphage Gdn
EC2 ....109 A3
St Alphage Highwalk
EC2 ....109 A3
St Alphonsus Rd
SW4 ....61 C3
St Andrew & St Francis
CE Prim Sch NW2 ...8 C2
St Andrew St EC4 ..107 C3
St Andrew's CE Prim
Sch
N1 ....85 A4
SW9 ....172 B1
St Andrew's Gr N16 ..6 C3
St Andrew's Greek Sch
NW1 ....13 B1
St Andrew's Hill
EC4 ....108 B1
St Andrew's Hospl
E3 ....27 A1
St Andrew's Mans
W1 ....103 B3

St Andrew's Mews
N6 ....3 C4
St Andrew's Pl
NW1 ....92 B2
St Andrew's Rd NW2 .9 A2
W3 ....29 A3
St Andrew's Rd
W14 ....154 B4
St Andrew's Sq
W11 ....31 A3
St Andrew's Wharf
SE1 ....139 A4
St Andrews Ct ⑧
SE16 ....40 A1
St Andrews Ct W4 ...45 B2
St Andrews Mews
SE3 ....53 C3
St Andrews Way E3 .27 A1
St Ann's Cres SW18 .59 B1
St Ann's Gdns NW5 .12 C2
St Ann's Hill SW18 ..59 B1
St Ann's Ho WC1 ....95 B3
St Ann's La SW1 ....133 C1
St Ann's Park Rd
SW18 ....59 B1
St Ann's Rd N15 ......30 C2
St Ann's St SW1 ....133 C2
St Ann's Terr NW8 ...79 C2
St Ann's Villas
W11 ....112 A1
St Anne St E14 ......33 B3
St Anne's Cl N6 ....3 C1
St Anne's Ct NW6 ...23 A4
St Anne's Ct W1 ....105 B1
St Anne's Flats
NW1 ....93 B4
St Anne's Pas E14 ..33 B3
St Anne's RC JMI Sch
E1 ....24 C1 99 B1
St Anne's Row E14 ..33 B3
St Anne's Trad Est
E14 ....33 B3
St Anns Rd SW13 ...46 B2
St Anselm's Pl W1 .104 A1
St Anselm's RC Prim Sch
SW17 ....72 C1
St Anthony's Cl E1 .125 B2
St Anthony's Ct
② SW12 ....60 C1
SW17 ....72 C2
St Anthony's Flats
NW1 ....83 B1
St Anthonys Cl
SW17 ....64 C1
St Asaph Ct SE4 .....65 C4
St Asaph Rd SE4 ....65 C4
St Aubins Ct N1 ......87 C4
St Augustine's CE Prim
& Sec Schs NW2 ....25 C3
St Augustine's CE Prim
& Sec Schs NW6 ....78 A2
St Augustine's RC Prim
Sch W6 ....154 B3
St Augustine's Rd
NW1 ....13 C1
St Austell Rd SE13 ..52 C1
St Barnabas & St Philip
CE Prim Sch W8 ...127 B1

St Barnabas CE Prim Sch SW1 ....145 C2
St Barnabas St SW1 ....145 C2
St Barnabas Terr E9 ....17 C3
St Barnabas Villas SW8 ....172 B4
St Bartholomew's Hospl EC1 ....108 B3
St Bede's RC Inf Sch SW12 ....73 C3
St Benet's Pl EC3 ..123 C4
St Benets Cl SW17 ..72 A2
St Bernadette RC Jun Mix Sch SW12 ....73 B4
St Bernard Ho **6** E14 ....42 B3
St Botolph St E1, EC3 ....110 C2
St Brelades Cl N1 ..87 C4
St Briavel's Ct **4** SE15 ....49 A3
St Bride St EC4 ....108 A2
St Bride's Ave EC4 ....108 A1
St Bride's Pas EC4 ....108 A1
St Catherine's Ct **8** W4 ....38 A3
St Catherine's Dr SE14 ....50 C1
St Catherines Cl SW17 ....72 A2
St Catherines Mews SW3 ....144 C4
St Chad's Pl WC1 ..94 C4
St Chad's St WC1 ...94 B4
St Charles Pl W10 .31 A4
St Charles RC Prim Sch W10 ....30 C4
St Charles RC Sixth Form Coll W10 ...30 C4
St Charles Sq W10 ..30 C4
St Charles' Hospl W10 ....30 C4
St Christina's RC Sch NW8 ....80 B2
St Christopher's Ho SW1 ....83 B1
St Christopher's Pl W1 ....103 C2
St Christopher's Sch NW3 ....11 C2
St Clair Ho **10** E3 ...26 B2
St Clare St EC3 ....110 C1
St Clement Danes CE Prim Sch WC2 ...106 C1
St Clement's La WC2 ....107 A1
St Clements & St James CE Prim Sch W11 ....31 A1 112 A2
St Clements Ct N7 ..14 B2
8 W11 ....30 C2
7 SE14 ....50 C4
St Clements Mans **3** SW6 ....47 C4
St Clements St N7 ..14 C1
St Columb's Ho **1** W10 ....31 A4
St Crispins Cl NW3 .12 A4
St Cross St EC1 ....107 C4

St Cuthbert with St Matthias Prim Sch SW5 ....142 A2
St Cuthbert's Rd NW2 ....10 B2
St David's Sq E14 ..42 A1
St Davids Cl **27** SE16 ....40 A1
St Dionis Rd SW6 .165 A2
St Dominic's RC JMI Schs E9 ....18 A2
St Dominic's RC Prim Sch NW5 ....12 B3
St Dunstan's Alley EC3 ....124 A3
St Dunstan's Ave W3 ....28 C2
St Dunstan's Ct EC4 ....107 C1
St Dunstan's Gdns W3 ....28 C2
St Dunstan's Hill EC3 ....124 A3
St Dunstan's La EC3 ....124 A3
St Dunstan's Rd W6 .39 C1
St Edmund's Cl NW8 ....80 C3
St Edmund's RC JMI Sch E14 ....41 C2
St Edmund's Terr NW8 ....80 C3
St Edmunds Cl SW17 ....72 A2
St Edward's RC Prim Sch NW1 ....90 B1
St Elizabeth's RC Prim Sch TW10 ....54 B1
St Elmo Rd W12 ....38 B4
St Elmos Rd SE16 ...41 A4
St Ermin's Hill SW1 ....133 B2
St Ervan's Rd W10 .31 B4
St Eugene de Mazenod RC Prim Sch NW6 .23 C4
St Faith's CE Prim Sch SW18 ....59 B2
St Faith's Rd SE24 ..75 A3
St Francesca Cabrini Prim Sch SE23 ..65 B1
St Francis RC Jun & Inf Sch SE15 ....49 C3
St Francis RC Prim Sch W11 ....30 C2
St Francis Rd SE22 ..64 A3
St Francis Xavier Sixth Form Coll SW12 ...61 A1
St Francis' Ho NW1 ....83 B1
St Gabriel's CE Prim Sch NW2 ....146 C1
St Gabriel's Rd NW2 .9 C3
St George Ho SW11 ....169 C3
St George St W1 ....118 B4
St George the Martyr CE Prim Sch WC1 ...95 A1
St George's Ave N7 .13 C4
St George's Battersea CE Prim Sch SW8 161 A1
St George's Cath SE1 ....135 C2

St George's Cath RC Jun & Inf Sch SE1 ....136 A2
St George's CE Jun & Inf Sch SE5 ....48 B3
St George's Circ SE1 ....136 A2
St George's Ct SW7 ....128 C1
SW3 ....136 A1
SW3 ....144 A4
St George's Dr SW1 ....146 B2
St George's Field W2 ....102 B1
St George's Gr SW17 ....71 C1
St George's Ho NW1 ....83 A1
St George's La EC3 ....124 A4
St George's Lo **5** SW2 ....51 A2
St George's Mews NW1 ....12 B1
St George's Mews SE1 ....135 C2
St George's RC Sec Sch W9 ....78 B1
St George's Rd TW9 .54 B4
St George's Rd SE1 ....136 A1
St George's Residences **4** SW2 ....62 C2
St George's Sq SW1 ....147 B1
St George's Square Mews SW1 ....147 B1
St George's Way SE15 ....49 A4
St Georges Ct SW5 58 B3
St Georges Hanover Sq Sch W1 ....117 C3
St Georges Rd W4 ..37 C4
St Georges Sq **1** E14 ....33 A2
St Georges's Ct EC4 ....108 A2
St Gerards Cl SW4 ..61 B2
St German's Pl SE3 .53 C2
St Giles Cir WC1 ...105 C2
St Giles Colls WC1 .106 B4
St Giles Ct WC2 ....106 A2
St Giles High St WC2 ....105 C2
St Giles Hospl SE5 .49 A2
St Giles Pas WC2 ..105 C1
St Giles Rd SE5 ....49 A2
St Giles Twr **3** SE5 .49 A2
St Gilles Ho **10** E2 .25 C3
St Gothard Rd SE21 .75 C1
St Helen's Gdns W10 ....30 C3
St Helen's Pl EC3 ..110 A2
St Helen's RC Prim Sch SW9 ....62 C4
St Helen's RC Prim Sch (Annexe) SW9 ..173 A2
St Helena Ho WC1 ...95 B3
St Helena Rd SE16 ..41 A2
St Helena St WC1 ...95 B3
St Helier Ct **5** N1 ..24 A4
St Hilda's Cl NW6 ...9 C1
St Hilda's Rd SW13 .47 A4
St Hilda's Cl SW17 .72 A2
St Hildas Wharf E1 ..32 B1
St Hubert's Ho **1** E14 ....41 C3

St Hughes Cl SW17 .72 A2
St James Ct E2 .....99 C3
10 W4 ....36 C1
St James Hatcham CE Prim Sch SE14 ...51 A2
St James Ind Mews SE1 ....153 C1
St James Mews E14 42 B3
St James School Flats **5** N7 ....14 C3
St James St W6 ....39 B1
St James the Less Prim Sch SW1 ....147 B2
St James' & St Michaels CE Sch W2 ....115 A4
St James' Ct **4** 37 C3
SW1 ....133 A2
St James' Mans NW6 ....10 C1
St James' Ave E2 ...25 A3
St James' CE Jun & Inf Sch SE16 ....139 B2
St James' Cl SW17 ..72 B2
St James' Cl NW8 ...80 C3
St James' Cloisters **2** SE22 ....64 B3
St James' Cres SW9 ....62 C4
St James' Dr SW17 .72 B3
SW12,SW17 ....72 B4
St James' Gdns W11 ....31 A1 112 A2
St James' Gr SW11 ....169 A2
St James' Market SW1 ....119 B3
St James' Palace ★ SW1 ....119 A1
St James' Park SW1 ....133 B3
St James' Park Sta SW1 ....133 B2
St James' Pas EC3 ....110 B1
St James' Pl SW1 ...118 C1
St James' Rd SE1, SE16 ....153 C4
St James' Sq SW1 ....119 A2
St James' Terr **2** SW12 ....72 C2
St James' Terr NW8 ....80 C3
St James' Terrace Mews NW8 ....80 C3
St James' Wlk EC1 ..96 A2
St Joan of Arc RC Prim Sch N5 ....15 B3
St John Angell Ston CE Prim Sch SW9 ..173 C1
St John CE Prim Sch SE17 ....151 A3
St John Cl SW6 .....155 B2
St John Evangelist RC Prim Sch N1 .....86 A2
St John of Jerusalem CE JMI Sch E9 ....17 B1
St John St EC1 .....96 A2

St John the Baptist JMI Sch N1 ....24 A3
St John the Baptist RC Jun Sch E2 ....25 B3
St John the Divine CE Jun Sch SE5 ...48 A3
St John's & St Clements CE Prim Sch SE15 64 C2
St John's (Highbury Vale) CE Prim Sch N5 ....6 A1
St John's (Upper Holloway) Prim Sch N19 ....4 C2
St John's Ave NW10 .21 B4
SW15 ....57 C2
St John's CE JMI Sch E2 ....25 B3
St John's Church Rd E9 ....17 B3
St John's Cres SW9 .62 C4
St John's Ct N4 .....6 A2
5 NW3 ....11 B2
N5 ....15 A4
W6 ....39 A2
SE8 ....52 B1
St John's Dr SW18 ..71 A3
St John's Est **1** N1 ..138 C3
St John's Gdns W11 ....31 B2 112 C3
St John's Gr N19 ....4 B2
3 SW13 ....46 B1
1 Richmond TW9 ..54 A3
St John's Hill SW11 .59 C3
St John's Hill Gr SW11 ....59 C3
St John's La EC1 ...108 A4
St John's Mans E5 ..17 B3
St John's Park Mans N19 ....4 B1
St John's Path EC1 ..96 A1
St John's Pk SE3 ...53 C3
St John's Pl EC1 ....96 A1
St John's RC Jun & Inf Sch SE16 ....41 A4
St John's Rd E16 ...35 C3
Richmond TW9 .....54 A3
SW11 ....60 A3
St John's Sch SW15 .96 A1
St John's Sta SE8 ...51 C1
St John's Terr W10 .22 C1
St John's Vale SE8 .51 C1
St John's Villas N19 .4 C2
St John's Villas W8 ....128 B1
St John's Wood Ct NW8 ....89 C3
St John's Wood High St NW8 ....80 A1
St John's Wood Jun Prep Sch NW8 ...90 A4
St John's Wood Pk NW8 ....79 B4
St John's Wood Rd NW8 ....89 C3
St John's Wood Sta NW8 ....79 B4
St John's Wood Terr NW8 ....80 A2
St Johns Concert Hall SW1 ....134 A1

St Johns Ho 5
SE17 ....48 C4
St Joseph's CI W10 .31 A4
St Joseph's Flats
NW1 ....93 B4
St Joseph's Ho W6 .39 C2
St Joseph's Hospice
E9,E8 ....25 A4
St Joseph's RC Jun & Inf
Sch
SE1 ....40 B3
SE5 ....48 B3
St Joseph's RC Jun &
Inf Sch
SE1 ....137 A4
SE16 ....139 B3
St Joseph's RC Jun & Inf
Schs NW10 ....10 A2
St Joseph's RC Prim Sch
N19 ....4 A3
SE10 ....43 A1
SE8 ....51 C3
St Joseph's RC Prim
Sch
W9 ....88 C3
WC2 ....106 B2
SW3 ....144 C3
St Joseph's St
SW8 ....170 B4
St Joseph's Vale
SE3 ....67 C4
St Josephs RC Prim Sch
SW18 ....58 C2
St Jude St N16 ......16 A3
St Jude's & St Paul's
Prim Sch N1 ....16 A2
St Jude's CE Prim Sch
SE24 ....63 A2
St Jude's Prim Sch
SE1 ....136 A1
St Jude's Rd E2 ......25 A3
St Julian's Rd NW6 .23 C4
St Katharine's Ho
N1 ....85 B2
St Katharine's Way
E1 ....125 B1
St Katherine's Dock *
E1 ....125 B2
St Katherine's Dock
(East Dock)* E1 .125 B2
St Katherine's Pier
E1 ....125 A2
St Katherine's Prec
NW1 ....82 A2
St Katherine's Row
EC3 ....110 B1
St Katherine's Way
E1 ....125 B1
St Kilda's Rd N16 .....7 A3
St Laurence's CI
NW6 ....22 C4
St Lawrence Ct N1 ..87 C4
St Lawrence Ho
SE1 ....138 B2
St Lawrence St E14 .34 B1
St Lawrence Terr
W10 ....31 A4
St Lawrence Way
SW9 ....173 C2
St Leonard's Ct N1 .97 C4
St Leonard's Hospl
N1 ....24 A1

St Leonard's Rd
NW10 ....20 C1
E14 ....34 B4
St Leonard's Sq
NW5 ....12 C2
St Leonard's St E3 .27 A2
St Leonard's Terr
SW3 ....145 A1
St Leonards Ct
SW14 ....55 B4
St Leonards Rd
SW14 ....55 B4
St Loo Ave SW3 ...158 B4
St Loo Ct SW3 .....158 C4
St Luke's Ave SW4 .61 C3
St Luke's CE JMI Sch
E14 ....42 C2
St Luke's CE Prim Sch
W9 ....23 B2
E16 ....35 B1
Richmond TW9 ....44 C2
St Luke's Ct E1 .....97 A2
St Luke's Ct W11 ...31 B3
St Luke's Hospl
W1 ....92 C1
St Luke's Mews
W11 ....31 B3
St Luke's Path
EC1 ....97 B4
St Luke's Rd W11 ...31 A4
St Luke's Sq E16 ...35 B1
St Luke's St SW3 ..144 B2
St Margaret St
SW1 ....134 A3
St Margaret's Cres
SW15 ....57 A2
St Margaret's Ct
SW15 ....57 A3
St Margaret's La
W8 ....128 A1
St Margaret's Rd
NW10 ....22 B2
SE4 ....66 B3
St Margaret's Sch
NW3 ....11 A4
St Margarets Lo
W3 ....37 A4
St Mark St E1 ......111 A1
St Mark's CE Prim Sch
SE11 ....163 A4
St Mark's Cres
NW1 ....81 C4
St Mark's Gr
SW10 ....156 B2
St Mark's Hospl
EC1 ....96 B4
St Mark's PI W11 ...31 A3
St Mark's Prim Sch
N19 ....4 C2
St Mark's Rd W10 ..30 C4
W11 ....31 A3
St Mark's Rise E8 ..16 B3
St Mark's Sq NW1 ..81 B3
St Marks CI SE10 ...52 B3
St Marks Gate E9 ...18 B1
St Marks Ho 6
SE17 ....48 C4
St Martin's Almshouses
NW1 ....82 C4
St Martin's CI NW1 .82 C4
St Martin's Ct SE27 .75 A2
St Martin's Ct
WC2 ....120 A4
St Martin's La
WC2 ....120 A3

St Martin's Le Grand
EC1 ....108 C2
St Martin's PI
WC2 ....120 A3
St Martin's Rd
SW9 ....172 C2
St Martin's St
WC2 ....119 C3
St Martin's Way
SW17 ....71 B1
St Martin-in-the-Fields
High Sch SW2 ....74 C3
St Mary & St Michael
Jun & Inf Sch E1 ...32 B3
St Mary & St Pancras CE
Prim Sch NW1 ......83 B1
St Mary Abbot's Ct
W14 ....126 C1
St Mary Abbot's PI
W8 ....127 A1
St Mary Abbots CE Prim
Sch W8 ....128 A3
St Mary Abbots Terr
W14 ....127 A1
St Mary at Hill
EC3 ....124 A3
St Mary Axe EC3 ...110 A2
St Mary Graces Ct
E1 ....125 A3
St Mary Magdalene CE
Prim Sch N7 ....14 C2
St Mary Magdalene CE
Sec Sch TW10 ......54 C2
St Mary Magdalene
Prim Sch SE15 ......50 A1
St Mary Magdalene's
CE Prim Sch W2 ..100 A4
St Mary Magdalens CE
Prim Sch SE4 ....66 A3
St Mary Magdalen's RC
Jun Sch NW2 ....9 A2
St Mary Newington CE
SE17 ....152 B2
St Mary of the Angels
Cath Prim Sch W2 .31 C3
St Mary's Bryanston
Square CE Sch
W1 ....102 C4
St Mary's CE Prim Sch
NW10 ....8 A2
SW15 ....57 C4
SE13 ....67 A2
St Mary's CE Prim Sch
N1 ....86 B4
St Mary's Gr W6 ....38 B3
St Mary's Est 2
SE16 ....40 B4
St Mary's Flats
NW1 ....93 B4
St Mary's Gate
W8 ....128 A1
St Mary's Gdns
SE11 ....149 C4
St Mary's Gr N1 .....15 C2
W4 ....45 A4
Richmond TW10,TW9 .54 B3
SW13 ....57 A4
St Mary's Ho N1 ....86 B4
St Mary's Hospl
W2 ....101 C2
St Mary's Kilburn CE
Prim Sch NW6 ......23 C4
St Mary's Mans
NW10 ....21 A4

St Mary's Mans
W2 ....101 B4
St Mary's Medical Sch
W2 ....101 C2
St Mary's Mews
NW6 ....11 A1
St Mary's Path N1 ..86 B4
St Mary's PI W8 ...128 A1
St Mary's RC Prim Sch
W10 ....23 A1
NW6 ....23 C3
W14 ....39 C3
W4 ....46 A4
SW4 ....61 B2
St Mary's RC Prim Sch
SW8 ....170 B4
St Mary's Rd NW11 ..1 A4
NW10 ....21 A4
SE15 ....50 B1
St Mary's
Hampstead NW3 ...11 C3
St Mary's Stoke
Newington CE JMI Sch
N16 ....7 A2
St Mary's Terr
W2 ....101 B4
St Mary's Twr EC1 ..97 A2
St Mary's Wlk
SE11 ....149 C4
St Mary-le-Park Ct
SW11 ....158 B1
St Marychurch St
SE16 ....40 B4
St Marylebone CE Sch
W1 ....103 C4
St Matthew St
SW1 ....133 B1
St Matthew's Ho 8
SE17 ....48 A4
St Matthew's Lo
NW1 ....83 A2
St Matthew's Rd
SW2 ....62 B2
St Matthew's Row
E2 ....24 C1 99 B2
St Matthews CE Prim
Sch SW1 ....133 C2
St Matthews Ct
SE1 ....136 C1
St Matthias CE Sch
E2 ....24 B1 99 A2
St Matthias's CE Prim
Sch N16 ....16 A4
St Maur Rd SW6 ..165 A3
St Michael's Alley
EC3 ....109 C1
St Michael's CE Prim
Sch N6 ....3 C4
St Michael's CE NW11 1 B4
St Michael's Flats
NW1 ....83 B1
St Michael's Gdns
W10 ....31 A4
St Michael's Prim Sch
SW18 ....70 B4
St Michael's RC Sec
Sch SE16 ....139 B3
St Michael's Rd
SW9 ....172 C2
W2 ....9 B4
St Michael's St
W2 ....102 A2

St Michaels Camden
Town CE Prim Sch &
Our Lady's RC Prim
Sch NW1 ....82 C4
St Michaels Ct E14 .34 B4
St Mildred's Ct
EC2 ....109 B1
St Monica's JMI Sch
N1 ....98 A4
St Nicholas Ho SE8 .51 C4
St Nicholas St SE8 .51 C2
St Nicholas' Flats
NW1 ....83 B1
St Norbert Gn SE4 .66 A3
St Norbert Rd SE4 .66 A3
St Olaf's Rd SW6 ..154 B1
St Olave's Ct EC2 ..109 B1
St Olave's Est SE1 .138 B4
St Olave's Gdns
SE11 ....149 B4
St Olave's Mans
SE11 ....149 B4
St Olaves Ct W2 ...114 A3
St Osmund's RC Prim
Sch SW13 ....46 B2
St Oswald's PI
SE11 ....148 C1
St Oswulf St SW1 .147 C3
St Owen Ho SE1 ...138 B2
St Pancras Almshouses
13 NW5 ....12 B3
St Pancras Commercial
Ctr NW1 ....83 B3
St Pancras Hospl
NW1 ....83 B3
St Pancras Sta WC1 .94 A4
St Pancras Way
NW1 ....83 B3
St Patrick's RC Inf Sch
E1 ....32 A1
St Patrick's RC Jun Sch
E1 ....32 A1
St Patrick's RC Prim Sch
NW5 ....13 A3
St Paul St N1 ....87 A3
St Paul's Ave NW2 ...9 B2
St Paul's Cath *
EC4 ....108 C1
St Paul's Cath Sch
EC4 ....108 C1
St Paul's CE JMI Sch
E1 ....125 C4
St Paul's CE Jun & Inf
Sch SE17 ....150 C1
St Paul's CE Prim Sch
NW3 ....12 B1
W6 ....39 B1
St Paul's Church Yd
EC4 ....108 C1
St Paul's Ct 8 N19 ...5 A2
St Paul's Dr E15 ....19 C3
St Paul's Girls' Sch
W6 ....39 C2
St Paul's PI N1 ......15 C2
St Paul's Rd SW3 .158 C1
St Paul's Terr SE17 .48 A4
St Paul's Way E3 ....33 C4
St Paul's Way Sec Sch
E3 ....33 C4
St Paul's with Lukes JMI
Sch E3 ....33 B4
St Pauls CI W5 ....36 B4
St Pauls Cres NW1 .13 C1
St Pauls Mews NW1 13 C1

St Pauls Rd TW9	54 B4
St Pauls View WC1	95 B3
St Pauls with St Michaels Haggerston CE JMI Sch E8	24 C4
St Peter's Alley EC3	109 C1
St Peter's CE Prim Sch W9	23 C1
W6	38 C1
St Peter's CI E2	24 C3
St Peter's Eaton Square CE Sch SW1	132 B1
St Peter's Gdns SE27	74 C1
St Peter's Gr W6	38 C2
St Peter's Ho N16	7 A4
4 SE17	48 C4
St Peter's PI W9	88 A1
St Peter's Prim Sch SE17	151 B1
St Peter's Rd W6	38 C1
St Peter's Sch E1	32 B1
St Peter's Sq E2	24 C3
W6	38 B1
St Peter's St N1	86 B3
St Peter's Street Mews N1	86 B2
St Peter's Terr SW6	154 B1
St Peter's Villas 5 W6	38 C2
St Peter's Way N1	16 A1
St Peters St Pauls RC Prim Sch E1	96 B2
St Peters CI SW17	72 A2
St Peters Ct E4	51 B1
St Peters Ho WC1	94 B3
St Petersburgh Mews W2	114 A4
St Petersburgh PI W2	114 A3
St Philip Ho N1	95 B3
St Philip Sq SW8	170 A1
St Philip St SW8	170 A1
St Philip's Rd E8	16 C2
St Philip's Way N1	87 A3
St Quentin Ho SW18	59 C1
St Quentin Ave W10	30 C4
St Quintin Gdns W10	30 B4
St Regis Hts NW3	2 A1
St Richard of Chichester RC Sec Sch NW1	13 B1
St Rule St SW8	170 C1
St Saviour's CE JMI Sch E14	34 A4
St Saviour's CE Prim Sch SE24	63 B4
St Saviour's CE Prim Sch W9	88 B1
St Saviour's RC Prim Sch SE13	67 B3
St Saviour's Rd SW2	62 B2
St Saviour's Wharf SE1	139 A4
St Saviours SW4	61 A3
St Saviours & St Olaves CE Sch SE1	138 A1
St Scholastica's RC JMI Sch E5	7 C2
St Silas PI NW5	12 C2
St Simon's Ave SW15	57 B2
St Stephen CE Prim Sch W12	39 B4
St Stephen's Ave W12	39 A4
St Stephen's CE Prim Sch W2	31 C4
SE8	51 C1
St Stephen's CE Prim Sch SW8	162 C2
St Stephen's CI NW5	12 B3
St Stephen's CI NW8	80 B3
St Stephen's Cres W2	31 C3
St Stephen's Gdns W2	31 C3
3 SW15	58 B2
St Stephen's Gr SE13	67 B4
St Stephen's Mews 4 W2	31 C4
St Stephen's Rd E3	26 B3
St Stephen's Row EC4	109 B1
St Stephen's Terr SW8	162 C1
St Stephens Ho 7 SE17	48 C4
St Swithin's La EC4	123 B4
St Swithun's Rd SE13	67 C2
St Thomas Ho 2 E1	32 C3
St Thomas of Canterbury RC Prim Sch SW6	154 C2
St Thomas Rd E16	35 C3
St Thomas St SE1	123 C1
St Thomas the Apostle Coll The SE15	50 B2
St Thomas' CE JMI Sch N16	7 C3
St Thomas' Gdns NW5	12 C2
St Thomas' Hospl SE1	135 A2
St Thomas' Rd W4	45 B4
St Thomas's CE Prim Sch SE1	23 A1
St Thomas's Hospital Medical Sch SE1	134 C1
St Thomas's Pas 9 E1	17 B1
St Thomas's Rd N4,N5	5 C1
NW10	21 A4
St Thomas's Sq E9	17 B1
St Thomas's Way SW6	155 A2
St Ursula's Convent Sch SE10	52 C3
St Vincent De Paul Ho 20 E1	32 B4
St Vincent De Paul Prim Sch SW1	132 C1
St Vincent St W1	138 C2
St Vincent's RC Prim Sch W3	28 A2
St Vincent's RC Prim Sch W1	103 C3
St William of York RC Sec Boys Sch (Upper) N1	14 A1
St. Paul's Sta EC2	108 C2
Stable Yd W10	30 B3
Stable Yd Rd SW1	133 A4
Stables Way SW11	149 B2
Stacey St WC2	105 C1
N7	5 C1
Stack Ho SW1	145 C3
Stackhouse St SW1	130 C2
Stacy Path SE5	49 A3
Stadium St SW10	157 A1
Stafford CI NW6	23 C2
Stafford Cripps Ho SW6	155 A3
20 E2	25 B2
Stafford Ct W8	127 C2
SW8	172 A4
Stafford Ho SE1	153 A2
Stafford Mans SW11	158 C1
13 W14	39 C3
Stafford PI SW1	132 C2
Stafford Rd NW6	23 C2
E3	26 B3
Stafford St W1	118 C2
Stafford Terr W8	127 B2
Staffordshire St SE15	49 C2
Stag La SW15	68 C2
Stag PI SW1	132 C2
Stagshaw Ho 17 SE22	64 A4
Stainer St SE1	123 C1
Staining La EC2	109 A2
Stainsbury St 22 E2	25 B3
Stainsby Rd E14	33 C3
Stainton Rd SE13	67 C1
Stalbridge Ho NW1	82 C1
Stalbridge St NW1	102 B4
Statham St SE16	40 A3
Stambourne Ho SW8	172 B4
Stamford Bridge Stadium (Chelsea FC) SW6	156 A2
Stamford Brook Ave W6	38 B3
Stamford Brook Gdns 1 W6	38 B3
Stamford Brook Mans 2 W6	38 B3
Stamford Brook Rd W6	38 B3
Stamford Brook Sta W6	38 C2
Stamford Grove E 1 N16	7 C3
Stamford Grove W 4 N16	7 C3
Stamford Hill N16	7 B3
Stamford Hill Mans 1 N16	7 A4
Stamford Lo 2 N16	7 B4
Stamford Mans 2 N16	7 C3
Stamford Rd N1	16 A2
Stamford St SE1	121 C2
Stanard CI N16	7 A4
Stanborough Ho 4 E3	27 A1
Stanborough Pas E8	16 B2
Stanbridge Mans SW11	57 B4
Stanbridge Rd SW15	57 B4
Stanbrook Ho 4	118 C2
Stanbury Ct 16 NW3	12 B2
Stanbury Rd SE15	50 A3
SE15	50 B1
Standard PI EC2	98 B3
Standard Rd NW10	20 C1
Standen Rd SW18	70 C4
Standish Ho 4 W6	38 C2
Standish Rd W6	38 C2
Stanesgate Ho 20 SE15	49 C3
Stanfield Ho NW8	89 C2
Stanfield Rd 15 E3	26 A3
Stanford Ct W8	128 B1
SW6	166 B3
Stanford PI SE1	152 A3
Stanford Rd W8	128 B2
Stanford St SW1	147 B3
Stanhope CI 28 SE16	40 C4
Stanhope Gate W1	117 C2
Stanhope Gdns SW7	143 A4
Stanhope Ho SE8	51 B3
4 SW15	57 B2
Stanhope Mews E SW7	143 A4
Stanhope Mews W SW7	143 A4
Stanhope PI W2	102 C1
Stanhope Rd N6	4 B4
Stanhope Row W1	118 A1
Stanhope St NW1	92 C3
Stanhope Terr W2	115 C4
Stanier CI SW5	141 A1
Stanlake Rd W12	30 B1
Stanlake Villas W12	30 B1
Stanley Bldgs NW1	84 A1
Stanley CI SW8	162 C3
Stanley Cres W11	31 B2 112 C4
NW2	9 A3
W3	38 A4
Stanley Gr SW11	169 C1
Stanley Ho 1 E1	25 B1
18 E14	33 C3
Stanley Mans SW10	157 A4
SW17	72 B2
Stanley Pas NW1	84 A1
Stanley Rd E15	27 C4
W3	37 B3
SW14	55 A3
Stanley St SE14,SE8	51 B3
Stanley Studios SW10	157 A4
Stanley Terr 1 N19	5 A2
Stanmer St SW11	168 B2
Stanmore Gdns TW9	54 B3
Stanmore Ho SW8	171 C2
Stanmore PI NW1	82 B4
Stanmore Rd TW9	54 B4
Stanmore St N1	84 C4
Stannard Cotts 23 E1	25 B1
Stannard Mews E8	16 C2
Stannard Rd E8	16 C2
Stannary PI SE11	149 C1
Stannary St SE11	149 C1
Stansbury Ho 3 W10	23 A2
Stansfeld Ho SE1	153 A3
Stansfield Rd SW9	62 B4
Stanstead Ho E3	27 B1
Stanswood Gdns SE5	49 A3
Stanton Ct N16	6 C4
Stanton Ho 8 SE10	52 B4
Stanton Rd SW13	46 B1
Stanway Ct 23 N1	24 A3
Stanway St N1	24 A3
Stanwick Rd W14	140 C3
Stapethurst Ho 3 E5	17 A3
Staple Inn WC2	107 B3
Staple Inn Bldgs WC2	107 B3
Staple St SE1	137 C3
Stapleford CI 3 SW2	74 A3
Stapleford CI SW19	70 A4
Staplehurst Ct	60 B1
Staples CI SE16	33 A1
Stapleton Hall N4	5 B4
Stapleton Hall Rd N4	5 B4
Stapleton Ho 10 E2	25 A2
Stapleton Rd SW17	72 C1
Star & Garter Mans SW15	57 C4
Star Alley EC3	124 B4
Star Rd W14	140 C1
Star St W2	102 A2
Star Works NW10	21 C2
Star Yd WC2	107 B2
Starboard Way E14	41 C3
Starcross St NW1	93 A3
Starfield Rd W12	38 C4
Starliner Ct N7	14 C2
Starling Ho NW8	80 A2
Statham Gr N16	6 C1
Statham Ho SW8	170 C4
Statham Ho 18 E1	25 B1
Station App NW10	21 B2
Richmond TW9	44 C2
SW6	58 A4
Station Approach Rd W4	45 B3
Station Ave SW9	63 A4
Station Cres SE3	43 C1
Station CI 5 SE15	50 B1
Station Gdns W4	45 B3
Station Par NW2	9 B2
Richmond TW9	44 C2
4 SW12	72 C3
Station Pas SE15	50 B2
Station PI N4	5 C2
Station Rd N19	4 B1
NW10	21 B3
SW13	46 B1
SE13	67 B4
Station Rise SE27	75 A2
Station St E15	19 C1
Station Terr NW10	22 C3

Station Terr *continued*
SE5 . . . . 48 B2
Stationers Hall Ct
EC4 . . . . 108 B1
Staunton Ho SE17 . . 152 A3
Staunton St SE8 . . . 51 B4
Stave Yard Rd SE16 . 33 A1
Staveley NW1 . . . . . . 92 C4
Staveley Cl N7 . . . . . 14 A4
E9 . . . . 17 B1
5 SE15 . . . . 50 A2
SE15 . . . . 50 B4
Staveley Gdns W4 . . 45 C2
Staveley Rd W4 . . . . 45 C3
Staverton Lo W14 . . 127 A2
Stavers Ho **10** E3 . . . 26 B3
Staverton Rd NW2 . . 9 B1
Staverdale Rd N5 . . . 15 A4
Stayner's Rd E1 . . . . . 25 C1
Stead St SE17 . . . . . 151 B3
Steadman Ct EC1 . . . 97 A2
Stean St E8 . . . . 24 B4
Stebbing Ho **8**
  W11 . . . . 30 C1
Stebon JMI Sch
  E14 . . . . 33 C4
Stebondale St E14 . . 42 B2
Stedham Pl WC1 . . . 106 A2
Steedman St SE17 . 150 C3
Steel's La **23** E1 . . . . 32 B3
Steele Rd NW10 . . . . 20 B3
  W4 . . . . 37 B3
Steele's Mews N
  NW3 . . . . 12 B2
Steele's Mews S
  NW3 . . . . 12 B2
Steele's Rd NW3 . . . 12 B2
Steen Way **7** SE22 . . 64 A2
Steep Hill SW16 . . . . 73 C1
Steeple Cl SW6 . . . . 164 B1
Steeple Ct **10** E1 . . . 25 A1
Steeple Wlk (off Maldon
  Cl) N1 . . . . 87 A4
Steerforth St SW18 . 71 B2
Steers Way SE16 . . . 41 A4
Stelfax Ho WC1 . . . . 95 A4
Stellman Cl E5 . . . . . . 7 C1
Stephan Cl E8 . . . . . . 24 C4
Stephen Ct **3** SW19 . 69 C3
Stephen Fox Ho **7**
  W4 . . . . 38 A1

Stepney Gn E1 . . . . . 32 C4
Stepney Green Boys Sec
  Sch E1 . . . . 32 C4
Stepney Green Ct **8**
  E1 . . . . 25 C1
Stepney Green Sta
  JMI Sch E14 . . . . . 33 B3
Stepney High St E1 . 32 C4
Stepney Way E1 . . . 32 B4
Sterling Cl NW10 . . . 8 C1
Sterling Gdns SE14 . 51 A4
Sterling Pl W5 . . . . . 36 A2
Sterling St SW7 . . . . 130 B2
Sterndale Rd W14 . . 39 C3
Sterne St W12 . . . . . 39 C4
Sternhall La SE15 . . 64 C4
Sternhold Ave
  SW12,SW2 . . . . 73 C2
Sterry St SE1 . . . . . . 137 B3
Steve Biko Ct W10 . . 22 C1
Steve Biko Rd N7 . . . 5 C1
Stevedore St **8** E1 . . 32 A1
Stevenage Rd SW6 . 47 C2
Stevens Ave E9 . . . . 17 B2
Stevens St SE1 . . . . 138 B2
Stevenson Cres
  SE16 . . . . 40 A1
Stevenson Ho NW8 . 78 C4
  SW11 . . . . 168 C1
Steventon Rd W12 . 29 B2
Stew La EC4 . . . . 122 C4
Steward St E1 . . . . . 110 B4
Stewart Headlam JMI
  Sch E1 . . . . 25 A1
Stewart Ho SE1 . . . 138 A1
Stewart Rd E15 . . . . 19 C4
Stewart St E14 . . . . 42 B4
Stewart's Gr SW3 . . 144 A2
Stewart's Rd SW8 . 170 C4
Steyne Rd W3 . . . . . 28 A1
Stifford Ho E1 . . . . . 32 B4
Stile Hall Gdns W4 . 36 C1
Stile Hall Par **6**
  W4 . . . . 36 C1
Stileman Ho **2** E3 . . 33 B4
Stillingfleet Rd
  SW13 . . . . 46 C4
Stillington St SW1 . . 147 A4
Stillness Prim Sch
  SE23 . . . . 66 A1
Stillness Rd SE23 . . . 66 B1
Stirling Ct WC2 . . . . 106 C1
Stirling Mans NW6 . 11 B2
Stirling Rd SW9 . . . 172 B1
  W3 . . . . 37 A3
Stoatley Ho **10**
  SW15 . . . . 68 C3
Stock Exchange
  EC2 . . . . 109 C1
Stock Orchard Cres
  N7 . . . . 14 B3
Stock Orchard St
  N7 . . . . 14 B3
Stockbeck NW1 . . . . 83 A1
Stockfield Rd SW16 . 74 B1
Stockholm Ho E1 . . 125 C4
Stockholm Rd SE16 . 40 B1
Stockholm Way E1 . 125 B2
Stockhurst Cl SW15 . 47 C1
Stockleigh Hall
  NW8 . . . . 80 B2
Stocks Ct **5** E1 . . . . 25 C1
Stocks Pl **10** E14 . . . 33 B2
Stockton Ho **18** E2 . 25 A2

Stockwell Ave SW9 . 62 B4
Stockwell Gdns
  SW9 . . . . 172 C3
Stockwell Gn SW9 . 172 C3
Stockwell Jun & Inf Sch
  SW9 . . . . 62 B4
Stockwell La SW9 . . 172 C3
Stockwell Park Cres
  SW9 . . . . 173 A3
Stockwell Park Rd
  SW9 . . . . 173 A3
Stockwell Park Sch
  SW9 . . . . 172 C3
Stockwell Park Wlk
  SW9 . . . . 62 C4
Stockwell Rd SW9 . 173 A1
Stockwell St SE10 . . 52 B4
Stockwell Sta SW9 . 172 B3
Stockwell Terr
  SW9 . . . . 172 C3
Stoddart Ho **8** SW8 163 A3
Stodmarsh Ho
  SW9 . . . . 173 C4
Stoford Cl SW19 . . . 70 A4
Stoke Newington
  Church St N16 . . . . 7 A2
Stoke Newington Comm
  N16 . . . . 7 B2
Stoke Newington High
  St N16 . . . . 7 B1
Stoke Newington Rd
  N16 . . . . 16 B4
Stoke Newington Sch
  N16 . . . . 6 C1
Stoke Newington Sta
  N16 . . . . 7 B2
Stoke Pl NW10 . . . . 21 B2
Stokenchurch St
  SW6 . . . . 166 A3
Stokesley St W12 . . 29 B3
Stondon Pk SE23 . . 66 A1
Stone Bldgs WC2 . . 107 A3
Stone Cl SW4 . . . . . 171 A1
Stone Gate **6** NW5 . 12 C2
Stonebridge Prim Sch
  The NW10 . . . . . . 20 C4
Stonecutter St
  EC4 . . . . 108 A2
Stonefield N4 . . . . . . 5 B2
Stonefield Mans N1 . 85 B3
Stonefield St N1 . . . 85 C4
Stonehill Cl SW14 . . 55 C2
Stonehill Rd W4 . . . 36 C1
  SW14 . . . . 55 A2
Stonehill's Mans **3**
  SW16 . . . . 74 A2
Stonehills Ct SE21 . 76 A1
Stonehouse NW1 . . 83 A3
Stonehouse Ho **27**
  W2 . . . . 31 C4
Stoneleigh Lo **13**
  TW9 . . . . 44 B2
Stoneleigh Pl W11 . 30 C2
Stoneleigh St W11 . 30 C2
Stonell's Rd SW11 . 60 B2
Stones End St SE1 . 136 C3
Stoney La E1 . . . . . . 110 B2
Stoney St SE1 . . . . . 123 B2
Stoneyard La E14 . . 34 A2
Stonhouse St SW4 . 61 C3
Stonnell's Rd SW11 . 60 B2
Stonor Rd W14 . . . . 140 C3
Stopes St SE15 . . . . 49 B3

Stopford Rd SE17 . . 150 B1
Stopher Ho SE1 . . . 136 B3
Storace Ho **6** SW4 . 62 A3
Store St WC1 . . . . . . 105 B4
Storers Quay E14 . . 42 C2
Storey Ct NW8 . . . . 89 B3
Storey Ho **2** E14 . . 34 A2
Storey's Gate
  SW1 . . . . 133 C3
Stories Rd SE5 . . . . 64 A4
Storks Rd SE16 . . . 139 C1
Stormont House Sch
  E5 . . . . 17 A4
Stormont Rd N6 . . . 3 B4
  SW11 . . . . 60 C3
Storrington WC1 . . . 94 B3
Story St N1 . . . . 14 B1
Stothard Pl E1 . . . . 110 B4
Stothard St **11** E1 . . 25 B1
Stoughton Cl SE11 . 149 A3
  SW15 . . . . 68 C3
Stour Rd E3 . . . . 18 C1
Stourcliffe Cl W1 . . 102 C2
Stourcliffe St W1 . . 102 C1
Stourhead Cl **6**
  SW19 . . . . 69 C4
Stowage SE8 . . . . . . 52 A4
Stowe Ho **11** N16 . . 7 A1
Stowe Rd W12 . . . . 39 A4
Stracey Rd NW10 . . 20 C4
Stradbroke Rd N5 . . 15 B4
Stradella Rd SE24 . . 63 B1
Straffan Lo **3** NW3 . 12 A2
Strafford Ho **9** SE8 . 41 B1
Strafford Rd W3 . . . 37 B4
Strafford St E14 . . . 41 C4
Strahan Rd E3 . . . . 26 A2
Straightsmouth
  SE10 . . . . 52 B3
Straker's Rd SE15 . . 65 B3
Strale Ho **10** N1 . . . 24 A4
Strand WC2 . . . . 120 C4
Strand La WC2 . . . . 121 A4
Strand on the Green
  Sch W4 . . . . 44 C4
Strand on the Green Jun
  Sch W4 . . . . 44 C4
Strand-on-the-Green
  W4 . . . . 44 C4
Strang Ho N1 . . . . . 86 C3
Strangways Terr
  W14 . . . . 126 C1
Stranraer Way N1 . . 14 A1
Strasburg Rd
  SW11 . . . . 169 C3
Stratford Bus Sta
  E15 . . . . 19 C1
Stratford Ctr E15 . . 19 C1
Stratford Gr SW15 . 57 C3
Stratford Pl W1 . . . 104 A1
Stratford Rd W8 . . . 127 C1
Stratford Sta E15 . . 19 C1
Stratford Studios
  W8 . . . . 128 A1
Stratford Villas
  NW1 . . . . 13 C1
Strath Terr SW11 . . 60 A3
Strathan Cl SE11 . . 58 A1
Strathblaine Rd
  SW11 . . . . 59 C3
Strathdon Dr SW17 . 71 C1
Strathearn Ho W2 . 116 A4
Strathearn Pl W2 . . 102 A1
  W2 . . . . 116 A4
Stratheden Par SE3 . 53 C3

Stratheden Rd SE3 . 53 C3
Strathleven Rd SW2 . 62 A2
Strathmore Ct NW8 . 90 A4
Strathmore Gdns
  W8 . . . . 113 C2
Strathmore Rd
  SW19 . . . . 70 C1
Strathnairn St SE1 . 153 C3
Strathray Gdns
  NW3 . . . . 12 A2
Strathville Rd SW18 . 71 A2
Stratton Ct **4** N1 . . 16 A1
Stratton St W1 . . . . 118 B2
Strattondale St E14 . 42 B3
Strauss Rd W4 . . . . 37 C4
Streatham & Tooting
  Adult Inst SW16 . . 74 B2
Streatham Cl SW16 . 74 A3
Streatham Ct SW16 . 74 A1
Streatham Hill SW2 . 74 A1
Streatham Hill &
  Clapham High Sch
  SW2 . . . . 74 B3
Streatham Hill Sta
  SW2 . . . . 74 A2
Streatham Pl SW2 . 74 A4
Streatham St WC1 . 106 A2
Streatbourne Rd
  SW17 . . . . 72 C2
Streathem Wells Prim
  Sch SW2 . . . . 74 C2
Streatley Par **4**
  SW16 . . . . 74 C2
Streatley Pl **10** NW3 . 11 B4
  NW3 . . . . 11 B4
Streatley Rd NW6 . . 10 B1
Streimer Rd E15 . . . 27 B3
Strelley Way W3 . . . 29 A2
Strickland Ct SE15 . 64 C4
Strickland Ho E2 . . 99 A3
Strickland Row
  SW18 . . . . 71 C4
Strickland St SE8 . . 51 C2
Stringer Hos **11** N1 . 24 A4
Strode Ho **3** SW2 . 74 C3
Strode Rd SW6 . . . 154 A2
  NW10 . . . . 8 C2
Strome Ho NW6 . . . 78 A1
Stronsa Rd W12 . . . 38 B4
Strood Ho SE1 . . . . 137 C3
Strood Cres SW15 . 68 C1
Stroud Green Prim Sch
  N4 . . . . 5 C3
Stroud Green Rd N4 . 5 C3
Stroud Ho SW9 . . . 173 C4
Stroudley Ho SW8 . 171 A4
Stroudley Wlk **10** E3 . 27 A2
Strout's Pl **3** E2 . . . 98 C4
Strudwick Ct SW4 . 172 B3
Strutton Ground
  SW1 . . . . 133 B1
Strype St E1 . . . . . . 110 C3
Stuart Ave W5 . . . . 36 B4
Stuart Ho W14 . . . . 140 A4
  1 E9 . . . . 17 C1
  SW4 . . . . 62 A3
Stuart Mill Ho N1 . . 84 C1
Stuart Rd NW6 . . . . 23 C2
  W3 . . . . 28 B1
  SE15 . . . . 65 B3
  SW19 . . . . 70 C1
Stubbs Dr SE16 . . . 40 A1
Stubbs Ho N2 . . . . . 2 C4
  E2 . . . . 25 C2
Stucley Pl **10** NW1 . 13 A1
Studd St N1 . . . . 86 A4

Studdridge St
SW6 ....165 C2
Studholme Ct NW1 ....10 C4
Studholme St SE15 ...50 A3
Studio Pl SW1 ....131 A3
Studios The SW8 ..171 C3
    4 SW4 ....61 B3
Studland SE17 ....151 B2
Studland Ho E14 ....33 A3
Studland St W6 ....39 A2
Studley Cl E5 ....18 A3
Studley Rd SW4 ......172 B2
Stukeley St WC2 .....106 B2
Stunnell Ho 23 SE14 ..50 C4
Sturdee Ho 22 E2 ....24 C3
Sturdy Ho 22 E3 ....26 A3
Sturdy Rd SE15 ....50 A1
Sturge St SE1 ....136 C4
Sturgeon Rd SE17 ..150 C1
Sturmer Way N7 ....14 B3
Sturminster Ho
    SW8 ....163 A1
Sturry St E14 ....34 A3
Sturt St N1 ....87 A1
Stutfield St E1 ....111 C1
Stuttle Ho E1 ....99 B1
Styles Gdns SW9 ......63 A4
Styles Ho SE1 ....122 A1
Sudbourne Prim Sch
    SW2 ....62 B2
Sudbourne Rd SW2 ..62 B2
Sudbrooke Rd
    SW12 ....60 C1
Sudbury Ct SW8 ......171 C4
    ....18 A4
Sudbury Ho SW18 ......59 A2
Sudeley St N1 ....86 B1
Sudlow Rd SW18 ....58 C2
Sudrey St SE1 ....136 C3
Suffield Ho SE17 ......150 B2
Suffolk La EC4 ....123 B4
Suffolk Pl SW1 ....119 C2
Suffolk Rd NW10 ....8 A1
    SW13 ....46 C3
Suffolk St SW1 ....119 C2
Sugar House La E15 27 B3
Sugar Loaf Wlk 6
    E2 ....25 B2
Sugden Ho SW11 ....149 A4
Sugden Rd SW11 ....60 C3
Sulby Ho SE4 ....66 A3
Sulgrave Gdns 11
    W6 ....39 B4
Sulgrave Rd W6 ....39 B3
Sulina Rd SW2 ....74 A4
Sulivan Ct SW6 ....165 B1
Sulivan Ent Ctr
    SW6 ....58 C4
Sulivan Prim Sch
    SW6 ....165 C1
Sulivan Rd SW6 ....58 C4
Sulkin Ho 11 E2 ....25 C2
Sullivan Cl SW11 ....60 A4
Sullivan Ct SW5 ......141 C4
    N16 ....7 B3
Sullivan Ho SE11 ...149 A3
    SW1 ....160 B4
Sullivan Rd SE11 ....149 C4
Sultan St SE5 ....48 B3
Sumatra Rd NW6 ....10 C2
Sumburgh Rd SW12 ..60 C1
Summer Ho SE13 ....67 C3
Summer Rd SE7 ....32 B3
Summercourt Rd
    E1 ....32 B3
Summerfield Ave
    NW6 ....23 A3

Summerhouse Rd
    N16 ....7 A2
Summerlands Ave
    W3 ....28 B2
Summerley St
    SW18 ....71 A2
Summers St EC1 ....95 B1
Summerstown
    SW17 ....71 B1
Summit Ho NW2 ....10 A3
Summit Est N16 ....7 C4
Sumner Ave SE15 ......49 B2
Sumner Bldgs SE1 ..122 C2
Sumner Ct SW8 ....172 A4
Sumner Ho 11 E3 ....34 A4
Sumner Pl SW7 ....143 C3
Sumner Place Mews
    SW7 ....143 C2
Sumner Rd SE15 ....49 B3
Sumner St SE1 ....122 C2
Sumpter Cl NW3 ....11 B2
Sun Alley 6 TW9 ....54 A3
Sun Ct EC3 ....109 C1
Sun Pas SE16 ....139 B2
Sun Rd W14 ....140 C1
Sun St EC2 ....109 C4
Sun St Pas EC2 ....110 A3
Sunbeam Cres W10 ...22 B1
Sunbeam Rd NW10 ...20 C1
Sunbury Ave SW14 ....55 C3
Sunbury Ct 3 SE14 ..50 C4
Sunbury Ho 22 E2 ....98 C3
Sunbury La SW11 ....167 C4
Sunbury Workshops
    E2 ....98 C3
Sunderland Ct SE22 ..76 C4
Sunderland Ho 20
    W2 ....31 C4
Sunderland Terr
    W2 ....100 A2
Sundew Ave W12 ....29 C2
Sundridge Ho 4 E9 17 C1
Sunningdale Ave
    W3 ....29 A2
Sunningdale Cl 22
    SE16 ....40 A1
Sunningdale Gdns
    W8 ....127 C1
Sunninghill Ct 9
    W3 ....37 B4
Sunninghill Rd
    SE13 ....52 A1
Sunnyhill Cl E5 ....18 A4
Sunnymead Rd
    SW15 ....57 A2
Sunnyside 3 NW2 ....1 B1
Sunnyside Ho 4
    NW2 ....1 B1
Sunnyside Rd N19 .....4 C4
Sunray Ave SE5,
    SE24 ....63 C3
Sunset Rd SE5 ....63 C3
Sunwell Cl SE15 ....50 A2
Surcot Ho SW4 ....171 C1
Surma Cl E1 ..24 C1 99 C1
Surr St N7 ....14 A3
Surrendale Pl W9 ......23 C1
Surrey Canal Rd
    SE14,SE16,SE8 ....50 C4
Surrey Commercial
    Wharf SE16 ....32 C1
Surrey Cres 11 W4 ...36 C1
Surrey Gr SE17 ....152 A1
Surrey Ho 8 SE16 ...32 C1
Surrey La SW11 ....168 B3

Surrey Quays Rd
    SE16 ....40 C4
Surrey Quays Sh Ctr
    SE16 ....40 C3
Surrey Quays Sta
    SE16 ....40 C2
Surrey Rd SE15 ....65 C2
Surrey Row SE1 ....136 B4
Surrey Sq SE17 ....152 B2
Surrey Square Inf Sch
    SE17 ....152 A2
Surrey Square Jun Sch
    SE17 ....152 A2
Surrey St WC2 ....121 A4
Surrey Terr SE17 .....152 B2
Surrey Water Rd
    SE16 ....32 C1
Surridge Ct SW9 ....172 B2
Susan Lawrence Jun &
    Inf Schs E14 ....34 B3
Susannah St E14 ....34 B3
Sussex Cl N19 ....5 A2
Sussex Ct W2 ....101 B1
    4 SW13 ....46 B1
    SE10 ....52 B4
Sussex Gdns W2 ......101 C1
    N6 ....3 B4
Sussex Ho NW3 ....12 A2
    Richmond TW9 ....44 B1
Sussex Lo W2 ....101 C1
Sussex Mans WC2 ...120 B4
    SW7 ....143 B3
Sussex Mews E
    W2 ....101 C1
Sussex Mews W
    W2 ....115 C4
Sussex Pl NW1 ....90 C2
    W2 ....101 C1
Sussex Sq W2 ....115 C4
Sussex St SW1 ....146 B2
Sussex Way N7,N19,
    N7,N19 ....5 A2
Sussex Wlk 18 SW9 ..63 A3
Sutherland Ave W9 ...88 B2
Sutherland Ct N16 ......6 C1
    2 W9 ....23 C1
Sutherland Gdns
    SW14 ....56 A4
Sutherland Gr SW18,
    SW19 ....70 B4
Sutherland Ho W8 ...128 A1
    6 NW6 ....10 C3
Sutherland Pl W2 ....31 C3
Sutherland Point 6
    E5 ....17 A4
Sutherland Row
    SW1 ....146 B2
Sutherland Sq
    SE17 ....150 C1
Sutherland St SW1 ..146 B2
Sutherland Wlk
    SE17 ....151 A1
Sutterton St N7 ....14 B2
Sutton Court Rd
    W4 ....45 B4
Sutton Ct 9 E5 ....17 A4
    W4 ....45 B4
Sutton Est SW3 ....144 B2
Sutton Est The W10 ..30 B4
Sutton La N W4 ....37 B1
Sutton La S W4 ....45 B4
Sutton Pl E9 ....17 B3
Sutton Row W1 ....105 C2

Sutton Sq E9 ....17 B3
Sutton St E1 ....32 B3
Sutton Way W10 ....30 B4
Suttons Way EC1 ......97 A1
Swaby Rd SW17, ...71 B2

Swaffield Prim Sch
    SW18 ....71 B4
Swaffield Rd SW18 ...71 B4
Swain's La N6 ....4 A2
Swainson Ho N7 ....14 C4
Swainson Rd W3 ....38 B4
Swallow Cl SE14 ....50 C2
Swallow Ct 4 W9 ....31 C4
Swallow Ho NW8 ....80 A2
Swallow Pl W1 ....104 B1
Swallow St W1 ....119 A3
Swallowfield NW1 ......92 B3
Swallowtail Ct SW3 .144 B4
    SW6 ....155 B1
    E14 ....33 B3
Swan Ctr SW17 ....71 B1
Swan Ho N1 ....15 C1
Swan La EC4 ....123 C3
Swan Lane Pier
    EC4 ....123 C3
Swan Mead SE1 ....138 A1
Swan Mews SW9 ......172 C2
Swan Pas E1 ....125 B3
Swan Pl SW13 ....46 B1
Swan Rd SE16 ....40 B4
Swan St SE1 ....137 A3
Swan Wlk SW3 ....158 C4
Swan Yd N1 ....15 A2
Swanage Ct 6 N1 ......16 A1
Swanage Ho SW8 ....162 C1
Swanage Rd SW18 ....59 B1
Swanbourne SE17 ....150 C3
Swanbourne Ho
    NW8 ....90 A2
Swandon Way
    SW18 ....59 A3
Swanfield St E2 ....99 A3
Swanlea Sec Sch
    E1 ....25 A1
Swanley Ho SE17 ....152 B2
Swanmore Ct SW18 ..59 B1
Swanne Ho 10 SE10 ..52 B3
Swanscombe Ho 9
    W11 ....30 C1
Swanscombe Point 7
    E16 ....35 B2
Swanscombe Rd
    W11 ....30 C1
    4 W4 ....38 A1
Swanton Gdns
    SW19 ....69 C3
Swanwick Cl SW15 ....68 B4
Swaton Rd E3 ....26 C1
Swaythling Ho 2
    SW15 ....56 B1
Sweden Gate SE16 ....41 A2
Swedenborg Gdns
    E1 ....32 A2
Swedish Schs W14 ....86 A3
Sweeney Cres SE1 ..139 A3
Sweyn Pl SE3 ....53 C1
Swift Ho SW9 ....163 C2
    N16 ....7 A1
Swift St SW6 ....164 C4
Swinbrook Rd W10 ....31 A4
Swinburne Ct 4
    SE5 ....63 C3
Swinburne Ho 19
    E2 ....25 B2

Swinburne Rd
    SW15 ....56 C3
Swindon St W12 ....30 B1
Swinford Gdns SW9 ..63 A4
Swingfield Ho 5
    E9 ....25 B4
Swinley Ho NW1 ....92 B4
Swinnerton St E9 ....18 A3
Swinton Ho E2 ....99 B3
Swinton Pl WC1 ....94 C4
Swinton St WC1 ....94 C4
Swiss Cottage NW3 ....11 C1
Swiss Cottage Sch
    NW8 ....79 C4
Swiss Cottage Sta
    NW3 ....11 C1
Swiss Terr 7 NW3 .....11 C1
Sybil Phoenix Cl
    SE8 ....40 C1
Sybil Thorndike Casson
    Ho SW5 ....141 C1
Sybil Thorndike Ho 7
    N1 ....15 B2
Sycamore Cl W3 ....29 A1
Sycamore Ct N19 ....4 C1
    NW6 ....23 C4
    4 SE5 ....48 B2
Sycamore Gdns W6,
    W12 ....39 A3
Sycamore Gr SE6 .....67 B1
Sycamore Ho N16 ......6 C2
    10 NW3 ....12 B2
    2 W6 ....39 A4
    6 SE16 ....40 C4
Sycamore Lo SW15 ....57 A4
Sycamore Mews 4
    SW4 ....61 B4
Sycamore St EC1 ....96 C1
Sycamore Wlk 11
    W10 ....23 A1
Sydenham Hill SE21,
    SE22,SE23,SE26,SE19 ..76 C1
Sydenham Hill Sta
    SE21 ....76 B1
Sydner Mews N16 ......16 B4
Sydner Rd N16 ....16 B4
Sydney Cl SW3 ....143 C3
Sydney Ho 4 W4 ....38 A2
Sydney Mews SW3 ..143 C3
Sydney Pl SW7 ....143 C3
Sydney Rd TW10,
    TW9 ....54 A3
Sydney St SW3 ....144 A2
Sylva Ct 3 SW15 ....69 C4
Sylvan Gr NW2 ....9 C4
    SE15 ....50 A4
Sylvester Ho 7 E8 ...18 A2
Sylvester Path 8
    E8 ....18 A2
Sylvester Rd E8 ....17 A2
Sylvia Cotts 3 SE8 ...51 C2
Sylvia Ct N1 ....87 B1
Sylvia Pankhurst Ho 4
    E2 ....25 C2
Symes Mews NW1 ......82 C2
Symington Ho SE1 ...137 B1
Symons St SW3 ....145 A3
Syringa Ho SE4 ....66 B4

T

Tabard Ct 3 E14 ....34 B3
Tabard Ho SE1 ....137 C2

Tabard St E1 .... 137 B2
Tabernacle St EC2 .. 97 C2
Tableer Ave SW4 .. 61 C2
Tabley Rd N7 ...... 14 A4
Tabor Rd W6 ...... 39 A3
Tachbrook Est
SW1 .... 147 C1
Tachbrook Mews
SW1 .... 146 C4
Tachbrook St SW1 .147 A3
Tack Mews SE4 ... 66 C4
Tadema Ho NW8 .. 89 C1
Tadema Rd SW10 .157 A1
Tadmor St W12 .... 30 C1
Tadworth Ho SE1 .136 A3
Taeping St E14 .... 42 A2
Taft Way W3 ...... 27 A2
Tait Ho SE1 ...... 171 C4
 3 .... 26 B4
Tait Ho SE1 ...... 121 C1
 2 N19 .... 13 B4
Talacre Rd NW5 .. 12 C2
Talbot Ct EC3 .... 123 C4
Talbot Grove Ho 9
W11 .... 31 A3
Talbot Ho N7 ...... 5 C1
E14 .... 34 A3
Talbot Pl SE3 ..... 53 A1
Talbot Rd W11 ..... 31 B3
W2 .... 31 C3
SE22 .... 64 A3
Talbot Sq W2 .... 101 B1
Talbot Wlk NW10 .. 8 A2
W11 .... 31 A3
Talbot Yd SE1 .... 123 B1
Talcott Path 12
SW2 .... 74 C3
Talfourd Pl SE15 .. 49 B2
Talfourd Rd SE15 .. 49 B2
Talgarth Rd W14 .140 B2
W6 .... 39 C1
Talia Ho E14 ..... 42 B3
Talina Ctr SW6 ...166 C3
Talleyrand Ho SE5 .48 B1
Tallis St EC4 ..... 121 C4
Talma Rd SW2 .... 62 C3
Talmud Torah Sch
N16 .... 7 C3
Talmudical Coll N16 .6 C4
Talwin St E3 ...... 27 A2
Tamar Cl E3 ...... 26 B4
Tamar Ho SE11 ...149 C2
Tamarind Ct 8
 W3 .... 28 B3
Tamarind Ho 5
SE15 .... 49 C3
Tamarind Yd E1 ...125 C2
Tamarisk Sq W12 .. 29 B2
Tamworth N7 ..... 14 A2
Tamworth St SW6 .155 B3
Tangier Rd TW10 .. 55 A4
Tangley Gr SW15 .. 68 B4
Tangmere WC1 .... 94 C3
Tanhurst Ho 27
SW2 .... 74 A4
Tankerton WC1 .... 94 B3
Tanner Ho SE1 ....138 B3
Tanner St SE1 ....138 B3
Tanner's Hill SE8 .. 51 C2
Tannington Terr N5 . 5 C1
Tansley Cl N7 ..... 13 C3
Tant Ave E16 ..... 35 B1

Tantallon Rd SW12 .72 C3
Tanza Rd NW3 .... 12 B4
Taplow Ho 5
SE15 .... 65 B4?
Taplow Ho 3 E2 .. 24 B2 C3
Taplow Rd SE17 .. 98 C2
Taplow St N1 ..... 87 A1
Tapp St E1 .... 25 A1
Tappesfield Rd
SE15 .... 65 B4
Taranto Ho 1 E1 .. 32 C4
Tarbert Ho SE22 .. 64 A2
Tarbert Rd SE22 .. 64 A2
Tarling Ho 6 E1 .. 32 A3
Tarling Rd E16 .... 35 B1
Tarling St E1 ..... 32 B3
Tarn St SE1 ......136 C1
Tarnbrook Ct SW1 145 B3
Tarns The NW1 ... 92 C4
Tarplett Ho 30 SE14 .50 C4
Tarragon Cl SE14 . 51 A3
Tarranbrae NW6 .. 10 A1
Tarrant Ho E2 .... 25 B2
Tarrant Pl W1 ....102 C3
Tarriff Cres SE8 .. 41 B2
Tarrington Cl SW16 .73 C1
Tartan Ho 6 E14 .. 34 B3
Tarver Rd SE17 ...150 B2
Tarves Way SE10 .. 52 A3
Tasker Ho 13 E14 .. 33 B4
Tasker Rd NW3 ... 12 B3
Tasman Ho 1 E1 .. 32 A1
Tasman Rd SW9 .. 62 A4
Tasso Rd W6 .....154 A4
Tasso Yd W6 .....154 A3
Tatchbury Ho 3
SW15 .... 56 B1
Tate Gallery
(Britain)The *
SW1 .... 148 A3
Tate Gallery of Modern
Art * SW1 ....122 B3
Tatham Pl NW8 ... 79 C2
Tatnell Rd SE23 .. 66 A1
Tatton Cres E5,N16 .7 B4
Tatum St SE17 ...151 C3
Tauheed Cl N4 .... 6 B2
Taunton Ho W2 ..100 C1
Taunton Mews NW1 .90 C1
Taunton Pl NW1 .. 90 C2
Taverner Sq 4 N5 .15 B4
Taverners Cl 11
W11 .... 112 A1
Tavistock Cl N16 .. 16 A3
Tavistock Cres 1
W11 .... 31 B4
Tavistock Ct WC2 .. 93 C2
Tavistock Ho 2
W11 .... 31 B4
Tavistock Mews 1
W11 .... 31 B3
Tavistock Pl WC1 .. 94 A2
Tavistock Rd NW10 .21 B3
W11 .... 31 B4
Tavistock Sq WC1 .120 B4?
Tavistock St WC2 .120 B4
Tavistock Terr N19 .. 4 C1
Tavistock Twr SE16 .41 A3
Taviton St WC1 ... 93 B2
Tavy Cl SE11 .....149 C2
Tawny Way SE16 .. 40 C2
Tayburn Cl E14 ... 34 B3
Tayler Ct NW8 .... 79 B4
Taylor Ave TW9 ... 45 A1
Taylor Ct E15 .... 76 B3

Taylor Ho 10 SW2 .74 C3
Taylor's Gn W3 ... 29 A3
Taylor's La NW10 .. 8 A1
Tayport Cl N1 .... 14 A1
Tayside Ct 6 SE5 .. 63 C3
Teak Cl SE16 ..... 33 A1
Teal Ct 30 SE8 .... 51 B4
Tealby Ct N7 ..... 14 B2
Teale St E2 ...... 24 C3
Teather St 20 SE5 .49 A3
Tebbs Ho 7 SW2 .. 74 C4
Ted Roberts Ho 24
E2 .... 25 A3
Tedworth Gdns
SW3 ....144 C1
Tedworth Sq SW3 144 C1
Tee The W3 ...... 29 A3
Teesdale Cl E2 .... 25 A3
Teesdale St E2 .... 25 A3
Teignmouth Cl 6
W4 .... 61 C3
Teignmouth Rd NW2 .9 C2
Telegraph Hill NW3 .2 A1
Telegraph Pl E14 .. 42 A2
Telegraph Rd SW15 .69 B4
Telegraph St EC2 .109 B2
Telfer Cl 4 W3 .... 37 B4
Telfer Ho EC1 .... 96 C3
Telferscot JMI Sch
SW12 .... 73 C3
Telferscot Rd SW12 .73 C3
Telford Ave SW2 .. 74 A3
SW2 .... 74 A3
Telford Ho SE1 ...136 C2
 8 W10 .... 31 A4
Telford Parade Mans 8
SW2 .... 74 A3
Telford Rd W10 ... 31 A4
Telford Terr SW1 .160 C4
Telford Way W3 ... 29 A4
Tell Gr SE22 ..... 64 B3
Telscombe Ho
SW11 ....169 B3
Temair Ho 1 SE10 .52 B3
Temeraire St SE16 .40 B4
Temperley Rd SW12 .72 C4
Templar Ho NW2 . 10 B2
Templar St SE5 ... 48 A1
Templars Ho E15 . 19 A3
Temple Ave EC4 ..121 C4
Temple Ct SW8 ...162 A1
Temple Dwellings 7
E2 .... 25 A3
Temple Ho 4 N7 .. 4 B1
SW11 .... 60 A4
Temple La EC4 ...107 C1
Temple Mills La
E10,E15 .... 76 B4
Temple Mills Rd E9 .18 C4
Temple Pl WC2 ...121 A4
Temple Rd W4 .... 37 B3
Richmond TW9 ... 54 B4
Temple Sheen
SW14 .... 55 B2
Temple Sheen Rd
SW14 .... 55 B3
Temple St E2 ..... 25 A3
Temple Sta WC2 ..121 B4
Temple West Mews
SE11 ....136 A1
Templecombe Rd
E9 .... 25 B4
Templemead Cl W3 .29 A3
Templemead Ho E9 .18 A4

Templeton Cl
N16 .... 16 A3
Templeton Pl SW5 141 C3
Templewood Ave
NW3 .... 2 A1
Templewood Gdns
NW3 .... 2 A1
Templewood Point
NW2 .... 1 B2
Tenbury Ct SW12 .73 C3
Tenby Ho W2 ....100 C1
Tench St E1 ...... 32 A1
Tenda Rd SE16 ... 40 A2
Tendring Ho SW2 . 62 C1
Tenham Ave SW2 .73 C2
Tenison Ct W1 ...118 C4
Tenison Way SE1 .121 B1
Tenniel Cl W2 ....114 B4
Tennis St SE1 ....137 B4
Tennyson Ho SE17 166 B3
Tennyson Rd NW6 .23 B4
Tennyson St SW8 .170 A1
Tensing Ho N1 ... 15 A2
Tent St E1 .... 25 A1
Tenter Ground E1 110 C3
Tenterden Ho
SE17 ....152 B1
Tenterden St W1 .104 B1
Terborah Way 8
SE22 .... 64 A2
Terling Ho W10 ... 30 B4
Terling Wlk N1 ... 86 C4
Terminus Pl SW1 .132 B1
Tern Ho 3 SE15 .. 49 B2
Terrace Ave NW10 .22 B2
Terrace Gdns SW13 .46 B1
Terrace La TW10 .. 54 A1
Terrace Rd E9 .... 17 B1
Terrace The EC4 ..107 C1
NW6 .... 23 C4
SW13 .... 46 A1
Terrace Wlk SW11 159 A2
Terrapin Ct SW17 .73 A1
Terrapin Rd SW17 .73 A1
Terrick St W12 ... 30 A3
Territorial Ho
SE11 ....149 C3
Terry Ho SW2 .... 74 C3
Tessa Sanderson Pl 1
SW8 .... 61 A4
Testerton Wlk 3
W11 .... 30 C2
Tetcott Rd SW10 .156 C1
Teversham La
SW8 ....172 B4
Teviot St E14 .... 34 B4
Teyham Ct SW11 .60 B1
Thackeray Ct W14 .126 A1
SW3 ....144 C2
Thackeray Ho WC1 .94 A2
Thackeray Mews E8 .16 C2
Thackeray Rd SW8 .170 B1
Thackeray St W8 .128 B2
Thalia Cl SE10 ... 52 C4
Thame Rd SE16 .. 40 C4
Thames Ave SW10 167 A4
Thames Bank SW14 .45 B1
Thames Circ E14 .. 41 C2
Thames Cres W4 .. 46 A3
Thames Ct 11 SE15 .49 B3
Thames St SE10 .. 52 A4
Thames Link Ho 7
TW9 .... 54 A3
Thames Pl SW15 .. 57 C4

Thames Quay
SW10 ....167 A3
E14 .... 42 A4
Thames Rd W4 ... 44 C4
Thames Reach W6 .47 B4
Thames St SE10 .. 52 A4
Thames Village W4 .45 B2
Thames Wlk SW11 148 A4
Thameside Ctr TW8 .44 B4
Thane Mans N7 ... 5 B1
Thane Villas N7 ... 5 B1
Thane Works N7 .. 5 B1
Thanet Ho WC1 .. 94 A3
 1 SE27 ....75 A1
Thanet Lo NW2 .. 10 A2
Thanet St WC1 ... 94 A3
Thavie's Inn EC1 .107 C2
Thaxted Ct N1 ...87 C1
Thaxted Ho SE16 .40 B2
Thaxton Rd W14 .155 A4
Thayer St W1 ....103 C2
Theatre Mus WC2 120 B4
Theatre St SW11 .60 B4
Theberton St N1 .. 86 A4
Theed St SE1 ....121 C1
Melbridge Ho 28
SE1 .... 152 B1
Theobald St SE1 .137 B1
Theobald's Rd
WC1 ....106 C4
Theobalds Ct N4 .. 6 B2
Theodore Ho 7
SW15 .... 56 C2
Theodore Rd SE13 .67 C1
Therapia Rd SE22 .65 B1
Theresa Rd W6 ... 38 C2
Therfield Ct N4 ... 6 B2
Thermopylae Gate
E14 .... 42 A2
Theseus Wlk N1 .. 86 B1
Thessaly Ho SW8 .160 C1
Thessaly Rd SW8 .171 A4
Thesus Ho 2 E14 .34 C3
Thetford Ho SE1 .138 C2
Thetis Terr TW9 .. 44 C4
Third Ave W10 ... 23 A2
W3 .... 29 B1
Thirleby Rd SW1 .133 A1
Thirlmere NW1 ... 92 B4
Thirlmere Ho 20
N16 .... 15 C4
Thirsk Rd SW11 .. 60 C3
Thistle Gr SW7 ...143 A1
Thistle Ho 6 E14 .. 34 B3
Thistlewood Cl 3 N7 .5 B2
Thomas Baines Rd
SW11 .... 59 C4
Thomas Burt Ho 8
E2 .... 25 A2
Thomas Buxton Jun &
Inf Sch E1 ...24 C1 99 C1
Thomas Doyle St
SE1 .... 136 B2
Thomas Fairchild JMI
Sch N1 .... 87 A2
Thomas Ho 3 E9 .17 B2
 4 SW4 .... 62 A3
Thomas Hollywood Ho
3 E2 .... 25 B3
Thomas Jones Prim Sch
W11 .... 31 A3
Thomas More Ho
EC2 ....108 C3
Thomas More Sq
E1 ....125 B3

Thomas More St
E1 . . . . .125 B2
Thomas North Terr **3**
E16 . . . . .35 C3
Thomas Pl W8 . . . . . .128 A1
Thomas Rd E14 . . . . . .33 C4
Thomas Road Ind Est
E14 . . . . .33 C3
Thomas's Prep Sch
SW11 . . . . .60 B2
Thomas's Prep Sch
SW11 . . . . .167 C3
Thompson Ave TW9 .54 C4
Thompson Ho
11 W10 . . . . .23 A2
SE14 . . . . .50 C4
Thompson Rd SE22 .64 B1
Thompson's Ave **6**
SE5 . . . . .48 B3
Thomson Ho SW1 . .147 C1
SE17 . . . . .152 A3
Thorburn Ho SW1 . .131 B3
Thorburn Sq SE1 . . .153 B3
Thoresby Ho N16 . . . . .6 C1
Thoresby St N1 . . . . . .97 A4
Thorn Ham Ho
SE1 . . . . .137 C2
Thornaby Ho **15** E2 . .25 A2
Thornbill Ho **1**
SE15 . . . . .49 C3
Thornbury Ho N16 . . .16 A3
Thornbury Ct W11 . .113 B4
Thornbury Ho N6 . . . . .4 B3
Thornbury Rd SW2 . .62 A1
Thornbury Sq N6 . . . . .4 B3
Thorncliffe Ct SW2 . .62 A1
Thorncliffe Rd SW2 . .62 A1
Thorncombe Rd
SE22 . . . . .64 A2
Thorncroft St SW8 .162 A1
Thorndale Ho N16 . . . .7 A3
Thorndean St SW18 .71 B2
Thorndike Cl
SW10 . . . . .156 C2
Thorndike Ho SW1 .147 B2
Thorndike St SW1 . .147 B3
Thorne Cl E16 . . . . . . .35 C3
Thorne Ho **34** E2 . . . .25 B2
4 E14 . . . . .42 A3
Thorne Pas **7**
SW13 . . . . .46 B1
Thorne Rd SW8 . . . .162 B1
Thorne St SW13,
SW14 . . . . .56 A4
Thorness Ct SW18 . .59 B1
Thornewill Ho **7**
E1 . . . . .32 B2
Thorney Cres
SW11 . . . . .157 C1
Thorney Ct W8 . . . . .128 C3
Thorney Hedge Rd
W4 . . . . .37 A2
Thornfield St SW1 . .148 A4
Thorneycroft Ho **1**
W4 . . . . .38 A1
Thornfield Ho **4**
E14 . . . . .33 C2
Thornfield Rd W12 . .39 A4
Thornford Rd SE13 . .67 B2
Thorngate Rd W9 . . .23 C1
Thornham Gr E15 . . .19 C3
Thornham St SE10 . .52 A4
Thornhaugh St
WC1 . . . . .93 C1
Thornhill Bridge Wharf
N1 . . . . .84 C3

Thornhill Cres N1 . . .14 B1
Thornhill Gr N1 . . . . .14 C1
Thornhill Ho N1 . . . . .14 C1
2 W4 . . . . .38 A1
Thornhill Prim Sch
N1 . . . . .14 C1
Thornhill Rd N1 . . . . .85 A4
Thornhill Sq N1 . . . . .85 A4
. . . . .14 B1
Thornicroft Ho
SW9 . . . . .173 A1
Thornley Pl **2** SE10 .43 A1
Thornsett Rd SW18 .71 A3
Thornton Ave W4 . . .38 A2
Thornton Ct N7 . . . . .14 A3
Thornton Gdns
SW12 . . . . .73 C3
Thornton Ho SE17 .152 A3
Thornton Pl W1 . . . .103 A4
Thornton Rd SW14 . .55 C4
SW12,SW2 . . . . .73 C3
Thornton St SW9 . .173 B2
Thornville St SE8 . . .51 C2
Thornycroft Ct TW9 .44 B1
Thorold Ho SE1 . . . .136 C4
6 SW2 . . . . .74 A4
Thorparch Rd
SW8 . . . . .161 C1
Thorpe Cl W10 . . . . .31 A3
Thorpe Ho N1 . . . . . .85 A3
Thorpebank Rd
W12 . . . . .29 C1
Thorpedale Rd N4 . . .5 B3
Thorverton Rd NW2 . .1 A1
Thoydon Rd E3 . . . . .26 A3
Thrale St SE1 . . . . . .123 A1
Thrasher Cl **20** E8 . .24 B4
Thrawl St E1 . . . . . . .111 A3
Thrayle Ho **2** SW9 . .62 B3
Threadgold Ho **8**
N1 . . . . .15 C2
Threadneedle St
EC2,EC3 . . . . .109 C1
Three Colt St E14 . . .33 B2
Three Colts La E2 . . .25 A1
Three Cups Yd
WC1 . . . . .107 A3
Three Kings Yd
W1 . . . . .118 A4
Three Mill La E3 . . . . .27 B2
Three Nun Ct EC2 . .109 A2
Three Oak La SE1 . .138 C4
Threshers Pl W11 . .112 A4
Thring Ho SW9 . . . . .172 C2
Throgmorton Ave
EC2 . . . . .109 C2
Throgmorton St
EC2 . . . . .109 C2
Thrush St SE17 . . . .150 C2
Thurland Ho **3**
SE16 . . . . .40 A2
Thurland Rd SE16 . .139 B2
Thurleigh Ave
SW12 . . . . .60 C1
Thurleigh Rd SW12 .60 C1
Thurloe Cl SW7 . . . .144 A4
Thurloe Ct SW3 . . . .144 A3
Thurloe Pl SW7 . . . .143 C4
Thurloe Place Mews
SW7 . . . . .143 C4
Thurloe Sq SW7 . . . .144 A4
Thurloe St SW7 . . . .143 C4
Thurlow Hill SE21 . . .75 B2

Thurlow Park Rd
SW16 . . . . .74 A1
Thurlow Park Sch
SE21,SE24 . . . . .75 B2
Thurlow Park Sch
SE27 . . . . .75 A2
Thurlow Rd NW3 . . .11 C3
Thurlow St SE17 . . .152 A1
Thurlow Terr NW5 . .12 C3
Thurlow Twrs SE27 . .74 C1
Thurnscoe NW1 . . . .82 C3
Thursley Gdns
SW19 . . . . .69 C2
Thursley Ho **10** SW2 .74 B4
Thurso Ho NW6 . . . . .78 A1
Thurston Ind Est
SE13 . . . . .67 A4
Thurston Rd SE8,
SE13 . . . . .52 A1
Thurtle Rd E2 . . . . . .24 B3
Tibbatt's Rd E3 . . . . .27 A1
Tibbet's Corner
SW19 . . . . .69 C4
Tibbet's Ride SW19 . .69 C4
Tibbets Ct SW19 . . . .69 C3
Tiber Gdns N1 . . . . . .84 B3
Tickford Ho NW8 . . .90 A3
Tidal Basin Rd E16 . .35 B2
Tidbury Ct SW8 . . . .160 C1
Tideswell **1** NW5 . .13 A3
Tideswell Rd SW15 . .57 B3
Tideway Ct **3** SE16 .32 C1
Tideway Ho E14 . . . . .41 C4
Tideway Ind Est
SW8 . . . . .161 A3
Tideway Wharf
SW13 . . . . .46 A1
Tideway Yd SW13 . . .46 A1
Tidey St E3 . . . . .33 C4
Tidworth Ho **15**
SE22 . . . . .64 A4
Tidworth Rd E3 . . . . .26 C1
Tierney Rd SW2 . . . .74 A3
Tierney Terr SW2 . . .74 A3
Tiger Way E5 . . . . . . .17 A4
Tilbury Cl **18** SE15 . .49 B3
Tilbury Ho **6** SE14 .50 C4
Tildesley Rd SW15 . .57 B1
Tile Kiln La N6 . . . . . .4 B3
Tilehurst NW1 . . . . . .92 B3
Tilehurst Rd SW17,
SW18 . . . . .71 C3
Tileyard Rd N7 . . . . . .14 A1
Tilford Gdns SW19 . .69 C2
Tilford Ho **5** SW2 . .74 B4
Tilia Rd E5 . . . . .17 A4
Tilleard Ho **4** W10 .23 A2
Tiller Ho **30** N1 . . . . .24 A4
Tiller Rd E14 . . . . . . .41 C3
Tillet Sq SE16 . . . . . .41 A4
Tillet Way E2 . . . . . . .99 B4
Tilling Ho **8** SE15 . .65 A4
Tillman Ho **3** SW2 . .74 B3
Tillman St E1 . . . . . .32 A3
Tillotson Ct SW8 . . .161 C1
Tilney Ct EC1 . . . . . . .97 A2
Tilney Gdns **12** N1 . .15 C2
Tilney St W1 . . . . . . .117 C2
Tilson Gdns SW2,
SW4 . . . . .74 A4
Tilson Ho SW2 . . . . . .74 A4
Tilton St SW6 . . . . . .154 B3
Tiltwood The W3 . . .28 B2

Timber Mill Way
SW4 . . . . .61 C4
Timber Pond Rd
SE16 . . . . .40 C4
Timber St EC1 . . . . . .96 C2
Timberland Cl **15**
SE15 . . . . .49 C3
Timberland Rd E1 . . .32 A3
Time Sq E8 . . . . .16 B3
Timothy Cl **1** SW4 . .61 B2
Timothy Rd E3 . . . . . .33 B4
Timsbury Wlk **5**
SW15 . . . . .68 C3
Tina Ct SW16 . . . . . .74 C1
Tindal St SW9 . . . . . .48 A2
Tinniswood Cl N5 . . .14 C3
Tinsley Rd E1 . . . . . .32 B4
Tintagel Cres SE22 . .64 B3
Tintern Cl SW15 . . . .58 A2
Tintern Ho NW1 . . . .82 B1
SW1 . . . . .146 A3
Tintern St SW4 . . . . .62 A3
Tinworth St SE11 . . .148 B2
Tipthorpe Rd SW11 . .60 C4
Tiptree **7** NW1 . . . . .13 A1
Tisbury Ct W1 . . . . . .119 B4
Tisdall Pl SE17 . . . . .151 C3
Tissington Ct **4**
SE16 . . . . .40 C2
Titan Bsns Est **3**
SE8 . . . . .51 C3
Titan Ct TW8 . . . . . . .36 B1
Titchborne Row
W2 . . . . .102 B1
Titchfield Rd NW8 . .80 C3
Titchwell Rd SW18 . .71 C3
Tite St SW3 . . . . .158 C4
Titmuss St **12** W12 .39 B4
Tiverton Rd NW6,
NW10 . . . . .22 C4
Tiverton St SE1 . . . .136 C2
Tivoli Ct SE16 . . . . . .33 B1
Tobago St E14 . . . . . .41 C4
Tobin Cl NW3 . . . . . .12 A1
Toby La E1 . . . . .26 A1
Todds Wlk N7 . . . . . . .5 B2
Tokenhouse Yd
EC2 . . . . .109 B2
Toland Sq SW15 . . . .56 C2
Tolchurch **2** W11 . .31 C3
Tolhurst Ho **5** W12 .30 A3
Tollbridge Cl W10 . . .23 A1
Tollet St E1 . . . . .25 C1
Tollgate Dr SE21 . . . .76 A2
Tollgate Ho NW6 . . .78 A2
Tollhouse Way N19 . .4 B2
Tollington Ct N4 . . . . .5 B2
Tollington Pk N4 . . . . .5 B2
Tollington Pl N4 . . . . .5 B2
Tollington Rd N7 . . . .14 B4
Tollington Way N7 . . .5 A1
Tolmers Sq NW1 . . . .93 A3
Tolpaide Ho SE11 . . .149 B3
Tolpuddle St N1 . . . . .85 C2
Tolsford Rd E5 . . . . . .17 A3
Tom Groves Cl E15 . .19 C3
Tom Hood Cl E15 . . .19 C3
Tom Jenkinson Rd **5**
E16 . . . . .35 C1
Tom Smith Cl SE10 . .53 A4
Tom Williams Ho
SW6 . . . . .154 C3
Tomkyns Ho SE11 . .149 B3
Tomlin's Gr E3 . . . . . .26 C2
Tomlin's Terr E14 . . .33 A3
Tomline Ho SE1 . . . .122 C1

Tomlins Wlk **4** N7 . . .5 B2
Tomlinson Cl E2 . . . . .99 A3
8 W4 . . . . .37 A1
Tompion Ho EC1 . . . .96 B2
Tompion St EC1 . . . . .96 B3
Tomson Ho SE1 . . . .138 C2
Tonbridge Hos WC1 . .94 A3
Tonbridge St WC1 . . .94 A3
Toneborough NW8 . .78 B3
Tonsley Hill SW18 . . .59 A2
Tonsley Pl SW18 . . . .59 A2
Tonsley Rd SW18 . . .59 A2
Tonsley St SW18 . . . .59 A2
Took's Ct EC4 . . . . . .107 B2
Tooley St SE1 . . . . . .124 A1
Tooting Bec SW17 . . .72 C1
Tooting Bec Sta
SW17 . . . . .72 C1
Topham Ho **3** SE10 .52 B3
Topham St EC1 . . . . .95 B2
Topiary Sq TW9 . . . . .54 B4
Topmast Point E14 . .41 C4
Topsham Rd SW17 . .72 C1
Tor Ct W8 . . . . .127 C4
Tor Gdns W8 . . . . . .127 B4
Torbay Ct **13** NW1 . .13 A1
Torbay Mans NW6 . .23 B4
Torbay Rd NW6 . . . . .10 B1
Torbay St **6** NW1 . . .13 A1
Tornay Ho N1 . . . . . .84 C2
E9 . . . . .17 B1
Toronto Rd E11 . . . . .19 C4
Torquay St W2 . . . . .100 A3
Torrens Ct SE5 . . . . .63 C4
Torrens Rd SW2 . . . .62 B2
Torrens St EC1 . . . . . .86 A1
Torriano Ave NW5 . . .13 C3
Torriano Cotts NW5 .13 B3
Torriano Jun & Inf Schs
NW5 . . . . .13 C3
Torridge Gdns SE15 .65 B3
Torridon Ho NW6 . . .78 A1
Torrington Pl WC1 . .105 B4
E1 . . . . .125 C2
Torrington Sq WC1 . .93 C1
Tortington Ho **1**
SE15 . . . . .50 A3
Torwood Rd SW15 . .56 C2
Tothill Ho SW1 . . . . .147 C4
Tothill St SW1 . . . . .133 C3
Totland Ho SW18 . . .59 A1
Tottan Terr E1 . . . . . .32 C3
Tottenhall **8** NW1 . .12 C1
Tottenham Court Rd **1**
W1 . . . . .105 A4
Tottenham Court Road
Sta W1 . . . . .105 C2
Tottenham Mews
W1 . . . . .105 A4
Tottenham Rd N1 . . .16 A2
Tottenham St W1 . . .105 A4
Totteridge Ho
SW11 . . . . .167 C2
Touchard Ho N1 . . . . .97 C3
Toulmin St SE1 . . . .136 C3
Toulon St SE5 . . . . . .48 B3
Toulouse Ct **2**
SE16 . . . . .40 A1
Tournay Rd SW6 . . .155 A2
Toussaint Wlk
SE16 . . . . .139 C2
Tovy Ho SE1 . . . . . . .153 B1

Towcester Rd E3 . . . .27 B1
Tower Bldgs 22 E1 . . .32 A1
Tower Br App E1,
EC3 . . . . .124 C3
Tower Br Piazza
SE1 . . . . .124 C2
Tower Bridge *
E1,EC3,SE1 . . . . . .124 C2
Tower Bridge Bsns
Complex SE16 . . . . .40 A3
Tower Bridge Bsns Sq
SE16 . . . . .40 A3
Tower Bridge Prim Sch
SE1 . . . . .138 C4
Tower Bridge Rd
EC3,SE1 . . . . .124 C1
Tower Bridge Sq
SE1 . . . . .138 C4
Tower Ct NW8 . . . . .80 B2
WC2 . . . . .106 A1
E5 . . . . .7 B4
Tower Gateway Sta
EC3 . . . . .124 B3
Tower Hamlets Coll
E1 . . . . .32 B4
E1 . . . . .32 C3
E14 . . . . .34 A2
E14 . . . . .34 A3
Tower Hill EC3 . . . .124 C3
Tower Hill Sta EC3 . .124 C3
Tower Hill Terr
EC3 . . . . .124 C3
Tower Mans SE1 . . .138 C1
Tower Mews E5 . . . .18 A3
Tower Millennium Pier
EC3 . . . . .124 B2
Tower Pl EC3 . . . . .124 B3
Tower Rd NW10 . . . . .8 C1
Tower Rise TW9 . . . .54 A4
Tower Royal EC4 . . .123 B4
Tower St WC2 . . . . .106 A1
Tower The * EC3 . . .124 C3
Tower Wharf SE1 . . .138 C4
Tower Wlk SE1 . . . .152 A4
Towergate SE1 . . . .152 A4
Towers Pl TW10 . . . .54 A2
Towers The NW5 . . . . .4 B1
 1 Richmond TW9 . . .54 B3
Town Hall Rd SW11 . .60 B4
Towncourt Path N4 . . .6 B3
Townhall Ave 3
W4 . . . . .37 C1
Townley Rd SE22 . . .64 A2
Townley St SE17 . . .151 B2
Townsend Bsns Ctr
SW6 . . . . .59 B4
Townmead Rd
SW6 . . . . .166 C3
SW6 . . . . .166 C3
Richmond TW9 . . . .45 A1
Townsend Ind Est
NW10 . . . . .20 B3
Townsend Prim Sch
SE17 . . . . .152 A4
Townsend St SE1,
SE17 . . . . .152 A4
Townsend Yd N6 . . . .4 A3
Townshend Ct NW8 . .80 B2
Townshend Est
NW8 . . . . .80 A2

Townshend Rd
NW8 . . . . .80 A3
Richmond TW9 . . . .54 B3
Townshend Terr
TW9 . . . . .54 B3
Towton Rd SE27 . . . .75 B2
Toxteth Ho N4 . . . . .6 B4
Toynbee St E1 . . . .110 C3
Tracey Ave NW2 . . . . .9 B3
Tracy Ho E3 . . . . . .26 B2
Trade Twr 8 SW11 . .59 B4
Trade Winds Ct E1 . .125 C2
Tradescant Ho 15
E9 . . . . .17 B1
Tradescant Rd
SW8 . . . . .162 B1
Trading Estate Rd
NW10 . . . . .20 B1
Traemore Ct SE16 . . .74 C1
Trafalgar Ave SE15 . .49 B4
Trafalgar Cl 1
SE16 . . . . .41 A2
Trafalgar Gdns
W8 . . . . .128 B2
E1 . . . . .32 C4
Trafalgar Gr SE10 . . .52 C4
Trafalgar Ho SE17 . .151 A2
Trafalgar Rd SE10 . . .43 A1
Trafalgar Sq SW1 . . .119 C2
Trafalgar St SE17 . . .151 C2
Trafalgar Way E14 . .34 B1
Trafford Cl E15 . . . .19 A3
Trafford Ho N1 . . . . .87 C2
Tragail SW15 . . . . . .58 A2
Traitors Gate EC3 . .124 C2
Tralee Ct 13 SE16 . . .40 A1
Tramway Ave E15 . . .19 C1
Trance Way W3 . . . .36 C3
Tranmere Ho 7 N7 . .14 C3
Tranmere Rd SW17,
SW18 . . . . .71 B2
Tranquil Pass SE3 . . .53 B1
Tranquil Vale SE3 . . .53 A1
Transept St NW1 . . .102 B3
Transom Cl SE16 . . . .41 A2
Transom Sq E14 . . . .42 A1
Tranton Rd SE16 . . .139 C2
SE16 . . . . .40 A3
Trappes Ho 2 SE16 . .40 A2
Travel Clinic, Hospl for
Tropical Diseases
WC1 . . . . .93 A1
Travers Ho 6 SE10 . .52 C4
Travers Rd N7 . . . . . .5 C1
Travis Ho SE10 . . . . .52 B2
Treadgold Ho W11 . .112 A4
 7 W11 . . . . .30 C2
Treadgold St W11 . .112 A4
Treadway St E2 . . . .25 A3
Treasury Buildings
SW1 . . . . .134 A4
Treaty St N1 . . . . . .84 C3
Trebeck St W1 . . . . .118 A1
Treborough Ho
W1 . . . . .103 B4
Trebovir Rd SW5 . . .141 C3
Treby St E3 . . . . . . .26 B1
Trecastle Way 3
N7 . . . . .13 C4
Tredegar Rd E3 . . . .26 B3
Tredegar Sq E3 . . . .26 B2
Tredegar Terr E3 . . .26 B2
Trederwen Rd E8 . . .24 C4
Treen Ave SW13 . . . .56 B4
Trees The N16 . . . . . .6 C4

Trefil Wlk N7 . . . . . .14 A4
Trefoil Rd SW18 . . . .59 B2
Tregarvon Rd SW11 . .60 C3
Trego Rd E9 . . . . . .18 C1
Tregothnan Rd SW9 . .62 A4
Tregunter Rd
SW10 . . . . .142 C1
Trehern Rd 12
SW14 . . . . .55 C4
Treherne Ct SW9 . . . .48 A2
Trehurst St E5 . . . . .18 A3
Trelawn Rd SW2 . . . .62 C2
Trelawney Est E9 . . .17 B2
Trelawney Ho SE1 . .136 C4
Trellis Sq 1 E3 . . . . .26 B2
Tremadoc Rd SW4 . . .61 C3
Tremaine Cl SE4 . . . .51 C1
Trematon Ho SE11 . .149 C2
Tremlett Gr N19 . . . . .4 B1
Tremlett Mews N19 . . .4 B1
Trenchard St SE10 . . .42 C1
Trenchold St SW8 . .162 A3
Trendell Ho 4 E14 . . .33 C3
Trenmar Gdns
NW10 . . . . .22 A2
Trenmar Lo NW10 . . .22 A2
Trent Ho SE15 . . . . .65 B3
Trent Rd SW2 . . . . . .62 B2
Trentham St SW18 . . .70 C3
Treport St SW18 . . . .71 A4
Tresco Ho SE11 . . . .149 B2
Tresco Rd SE15 . . . . .65 A3
Tresham Cres NW8 . .90 A2
Tresham Wlk E9 . . . .17 B3
Tresidder Ho 6
SW4 . . . . .73 C4
Tressel Cl 20 N1 . . . .15 A1
Tressillian Cres SE4 . .66 C4
Tressillian Rd SE4 . . .66 C4
Trevanion Rd W14 . .140 B2
Trevelyan Gdns
NW10 . . . . .22 B4
Trevelyan Ho 16 E2 . .25 C2
 3 SE5 . . . . .48 A3
Treveris St SE1 . . . .122 B1
Treverton St W10 . . .22 C1
Treverton Twr W10 . .30 C4
Treves Ho E1 . . . . . .24 C1 99 C1
Treville St SW15 . . . .69 A4
Trevithick Ho SW8 . .171 B4
 B SE16 . . . . .40 A2
Trevithick St SE8 . . .51 C4
Trevor Pl SW7 . . . . .130 B3
Trevor Sq SW7 . . . .130 B3
Trevor St SW7 . . . . .130 B3
Trevose Ho SE11 . . .149 A2
Trewint St SW18 . . . .71 B2
Triangle Pl SW4 . . . .61 C3
Triangle Rd 7 E8 . . . .25 A4
Triangle The EC1 . . . .96 B2
N19 . . . . .4 C4
E8 . . . . .25 A4
Trident Ho 13 E14 . . .34 B3
Trident St SE16 . . . . .40 C2
Trigon Rd SW8 . . . .163 A2
Trim St SE8 . . . . . . .51 B4
Trimdon NW1 . . . . . .83 A3
Trimmer Wlk 11
TW8 . . . . .44 A4
Trinder Rd N4,N19 . . .5 A3
Tring Ave 5 W5 . . . . .36 B4
Trinidad Ho 13 E14 . .33 B2
Trinidad St E14 . . . . .33 B2
Trinity Church Rd
SW13 . . . . .47 A4

Trinity Church Sq
SE1 . . . . .137 A2
Trinity Cl 3 SW4 . . . .61 B3
SE13 . . . . .67 C3
Trinity Coll of Music
W1 . . . . .103 C2
Trinity Cotts TW9 . . .54 B4
Trinity Cres SW17 . . .72 C2
Trinity Ct WC1 . . . . .94 C2
 2 N1 . . . . .24 A4
SE16 . . . . .41 A4
Trinity Gdns E16 . . . .35 B2
SW2,SW9 . . . . . . .62 B3
Trinity Gn 1 E1 . . . .32 B4
Trinity Gr 8 SE10 . . .52 B2
Trinity Ho SE1 . . . .137 A2
Trinity Homes 14
SW2 . . . . .62 B3
Trinity Pl EC3 . . . . .124 C3
Trinity Rd
Richmond TW9 . . . .54 B4
SW18 . . . . .72 A3
Trinity Rise SE24,
SW2 . . . . .75 A4
Trinity Sq EC3 . . . .124 B4
Trinity St SE1 . . . . .137 B2
 1 E16 . . . . .35 C4
Trinity St Mary's CE
Prim Sch SW12 . . . .72 C3
Trinity Way W3 . . . . .29 B2
Trinity Wharf Bsns Ctr
SE16 . . . . .41 B4
Trio Pl SE1 . . . . . . .137 A3
Tristan Ct 42 SE8 . . . .51 B4
Triton Ho E14 . . . . . .42 A2
Triton Sq NW1 . . . . .92 C2
Tritton Rd SE21,
SE27 . . . . .75 C1
Trocette Mans SE1 . .138 B2
Trojan Ct NW6 . . . . .10 A1
Troon Cl 13 SE16 . . . .40 A1
Troon Ho 11 E14 . . . .33 A3
Troon St E1 . . . . . . .33 A3
Tropical Ct 3 W10 . . .22 C2
Trossachs Rd SE22 . . .64 A2
Trothy Rd SE1 . . . .153 C3
Trotman Ho SE14 . . .50 B2
Trott St SW11 . . . . .168 A3
Trotwood Ho 3
SE16 . . . . .40 A4
Troutbeck NW1 . . . . .92 B3
Troutbeck Rd SE14 . .51 A2
Trouville Rd SW4 . . . .61 B1
Trowbridge Rd E9 . . .18 B2
Trower Ho 5 E9 . . . .18 A2
Troy Ct W8 . . . . . . .127 B2
Troy Town SE15 . . . .64 C4
Troy Town Flats
SE15 . . . . .64 C4
Troyes Ho NW3 . . . .12 B3
Truman's Rd 24 N16 . .16 A3
Trump St EC2 . . . . .109 A1
Trundle St SE1 . . . .136 C4
Trundle's Ct SE8 . . . .40 C1
Trundley's Terr SE8 . .40 C2
Trundleys Rd SE8 . . .51 A4
Truro Ho 25 W2 . . . .31 C4
Truro St NW5 . . . . . .12 C2
Trussley Rd W6 . . . . .39 B3
Trust Wlk SE21 . . . . .75 A3
Tryon St SW3 . . . . .144 C2
Tubbs Rd NW10 . . . .21 B3
Tudor Cl N6 . . . . .4 B4
NW3 . . . . .12 A2

Tudor Cl *continued*
 . . . . .62 B1
Tudor Ct N1 . . . . . . .16 A2
 B SE16 . . . . .32 C1
Tudor Est NW10 . . . .20 A3
Tudor Gdns SW13 . . .56 A4
Tudor Gr E9 . . . . . .17 B1
Tudor Ho 34 E9 . . . .17 B1
W14 . . . . .39 C2
Tudor Mews 2
NW10 . . . . .8 C2
Tudor Rd E9 . . . . . .25 A4
Tudor St EC4 . . . . .121 C4
Tudor Way W3 . . . . .36 C4
Tufnell Ct 12 E3 . . . .26 B4
Tufnell Park Mans 1
N7 . . . . .5 A1
Tufnell Park Prim Sch
N7 . . . . .13 C4
Tufnell Park Rd
N19,N7 . . . . .13 C4
Tufnell Park Sta
N19 . . . . .13 B4
Tufton Ct SW1 . . . .134 A1
Tufton St SW1 . . . .134 A1
Tullis Ho 10 E9 . . . .17 B1
Tulse Hill SW2,SE24 . .74 C4
SW2 . . . . .75 A2
Tulse Hill Ho SW2 . . .62 C1
Tulse Ho SW2 . . . . .62 C1
Tulsemere Rd SE21,
SE27 . . . . .75 B2
Tunbridge Ct 1
SE26 . . . . .76 C1
Tunbridge Ho EC1 . . .96 A4
Tunis Ho E1 . . . . . . .33 A4
Tunis Rd W12 . . . . . .30 A1
Tunley Gn 18 E14 . . .33 B4
Tunley Rd NW10 . . . .21 A4
SW12,SW17 . . . . . .72 C2
Tunnel Ave SE10 . . . .42 C4
SE10 . . . . .43 B2
Tunnel Avenue Trad Est
SE10 . . . . .42 C4
Tunnel Rd SE16 . . . . .40 B4
Tunstall Ct 14 TW9 . .44 B2
Tunstall Rd SW9 . . . .62 B3
Tunstall Wlk 10
TW8 . . . . .44 A4
Tunworth Cres
SW15 . . . . .56 B1
Tupman Ho SE16 . . .139 B3
Turberville Ho 1
SW9 . . . . .173 B4
Turene Ct SW18 . . . .59 B3
Turin St E2 . . . .24 C2 99 B3
Turks Row SW3 . . . .145 A2
Turle Rd N4 . . . . .5 B2
Turlewray Cl N4 . . . . .5 B3
Turnagain La EC4 . . .108 A2
Turnberry Cl 24
SE16 . . . . .40 A1
Turnbull Ho N1 . . . . .86 B4
Turnchapel Mews 1
SW4 . . . . .61 A4
Turner Cl 7 SW9 . . . .48 A2
Turner Ct 19 SE16 . . .40 A8
 B SE5 . . . . .48 B3
Turner Ho NW8 . . . . .80 A2
WC2 . . . . .120 B3
SW1 . . . . .147 C3
N4 . . . . .5 B3

Turner Lo [10] W19 ...69 C3
Turner St E1 ...32 A4
E16 ...35 B1
Turner's Rd E3 ...33 B4
Turneville Rd W14 .154 C4
Turney Rd SE21 ...75 C4
Turney Sch SE21 ...75 C4
Turnham Green Sta
W4 ...38 A2
Turnham Green Terr
W4 ...38 A2
Turnham Ho SE4 ...66 A3
Turnham Prim Sch
SE4 ...66 A3
Turnham Rd SE4 ...66 A3
Turnmill Ho [8] SW2 .62 C2
Turnmill St EC1 ...108 A4
Turnour Ho [22] E1 ...32 A3
Turnpike Cl SE8 ...51 B3
Turnpike Ho EC1 ...96 B3
Turnpin La [3] SE10 .52 B4
Turnstone Ct [22] ...51 B4
SE8
Turpentine La
SW1 ...146 B1
Turpin Ho SW11 ...170 A4
Turpin Way N19 ...4 C3
Turquand St SE17 .151 A3
Turret Gr SW4 ...61 B4
Turville Ho NW8 ...90 A2
Turville St E2 ...98 C2
Tuscan Ho [30] E2 ...25 B2
Tuskar St SE10 ...43 A1
Tutshill Ct [5] SE15 ..49 B3
Tuttle Ho SW1 ...147 C1
Tweed Ho E14 ...34 B1
Tweedale Ct E15 ...76 B3
Tweezer's Alley
WC2 ...121 B4
Twelvetrees Cres
E3 ...27 B1
Twig Folly Cl E2 ...25 C3
Twilley St SW18 ...71 A4
Twine Ct E1 ...32 B2
Twisden Rd NW5 ...13 A4
Twyford CE High Sch
W3 ...28 A1
Twyford Ho N5 ...6 A1
Twyford Pl WC2 ...106 C2
Twyford St N1 ...84 C4
Twynholm Mans
SW6 ...154 A2
Tyburn RC Inf Sch
NW8 ...89 C2
Tyburn Tree (site of)
...116 C3
Tyburn Way NW1 ...117 A4
Tyer's Est SE1 ...138 A4
Tyers Gate SE1 ...138 A3
Tyers St SE11 ...148 C2
Tyers Terr SE11 ...149 A1
Tyler Cl E2 ...24 B3
Tyler St SE10 ...43 A1
Tylney Ho [6] E1 ...32 A3
Tymperley Ct [3] ...70 A3
SW19
Tyndale La N1 ...15 A1
Tyndale Mans N1 ...15 A1
Tyndale Terr [13] N1 ..15 A1
Tyne St E1 ...111 A2
Tynedale Cl E14 ...42 A1
Tynemouth Cl [10] ...60 C4
E6
Tyneham Cl [11] ...60 C4
SW11
Tynemouth St
SW6 ...166 C2
Tynte Ct E9 ...18 A3

Tynwald Ho [14] SE26 76 C1
Type St E2 ...25 C3
Tyrawley Rd SW6 .166 A4
Tyrrell Ho [11] SW1 ..161 A4
Tyrrell Rd SE22 ...64 C3
Tyrwhitt Rd SE4 ...66 C4
Tysoe St EC1 ...95 C3
Tyssen JMI Sch N16 ..7 C3
Tyssen Rd N16 ...7 B1
Tyssen St E8 ...16 B2
N1 ...24 A3
Tytherton [6] E2 ...25 B3
Tytherton Rd N19 ...4 C1

U

Uamvar St E14 ...34 A4
Udall St SW1 ...147 A3
Udimore Ho W10 ...30 B4
Uffington Rd NW10 ..22 A4
Ufford St SE1 ...135 C4
Ufton Gr N1 ...15 C1
Ufton Rd N1 ...16 A1
Uhura Sq [1] N16 ...7 A1
Ujima Ct N19 ...5 A3
Ullin St E14 ...34 B4
Ullswater SW15 ...57 C1
Ullswater Ho SE15 ..50 B4
Ullswater Rd SW13 .46 C3
SE27,SW16 ...75 A2
Ulster Pl NW1 ...92 A1
Ulundi Rd SE3 ...53 A4
Ulva Rd SW15 ...57 C3
Ulverscroft Rd SE22 .64 C2
Ulverstone Rd SE27 .75 A2
Ulysses Rd NW6 ...10 B3
Umberston St E1 ...32 A3
Umbria St SW15 ...56 C1
Una Ho [7] NW5 ...13 A2
Under Cliff SE10 ...52 B2
Undercliff Rd SE13 ..67 A4
Underhill Ho [7] E14 ..33 C4
Underhill Pas NW1 ..82 B4
Underhill Rd SE22 ...65 A1
Underhill St NW1 ...82 B3
Undershaft EC3 ...110 A1
Underwood Ho W6 ..39 A3
Underwood Rd
E1 ...24 C1 99 C1
Underwood Row
N1 ...97 A4
Underwood St N1 ...97 A4
Undine Rd E14 ...42 A2
Unicorn Bldg [10] E1 ..32 C2
Unicorn Sch TW9 ...44 B2
Union Cl SW4 ...172 A1
E15 Richmond TW10 ..54 A2
Union Dr E1 ...26 A1
Union Gr SW8 ...171 C2
Union Mews SW9 ...172 A1
Union Rd SW4 ...171 C1
Union Sq N1 ...87 A3
Union St SE1 ...122 C1
E15 ...27 C4
Union Wlk E2 ...98 C4
Union Yd W1 ...104 B1
Unity Cl NW10 ...8 C2
Unity Mews NW1 ...83 B2
Univ Coll Hosp
WC1 ...93 A1
Univ Coll Jun Sch
NW3 ...11 B4
Univ Coll London
WC1 ...93 B2
WC1 ...93 C1
WC1 ...94 B3

Univ Coll London
continued
W1 ...105 A4
Univ College Hospl
(Annexe) W1 ...103 C4
Univ of East London
E15 ...27 C4
Univ of Greenwich
Maritime Campus
SE10 ...52 C4
Univ of Greenwich
Rachel Mcmillan
Campus SE8 ...51 C4
Univ of Greenwich The
SW15 ...68 C4
Univ of London
WC1 ...94 A3
Univ of London (King's
Coll Hall) SE5 ...63 C4
Univ of London (Queen
Mary & Westfield Coll)
E1 ...26 A1
Univ of London
(Raymont Hall)
SE4 ...66 B4
Univ of London
Goldsmith's Coll
SE14 ...51 A2
Univ of North London
N7 ...14 C3
Univ of North London
(Carleton Grange Hall)
NW8 ...90 A1
W1 ...92 C2
W1 ...103 B4
W1 ...104 B3
W1 ...104 C2
W1 ...104 C3
W1 ...105 A3
University College Sch
NW3 ...11 B3
University Mans
SW15 ...57 C4
University of North
London (Tufnel Park
Hall) N7 ...4 A1
University St WC1 ...93 A1
Unwin Cl SE15 ...49 C4
Unwin Rd SW7 ...129 C2
Upbrook Mews
W2 ...101 A1
Upcerne Rd SW10 .157 A1
Upcott Ho [4] E9 ...17 B1
[33] E3 ...26 B2
Upgrove Manor Way [12]
SE24 ...74 C4
Upham Park Rd W4 .38 A2
Upland Rd SE22 ...64 C1
Uplands Cl SW14 ...55 A2
Upnall Ho [6] SE15 ..50 B4
Upnor Way SE17 ...152 B2
Upper Addison Gdns
W14 ...126 A4
Upper Belgrave St
SW1 ...131 C2
Upper Berkeley St
W1 ...103 A1
Upper Brockley Rd
SE4 ...51 B1
Upper Brook St
W1 ...117 B4
Upper Caldy Wlk [7]
N1 ...15 B2

Upper Cheyne Row
SW3 ...158 A4
Upper Dengie Wlk (off
Maldon Cl) N1 ...86 C4
Upper Grosvenor St
W1 ...117 B3
Upper Ground SE1 .121 B2
Upper Gulland Wlk [8]
N1 ...15 B2
Upper Harley St
NW1 ...91 C1
Upper Hawkwell Wlk
(off Maldon Cl) N1 87 A4
Upper Holloway Sta
N19 ...4 C2
Upper James St
W1 ...119 A4
Upper John St W1 .119 A4
Upper Mall W6 ...39 A1
Upper Marsh SE1 .135 A2
Upper Montague St
W1 ...102 C3
Upper North St E3,
E14 ...33 C4
Upper Park Rd NW3 .12 B3
Upper Phillimore Gdns
W8 ...127 B3
Upper Rawreth Wlk (off
Basire St) N1 ...87 A4
Upper Richmond Rd
SW15 ...57 B3
Upper Richmond Rd W
TW10,SW14,SW15 ...55 B3
Upper St N1 ...86 A3
Upper St Martin's La
WC2 ...120 A4
Upper Tachbrook St
SW1 ...147 A3
Upper Terr NW3 ...2 B1
Upper Thames St
EC4 ...123 A4
Upper Tollington Pk
N4 ...5 C3
Upper Tooting
Independent High Sch
SW17 ...72 B2
Upper Tooting Park
Mans [1] SW17 ...72 C2
Upper Tooting Pk
SW17 ...72 C2
Upper Tooting Rd
SW17 ...72 B1
Upper Tulse Hill
SW2 ...74 B3
Upper Wimpole St
W1 ...103 C4
Upper Woburn Pl
WC1 ...93 C2
Upstall St SE5 ...48 A2
Upton Cl NW2 ...1 A1
Urbank St SE5 ...48 B4
Urlwin Wlk SW9 ...48 A3
Urmston Dr SW19 ...70 A3
Urmston Ho [3] E14 ..42 B2
Ursula Mews N4 ...6 B3
Ursula St SW11 ...168 A3
Urswick Rd E5,E9 ...17 B3
Usborne Mews
SW8 ...163 A2
Usher Rd E3 ...26 B3
Usk Rd SW11 ...59 B3
Usk St E2 ...25 C2
Utopia Village NW1 .81 B4
Uverdale Rd SW10 .157 A1
Uxbridge Rd W12 ...30 A1
W8 ...31 C1 113 B2

V

Vaine Ho [4] E9 ...18 A2
Vale Cl W9 ...88 C3
Vale Cres SW15 ...68 A1
Vale Ct W9 ...88 C3
W3 ...29 B1
Vale End SE22 ...64 B3
Vale Est The W3 ...29 A1
Vale Gr N4 ...6 A4
W3 ...28 C1
Vale of Health NW3 ...2 C1
Vale Rd N4 ...6 A4
Vale Rise NW11 ...1 B3
Vale Row N5 ...6 A1
Vale Royal N7 ...14 A1
Vale The SW3 ...157 C4
NW11 ...1 C2
W3 ...29 A2
Valens Ho [1] SW2 ...74 C3
Valentia Pl SW9 ...62 C3
Valentine Ho [1]
SW4 ...61 B1
Valentine Pl SE1 ...136 A4
Valentine Rd E9 ...17 C2
Valentine Row
SE1 ...136 A3
Valetta Rd W3 ...38 A4
Valette Ho E9 ...17 B2
Valette St E9 ...17 A2
Valiant Ho SW11 ...167 C3
Vallance Rd
E1 ...24 C1 99 C1
Valliere Rd NW10 ...21 C2
Valmar Rd SE5 ...48 B2
Valmar Trad Est [2]
SE5 ...48 B2
Valois Ho SE1 ...138 C2
Van Gogh Ct E14 ...42 C3
Vanbern Ho NW5 ...12 C2
Vanbrugh Ct SE11 .149 C3
Vanbrugh Fields
SE3 ...53 B3
Vanbrugh Hill SE10,
SE3 ...53 B3
Vanbrugh Ho [8] E9 ..17 B1
Vanbrugh Park Rd
SE3 ...53 B3
Vanbrugh Park Rd W
SE3 ...53 B3
Vanbrugh Pk SE3 ...53 B3
Vanbrugh Rd W4 ...37 C3
Vanbrugh Terr SE3 ..53 B2
Vanbrugh Ho E11 ...110 C4
Vancover Ho [6] E1 ..32 A1
Vanderbilt Rd SW18 .71 B3
Vanderbilt Villas [1]
W12 ...39 C4
Vandon Ct SW1 ...133 A2
Vandon Pas SW1 ...133 A2
Vandon St SW1 ...133 A2
Vandy St EC2 ...98 A1
Vandyke Cl SW15 ...57 C1
Vane Cl NW3 ...11 C3
Vane St SW1 ...147 A4
Vange Ho W10 ...30 B4
Vanguard St SE8 ...51 C2
Vanneck Sq SW15 ...56 C2
Vansittart St [7]
SE14 ...51 A3
Vanston Pl SW6 ...155 C2

Vantage Mews E14 . . . . .34 B1
Vantrey Ho SE11 . . . .149 B3
Varcoe Rd SE16 . . . . . .40 B1
Varden St E1 . . . . .32 A3
Vardens Rd SW11 . . . . .59 C3
Vardon Cl W3 . . . . .28 C3
Vardon Ho SE10 . . . . . .52 B2
Varey Ho E1 . . . . .26 A2
Varley Ho **5** NW6 . . . .23 C4
Varna Rd SW6 . . . . . .154 C1
Varndell St NW1 . . . . . .92 C4
Varsity Row SW14 . . . . .45 B1
Vassal Ho E3 . . . . .26 A2
Vassall Rd SW9 . . . . .163 C1
Vat Ho SW8 . . . . .162 B2
Vauban Est SE16 . . . .139 A1
Vauban St SE16 . . . . .139 A1
Vaudeville Ct N4 . . . . . .5 C2
Vaughan Ave W6 . . . . .38 B2
Vaughan Est E2 . . . . . .98 C4
Vaughan Ho **1** SE1 . .136 A4
Vaughan Ho SE5 . . . . . .63 B4
Vaughan St SE16 . . . . .41 B4
Vaughan Way E1 . . . .125 C2
Vaughan Williams Cl
  SE8 . . . . .51 C3
Vauxhall Bridge Rd
  SW1 . . . . .147 A3
Vauxhall Cross
  SE1,SW8 . . . . .148 B1
Vauxhall Gr SW8 . . . .162 C4
Vauxhall Prim Sch
  SE11 . . . . .149 A2
Vauxhall Sta SE11 . . . .148 B1
Vauxhall Wlk SE11 . . .148 C2
Vawdrey Cl E1 . . . . . . .25 B1
Vaynor Ho N7 . . . . . . .14 A4
Vectis Ct SW18 . . . . . .59 A1
Veda Rd SE13 . . . . . . .66 C3
Velde Way **2** SE22 . . .64 A2
Vellacott Ho W12 . . . . .30 A3
Velletri Ho **17** E2 . . . . .25 C3
Venables St NW8 . . . .101 C4
Vencourt Pl W6 . . . . . .38 C2
Venetian Rd SE5 . . . . .48 B1
Venice Ct **14** SE5 . . . . .48 B3
Venn Ho N1 . . . . .85 A3
Venn St SW4 . . . . .61 B3
Ventnor Rd SE14 . . . . .50 C3
Venue St E14 . . . . .34 B4
Vera Ct W2 . . . . .100 A2
Vera Rd SW6 . . . . . . .164 B4
Verbena Gdns W6 . . . .38 C1
Verdi Ho **2** NW6 . . . . .23 A3
Verdun Rd SW13 . . . . .46 C3
Vere Bank SW19 . . . . .70 B3
Vere St W1 . . . . .104 A1
Vereker Rd W14 . . . . .140 B1
Verity Cl W11 . . . . . . .112 A4
  W11 . . . . .31 A3
Verity Ho **13** E3 . . . . . .26 B2
Vermeer Ct E14 . . . . . .42 C2
Vermont Rd SW18 . . . .59 A1
Verne Ct **8** W3 . . . . . .37 B3
Verney Ho NW8 . . . . . .90 A2
Verney Rd SE16 . . . . . .40 A1
Verney Way SE16 . . . . .40 A1
Vernon Ct NW2 . . . . . . .1 B1
Vernon Mews W14 . . .140 B3
Vernon Pl WC1 . . . . . .106 B3
Vernon Rd E3 . . . . .26 B3

Vernon Rd continued
Vernon Rd SW14 . . . . .55 C4
Vernon Rise WC1 . . . . .95 A4
Vernon Sq WC1 . . . . . .95 A4
Vernon St W14 . . . . . .140 B3
Vernon Yd
  W11 . . . . . . .31 **B2** 112 C4
Verona Ct **13** SE14 . . .50 C4
Veronica Ho SE4 . . . . .66 B4
Veronica Rd SW17 . . . .73 A2
Verran Rd SW12 . . . . . .73 A4
Verulam Ho **5** W6 . . . .39 B4
Verulam St WC1 . . . . .107 B4
Vervain Ho **2** SE15 . . .49 C3
Verwood Ho SW8 . . . .163 A1
Verwood Lo **1** E14 . . .42 C2
Vesage Ct EC1 . . . . . .107 C3
Vesey Path **1** E14 . . . .34 A3
Vespan Rd W12 . . . . . .38 C4
Vesta Rd SE4,SE14 . . . .51 A1
Vestry Mews **15** SE5 . .49 A2
Vestry Rd SE5 . . . . . . .49 A2
Vestry St N1 . . . . .97 B4
Viaduct Pl **28** E2 . . . . .25 A2
Viaduct St E2 . . . . .25 A2
Vian St SE13 . . . . .67 A4
Vibart Gdns SW2 . . . . .74 B4
Vibart Wlk N1 . . . . .84 B4
Vic Johnson Ho **4** E3 . . .
  . . . . .26 B4
Vicar's Cl E9 . . . . .25 B4
Vicar's Rd NW5 . . . . . .12 C3
Vicarage Ave SE3 . . . . .53 C3
Vicarage Cres
  SW11 . . . . .167 B3
Vicarage Ct W8 . . . . . .128 A4
  SW15 . . . . .68 C4
Vicarage Dr SW14 . . . . .55 C2
Vicarage Gate W8 . . . .114 A1
Vicarage Gdns **1** W8 .113 C1
  SW14 . . . . .55 C2
Vicarage Gr SE5 . . . . . .48 C2
Vicarage Mans
  SW4 . . . . .170 A1
Vicarage Rd SW14 . . . .55 C2
Vicarage Wlk
  SW11 . . . . .167 C4
Vicars Cl E9 . . . . .25 B4
Vicars Hill SE13 . . . . . .67 A3
Viceroy Ct NW8 . . . . . .80 B2
Viceroy Rd SW8 . . . . .172 A4
Vickery Ct EC1 . . . . . . .97 A2
Victor Cazalet Ho
  N1 . . . . .86 A4
Victoria & Albert Mus ★
  SW7 . . . . .129 C1
Victoria Arc SW1 . . . .132 B1
Victoria Ave EC2 . . . . .110 B3
Victoria Bldgs **13**
  E8 . . . . .25 A4
Victoria Coach Sta
  SW1 . . . . .146 A3
Victoria Cotts E1 . . . . .111 B4
  7 Richmond TW9 . . .44 C2
Victoria Ct E1 . . . . . . .125 B3
  W3 . . . . .36 C4
  5 SW4 . . . . .61 C1
Victoria Dr SW19 . . . . .69 C3
Victoria Emb SW1 . . . .120 B2
Victoria Gdns
  W11 . . . . . . .31 C1 113 B2
Victoria Gr W8 . . . . . .128 C2
Victoria Gr Mews
  W2 . . . . .114 A3
Victoria Ho SW1 . . . . .146 A2

Victoria Ho continued
2 W12 . . . . .38 C4
6 SW4 . . . . .61 C1
Victoria Ind Est W3 . . . .29 A4
Victoria Mans NW10 . . . .9 A1
  N7 . . . . .14 C3
Victoria Mews NW6 . . .23 C4
  SW18 . . . . .71 B3
Victoria Park Ct **11**
  E9 . . . . .17 B1
Victoria Park Ind Ctr
  E9 . . . .
Victoria Park Rd E9 . . .17 C1
Victoria Park Sq E2 . . . .25 B2
Victoria Pas NW8 . . . . .89 B2
Victoria Rd W8 . . . . . .128 C2
  N4 . . . . .5 B3
  NW6 . . . . .23 B3
  NW10 . . . . .21 A1
  SW14 . . . . .55 C4
Victoria Rise SW4 . . . . .61 A4
Victoria Sq SW1 . . . . .132 B2
Victoria St SW1 . . . . .133 A1
Victoria Sta SW1 . . . .146 B4
Victoria Terr N4 . . . . . . .5 C3
  NW10 . . . . .21 A1
Victorian Gr N16 . . . . . .7 A1
Victorian Rd N16 . . . . . .7 B1
Victory Pl SE17 . . . . . .151 B4
  6 E14 . . . . .33 A2
Victory Prim Sch
  SE17 . . . . .151 A4
Victory Way SE16 . . . . .41 A4
Victory Wharf E14 . . . . .33 A2
Victory Wlk SE8 . . . . . .51 C2
Video Ct N4 . . . . .5 A4
View Ct N6 . . . . .4 B4
Viewfield Rd SW18 . . . .58 B1
Vigo St W1 . . . . .118 C3
Viking Cl **19** E3 . . . . . .26 A3
Viking Ho **3** SE5 . . . . .48 B1
Villa Rd SW9 . . . . .62 C4
Villa St SE17 . . . . .151 C1
Village Cl NW3 . . . . . . .11 C3
Village Mount **18**
  NW3 . . . . .11 B4
Village Sch The
  NW3 . . . . .12 B2
Village The SW11 . . . . .60 A4
Village Way SE21 . . . . .63 C1
Villas Rd SE18 . . . .
Villiers Ho **16** E9 . . . . .25 B4
Villiers Rd NW2 . . . . . . .8 C2
Villiers St WC2 . . . . . .120 B2
Vince Ct N1 . . . . .97 C3
Vince St EC1 . . . . .97 C3
Vincent Ct W1 . . . . . .102 C2
  N4 . . . . .5 A3
Vincent Rd W3 . . . . . . .37 B3
Vincent Sq SW1 . . . . .147 B4
Vincent St SW1 . . . . . .147 C4
  E16 . . . . .35 B2
Vincent Terr N1 . . . . . .86 B2
Vincents Cl SE16 . . . . .41 A4
Vine Ct E1 . . . . .111 C3
Vine Hill EC1 . . . . .95 B1
Vine La SE1 . . . . .124 B1
Vine Sq SW13 . . . . .56 B4
Vine St W1 . . . . .141 A1
Vine St EC3 . . . . .110 C1
  E1 . . . . .110 C1
Vine St Bridge EC1 . . . .95 C1
Vine Yd SE1 . . . . .137 A4
Vinegar St E1 . . . . .32 A1

Vinegar Yd SE1 . . . . .138 A4
Vines Prim Sch The
  SW11 . . . . .60 C3
Viney Ct **3** SW4 . . . . . .61 C1
Viney Rd SE13 . . . . . . .67 A4
Vineyard Hill Rd
  SW19 . . . . .70 C1
Vineyard Path
  SW14 . . . . .55 C4
Vineyard Sch The
  TW10 . . . . .54 A1
Vineyard The TW10 . . .54 A2
Vineyard Wlk EC1 . . . . .95 B2
Vining St SW2,SW9 . . . .62 C3
Vinson Ho N1 . . . . .87 C1
Vintners Ct EC4 . . . . .123 A4
Viola Sq W12 . . . . .29 B2
Violet Hill NW8 . . . . . . .78 C1
Violet Hill Ho NW8 . . . .78 C1
Violet Rd E3 . . . . .27 A1
Violet St E2 . . . . .25 A1
Virgil Pl W1 . . . . .102 C3
Virgil St SE1 . . . . .135 A2
Virginia Ct **7** SE16 . . .40 C4
Virginia Ho **3** E14 . . . .34 B2
Virginia JMI Sch E2 . . .98 C3
Virginia Rd E2 . . . . .98 C3
Virginia St E1 . . . . . . .125 C3
Virginia Wlk SW2 . . . . .62 B1
Viscount Ct **9** W11 . . .31 C3
Viscount St EC1 . . . . .108 C4
Vittoria Ho N1 . . . . . . .85 A3
Vittoria Prim Sch
  N1 . . . . .85 B2
Vivian Ho NW6 . . . . . . .78 A2
Vivian Ho N4 . . . . .6 C4
Vivian Rd E3 . . . . .26 A3
Vivian Sq SE15 . . . . . . .65 A4
Vogans Mill SE1 . . . . .139 A4
Vogler Ho **2** E1 . . . . . .32 B2
Vollasky Ho E1 . . . . . .111 B4
Voltaire
  15 Richmond TW9 . . .44 B2
  2 SE5 . . . . .49 B2
Voltaire Ct SW11 . . . .169 C2
Voltaire Rd SW4 . . . . . .61 C4
Vorley Rd N19 . . . . .4 B2
Voss St E2 . . . . . .24 C2 99 C3
Voyager Bsns Est
  SE16 . . . . .139 B2
Vulcan Rd SE4 . . . . . . .51 B1
Vulcan Sq E14 . . . . . . .41 C2
Vulcan Terr SE4 . . . . . .51 B1
Vulcan Way N7 . . . . . . .14 B2
Vyner Ct E5 . . . . .7 C2
Vyner Rd W3 . . . . .28 C2
Vyner St E2 . . . . .25 A4

W

Wadding St SE17 . . . . .151 B3
Waddington Rd E15 . . .19 C2
Waddington St E15 . . . .19 C2
Wade Ho SE1 . . . . . . .139 B3
Wadeson St E2 . . . . . . .25 A3
Wadham Gdns NW3 . . .80 A4
Wadham Rd SW15 . . . .58 A3
Wadhurst Rd W4 . . . . . .37 C3
Wager St E3 . . . . .26 B1
Waghorn St SE15 . . . . .64 C4
Wagner St SE15 . . . . . .50 B3
Wainford Cl SW19 . . . . .69 C3
Wainwright Ho
  SW8 . . . . .171 B3
  3 E1 . . . . .32 B1

Waite St SE15 . . . . .49 B4
Waithman St EC4 . . . .108 A1
Wakefield Ho **8**
  SE15 . . . . .49 C2
Wakefield Mews
  WC1 . . . . .94 B3
Wakefield St WC1 . . . . .94 B3
Wakeham St **1** N1 . . .15 C2
Wakehurst Rd SW11 . . .60 B2
Wakelin Ho **19** N1 . . . .15 A1
Wakeling Ho **8**
  SE27 . . . . .75 A1
Wakeling St **1** E14 . . .33 A3
Wakelyn Ho **14** E9 . . . .25 B4
Wakeman Rd NW10 . . .22 C2
Wakley St EC1 . . . . . . .96 A4
Walberswick St
  SW8 . . . . .162 B1
Walbrook EC4 . . . . . . .123 B4
Walburgh St E1 . . . . . .32 A3
Walcorde Ave
  SE17 . . . . .151 A3
Walcot Gdns SE11 . . .149 B4
Walcot Ho **9** SE22 . . . .64 A4
Walcot Sq SE11 . . . . .149 C4
Walcott St SW1 . . . . . .147 A4
Waldeck Gr SE27 . . . . .75 A1
Waldeck Rd W4 . . . . . .44 C4
  SW14 . . . . .55 B4
Waldeck Terr SW14 . . . .55 B4
Waldegrave Ho **5**
  SW15 . . . . .57 B2
Waldemar Ave
  SW6 . . . . .164 B2
Waldemar Avenue Mans
  SW6 . . . . .164 A3
Walden Ct SW8 . . . . .171 C4
Walden Ho NW1 . . . . .145 C3
  SW11 . . . . .169 B2
Walden St E1 . . . . .32 A3
Waldo Cl SW4 . . . . . . .61 B2
Waldo Rd NW10 . . . . . .22 A2
Waldron Ho **4** SW2 . . .62 B2
Waldron Mews
  SW3 . . . . .157 C4
Waldron Rd SW18 . . . .71 B1
Waleran Flats SE1 . . . .152 A4
Waleran Rd SE13 . . . . .52 B1
Wales Farm Rd W3 . . . .28 C4
Waley St **1** E1 . . . . . . .33 A4
Walford Ct SE1 . . . . . .138 B2
Walford Ho **4** E1 . . . . .32 A3
Walford Rd N16 . . . . . .16 A4
Walham Ct **15** NW3 . . .12 B3
Walham Gr SW6 . . . . .155 C2
Walham Green Arc
  SW6 . . . . .155 C2
Walker Ho NW1 . . . . . .83 B1
Walker's Ct W1 . . . . . .119 B4
Walker's Pl SW15 . . . . .58 A3
Walkerscroft Mead
  SE21 . . . . .75 B3
Walkinshaw Ct **14**
  N1 . . . . .15 B1
Walkynscroft **1**
  SE15 . . . . .50 A1
Wall Ct N4 . . . . .5 B3
Wall St N1 . . . . .15 C2
Wallace Collection ★
  W1 . . . . .103 B2
Wallace Ho N7 . . . . . . .14 B2
Wallace Rd N1,N5 . . . .15 B2
Wallbutton Rd SE4 . . . .51 A1
Waller Rd SE14 . . . . . .50 C1
Wallett Ct **9** NW1 . . . .13 B1

Wallflower St W12 ...29 B2
Wallgrave Rd SW5 ..142 A3
Wallingford Ave
W10 ....30 C3
Wallis Alley SE1 ..137 A4
Wallis Ct SW11 ......59 C4
Wallis Rd E9 ....18 C2
Wallorton Gdns
SW14 ....55 C3
Wallwood St E14 ....33 B4
Walm La NW2 ....9 B2
Walmer Ho ☑ W10 ..30 C3
Walmer Pl W1 ....102 C4
Walmer Rd
W11 ....31 A2 112 A3
W10 ....30 B3
Walmer St NW1 .....102 C4
Walnut Cl SE8 ....51 B4
Walnut Tree Cl
SW13 ....46 B2
Walnut Tree Ho
SW10 ....156 B4
Walnut Tree Rd
SE10 ....43 A1
Brentford TW8 ....44 A4
Walnut Tree Walk Prim
Sch SE11 ....149 B4
Walnut Tree Wlk
SE11 ....149 B4
Walpole Ave TW9 ...44 B1
Walpole Ct NW6 .....11 B1
☑ W14 ....39 C3
Walpole Gdns w4 ...37 B1
Walpole Mews NW8 79 B3
Walpole St SW3 ....145 A2
Walsham Cl N16 ......7 C3
Walsham Ho SE17 ..151 B2
SE14 ....50 C1
Walsingham NW8 ....79 C4
Walsingham Lo
SW6 ....156 B2
Walsingham Mans
SW6 ....156 B2
Walsingham Pl
SW4,SW11 ....60 C1
Walsingham Rd E5 ...7 C1
Walt Whitman Cl ☑
SE24 ....63 A3
Walter Besant Ho ☑
E1 ....25 C2
Walter Ct ☑ W3 ....28 B3
Walter Green Ho
SE15 ....50 B2
Walter Ho SW10 ...157 B2
Walter Northcott Ho ☑
NW6 ....10 C3
Walter St E2 ....25 C2
Walter Terr E1 ....32 C3
Walters Cl SE17 ....151 A3
Walters Ho ☑ SE17 48 A4
☑ SE5 ....49 A1
Walters Way SE23 ..65 C1
Walterton Rd W9 ...23 C1
Waltham Green Ct
SW6 ....156 A1
Waltham Ho NW8 ....78 C4
SW9 ....173 B4
Walton Cl SW8 ......162 B2
Walton Gdns W3 ....28 A4
Walton Ho E2 ....99 A4
N 5 B1
SW18 ....58 C1
Walton Pl SW3 .....130 C1
Walton St SW3 ......130 B1

Walton Way W3 .....28 A4
Walworth Lower Sch
SE17 ....151 C2
Walworth Pl SE17 ..151 A1
Walworth Rd SE17 ..151 A4
Walworth Sch
SE17 ....152 B1
Walworth Upper Sch
SE17 ....152 B1
Wanborough Dr
SW15 ....69 A3
Wandle Ct ☑ W12 ..38 A4
Wandle Ho NW8 ....102 A4
SW18 ....71 A4
Wandle Prim Sch
SW18 ....71 A3
Wandle Rd SW17 ....72 A2
Wandle Way SW18 ..71 A3
Wandon Rd SW6 ...156 B1
Wandsworth Bridge Rd
SW6 ....166 A2
Wandsworth Common
Sta SW12 ....72 B4
Wandsworth Common
West Side SW18 ....59 B2
Wandsworth Gyratory
SW18 ....59 A2
Wandsworth High St
SW18 ....59 A2
Wandsworth Mus
SW15 ....58 A3
Wandsworth Plain
SW18 ....59 A2
Wandsworth Rd
SW8 ....162 A1
Wandsworth Road Sta
SW4 ....171 A1
Wandsworth Town Sta
SW18 ....59 B3
Wangford Ho ☑
SW9 ....63 A3
Wanless Rd SE24 ...63 B3
Wanley Rd SE5 ......63 C3
Wansbeck Rd E3,E9 18 B1
Wansdown Pl SW6 156 A2
Wansey St SE17 ....151 A3
Wapping Dock St ☑
E1 ....32 A1
Wapping High St
E1 ....32 A1
Wapping La E1 ......32 A1
Wapping Sta E1 .....32 B1
Wapping Wall E1 ....32 B1
War Memorial Homes
W4 ....45 C3
Warbeck Rd W12 ...39 A4
Warburg Ho E2 ......99 B3
Warburton Ct SE15 64 C4
Warburton Ho ☑
E8 ....25 A4
Warburton Rd ☑ E8 25 A4
Warburton St ☑ E8 25 A4
Ward Point SE11 ...149 B3
Ward Rd N19 ....4 B1
E15 ....
Wardalls Ho ☑ SE8 51 B4
Wardell Ho ☑ SE10 52 B4
Warden Rd NW5 .....12 C2
Wardens Gr SE1 ...122 C1
Wardle St E9 ....17 C3
Wardley St SW18 ...71 A4
Wardlow ☑ NW5 ...13 A4
Wardo Ave SW6 ....164 A4
Wardour Mews
W1 ....105 A1

Wardour St W1 .....105 B1
Wardrobe Pl EC4 ...108 B1
Wardrobe Terr
EC4 ....122 B4
Wareham Ct ☑ N1 ..16 A1
Wareham Ho SW8 ..162 C2
Warfield Rd NW10 ..22 C2
Warfield Yd ☑
NW10 ....22 C2
Wargrave Ho ☑ E2 .98 C3
Warham St SE5 ......48 A3
Waring Ho E2 ....99 C3
Warley Ho N1 ....15 C2
Warley St E2 ....25 C2
Warlock Rd W9 ......23 C1
Warlters Cl N7 ....14 A4
Warlters Rd N7 ......14 A4
Warltersville Mans
N19 ....5 A4
Warltersville Rd N4,
N19 ....5 A4
Warmington Rd
SE24 ....63 B1
Warmley Ct ☑ SE15 49 A4
Warmsworth NW1 ...82 C4
Warncliffe Ho ☑
SW15 ....57 B2
Warndon St SE16 ...40 B2
Warneford St E9 .....25 A4
Warner Ho NW8 ....88 C4
☑ E9 ....17 C2
SE13 ....52 A1
Warner Rd SE5 ......48 B2
Warner St EC1 ....95 B1
Warner Yd EC1 ......95 B1
Warnford Ho SW15 56 A4
Warnham WC1 ....94 C3
Warnham Ho ☑
SW2 ....74 B4
Warple Mews W3 ...38 A4
Warple Way W3,
W3 ....38 A4
Warren Ave SW14,
TW10 ....55 A3
Warren Cl SE21 .....75 B4
Warren Ct N1 ....85 B2
Warren Gdns E15 ...19 C3
Warren Ho ☑ E3 ....27 A2
Warren Mews W1 ...92 C1
Warren Street Sta
NW1 ....93 A2
Warrender Rd N19 ..13 B4
Warriner Gdns
SW11 ....169 B3
Warrington Cres
W9 ....88 C2
Warrington Gdns
W9 ....88 C1
Warrington Pl E14 ..34 B1
Warspite Ho ☑ E14 42 A2
Warton Rd E15 ....27 B4
Warwick W14 ....141 A3
Warwick Ave W9 ....88 C1
Warwick Avenue Sta
W9 ....88 C1
Warwick Chambers
W8 ....127 B2
Warwick Cres W2 ..100 C4
Warwick Ct WC1 ...107 A3
SW15 ....57 A4
Warwick Dr SW15 ..57 A4
Warwick Gdns
W14 ....141 A4
Warwick Ho SW9 ..173 B1
N4 ....6 B3

Warwick Ho continued
☑ SW15 ....69 B4
Warwick House St
SW1 ....119 C2
Warwick La EC4 ....108 B1
Warwick Mans
SW5 ....141 B4
Warwick Park Sch
SE15 ....49 B2
Warwick Pas EC4 ..108 B2
Warwick Pl W9 .....100 C4
Warwick Pl N SW1 146 C3
Warwick Rd W14 ...141 A4
Warwick Row SW1 132 B2
Warwick Sq EC4 ...108 B2
SW1 ....146 C2
Warwick Sq Mews
SW1 ....146 C3
Warwick St W1 .....119 A4
Warwick Way SW1 146 B3
Warwick Yd EC1 ....97 A1
Warwickshire Path
SE8 ....51 B3
Warwickshire Rd
N16 ....16 A4
Wasdale NW1 ....92 B3
Washbrook Ho SW2 62 C1
Washington Ho
SW1 ....130 C3
Washington Rd
SW13 ....46 C3
Wat Tyler Rd SE10 ..52 C2
Watchfield Ct ☑
W4 ....37 B1
Watcombe Cotts
TW9 ....44 C4
Water Gdns The
W2 ....102 B2
Water La SE14 ....50 B3
Water Mews SE15 ..65 B3
Water St WC2 ....121 B4
Water Tower Ho
W8 ....113 B1
Water Tower Pl N1 ..86 A3
Watercress Pl N1 ...16 A1
Waterden Rd E15 ...18 C2
Waterford Ho ☑
W11 ....31 B2 113 A4
Waterford Rd SW6 156 A1
Watergate EC4 .....122 A4
Watergate Sch
SE13 ....67 A3
Watergate St SE8 ..51 C4
Watergate Wlk
WC2 ....120 B2
Waterhead NW1 ....92 C4
Waterhouse Cl
NW3 ....11 C3
W6 ....39 C1
Wateridge Cl E14 ...41 C3
Waterloo Bridge
SE1,WC2 ....121 A3
Waterloo Cl E9 ....17 B3
Waterloo East Sta
SE1 ....121 C1
Waterloo Gdns ☑ E2 25 B3
Waterloo Int Sta
SE1 ....135 A4
Waterloo Pier SE1 134 C4
Waterloo Pl SW1 ...119 B2
Richmond TW9 ....44 C4
Waterloo Rd SE1 ..135 C4
Waterloo Sta SE1 ..135 B4
Waterloo Terr N1 ...15 A1
Waterlow Ct NW11 ...2 A4
Waterlow Rd N19 ...4 B3
Waterman St SW15 57 C4

Waterman Way E1 ...32 A1
Watermead Ho E9 ..18 B3
Watermeadow La
SW6 ....166 C1
Watermint Quay N16 7 C4
Waters Pl SW15 .....47 B1
Waterside Cl SE16 139 C3
E3 ....26 B4
Waterside Pl NW1 ..81 C4
Waterside Point
SW11 ....158 B2
Waterson St E2 ......98 C4
Waterview Ho E14 ..33 A4
Waterworks Rd
SW2 ....62 B1
Watford Cl SW11 ...168 B4
Watford Rd E16 ......35 C4
Watkin Ho N16 ....7 B4
Watling Ct EC4 .....109 A1
Watling Gdns NW2 ..10 A2
Watling St EC4 .....109 A1
Watney Cotts SW14 55 B4
Watney Mkt E1 ....32 A3
Watney Rd SW14 ...55 B4
Watney St E1 ....32 A3
Watson Cl N16 ....15 C3
Watson Ho ☑ SW2 ..74 A4
Watson's Mews
W1 ....102 B3
Watson's St SE8 ....51 C3
Watts Gr E3 ....34 A4
Watts Ho ☑ W10 ...31 A4
Watts St E1 ....32 A1
SE15 ....49 B2
Wavel Ct ☑ E1 ......32 B1
☑ SW16 ....74 A1
Wavel Mews NW6 ..11 A1
Wavendon Ave W4 .37 C1
Waveney Ave SE15 65 B3
Waveney Cl E1 .....125 C2
Waveney Ho SE15 ..65 A3
Waverley Ct NW3 ..11 A3
☑ NW6 ....10 A1
Waverley Ho NW8 ..79 B2
N4 ....5 A4
Waverley Pl N4 ....6 A3
SW6 ....
Waverley Sch (Upper)
SE15 ....65 B2
Waverley Ct NW3 ...12 B3
Waverton Ho ☑ E3 26 B4
Waverton Rd SW18 71 B4
Waverton St W1 ....118 A2
Wavertree Ct ☑
SW2 ....74 A3
Wavertree Rd SW2 74 B3
Waxham NW5 ....12 B3
Waxlow Rd NW10 ..20 C3
Wayford St SW11 ..168 B1
Wayland Ave ☑ E8 16 C3
Wayland Ho SW9 ..173 B2
Waylett Ho SE11 ..149 B1
Waylett Pl SE27 ....75 A1
Wayman Ct E8 ....17 A2
Waynflete Sq ☑
W10 ....30 C3
Waynflete St SW18 71 B2
Weald Cl ☑ SE16 ...40 A1
Wear Pl ☑ E2 ....25 A2
Weald Cl ☑ SE16 ...40 A1
Weald Cl ☑ SE16 ...40 A1
Weardale Ho N4 .....6 B4
Weardale Rd SE13 .67 C3

Wearmouth Ho **1**
E3 . . . . 33 B4
Wearside Rd SE13 . . 67 A3
Weatherbury **6** W2 31 C3
Weatherbury Ho **3**
N19 . . . . 4 C1
Weatherley Cl E3 . . 33 B4
Weaver Ct **2** E2 . . . 25 A1
Weaver Ho **1** 99 B1
Weaver St E1 . 24 C1 99 B1
Weaver's Field Sch
E2 . . . . 25 A1
Weaver's La SE1 . . 124 B1
Weavers Way NW1 . 83 B4
6 NW1 . . . . 13 C1
Webb Ct W3 . . . . 37 A4
Webb Est E5 . . . . 7 C4
Webb Ho SW8 . . . . 161 C1
Webb Pl NW10 . . . . . 21 B2
Webb Rd SE3 . . . . . . 53 B4
Webb St SE1 . . . . . 138 A1
Webb's Rd SW11 . . . 60 B2
Webber Row E1 . . . 136 A3
Webber St SE1 . . . . 136 A3
Webheath **6** NW6 . . 10 B1
Webster Ho **16** N16 16 A3
Webster St SE16 . . 139 C1
Weddell Ho **21** E3 . . 26 C3
Wedderburn Rd
NW3 . . . . 11 C3
Wedgewood Ho
SW1 . . . . 146 C1
Wedgewood Mews
W1 . . . . 105 C2
Wedgwood Ho
SE11 . . . . 135 B1
11 E2 . . . . 25 C2
Wedlake St W10 . . . 23 A1
Wedmore Gdns N19 . 4 C2
Wedmore St N19 . . . . 4 C1
Weech Rd NW6 . . . . 10 C4
Weedington Rd
NW5 . . . . 12 C3
Weedon Ho W12 . . . 29 C3
Weekley Sq SW11 . . 59 C4
Weighhouse St
W1 . . . . 103 C1
Weimar St SW15 . . . 58 A4
Weir Ho **8** SW12 . . . 73 B4
Weir Rd SW18,SW19 71 A1
SW12 . . . . 73 B4
Weir's Pas NW1 . . . . 93 C4
Weiss Rd SW15 . . . . 57 C4
Welbeck Ct W14 . . 140 C4
Welbeck Mans **10**
NW6 . . . . 10 C3
Welbeck St W1 . . . 104 A2
Welbeck Way W1 . . 104 A2
Welby Ho N19 . . . . . . 4 C4
Welby St SE5 . . . . . . 48 A2
Welford Ct SW8 . . . 170 C1
12 NW1 . . . . 13 A1
Well Ct EC4 . . . . . . 109 A1
Well La SW14 . . . . . . 55 B2
Well Rd NW3 . . . . 2 C1
Well St E9 . . . . 17 B1
Well Wlk NW3 . . . . . . 2 C1
Welland Ho SE15 . . . 65 B3
Welland Mews E1 . 125 C2
Welland St SE10 . . . 52 B4
Wellclose Sq E1 . . 125 C4
Wellclose St **2** E1 . 125 C3
Wellday Ho **2** E9 . . 18 A2

Weller Ho SE16 . . . 139 B3
Weller St SE1 . . . . . 136 C4
Wellers Ct NW1 . . . . 84 A1
Wellesley Ave W6 . . 39 A3
Wellesley Ct W9 . . . 88 C4
Wellesley Ho NW1 . . 93 B3
Wellesley Pl NW1 . . 93 B3
Wellesley Rd NW5 . . 12 C3
W4 . . . . 37 A1
Wellesley St E1 . . . . 32 C4
Wellesley Terr N1 . . 97 A4
Wellfit St **16** SE24 . . 63 A4
Wellgarth Rd NW11 . . 2 A3
Welling St 131 C1
Wellington Bldgs
SW1 . . . . 145 C1
14 E3 . . . . 26 C2
Wellington Cl W11 . . 31 C3
SE14 . . . . 50 C2
Wellington Ct NW8 . 79 C1
WC2 . . . . 120 A4
SW1 . . . . 130 C3
SW6 . . . . 166 B3
SW18 . . . . 59 A2
Wellington Gr SE10 . 52 C3
Wellington Ho **18**
NW3 . . . . 12 B3
Wellington Hospl
(North) NW8 . . . . . 79 C1
Wellington Hospl
(South) NW8 . . . . . 79 C1
Wellington JMI Sch
E3 . . . . 26 C2
Wellington Mans
N16 . . . . 16 B4
Wellington Mews
SE22 . . . . 64 C3
Wellington Mus (Apsley
Ho) SW1 . . . . 131 C4
Wellington Pl NW8 . 89 C4
Wellington Rd NW8 . 79 C1
NW10 . . . . 22 C2
SW19 . . . . 70 C2
Wellington Row
E2 . . . . 24 C2 99 B4
Wellington Sq
SW3 . . . . 144 C2
Wellington St
WC2 . . . . 120 C4
Wellington Terr **2**
E1 . . . . 32 A1
Wellington Way E3 . 26 C2
Wells Ct **3** NW6 . . . 23 C3
Wells House Rd
NW10 . . . . 29 A4
Wells Mews W1 . . . 105 A2
Wells Park Rd SE26 . 76 C1
Wells Rd W12 . . . . . 39 B4
Wells Rise NW8 . . . . 80 C3
Wells Sq WC1 . . . . . 95 A3
Wells St W1 . . . . . . 105 A2
Wells Terr N4 . . . . 5 C2
Wells Way SW7 . . . 129 B2
SE5 . . . . 49 A4
Wells Yd **2** N7 . . . . 14 C3
Wellside Gdns
SW14 . . . . 55 B2
Wellwood Ct SW15 . 57 B3
Welsford St SE1 . . . 153 B3

Welsh Ho **14** E1 . . . 32 A1
Welshpool Ho **22**
E8 . . . . 24 C4
Welshpool St **1** E8 25 A4
Welstead Ho **1** E1 . 32 A3
Welstead Way W4 . . 38 B2
Weltje Rd W6 . . . . . . 38 C1
Welton Ho E1 . . . . . . 32 C4
SE5 . . . . 49 A2
Welwyn St E2 . . . . . 25 B2
Wembury Rd N6 . . . . 4 A4
Wemyss Rd SE3 . . . 53 B1
Wendell Park Prim Sch
W12 . . . . 38 B4
Wendell Rd W12 . . . 38 B4
Wendle Ct SW8 . . . 162 A3
Wendling NW5 . . . . 12 B3
Wendon St E3 . . . . . 26 B4
Wendover SE17 . . . 152 A1
Wendover Ct W1 . . 103 B3
4 NW2 . . . . 1 C1
W3 . . . . 20 B1
Wendover Ho W1 . . 103 B3
Wendover Rd NW10 21 B3
Wengham Ho W12 . . 29 C2
Wenham Ho SW8 . . 160 C1
Wenlake Ho EC1 . . . 96 C2
Wenlock Ct N1 . . . . . 87 C1
Wenlock Rd N1 . . . . 87 A1
Wenlock St N1 . . . . . 87 B1
Wennington Rd E3 . . 25 C3
Wensdale Ho E5 . . . . 7 C2
Wensleydale Ho **8**
N4 . . . . 6 B4
Wentworth Cres
SE15 . . . . 49 C3
Wentworth Ct W6 . 154 A3
SW18 . . . . 59 B4
Wentworth Dwellings
E1 . . . . 110 C2
Wentworth Mews
E3 . . . . 26 B2
Wentworth St E1 . . 111 A3
Werrington St NW1 . 83 A1
Werter Rd SW15 . . . 58 A3
Wesley Ave NW10 . . 20 C2
Wesley Cl SE17 . . . 150 B3
N7 . . . . 5 B2
Wesley Ho SE24 . . . 63 C1
Wesley Rd NW10 . . . 20 B4
Wesley Sq W11 . . . . 31 A3
Wesley St W1 . . . . . 103 C3
Wesleyan Pl NW5 . . 13 A4
Wessex Ct SW15 . . . 57 C2
Wessex Gardens Prim
Sch NW11 . . . . 1 A3
Wessex Gdns NW11 . 1 A3
Wessex Ho SE1 . . . 153 A1
4 N19 . . . . 4 C1
Wessex St E2 . . . . . 25 B2
Wessex Way NW11 . . 1 A3
West Acton Prim Sch
W3 . . . . 28 A3
West Arbour St E1 . . 32 C3
West Bank N16 . . . . . 7 A4
West Block **11** E1 . . 32 B2
West Brompton Sta
SW5 . . . . 141 C1
West Carriage Dr
W2 . . . . 116 A2
West Central Ave . . . 22 A2
West Central St
WC1 . . . . 106 A2
West Cotts NW6 . . . 10 C3

West Cromwell Rd
W14 . . . . 141 A2
West Cross Route
W10,W11 . . . . 30 C2
West Dulwich Sta
SE21 . . . . 75 C1
West Eaton Pl
SW1 . . . . 145 B4
West Eaton Pl Mews
SW1 . . . . 145 B4
West Ella Rd NW10 . . 8 A1
West End Ct NW6 . . . 11 A1
West End La NW6 . . 78 A4
NW6 . . . . 11 A2
West Garden Pl
W2 . . . . 102 B1
West Gdns **1** E1 . . . 32 A2
West Gr SE10 . . . . . . 52 C2
West Halkin St
SW1 . . . . 131 B2
West Hall Rd TW9 . . 45 A2
West Hampstead Mews
NW6 . . . . 11 A2
West Hampstead Sta
NW6 . . . . 10 C2
West Hampstead
Thameslink Sta
NW6 . . . . 10 C2
West Harding St
EC4 . . . . 107 C2
West Heath Ave
NW11 . . . . 1 C3
West Heath Cl NW3 . . 1 C1
West Heath Ct NW11 . 1 C3
West Heath Dr NW11 . 1 C3
West Heath Gdns
NW3 . . . . 1 C1
West Heath Rd NW3 . 2 A1
West Hill N6 . . . . 3 C3
SW15 . . . . 58 A1
West Hill Ct N6 . . . . . 3 C2
West Hill Prim Sch
SW18 . . . . 58 C2
West Hill Rd SW18 . . 58 B1
West Ho **6** SW12 . . 73 B4
West House Cl
SW19 . . . . 70 A3
West India Ave E14 . 33 C1
West India Dock Rd
E14 . . . . 33 C2
West India Ho **1**
E14 . . . . 33 C2
West India Quay Sta
E14 . . . . 33 C2
West Kensington Ct
W14 . . . . 140 C2
West Kensington Mans
W14 . . . . 140 C1
West Kensington Sta
W14 . . . . 140 C2
West La SE16 . . . . . . 40 A4
West London Stad The
SW6 . . . . 30 A4
West Mall W11 . . . . 113 C2
West Mews SW1 . . 146 C3
West Norwood Sta
SE27 . . . . 75 A1
West Park Ave TW9 . 45 A2
West Park Rd TW9 . . 44 C2
West Point SE1 . . . . 153 B2
West Poultry Ave
EC1 . . . . 108 A3
West Quarters W12 . 29 C3
West Rd SW3 . . . . . 159 A4
SW4 . . . . 61 C2
West Row W10 . . . . . 23 A1

West Sheen Vale
TW9 . . . . 54 B3
West Smithfield
EC1 . . . . 108 B3
West Sq SE11 . . . . . 136 A1
West St WC2 . . . . . . 105 C1
2 E2 . . . . 25 A3
West Temple Sheen
SW14 . . . . 55 A2
West Tenter St E1 . . 111 A1
West Warwick Pl
SW1 . . . . 146 C2
Westacott Cl N19 . . . 4 C3
Westbere Rd NW2 . . 10 A3
Westbourne Ave
W3 . . . . 28 C3
W2 . . . . 100 C3
Westbourne Cres
W2 . . . . 115 B4
Westbourne Ct
W2 . . . . 100 C2
Westbourne Gdns
W2 . . . . 100 A2
Westbourne Gr
W2 . . . . 100 A1
W2,W11 . . . 31 C3 113 A4
Westbourne Gr Mews **7**
W11 . . . . 31 C3
Westbourne Grove Terr
W2 . . . . 100 A1
Westbourne Ho
SW1 . . . . 146 A1
Westbourne Park Rd
W11 . . . . 31 B3
W2 . . . . 31 C3
Westbourne Park Sta
W11 . . . . 31 B4
Westbourne Park Villas
W2 . . . . 100 A3
Westbourne Rd N7 . . 14 B2
Westbourne St
W2 . . . . 115 B4
Westbourne Terr
W2 . . . . 101 A2
Westbourne Terr Mews
W2 . . . . 100 C2
Westbourne Terr Rd
W2 . . . . 100 C3
Westbridge Cl W12 . 29 C1
Westbridge Rd
SW11 . . . . 168 A3
Westbrook Ho
5 E2 . . . . 25 B2
5 SW4 . . . . 61 B2
Westbury Ct SW4 . . 61 A1
Westbush Ct **1**
W12 . . . . 39 A4
Westchester Ho
W2 . . . . 102 C1
Westcliff Ho **13** N1 . 15 C2
Westcombe Ct **1**
SE3 . . . . 53 B3
Westcombe Hill
SE3,SE10 . . . . 53 B4
Westcombe Park Rd
SE3 . . . . 53 B3
Westcombe Park Sta
SE3 . . . . 43 C1
Westcott Ho **11** E14 33 C2
Westcott Rd SE17 . . 48 A4
Westcott Road
SE17 . . . . 150 B1
Westcroft Cl NW2 . . 10 A4
Westcroft **3** W6 . . 38 C2

Westcroft Sq W6 ... 38 C2
Westcroft Way NW2 10 A4
Westdean Cl SW18 ... 59 A1
Westdown Rd E15 ... 76 B4
Westerdale Ct N5 ... 15 A4
Westerdale Rd 2 SE10 ... 43 C1
Westerham NW1 ... 82 C3
Westerham Ho SE1 ... 137 C2
Western Ave W3 ... 28 C3
Western Ct 3 W9 ... 23 B3
4 W3 ... 28 C3
Western Eye Hospl The NW1 ... 102 C4
Western La SW12 ... 72 C4
Western Mews W9 ... 23 B1
Western Pl 13 SE16 ... 40 B4
Western Rd NW10 ... 20 B1
SW9 ... 62 C4
Western Terr W6 ... 38 C1
Western Wharf 2 SE15 ... 49 C4
Westferry Cir E14 ... 33 C1
Westferry Rd E14 ... 41 C3
Westferry Sta E14 ... 33 C2
Westfield Cl SW10 ... 156 C1
Westfield Ct 1 W10 ... 22 C2
Westfield Ho 6 SE16 ... 40 C2
Westfield Way E1 ... 26 A1
Westfields SW13 ... 56 B4
Westfields Ave SW13 ... 56 A4
Westfields Rd W3 ... 28 A4
Westfields Sch SW13 ... 56 B4
Westgate Bsns Ctr W10 ... 22 C1
2 W10 ... 23 A1
Westgate Ct 16 SW9 ... 62 C4
Westgate St E8 ... 25 A4
Westgate Terr SW10 ... 156 B4
Westgrove La SE10 ... 52 B2
Westhay Gdns SW14 ... 55 A2
Westhill Ct W11 ... 113 A4
Westhill Pk N6 ... 3 C2
Westhope Ho E2 ... 99 C3
Westhorpe Rd SW15 ... 57 B4
Westlake 10 SE16 ... 40 B2
Westland Pl N1 ... 97 B4
Westlands Terr 3 SW12 ... 61 B1
Westleigh Ave SW15 ... 57 B2
Westly Ct NW2 ... 9 C2
Westmacott Ho NW8 ... 89 C1
Westmark Point 13 SW15 ... 69 A3
Westmead SW15 ... 57 A1
Westmill Ct N4 ... 6 B2
Westminster Abbey* SW1 ... 134 A2
Westminster Abbey Choir Sch SW1 ... 133 C2
Westminster Boating Base SW1 ... 161 B4
Westminster Bridge SE1,SW1 ... 134 B3
Westminster Bridge Rd SE1 ... 135 B2
Westminster Cath* SW1 ... 132 C1
Westminster Cath Choir Sch SW1 ... 147 A4
Westminster Cath RC Prim Sch SW1 ... 147 C2
Westminster City CE Sch SW1 ... 133 A2
Westminster City Hall SW1 ... 133 A2
Westminster Coll W1 ... 119 B4
SW1 ... 133 A2
SW1 ... 147 B4
SW11 ... 169 C4
Westminster Ct 22 SE16 ... 32 C1
5 SW18 ... 58 C2
Westminster Gdns SW1 ... 148 A4
Westminster Sch SW1 ... 134 A2
Westminster Sta SW1 ... 134 B3
Westmore Ct SW15 ... 58 A2
Westmoreland Ho NW10 ... 21 C2
Westmoreland Pl SW1 ... 146 B1
Westmoreland Rd SW13 ... 46 C2
SE17 ... 48 C4
Westmoreland St W1 ... 103 C3
Westmoreland Terr SW1 ... 146 B1
Weston Ct N4 ... 6 B1
Weston Ed Ctr The SE5 ... 48 B1
Weston Ho 4 NW6 ... 10 A1
9 E9 ... 25 B4
Weston Rd W4 ... 37 B3
Weston Rise N1, WC1 ... 95 A4
Weston St SE1 ... 137 C4
Weston Wlk 3 E8, E9 ... 17 A1
Westonbirt Ct 6 SE15 ... 49 B4
Westover Hill NW3 ... 1 C2
Westover Rd SW18 ... 59 B1
Westpoint SW15 ... 57 C1
Westpoint Trad Est W3 ... 28 A4
Westport St E1 ... 32 C3
Westrow SW15 ... 57 B1
Westside Ct 1 W9 ... 23 C1
Westview Cl NW10 ... 8 B3
W10 ... 30 B3
Westville Rd W12 ... 38 C4
Westway W2 ... 100 C3
W10,W12 ... 29 C2
Westway (Elevated Rd) W10 ... 31 B4
Westwell 4 NW5 ... 12 C2
Westwick Gdns W14 ... 39 C4
Westwood Gdns SW13 ... 56 B4
Westwood Ho 5 N4 ... 6 C4
W12 ... 30 B1
Westwood Rd SW13 ... 56 B4
Wetherby Gdns SW5 ... 142 C3
Wetherby Mans SW5 ... 142 A2
Wetherby Mews SW5 ... 142 B2
Wetherby Pl SW7 ... 143 A3
Wetherell Rd E9 ... 25 C4
Wetland Centre The SW13 ... 47 A3
Wevco Wharf SE15 ... 50 A4
Wexford Ho 9 E1 ... 32 B4
Wexford Rd SW12 ... 72 B4
Wey Ho NW8 ... 89 C1
Weybourne St SW18 ... 71 B2
Weybridge Ct 19 SE16 ... 40 A1
Weybridge Ho N4 ... 6 B4
Weybridge Point SW11 ... 169 A2
Weydown Cl SW19 ... 70 A3
Weyhill Ho 27 SE5 ... 48 B1
Weyhill Rd E1 ... 111 C2
Weymouth Ct 5 E2 ... 24 B3
15 SW2 ... 74 B4
Weymouth Ho SW8 ... 162 C1
Weymouth Mews W1 ... 104 A4
Weymouth St W1 ... 104 A4
Weymouth Terr E2 ... 24 B3
Whadcoat St N4 ... 5 C2
Whadden Ho 10 SE5 ... 64 A4
Whaddon Ho SW1 ... 131 A3
Wharf Pl E2 ... 25 A4
Wharf Rd NW1 ... 83 C3
N1 ... 86 C1
E15 ... 27 C4
Wharf St E16 ... 35 A4
Wharfdale Rd N1 ... 84 B2
Wharfedale Ct 5 E5 ... 17 C4
Wharfedale St SW10 ... 142 A1
Wharfside Rd E16 ... 35 A3
Wharton Cl NW10 ... 8 A2
Wharton Ho SE1 ... 138 C2
Wharton St WC1 ... 95 A3
Whateley Rd SE22 ... 64 B2
Wheat Sheaf Cl E14 42 A2
Wheatland Ho 7 SE22 ... 64 A4
Wheatlands Rd SW17 ... 72 C1
Wheatley Ho NW5 ... 13 A4
3 SW15 ... 68 C4
Wheatley St W1 ... 103 C3
Wheatsheaf La SW8 ... 162 B2
SW6 ... 47 B3
Wheatsheaf Terr SW6 ... 155 A1
Wheatstone Ho 7 W10 ... 31 A4
Wheatstone Rd W10 ... 31 A4
Wheeler Ct 5 SW11 ... 59 C4
Wheeler Gdns N1 ... 84 B4
Wheeler La E1 ... 110 C4
Wheelwright St N7 ... 14 B1
Wheldon Ct SE1 ... 138 C4
Wheler Ho E1 ... 98 C1
Wheler St E1 ... 24 98 C1
Whellock Rd W4 ... 38 A3
Whetstone Pk WC2 ... 106 C2
Whewell Rd N19 ... 5 A2
Whichcote St SE1 ... 121 B1
Whidborne Bldgs WC1 ... 94 A3
Whidborne Cl SE8 ... 51 C1
Whidborne St WC1 ... 94 B3
Whippingham Ho 17 E3 ... 26 B2
Whiskin St EC1 ... 96 A3
Whistler St N5 ... 15 A3
Whistler Twr SW10 ... 156 C1
Whistler Wlk SW10 ... 157 A2
Whistlers Ave SW11 ... 157 C1
Whiston Ho 18 N1 ... 15 A1
Whiston Rd E2 ... 24 C4
Whitbread Ctr EC1 ... 97 B1
Whitbread Rd SE4 ... 66 B3
Whitburn Rd SE13 ... 67 B3
Whitby Ave NW10 ... 20 A2
Whitby Ct N7 ... 14 A4
Whitby Ho NW8 ... 78 C3
Whitby St E1 ... 98 C2
Whitcher Cl SE14 ... 51 A4
Whitcher Pl NW1 ... 13 B2
Whitchurch Ho 16 W10 ... 30 C3
Whitchurch Rd W11 30 C2
Whitcomb Ct W1 ... 119 C3
Whitcomb St WC2 ... 119 C3
White Bear Pl NW3 ... 11 C4
White Bear Yd EC1 ... 95 B1
White City W10 ... 30 B3
White City Cl W12 ... 30 B2
White City Rd W12 ... 30 B2
White City Sta W12 ... 30 B2
White Conduit St N1 ... 85 C2
White Hart Ct EC2 ... 110 A3
White Hart La NW10 ... 8 B2
SW13 ... 56 A4
White Hart St SE11 ... 149 C2
White Hart Yd SE1 ... 123 B1
White Ho SW11 ... 167 C2
3 SW4 ... 73 C4
White Ho The NW1 ... 92 B2
White Horse La E1 ... 32 C4
White Horse Rd E1 ... 33 A3
White Horse St W1 ... 118 B1
White Horse Yd EC2 ... 109 B2
White Kennett St E1 ... 110 B2
White Lion Ct EC3 ... 110 A1
White Lion Hill EC4 ... 122 B4
White Lion St N1 ... 85 C1
White Lion Yd W1 ... 118 A4
White Post La E9 ... 18 C2
White Post St SE14, SE15 ... 50 B3
White's Grounds SE1 ... 138 B4
White's Grounds Est SE1 ... 138 B4
White's Row E1 ... 110 C3
White's Sq SW4 ... 61 C3
Whiteadder Way E14 ... 42 A2
Whitear Wlk E15 ... 19 C2
Whitebeam Cl SW9 ... 163 A1
Whitebeam Ho 3 NW3 ... 12 B2
Whitechapel High St E1 ... 111 A2
Whitechapel Rd E1 ... 111 B3
E1 ... 32 A4
Whitechapel Sta E1 32 A4
Whitecliff Ho SW18 ... 59 A1
Whitecross Pl EC2 ... 109 C4
Whitecross St EC1 ... 97 A1
Whitefield Cl SW15 ... 58 A1
Whitefriars St EC4 ... 107 C1
Whitehall SW1 ... 134 A4
Whitehall Ct SW1 ... 120 B1
Whitehall Gdns SW1 ... 120 A1
W4 ... 45 A4
Whitehall Mans 3 N19 ... 4 B3
Whitehall Park Rd W4 ... 45 A4
Whitehall Pk N19 ... 4 B3
Whitehall Pl WC2, SW1 ... 120 A1
Whitehaven St NW8 ... 90 A1
Whitehead Cl SW18 ... 71 B4
Whitehead Ho 8 SW15 ... 57 C2
Whitehead's Gr SW3 ... 144 B3
Whitehorn Ho 6 E1 32 B1
Whitehorse Mews SE1 ... 136 A2
Whitehorse Rd E1 ... 33 A4
Whitelands Coll, Roehampton Inst SW18 ... 70 A4
Whitelands Ho SW3 ... 145 A2
Whiteley Ho 9 SW4 ... 73 C4
Whitelock Ho 21 E9 ... 17 C2
Whiteness Ho SW9 173 B4
Whitestone La NW3 ... 2 B1
Whitestone Wlk NW3 2 B1
Whitethorn St E3 ... 33 C4
Whitfield Ct SW4 ... 172 A3
Whitfield Gdns W1 ... 105 A4
Whitfield Ho NW8 ... 90 A1
Whitfield Pl W1 ... 93 A1
Whitfield Rd SE10, SE13 ... 52 C2
Whitfield St W1 ... 105 A4
Whitgift Ho SE11 ... 148 C4
SW11 ... 168 A4
Whitgift St SE11 ... 148 C4
Whitington Ave EC3 ... 110 A1
Whitley Ho SW1 ... 161 A4
Whitlock Dr SW19 ... 70 A3
Whitman Ho 20 E2 ... 25 B2
Whitman Rd E3 ... 26 A1
Whitmore Gdns NW10 ... 22 B3
Whitmore Ho 20 E1 ... 24 A4
Whitmore Jun & Inf Sch N1 ... 87 C3
Whitmore Rd N1 ... 24 A4

Whitnell Ct **7**
SW15 ....57 C2
Whitnell Way SW15 .57 C2
Whitney Ho **6** SE2 64 A4
Whitstable Ho **11**
W10 ....30 C3
Whitsters Ho SE1 .138 C4
Whittaker Ct SW15 .69 B4
Whittaker St SW1 .172 B3
Whittaker St SW1 .145 B3
Whittingham Ct W4 46 A3
Whittingstall Mans
SW6 ....165 A3
Whittingstall Rd
SW6 ....165 A3
Whittington Hospl The
N19 ....4 B2
Whittlebury Ho N4 ..6 B4
Whittlesey St SE1 .121 C1
Whitton W3 ....28 B3
Whitton Wlk E3 ....26 C2
Whitworth Ho SE1 .137 A1
Whitworth St SE10 .43 A1
Whorlton Rd SE15 .65 A4
Whytlaw Ho **11** E3 .33 B4
Wick La E15 ....18 B1
E3 ....18 C1
Wick Mews **1** E9 .18 A2
Wick Rd E9 ....18 A2
Wick Sq E9 ....18 B2
Wicker St **2** E1 ...32 A3
Wickersley Rd
SW11 ....169 C1
9 SW11 ....60 C4
Wickfield Ho SE16 .139 C3
Wickford Ho **4** E1 .25 B1
Wickford St E1 ....25 B1
Wickham Gdns SE4 .66 B4
Wickham Ho E1 ....32 B4
SW15 ....57 C1
Wickham Mews SE4 51 B1
Wickham Rd SE4 ...66 B3
Wickham Rd SE4 ..148 C2
Wicklow Ho N16 ....7 B3
Wicklow St WC1 ...94 C4
Wickstead Ho TW8 .36 B1
Wicksteed Ho SE1 .137 A1
Wickway Ct **7** SE15 49 B4
Wickwood St SE5 ..48 A1
Widdenham Rd N7 .14 B4
Widecombe Ho **53**
SE5 ....48 B1
Widegate St E1 ...110 B3
Widford **8** NW1 ...13 A2
Widford Ho N1 .....86 A1
Widley Rd W9 .....23 C1
Widnes Ho **7** N7 ..14 C3
Wigmore Hall W1 ..104 A2
Wigmore Pl W1 ....104 A2
Wigmore St W1 ....103 C2
Wigram Ct SW11 ..168 A4
Wigram Ho **6** E14 .34 A2
Wigton Pl SE11 ...149 C1
Wilberforce Ho **4**
SW11 ....59 C4
Wilberforce Prim Sch
W10 ....23 A2
Wilberforce Rd N4 ..6 A2
N4,N5 ....6 B1
Wilbraham Ho
SW8 ....162 A1
Wilbraham Pl SW1 145 B4
Wilby Mews
W11 .....31 B1 113 A2

Wilcox Cl SW8 ....162 B2
Wilcox Ho **6** E3 ...33 B4
Wilcox Pl SW1 ....133 A1
Wilcox Rd SW8 ...162 A2
Wild Ct WC2 ......106 C2
Wild Goose Dr SE14 50 B2
Wild St WC2 ......106 C1
Wild's Rents SE1 ..138 A2
Wildcroft Manor
SW15 ....69 B4
Wildcroft Rd SW15 .69 B4
Wilde Cl E8 ....24 C4
Wilde Pl SW18 ....71 C4
Wilderton Rd N16 ...7 A4
Wilding Ho **6** E9 ..17 C2
Wildwood Gr NW3 ...2 B3
Wildwood Rd NW11 ..2 B3
Wildwood Terr NW3 .2 B3
Wilfred Fienburgh Ho
N7 ....13 C4
Wilfred St SW1 ....132 C2
Wilfrid Gdns W3 ...28 B4
Wilkes Rd **3** TW8 .44 A4
Wilkes St E1 ......111 A4
Wilkie Ho SW1 ....147 C2
Wilkin St NW5 .....13 A2
Wilkins Ho SW1 ...160 C4
Wilkinson Ho N1 ...87 C1
7 E14 ....33 A4
Wilkinson St SW8 .162 C1
Wilkinson Way W4 .37 C4
Wilks Pl N1 ....24 A3
Willan Wall E16 ...35 B2
Willard St SW8 ....61 A4
Willbury Ho **7** N7 .13 C3
Willcott Rd W3 ....28 A1
Willenfield Rd
NW10 ....20 B3
Willes Rd NW5 ....13 A2
Willesden Community
Hospl The NW10 ....8 C1
Willesden High Sch
NW10 ....22 A4
Willesden Junction Sta
NW10 ....21 B2
Willesden La NW2,
NW6 ....9 C1
Willett Ho SW9 ....62 C4
William Banfield Ho
SW6 ....164 C2
William Booth Meml
Training Coll SE5 ..48 C1
William Brown Ct
SE27 ....75 A2
William Caslon Ho **28**
E2 ....25 A3
William Channing Ho **6**
E2 ....25 A2
William Cl SE13 ...67 B4
William Davis Prim Sch
E2 ....24 C1 99 B2
William Dromey Ct
NW6 ....10 B1
William Dunbar Ho
NW6 ....23 B3
William Ellis Sch
NW5 ....3 C1
William Ellis Way
SE16 ....139 C1
William Evans Ho **8**
SE8 ....40 C2
William Gdns SW15 57 A2

William Guy Gdns **47**
E3 ....27 A2
William Harvey Ho **1**
SW19 ....70 A3
William IV St WC2 .120 A3
William Margrie Cl **1**
SE15 ....49 C1
William Mews
SW1 ....131 A3
William Morris Acad
W6 ....39 C1
William Morris Ho
W6 ....47 C4
William Morris Way
SW6 ....166 C1
William Patten JMI Sch
N16 ....7 B2
William Rathbone Ho **7**
E2 ....25 A2
William Rd NW1 ...92 C3
William Rushbrooke Ho
SE16 ....153 B4
William Saville Ho **2**
NW6 ....23 B3
William Sq **15** SE16 .33 A2
William St SW1 ...131 A3
William Tyndale Prim
Sch N1 ....15 A1
William's Bldgs **1**
E2 ....25 B1
Williams Ho **9** E9 .25 C2
6 E14 ....26 C2
E14 ....33 A3
14 SW2 ....74 C3
Williams La SW14 .45 B1
Williamson Cl SE10 43 B1
Williamson Ct
SE17 ....150 C1
Williamson St N7 ..14 A4
Willingham Cl **4**
NW5 ....13 B3
Willingham Terr
NW5 ....13 B3
Willington Rd SW9 .62 A4
Willis Ho **7** E14 ...34 A2
Willis St E14 ......34 A3
Willoughby Ho
EC2 ....109 B3
Willoughby Rd NW3 11 C4
Willoughby St
WC1 ....106 A3
Willoughbys The
SW14 ....56 A3
Willow Ave SW13 ..46 B1
Willow Bridge Rd
N1 ....15 B2
Willow Cotts TW9 ..44 C4
Willow Ct EC2 .....98 A2
SW9 ....173 B3
7 W4 ....45 B3
3 SW16 ....74 B1
Willow Farm La
SW15 ....57 A4
Willow Hall NW3 ...11 C4
Willow Ho **8** W10 .23 B2
NW3 ....11 C1
Willow Lo SW6 ....47 C2
Willow Rd NW3 ....11 C4
W5 ....36 A4
Willow St
EC2 ....24 A1 98 A2
Willow Tree Cl E3 ..26 B4

Willow Tree Cl continued
SW18 ....71 A3
Willow Vale W12 ..29 C1
Willow Way **9** W11 30 C2
Willow Wlk SE1 ...152 C4
Willowbank SW6 ..58 A4
Willowbrook Rd
SE15 ....49 B4
Willowdene N6 .....3 B4
1 SE15 ....50 A2
5 SE15 ....50 A2
Willows Terr NW10 .21 B3
Willsbridge Ct **1**
SE15 ....49 B4
Willshaw St SE14 .51 C2
Wilman Gr E8 .....16 C1
Wilmcote Ho W2 ..100 A4
Wilmer Gdns N1 ...24 A4
Wilmer Ho **3** E3 ..26 A3
Wilmer Lea Cl E15 .19 C1
Wilmer Pl N16 .....7 B2
Wilmers Ct **5**
NW10 ....20 C4
Wilmington Ave W4 45 C3
Wilmington Sq WC1 95 B3
Wilmington St WC1 95 B3
Wilmot Cl SE15 ...49 C3
Wilmot Pl NW1 ....13 B1
Wilmot St E2 ......25 A1
Wilna Rd SW18 ...71 B4
Wilsham St
W11 .....31 A1 112 A2
Wilshaw Ho **6** SE8 51 C3
Wilson Gr SE16 ...40 A4
Wilson Ho SW8 ...171 B1
3 SW1 ....146 B4
Wilson Rd SE5 ....49 A2
Wilson St EC2 ....109 C4
Wilson's Pl E14 ....33 B3
Wilson's Rd W6 ...39 C1
Wilston Ct NW2 ...10 A2
Wilton Ave W4 ....38 A1
Wilton Cres SW1 ..131 B3
Wilton Ct **3** E1 ...32 A3
1 Richmond TW10 54 A2
Wilton Est E8 .....16 C2
Wilton Ho **8** SE22 64 A4
Wilton Mews SW1 .131 C2
Wilton Pl SW1 ....131 B3
Wilton Rd SW1 ...146 C4
Wilton Row SW1 ..131 B3
Wilton Sq N1 .....87 B4
Wilton St SW1 ....132 A2
Wilton Terr SW1 ..131 B2
Wilton Villas N1 ...87 B3
Wilton Way E8 ....16 C2
Wiltshire Cl SW3 ..144 C3
Wiltshire Ct **4** N4 .5 B3
Wiltshire Rd SW9 ..62 C4
Wiltshire Row N1 ..87 C3
Wimbart Rd SW2 ..74 B4
Wimbledon Common
SW19 ....69 C4
Wimbledon Lawn Tennis
Mus SW19 ....70 A1
Wimbledon Park Ct
SW19 ....70 B3
Wimbledon Park Prim
Sch SW19 ....71 A2
Wimbledon Park Rd
SW18,SW19 ......70 B3
Wimbledon Park Side
SW19 ....69 C3
Wimbledon Park Sta
SW19 ....70 C1

Wimbledon Stadium
Bsns Ctr SW17 ....71 A1
Wimbledon Windmill
Mus SW19 ....69 B1
Wimbolt St
E2 ....24 C2 99 B4
Wimborne Ho NW1 .90 B1
SW8 ....163 A1
SW12 ....73 B1
Wimborne Ct **1**
SW1 ....87 B2
Wimborne St N1 ...87 B2
Wimpole Mews
W1 ....104 A3
Wimpole St W1 ...104 A2
Winans Wlk SW9 ..173 B1
Winant Ho **17** E14 .34 A2
Wincanton Rd
SW18 ....70 B4
Winch Ho SW10 ..157 A2
Winchcombe Ct **6**
SE5 ....49 A4
Winchelsea Cl
SW15 ....57 C2
Winchelsea Ho **11**
SE16 ....40 B4
Winchelsea Rd
NW10 ....20 C4
Winchendon Rd
SW6 ....165 A4
Winchester Ave
NW6 ....10 A1
Winchester Cl
SE17 ....150 B3
Winchester Ct W8 .128 A4
Winchester Ho
W2 ....100 C1
SW3 ....157 C3
13 E3 ....26 B2
Winchester Pl N6 ...4 A3
E8 ....16 B3
Winchester Rd N6 ..4 A3
NW3 ....11 C1
Winchester Sq
SE1 ....123 B2
Winchester St
SW1 ....146 B2
W3 ....37 B4
Winchester Wlk
SE1 ....123 B2
Winchfield Ho
SW15 ....56 B1
Winchilsea Ho NW8 89 C3
Wincott St SE11 ..149 C3
Windermere NW1 ..92 B4
12 SW15 ....57 C1
Windermere Ave
NW6 ....23 A4
SW19 ....70 C1
Windermere Ct
SW13 ....46 B4
Windermere Ho E3 .26 B1
Windermere Point **3**
SE15 ....50 B3
Windermere Rd N19 .4 B2
Winders Rd SW11 .168 A2
Windham Rd TW9 ..54 B4
Windlass Pl SE8 ...41 A2
Windlesham Gr
SW19 ....69 C3
Windmill W1 ......106 C4
Windmill Alley **7**
W4 ....38 A2
Windmill Cl SE1 ..153 C4
8 SE13 ....52 B1
Windmill Ct NW2 ..10 A2
Windmill Dr SW4 ..61 A2
Windmill Hill NW3 ..2 B1

Windmill Hill continued
1 NW3 ....11 B4
Windmill Ho SE1 ...121 C1
Windmill La E15 ...19 C2
Windmill Pas 10
W4 ....38 A2
Windmill Rd W4 ...38 A2
SW18 ....59 C1
SW19 ....69 A1
Windmill Row
SE11 ....149 B1
Windmill Sch2 SE2 ...62 A2
Windmill St SW1 ...105 B3
Windmill Wlk SE1 ...121 C1
Windrose Cl SE16 ...40 C4
Windrush Cl W4 ...45 B3
SW11 ....59 C3
Windrush Ho NW8 101 C4
Windsock Cl 1
SE16 ....41 B2
Windsor Ct W2 ...114 A4
SW3 ....144 B2
SW11 ....167 C2
NW3 ....10 C1
20 SE16 ....32 C1
SW6 ....58 A4
4 SW18 ....58 B2
2 SW4 ....61 B3
Windsor Gdns W9 ...23 C1
Windsor Ho N1 ...87 A2
NW1 ....92 B4
N4 ....6 B3
NW2 ....10 A2
4 E2 ....25 C2
4 W4 ....37 B1
Richmond TW9 ...44 B1
Windsor Pl SW1 147 A4
Windsor Rd N7 ...5 A1
NW2 ....9 A2
Richmond TW9 ...44 B1
Windsor St N1 ...86 B4
Windsor Terr N1 ...97 A4
Windsor Way W14 140 A4
Windsor Wharf E9 ...18 B3
Windsor Wlk SE5 ...48 C1
Windspoint Dr SE15 50 A4
Windus Rd N16 ...7 B3
Windus Wlk N16 ...7 B3
Wine Cl E1 ...32 B2
Wine Office Ct
EC4 ....107 C2
Winfield Ho SW11 167 C3
Winford Ct 15 ...49 C2
Winford Ho E3 ...26 B4
Winforton St SE10 52 B2
Winfrith Rd SW18 71 B3
Wingate Ho 8 N16 ...15 C4
26 E3 ....27 A2
Wingate Rd W6 ...39 A3
Wingfield Ho NW6 78 A2
E2 ....98 C3
Wingfield Mews
SE15 ....64 C4
Wingfield St SE15 ...64 C4
Wingford Rd SW2 ...62 A1
Wingham 3 NW5 ...12 C2
Wingrave SE17 ...151 B3
Wingrave Ho NW8 ...90 A1
Wingrave Rd W6 ...47 B4
Wingreen NW8 ...78 B4
Winifrede Paul Ho 7
NW5 ....13 A4
Winkley St 6 E2 ...25 A3
Winkworth Cotts 18
E1 ....25 B1

Winnett St W1 ...119 B4
Winnington Ho 8
SE5 ....48 B3
Winscombe St N19 ...4 A2
Winsham Gr SW11 ...60 C2
Winsham Ho NW1 ...93 C4
Winslade Rd SW2 ...62 A2
Winsland Mews
W2 ....101 B2
Winsland St W2 ...101 B2
Winsley St W1 ...105 A2
Winslow SE17 ...152 A1
Winslow Ho SW4 ...171 C2
Winslow Rd W6 ...47 B4
Winstanley Rd
SW11 ....59 C4
Winston Rd N16 ...15 C4
Winston Wlk 4 W4 ...37 C2
Winter Box Wlk
SW11 ....54 B2
Winter Lo SE16 ...153 C1
Winterbourne Ho
W11 ....112 A3
Winterbrook Rd
SE24 ....63 B1
Winterfold Cl SW19 70 A2
Winterleys 7 NW6 ...23 B3
Winterslow Ho 20
SE5 ....48 B1
Winterton Ho 8 E1 32 B3
Winterton Pl
SW10 ....157 A4
Winterwell Rd SW2 62 A2
Winthorpe Rd SW15 58 A3
Winthrop Ho 10
W10 ....30 A2
Winthrop St 4 E1 ...32 A4
Winton Prim Sch
N1 ....84 C1
Wirrall Ho 5 SE26 76 C1
Wisden Ho N16 ...7 C4
Wise Rd E15 ...27 C4
Wiseton Rd SW17 ...72 B3
Wisley Ho SW1 ...147 B2
Wisley Rd SW11 ...60 C2
Wisteria Rd SE13 ...67 C3
Wistow Ho 14 E2 ...24 C4
Witan St E2 ...25 A2
Witanhurst La N6 ...3 C3
Witchwood Ho 11
SW9 ....62 C4
Witcombe Point 18
SE15 ....49 C2
Witham Ho 19 SE5 ...48 B1
Witherington Rd
N5 ....14 C3
Withers Pl EC1 ...97 A2
Withy Ho 4 E1 ...25 C1
Witley Ho 2 SW2 ...74 B4
Witley Point 8
SW15 ....69 A3
Witley Rd N19 ...4 B2
Wittering Ho
SW11 ....169 A2
Wivenhoe Cl SE15 ...65 A4
Wix Prim Sch SW4 ...61 A3
Wix's La SW4 ...61 A3
Woburn Ct 23 SE16 ...40 A1
Richmond TW9 ...54 B4
Woburn Pl WC1 ...94 A1
Woburn Sq WC1 ...93 C1
Woburn Wlk WC1 ...93 C3
Wodehouse Ave
SE15 ....49 B2
Wodehouse Ct 10
W3 ....37 B3

Woking Cl SW15 ...56 B3
Wolcot Ho NW1 ...83 A1
Wolfe Cres 34 SE16 ...40 C4
Wolfe Ho 11 W12 ...30 A2
Wolfson Ct SE1 ...139 A4
NW11 ....1 A4
Wolftencroft Cl
SW11 ....59 C4
Wollaston Cl SE1 ...150 C4
Wolseley Ave SW18,
SW19 ....70 C2
Wolseley Gdns W4 ...45 A4
Wolseley Rd W4 ...37 B2
Wolseley St SE1 ...139 A3
Wolsey Ct NW6 ...11 B1
Wolsey Mews NW5 ...13 B2
Wolsey Rd N1 ...15 C3
Wolsey St E1 ...32 B4
Wolverley St E2 ...25 A2
Wolverton SE17 ...152 A2
Wolverton Gdns
W6 ....39 C2
Womersley Rd N8 ...5 A4
Wontner Cl 5 N1 ...15 B1
Wontner Rd SW12,
SW17 ....72 B2
Wood Cl E2 ...24 C1 99 B2
Wood Dene 8 SE15 50 A2
Wood Field NW3 ...12 B3
Wood Ho 3 SW4 ...171 C2
4 NW6 ....23 B3
Wood La W12 ...30 A3
Wood Lane Sch
W12 ....30 A3
Wood Point 8 E16 35 C4
Wood St EC2 ...109 A2
W4 ....38 A1
Wood Vale SE22 ...65 A1
Wood Wharf SE10 ...52 B4
Wood's Mews W1 ...117 B4
Wood's Pl SE1 ...138 B1
Wood's Rd SE15 ...50 A2
Woodberry Down N4 6 B4
Woodberry Down JMI
Schs N4 ...6 B4
Woodberry Gr N4 ...6 B4
Woodbine Terr 9 E9 17 B2
Woodborough Rd
SW15 ....57 A3
Woodbourne Ave
SW16 ....73 C1
Woodbourne Cl
SW16 ....74 A1
Woodbridge Cl 10 N7 5 B2
Woodbridge Ct N16 ...6 C1
Woodbridge St EC1 96 A2
Woodchester Sq
W2 ....100 A4
Woodchurch Ho
SW9 ....173 B4
Woodchurch Rd
NW6 ....11 A1
Woodcock Ho 4
E14 ....33 C4
Woodcote Ho 2
SE8 ....51 B4
Woodcroft Mews
SE8 ....41 A2
Woodfall Rd N4 ...5 C2
Woodfall St SW3 ...144 C1
Woodfarrs SE5 ...63 C3
Woodfield Ave
SW16 ....73 C1
Woodfield Gr SW16 73 C1
Woodfield Pl W9 ...23 B1

Woodfield Rd W9 ...31 B4
Woodger Rd W12 ...39 B4
Woodhall NW1 ...92 C3
Woodhall Ave SE21 76 B1
Woodhall Dr SE21 ...76 B1
Woodhall Ho SW18 59 C1
Woodheyes Rd NW10 8 A2
Woodhurst Rd W3 ...28 B2
Woodison St E3 ...26 A1
Woodland Cres
16 SE16 ....40 C4
SE10 ....53 A4
Woodland Gr SE10 ...43 A1
Woodland St 2 E8 ...16 B2
Woodland Wlk NW3 12 A3
SE10 ....43 A1
Woodlands SW4 ...61 A3
Woodlands Ave W3 28 A1
Woodlands Ct
NW10 ....22 C4
Woodlands Gr SE10 43 A1
Woodlands Park Rd
SE10 ....53 A4
Woodlands Rd
SW13 ....56 B4
Woodlands St SE13 67 C1
Woodlands The N5 15 B4
Woodlands Way
SW15 ....58 B2
Woodlawn Cl SW15 58 B2
Woodlawn Rd SW6 47 C2
Woodlea Rd N16 ...7 A1
Woodleigh Gdns
SW16 ....74 A1
Woodmans Gr NW10 8 B3
Woodmans Mews
W12 ....30 A4
Woodquest Ave
SE24 ....63 B2
Woodruff Ho SW2 ...62 C1
Woodrush Cl 4
SE14 ....51 A3
Woods Ho SW8 ...170 C4
Woodseer St E1 ...111 B4
Woodsford Sq
W14 ....126 B4
Woodspring Rd
SW19 ....70 A2
Woodstar Ho 3
SE15 ....49 C3
Woodstock Ave
NW11 ....1 A4
Woodstock Ct
SE11 ....149 A2
Woodstock Gr W12 39 C4
Woodstock Ho 2
N5 ....15 B4
Woodstock Mews
W1 ....103 C3
Woodstock Rd NW11 1 B3
N4 ....5 C4
W4 ....38 A3
Woodstock St W1 ...104 A1
Woodstock Terr
E14 ....34 A2
Woodsyre SE26 ...76 B1
Woodthorpe Rd
SW15 ....57 B3
Woodview Cl N4 ...6 A4
Woodville 3
SE10 ....52 B2
Woodville Ho SE1 138 C2
Woodville Rd NW11 1 A4
N16 ....16 A3

Woodville Rd continued
NW6 ....23 B3
Woodwarde Rd
SE22 ....64 A1
Woodwell St SW18 59 B2
Woodyard Cl NW5 ...12 C3
Woodyard La SE21 ...76 A4
Woolcombes Ct 4
SE16 ....32 C1
Wooler St SE17 ...151 C2
Woolf Cl 2 SE16 ...37 B3
Woolley Ho SW9 ...63 A4
Woollon Ho 1 E1 ...32 B3
Woolmore JMI Sch
E14 ....34 B2
Woolmore St E14 ...34 B2
Woolneigh St SW6 166 A1
Woolpack Ho 6 E9 ...17 B2
Woolridge Way E9 ...17 B1
Woolstaplers Way
SE16 ....153 B4
Woolstone Ho 7
E2 ....24 C4
Woolven Ho SE3 ...53 B4
Woolwich Rd SE10 ...43 C1
Wooster Gdns E14 ...34 C3
Wootton St SE1 ...121 C1
Worcester Dr W4 ...38 A3
Worcester Gdns
SW11 ....60 B2
Worcester Ho W2 ...100 C1
SE11 ....135 B1
9 SW15 ....69 B4
Worcester Mews 2
NW6 ....11 A2
Wordsworth Ho
NW6 ....23 C2
Wordsworth Pl 11
NW3 ....12 B3
Wordsworth Rd
SE1 ....153 A3
N16 ....16 A4
Worfield St SW11 ...158 B1
Worgan St SE11 ...148 C2
SE16 ....40 C2
Working Men's Coll
NW1 ....83 A2
World's End Pas
SW10 ....157 B2
World's End Pl
SW10 ....157 A2
Worlidge St W6 ...39 B1
Worlingham Rd
SE22 ....64 B3
Wormholt Park Prim
Sch W12 ...29 C2
Wormholt Rd W12 ...29 C1
Wormwood St EC2 110 A2
W10 ....31 A4
Wornum Ho 3
NW6 ....23 A3
Woronzow Rd NW8 80 A3
Worple St SW14 ...55 C4
Worple Way TW10 ...54 A3
Worship St
EC2 ....24 A1 98 A1
Worsopp Dr SW4 ...61 B2
Worth Gr SE17 ...151 B1
Worthington Ho
EC1 ....95 C4
18 SW2 ....62 C2
Wotton Rd 18 SE8 ...51 B4

Wouldham Rd E16 ....35 B1
Wray Cres N4 ....5 B2
Wray Ct N4 ....5 B2
Wray Ho 11 SW2 ...74 A3
Wrayburn Ho SE16 139 C3
Wren Ave NW2 ....9 B4
Wren Cl E16 ....35 B1
Wren Ho SW1 .....147 B1
27 E3 ....26 A3
Wren Landing E14 ..33 C1
Wren Rd SE5 ....48 C2
Wren St WC1 ....95 A2
Wren View N6 ....4 B3
Wrentham Ave
NW10 ....22 C3
Wrestlers Ct EC3 ..110 A2
Wrexham Rd E3 .....26 C3
Wrigglesworth St
SE14 ....50 C3
Wright Cl SE13 .....67 C3
Wright Ho SW15 ....57 A2
Wright's Gn SW4 ...61 C3
Wright's La W8 ....128 A2
Wright's Rd E3 .....26 B3
Wrotham Ho SE1 ..137 C2
Wrotham Rd 11
NW1 ....13 B1
Wrottesley Rd
NW10 ....21 C3
Wroughton Rd
SW11 ....60 B1
Wroxton Rd SE15 ..50 B1
Wulfstan St W12 ...29 B3
Wyatt Cl SE16 ......41 B4
Wyatt Dr SW13 .....47 A3
Wyatt Ho NW8 ......89 C1
SE3 ....53 B1
Wyatt Park Mans 11
SW2 ....74 A2
Wyatt Park Rd SW2 74 B2
Wyatt Rd N5 ....6 B1
Wybert St NW1 ....92 C2

Wycherley Cl SE3 ...53 B3
Wychwood End N6 ...4 B4
Wychwood Ho N4 ....6 B4
Wyclif Ct EC1 ......96 A3
Wyclif St EC1 ......96 A3
Wycliffe Ho 11 N16 .16 A4
Wycliffe Rd SW11 169 C1
Wycombe Ct SE3 ...53 C3
Wycombe Gdns
NW11 ....1 C2
Wycombe Ho NW8 ..90 A2
Wycombe Pl SW18 ..59 B1
Wye St SW11 ......167 C1
Wyersdale Ho N4 ....6 B4
Wyfold Rd SW6 ...154 A1
Wyke Rd E3 ....18 C1
Wyldes Cl NW11 .....2 B3
Wyleu St SE23 ......66 A1
Wyllen Cl E1 ....25 B1
Wymering Mans 6
W9 ....23 C2
Wymering Rd W9 ...23 C2
Wymond St SW15 ..57 B4
Wymondham Ct
NW8 ....79 CA
Wynan Rd E14 ......42 A1
Wynard Terr SE11 149 A2
Wyndham Cres N19 ..4 B1
Wyndham Deedes Ho 37
E2 ....24 C3
Wyndham Ho SW1 145 B3
Wyndham Mews
W1 ....102 C3
Wyndham Pl W1 ...102 C3
Wyndham Rd SE5 ..48 B3
Wyndham St W1 ...102 C4
Wyndham Yd W1 ..102 C3
Wyneham Rd SE24 .63 C2
Wynford Ho N1 .....85 A2
Wynford Rd N1 .....85 A2
Wynne Ho SE14 ....50 C2
Wynne Rd SW9 ...173 B1
Wynnstay Gdns
W8 ....127 C2

Wynter Ho SW9 ...173 A1
Wynter St SW11 ....59 B3
Wynton Pl W3 ......28 A3
Wynyard Ho SE11 .149 A2
Wynyatt St EC1 .....96 A4
Wytham Ho NW8 ...89 C1
Wythburn Ct W1 ..102 C2
Wythburn Pl W1 ..102 C2

Wyvil Prim Sch
SW8 ....162 B2
Wyvil Rd SW8 ....162 A2
Wyvis St E14 ....34 A4

Y

Yabsley St E14 .....34 B1
Yaldam Ho SE1 ...152 A3
Yalding Ho 20 E5 ...17 A3
Yalding Rd SE16 ..153 B4
Yale Ct NW6 ....11 A3
Yardley St WC1 .....95 B3
Yarmouth Pl W1 ..118 A1
Yarnfield Sq 14
SE15 ....49 C2
Yarrow Ho W10 ....30 B4
11 E14 ....42 B3
Yates Ct NW2 ....9 C2
Yates St SE17 ......18 A3
Yatesbury Ct E5 ...18 A3
Yatton Ho W10 .....30 B4
Yeadon Ho W10 ....30 B4
Yearby Ho W10 .....22 B1
Yeate St N1 ....15 C1
Yeats Cl NW10 ......8 A2
Yeldham Ho W6 ....39 C1
Yeldham Rd W6 ....39 C1
Yelverton Rd
SW11 ....167 C1
Yeo St E3 ....34 A4
Yeoman Cl SE27 ...75 A1
Yeoman Ho SE1 ...153 A2
Yeoman St SE8 .....41 A2
Yeoman's Row
SW3 ....130 B1
Yeoman's Yd E1 ..125 A4

Yeovil Ho N7 ....5 B2
W10 ....22 B1
Yerbury Prim Sch
N19 ....4 C1
Yerbury Rd N19 .....4 C1
Yesodey Hatorah Gram
Sch N16 ....7 B4
Yew Gr NW2 ....9 C4
Yew Ho SE14 ....51 B1
Yew Tree Rd W12 ..29 B2
Yewfield Rd NW10 ..8 B2
Yoakley Rd N16 .....7 A2
Yoke Cl N7 ....14 A2
Yonge Pk N4,N7 .....5 C1
York Ave SE17 ....151 A2
SW14 ....55 B2
York Bldgs WC2 ...120 B3
York Bridge NW1 ...91 B2
York Cl 17 SE5 .....48 B1
York Gate NW1 .....91 C1
York Gr SE15 ....50 B2
York Hill SE27,SW16 75 A1
York Ho N21 ....84 C1
W1 ....102 C4
W8 ....128 A4
SE1 ....135 A1
SW3 ....145 A2
11 N7 ....13 C2
SW11 ....14 C3
W3 ....28 B2
Richmond TW9 ....44 C2
Richmond TW10 ...54 C2
York House Pl W8 128 A4
York Mans W1 ....103 B4
SW11 ....169 C4
York Mews NW5 ...13 A3
York Pl WC2 ......120 B3
SW11 ....59 C4
York Place Mans
NW1 ....103 A4
York Rd SE1 ......135 A4
W3 ....28 C3
4 Richmond TW10 54 B2
SW11,SW18 ....59 C4

York Rd Bsns Ctr
SW11 ....167 C1
York Rise NW5 ......4 A1
York Sq 14 E14 ....33 A3
York St W1 ....103 A4
York St Chambers
W1 ....102 C4
York Terr E NW1 ...91 C1
York Terr W NW1 ...91 B1
York Way N1 ....84 B3
N1,N7,NW1 ....14 A1
York Way Ct N1 ....84 B3
Yorkley Ho W10 ...22 B1
Yorkshire Cl N16 ...7 A1
Yorkshire Grey Yd
WC1 ....106 C3
Yorkshire Rd E14 ..33 A3
Yorkton St E2 ......24 C3
Young St W8 ......128 A3
Young's Bldgs EC1 .97 A2
Youngs Ct SW11 ..169 C3
Yoxall Ho W10 .....22 B1
Yukon Rd SW12 ...73 A4
Yuletide Cl NW10 ...8 A2

Z

Zampa Rd SE16 ....40 B1
Zander Ct E2 24 C2,99 C4
Zangwill Ho NW6 ..23 B3
Zealand Ho 11 SE5 .48 B1
Zealand Rd E3 .....26 A3
Zennor Rd SW12 ...73 B3
Zenoria St SE22 ...64 B3
Zetland Ho W8 ....128 A2
Zetland St E14 .....34 B4
Zion Ho 6 E1 ......32 B3
Zoar St SE1 ....122 C2
Zodiac Ho 3 E3 ...26 C1
Zoffany St N19 ......4 C2

List of numbered locations

This atlas shows thousands more place names than any other London street atlas. In some busy areas it is impossible to fit the name of every place.

Where not all names will fit, some smaller places are shown by a number. If you wish to find out the name associated with a number, use this listing.

34

A5 **8** St James's Ct

Page number | Grid square | Location number | Place name

1

B1 **1** Mortimer Cl
2 Sunnyside Ho
3 Sunnyside
4 Prospect Pl
B4 **1** Berkeley Ct
2 Exchange Mans
3 Beechcroft Ct
4 Nedahall Ct
C1 **1** Portman Hts
2 Hermitage Ct
3 Moreland Ct
4 Wendover Ct

4

B1 **1** Hunter Ho
2 Fisher Ho
3 Lang Ho
4 Temple Ho
5 Palmer Ho
B2 **1** Flowers Mews
2 Sandridge St
3 Bovingdon Cl
4 Laurel Cl
5 Forest Way
6 Larch Cl
7 Pine Cl
8 Alder Mews
9 Aspen Cl
B3 **1** Calvert Ct
2 Academy The
3 Whitehall Mans
4 Pauntley St
5 Archway Hts
6 Pauntley Ho
C1 **1** Melchester Ho
2 Norcombe Ho
3 Weatherbury Ho
4 Wessex Ho
5 Archway Bsns Ctr
C2 **1** Bowerman Ct
2 Hargrave Mans
3 Church Garth
4 John King Ct
C3 **1** Louise White Ho
2 Levison Way
3 Sanders Way
C4 **1** Eleanor Rathbone Ho

2 Christopher Lo
3 Monkridge
4 Marbleford Ct
5 High London
6 Garton Ho
7 Hilltop Ho
8 Caroline Martyn Ho
9 Arthur Henderson Ho
10 Margaret Mcmillan Ho
11 Enid Stacy Ho
12 Mary McArthur Ho
13 Bruce Glasier Ho
14 John Wheatley Ho
15 Keir Hardie Ho
16 Monroe Ho
17 Iberia Ho
18 Lygoe Ho
19 Lambert Ho
20 Shelbourne Ho
21 Arkansas Ho
22 Lafitte Ho
23 Shreveport Ho
24 Packenham Ho
25 Orpheus Ho
26 Fayetville Ho
27 Bayon Ho

5

A1 **1** Northview
2 Tufnell Park Mans
A2 **1** Christie Ct
2 Ringmer Gdns
3 Kingsdown Rd
4 Cottenham Ho
5 St Paul's Ct
6 Rickthorne Rd
7 Stanley Terr
A3 **1** Beeches The
2 Lambton Ct
A4 **1** Marie Lloyd Gdns
2 Jessie Blythe La
3 Leyden Mans
4 Brambledown
5 Lochbie
B2 **1** Berkeley Wlk
2 Lazar Wlk
3 Thistlewood Cl

4 Tomlins Wlk
5 Andover Ho
6 Barmouth Ho
7 Chard Ho
8 Methley Ho
9 Rainford Ho
10 Woodbridge Cl
11 Allerton Wlk
12 Falconer Wlk
13 Sonderburg Rd
B3 **1** Lawson Ct
2 Wiltshire Ct
3 Hutton Ct
C2 **1** Brookfield
2 Churnfield

6

B4 **1** Finmere Ho
2 Keynsham Ho
3 Kilpeck Ho
4 Knaresborough Ho
5 Leighfield Ho
6 Lonsdale Ho
7 Groveley Ho
8 Wensleydale Ho
9 Badminton Ct
C2 **1** Chestnut Cl
2 Sycamore Ho
3 Lordship Ho
4 Clissold Ho
5 Beech Ho
6 Laburnum Ho
7 Ormond Ho
C4 **1** Selwood Ho
2 Mendip Ho
3 Ennerdale Ho
4 Delamere Ho
5 Westwood Ho
6 Bernwood Ho
7 Allerdale Ho
8 Chattenden Ho
9 Farningham Ho
10 Oakend Ho

7

A1 **1** Gujarat Ho
2 Marton Rd
3 Painsthorpe Rd
4 Selkirk Ho

5 Defoe Ho
6 Edward Friend Ho
7 Sheridan Ho
8 Barrie Ho
9 Arnold Ho
10 Macaulay Ho
11 Stowe Ho
12 Carlyle Ho
13 Shaftesbury Ho
14 Lillian Cl
15 Swift Ho
16 Dryden Ho
17 Scott Ct
18 Kingsfield Ho
19 Uhura Sq
A3 **1** Godstone Ct
2 Farnham Ct
3 Milford Ct
4 Cranleigh Ct
5 Haslemere Ct
6 Belmont Ct
7 Hockworth Ho
8 Garratt Ho
9 Fairburn Ho
B1 **1** Lawrence's Bldgs
2 Cottage Wlk
3 Batley Pl
B2 **1** Garnham St
2 Garnham Ct
3 Sanford La
4 Sanford Wlk
B3 **1** Stamford Hill Mans
2 Montefiore Ct
3 Berwyn Ho
4 Clent Ho
5 Chiltern Ho
6 Laindon Ho
7 Pentland Ho
B4 **1** Regent Ct
2 Stamford Lo
3 Holmwood Ct
C1 **1** Ravenscourt
2 Mellington Ct
3 Rendlesham Ho
4 Florence Ct
5 Burnaston Ho
C2 **1** Cazenove Mans
2 Chedworth Ho
3 Aldergrove Ho
4 Abbotstone Ho

5 Briggeford Cl
6 Inglethorpe Ho
7 Ashdown Ho
C3 **1** Stamford Grove E
2 Stamford Mans
3 Grove Mans
4 Stamford Grove W

8

C2 **1** Regency Mews
2 Tudor Mews

10

A1 **1** Fountain Ho
2 Kingston Ho
3 Waverley Ct
4 Weston Ho
5 Mapes Ho
6 Athelstan Gdns
7 Leff Ho
B1 **1** Alma Birk Ho
2 Brooklands Ct
3 Brooklands Court Apartments
4 Cleveland Mans
5 Buckley Ct
6 Webheath
C1 **1** Linstead St
2 Embassy Ho
3 Acol Ct
4 Kings Wood Ct
5 Douglas Ct
6 King's Gdns
7 Carlton Mans
8 Smyrna Mans
9 New Priory Ct
10 Queensgate Pl
11 Brondesbury Mews
C2 **1** Dene Mans
2 Sandwell Cres
3 Sandwell Mans
4 Hampstead West
5 Redcroft
C3 **1** Melaris Mews
2 Walter Northcott Ho
3 Polperro Mans
4 Lyncroft Mans
5 Marlborough Mans

6 Alexandra Mans
7 Cumberland Mans
8 Cavendish Mans
9 Ambassador Ct
10 Welbeck Mans
11 Inglewood Mans

11

A2 **1** Beswick Mews
2 Worcester Mews
3 Minton Mews
4 Doulton Mews
5 Laurel Ho
6 Sandalwood Ho
7 Iroko Ho
8 Banyan Ho
9 Rosewood Ho
10 Ebony Ho
11 Rosemont Mans
B1 **1** Harrold Ho
2 Glover Ho
3 Byron Ct
4 Nalton Ho
B2 **1** Petros Gdns
2 Heath Ct
3 Imperial Twrs
4 Fairhurst
5 St John's Ct
6 New College Ct
B4 **1** Windmill Hill
2 Highgrove Point
3 Gainsborough Ho
4 Heath Mans
5 Pavilion Ct
6 Holly Berry La
7 New Campden Ct
8 Benham's Pl
9 Holly Bush Vale
10 Gardnor Mans
11 Mansfield Pl
12 Streatley Pl
13 New Ct
14 Bird In Hand Yd
15 Spencer Wlk
16 Wells Ct
17 Perrin's Ct
18 Village Mount
19 Prince Arthur Ct
20 Prince Arthur Mews
21 Monro Ho
C1 **1** New College Par
2 Northways Par
3 Noel Ho
4 Campden Ho
5 Centre Hts
6 Hickes Ho
7 Swiss Terr
8 Leitch Ho
9 Jevons Ho
10 Langhorne Ct
11 Park Lo
12 Avenue Lo
C2 **1** Belsize Park Mews
2 Baynes Mews
3 McCrone Mews
C3 **1** Belsize Court Garages
2 Roscommon Ho
3 Akenside Ct

12

A2 **1** Banff Ho
2 Glenloch Ct
3 Havercourt
4 Holmfield Ct
5 Gilling Ct
6 Howitt Cl
7 Manor Mans
8 Straffan Lo
9 Romney Ct
10 Lancaster Stables
11 Eton Garages
B1 **1** Hancock Nunn Ho
2 Higginson Ho
3 Duncan Ho
4 Mary Wharrie Ho
5 Rockstraw Ho
6 Cleaver Ho
7 Chamberlain Ho
8 Sharples Hall St
9 Primrose Mews
10 Rothwell St
B2 **1** Alder Ho
2 Hornbeam Ho
3 Whitebeam Ho
4 Aspen Ho
5 Rowan Ho
6 Beech Ho
7 Chestnut Ho
8 Oak Ho
9 Willow Ho
10 Sycamore Ho
11 Maple Ho
12 Hazel Ho
13 Elaine Ct
14 Faircourt
15 Stanbury Ct
16 Priory Mans
17 Grange The
B3 **1** Cayford Ho
2 Du Maurier Ho
3 Isokon Flats
4 Palgrave Ho
5 Garnett Ho
6 Stephenson Ho
7 Park Dwellings
8 Siddons Ho
9 Mall Studios
10 Park Hill Wlk
11 Wordsworth Pl
12 Fraser Regnart Ct
13 St Pancras Almshouses
14 Walham Ct
15 Wellington Ho
C1 **1** Bridge Ho
2 Hardington
3 Mead Cl
4 Rugmere
5 Tottenhall
6 Beauvale
7 Broomfield
C2 **1** Silverbirch Wlk
2 Penshurst
3 Wingham
4 Westwell
5 Chislet
6 Burmarsh
7 Shipton Ho
8 Stone Gate
9 Leysdown
10 Headcorn
11 Lenham
12 Halstow
13 Fordcombe

14 Cannington
15 Langridge
16 Athlone Ho
17 Pentland Ho
18 Beckington
19 Hawkridge
20 Edington

13

A1 **1** Ferdinand Ho
2 Harmood Ho
3 Hawley Rd
4 Hawley Mews
5 Leybourne St
6 Barling
7 Tiptree
8 Havering
9 Candida Ct
10 Lorraine Ct
11 Donnington Ct
12 Welford Ct
13 Torbay Ct
14 Bradfield Ct
15 Torbay St
16 Leybourne Rd
17 Haven St
18 Stucley Pl
A2 **1** Ashington
2 Priestley Ho
3 Leonard Day Ho
4 Old Dairy Mews
5 Monmouth Ho
6 Alpha Ct
7 Una Ho
8 Widford
9 Hey Bridge
10 Roxwell
A4 **1** Denyer Ho
2 Stephenson Ho
3 Trevithick Ho
4 Brunel Ho
5 Newcomen Ho
6 Faraday Ho
7 Winifrede Paul Ho
8 Wardlow
9 Fletcher Ct
10 Tideswell
11 Grangemill
12 Hambrook Ct
13 Calver
B1 **1** Durdans Ho
2 Philia Ho
3 Bernard Shaw Ct
4 Foster Ct
5 Bessemer Ct
6 Hogarth Ct
7 Rochester Ct
8 Soane Ct
9 Wallett Ct
10 Inwood Ct
11 Wrotham Rd
12 Caulfield Ct
13 Bruges Pl
14 Reachview Cl
15 Hightstone Mans
B3 **1** Eleanor Ho
2 Falkland Pl
3 Kensington Ho
4 Willingham Cl
5 Kenbrook Ho
6 Aborfield
7 Great Field
8 Appleford
9 Forties The
B4 **1** Benson Ct

2 Tait Ho
3 Manorfield Cl
4 Greatfield Cl
5 Longley Ho
6 Lampson Ho
7 Davidson Ho
8 Palmer Ho
9 Lambourn Cl
10 Morris Ho
11 Owen Ho
C1 **1** Hillier Ho
2 Gairloch Ho
3 Cobham Mews
4 Bergholt Mews
5 Blakeney Cl
6 Weavers Way
7 Allensbury Pl
C2 **1** Rowstock
2 Carters Cl
3 York Ho
4 Hungerford Rd
5 Cliff Ct
6 Camelot Ho
C3 **1** Blake Ho
2 Quelch Ho
3 Lee Ho
4 Willbury Ho
5 Howell Ho
6 Holmsbury Ho
7 Leith Ho
8 Betchworth Ho
9 Rushmore Ho
10 Dugdale Ho
11 Horsendon Ho
12 Colley Ho
13 Coombe Ho
14 Ivinghoe Ho
15 Buckhurst Ho
16 Saxonbury Ct
17 Charlton Ct
18 Apollo Studios
19 Barn Cl
20 Long Meadow
21 Landleys Field
22 Margaret Bondfield Ho
23 Haywood Lo
C4 **1** Fairlie Ct
2 Univ of North London (Carleton Grange Hall)
3 Trecastle Way
4 Hilldrop Est
5 Hyndman Ho
6 Carpenter Ho
7 Graham Ho

14

A3 **1** Kimble Ho
2 Saxonbury Ct
3 Poynder Ct
4 Pangbourne Ho
5 Moulsford Ho
A4 **1** Arcade The
2 Macready Pl
B1 **1** Kerwick Cl
2 Rydston Cl
3 Skegness Ho
4 Frederica St
5 Ponder St
6 Kings Ct
7 Freeling St
B4 **1** Buckmaster Ho
2 Loreburn Ho
3 Cairns Ho

4 Halsbury Ho
5 Chelmsford Ho
6 Cranworth Ho
C1 **1** Mountfort Terr
2 Davey Lo
3 Carfree Cl
C3 **1** Blaney Pl
2 Wells Yd
3 Milton Pl
4 Hartnoll Ho
5 St James School Flats
6 Widnes Ho
7 Tranmere Ho
8 Victoria Mans
9 Formby Ct
10 Mersey Ho
11 Birkenhead Ho

15

A1 **1** Islington Park Mews
2 Evelyn Denington Ct
3 Bassingbourn Ho
4 Cadmore Ho
5 Adstock Ho
6 Garston Ho
7 Flitton Ho
8 Datchworth Ho
9 Battishill St
10 Almeida St
11 Edward's Cotts
12 Hyde's Pl
13 Tyndale Terr
14 Spriggs Ho
15 Barratt Ho
16 Spencer Pl
17 Chadston Ho
18 Whiston Ho
19 Wakelin Ho
20 Tressel Cl
21 Canonbury Ct
22 Shillingford St
23 Halton Ho
A4 **1** Chestnuts The
2 Bowen Ct
3 Peckett Sq
B1 **1** Haslam Ho
2 Horsfield Ho
3 Astey's Row
4 Melville Pl
5 Wontner Cl
6 Hedingham Cl
7 Eric Fletcher Ct
8 Ashby Ho
9 Annette Cres
10 Bentham Ct
11 New Bentham Ct
12 Cardigan Wlk
13 Lindsey Mews
14 Walkinshaw Ct
B2 **1** Crowline Wlk
2 Bardsey Wlk
3 Handa Wlk
4 Lismore Wlk
5 Sark Ho
6 Clephane Rd
7 Sybil Thorndike Ho
8 Guernsey Rd
9 Guernsey Ho
10 Herm Ho
11 Florence Nightingale Ho
12 Jersey Ho

13 Jethou Ho
14 Upper Caldy Wlk
15 Caldy Wlk
16 Alderney Ho
17 Marquess Rd S
18 Oronsay Wlk
19 Upper Gulland Wlk
20 Gulland Wlk

B3 1 Pearfield Ho
2 Larchfield Ho
3 Beresford Terr
4 Pondfield Ho
5 Ashfield Ho
6 Elmfield Ho

B4 1 Fountain Mews
2 Woodstock Ho
3 Henson Ct
4 Taverner Sq

C2 1 John Kennedy Ct
2 John Kennedy Lo
3 Ball's Pond Pl
4 Haliday Wlk
5 Mason Chamber Ct
6 Ramsey Wlk
7 Rona Wlk
8 Threadgold Ho
9 Wakeham St
10 Saffron Ct
11 Callaby Terr
12 Tilney Gdns
13 Westcliff Ho
14 Ilford Ho
15 Ongar Ho
16 Greenhills Terr
17 Romford Ho

C4 1 Ledo Ho
2 Salween Ho
3 Prome Ho
4 Arakan Ho
5 Rangoon Ho
6 Mandalay Ho
7 Karen Ho
8 Wingate Ho
9 Jubet Ho
10 Orde Ho
11 Chindit Ho
12 Mabel Thornton Ho
13 Crawshay Ho
14 Avon Ho
15 Connaught Mans
16 Jonson Ho
17 Herrick Ho
18 Donne Ho
19 Grasmere Ho
20 Thirlmere Ho

16

A1 1 Dorchester Ct
2 Wareham Ct
3 Dorset Ct
4 Stratton Ct
5 Swanage Ct
6 Blandford Ct
7 Portland Ct
8 Oscar Faber Pl
9 Lancaster Ct

A2 1 Kingsland Gn
2 Kingsland Pas
3 Metropolitan Benefit Societies Almshouses
4 Nimrod Pas
5 De Beauvoir Pl

A3 1 Hewling Ho
2 Matthias Ho

3 Port Royal Pl
4 Cressington Cl
5 King Henry's Yd
6 Bronte Ho
7 Sewell Ho
8 Lydgate Ho
9 Patmore Ho
10 Congreve Ho
11 Elton St
12 Conrad Ho
13 Southwell Ho
14 Neptune Ho
15 Campion Ho
16 Webster Ho
17 Meredith Ho
18 Beckford Ho
19 Ashley Ct
20 Hayling Cl
21 Millard Cl
22 Lydford Cl
23 Salcombe Rd
24 Truman's Rd
25 Templeton Cl
26 John Campbell Rd
27 Gillett Pl
28 Bradbury St

A4 1 Londesborough Ho
2 Knebworth Ho
3 Knebworth Rd
4 Bransby Ct
5 Imperial Ave
6 Leonard Pl
7 Shakspeare Mews
8 Binyon Ho
9 Shelley Ho
10 Browning Ho
11 Burns Ho
12 Andrew Marvell Ho
13 Wycliffe Ho
14 Blake Ho
15 Marlowe Ho
16 Fletcher Ho
17 Chaucer Ct

B1 1 Hilborough Rd
2 Shoreditch Ct

B2 1 Prospect Ho
2 Woodland St
3 Crosby Wlk
4 Kirkland Wlk
5 Bowness Cl
6 Carlisle Wlk
7 Skelton Cl
8 Camerton Cl
9 Buttermere Wlk
10 Houghton Cl

B3 1 Miller's Terr
2 Chow Sq
3 Drysdale Flats
4 Gateway Mews
5 Birkbeck Mews
6 Winchester St

B4 1 Coronation Ave
2 Morris Blitz Ct
3 Shacklewell Ho
4 Alexandra Ct

C1 1 Aldington Ct
2 Bayton Ct
3 Rochford Wlk

C3 1 Kingsdown Ho
2 Glendown Ho
3 Moredown Ho
4 Blakeney Cl
5 Beeston Cl
6 Benabo Ct
7 David Devine Ho
8 Kreedman Wlk

9 Hermitage Row
10 Grafton Ct
11 Lushington Terr

17

A1 1 Fortescue Ave
2 Pemberton Pl
3 Weston Wlk
4 Bayford St Ind Ctr
5 Bayford St
6 Sidworth St
7 Helmsley St

A2 1 Bohemia Pl
2 Graham Mans
3 Marvin St
4 Boscobel Ho
5 Royal Oak Rd
6 Colonnades The
7 Sylvester Ho
8 Sylvester Path
9 Doctor Spurstowe Almshouses
10 Great Eastern Bldgs
11 Sojourner-Truth Cl

A3 1 Birchington Ho
2 Bicknor Ho
3 Boxley Ho
4 Adisham Ho
5 Cranbrook Ho
6 Marden Ho
7 Broome Ho
8 Crandale Ho
9 Cheriton Ho
10 Ditton Ho
11 Langley Ho
12 Dymchurch Ho
13 Elham Ho
14 Bodney Mans
15 Pembury Ct
16 Downs Ct
17 Perrywood Ho
18 Stapelhurst Ho
19 Pegwell Ho
20 Yalding Ho
21 Northbourne Ho
22 Monkton Ho
23 Milsted Ho
24 Athlone Cl
25 Clarence Pl
26 Gould Terr
27 Quested Ct
28 Brett Pas
29 Marcon Ct

A4 1 Sutherland Point
2 Embley Point
3 Downs La
4 Gaviller Pl
5 Robert Owen Lo
6 Apprentice Way
7 Arrowe Ct
8 Gilwell Ct
9 Sutton Ct
10 Kinnoull Mans
11 Rowhill Mans
12 Sladen Pl
13 Mothers Sq The
14 Richborough Ho
15 Sandgate Ho

B1 1 Pitcairn Ho
2 Lyme Grove Ho
3 Shakespeare Ho
4 Upcott Ho
5 Loddiges Ho

6 Parkinson Ho
7 Sloane Ho
8 Vanbrugh Ho
9 Cambridge Pas
10 Lyttleton Ho
11 Victoria Park Ct
12 Tullis Ho
13 Fairchild Ho
14 Forsyth Ho
15 Tradescant Ho
16 Mason Ho
17 Capel Ho
18 Cordwainers Ct
19 Bridgeman Ho
20 St Thomas's Pas
21 Barclay Ho
22 Clayton Ho
23 Danby Ho
24 Sherard Ho
25 Catesby Ho
26 Petiver Cl
27 Leander Ct
28 Philip Turner Est
29 Grendon Ho
30 Shore Mews
31 Shore Bsns Ctr
32 Kendal Ho
33 Classic Mans
34 Tudor Ho
35 Park Ho

B2 1 Woolpack Ho
2 Elvin Ho
3 Thomas Ho
4 Hockley Ho
5 Retreat Ho
6 Butfield Ho
7 Brooksbank Ho
8 Cresset Ho
9 Brooksbank St
10 Lennox Ho
11 Milborne Ho
12 Collent Ho
13 Middlesex Pl
14 Devonshire Hall
15 Brent Ho

C1 1 Stuart Ho
2 Gascoyne Ho
3 Chelsfield Point
4 Sundridge Ho
5 Banbury Ho

C2 1 Musgrove Ho
2 Cheyney Ho
3 Haynes Ho
4 Warner Ho
5 Gilby Ho
6 Gadsden Ho
7 Risley Ho
8 Baycliffe Ho
9 Sheldon Ho
10 Offley Ho
11 Latimer Ho
12 Ribstone Ho
13 Salem Ho
14 Fieldwick Ho
15 Lever Ct
16 Matson Ho
17 Wilding Ho
18 Rennell Ho
19 Dycer Ho
20 Granard Ho
21 Whitelock Ho
22 Harrowgate Ho
23 Cass Ho

C4 1 Cromford Path
2 Longford Ct
3 Overbury Ho

23 A2   269

4 Heanor Ct
5 Wharfedale Ct
6 Ladybower Ct
7 Ilkeston Ct
8 Derby Ct
9 Rushmore Cres
10 Blackwell Cl

18

A2 1 Wick Mews
2 Wellday Ho
3 Selman Ho
4 Vaine Ho
5 Trower Ho

19

C4 1 Mulberry Ct
2 Rosewood Ct
3 Gean Ct
4 Blackthorn Ct
5 Cypress Ct

20

1 Fitzsimmons Ct
2 Bernard Shaw Ho
3 Longlents Ho
4 Mordaunt Ho
5 Wilmers Ct

22

C2 1 Westfield Ct
2 Tropical Ct
3 Chamberlayne Mans
4 Quadrant The
5 Queens Park Ct
6 Warfield Yd
7 Cherrytree Ho

23

A1 1 Sycamore Wlk
2 Westgate Bsns Ctr
3 Buspace Studios
4 Bosworth Ho
5 Golborne Gdns
6 Appleford Ho
7 Adair Twr
8 Gadsden Ho
9 Southam Ho
10 Norman Butler Ho
11 Thompson Ho
12 Wells Ho
13 Paul Ho
14 Olive Blythe Ho
15 Katherine Ho
16 Breakwell Ct
17 Pepler Ho
18 Edward Kennedy Ho

A2 1 Onslow Ho
2 Slomon Ho
3 Stansbury Ho
4 Tilleard Ho
5 Selby Ho
6 Tolhurst Ho
7 Severn Ho
8 Mundy Ho
9 Macfarren Ho
10 Mounsey Ho
11 Courtville Ho

12 Croft Ho
13 Batten Ho
14 Bantock Ho
15 Banister Ho
A3 1 Lancefield Ct
2 Verdi Ho
3 Wornum Ho
B2 1 Boyce Ho
2 Farnaby Ho
3 Danby Ho
4 Purday Ho
5 Naylor Ho
6 Novello Ho
7 Leeve Ho
8 Longhurst Ho
9 Harrington Ct
10 Mulberry Ct
11 Quilter Ho
12 Romer Ho
13 Kilburn Ho
B3 1 Claremont Ct
2 William Saville Ho
3 Western Ct
4 Bond Ho
5 Crone Ct
6 Wood Ho
7 Winterleys
8 Carlton Ho
9 Fiona Ct
C1 1 Westside Ct
2 Sutherland Ct
C2 1 Masefield Ho
2 Austen Ho
3 Fielding Ho
4 Park Bsns Ctr
5 John Ratcliffe Ho
6 Wymering Mans
C3 1 Wells Ct
2 Cambridge Ct
3 Durham Ct
C4 1 Ryde Ho
2 Glengall Pass
3 Leith Yd
4 Daynor Ho
5 Varley Ho
6 Sandby Ho
7 Colas Mews
8 Bishopsdale Ho
9 Lorton Ho
10 Marshwood Ho
11 Ribblesdale Ho
12 Holmesdale Ho
13 Kilburn Vale Est
14 Kilburn Bridge

24

A3 1 Bracer Ho
2 Scorton Ho
3 Fern Cl
4 Macbeth Ho
5 Oberon Ho
6 Buckland Ct
7 Crondall Ct
8 Osric Path
9 Caliban Twr
10 Celia Ho
11 Juliet Ho
12 Bacchus Wlk
13 Malcolm Ho
14 Homefield St
15 Crondall Ho
16 Blanca Ho

17 Miranda Ho
18 Falstaff Ho
19 Charmian Ho
20 Myrtle Wlk
21 Arden Ho
22 Sebastian Ho
23 Stanway Ct
24 Jerrold St
25 Rosalind Ho
26 Cordelia Ho
27 Monteagle Ct
28 John Parry Ct
29 James Anderson Ct
30 Ben Jonson Ct
A4 1 Sara Lane Ct
2 Portelet Ct
3 Trinity Ct
4 Rozel Ct
5 St Helier Ct
6 Corbiere Ho
7 Kenning Ho
8 Higgins Ho
9 Cavell Ho
10 Girling Ho
11 Fulcher Ho
12 Francis Ho
13 Norris Ho
14 Kempton Ho
15 Nesham Ho
16 Crossbow Ho
17 Catherine Ho
18 Strale Ho
19 Horner Hos
20 Stringer Hos
21 Whitmore Ho
22 Nightingale Ho
23 Fletcher Ho
24 Arrow Ho
25 Archer Ho
26 Meriden Ho
27 Rover Ho
28 Bowyer Ho
29 Longbow Ho
30 Tiller Ho
31 Canalside Studios
32 Bishopgate
33 Holburn
34 Fenchurch
B3 1 Queensbridge Ct
2 Godwin Ho
3 Kent Ct
4 Brunswick Ho
5 Weymouth Ct
6 Sovereign Mews
7 Dunloe Ct
8 Cremer Bsns Ctr
9 James Hammett Ho
10 Allgood St
11 Horatio St
12 Cadell Ho
13 Horatio Ho
14 Shipton Ho
B4 1 Hilborough Ct
2 Scriven Ct
3 Livermere Ct
4 Angrave Ct
5 Angrave Pas
6 Benfleet Ct
7 Belford Ho
8 Orme Ho
9 Clemson Ho
10 Longman Ho
11 Lowther Ho
12 Lovelace Ho
13 Harlowe Ho

14 Pamela Ho
15 Samuel Ho
16 Acton Ho
17 Loanda Cl
18 Phoenix Cl
19 Richardson Ct
20 Thrasher Cl
21 Mary Secole Cl
22 Canal Path
23 Pear Tree Ct
24 Hebden Ct
25 Charlton Ct
26 Laburnum Ct
27 Mansfield Ct
C3 1 London Terr
2 Sturdee Ho
3 Maude Ho
4 Haig Ho
5 Jellicoe Ho
6 Ropley St
7 Guinness Trust Bldgs
8 Ion Sq
9 Moye Cl
10 Morrel Ct
11 Courtauld Ho
12 Drummond Ho
13 Atkinson Ho
14 Gurney Ho
15 Halley Ho
16 Goldsmith's Sq
17 Ken Wilson Ho
18 Shahjalal Ho
19 Crofts Ho
20 April Ct
21 Sebright Ho
22 Beechwood Ho
23 Gillman Ho
24 Cheverell Ho
25 Besford Ho
26 Dinmont Ho
27 Wyndham Deedes Ho
28 Sheppard Ho
29 Mary James Ho
30 Hadrian Est
31 Blythendale Ho
32 George Vale Ho
33 Lion Mills
34 Pritchard Ho
C4 1 Broke Wlk
2 Rochemont Wlk
3 Marlborough Ave
4 Warburton Ho
5 Magnin Ct
6 Gloucester Sq
7 Woolstone Ho
8 Marsworth Ho
9 Cheddington Ho
10 Linslade Ho
11 Cosgrove Ho
12 Blisworth Ho
13 Eleanor Ct
14 Wistow Ho
15 Muscott Ho
16 Boxmoor Ho
17 Linford Ho
18 Pendley Ho
19 North Church Ho
20 Debdale Ho
21 Broadway Market Mews
22 Welshpool Ho
23 Ada Ho

25

A1 1 Rochester Ct
2 Weaver Ct
3 Greenheath Bsns Ctr
4 Glass St
5 Herald St
6 Northesk Ho
7 Codrington Ho
8 Heathpool Ct
9 Mocatta Ho
10 Harvey Ho
11 Blackwood Ho
12 Rutherford Ho
13 Bullen Ho
14 Fremantle Ho
15 Pellew Ho
16 Ashington Ho
17 Dinnington Ho
18 Bartholomew Sq
19 Steeple Ct
20 Orion Ho
21 Fellbrigg St
22 Eagle Ho
23 Sovereign Ho
24 Redmill Ho
25 Berry Ho
26 Grindall Ho
27 Collingwood Ho
A2 1 Charles Dickens Ho
2 Adrian Bolt Ho
3 William Rathbone Ho
4 Southwood Smith Ho
5 Rushmead
6 William Channing Ho
7 John Cartwright Ho
8 Charles Darwin Ho
9 Thomas Burt Ho
10 John Fielden Ho
11 Gwilym Maries Ho
12 Joseph Priestley Ho
13 Wear Pl
14 John Nettleford Ho
15 Thornaby Ho
16 Stockton Ho
17 Barnard Ho
18 Gainford Ho
19 Stapleton Ho
20 James Middleton Ho
21 Kedleston Wlk
22 Queen Margaret Flats
23 Hollybush Ho
24 Horwood Ho
25 Norden Ho
26 Newcourt Ho
27 Seabright St
28 Viaduct Pl
A3 1 Dinmont St
2 Marian St
3 Claredale Ho
4 Bradley Ho
5 Connett Ho
6 Winkley St
7 Temple Dwellings
8 Argos Ho
9 Helen Ho
10 Lysander Ho

11 Antenor Ho
12 Paris Ho
13 Nestor Ho
14 Hector Ho
15 Ajax Ho
16 Achilles Ho
17 Priam Ho
18 Peabody Est
19 Felix St
20 Cambridge Cres
21 Peterley Bsns Ctr
22 Beckwith Ho
23 Parminter Ind Est
24 Ted Roberts Ho
25 Cambridge Ct
26 West St
27 Millennium Pl
28 William Caslon Ho
29 Hugh Platt Ho
30 Mayfield Ho
31 Apollo Ho
A4 1 Welshpool St
2 Broadway Ho
3 Regents Wharf
4 London Wharf
5 Warburton Ho
6 Warburton St
7 Triangle Rd
8 Warburton Rd
9 Williams Ho
10 Booth Cl
11 Albert Cl
12 King Edward Mans
13 Victoria Bldgs
B1 1 William's Bldgs
2 Donegal Ho
3 Frederick Charrington Ho
4 Wickford Ho
5 Braintree Ho
6 Doveton Ho
7 Doveton St
8 Cephas Ho
9 Sceptre Ho
10 Bancroft Ho
11 Stothard St
12 Redclyf Ho
13 Winkworth Cotts
14 Ryder Ho
15 Hadleigh Ho
16 Hadleigh Cl
17 Amiel St
18 Stathard Ho
19 Barbanel Ho
20 Colebert Ho
21 Kenton Ho
22 Ibbott St
23 Stannard Cotts
24 Rennie Cotts
25 Rickman St
26 Rickman Ho
27 Pemell Cl
28 Pemell Ho
29 Leatherdale St
30 Gouldman Ho
31 Lamplighter Cl
32 Hamilton Lo
33 Cleveland Gr
34 Montgomery Lo
35 Bardsey Pl
36 Cromwell Lo
37 Colin Winter Ho
38 Hayfield Ho
B2 1 Mulberry Ho
2 Gretton Ho
3 Merceron Ho

B1
9 Mill Hill Terr
B1
1 Rectory Rd
2 Derwentwater Mans
3 Market Pl
4 Hooper's Mews
5 Cromwell Pl
6 Locarno Rd
7 Edgecote Cl
8 Harleyford Manor
B3
1 Avon Ct
2 Bromley Lo
3 Walter Ct
4 Lynton Terr
5 Acton Ho
6 Fells Haugh
7 Springfield Ct
8 Tamarind Ct
9 Lynton Ct
C3
1 Rosebank Gdns
2 Rosebank
3 Edinburgh Ho
4 Western Ct
5 Kilronan

30
A2
1 Abercrombie Ho
2 Bathurst Ho
3 Brisbane Ho
4 Bentinck Ho
5 Ellenborough Ho
6 Lawrence Ho
7 Mackenzie Ct
8 Carteret Ho
9 Calvert Ho
10 Winthrop Ho
11 Auckland Ho
12 Blaxland Ho
13 Havelock Cl
14 Hargraves Ho
15 Hudson Ct
16 Phipps Ho
17 Lawson Ho
18 Hastings Ho
19 Wolfe Ho
20 Malabar Ct
21 Commonwealth Ave
22 Charnock Ho
23 Canning Ho
24 Cornwallis Ho
25 Champlain Ho
26 Grey Ho
27 Durban Ho
28 Baird Ho
29 Campbell Ho
30 Mitchell Ho
31 Denham Ho
32 Mackay Ho
33 Evans Ho
34 Daws Ho
35 Mandela Cl
C1
1 Katherine's Wlk
2 Dorrit Ho
3 Pickwick Ho
4 Dombey Ho
5 Saunders Ho
6 Mortimer Ho
7 Nickleby Ho
8 Stebbing Ho
9 Boxmoor Ho
10 Poynter Ho

11 Swanscombe Ho
12 Darnley Terr
13 Norland Ho
14 Hume Ho
C2
1 Frinstead Ho
2 Hurstway Wlk
3 Testerton Wlk
4 Grenfell Wlk
5 Grenfell Tower
6 Barandon Wlk
7 Treadgold Ho
8 St Clements Ct
9 Willow Way
10 Florence Ho
11 Dora Ho
12 Carton Ho
13 Agnes Ho
14 Marley Ho
C3
1 Kelfield Ct
2 Downing Ho
3 Crosfield Ct
4 Robinson Ho
5 Scampston Mews
6 Girton Villas
7 Ray Ho
8 Walmer Ho
9 Goodrich Ct
10 Arthur Ct
11 Whitstable Ho
12 Kingsnorth Ho
13 Bridge Cl
14 Prospect Ho
15 Whitchurch Ho
16 Blechynden Ho
17 Wayneflete Sq
18 Bramley Ho

31
A3
1 Malton Mews
2 Lancaster Lo
3 Manning Ho
4 Galsworthy Ho
5 Hudson Ho
6 Cambourne Mews
7 Camelford Ct
8 Camelford Wlk
9 Talbot Grove Ho
10 Clarendon Wlk
11 Kingsdown Cl
A4
1 Murchison Ho
2 Macaulay Ho
3 Chesterton Ho
4 Chiltern Ho
5 Lionel Ho
6 Watts Ho
7 Wheatstone Ho
8 Telford Ho
9 Golborne Mews
10 Millwood St
11 St Columb's Ho
B3
1 Tavistock Mews
2 Silvester Ho
3 Clydesdale Ho
4 Colville Sq Mews
5 Denbigh Ho
B4
1 Blagrove Rd
2 Tavistock Ho
3 Leamington Ho
C3
1 Shottsford
2 Tolchurch
3 Casterbridge
4 Sandbourne
5 Anglebury

6 Weatherbury
7 Westbourne Gr Mews
8 Rosehart Mews
9 Viscount Ct
10 Hereford Mans
11 Hereford Mews
C4
1 Ascot Ho
2 Ashgrove Ct
3 Lockbridge Ct
4 Swallow Ct
5 Nightingale Lo
6 Hammond Lo
7 Penfield Lo
8 Harvey Lo
9 Hunter Lo
10 Barnard Lo
11 Falcon Lo
12 Johnson Lo
13 Livingstone Lo
14 Nuffield Lo
15 Finch Lo
16 Polesworth Ho
17 Oversley Ho
18 Derrycombe Ho
19 Buckshead Ho
20 Combe Ho
21 Culham Ho
22 Dainton Ho
23 Devonport Ho
24 Hanwell Ho
25 Truro Ho
26 Sunderland Ho
27 Stonehouse Ho
28 Riverford Ho
29 Portishead Ho
30 Mickleton Ho
31 Keyham Ho
32 Moulsford Ho
33 Shrewsbury Mews
34 St Stephen's Mews

32
A1
1 China Ct
2 Wellington Terr
3 Stevedore St
4 Portland Sq
5 Reardon Ho
6 Lowder Ho
7 Meeting House Alley
8 Farthing Fields
9 Oswell Ho
10 Park Lo
11 Doughty Ct
12 Inglefield Sq
13 Chopin's Ct
14 Welsh Ho
15 Hilliard Ho
16 Clegg St
17 Tasman Ho
18 Ross Ho
19 Wapping Dock St
20 Bridewell Pl
21 New Tower Bldgs
22 Tower Bldgs
23 Chimney Ct
24 Jackman Ho
25 Fenner Ho
26 Franklin Ho
27 Frobisher Ho
28 Flinders Ho
29 Chancellor Ho
30 Beechey Ho
31 Reardon Path

32 Parry Ho
33 Vancover Ho
34 Willoughby Ho
35 Sanctuary The
36 Dundee Ct
37 Pierhead Wharf
38 Scandrett St
A2
1 Newton Ho
2 Richard Neale Ho
3 Maddocks Ho
4 Cornwall St
5 Brockmer Ho
6 Dellow Ho
7 Bewley Ho
8 Artichoke Hill
A3
1 Jacob Mans
2 Wicker St
3 Langdale St
4 Walford Ho
5 Welstead Ho
6 Peter Best Ho
7 Barnett St
8 Kinder St
9 Richard St
10 Sarah Ho
11 Mellish Ho
12 Dickson Ho
13 Joscoyne Ho
14 Bridgen Ho
15 Wilton Ct
16 Silvester Ho
17 Greenwich Ct
18 Tylney Ho
19 Damien Ct
20 Siege Ho
21 Melwood Ho
22 Colstead Ho
23 Hungerford St
24 Burwell Cl
25 Chapman Ho
26 Tarling Ho
27 Sheridan St
28 Brinsley St
29 Dunch St
30 Luke Ho
31 Turnour Ho
32 Norton Ho
B1
1 John Rennie Wlk
2 Malay Ho
3 Wainwright Ho
4 Riverside Mans
5 Shackleton Ho
6 Whitehorn Ho
7 Wavel Ct
8 Prusom's Island
B2
1 Gosling Ho
2 Vogler Ho
3 Donovan Ho
4 Knowlden Ho
5 Chamberlain Ho
6 Moore Ho
7 Thornewill Ho
8 Fisher Ho
9 All Saints Ct
10 Coburg Dwellings
11 Lowood Ho
12 Solander Gdns
13 Chancery Bldgs
14 Ring Ho
15 Juniper St
16 Gordon Ho
17 West Block
18 North Block
19 South Block
B3
1 Woollon Ho

2 Dundalk Ho
3 Anne Goodman Ho
4 Newbold Cotts
5 Kerry Ho
6 Zion Ho
7 Longford Ho
8 Bromehead St
9 Athlone Ho
10 Jubilee Mans
11 Harriott Ho
12 Brayford Sq
13 Clearbrook Way
14 Rochelle Ct
15 Winterton Ho
16 Sheridan Ho
17 Brinsley Ho
18 Dean Ho
19 Foley Ho
20 Robert Sutton Ho
21 Montpelier Pl
22 Masters Lo
23 Steel's La
B4
1 Fulneck
2 Gracehill
3 Ockbrook
4 Fairfield
5 Dunstan Hos
6 Cressy Ct
7 Cressy Hos
8 Callahan Cotts
9 Wexford Ho
10 Sandhurst Ho
11 Colverson Ho
12 Beckett Ho
13 Jarman Ho
14 Wingrad Ho
15 Armsby Ho
16 Miranda Cl
17 Drake Ho
18 Louise De Marillac Ho
19 Sambrook Ho
20 St Vincent De Paul Ho
21 Jean Pardies Ho
22 Clichy Ho
23 Le Moal Ho
24 Odette Duval Ho
25 Dagobert Ho
26 Charles Auffray Ho
27 Boisseau Ho
28 Paymal Ho
29 Ewhurst Ho
C1
1 Clarence Mews
2 Raleigh Ct
3 Katherine Cl
4 Woolcombes Ct
5 Tudor Ct
6 Quayside Ct
7 Princes Riverside Rd
8 Surrey Ho
9 Tideway Ct
10 Edinburgh Ct
11 Falkirk Ct
12 Byelands Cl
13 Gwent Ct
14 Lavender Ho
15 Abbotshade Rd
16 Bellamy's Ct
17 Blenheim Ct
18 Sandringham Ct
19 Hampton Ct
20 Windsor Ct
21 Balmoral Ct
22 Westminster Ct

C2 1 Barnardo Gdns
2 Roslin Ho
3 Glamis Est
4 Peabody Est
5 East Block
6 Highway Trad Ctr The
7 Highway Bsns Pk The
8 Cranford Cotts
9 Ratcliffe Orch
10 Scotia Bldg
11 Mauretania Bldg
12 Compania Bldg
13 Sirius Bldg
14 Unicorn Bldg
C3 1 Pattison Ho
2 St Thomas Ho
3 Arbour Ho
4 Bladen Ho
5 Antill Terr
6 Billing Ho
7 Dowson Ho
8 Lipton Rd
9 Chalkwell Ho
10 Corringham Ho
11 Ogilvie Ho
12 Edward Mann Cl
13 Lighterman Mews
C4 1 Roland Mews
2 Morecambe Cl
3 Stepney Green Ct
4 Milrood Ho
5 Panama Ho
6 Galway Ho
7 Caspian Ho
8 Darien Ho
9 Rigo Ho
10 Flores Ho
11 Taranto Ho
12 Aden Ho
13 Frances Grey Ho
14 Master's St
15 Searle Ho
16 Diggon St

33
A2 1 St Georges Sq
2 Drake Ho
3 Osprey Ho
4 Fleet Ho
5 Gainsborough Ho
6 Victory Pl
7 Challenger Ho
8 Conrad Ho
9 Lock View Ct
10 Shoulder of Mutton Alley
11 Frederick Sq
12 Helena Sq
13 Elizabeth Sq
14 Sophia Sq
15 William Sq
A3 1 Coltman Ho
2 Repton Ho
3 Causton Cotts
4 Delmane Ho
5 Culpepper Ho
6 Shaw Ho
7 Williams Ho
8 Jerome Ho
9 Darnley Ho
10 Mercer's Cotts
11 Troon Ho
12 Ratcliffe Ho

13 Wakeling St
14 York Sq
15 Anglia Ho
16 Cambria Ho
17 Caledonia Ho
18 Ratcliffe La
19 Bekesbourne St
20 John Scurr Ho
21 Regents Canal Ho
A4 1 Waley St
2 Edith Ramsay Ho
3 Andaman Ho
4 Atlantic Ho
5 Pevensey Ho
6 Solent Ho
7 Lorne Ho
8 Cromarty Ho
9 Hearnshaw Ho
10 Hawksmoor Ho
11 Hemlington Ho
12 Greaves Cotts
13 Donaghue Cotts
14 Ames Cotts
15 Maroon Ho
16 Blount Ho
17 Wilkinson Ho
18 Aylward Ho
B2 1 Hamilton Ho
2 Imperial Ho
3 Oriana Ho
4 Queens Ct
5 Brightlingsea Pl
6 Faraday Ho
7 Ropemaker's Fields
8 Oast Ct
9 Mitre The
10 Bate St
11 Joseph Irwin Ho
12 Padstow Ho
13 Bethlehem Ho
14 Saunders Cl
15 Roche Ho
16 Stocks Pl
17 Trinidad Ho
18 Grenada Ho
B3 1 Dora Ho
2 Flansham Ho
3 Gatwick Ho
4 Ashpark Ho
5 Newdigate Ho
6 Midhurst Ho
7 Redbourne Ho
8 Southwater Cl
9 Aithan Ho
10 Britley Ho
11 Cheadle Ho
12 Elland Ho
13 Butler Ho
14 Fitzroy Ho
B4 1 Wearmouth Ho
2 Elmslie Point
3 Grindley Ho
4 Stileman Ho
5 Baythorne St
6 Wilcox Ho
7 Robeson St
8 Couzens Ho
9 Perley Ho
10 Whytlaw Ho
11 Printon Ho
12 Perkins Ho
13 Booker Cl
14 Tunley Gn
15 Callingham Cl

18 Tasker Ho
C2 1 West India Ho
2 Birchfield Ho
3 Elderfield Ho
4 Thornfield Ho
5 Gorsefield Ho
6 Arborfield Ho
7 Colborne Ho
8 East India Bldgs
9 Compass Point
10 Salter St
11 Kelly Ct
12 Flynn Ct
13 Mary Jones Ho
C3 1 Landin Ho
2 Charlesworth Ho
3 Gurdon Ho
4 Trendell Ho
5 Menteath Ho
6 Minchin Ho
7 Donne Ho
8 Dennison Ho
9 Anglesey Ho
10 Gough Wlk
11 Baring Ho
12 Hopkins Ho
13 Granville Ho
14 Gladstone Ho
15 Russell Ho
16 Pusey Ho
17 Overstone Ho
18 Stanley Ho
C4 1 Bredel Ho
2 Linton Ho
3 Matthews Ho
4 Woodcock Ho
5 Limborough Ho
6 Maydwell Ho
7 Underhill Ho
8 Meyrick Ho
9 Ambrose Ho
10 Carpenter Ho
11 Robinson Ho
12 Bramble Ho
13 Bilberry Ho
14 Bracken Ho
15 Berberis Ho
16 Busbridge Ho

34
A2 1 Westcott Ho
2 Corry Ho
3 Malam Gdns
4 Devitt Ho
5 Leyland Ho
6 Wigram Ho
7 Willis Ho
8 Balsam Ho
9 Finch's Ct
10 Poplar Bath St
11 Lawless St
12 Storey Ho
13 Abbot Ho
14 Landon Wlk
15 Goodhope Ho
16 Goodfaith Ho
17 Winant Ho
18 Lubbock Ho
19 Goodwill Ho
20 Martindale Ho
21 Norwood Ho
22 Constant Ho
A3 1 Colebrook Ho
2 Essex Ho

3 Salisbury Ho
4 Maidstone Ho
5 Osterley Ho
6 Norwich Ho
7 Clarissa Ho
8 Elgin Ho
9 Shaftesbury Lo
10 Shepherd Ho
11 Jeremiah St
12 Elizabeth Cl
13 Chilcot Cl
14 Fitzgerald Ho
15 Vesey Path
16 Ennis Ho
17 Kilmore Ho
A4 1 Sumner Ho
2 Irvine Ho
3 David Ho
4 Brushwood Ho
5 Limehouse Cut
6 Colmans Wharf
7 Foundary Ho
8 Radford Ho
B2 1 Discovery Ho
2 Mountague Pl
3 Virginia Ho
4 Collins Ho
5 Lawless Ho
6 Carmichael Ho
7 Commodore Ho
8 Mermaid Ho
9 Bullivant St
10 Anderson Ho
11 Mackrow Wlk
12 Robin Hood Gdns
B3 1 Langdon Ho
2 Balfron Twr
3 Tabard Ct
4 Delta Bldg
5 Kilbrennan Ho
6 Thistle Ho
7 Heather Ho
8 Tartan Ho
9 Trident Ho
C3 1 Lansbury Gdns
2 Thesus Ho
3 Adams Ho
4 Jones Ho
5 Sam March Ho
6 Arapiles Ho
7 Athenia Ho
8 Jervis Bay Ho
9 Helen Mackay Ho
10 Gaze Ho
11 Ritchie Ho
12 Circle Ho
13 Dunkeld Ho
14 Braithwaite Ho
15 Rosemary Dr
16 Sorrel La
17 East India Dock Road Tunnel

35
B1 1 Newton Point
2 Sparke Terr
3 Montesquieu Terr
4 Crawford Point
5 Rathbone Ho
6 George St
7 Emily St
8 Fendt Cl
B2 1 Radley Terr
2 Rathbone Mkt
3 Thomas North Terr

37 B1 273

4 Bernard Cassidy St
5 Mary St
6 Hughes Terr
7 Swanscombe Point
8 Rawlinson Point
9 Kennedy Cox Ho
10 Cooper St
C1 1 Capulet Mews
2 Pepys Cres
3 De Quincey Mews
4 Hardy Ave
5 Tom Jenkinson Rd
6 Hanamel St
7 Kennacraig Cl
8 Charles Flemmell Mews
9 Gatcombe Rd
10 Badminton Mews
11 Holyrood Mews
12 Britannia Gate
13 Dalemain Mews
C2 1 Clements Ave
2 Martindale Ave
C4 1 Odeon Ct
2 Edward Ct
3 Newhaven Ct
4 Ravenscroft Cl
5 Douglas Rd
6 Ferrier Point
7 Harvey Point
8 Wood Point
9 Trinity St
10 Pattinson Point
11 Clinch Ct
12 Mint Bsns Pk

36
A1 1 Burford Ho
2 Hope Ct
3 Centaur Ct
4 Phoenix Ct
C1 1 Surrey Cres
2 Forbes Ho
3 Haining Cl
4 Melville Ct
5 London Stile
6 Stile Hall Par
7 Priory Lo
8 Kew Bridge Ct
9 Meadowcroft
10 St James Ct

37
A1 1 Churchdale Ct
2 Cromwell Cl
3 Cambridge Rd S
4 Oxbridge Ct
5 Tomlinson Cl
6 Gunnersbury Mews
7 Grange The
8 Gunnersbury Cl
A4 1 Cheltenham Pl
2 Beaumaris Twr
3 Arundel Ho
4 Pevensey Ct
5 Jerome Twr
6 Anstey Ct
7 Bennett Ct
8 Gunnersbury Ct
B1 1 Arlington Park Mans
2 Sandown Ho

37 B2

3 Goodwood Ho
4 Windsor Ho
5 Lingfield Ho
6 Ascot Ho
7 Watchfield Ct
8 Belgrave Ct
9 Beverley Ct
10 Beaumont Ct
11 Harvard Rd
B2 1 Church Green Ho
2 Bell Ind Est
3 Fairlawn Ct
4 Dukes Gate
5 Dewsbury Ct
6 Chiswick Terr
B3 1 Blackmore Twr
2 Bollo Ct
3 Kipling Twr
4 Lawrence Ct
5 Maugham Ct
6 Reade Ct
7 Woolf Ct
8 Shaw Ct
9 Verne Ct
10 Wodehouse Ct
11 Greenock Rd
12 Garden Ct
13 Barons Gate
14 Cleveland Rd
15 Chapter Cl
16 Beauchamp Cl
17 Holmes Ct
B4 1 Belgrave Cl
2 Buckland Wlk
3 Frampton Ct
4 Telfer Cl
5 Harlech Twr
6 Corfe Twr
7 Barwick Ho
8 Charles Hocking Ho
9 Sunninghill Ct
10 Salisbury St
C1 1 Chatsworth Lo
2 Prospect Pl
3 Townhall Ave
4 Devonhurst Pl
5 Heathfield Ct
6 Horticultural Pl
7 Merlin Ho
8 Garth Rd

38

A1 1 Glebe Cl
2 Devonshire Mews
3 Binns Terr
4 Ingress St
5 Swanscombe Rd
6 Brackley Terr
7 Stephen Fox Ho
8 Manor Gdns
9 Coram Ho
10 Flaxman Ho
11 Thorneycroft Ho
12 Thornhill Ho
13 Kent Ho
14 Oldfield Ho
A2 1 Chestnut Ho
2 Bedford Ho
3 Bedford Cnr
4 Sydney Ho
5 Bedford Park Cnr
6 Priory Gdns
7 Windmill Alley
8 Castle Pl
9 Jonathan Ct
10 Windmill Pas
11 Chardin Rd
12 Gable Ho
A3 1 Fleet Ct
2 Ember Ct
3 Emlyn Gdns
4 Clone Ct
5 Brent Ct
6 Abbey Ct
7 Ormsby Lo
8 St Catherine's Ct
A4 1 Longford Ct
2 Mole Ct
3 Lea Ct
4 Wandle Ct
5 Beverley Ct
6 Roding Ct
7 Crane Ct
B1 1 Miller's Ct
2 British Grove Pas
3 British Grove S
4 Berestede Rd
5 North Eyot Gdns
B2 1 Flanders Mans
2 Stamford Brook Mans
3 Linkenholt Mans
4 Prebend Mans
5 Middlesex Ct
B3 1 Stamford Brook Gdns
2 Hauteville Court Gdns
3 Ranelagh Gdns
C2 1 Hamlet Ct
2 Derwent Ct
3 Westcroft Ct
4 Black Lion Mews
5 St Peter's Villas
6 Standish Ho
7 Chambon Pl
8 Court Mans
C4 1 Becklow Gdns
2 Victoria Ho
3 Lycett Pl
4 Kylemore Ct
5 Alexandra Ct
6 Lytten Ct
7 Becklow Mews
8 Northcroft Ct
9 Bailey Ct
10 Spring Cott
11 Landor Wlk
12 Laurence Mews
13 Hadyn Park Ct
14 Askew Mans

39

A2 1 Albion Gdns
2 Flora Gdns
3 Lamington St
4 Felgate Mews
5 Galena Ho
6 Albion Mews
7 Albion Ct
8 King Street Cloisters
9 Dimes Pl
10 Clarence Ct
11 Hampshire Hog La
12 Marryat Ct
A4 1 Westbush Ct
2 Goldhawk Mews
3 Sycamore Ho
4 Shackleton Ct
5 Drake Ct
6 Scotts Ct
B1 1 Bridge Avenue Mans
2 Bridgeview
3 College Ct
4 Beatrice Ho
5 Amelia Ho
6 Edith Ho
7 Joanna Ho
8 Mary Ho
9 Adela Ho
10 Sophia Ho
11 Henrietta Ho
12 Charlotte Ho
13 Alexandra Ho
14 Bath Pl
15 Elizabeth Ho
16 Margaret Ho
17 Peabody Est
18 Eleanor Ho
19 Isabella Ho
20 Caroline Ho
21 Chancellors Wharf
B2 1 Phoenix Lodge Mans
2 Samuel's Cl
3 Broadway Arc
4 Brook Ho
5 Hammersmith Broadway
B4 1 Verulam Ho
2 Grove Mans
3 Frobisher Ct
4 Library Mans
5 Pennard Mans
6 Lanark Mans
7 Kerrington Ct
8 Granville Mans
9 Romney Ct
10 Rayner Ct
11 Sulgrave Gdns
12 Bamborough Gdns
C3 1 Grosvenor Residences
2 Blythe Mews
3 Burnand Ho
4 Bradford Ho
5 Springvale Terr
6 Ceylon Rd
7 Walpole Ct
8 Bronte Ct
9 Boswell Ct
10 Souldern Rd
11 Brook Green Flats
12 Haarlem Rd
13 Stafford Mans
14 Lionel Mans
C4 1 Vanderbilt Villas
2 Bodington Ct
3 Kingham Cl
4 Clearwater Terr
5 Lorne Gdns
6 Cameret Ct
7 Bush Ct
8 Shepherds Ct
9 Rockley Ct
10 Grampians The
11 Charcroft Ct
12 Addison Park Mans
13 Sinclair Mans

40

A1 1 Hockney Ct
2 Toulouse Ct
3 Lowry Ct
4 Barry Ho
5 Lewis Ct
6 Gainsborough Ct
7 Renoir Ct
8 Blake Ct
9 Raphael Ct
10 Rembrandt Ct
11 Constable Ct
12 Da Vinci Ct
13 Gaugin Ct
14 Michelangelo Ct
15 Monet Ct
16 Weald Cl
17 Jasmin Lo
18 Birchmere Lo
19 Weybridge Ct
20 Florence Ho
21 Gleneagles Cl
22 Sunningdale Cl
23 Muirfield Cl
24 Turnberry Cl
25 St Andrews Cl
26 Kingsdown Cl
27 St Davids Cl
28 Galway Cl
29 Edenbridge Cl
30 Birkdale Cl
31 Tralee Ct
32 Woburn Ct
33 Belfry Cl
34 Troon Cl
35 Holywell Cl
A2 1 Market Pl
2 Trappes Ho
3 Thurland Ho
4 Ramsfort Ho
5 Hambley Ho
6 Holford Ho
7 Pope Ho
8 Southwell Ho
9 Mortain Ho
10 Radcliffe Ho
11 Southwark Park Est
12 Galleywall Road Trad Est
13 Trevithick Ho
14 Barlow Ho
15 Donkin Ho
16 Landmann Ho
17 Fitzmaurice Ho
18 Dodd Ho
A3 1 Perryn Rd
2 Chalfont Ho
3 Prestwood Ho
4 Farmer Ho
5 Gataker Ho
6 Gataker St
7 Cornick Ho
8 Glebe Ho
9 Matson Ho
10 Hickling Ho
A4 1 Butterfield Cl
2 Janeway Pl
3 Trotwood Ho
4 Cranbourn Ho
5 Cherry Garden Ho
6 Burton Ho
7 Morriss Ho
8 King Edward The Third Mews
9 Cathay St
10 Rotherhithe St
B2 1 Damory Ho
2 Antony Ho
3 Roderick Ho
4 Pedworth Gdns
5 Beamish Ho
6 Gillam Ho
7 George Walter Ho
8 Richard Ho
9 Adron Ho
10 Westlake
11 McIntosh Ho
B3 1 Blick Ho
2 Neptune Ho
3 Scotia Ct
4 Murdoch Ho
5 Edmonton Ct
6 Niagara Ct
7 Columbia Point
8 Ritchie Ho
9 Wells Ho
10 Helen Peele Cotts
11 Orchard Ho
12 Dock Offices
13 Landale Ho
14 Courthope Ho
B4 1 Mayflower St
2 St Mary's Est
3 Rupack St
4 Frank Whymark Ho
5 Adams Gardens Est
6 Hatteraick St
7 Hythe Ho
8 Seaford Ho
9 Sandwich Ho
10 Rye Ho
11 Winchelsea Ho
12 Kenning St
13 Western Pl
14 Ainsty St
15 Pine Ho
16 Beech Ho
17 Larch Ho
18 Seth St
19 Turner Ct
20 Risdon Ho
21 Risdon St
22 Aylton Est
23 Manitoba Ct
24 Calgary Ct
25 Irwell Est
26 City Bsns Ctr
C2 1 John Kennedy Ho
2 Brydale Ho
3 Balman Ho
4 Tissington Ct
5 Harbord Ho
6 Westfield Ho
7 Albert Starr Ho
8 John Brent Ho
9 William Evans Ho
10 Raven Ho
11 Egret Ho
12 Fulmar Ho
13 Dunlin Ho
14 Siskin Ho
15 Sheldrake Ho
16 Buchanan Ct
17 Burrage Ct
18 Biddenham Ho
19 Ayston Ho
20 Empingham Ho
21 Deanshanger Ho
22 Codicote Ho
C4 1 Schooner Cl

2 Milton Ho
3 Pope Ho
4 Chester Ct
5 Marvel Ho
6 Flecker Ho
7 Landor Ho
8 Evelina Mans
9 Habington Ho
10 Langland Ho
11 Drinkwater Ho
12 Procter Ho
13 Shirley Ho
14 Drayton Ho
15 Bridges Ho
16 Cunningham Ho
17 Hood Ho
18 Herrick Ho
19 Dekker Ho
20 Sansom St
21 Housman Way
22 Coleby Path
C4 1 Queens Ho
2 Arnside Ho
3 Horsley St
4 St Peter's Ho
5 St Johns Ho
6 St Marks Ho
7 St Stephens Ho
8 St Matthew's Ho
9 Red Lion Ct
10 Boyson Rd
11 Bradenham

49

A1 1 Springfield Ho
2 Craston Ho
3 Walters Ho
4 Edgecombe Ho
5 Fowler Ho
6 Rignold Ho
7 Chatham Ho
A2 1 Barnwell Ho
2 Brunswick Villas
3 St Giles Twr
4 Bentley Ho
5 Dawson Ho
6 Dryden Ho
7 Mayward Ho
8 Longleigh Ho
9 Fairwall Ho
10 Bodeney Ho
11 Sandby Ho
12 Vestry Mews
13 Netley
14 Lakanal
15 Racine
A3 1 Kemble Ct
2 Dursley Ct
3 Dymock Ct
4 St Briavel's Ct
5 Tutshill Ct
6 Lasborough Ct
7 Almondsbury Ct
8 Granville Sq
9 Alderholt Way
10 Farnborough Way
11 Blendworth Way
12 Clanfield Way
13 Hordle Promenade W
14 Copnor Way

16 Samuel Jones Ind Est
17 Dibden Ho
18 Marchwood Cl
19 Pilgrims Cloisters
20 Beacon Ho
21 Teather St
22 Stacy Path
22 Rumball Ho
23 Ballow Cl
24 Rill Ho
A4 1 Elkstone Ct
2 Northleach Ct
3 Nailsworth Ct
4 Patchway Ct
5 Warmley Ct
6 Winchcombe Ct
7 Andoversford Ct
8 Downend Ct
B2 1 Colbert
2 Voltaire
3 Finch Mews
4 Charles Coveney Way
5 Crane St
6 Curlew Ho
7 Mallard Ho
8 Tern Ho
9 Crane Ho
10 Falcon Ho
11 Bryanston Ho
12 Basing Ct
13 Marcus Ho
14 Sheffield Ho
B3 1 Painswick Ct
2 Sharpness Ct
3 Hordle Promenade N
4 Mattingly Way
5 Gosport Way
6 Quarley Way
7 Hordle Promenade S
8 Havant Way
9 Shannon Ct
10 Thames Ct
11 Amstel Ct
12 Danube Ct
13 Tilbury Ct
14 Hordle Promenade E
15 Indus Ct
16 Oakcourt
17 Palm Ct
18 Rowan Ct
19 Blackthorn Ct
20 Pear Ct
B4 1 Willsbridge Ct
2 Cam Ct
3 Quedgeley Ct
4 Saul Ct
5 Quenington Ct
6 Westonbirt Ct
7 Wickway Ct
C1 1 William Margrie Cl
2 Choumert Sq
3 Parkstone Rd
4 Atwell Rd
C2 1 Lagan Ho
2 Angelina Ho
3 Jarvis Ho
4 Richland Ho
5 Heywood Ho
6 Wakefield Ho
7 Primrose Ho

8 Hardcastle Ho
9 Dunstall Ho
10 Purdon Ho
11 Flamborough Ho
12 Lambrook Ho
13 Witcombe Point
14 Yarnfield Sq
15 Winford Ct
16 Portbury Cl
17 Robert Keen Cl
C3 1 Thornbill Ho
2 Vervain Ho
3 Woodstar Ho
4 Tamarind Ho
5 Hereford Retreat
6 Haymerle Ho
7 Furley Ho
8 Applegarth Ho
9 Freda Corbett Cl
10 Rudbeck Ho
11 Henslow Ho
12 Lindley Ho
13 Collinson Ho
14 Sister Mabel's Way
15 Timberland Ct
16 Hastings Ct
17 Neville Cl
18 Sidmouth Ho
19 Budleigh Ho
20 Stanesgate Ho
21 Braemore Ho
22 Ely Ho
C4 1 Bowles Rd
2 Western Wharf
3 Northfield Ho
4 Millbrook Ho
5 Denstone Ho
6 Deerhurst Ho
7 Caversham Ho
8 Battle Ho
9 Cardiff Ho
10 Bridgnorth Ho
11 Exeter Ho
12 Grantham Ho
13 Aylesbury Ho
14 Royston Ho

50

A1 1 Walkynscroft
2 Ryegates
3 Hathorne Cl
4 Pilkington Rd
5 Russell Ct
6 Heaton Ho
7 Magdalene Cl
A2 1 Willowdene
2 Pinedene
3 Oakdene
4 Beechdene
5 Hollydene
6 Wood Dene
7 Staveley Cl
8 Carnicot Ho
9 Martock Ct
A3 1 Tortington Ho
2 Credenhill Ho
3 Bromyard Ho
4 Hoyland Ct
5 Willowdene
6 Ashdene
7 Acorn Par
8 Carlton Gr
9 Springall St
10 Harry Lambourn Ho

B1 1 Honiton Gdns
2 Selden Ho
3 Hathway Ho
4 Hathway St
5 Station Ct
B3 1 Ambleside Point
2 Grasmere Point
3 Windermere Point
4 Roman Way
5 Laburnham Ct
6 Romney Ct
7 Hammersley Ho
8 Hutchinson Ho
9 Hammond Ho
10 Fir Tree Ho
11 Glastonbury Ct
12 Highbridge Ct
13 Filton Ct
14 Chiltern Ct
15 Cheviot Ct
B4 1 Penshurst Ho
2 Reculver Ho
3 Mereworth Ho
4 Camber Ho
5 Chilam Ho
6 Otford Ho
7 Olive Tree Ho
8 Aspen Ho
9 Lewis Silkin Ho
10 Richborough Ho
11 Dover Ho
12 Eynsford Ho
13 Horton Ho
14 Lamberhurst Ho
15 Canterbury Ind Pk
16 Upnall Ho
17 Sissinghurst Ho
18 Rochester Ho
19 Leybourne Ho
20 Lullingstone Ho
C3 1 Richard Anderson Ct
2 Palm Tree Ho
3 Edward Robinson Ho
4 Antony Ho
5 Gerrard Ho
6 Palmer Ho
7 Pankhurst Cl
C4 1 Harrisons Ct
2 Grantley Ho
3 Sunbury Ct
4 Tilbury Ho
5 Graham Ct
6 Connell Ct
7 St Clements Ct
8 Henderson Ct
9 Jemotts Ct
10 Verona Ct
11 Heywood Ho
12 Francis Ct
13 Hind Ho
14 Donne Ho
15 Carew Ct
16 Burbage Ho
17 Newland Ho
18 Dobson Ho
19 Dalton Ho
20 Greene Ct
21 Redrup Ho
22 Tarplett Ho
23 Stunnell Ho
24 Gasson Ho
25 Bryce Ho
26 Barnes Ho
27 Barkwith Ho

28 Bannister Ho
29 Apollo Ind Bsns Ctr

51

A3 1 Batavia Ho
2 Marlowe Bsns Ctr
3 Batavia Mews
4 Woodrush Cl
5 Alexandra St
6 Orpheus Twr
7 Vansittart St
8 Granville Ct
9 Cottesbrook St
A4 1 Portland Ct
2 Phoenix Ct
3 Rainbow Ct
4 Hawke Twr
5 Snipe Ct
B3 1 Austin Ho
2 Exeter Way
3 Crossleigh Ct
4 Mornington Pl
5 Maple Ho
B4 1 Chester Ho
2 Lynch Wlk
3 Arlington Ho
4 Woodcote Ho
5 Cornbury Ho
6 Prospect Pl
7 Akintaro Ho
8 Mulberry Ho
9 Laurel Ho
10 Linden Ho
11 Ashford Ho
12 Wardalls Ho
13 Magnolia Ho
14 Howard Ho
15 Larch Cl
16 Ibis Ct
17 Merganser Ct
18 Wotton Rd
19 Kingfisher Sq
20 Sanderling Ct
21 Dolphin Twr
22 Mermaid Twr
23 Scoter Ct
24 Shearwater Ct
25 Brambling Ct
26 Kittiwake Ct
27 Kestrel Ct
28 Guillemot Ct
29 Marine Twr
30 Teal Ct
31 Lapwing Twr
32 Turnstone Ct
33 Goosander Ct
34 Cormorant Ct
35 Moorhen Ct
36 Shelduck Ct
37 Plover Ct
38 Grebe Ct
39 Elder Ct
40 Pintail Ct
41 Tristan Ct
42 Skua Ct
C2 1 Admiralty Cl
2 Harton Lo
3 Sylvia Cotts
4 Pitman Ho
5 Heston Ho
C3 1 Sandpiper Ct
2 Flamingo Ct
3 Titan Bsns Est
4 Rochdale Way
5 Speedwell St

6 Reginald Pl
7 Fletcher Path
8 Frankham Ho
9 Cremer Ho
10 Wilshaw Ho
11 Castell Ho
12 Holden Ho
13 Browne Ho
C4 1 Dryfield Wlk
2 Blake Ho
3 Hawkins Ho
4 Grenville Ho
5 Langford Ho
6 Mandarin Ct
7 Peregrine Ct
8 Bittern Ct
9 Lamerton St
10 Armada St
11 Armada Ct
12 Benbow Ho
13 Oxenham Ho
14 Caravel Mews
15 Hughes Ho

52
A3 1 Finch Ho
2 Jubilee The
3 Gordon Ho
4 Haddington Ct
5 Maitland Ct
6 Ashburnham Retreat
B1 1 Ellison Ho
2 Pitmaston Ho
3 Windmill Ct
4 Hertmitage The
5 Burnett Ho
6 Lacey Ho
B2 1 Penn Almshouse
2 Jarvis Ct
3 Woodville Ct
4 Darnell Ho
5 Renbold Ho
6 Lindsell St
7 Plumbridge St
8 Trinity Gr
9 Hollymount Cl
10 Cade Tyler Ho
11 Robertson Ho
B3 1 Temair Ho
2 Glaisher St
3 Prince of Orange La
4 Lombard Ho
5 St Marks Cl
6 Ada Kennedy Ct
7 Arlington Pl
8 Topham Ho
9 Darnell Ho
10 Hawks Mews
11 Royal Pl
12 Swanne Ho
13 Maribor
14 Serica Ct
B4 1 Greenwich Mkt
2 Turnpin La
3 Durnford St
4 Sexton's Ho
5 Bardsley Ho
6 Wardell Ho
7 Clavell St
8 Stanton Ho
9 Macey Ho
10 Boreman Ho
C4 1 Frobisher Sq

2 Hardy Cotts
3 Palliser Ho
4 Bernard Angell Ho
5 Corvette Sq
6 Travers Ho
7 Reade Ho
8 Maze Hill Ho

53
B3 1 Westcombe Ct
2 Kleffens Ct
3 Ferndale Ct
4 Combe Mews
5 Mandeville Cl
6 Heathway
7 Pinelands Cl
C3 1 Mary Lawrenson Pl
2 Bradbury Ct
3 Dunstable Ct
C4 1 Nethercombe Ho
2 Holywell Cl

54
A1 1 Lancaster Cotts
2 Lancaster Mews
3 Bromwich Ho
4 Priors Lo
5 Richmond Hill Ct
6 Glenmore Ho
7 Hillbrow
8 Heathshot
9 Friars Stile Pl
10 Spire Ct
11 Ridgeway
12 Matthias Ct
A2 1 Lichfield Terr
2 Union Ct
3 Carrington Lo
4 Wilton Ct
5 Egerton Ct
6 Beverley Lo
7 Bishop Duppa's Almshouses
8 Regency Wlk
9 Clearwater Ho
10 Onslow Avenue Mans
11 Michels Almshouses
A3 1 St John's Gr
2 Michel's Row
3 Michelsdale Dr
4 Blue Anchor Alley
5 Clarence St
6 Sun Alley
7 Richmond Adult Coll
8 Thames Link Ho
B1 1 Chester Cl
2 Grosvenor Ct
3 Queen's Ct
4 Russell Wlk
5 Charlotte Sq
6 Jones Wlk
7 Hildrich Ho
8 Isabella Ct
9 Hobart Pl
10 Damer Ho
11 Eliot Ho
12 Fitzherbert Ho
13 Reynolds Pl
14 Chisholm Rd
B2 1 Alberta Ct
2 Beatrice Rd
3 Lorne Rd

4 York Rd
5 Connaught Rd
6 Albany Terr
7 Kingswood Ct
8 Selwyn Ct
B3 1 Towers The
2 Longs Ct
3 Sovereign Ct
4 Robinson Ct
5 Calvert Ct
6 Bedford Ct
7 Hickey's Almshouses
8 Church Almshouses

55
A3 1 Hershell Ct
2 Deanhill Ct
3 Park Sheen
4 Furness Lo
5 Merricks Ct
C4 1 Rann House
2 Craven Ho
3 John Dee Ho
4 Kindell Ho
5 Montgomery Ho
6 Avondale Ho
7 Addington Ct
8 Dovecote Gdns
9 Firmston Ho
10 Glendower Gdns
11 Chestnut Ave
12 Trehern Rd
13 Rock Ave

56
B1 1 Allenford Ho
2 Swaythling Ho
3 Tatchbury Ho
4 Penwood Ho
5 Bramley Ho
6 Shalden Ho
7 Dunbridge Ho
8 Denmead Ho
9 Charcot Ho
10 Portswood Ho
11 Brockbridge Ho
12 Hurstbourne Ho
C2 1 Theodore Ho
2 Nicholas Ho
3 Bonner Ho
4 Downing Ho
5 Johsen Ho
6 Fairfax Ho
7 Devereux Ho
8 David Ho
9 Leigh Ho
10 Clipstone Ho
11 Mallet Ho
12 Arton Wilson Ho

57
B2 1 Inglis Ho
2 Ducie Ho
3 Warncliffe Ho
4 Stanhope Ho
5 Waldegrave Ho
6 Mildmay Ho
7 Mullens Ho
C1 1 Balmoral Ho
2 Glenalmond Ho
3 Selwyn Ho

4 Keble Ho
5 Bede Ho
6 Gonville Ho
7 Magdalene Ho
8 Armstrong Ho
9 Newnham Ho
10 Somerville Ho
11 Balliol Ho
12 Windermere
13 Little Combe Cl
14 Classinghall Ho
15 Chalford Ct
16 Garden Royal
17 South Ct
18 Anne Kerr Ct
19 Ewhurst
C2 1 Geneva Ct
2 Laurel Ct
3 Cambalt Ho
4 Langham Ct
5 Lower Pk
6 King's Keep
7 Whitnell Ct
8 Whitehead Ho
9 Halford Ho
10 Humphry Ho
11 Jellicoe Ho
C3 1 Olivette St
2 Mascotte Rd
3 Glegg Pl
4 Crown Ct
5 Charlwood Terr

58
A2 1 Claremont
2 Downside
3 Cavendish Cl
4 Ashcombe Ct
5 Carltons The
6 Draldo Ho
7 Millbrooke Ct
8 Coysh Ct
9 Keswick Hts
10 Lincoln Ho
11 Avon Ct
B2 1 Burlington Mews
2 Cumbria Ho
3 St Stephen's Gdns
4 Atlantic Ho
5 Burton Lo
6 Manfred Ct
7 Meadow Bank
8 Hooper Ho
C2 1 Pembridge Pl
2 Adelaide Rd
3 London Ct
4 Windsor Ct
5 Westminster Ct
6 Fullers Ho
7 Bridge Pk
8 Lambeth Ct
9 Milton Ct
10 Norfolk Mans
11 Francis Snary Lo
12 Bush Cotts
13 Downbury Mews
14 Newton's Yd

59
A2 1 Fairfield Ct
2 Blackmore Ho
3 Lancaster Mews
4 Cricketers Mews
B4 1 Molasses Ho
2 Molasses Row

3 Cinnamon Row
4 Calico Ho
5 Calico Row
6 Port Ho
7 Square Rigger Row
8 Trade Twr
9 Ivory Ho
10 Spice Ct
11 Sherwood Ct
12 Mendip Ct
13 Chalmers Ho
C3 1 Burke Ho
2 Fox Ho
3 Buxton Ho
4 Pitt Ho
5 Romsey Ho
6 Beverley Ho
7 Florence Ho
8 Linden Ct
9 Dorcas Ct
10 Johnson Ct
11 Agnes Ct
12 Hilltop Ct
13 Courtyard The
14 Old Laundry The
15 Oberstein Rd
16 Fineran Ct
17 Sangora Rd
18 Harvard Mans
C4 1 Benham Cl
2 Milner Ho
3 McManus Ho
4 Wilberforce Ho
5 Wheeler Ct
6 Sporle Ct
7 Holliday Sq
8 John Parker Sq
9 Carmichael Ct
10 Fenner Sq
11 Clark Lawrence Ct
12 Shaw Ct
13 Sendall Ct
14 Livingstone Rd
15 Farrant Ho
16 Jackson Ho
17 Darien Ho
18 Sheppard Ho
19 Ganley Ct
20 Arthur Newton Ho
21 Chesterton Ho
22 John Kirk Ho
23 Mantua St
24 Heaver Rd

60
A4 1 Kiloh Ct
2 Lanner Ho
3 Grifton Ho
4 Kestrel Ho
5 Kite Ho
6 Peregrine Ho
7 Hawk Ho
8 Inkster Ho
9 Harrier Ho
10 Eagle Hts
11 Kingfisher Ct
12 Lavender Terr
13 Temple Ho
14 Ridley Ho
15 Eden Ho
16 Hertford Ct
17 Nepaul Rd

278 60 C1

C1
1 Rayne Ho
2 St Anthony's Ct
3 Earlsthorpe Mews
C4 1 Shaftesbury Park Chambers
2 Selborne
3 Rush Hill Mews
4 Marmion Mews
5 Crosland Pl
6 Craven Mews
7 Wycliffe Rd
8 Basnett Rd
9 Wickersley Rd
10 Tyneham Cl

61

A4 1 Turnchapel Mews
2 Redwood Mews
3 Phil Brown Pl
4 Bev Callender Cl
5 Keith Connor Cl
6 Tessa Sanderson Pl
7 Daley Thompson Way
8 Rashleigh Ct
B1 1 Joseph Powell Cl
2 Cavendish Mans
3 Westlands Terr
4 Cubitt Ho
5 Hawkesworth Ho
6 Normanton Ho
7 Eastman Ho
8 Couchman Ho
9 Poynders Ct
10 Selby Ho
11 Valentine Ho
12 Gorham Ho
13 Deauville Mans
14 Deauville Ct
B2 1 Timothy Cl
2 Shaftesbury Mews
3 Brook Ho
4 Grover Ho
5 Westbrook Ho
6 Hewer Ho
7 Batten Ho
8 Mandeville Ho
9 George Beare Lo
B3 1 Polygon Ct
2 Windsor Ct
3 Trinity Cl
4 Studios The
5 Bourne Ho
B4 1 Clapham Manor Ct
2 Clarke Ho
3 Gables The
4 Sycamore Mews
5 Maritime Ho
C1 1 Parrington Ho
2 Savill Ho
3 Blackwell Ho
4 Bruce Ho
5 Victoria Ct
6 Victoria Ho
7 Belvedere Ct
8 Ingram Lo
9 Viney Ct
10 Bloomsbury Ho
11 Belgravia Ho
12 Barnsbury Ho
C3 1 Kendoa Rd
2 Felmersham Cl

3 Abbeville Mews
4 Saxon Ho
5 Gifford Ho
6 Teignmouth Cl
7 Holwood Pl
8 Oaklands Pl
C4 1 Chelsham Ho
2 Lynde Ho
3 Greener Ho
4 Towns Ho
5 Hugh Morgan Ho
6 Roy Ridley Ho
7 Lendal Terr
8 Slievemore Cl

62

A2 1 King's Mews
2 Clapham Court Terr
3 Clapham Ct
4 Clapham Park Terr
5 Queenswood Ct
A3 1 Morris Ho
2 Gye Ho
3 Clowes Ho
4 Thomas Ho
5 Stuart Ho
6 Storace Ho
7 Bedford Ho
8 Ascot Ct
9 Ascot Par
10 Ashmere Ho
11 Ashmere Gr
A4 1 Callingham Ho
2 Russell Pickering Ho
3 Lopez Ho
B2 1 Beatrice Ho
2 Florence Ho
3 Evelyn Ho
4 Diana Ho
5 Brixton Hill Ct
6 Austin Ho
7 Manor Ct
8 Camsey Ho
9 Romer Ho
10 Gale Ho
11 Byrne Ho
12 Farnfield Ho
13 Marchant Ho
14 Rainsford Ho
15 Springett Ho
16 Mannering Ho
17 Waldron Ho
B3 1 Freemens Hos
2 Roger's Almshouses
3 Gresham Almshouses
4 Exbury Ho
5 Glasbury Ho
6 Dalbury Ho
7 Fosbury Ho
8 Chalbury Ho
9 Neilson-Terry Ct
10 Pavilion Mans
11 Daisy Dormer Ct
12 George Lashwood Ct
13 Marie Lloyd Ct
14 Trinity Homes
B4 1 Turberville Ho
2 Thrayle Ho
C1 1 Eccleston Ho
2 Scarsbrook Ho
3 Purser Ho

4 Rudhall Ho
5 Hardham Ho
6 Heywood Ho
7 Haworth Ho
8 Birch Ho
9 Lonsdell Ho
10 Lomley Ho
11 Laughton Ho
C2 1 Crownstone Ct
2 Brockwell Ct
3 Nevena Ct
4 St George's Residences
5 Hanover Mans
6 Fleet Ho
7 Langbourne Ho
8 Turnmill Ho
C3 1 Electric Mans
2 Electric La
3 Connaught Mans
4 Clifton Mans
5 Hereford Ho
6 Chaplin Ho
7 Brixton Oval
8 Lord David Pitt Ho
9 Marcus Garvey Way
10 Montgo Cl
11 Bob Marley Way
12 Leeson Ho
C4 1 Buckmaster Ho
2 Barret Ho
3 Albermarle Ho
4 Goodwood Mans
5 Angell Park Gdns
6 Fyfield Rd
7 Howard Ho
8 Harris Ho
9 Broadoak Ct
10 Burgate Ct
11 Witchwood Ho
12 Blacktree Mews
13 Chartham Ct
14 Chilham Ct
15 Northgate Ct
16 Westgate Ct
17 Dover Mans

63

A3 1 Mahatma Ganhi Ind Est
2 Dylan Rd
3 Bessemer Park Ind Est
4 Pablo Neruda Cl
5 Langston Hughes Cl
6 Walt Whitman Cl
7 James Joyes Wlk
8 Alice Walker Cl
9 Louise Bennett Cl
10 Chaddacre Ho
11 Burwood Ho
12 Pyrford Ho
13 Wangford Ho
14 Ashford Ho
15 Kenwood Ho
16 Moyne Ho
17 Elveden Ho
18 Sussex Wlk
19 Carrara Wlk
20 Broughton Dr
21 Angela Davis Ind Est
A4 1 Mallams Mews

2 Amberley Ho
3 Harper Ho
4 Leicester Ho
5 Station Ave
6 Wellfit St
7 Loughborough Ct
8 Belinda Rd
9 Higgs Ind Est
C3 1 Shaftesbury Ct
2 Mayhew Ct
3 Morris Ct
4 Swinburne Ct
5 Perth Ct
6 Tayside Ct
7 Matlock Ct
8 Hunter Ct
9 Turner Ct

64

A2 1 Velde Way
2 Delft Way
3 Arnhem Way
4 Isel Way
5 Kempis Way
6 Terborah Way
7 Steen Way
8 Deventer Cres
9 Nimegen Way
10 Hilversum Cres
A4 1 Harfield Gdns
2 Karen Ct
3 Seavington Ho
4 Appleshaw Ho
5 Birdsall Ho
6 Whitney Ho
7 Wheatland Ho
8 Wilton Ho
9 Walcot Ho
10 Whadden Ho
11 Melbrook Ho
12 Ledbury Ho
13 Tidworth Ho
14 Riseholme Ho
15 Ringmer Ho
16 Petworth Ho
17 Stagshaw Ho
18 Ivybridge Ho
19 Inwood Ho
20 Gatcombe Ho
21 Gatebeck Ho
22 Felbridge Ho
23 Cowdray Ho
B3 1 Dulwich Mews
2 St James's Cloisters
C2 1 Dorothy Charrington Ho
2 Keswick Ct
3 Kendall Ct
4 Halliwell Ct

65

A4 1 Tilling Ho
2 Goodwin Ho
3 Citron Terr
4 Cheam St
5 Linden Ho
C3 1 Laxton Path
2 Barlings Ho
3 Bayfield Ho
4 Coston Wlk
5 Coverham Ho
6 Gateley Ho
7 Dereham Ho
8 Greenwood Ho

9 Hilton Ho
10 Goodall Ho
11 Horsley Ho
12 Jordan Ho

68

1 Farnborough Ho
2 Rushmere Ho
3 Horndean Cl
4 Highcross Way
5 Timsbury Wlk
6 Foxcombe Rd
7 Ryefield Path
8 Greatham Wlk
9 Gosport Ho
10 Stoatley Ho
11 Milland Ho
12 Clanfield Ho
13 Fareham Ho
14 Grayswood Point
C4 1 Woodcott Ho
2 Lyndhurst Ho
3 Wheatley Ho
4 Allbrook Ho
5 Bordon Wlk
6 Chilcombe Ho
7 Vicarage Ct
8 Shawford Ct
9 Eastleigh Wlk
10 Kings Ct

69

A3 1 Ramsdean Ho
2 Purbrook Ho
3 Portsea Ho
4 Blendworth Point
5 Eashing Point
6 Hindhead Point
7 Hilsea Point
8 Witley Point
9 Buriton Ho
10 Grately Ho
11 Hascombe Ho
12 Dunhill Point
13 Westmark Point
14 Longmoor Point
15 Cadnam Point
B4 1 Cumberland Ho
2 Devonshire Ho
3 Cornwall Ho
4 Norfolk Ho
5 Leicester Ho
6 Warwick Ho
7 Sutherland Ho
8 Carmarthen Ho
9 Worcester Ho
10 Rutland Ho
C3 1 Sandringham Cl
2 Eastwick Ct
3 Oatlands Ct
4 Banning Ho
5 Grantley Ho
6 Caryl Ho
7 Duncombe Ho
8 Chilworth Ct
9 Kent Lo
10 Turner Lo
11 Marlborough
12 Parkland Gdns
13 Lewesdon Cl
14 Pines Ct
15 Ashtead Ct
16 Mynterne Ct
17 Arden
18 Stephen Ct

19 Marsham Ct
20 Doradus Ct
21 Acorns The
22 Heritage Ho
23 Conifer Ct
24 Spencer Ho
25 Chartwell
26 Blenheim
27 Chivelston
28 Greenfield Ho
29 Oakman Ho
30 Radley Lo
31 Simon Lo
32 Admirals Ct
C4 1 Brett Ho
2 Brett House Cl
3 Sylva Ct
4 Ross Ct
5 Stourhead Cl
6 Fleur Gates
7 Greenwood

70
A3 1 William Harvey Ho
2 Highview Ct
3 Cameron Ct
4 Galgate Ct
5 Green Ho The
6 King Charles Wlk
7 Florys Ct
8 Augustus Ct
9 Albert Ct
10 Hertford Lo
11 Mortimer Lo
12 Allenswood
13 Ambleside

72
C2 1 Upper Tooting Park
Mans
2 Cecil Mans
3 Marius Mans
4 Boulevard The
5 Elmfield Mans
6 Holdernesse Rd
C3 1 Heslop Ct
2 St James's Terr
3 Boundaries Mans
4 Station Par
C4 1 Hollies Way
2 Endlesham Ct

73
A3 1 Holbeach Mews
2 Hildreth Street
Mews

3 Coalbrook Mans
A4 1 Meyer Ho
2 Faraday Ho
3 Hales Ho
4 Frankland Ho
5 Graham Ho
6 Gibbs Ho
7 Dalton Ho
8 Anslie Wlk
9 Rokeby Ho
10 Caister Ho
11 Ivanhoe Ho
12 Catherine Baird Ct
13 Marmion Ho
14 Devonshire Ho
B4 1 Limerick Ct
2 Homewoods
3 Jewell Ho
4 Glanville Ho
5 Dan Bryant Ho
6 Olding Ho
7 Quennel Ho
8 Weir Ho
9 West Ho
10 Neville Ho
C3 1 Sinclair Ho
2 MacGregor Ho
3 Ingle Ho
C4 1 Riley Ho
2 Bennett Ho
3 White Ho
4 Rodgers Ho
5 Dumphreys Ho
6 Homan Ho
7 Prendergast Ho
8 Hutchins Ho
9 Whiteley Ho
10 Tresidder Ho
11 Primrose Ct
12 Angus Ho
13 Currie Ho

74
A1 1 De Montfort Par
2 Leigham Hall Par
3 Leigham Hall
4 Endsleigh Mans
5 John Kirk Ho
6 Raebarn Ct
7 Wavel Ct
8 Homeleigh Ct
9 Howland Ho
10 Beauclerk Ho
11 Bertrand Ho
12 Drew Ho
13 Dowes Ho
14 Dunton Ho
15 Raynald Ho

16 Sackville Ho
17 Thurlow Ho
18 Astoria Mans
A2 1 Wyatt Park Mans
2 Broadlands Mans
3 Stonehill's Mans
4 Streatleigh Par
5 Dorchester Ct
A3 1 Beaumont Ho
2 Christchurch Ho
3 Staplefield Cl
4 Chipstead Ho
5 Coulsdon Ho
6 Conway Ho
7 Telford Avenue
Mans
8 Telford Parade
Mans
9 Wavertree Ct
10 Hartswood Ho
11 Wray Ho
A4 1 Picton Ho
2 Rigg Ho
3 Watson Ho
4 MacArthur Ho
5 Sandon Ho
6 Thorold Ho
7 Pearce Ho
8 Mudie Ho
9 Miller Ho
10 Lycett Ho
11 Lafone Ho
12 Lucraft Ho
13 Freeman Ho
14 New Park Par
15 Argyll Ct
16 Dumbarton Ct
17 Kintyre Ct
18 Cotton Ho
19 Crossman Hos
20 Cameford Ct
21 Parsons Ho
22 Brindley Ho
23 Arkwright Ho
24 Perry Ho
25 Brunel Ho
26 New Park Ct
27 Tanhurst Ho
B1 1 Carisbrook Ct
2 Pembrook Lo
3 Willow Ct
4 Poplar Ct
5 Mountview
6 Spa View
B3 1 Charlwood Ho
2 Earlswood Ho
3 Balcombe Ho
4 Claremont Cl
5 Holbrook Ho

6 Gwynne Ho
7 Kynaston Ho
8 Tillman Ho
9 Regent Lo
10 Hazelmere Ct
B4 1 Archbishop's Pl
2 Witley Ho
3 Outwood Ho
4 Dunsfold Ho
5 Deepdene Lo
6 Warnham Ho
7 Albury Lo
8 Tilford Ho
9 Elstead Ho
10 Thursley Ho
11 Brockham Ho
12 Capel Lo
13 Leith Ho
14 Fairview Ho
15 Weymouth Ct
16 Ascalon Ct
C3 1 Valens Ho
2 Loveday Ho
3 Strode Ho
4 Ethelworth Ct
5 Harbin Ho
6 Brooks Ho
7 Godolphin Ho
8 Sheppard Ho
9 McCormick Ho
10 Taylor Ho
11 Saunders Ho
12 Talcott Path
13 Derrick Ho
14 Williams Ho
15 Baldwin Ho
16 Berkeley Ct
17 Churston Cl
18 Neil Wates Cres
19 Burnell Ho
20 Portland Ho
C4 1 Ellacombe Ho
2 Booth Ho
3 Hathersley Ho
4 Brereton Ho
5 Holdsworth Ho
6 Dearmer Ho
7 Cherry Cl
8 Greenleaf Cl
9 Longford Wlk
10 Scarlette Manor
Wlk
11 Chandlers Way
12 Upgrove Manor
Way
13 Ropers Wlk
14 Tebbs Ho
15 Bell Ho

16 Worthington Ho
17 Courier Ho
18 Mackie Rd
19 Hamers Ho
20 Kelyway Ho
21 Harriet Tubman Cl
22 Estoria Cl
23 Leckhampton Pl
24 Scotia Rd

75
A1 1 Thanet Ho
2 Chapman Ho
3 Beaufoy Ho
4 Easton Ho
5 Roberts Ho
6 Lloyd Ct
7 Kershaw Ho
8 Wakeling Ho
9 Edridge Ho
10 Jeston Ho
11 Lansdowne Wood
Cl
C2 1 Coppedhall
2 Shackleton Ct
3 Bullfinch Ct
4 Gannet Ct
5 Fulmar Ct
6 Heron Ct
7 Petrel Ct
8 Falcon Ct
9 Eagle Ct
10 Dunnock Ct
11 Dunlin Ct
12 Cormorant Ct

76
C1 1 Tunbridge Ct
2 Harrogate Ct
3 Bath Ct
4 Leamington Ct
5 Porlock Ho
6 Cissbury Ho
7 Eddisbury Ho
8 Dundry Ho
9 Silbury Ho
10 Homildon Ho
11 Highgate Ho
12 Richmond Ho
13 Pendle Ho
14 Tynwald Ho
15 Wirrall Ho
16 Greyfriars

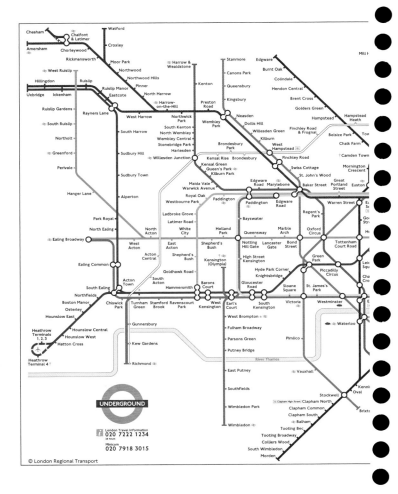

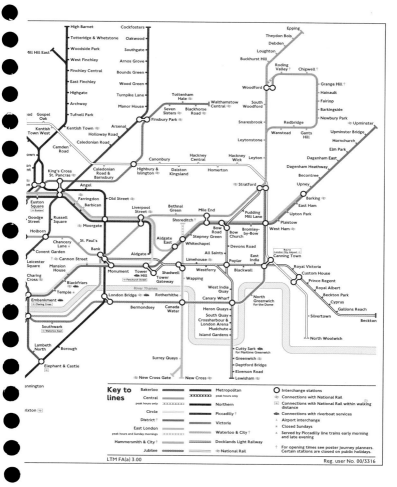

Key to lines

Bakerloo
Central — peak hours only
Circle
District † — peak hours and Sunday mornings
East London
Hammersmith & City †
Jubilee

Metropolitan — peak hours only
Northern
Piccadilly †
Victoria
Waterloo & City †
Docklands Light Railway
National Rail

○ Interchange stations
≷ Connections with National Rail
⊟ Connections with National Rail within walking distance
⛴ Connections with riverboat services
✈ Airport interchange
✷ Closed Sundays
Served by Piccadilly line trains early morning and late evening

† For opening times see poster journey planners. Certain stations are closed on public holidays.

LTM FA(a) 3.00

Reg. user No. 00/3316

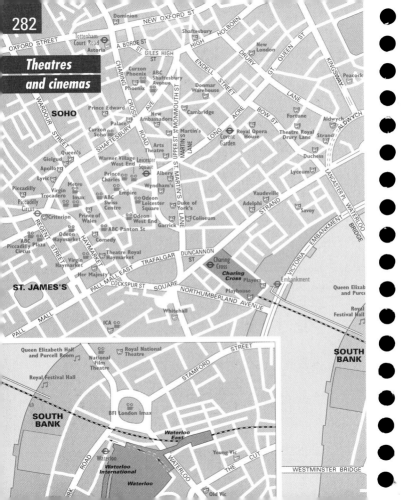

Theatres and cinemas

OXFORD STREET
Dominion
NEW OXFORD ST
Tottenham
Court Road
Astoria
A BORDE ST
GILES HIGH ST
Shaftesbury
HIGH
HOLBORN
New
London
DRURY
Peacock

SOHO

WARDOUR STREET

CHARING CROSS ROAD

Curzon
Phoenix
Phoenix
ABC
Shaftesbury
Avenue

ENDELL STREET

GT. QUEEN ST
KINGSWAY

Prince Edward
Palace
Curzon
Soho

New
Ambassadors
Arts
Theatre

Donmar
Warehouse

Cambridge

LANE

LONG ACRE
BOW ST
Fortune

St Martin's
Covent
Garden

Royal Opera
House

Aldwych
ALDWYCH
Theatre Royal
Drury Lane
Strand

Gielgud
Queen's
Apollo
Lyric

SHAFTESBURY AVE
Warner Village
West End

Prince
Charles

Leicester
square

Empire
Odeon
Leicester
Square

Albery

ST MARTIN'S LANE
Wyndham's

Duke of
York's

Duchess
Lyceum

LANCASTER PL
WATERLOO BRIDGE

Piccadilly
Virgin
Trocadero
Metro
Imax
Piccadilly
Circus
Criterion
Prince of
Wales
ABC
Swiss
Centre

Odeon
West End
ABC Panton St
Comedy

Garrick

Coliseum

Vaudeville
Adelphi
STRAND
Savoy

VICTORIA EMBANKMENT

ABC
Piccadilly
Plaza
Circus
Odeon
Haymarket
Virgin
Haymarket

REGENT STREET
HAYMARKET

Theatre Royal
Haymarket

Her Majesty's

DUNCANNON ST
TRAFALGAR

Charing
Cross

Charing
Cross
Players

Embankment

ST. JAMES'S

PALL MALL EAST
COCKSPUR ST
SQUARE

NORTHUMBERLAND AVENUE

Playhouse

Queen Elizab
and Purc

Royal
Festival Hall

PALL MALL

Whitehall

ICA

Queen Elizabeth Hall
and Purcell Room

National
Film
Theatre

Royal National
Theatre

STREET

STAMFORD

**SOUTH
BANK**

Royal Festival Hall

**SOUTH
BANK**

BFI London Imax

Waterloo
East

Young Vic
THE CUT

ROAD
Waterloo
International
WATERLOO

Waterloo

Old Vic

WESTMINSTER BRIDGE